T0314245

MAKING MONEY IN SIXTEENTH-CENTURY FRANCE

MAKING MONEY IN SIXTEENTH-CENTURY FRANCE

CURRENCY, CULTURE, AND THE STATE

JOTHAM PARSONS

CORNELL UNIVERSITY PRESS
Ithaca and London

First published 2014 by Cornell University Press

Printed in the United States of America

Library of Congress Cataloging-in-Publication Data

Parsons, Jotham, author.
   Making money in sixteenth-century France : currency, culture, and the state / Jotham Parsons.
      pages cm
   Includes bibliographical references.
   ISBN 978-0-8014-5159-1 (cloth : alk. paper)
   1. Money—France—History—16th century. I. Title.
   HG976.P37   2015
   332.4'94409031—dc23   2014021596

Cornell University Press strives to use environmentally responsible suppliers and materials to the fullest extent possible in the publishing of its books. Such materials include vegetable-based, low-VOC inks and acid-free papers that are recycled, totally chlorine-free, or partly composed of nonwood fibers. For further information, visit our website at www.cornellpress.cornell.edu.

Cloth printing   10 9 8 7 6 5 4 3 2 1

For Elaine

Contents

Acknowledgments   ix

Introduction   1

1. The Cour des Monnaies   17

2. The Logic of Economic Regulation   60

3. The Inflationary Crisis and the
   Reforms of 1577   104

4. Money and Sovereignty   153

5. Crimes against the Currency   193

6. The Monetary Imaginary of
   Renaissance France   237

   Conclusion: The Court and the Queen   282

Bibliography   289

Index   319

ACKNOWLEDGMENTS

This book has been a long time in the making, and I have incurred many debts of gratitude along the way. Financial support was provided by Roosevelt University, Duquesne University, the Stanford University Libraries (Gustave Gimon Visiting Scholar Fellowship), and the National Endowment for the Humanities (N.E.H. Summer Stipend). Publication of this volume was generously assisted by a subvention from Duquesne University and its MacAnulty College of Liberal Arts. The list of libraries and archives on whose facilities and staff I have depended is very long; aside from the institutions just mentioned, they include the Bibliothèque Nationale and Archives Nationales of France, the Archives Municipales de Lyon, the Newberry Library, the Harvard University Libraries, and the University of Wisconsin and University of Pittsburgh libraries, among others. Two seminars provided especially valuable occasions to reflect on and discuss aspects of this project: a 2003 N.E.H. Summer Seminar, "Surveying Paris: Urban Space and Urban Culture in the Early Modern City," directed by Karen Newman; and a 2008 Folger Library Faculty Seminar, "Connections, Trust, and Causation in Economic History," directed by Craig Muldrew. I have also received valuable feedback from a variety of presentations of material from this project, at meetings of the Sixteenth Century Studies Conference, the Society for French Historical Studies, the Western Society for French History, the Pittsburgh Area Early Modern Group, and the West Virginia University History Graduate Colloquium.

Portions of chapter 3 appeared as "Governing Sixteenth-Century France: The Monetary Reforms of 1577," in *French Historical Studies*, vol. 26, no. 1, pp. 1–30, copyright 2003, Society for French Historical Studies, all rights reserved, and are reprinted by permission of the present publisher, Duke University Press. Portions of chapters 3 and 4 appeared as "Money and Sovereignty in Early Modern France," in *Journal of the History of Ideas*, vol. 62, no. 1, pp. 59–79, copyright 2001, *Journal of the History of Ideas*, all rights reserved, and are reprinted by permission of the present publisher, the University of Pennsylvania Press.

Any attempt to list all the colleagues whose advice and criticism have contributed to this book would inevitably be both tedious and incomplete. I will content myself with singling out my editor, John Ackerman, and the anonymous reviewers he recruited for Cornell, who provided unusually careful and valuable feedback. To the extent that this book is readable at all, they deserve credit, while I reserve blame for remaining faults. Orest Ranum not only taught me most of what I know about history but also provided help, encouragement, and detailed criticism throughout this book's long gestation. Finally, while it is customary to thank one's family in this space, I have more than the usual reason to do so. My parents, Charles and Marjorie, read drafts, provided advice, and in one case retrieved an errant microfilm from the Archives Nationales. My sister Sylvia gave invaluable aid with some tricky Latin. My children, Charlotte and Nathaniel, were both inspirational and cooperative through a project that began before either of them was born. Elaine, on the other hand, has been my wife, my colleague, and my closest friend since before I undertook this project.

MAKING MONEY IN SIXTEENTH-CENTURY FRANCE

Introduction

> The bourgeoisie . . . has pitilessly torn asunder the motley feudal ties that bound man to his "natural superiors," and has left remaining no other nexus between man and man than naked self-interest, than callous "cash payment."
>
> —Karl Marx

The *Communist Manifesto*'s famous diagnosis of nineteenth-century society is in no way distinctively communist.[1] Indeed, social theorists from Marx's day to ours have been nearly unanimous in connecting what Karl Polanyi called the "great transformation" of modern society and economy with an equally profound transformation in the social and political role of money. Abstract, impersonal, subject to mathematical manipulation and analysis, money has encouraged or enabled many of the relationships and attitudes characteristic of modernity. Bearing only a formal relationship to those who possessed it, those who received it, or goods for which it was exchanged, it suited, if it did not actually create, a world of formally equal persons, arbitrarily contractual relations, and identities formed from the consumption of a boundlessly increasing variety of goods. The indispensable technology of the disinterestedly calculating "spirit of capitalism," it might subsume and secularize even the most powerful religious impulses.[2] Enabling an "industrious revolution" in which wage labor and its complement, market consumption, replaced work and exchange that had previously occurred within households, it had in fact, as Marx said, "torn

---

1. Karl Marx, *The Communist Manifesto*, ed. Frederic L. Bender (New York: Norton, 1988), 57.
2. Max Weber, *The Protestant Ethic and the Spirit of Capitalism*, trans. Talcott Parsons (London: Routledge, 2001).

away from the family its sentimental veil, and . . . reduced [it] to a mere money relation."[3] Already by the late eighteenth century, and increasingly since, the study of monetary exchange had become the master key to understanding all of society—a development that Marx deplored but in which he saw no alternative to participating, if only to turn the science of political economy and ultimately the capitalist order itself to its own destruction.[4] As of yet, that project has not succeeded.

In sixteenth-century Europe these developments were still at an early stage, but their effects were already felt. The major instruments of this incipient transformation are familiar: the expansion of global and internal commerce following the voyages of discovery; the influx of precious metal from central European, South American, and Japanese mines; the exponentially increasing fiscal demands of warfare in the age of the military revolution; and the concomitant emergence of the European state system. Though the general shape of this transformation is well known, it is harder to discover how those who lived through it experienced it, understood it, and attempted to shape it. Tracking money, as it circulated, is one of the best ways to get at how a broad array of people lived with the state in transformation. Money was at the heart of much fundamental change in early modern European society, but it also is especially fertile ground for reflection on life at the ground level. Most obviously, it was ubiquitous, both as an abstract entity and in the physical form of the coinage. It was "good to think with," serving admirably then as now as a literary and philosophical metaphor. It also posed more or less acute problems in the course of the so-called great inflation, provoking explicit and public reflection. And currency was both a creation and a vital tool of the state's rapidly expanding machinery, linking it intimately to broader issues of governance.

While the early modern transformation of the money economy was a long-term European and even global phenomenon, this book will focus on France from the mid-sixteenth through the early seventeenth century. In the second half of the sixteenth century, France was still Europe's largest and most powerful state, but it faced daunting challenges. Wars with the Spanish and German Habsburgs sapped French political, economic, and military stability from 1498 to 1559. The death of Henri II in that year led to a weak regency, factional strife, and civil war, largely motivated and certainly inflamed by conflict

---

3. Jan de Vries, *The Industrious Revolution: Consumer Behaviour and the Household Economy, 1650 to the Present* (Cambridge: Cambridge University Press, 2008).

4. See in particular the early sections of Karl Marx, *Capital: A Critique of Political* Economy, 3 vols. (New York: International Publishers, 1967).

between Catholics and followers of Reformed Protestantism. The political and reproductive difficulties of Henri II's four sons—François II (r. 1559–1560), Charles IX (r. 1560–1574), Henri III (r. 1574–1589), and François d'Anjou (d. 1584)—allowed civil war to fester for a quarter century before it erupted in a paroxysm of violence when their cousin Henri, king of Navarre and head of the Protestant party, became heir to the throne. Only at the end of the century was he able to restore an order that was threatened but not destroyed by his assassination in 1610.[5]

This combination of power, centrality, and wild instability, along with a vibrant literary and political culture, encouraged French intellectuals to reflect on money, society, and governance. Several structural features of the French monarchy also helped make it a good subject for this kind of historical investigation. Most important, administration of the complex and sprawling French mint system was centralized in a Parisian judicial and advisory body, the Chambre, later Cour des Monnaies (Chamber or Court of Moneys), whose archives are well preserved. There was no equivalent situation anywhere in western Europe: minting and monetary policy were highly decentralized in the German Empire and Italy; the Low Countries were falling apart; and while the Spanish currency was centrally administered, it was dominated by the mines and mints of the New World. England, also a good-sized, centralized monarchy, was most comparable, though it was much smaller and more geographically marginal than France and relied almost entirely on a single mint located in the Tower of London.[6] So while the French case is not entirely typical, it generated many ideas and institutions crucial to the unfolding European system. To clarify both the uniqueness and the exemplarity of the French case, and more generally to give a better idea of how French money worked in a European context, this book will turn fairly regularly to the example of England in particular.

At time same time, it will range broadly from the administrative details of the coinage to its uses as a literary metaphor, with detours into political and economic thought, policymaking, and the criminal underworld. This diverse landscape, though, is surprisingly consistent. Early modern Europeans believed that money was dangerous—not just because it was the biblical

---

5. There are numerous surveys of this period of French history. Mack Holt, ed., *Renaissance and Reformation France, 1500–1648* (Oxford: Oxford University Press, 2002), offers a good, compact introduction to current scholarship on the subject.

6. Technically, the mint of the episcopal palatinate of Durham was still in operation at the beginning of our period, and a couple of satellite mints opened during the Elizabethan recoinage of 1561, but their contribution to the English monetary system was trivial.

"root of all evil" but because they feared (not unlike Marx) that it threatened to disrupt social organization and human relations. But they also believed that the government had the ability to solve the dangers money posed. The right policies could transform money from a threat into a real instrument of the common good. Renaissance monarchy, to their minds, was well suited to this task. Intimately tied to royal sovereignty on many levels, the currency was a microcosm of how the French thought their society could and should work. Not only was it practically connected to almost every area of governance, but it tended to serve metonymically as a symbol of the process of governance as a whole.

At the same time, money was a product of both foreign and domestic forces beyond the king's control. The turn of the century saw the emergence of an idea that would become central to classical and current political economy—that money existed in the context of an international state system and an autonomous market. This did not mean that people stopped interpreting the success of the currency as a test of sovereign governance, but it did encourage both states and their subjects to seek other sources of stability in the dangerous flux of ungoverned value. This was still very far from laissez-faire theory, utopian socialism, or the like, but it did generate increasingly sophisticated reflections on how societies measure value and what the limits or appropriate models of regulation might be for that kind of measurement, which might well be only metaphorically monetary. Money always exists at the border between law and anarchy, freedom and coercion, society and the individual. In trying to understand and control it, the people of sixteenth-century France were grappling with the most basic questions of social life.

Meanings of Money

But "money" is an inexact word—even more in French than in English, since *monnaie* can mean money in general, coins, a mint, or the change returned in a transaction. Economically, it is traditionally defined as whatever functions as a medium of transactions or a store of value.[7] More important, money subsisted, at least from the Hellenistic period to the late nineteenth century, as part of a complex relationship among the precious metals (gold and silver, with an occasional cameo by copper), those same metals alloyed and stamped

---

7. As far as I know, only fairly radical libertarians have taken the possibility of disaggregating those two functions at all seriously. On this subject, which is far beyond my expertise, see Tyler Cowen and Randall Kronzsner, "The Development of the New Monetary Economics," *Journal of Political Economy* 95 (1987): 567–90.

into coins by multiple authorities at different times, and various abstract units of account. No less an authority than John Maynard Keynes argued that the last of these was the most important. "Money-of-account," he says at the beginning of his *Treatise on Money*, "namely that in which Debts and Prices and General Purchasing Power are *expressed*, is the primary concept of a Theory of Money." This money of account is, as its name implies, the result of the abstract expression of prices and debts, "whether they are recorded . . . in book entry on baked bricks or paper documents." The unit of those debts will in turn generally be controlled by the organism responsible for enforcing them—in the (early) modern world, the state, which is also likely to be the largest and most powerful debtor and maker and receiver of payments within its territory. That "chartalist" account of money, pioneered (like so much eccentric monetary theory) by an Austrian, Georg Friedrich Knapp, has aroused only spotty interest among economists, but its illumination of the intimate link between governance and money makes it a valuable starting place for our purposes.[8]

Chartalism also draws attention to the intimate relationship between money and debts, both public and private; and debt, and the social relations within which it was embedded, has in recent years become a major focus of the study of early modern society.[9] Debt turns out to have been astonishingly and, most likely, increasingly pervasive throughout western Europe between 1500 and 1800. Retail transactions were predominantly on credit, even moderately prosperous households usually carried significant long-term debt, and the judicial treatment of debt and default was a perennial matter of urgent concern under the old regime. Almost all relationships, including those of family, political institutions, and patronage, were also frequently relationships of credit and debt. Thus, hardly any area of life in early modern Europe was not permeated by money-as-debt; yet much less scholarly attention has been

---

8. See Georg Friedrich Knapp, *The State Theory of Money*, ed. H. M. Lucas and J. Bonar (London: Macmillan, 1924). This is an abridged translation of Knapp, *Staatliche Theorie des Geldes*, 4th ed. (Munich: Dunker and Humblot, 1923). There is a highly partisan but useful discussion of chartalism and economic theories of money in David Graeber, *Debt: The First 5,000 Years* (New York: Melville House, 2011), 21–42. This book is, however, largely worthless on the post-classical history of money.

9. In addition to Graeber, *Debt*, see Laurence Fontaine, *L'Economie morale. Pauvreté, crédit et confiance dans l'Europe préindustrielle* (Paris: Gallimard, 2008); Craig Muldrew, *The Economy of Obligation: The Culture of Credit and Social Relations in Early Modern England* (London: St. Martin's, 1998); Philip T. Hoffman, Gilles Postel-Vinay, and Jean-Laurent Rosenthal, *Priceless Markets: The Political Economy of Credit in Paris, 1660–1870* (Chicago: University of Chicago Press, 2000); Julie Hardwick, *Family Business: Litigation and the Political Economies of Daily Life in Early Modern France* (Oxford: Oxford University Press, 2009); and, on the period preceding ours, Julie Claustre, *Dans les geôles du roi: L'emprisonnement pour dette à Paris à la fin du Moyen-Âge* (Paris: Publications de la Sorbonne, 2007).

focused on its logical concomitant of money-as-money. For in practice, early modern economic actors needed physical tokens, "by the delivery of which debt-contracts and price-contracts are *discharged*, and in the shape of which a store of General Purchasing Power is *held*."[10] Governments faced the task not so much of dictating as of stabilizing (or, occasionally, manipulating) the relationship among those tokens, the gold or silver they contained, and the prices and obligations they represented. This was the central problem of pre-industrial money, and its seemingly endless implications and complications are the central issue of this book.

In early modern France, the money of account was generally the *livre tournois* (pound of Tours), sometimes called the *franc* after a coin that was intermittently struck at that face value. There was also a *livre parisis* (pound of Paris), whose value was fixed at 1.25 livres tournois and which went almost entirely out of use in the course of the sixteenth century; in this book, the term *livre* by itself will always refer to the livre tournois. From 1577 to 1602 the money of account was changed to the *écu*, named after a gold coin, whose value was set at three livres. As in other countries that maintained the Carolingian nomenclature, the livre was divided into twenty *sols* (shillings; the écu of account thus contained sixty sols), each of which was further divided into twelve *deniers* (pennies). Actual coins, domestic and foreign, were assigned and periodically reassigned face values in the money of account. A coin could thus function as a simple token of the money of account, as an object of commerce bought or sold for a sum in the money of account other than the one officially assigned, or as an object of barter, exchanged for goods without direct or necessary reference to the money of account.

The early modern European public faced a truly bewildering variety of these coins, and the sixteenth-century French probably had it worse than most. For one thing, they accumulated over time: metal tokens were very durable and could in principle continue to circulate for well over a century. From time to time puzzled consumers would write in to the Cour des Monnaies asking for an official valuation of some truly archaic coin that had showed up in their purse or was mentioned in an old contract.[11] Europe's huge number of states and statelets gave rise to a corresponding variety of coinage, and even in the best of times a country with borders as long and

---

10. John Maynard Keynes, *A Treatise on Money*, 2 vols. (New York: Harcourt, Brace, 1930) 1:3 (emphasis and eccentric capitalization in original).

11. See, e.g., Archives Nationales de France (AN), Z^{1B} 370, piece dated 24 March 1556 (petition of Jehan de la Primaudaye), asking about the *écu couronne* of 1516; a similar petition by one Marguerite Durant fifty years later (AN, Z^{1B} 396, piece dated 30 August 1606) inquired about coins going back to 1466!

porous as France's would have had difficulty keeping foreign coin out. (Not that it was always entirely clear what "foreign" meant: for political reasons, the coinage of some tiny client principalities—notably Dombes, Trèves, and Béarn/Navarre—was allowed to circulate freely in France, to the great distress of the monetary authorities.)[12] This was all the more true in the sixteenth century, when the vast flood of overseas precious metal coming into Europe through the Iberian Peninsula was at its height. Indeed, throughout our period, it is almost certain that the majority of the money circulating in France took the form of Spanish (and, to a much lesser extent, Portuguese) gold *pistoles* (double *escudos* in Spanish; in English, doubloons) and silver *reals* (the "pieces of eight" of popular legend). Despite strong misgivings, successive governments saw no alternative to allowing them to circulate legally. The French equivalents in fairly pure gold and silver—the écu and *henric* on the one hand and the *teston* and franc on the other—had trouble competing. Small-denomination coins, worth less than a sol, did not necessarily benefit from similar toleration, but for technical reasons they were always in short supply, and consumers were frequently willing to accept even the most dubious and illegal specimens, domestic or foreign, so that on this end too variety was often bewildering.

In sixteenth-century Europe, the production of money was essentially an artisanal business.[13] That had been true, of course, for better than two thousand years, since the emergence of coinage in archaic Lydia. The process of coining had in fact barely changed since the time of Cyrus the Great, and it is worth describing it in some detail, given its centrality to all the issues surrounding early modern money. Coining had two purposes: to create consistent units of precious metal and to mark those units in such a way that they would be readily identifiable and readily accepted by the public. Neither of these tasks was particularly easy, given the available technology. Achieving consistency in the amount of precious metal in each coin required converting whatever materials were available—ores, worn or foreign coin, plate, jewelry, counterfeit pieces, etc.—into a single alloy. While it was possible to refine a poor alloy into a richer one, this was a very expensive process: labor intensive, often requiring costly materials like mercury, and usually resulting in the loss

---

12. For objections to such arrangements, see, e.g., AN, Z[1B] 376, piece dated 31 March 1576 (Trèves); AN, Z[1B] 387, piece dated 19 November 1596 (still Trèves); AN, Z[1B] 379, pieces dated 30 July and 4 April 1582 and 14 April 1583 (Navarre); and AN, Z[1B] 389, pieces dated 12 and 21 January 1598 (Dombes).

13. The best introduction to the mint system of old-regime France is Adrien Blanchet and Adolphe Dieudonné, *Manuel de numismatique française*, 4 vols. (Paris: Picard, 1912–36) 2:12–24.

of a substantial fraction of the precious metal in question. Whenever possible, mints preferred to coin at the same or a lesser alloy than the (average of) the material they were receiving—though, needless to say, this could depend on unpredictable factors affecting what was brought to the mints. Assaying and refining were, however, quite well-understood and precise procedures by the sixteenth century, and thus in a well-run mint the margin of error in the alloy of coins was relatively small: the limit of variation, called the "remedies," was set by law.[14]

This was important for a couple of reasons. First (as was well known in the sixteenth century), consumers tended to hoard or melt down coins of a given nominal value if they contained an excessive amount of specie while passing on those that had less. The mid-sixteenth-century English financier Thomas Gresham gave his name to this phenomenon as Gresham's law—"bad money drives out good"—though it had already been formulated in Poland by none other than Nicolas Copernicus.[15] Second, because there was a lower limit on how much metal could make a usable, durable coin, small change had to be struck from alloys that consisted largely of copper or other cheap base metals. These alloys and the coins made from them (*liards* at 3 deniers, *doubles* at 2d., and deniers or *douzains* at 1d. being the most common) were generically called *billon* in French. Because their precious metal content was not at all easy to evaluate, they were ripe for fraud and abuse. Indeed, criminals who committed fraud against the coinage were frequently termed *billoneurs*. Unless one was to cut the Gordian knot and mint such coins out of pure copper, the billon required especially careful supervision.

At any rate, whatever alloy was being used then had to be worked into coin-shaped blanks of uniform weight. This was a technically straightforward process of clipping, filing, and weighing, but it was vulnerable to sloppiness or fraud. Finally, workers stamped blank metal disks with dies that imprinted their distinctive images on the obverse and reverse. There were machines that could do this more precisely than any human equipped with a hammer, but in the sixteenth century they were expensive, unreliable, and

---

14. It was a matter of frequent dispute whether a mint should be allowed to produce coins that fell on average below the standard specie content as long as each individual coin was within the *remèdes*, or whether the mean should be at the standard, "le fort portant le faible." Improved assaying techniques had made this a viable way for mint masters to improve their returns; it was extensively litigated in England in the 1570s and played a part in French public controversies in 1609–1610. See C. E. Challis, *The Tudor Coinage* (Manchester, UK: Manchester University Press, 1978), 135–40; and chapter 4, below.

15. In his 1528 tract *Monetæ cudendæ ratio,* though it had been suggested two centuries earlier by Nicole Oresme. See M. L. Wolowski, ed., *Traictie de la premiere invention des monnoies de Nicole Oresme . . . et Traité de la monnaie de Copernic* (Paris: Librairie de Gillaumin, 1864).

little used. Although striking the coins was a relatively unskilled task, engraving the dies was not, especially given the exigencies of the French system. Multiple mints often had to strike the same coin: if the different issues were not substantially identical, they risked confusing and alienating the public. If they were not somehow differentiated, it would be impossible to assign blame for defects in individual coins. In practice, a master engraver in Paris made (hopefully) standard punches for lettering, portraits, and other necessary designs, which were then distributed to the mints, where local engravers used them to create coining dies, adding to each a tiny unique letter, the "difference" of that mint.

The technology of coining, then, was fairly simple in its components but not easy to manage as a system. The capital requirements, apart from the raw materials, were moderate. Only the furnaces needed for smelting and refining the metals and, of course, suitable space for working required significant investment.[16] Both engraving and refining were specialized skills but were fairly widespread among metal craftsmen: not only goldsmiths but locksmiths, swordsmiths, and tinsmiths, not to mention sculptors and alchemists. The other steps in the process required practice if they were to be conducted quickly and precisely, but they were not otherwise challenging. There was, then, no easy way to prevent unauthorized persons from issuing coins: barriers to entry, to use the technical term, were low, and only efficient legal repression (which imposed additional costs both directly, through the possibility of fines, imprisonment, exile, or death, and indirectly, through the need for stealth and concealment) combined with attention to consumer demand would allow the state to maintain anything like a monopoly on coinage.

Besides such repression, the government also faced the challenge of keeping the mints reasonably honest and competent. This was uniquely difficult in the largest and most diverse kingdom in Europe, as well as one of the wealthiest and most commercially active. It would have been impossible to supply all of France from a single mint, as was done in England.[17] Instead, about twenty mints operated at any given time, their locations determined by trade routes, political pressures, and tradition. They tended to cluster on the edges of the kingdom, a particularly inconvenient arrangement from the point of view of centralized control: taken together, the French mint system

16. A 1555 inventory of the Paris mint valued the movable equipment therein (including the furnaces) at just over 380 livres: see AN, Z^{1B} 369, piece dated 5 May 155 (procès-verbal of the transfer of the Paris mint from Bernard de Riberolles to Estienne Bergeron).

17. On English mint administration in this period, see Challis, *Tudor Coinage*; and Challis, ed., *A New History of the Royal Mint* (Cambridge: Cambridge University Press, 1992), chap. 3.

and the Cour des Monnaies would have about five hundred active employees at a time by the end of the sixteenth century, making it a very large industrial operation by contemporary standards. This was a problem, given the obvious rewards of dishonesty in the mints, and it was exacerbated by the way individual mints were managed.

Administratively, the French monarchy treated its mints as a revenue source. Like almost all taxes and the royal domain, the mints were periodically farmed out to contractors who paid out a portion of the expected receipts up front. The mint farmers were generally local businessmen, often goldsmiths, who frequently renewed their leases over quite long terms. Kings periodically considered combining many or all of their mints into a single farm, but this never actually happened and would almost certainly have been a disaster.[18] Even so, while the system of farming brought outside capital into government operations and, at least in principle, eased administrative burdens, it led to corruption and conflict of interest. Those who leased the farms as mint masters had a strong incentive to produce substandard currency, both because using less precious metal was cheaper and because they usually contracted to produce specified amounts of coin and might find it difficult to live up to those obligations honestly. The mint farmers were also of highly varying degrees of competence.[19] This was why the generals of the moneys served, above all, as auditors.

The system in place, roughly, was as follows. Within every mint, employees were supposed to keep an eye on each other: in particular, the mint master, the guard, a royal officer, and his counterguard had to cooperate or countersign on most significant actions. Together, they were to keep a register of all metals purchased and how they were coined, while an assayer, another independent royal officer, tested the coins for weight and alloy.[20] Most important, a sample of the mint's output was to be placed in a box, sealed by master, provost, and assayer, and brought to Paris at the end of the year, along with certified copies of the registers, to be assayed by the Monnaies. The contents of these "boxes" (*boestes* or *boîtes*: the English called them

---

18. See chapter 4, below.

19. An extreme case is Denis Faulcheur, master of the mint of Troyes in 1584, who, on being reprimanded for allowing coins marked "1568" to be produced in his mint, "a dit quil ne scet lire et que sil eust congneu la faulte ne la eust souffert." AN, Z^{1B} 380, piece dated 3 March 1584 (interrogatory of Faulcheur). His engraver had died, and the man's preadolescent son was doing the work.

20. This did not exhaust the system of internal checks and balances: there was also a provost, originally elected by the mint workers but later a royal officer, who oversaw law enforcement for each mint, as well as an official engraver (*tailleur*) and sometimes a comptroller (*contrerolleur*) who double-checked the books.

"pyxes," a term we might as well use), which also conveniently served as at least partial payment of the farm of the mint, would be compared with coins of the same denomination, mint, and year taken from circulation—usually from the receipts of the royal tax officials, who brought in coin from all over the kingdom—and any major discrepancy would be investigated.[21] The registers were also audited, either in Paris or by generals of the moneys sent out into the provinces. In principle this system should have worked, and indeed, when properly administered it did well under ordinary circumstances. As we shall see, however, there was a great deal that could, and did, go wrong.

Money in Theory

Given its centrality to so many aspects of human experience, it is no surprise that money has been the subject of an enormous amount of theoretical reflection. This is a tradition that goes back to antiquity and continued through the Middle Ages and our period. While a detailed consideration of modern theory about money would take us well out of our way, a few remarks seem helpful in clarifying this book's orientation. In general, the mainstream of modern monetary and macro economics has little to offer a nonquantitative study like this one.[22] This book does draw on schools of thought that have concentrated on the institutional foundations of money and economy: the classic tradition of nineteenth- and early-twentieth-century German social theory and the various ideas grouped under the broad rubric of "institutional economics," many of which grow directly from those Teutonic roots.

Marx and Polanyi, who appeared in the first paragraph of this introduction, represent strains of German theory deeply at odds with actually existing systems of exchange and hence, of money. Since this book's aim is analysis rather than critique of early modern political economy, though, their writings are less relevant than those of a number of compatriots with broadly overlapping ideas. Foremost among them, unsurprisingly, is Max Weber, who had a great deal to say about money in his general attempt to construct a sociological model of human economy and society in historical

---

21. For a description of the English auditing procedure in a particularly baroque elaboration, see Simon Wortham, "Sovereign Counterfeits: The Trial of the Pyx," *Renaissance Quarterly* 49 (1996): 334–59.

22. The major exception is Thomas J. Sargent and François R. Velde. *The Big Problem of Small Change* (Princeton: Princeton University Press, 2002), though certainly no one should attempt to write the history of money in any period without consulting Milton Friedman and Anna Schwartz, *A Monetary History of the United States, 1867–1960* (Princeton: Princeton University Press, 1963).

times.[23] Much of his discussion is devoted to the development of his famous concept of "market rationality," of which money and the mathetic reasoning it enabled were constitutive parts.

While the general idea (partially derived from Werner Sombart) that the increasing monetization of the modern economy led to profoundly important intellectual and psychological transformations serves as one of the main justifications for this project, many details of such transformations will not appear in the limited geographic and chronological space we are considering.[24] Instead, this book analyzes a relatively stable (though by no means static) configuration of money and society, such that synchronic analysis is more important than diachronic analysis. Weber's anatomy of the diversity of social groups potentially involved in enabling the value and function of money is useful to this project if only to provide an idea of what such a social configuration might look like. Even more valuable is his account of the broad range of means, both coercive and normative, these (broadly speaking) economic actors had at their disposal.[25] This helps place money and monetary exchange in the broad context of social relations and social action. For Weber, economic activity within society consists largely in establishing the social facts of what he terms *Verfügungsgewalt,* a right to control or dispose of resources, human or otherwise. Money, as a "means of payment," is a special case of such a right, providing a guarantee (by law or custom) that it may be exchanged for resources in the future. Money, in this sense, is a technology of power.[26] Not surprisingly, Weber was particularly attracted to Knapp's *State Theory*—"one of the greatest masterpieces of German literary style and scientific acumen"—with its stress on money's roots in contract and debt and on the role of the state's coercive power in defining it.[27]

---

23. This is probably the time to admit that I am a grandson of the sociologist Talcott Parsons, whose generally Weberian "social-relations theory" I imbibed more or less with my mother's milk. The reader will have to make his or her own judgment as to how well it fits the phenomena discussed in this book.

24. See Werner Sombart, *Der moderne Kapitalismus: Historisch-systematische Darstellung des gesamteuropäischen Wirtschaftslebens von seinen Anfängen bis zur Gegenwart,* 3rd ed., 3 vols. (Leipzig: Duncker & Humblot, 1919).

25. For what follows, see especially Max Weber, *Economy and Society,* ed. Guenther Roth and Claus Wittich, 2 vols. (Berkeley: University of California Press, 1968) 1:63–211.

26. Weber's analysis also implies that money will mean different things to different social groups or in different social contexts, an insight that has been followed up by more recent sociologists, particularly Viviana Zelizer, in *The Social Meaning of Money* (New York: Basic Books, 1994), and subsequent work.

27. Weber, *Economy,* 179.

Money is at least partially fungible with other forms of social power—not just economic ones, like productive potential, but physical force, political authority, social prestige, and cultural influence. This could be a source of legitimacy—Giacomo Todeschini has argued, for example, that late-medieval Francisans thought that money was a positive force in society precisely when it could be controlled by and serve to confirm an existing Christian social order—but more often it was a source of profound social anxiety, as it threatened to dissolve or transform all other comparable relations. Perhaps the best anatomist of that ambiguity was the turn-of-the-century German philosopher and sociologist Georg Simmel.[28] To oversimplify a complex argument, Simmel sees money as essentially a symbolic externalization of the quality of value, which is originally a private, psychological phenomenon. Over time, he suggests, the phenomenon of money reshapes both the societies and the psychological processes that gave it birth. Becoming itself ever more abstract and dissociated from individual commodities and physical forms (gold, coins, etc.), it encourages a detached, calculating attitude akin to but broader than Weber's capitalist rationality. While money supplants the embodied human as the measure of all things, Simmel is inclined to see gain as well as loss in this process: it brings, relatively to its absence, a comprehensible society, a universal outlook, and an increase in individual autonomy.

What Simmel (unlike Weber) tended to neglect was the fact that, as a key—in modern societies, arguably *the* key—technology of power, money is implicated in and relies on all other manifestations and institutions of power. That is why control of the currency is inseparable from modern governance; it is also why money has profound intellectual and cultural dimensions. This is not a unique insight: literary critics, for example, have been increasingly sensitive to it for some years now, inspired in part by French theorists' explorations of the homologies among economic, linguistic, sexual, and other systems of exchange.[29] My project, though, is more straightforward: I trace an outline of the vast web of primarily noneconomic (or not primarily economic) structures within which French Renaissance money operated and on which it depended for its existence. The administrative, intellectual, and political aspects of monetary regulation were connected to law enforcement and cultural production by the fact that regulation, enforcement, and culture alike helped create, preserve, or restore money as an effective social force. All helped control it when it threatened to overwhelm other forms of social

---

28. See Georg Simmel, *The Philosophy of Money*, trans. Tom Bottomore, David Frisby, and Kaethe Mengelberg, 2nd ed. (London: Routledge, 1990).

29. This will be discussed in detail in chapters 2 and 6.

relation and identity. Each, to some degree, relied on the others to accomplish those tasks.

The Structure of the Argument

No single narrative will encapsulate this complex structure of ideas and practices: there is no one chronological story that this book sets out to tell. It is organized in a series of interrelated essays, centered on the different ways in which the operation of the currency was governed. The book begins with governmental institutions, which constituted the most basic technology by which currency was created and regulated. From there it moves to the ideological and practical considerations that shaped policy within those institutions but also within the larger governing class. Covering the first two-thirds of the book, this section is largely an account of how political elites responded to a range of challenges raised by the currency and how they in turn used the currency to further their own projects of governance. The last third of the book takes a broader social perspective, looking at engagement with the currency through the lenses of criminality and literature. Though here money played a metaphorical role in reflections on social order, it still proved to be inseparable from royal governance; writers may not have felt much freer of state control than did the counterfeiters to whom they compared themselves.

The first chapter examines the institutional structure of control over coinage and precious metals in France in the second half of the sixteenth century. Though coinage was overseen by the royal council, which made most executive decisions, day-to-day control was vested in the Cour des Monnaies, which administered, audited, and disciplined the mints and their workers, regulated goldsmiths and other craftsmen in precious metals, enforced laws against tampering with the coinage, and advised the royal council on policy. Particularly under King Henri II (r. 1547–1559) it increased substantially in size, power, and prestige, weathering a number of attacks and scandals, and its members remained individually and collectively influential into the seventeenth century. The second chapter turns to intellectual history, arguing that the dominant understanding of money in sixteenth-century France was Aristotelian, seeing it as the inevitable but dangerous and destabilizing product of commerce between households and polities, constantly threatening to inflate and unchain the illegitimate ambitions of nobles and commoners alike.

The third and fourth chapters cover the history of French monetary policy from the accession of Henri II to the assassination of Henri IV as successive governments confronted the Great Inflation and the increasing damage that the Wars of Religion inflicted on the currency and on centralized control of the coinage. Despite some shortcomings, the government's responses were frequently creative, effective, and broadly supported, belying the common portrayal of the early modern French government as weak and tightly constrained in its actions. This was a function of the institutional development already portrayed, but it was also supported by a developing discourse of expertise and technical mastery over this dangerous force, as well as a dawning understanding of the radical modernity of a world populated by autonomous, commercial sovereignties. Indeed, one of the most interesting aspects of this story is the tight dialectic it reveals between the way money was theorized and the ways the government managed it.

The Cour des Monnaies' law enforcement activities, which form the subject of chapter 5, were equally popular. They also revealed tantalizing details of the seldom-studied underworld of coiners and counterfeiters, a picaresque criminal elite of skilled but desperate craftsmen, crooked merchants, and marginal nobles from as far afield as Spain and Italy. Such criminality made real all the contemporary fears of the artificial and unstable nature of money, its involvement in social ambition and avarice, and its dangerous links to the heart of royal sovereignty. In the sixth and final chapter, I argue that French literature down to the 1630s frequently thematized the social danger of money, particularly when it dealt with social mobility—which in practice was usually facilitated by the purchase of royal office, a method of turning the fruits of avarice to the uses of ambition that proved as ineradicable as it was unpopular. Writers from the age of Henri II through the first years of the seventeenth century tended to stress the role of money and precious metals as both expressions and synecdoches of royal or even divine majesty. In the half century that followed the death of Henri IV, though, monetary themes became the province of comic and libertine writers such as Pierre Corneille, Tristan l'Hermite, and Charles Sorel, who flourished in the reign of Louis XIII (1610–1643), and their successors, such as Molière and Antoine Furetière, under Louis XIV (r. 1643–1715). Their focus was on the dangers and instability of money, often presented in a context of disguise, counterfeit, and the satirical exchange that the French call "monkey money" (*monnaie de singe*).

Concluding with literary analysis serves as a reminder that money was meaningful only insofar as it responded to the needs, desires, and anxieties of individuals in concrete situations. Currency in early modern Europe was not just a technology by which authorities sought to govern populations or render them amenable to government but (outside of vague pieties like peace, justice, and religion) the element of governance most consistently in demand by the population at large. Nor was this simply a matter of economic pragmatism: in theoretical and literary reflections, in the statements of local officials and crime victims alike, currency appears as a favored site of governmental intervention to order and regulate social relations. People were often dissatisfied with actual government policies in those areas, but all agreed that active, centralized governance was required. Money might well be the root of all evil, a profoundly dangerous technology that promoted the individual's worst instincts and dissolved the sacred bonds of society, but it also, and more powerfully, represented the possibility of collective political action to produce harmony, stability, and justice.

CHAPTER 1

The Cour des Monnaies

> The memory of the reasons for its suppression were
> still fairly recent, and one had not forgotten about the
> adventure of Pinatel who, having had light doubles and
> pennies struck under color of a commission obtained
> from the Chamber of the Generals of the Moneys by
> underhanded means in 1552, was convicted of hav-
> ing stolen very considerable sums—including fifty
> thousand livres given to a lady to get himself pardoned,
> which were enough to defer his execution but not to
> spare him from it.
>
> —Jean de Colenges

In 1581 Jean de Colenges, president of a royal
court in Villefranche-de-Rouergue, attempted to reestablish the long-suppressed
mint of his small, remote town in the South of France, only to be thwarted by
the queen mother, Catherine de Médicis.[1] She, like him, remembered all too
well the incident he mentioned, which was, if not the most damaging, perhaps
the most disgraceful misfortune to befall the French currency in the sixteenth
century. That scandal, already a bit obscure though far from forgotten after
thirty years, may seem an odd place to begin an investigation of the entire practical and cultural system of money. But it is in fact as revealing as it was colorful.
By studying a case in which the system that regulated the coinage failed utterly,
we can get an understanding of the practical challenges that system faced and
of the experience and reasoning behind both the structure of that system and
various attempts to reform it.

---

1. Jean de Colenges, *Mémoires* (Rodez: Société des Lettres, 2011), 38: "La mémoire estoit encore
assès récente de la cause de la suppression, et on ne l'avoit pas oublié l'avanture de Pinatel, lequel, en
vertu d'une commission obtenu sous main de la chambre des généraux des monnoyes en 1552, ayant
fait forger des doubles et deniers faibles, fut convaincu d'avoir desrobé des sommes très considérables,
dont cinquante mille livres, donnés à une dame pour luy faire obtenir sa grâce, eurent bien le pouvoir
de différer son supplice mais non pas de l'en garantir." The memoirist was incorrect on almost every
point of detail in this brief account. My thanks to Orest Ranum for this citation.

Among other things, this incident dramatized a fundamental problem of governing or controlling money. As a social construct, money can be created, but if individuals are able to create it at will, it is in danger of becoming economically worthless and socially meaningless. The process of coining, which abstracted and partially detached monetary value from the commodity value of gold and silver, was a fertile ground for such issues. No one could count on the powerful operations of coining always being carried out with perfect integrity and disinterestedness, so the social control of money had to begin very practically with control of the mints. Given the limited technical and institutional resources of early modern European governments and the rapid expansion of the cash nexus in the Renaissance period, that control was necessarily imperfect, but it admitted many degrees of imperfection. It also admitted a number of different strategies. Minting might be centralized in a single location for better supervision or be contracted out to private enterprise and subjected to market discipline—both were attempted in England. Or minting could be integrated with the process of mining, as the Spanish did in Peru or various German princes did in east-central Europe, which worked well enough to give German thalers and Spanish reals circulation throughout the West. France, which was large, geographically diverse, and generally lacking in mines, could not practically adopt any of those systems. Instead, it possessed a dozen or so mints at any time, spread through the country and supervised from Paris. It was a real question whether this could be made to work.

The Pinatel Affair

It was widely assumed that what we now call corruption—self-interested violation of broadly accepted norms of official conduct—was common among the magistrates of early modern Europe. But details tend to be sparse, and historians have not done as much as they might to clarify an inherently murky subject.[2] That very murkiness, however, as frustrating as it is, is a vital element of the nature of corruption. Corruption is at least formally illegal,

---

2. On public opinion concerning judicial corruption in the first third of the seventeenth century (when, seemingly, little had changed since the mid-sixteenth century), see Jeffrey Sawyer, "Judicial Corruption and Legal Reform in Early Seventeenth-Century France," *Law and History Review* 6 (1988): 95–117. On the general neglect of corruption by historians of the French old regime, see the polemical but not unjust remarks of Jean-Claude Waquet, *Corruption: Ethics and Power in Florence, 1600–1770*, trans. Linda McCall (University Park: Pennsylvania State University Press, 1992), 1–18. The only explicit discussion I know of corruption and the law in old-regime France is Maryvonne Génaux, "La corruption avant la lettre: La vocabulaire de la déviance public dans l'ancien droit pénal," *Révue historique de droit français et étranger* 81 (2003): 15–32.

and an elementary sense of self-preservation will suggest that its perpetrators leave as few written traces of their activities as possible. This is a general problem in the historical study of criminality, but in the case of corruption it is compounded by the fact that such criminality is generally interior to the state apparatus charged with suppressing it and with recording that suppression. This tended to make corruption less likely to be caught than many other crimes, but it also tended to make even prosecuted cases exceedingly murky. Corruption accusations could easily be trumped up wholly or in part in ways subsequently impossible to disentangle. To take a famous example, not just in spite but largely because of a massive trial record, we will never know the full truth about Sir Francis Bacon's alleged crimes.[3]

And even if properly detected and punished, corruption might be minimized both publicly and in the official record. For corruption is, as Jean-Claude Waquet has put it, "the fragility of the state," and states are disinclined to admit weakness.[4] This was all the more true in old-regime France, where the state as a whole had only modest coercive powers, resting to a large extent on the uncertain and intangible pillars of prestige and symbolism; at the same time the many component bodies of which the monarchy was composed engaged in a vicious, high-stakes competition for their own status and symbolic capital, all of which could be put in jeopardy by the public humiliation of a scandal. The authorities' desire to repress corruption therefore struggled with an impulse to deny or conceal it, and even proceedings designed for public display could simultaneously operate as partial cover-ups. All of this was at work in the Pinatel scandal, which means that the story that comes down to us has a certain number of gaps but also that those gaps themselves are informative about the weaknesses and sensitivities of the governmental systems in question.

The scandal touched both provincial mints and the central administration in Paris, but we are better informed about the former than the latter. The greatest detail concerns the small, isolated mint of Villefranche-de-Rouergue, where efforts to bring the culpable to justice were most intense. Villefranche was not a typical mint in that it was not located in a major commercial center (like nearby Toulouse, for example, which had a mint of its own); instead, it was one of a small group of mints that existed to serve specialized economic or political needs. Villefranche was the center of France's small silver-mining industry, and it is probably not coincidental that the other special-purpose mints (Villeneuve-les-Avignon, which existed to recoin money from the

---

3. See on this question Lisa Jardine and Alan Stewart, *Hostage to Fortune: The Troubled Life of Francis Bacon* (New York: Hill and Wang, 1999).

4. This is the title of the concluding chapter of Waquet, *Corruption.*

papal Comtat Venaissin; Chambéry, capital of a region briefly conquered from the duke of Savoy; and Morlaas, not technically in France but serving the rump client kingdom of Navarre and run by Frenchmen on the French model) were all deeply touched by the corruption scandal.[5] Because of their size and location, these towns were difficult to supervise, while their tight elites allowed cultures of impunity to develop with relative ease.

Villefranche, at least, also seems to have had trouble attracting high-quality personnel. When its longtime master Jehan de Pomeyrol (himself not a man entirely above suspicion) left in 1528 to take charge of Morlaas, he was replaced by a series of substitutes working for one Jehan Blanc, whose tenure ended abruptly in 1535 when, it seems, he was arrested and ultimately condemned to be burned to death for incest with his mother- (or perhaps sister-) in-law.[6] Blanc's replacement was Pierre Colom, a member of a large local clan that had long been deeply involved with the mint.[7] According to later testimony, from about 1542 on, he and his associates turned to large-scale looting.[8] They minted huge quantities of small change well below the required weight and alloy. To keep doing this, the conspirators relied on intimidation of the other mint officers, on cooperative merchants who would pass the bad coin at some distance from Villefranche, and, initially, on the collusion of the local "subsidiary general" of the moneys, one Robin. These officers, resident in various provinces far from Paris, were supposed to bring the authority of the Chambre des Monnaies closer to where the action was. In fact, by leaving them isolated with no institutional support or norms, this system seems to have made them liable to what might politely be called

---

5. There is a detailed historical study of the Villefranche mint: Urbain Cabrol, *Histoire de l'atelier monétaire royal de Villefranche-de-Rouergue* (Villefranche: Société Anonyme d'Imprimerie, 1913).

6. See Etienne Cabrol, *Annales de Villefranche de Rouergue*, 2 vols. (Villefranche: Imprimerie de veuve Cestan, 1860), 1:620–21: "Jeanne Vedelle mère d'Orable Briansonne estant prevenuës de crime d'inceste et autres deshonnestes malversations en paillardise, et fille lubrique, pour avoir malversé avec Jean Blanc jadis maistre particulier de la monnoye en la présente ville lequel fut condamné à estre bruslé et exécuté, qui avoit épousé auparavant une autre fille de la ditte Jeanne de Vedel, laquelle avoit fait briser portes de la prison, feurent bannies et leurs biens confisquez en 1542 le 28 juin." This volume seems to reproduce a late sixteenth- or early seventeenth-century calendar of the city archives.

7. The following is drawn from AN, Z^{1B} 678, piece dated 26 August 1557 (a series of depositions— most significantly by Beraud Dozolet, former *contregarde* of the Villefranche mint—labeled on the back "Jugement secret pour estre presente a treshonore seigneur monsieur latony conseiller & president en la court de parlement de tholoze"). How this wound up in the archives of the Cour des Monnaies is unclear; by 1557 that body played no part in the criminal prosecution of this affair. On the Colom brothers (who, during a visitation of the plague, had once moved the mint lock, stock, and barrel to one of their country properties), see Cabrol, *Atelier*, passim.

8. This was also the story told by sometime mint master Antoine du Rieu in his letters of remission: AN, Z^{1B} 38, fol. 288, published in Cabrol, *Atelier*, 271–77.

"regulatory capture"; this was even more true of the on-site mint supervisors (especially the *gardes*), who were closely linked to the masters.

Colom made thorough and ingenious use of these inbred structures. After a period of alternating the lease of the Villefranche mint with his coconspirator, Antoine de Rieu, he handed it over to a straw man, "a certain Maître Anthoine Pojery, master pedagogue of Colom's brother." When an official of the Paris Monnaies visited in 1544, the mint temporarily went back to producing honestly. Two years later, when the president of the Chambre des Monnaies, Loys Vachot, arrived, the conspirators "spoke slightingly of the said president and the other generals [as the members of the Chambre were called], saying that as soon as they arrived and began any proceeding, they were stopped with a big purse full of money."[9] This corrupt relationship continued and flourished: the conspirators could well afford bribery, since by an informed account their operation cleared on the order of twenty-four thousand livres a year (which was, by way of comparison, double the salary of a provincial governor, a vital office generally held by members of the very highest nobility).[10] In fact, the governor of Guyenne, Henri II d'Albret, king of Navarre, became suspicious of the goings-on in Villefranche.[11] It was perhaps at his instance that proceedings were brought against some of the Colom gang in Toulouse and maybe also in Paris. But, through Vachot's good offices, the conspirators managed to have them quashed.[12]

It is not coincidental that the Villefranche mint moved from retail dishonesty to wholesale fraud during the unhappy final years of François I's life, when the 1541 disgrace of the constable Anne de Montmorency was followed by a revival of the Habsburg-Valois wars.[13] This was a period when oversight slackened, royal finances were even more disastrous than usual, and

---

9. Ibid., fols. 3v, 6v: "ung nome me anthoine pojery maistre padagogue de frere dudict colom"; "se moquoyent dudict president et dautres generaulx disant que si tost quilz estoyent arrives et commencoyent faire quelque procedure que avec une grosse bourse dargent lon les assomoyt Et ne y veoyent plus pour y prendre."

10. For the figure of twelve thousand livres for a governor's *plat*, see David Potter, "A Treason Trial in Sixteenth-Century France: The Fall of Marshal du Biez, 1549–51," *English Historical Review* 105 (1990): 611.

11. The Rouergue was under the governorship of Guyenne: for a map and for Henri II d'Albret (king of Navarre)'s tenure of the governorship, see Robert Harding, *Anatomy of a Power Elite: The Provincial Governors of Early Modern France* (New Haven: Yale University Press, 1978), 30, 223.

12. See AN, Z[1B] 63, fols. 267v–269v: "Lettres patentes . . . pour faire le proces de michel amat et aultres officiers de la monnoye de villefranche en Rouergue," evoking the trial of another of Colom's straw men from the Parlement of Toulouse to the Chambre des Monnaies. The 1557 deposition mentions proceedings in the Parlement of Paris, but it might well be mistaken.

13. On the political background of this period, see R. J. Knecht, *Renaissance Warrior and Patron: The Reign of Francis I* (Cambridge: Cambridge University Press, 1994), 478–560.

factional politics flourished in expectation of a new reign. And the loss of control over the mints seemed to become general. In 1542, the king issued a pardon ("letters of remission") to a man named Jacques Pinatel, who, while master of a mint at the small town of Crémieu, had "through ignorance, evil counsel, or otherwise, committed various crimes and malversations in the debasement and deformation of our moneys, and other infractions, even escaping and breaking out of the prison where he had been made prisoner, for which he was again made prisoner and tried on those charges."[14] Simultaneously, Pinatel took up the farm of the new mint of Chambéry, the capital of recently conquered Savoy.[15] The Chambre des Monnaies refused to approve the lease, and Pinatel was left to wait for a more sympathetic audience. This he did not receive until François I died and his son, Henri II, came to the throne. At that point the Monnaies registered new letters of remission specifically allowing him to hold the lease of mints, "but under the condition," as an attached paper noted, "that the Chamber should bear in mind and record in its registers that he may never be appointed or received in the estate of a president or general of the said moneys."[16] This reservation, however, apparently did not apply to Pinatel's brother, also named Jacques, who was already or soon became a general and proved entirely capable of upholding the family tradition of flagrant dishonesty.[17] And at about the same time,

---

14. AN, Z[1B] 483, dossier dated 19 January 1548, piece no. 3 (letters of remission of 30 September 1548 in favor of Jacques Pinatel): "auroit par ignorence maulvays conseil ou autrement commis aulcunes faulte & malversation en billongnaiges difformations de noz monnoyes et aultres cas mesmement evader & brise les prisons ou il feust pour raison de ce constitue prisonnier dont de rechef il fust emprisonne & sur iceulx cas son proces faict." The Crémieu mint, supposedly abolished in 1540, actually ceased production in 1551. See Blanchet and Dieudonné, *Manuel* 2:402. The 1542 letters referred to here were registered by then general Gabriel Chicot while he was on commission and do not survive. They were never recorded in the court's registers, as they ought to have been. Pinatel had been a *maître particulier* in a number of mints in the Midi in the 1530s. See F. de Saulcy, *Histoire numismatique du règne de François I, roi de France* (Paris: Librairie numismatique C. van Peteghem, 1876), 224–25.

15. The Chambéry mint was opened by letters patent of 5 June 1542. See AN, Z[1B] 63, fols. 267v–269v.

16. Ibid., piece no. 4 (conclusions of the *procureur général*): "A la charge toutesfoys quil soit reserve in mente de la chambre et enregistre en icelle quil ne pourra a jamais estre pourveu ne receu a lestat de president ou general des monnoyes."

17. That the Jacques Pinatel referred to in the letters of remission was the brother of the general of the moneys I infer from a reference in a deposition by one of his colleagues, Sebastien de Riberolles, who refers to his having acted improperly to obtain for his brother a position as mint master. AN, Z[1B] 485, piece dated 22 June 1554, fol. 4. It is not completely impossible that the Jacques were in fact the same, but it seems more likely that they just had unimaginative parents, as did their almost exact contemporaries, the brothers Jehan du Tillet (bishop of Meaux and clerk of the Parlement of Paris—the latter had a civil suit in the Grand Conseil while Pinatel was being tried there: see AN, V[5] 39, piece dated 10 July 1554) and the two brothers Pierre Colom. No record survives of when Pinatel was appointed to the Monnaies.

in the summer of 1549, we find the generals Simon Radin and Charles le
Prevost being sent to Grenoble (not far from Crémieu and Chambéry) to
investigate large-scale production of underweight coin.[18] A year later, Alexandre de la Tourette and Antoine de la Primaudaye were investigating similar
matters in Marseilles.[19]

The effects of all this malfeasance, aggravating and aggravated by the
inflation then beginning to make itself felt in Europe, eventually did catch
the king's attention. As early as 1543, complaints arose about the excessive
quantity of small change presented to the royal tax receivers—coins of no
use to the foreign mercenaries France needed to hire in order to pursue its
foreign wars.[20] Little was done, however, until 1549. At that point the new
king undertook a preliminary centralizing measure—namely, the elimination
of the provincial generals, who had proven themselves worse than useless.[21]
As early as June 1549, the master of the Chambéry mint had been arrested
by order of the chancellor (who, as the head of the judicial system, oversaw the Chambre des Monnaies).[22] That winter, King Henri undertook to
close all but twelve of France's mints, eliminating among others the mints
of Chambéry, Villefranche, and Villeneuve-lès-Avignon.[23] But most of the
closed mints reopened within a few months as local interests brought pressure to bear on Paris.

Thus, it was in a context of gradually appearing chaos, criminality, and
inflation that Henri II decided, beginning in the winter of 1549–1550, to
proceed dramatically with the policy of centralization and of strengthening the supervisory Chambre des Monnaies. In the short run, at least, this
was exactly the wrong idea, since the Monnaies itself was a large part of

18. See AN, Z[1B] 537, piece dated 16 August 1549 (documents on a quarrel with the sovereign
courts of Grenoble concerning that mission). Another royal command of the same date had ordered
the generals "informer contre les maistres des monnoies du royaulme sur louvrage par eulx faict de
xxii[ains] eschars de loy & de poix, liards, doubles & petis tournois." AN, Z[1B] 64, fol. 26.

19. See AN, Z[1B] 537, piece dated 10 September 1550 (letters patent of that date).

20. See Philippe Hamon, L'argent du roi: Les finances sous François Ier (Paris: Comité pour l'Histoire
Economique et Financière de la France, 1994), 80–81. Hamon may well be wrong in supposing that
the situation had not degraded much since 1538: a flood of poor coin would, by Gresham's law, push
gold out of circulation, at least where, as in the royal tax offices, both types passed at their nominal
values in the money of account.

21. See AN, Z[1B] 64, fols. 48v–49v (letters patent of early March 1550, "Suppression des generaulx subsidiaires").

22. See AN, Z[1B] 37, 26 June 1549. The case was reported by Vachot and Philippe de Lauthier.

23. See AN, Z[1B] 64, fols. 1v–3r ("Lettres pour clorre les monnoyes de france"); and 6r–8r
("Lettres patentes de louverture des douze monnoyes de ce royaulme"). The mints to be retained
were Paris, Rouen, Lyons, Poitiers, la Rochelle, Bayonne, Montpellier, Dijon, Troyes, Grenoble,
Marseilles, and Rennes.

the problem. The behavior of President Vachot and of the general Jacques Pinatel, in particular, seems to have become ever more brazen. They began to loot the Paris mint, with Pinatel forcing its master to buy silver at an elevated price, "threatening, if he did not do so, to so impede him that . . . he would not have dared disobey him," while Vachot would simply walk in and take "sometimes ten écus or ten *testons* [large silver coins], and he said that it was to show the king, and he never brought any of them back," to a total of five or six hundred livres.[24] When the mint of Villeneuve reopened in October 1552, Pinatel was in the area, and as it later developed, he gave the master, one Jehan Chantal, permission to coin small change, though the Monnaies, smelling a rat, had refused to receive the royal letters patent Chantal had presented. Pinatel then proceeded to Villefranche, where he further obstructed the developing case against the officers of that mint.[25]

At this point, however, something happened. Even those members of the Monnaies not personally implicated in corrupt activities must have been aware of them; Chantal was accused of having "organized an assembly of some of the generals in Paris at the house of the said Pinatel or of . . . President Vachot, to have the said letters verified outside of the said court."[26] Still, they were presumably reluctant to pursue the matter vigorously, both because of their personal interest in the court's reputation and because Loys Vachot had the power to make their lives miserable. But with royal attention focusing on monetary affairs (especially after the very active 1552 military campaigning season came to an end), and with matters going from bad to worse, some action became unavoidable. When it came, it was decisive. The generals of the moneys chose not to record the details of the sordid affair, but a few traces remain. On 3 January 1553, after

> having heard . . . the report and declaration made in the said court by Maître Loys Vachot, president therein, on his return from Lyons, who had declared that Maître Jacques Pinatel had given the master of the mint of Villeneuve-St.-André-lès-Avignon permission to make

---

24. AN, Z[1B] 485, piece dated 22 June 1554 (deposition of Sébastien de la Riberolles, a general of the moneys who had previously been master of the Paris mint), fols. 3r: "le menassant sil faisoit le contraire de le fascher tellement quil . . . ne luy eust ose desobeyr"; 6v: "quelques fois dis escus dix testons et disoit que cestoit pour monstrer au Roy et nen rapportoit jamais rien."

25. See AN, Z[1B] 487, piece dated 28 May 1558 (arrêt of that date); and AN, Z[1B] 38, fol. 132 (arrêt of 11 October 1552, "contre les officiers de la monnoye de Villefranche de Rouergue & Pierre Robert"), which referred the case brought from Toulouse to Pinatel.

26. AN, Z[1B] 487, piece dated 3 May 1558 (interrogatory of Jehan Chantal): "Enquis sil se fiest une assemblee daucuns desdicts generaulx a paris en la maison dudict pinatel ou du . . . president vachot pour veriffier lesdictes lettres du xxiiie nov. hors le lieu de ladicte court."

doubles and small pennies, and having also examined certain letters missive sent by the said Pinatel for that purpose, and the report of the beadle [*huissier*] Dain, the said court has ordained and ordains that the said Pinatel will be denied entry to the court and its bureau, and will have no deliberative voice in the proceedings begun in the said court concerning small change against the officers of Villefranche and Villeneuve until the king or the court orders otherwise.[27]

On the sixteenth, the Monnaies ordered production stopped at Villeneuve and sent Alexandre de la Tourette and Joseph du Maignet to make sure its orders were obeyed.[28] On the twenty-second, they obtained a royal ordinance removing the small change of Villefranche and Villeneuve from circulation.[29]

When Pinatel returned and heard all this, he did not take it well: "Rising in anger from the bar, he said and offered these and similar words: 'I would that this Chamber be abolished, if it cost me [the substantial sum of] a thousand écus and my office,' and that he would avenge himself for what had been said about him, and that it was very wrong to have advised that the doubles be cried down, and that he would burn his books if he could not have them put back in circulation" (the "doubles" were the small coins that had recently been demonetized).[30] Unsurprisingly, Pinatel was immediately barred from the court. The king must then have demanded some answers, for in April 1553, he sent Claude Bourgeois, a councillor in the Grand Conseil—another Parisian sovereign court with a broad jurisdiction and close ties to the central organs of royal governance—into the South to investigate.[31] Later, he commissioned Jehan d'Auvason, a president in that court, and Réné Baillet, a

---

27. AN, Z¹ᴮ 38, fol. 137r: "avoir oy par la court le rapport & declaration faicte en ladicte court par me Loys de Vachot president en icelle a son retour de lyon qui a declare me Jacques pinatel avoyr baille au me de la monnoye de Villeneufve sainct andre les avignon permission de faire doubles & petitz deniers tz Et apres avoyr aussy veu certains lettres missives a ceste fin envoyees par ledict pinatel & proces verbal de lhuissier dain Ladicte court a ordonne & ordonne que lentree & bureau dicelle sera deffendue audict pinatel et naura aulcune voix deliberative es proces introduictz en ladicte court sur les menuz ouvraiges contre les officiers de Villefranche & Villeneufve jusques ad ce que par le roy ou ladicte court aultrement en soyt ordonne."

28. AN, Z¹ᴮ 368, pieces dated 16 January 1552 (arrêts of that date).

29. See AN, Z¹ᴮ 64, fols. 157v–158r ("Ordonnance du descry des doubles & petitz tournois a la petite croix faictz nouvellement").

30. AN, Z¹ᴮ 368, piece dated 20 February 1552: "soy levant en collere du bureau A dict & profere telles & semblables parolles Je vouldroys quil meust couste mils escuz et mon office que ladicte chambre fust suprimee Et quil se vangeroit des propoz que lon avoit tenuz de luy Et que lon avoit grand tort davoir baille advis du descry des doubles Et quil brusleroit ses livres ou quil feroit remectre la cours diceulx."

31. See AN, Z¹ᴮ 368, piece dated 9 April 1553 (commission of that date for Claude Bourgeois).

president in the Parlement of Paris, the most powerful and prestigious court in France, to prosecute offenders in the sovereign courts of Paris.[32]

By the summer of 1554, Vachot was a prisoner, on trial at the Grand Conseil along with Pinatel, de Lauthier, Radin, Guy Bedant, and Alexandre Faucon.[33] On 24 September 1554, the Grand Conseil issued its verdict, which does not survive, though other documents make its outlines fairly clear. Bedant and Faucon were exonerated, but the others were convicted, deprived of their offices, and doubtless subjected to other penalties as well.[34] Pinatel, for whom such behavior ran in the family, had already broken out of jail and fled.[35] More important for the surviving members of the court and for the French monetary administration as a whole, Pinatel seemed to have made good on his threat to bring down the court if it cost him his office: the Grand Conseil strongly recommended that the Monnaies be dissolved and its responsibilities transferred elsewhere. Their view was that the French monetary administration, and the king's policy toward it, had faced a major test and had failed.

The Sovereignty of the Moneys

To understand the nature of that test and its ultimate outcome, we must return to the set of initially ineffective reforms, to which we have already alluded, early in the reign of Henri II.[36] They began rather unremarkably

---

32. See AN, V⁵ 39, pieces dated 28 August 1554 and 3 October 1554 (procedural arrêts from the case of Béranger Portail). It was a matter of sometimes bitter dispute whether the Parlement or the Grand Conseil had jurisdiction in cases of the potential destitution of royal officers: see Eduard Maugis, *Histoire du Parlement de Paris de l'avènement des rois Valois à la Mort de Henri IV*, 3 vols. (Paris: A. Picard, 1913–1916), 1:380–82. Including a prominent *parlementaire* like Baillet among the instructors of the case may have served to head off disputes on that head. No records appear to survive of the final results of their activities.

33. The registers of the Grand Conseil for this period do not survive, and the minutes from September 1554 are also missing, perhaps suspiciously. A few procedural pieces from before and after that month relate to the administration of the sequestered goods of Vachot, Pinatel, Lauthier, and Radin, while one demonstrates that one of the Colom brothers and a merchant from Villefranche had been detained, apparently as witnesses. AN V⁵ 39, piece dated 29 November 1554.

34. For Bedant and Faucon's exoneration, see AN, Z¹ᴮ 38, fol. 188r ("Arrest portant permission a messieurs de Bedante & Faulcon de exercer leurs estats en la court de ceans comme ils auroit accoustumez," 5 October 1554).

35. AN, Z¹ᴮ 487, piece dated 23 July 1558: "Inventaire des pieces & procedures faictes sur le brise de prison de me jacques pinatel nagueres general des monnoyes mises au greffe de la court des monnoyes par me claude bourgeois." A piece from the minutes of the Grand Conseil, AN, V⁵ 38, 22 June 1554, shows him failing to appear for a proceeding on that date.

36. The only discussion of these reforms that I know of, a very brief mention in Frederick Baumgartner, *Henry II, King of France* (Durham, NC: Duke University Press, 1988), 80–81 and 87–88, is incorrect in almost every particular.

with an "Edict and Ordinance on Monetary Affairs," dated 14 January 1550, the first since he had come to the throne more than two years earlier. The edict was innovative in several ways, notably in creating a new flagship gold coin for the kingdom—the *Henrique d'or*—which was to be adorned with the king's portrait and manufactured by a new mechanical process in a new mint on the Île de la Cité, in central Paris.[37] While that particular idea was not destined to have a great future—the Henrique d'or never really circulated, a victim of high costs and Gresham's law—the edict did demonstrate that Henri was determined to act energetically in controlling his coinage and in projecting his power and glory through it. A much less prominent but in the long run much more important aspect of his program was an attempt to shore up the jurisdiction of Chambre des Monnaies. Articles 10 and 22 of the 1550 edict reserved to the Monnaies, rather than local officials, the auditing of mints on the periphery of the kingdom (supposedly already implemented by an edict of 1540, which had not been followed in practice) and allowed the Monnaies to complete criminal trials even when its competence in a case was under appeal.

The Chambre des Monnaies at that point was a semiautonomous appendage of another body, the Chambre des Comptes of Paris, which audited the accounts of those elements of the royal government located in all but a few distant provinces of France.[38] Among the organizations that needed to be audited were the royal mints, and since this was a particularly specialized, laborious, and delicate task, it had gradually devolved onto a group of experts. Once constituted, that group had drawn to itself a number of additional duties, including trying counterfeiters whom the generals of the moneys (as they were termed) might come across in the course of their business and supervising changers, goldsmiths, and others who worked with coins and precious metals.[39] In January 1552, two years after his first monetary edict,

---

37. *Edict et ordonnance sur le faict des monoyes & nouvelle fabrication poids alloy & prix, ouverture & jugement des boettes d'icelles* (Paris: Pierre Haultin and Jean Dallier, 1550). On the so-called Monnaie des Etuves see below, chapter 3; for its opening, see AN, Z^{1B} 64, fols. 106r–108r ("Ouverture des engins de marilac").

38. The best summary description of the system of sixteenth-century fiscal courts (minus the Cour des Monnaies) is Martin Wolfe, *The Fiscal System of Renaissance France* (New Haven: Yale University Press, 1972), app. C (pp. 269–78). The provinces with their own Chambres des Comptes were Provence, Dauphiné, Burgundy, and Brittany: see Roger Doucet, *Les institutions du France au XVIe siècle*, 2 vols. (Paris: J. Picard, 1948), 1:192. The archives of the Paris Chambre des Comptes were entirely destroyed by a fire in 1776.

39. This distinctive character led to a certain amount of tension between the Chambre des Monnaies and its parent body. In February 1543, for example, their respective *procureurs du roi* exchanged rather bitter memorandums on the authority of the Chambre. See AN, Z^{1B} 63, fols. 31r–36v.

Henri II, apparently unsatisfied with its results, issued another edict "creating, establishing, and erecting" the "Chambre des Monnaies sitting at Paris into a sovereign and superior court and jurisdiction," removing it from and making it coequal with the Chambre des Comptes.[40]

This edict had broader implications than just emancipating the Chambre des Monnaies from what had become a somewhat anomalous tutelage. For this was not an isolated initiative: it was part of a substantial program to expand and centralize the French judicial and fiscal system. Aside from the elevation of the Chambre des Monnaies, the major elements of this program were the creation of intendants of finances to manage fiscal matters within the royal council; the creation of the *présidiaux*, a new layer of intermediate appellate courts; and measures to strengthen the authority of the Cour des Aides, which oversaw the revenues from royal property and certain indirect taxes.[41] These four major initiatives, along with a number of smaller ones, had two things in common. Their first (and from Henri's view probably more important) commonality was that they helped channel more money to the king's very aggressive military enterprises. The reform of the fiscal administration was clearly targeted at increasing revenue; in the case of the presidial courts the offices in them could be sold. The case of the Monnaies was more complex: several new offices (a second president and three generals) would be created and sold, existing officers would have to pay for their newfound prestige, and the king presumably hoped that the new arrangement would be more efficient at extracting whatever revenues were to be had from the currency.[42] This was a fine example of what Ranke called the *Primat der Außenpolitik*, the mechanism whereby the exigencies of foreign policy and of survival in a violent international system drove the internal development

---

40. *Edict du Roy pour la souvereineté de la Cour des monnoyes en l'annee 1551* (Paris: Jean Dalier, [1555]), 5: "avons cree erigé & estably, creons erigons & establissons par ces presentes. Nostredicte Chambre des monnoyes sceant a Paris en Cour & jurisdiction souveraine & superieure."

41. On the fiscal reforms and their logic, see Michel Antoine, *Le cœur de l'état: Surintendance, contrôle général et intendance des finances 1552–1791* (Paris: Fayard, 2003), 21–34. Little has been written about the *présidiaux*, but see Gaspard Zeller, *Les institutions de la France au XVIe siècle* (Paris: Presses universitaires de France, 1987), 175–77; and Doucet, *Les insitutions*, 1:264–70. On the Aides, see the "Edit sur la compétence et juridiction de la cour des aides" (March 1552), in *Recueil général des anciennes lois françaises, depuis l'an 420 jusqu'à la révolution de 1789*, ed. François-André Isambert et al., 29 vols. (Paris: Plon, 1821–1833), 13:264–68; and Maugis, *Histoire du Parlement*, 1:408–9.

42. By an edict of June 1552, the wages of the presidents of the Monnaies were raised to one thousand livres and of the generals to five hundred livres, for which the existing president would have had to pay about one thousand livres and the generals five hundred livres each (capitalizing at twenty years' purchase). AN, Z^{1B} 64, fols. 142r–143v.

of modern governments.[43] It is not really a coincidence that Henry VIII of England had reorganized his mint administration a few years earlier (in 1544), bringing it under the treasury bureaucracy precisely in search of funds for his foreign policy.[44]

But Henri II's reforms also had in common an element of centralization and rationalization that went beyond mere short-term fiscal expediency and contributed to making this, despite its relative brevity, one of the most important reigns of the old regime in terms of administrative development.[45] All three of the reforms mentioned were notable for establishing a more uniform administration throughout the kingdom and for extending the reach of the central government, whether judicial or administrative, more deeply into important localities. They were, in other words, *rationalizing* in the traditional sense of the term. This need not imply either that they *succeeded* in substantially rationalizing the French government or even that they were in any particularly conscious way intended to do so: simply, there was a tendency, whatever its source, in this direction. That tendency was both confirmed and diverted by the other important element of the reform of the Monnaies: its new status as a sovereign court.

Even at the time, it was not quite clear what the status of "sovereign" meant, though this bothered people remarkably little. On one level, it meant that appeals would lie only to the king himself in his Conseil Privé, the judicial instance of the royal council. For the Monnaies, which had already been part of a sovereign court, the practical implication of this fact was that its criminal sentences could (in theory) no longer be appealed to the Parlement of Paris. Much more important was the prestige that accrued to a sovereign court in a society that placed enormous value on symbolic capital. The very term suggested, in an undefined way, that such courts participated in royal sovereignty.[46] They were among those, as an eighteenth-century jurist put it,

---

43. For a clear discussion of this principle and its use in German historiography, see Brendan Simms, "The Return of the Primacy of Foreign Policy," *German History* 21 (2003): 275–91; for a recent application of this model to early modern France (which I by no means entirely endorse), see Thomas Ertman, *Birth of the Leviathan: Building States and Regimes in Medieval and Early Modern Europe* (Cambridge: Cambridge University Press, 1997), 91–110.

44. See C. E. Challis, ed., *A New History of the Royal Mint* (Cambridge: Cambridge University Press, 1992), 230–32; this was a prelude to Henry's debasements.

45. This aspect of Henri II's reign has been badly neglected by historians with the major exception of Michel Antoine, but for a reasonable overview of the reform process (which does not, however, mention the Monnaies), see Ivan Cloulas, *Henri II* (Paris: Fayard, 1985), 520–24.

46. The magistrates in the newly sovereign Cour des Monnaies did not, however, share the privilege of the Parlement of Paris of attending royal funerals in their red robes of office rather than in mourning, which symbolized the Parlement's dependence on the immortal Crown rather than the mortal king. See Ralph Giesey, *The Royal Funeral Ceremony in Renaissance France* (Geneva: Droz, 1960), 52–61.

"who represent the person of the king, and who *give judgment in the place of the prince's sacred duty*."[47] Sovereign courts also claimed extensive power to judge at equity rather than at law and to adjust criminal penalties arbitrarily.[48] And as the fact that their offices commanded a premium on the market attested, sovereign courts were simply prestigious.

In elevating the Cour des Monnaies to this status, then, Henri II was not only raising money for his wars and trying to strengthen his control over the far-flung system of mints but also (perhaps unintentionally, since the issue was not broached in the text of the edict) raising the currency to a central position within the mechanism of the Crown itself. For at least the next seventy-five years, as inflation persisted and the French government lurched from crisis to crisis, money and monetary policy retained the key role in the French state that the Cour des Monnaies' new position implied. Ultimately, the crisis of the Pinatel affair proved to be a passing one, and the institutions of the currency recovered and continued to develop, if without the clear direction they had had from 1540 to 1559. By the beginning of the seventeenth century they received in actuality at least a large measure of the respect and deference to which Henri II's reforms in principle entitled them. This was not, however, a simple or straightforward process—it was nearly twenty-five years before the generals of the moneys could feel secure in their sovereign status. Aside from the vagaries of individual actors, this insecurity and its eventual resolution resulted from the structure of the French government itself, and more particularly from the enormous challenges of managing an early modern currency.

Rebuilding the Monnaies

In the end, the logic of governmental centralization and rationalization won out over the shock of the corruption revealed in 1552, though this outcome was at least as dependent on contingent factors of chance and personality as it was on any broader logic of modernity. For Henri II showed more confidence in his reforms, and in the remaining generals of the moneys, than did

---

47. Claude-Joseph de Ferrière, quoted by Jacques Krynen, *L'idéologie de la magistrature ancienne* (Paris: N.R.F. Gallimard, 2009), 171: "les juges souverains, qui représentent la personne du roi, et qui *vice sacra Principis judicant*." Ferrière drew on a tradition extending far back into the Middle Ages.

48. On equity and arbitrary justice, see the extensive discussion in Krynen, *L'idéologie,* esp. 62–78 and 139–90; William Monter, *Judging the French Reformation: Heresy Trials by Sixteenth-Century Parlements* (Cambridge, MA: Harvard University Press, 1999), 17–24; and Bernard Schnapper, *Les peines arbitraires du XIIIe au XVIIIe siècle (doctrines savants et usages français)* (Paris: R. Pichon et R. Durand-Auzias, 1974), 54–61.

his Grand Conseil. This probably indicates a genuine commitment to the new order, but it was also a testament to the political skill of the Monnaies and particularly of the man who had obtained the newly created office of second president when the court was elevated to sovereign status, Alexandre de la Tourette.[49] Originally from Dauphiné, he had joined the court shortly before its elevation.[50] He took up the office of president in September 1553, about the time of Vachot's fall, but even before that his personal qualities had given him a leadership role in the court. Through much of the summer and fall of 1552, for example, he was engaged in the vital but unpleasant task of following the royal court around northern France—"it is an unbelievable effort and trouble to follow in this court now, and no one can understand it who does not try it," he wrote—waiting for the king to turn his attention to the Monnaies, the deteriorating currency, and the corruption eating away at both.[51] It is possible that he was himself not entirely immune to corruption: a decade later, he lost his office in a rather mysterious process.[52]

Whatever his personal failings, though—and he never suffered a conviction or long-term disgrace—he was an effective advocate. Aside from whatever hopes he may have had of managing the brewing scandal, de la Tourette's main business at court in 1552 was to bring the elevation of the Monnaies

---

49. Returning the Monnaies to its old status would not have cost the king any money, since the newly created offices had escheated to the Crown on the deprivation of their holders and would not have had to be reimbursed. Indeed, it might have saved some money, either in reduced overhead or from the possibility of later re-elevating the court and collecting the attendant revenue.

50. On what little is known of his background, see Marie-Noëlle Baudouin-Matuszek, "Un tour de France des généraux des monnaies (1556)," in *Etudes sur l'ancienne France offertes en hommage à Michel Antoine*, ed. Bernard Barbiche and Yves-Marie Bercé (Paris: Ecole des Chartes, 2003), 28.

51. AN, Z[1B] 368, piece dated 22 September 1552 (de la Tourette to the Monnaies from la Fère of that date, orig.): "cest peyne et enuy incredible de poursuyvre maintenant en ceste court, & nul ne le scaist que ne lessaye." Court business had been badly interrupted by the invasion of the Rhineland that summer.

52. The office of second president was suppressed and reimbursed by letters patent of 22 July 1564. The Monnaies at first asked the Chambre des Comptes *not* to register those letters. AN, Z[1B] 65, fol. 224v (19 July 1565). By March 27 it had changed course, asking the Comptes to proceed as it saw fit. Ibid., fol. 226r. It was not until 20 July 1567, however, that the Monnaies registered the letters and they took full effect. Ibid., fols. 247r–248r. De la Tourette seems to have been absent from the court for this entire period. While sixteenth-century kings regularly expressed a pious intention of suppressing some of the many offices they created, and while article 41 of the Edict of Orleans had established a procedure for it, to have it actually happen was almost unheard-of and requires some explanation—particularly since First President Jehan le Lieur's chronic absenteeism made de la Tourette's services helpful. Two not mutually exclusive possibilities suggest themselves. The first is that de la Tourette was eased out on suspicion of corruption; the second, that his financial condition required him to liquidate his office but that enemies somewhere prevented him from selling it on, which would likely have been more profitable. At any rate, he seems to have moved his permanent residence back to Grenoble at this point. De la Tourette's financial problems are discussed below.

into its full effect. He needed to complete the process of registering the edict of sovereignty, get the edict of creation of new offices and augmentation of salary approved, and more generally fight off the importunities of the Chambre des Comptes and of regional sovereign courts that had traditionally been outside the jurisdiction of Paris. He was ultimately successful in these attempts, which at least partially validated his claims to skill in court maneuvering, whether in just showing up at the right time and properly briefed (unlike the "gentlemen of the Comptes, rather inexperienced courtiers") or knowing how to judge the chancellor's mood or obtain an audience with the all-powerful constable.[53] In the fluid and personalized world of a sixteenth-century royal court, such skills were essential even—perhaps especially—for Parisian bureaucrats.

De la Tourette made a more significant appearance before the king's council two years later, along with his colleagues Joseph du Maignet and Jehan le Mestayer. There they sought not only to dissuade the king from following the Grand Conseil's advice that he "close the said Cour and Chambre des Monnaies for such time as shall please [His Majesty], and similarly deprive the said generals in perpetuity of their sovereignty and judgment in last resort" but literally to erase the stain that this call had left on the company. They asked "that the clause concerning that advice be removed and struck out from the said ruling and from the registers of the Conseil," a procedure traditionally imposed against decisions that the king felt were severely prejudicial to his own sovereignty. In the event, the royal council did not go that far, but by ruling "that the oral delivery made of it containing the said clause of closure and privation of sovereignty and last resort may not carry any note of infamy to the suppliants, but rather we intend that it is necessary to exempt them therefrom, and do exempt them, and have ordered and do order that the ruling be distributed without the clause containing the said advice," it acceded to the essentials of de la Tourette's request.[54]

---

53. AN, Z^{1B} 368, piece dated 22 September 1552: "lesdicts sieurs des comptes, assez nouveaulx courtisans." The other maneuvers are from a subsequent letter (la Tourette to the Monnaies from Villers-Côterets, 22 September 1552, orig.).

54. AN, Z^{1B} 64, fol. 200r (extrait des registres du conseil du roy, 28 September 1554): "clorre ladicte court & chambre des monnoyes pour tel temps que bon luy sembleroit Et pareillement de priver lesdicts generaulx a perpetuite de la souverainete & dernier ressort"; "que la clause concernant ledict advis fust rentree & rayee tant dudict arrest que des registres dudict conseil"; "que la prononciation verballe faicte dicelluy avec la clause contenante ladicte closture & privation de ladicte souverainté & dernier ressort ne puisse porter aulcune notte dynfamye ausdicts supplyans Ains entent que besoing seroit les en a exemptez & exempte Et a ordonné & ordonne que les arrestz seront expediez sans ladicte clause contenante ledict advis."

This was a complex transaction, in which all involved aggressively asserted their own honor and influence and, with the notable exception of the convicted officials, increased or maintained it. By successfully (and by the standards of the day, rapidly) concluding the case and by, in advising the dissolution of the Monnaies, offering authoritative counsel to the king on a matter directly touching his sovereignty, the Grand Conseil and the individual magistrates involved in its proceedings certainly raised their stature. By refusing that counsel, the king and his personal advisers maintained their own but without attacking the Grand Conseil in the way de la Tourette had suggested. By successfully opposing their own dissolution and by obtaining an emphatic statement that neither legal nor moral responsibility extended beyond the individuals convicted, the generals of the moneys preserved both their institution and their personal stake in it. And through the whole transaction Henri II maintained, if in a somewhat battered form, a set of initiatives about which he seems to have actually been serious. The minuet did not stop there, however, for the loss of confidence in the Monnaies was very real and did have to be addressed. So the king's final action in the affair was to appoint as Vachot's replacement at the head of the Monnaies Claude Bourgeois, the man who had overseen the investigation of the Monnaies in the Grand Conseil.

This caused a certain amount of trepidation in the court. De la Tourette took the view that he ought to be first president by right of seniority; more important, the court as a whole felt compelled to ask Bourgeois "if he had anything to say individually against any members of the body, or against the corporation." He replied "that as for himself, he holds the corporation and its members in good repute, and that if he felt otherwise he would not wish to join it."[55] That was, indeed, the genius of Bourgeois's appointment: by incorporating the Monnaies' main critic, it simultaneously disciplined and rehabilitated the court. The new first president brought with him a comprehensive internal regulation in the form of royal letters patent. Without being particularly innovative, the new regulations strongly underlined the need for the Monnaies to act corporately, requiring a quorum of seven

---

55. Ibid., fol. 210r ("Remonstrances fetes par la court de ceans A me Claude bourgeois premier president en icelle a la reception dudict estat," 19 March 1555): "sil avoit quelque chose a dire particullierement contre aulcuns du corps ou contre ledict corps Quil eust a le declarer Et aussi sil entendoit pas payer les droiz deubz a sadicte reception comme ont faict les autres presidens et conseillers de ladicte court. A dict quil nestoit tenu de respondre aux remonstrances sudictes Mais que de soy quil a la compaigne au corps & aux membres en bonne reputation et sil en sentoit autre chose quil ny vouldroit entrer."

members for most important actions, discouraging fraternization with mint officials, and raising the wages and hence the status of the attorneys who represented the Crown in the court. The regulation also restated with great emphasis the principle that only the king in council could authorize the minting of small change; and even if he did so, the Monnaies was urged to contact the council with any doubts. The preamble of the regulation stated, without unnecessary subtlety (but neatly associating the physical and institutional bases of the currency), that "it is most required and necessary that the state of our moneys and the officers established therein should be maintained and confirmed in such a state that, if possible, no corruption, alteration, or change should come about in them," and the court was certainly in no position to object.[56] The Pinatel affair thus ended as something of a triumph of royal state building: corruption had been repressed, and the institutional structure the king had laboriously built was preserved and strengthened.

By the time Henri II died prematurely in 1559, the Cour des Monnaies had surmounted the worst of its troubles and was reasonably well established in its sovereign status. In 1555, reaffirming his confidence in the court, the king had begun the process of forcing through registration of the edict of its sovereignty in the provinces traditionally outside the jurisdiction of the Paris Chambre des Comptes.[57] He had also promulgated an edict placing goldsmiths and other workers in precious metals throughout the kingdom under the jurisdiction of the Monnaies.[58] Predictably, the elevation of the Monnaies had also given rise to a general uncertainty as to its status within the hierarchies of government, and particularly precedence disputes with other bodies of Parisian magistrates: a royal decision of 1557 more or less

---

56. Ibid., fols. 217r–222r (letters patent given at Fontainebleau, March, 1555): "Il soyt tresrequis & necessaire que le faict de noz monnoyes & des officiers establys en icelles soit entretenu & conferme en tel estat que sil est possible il ny puisse advenir aulcune corruption alteration ou changement."

57. "Arrest du Conseil Privé du Roy, donné pour la Souveraineté & Jurisdiction de sa Cour des Generaux des Monnoyes, à Paris, le 5. jour de Septembre 1555," in *Recueil d'aucuns Edicts, Declarations, Lettres Patentes, & Arrests du Conseil d'Estat & Privé de nos Roys touchant la Souveraineté & Jurisdiction privative & cumulative de la Cour des Monnoyes, Juges Gardes, Officiers & Justiciables d'icelle* (Paris, 1635), separately paginated.

58. *Edict faict par le Roy sur la reformation, reduction, & reiglement des Orfevres, Joyauliers, Affineurs, Departeurs, Batteurs, & Tireurs d'or, & d'argent se don Royaulme, pays, terres, & seigneuries de son obeissance* (Paris: Jean Dallier, 1555). The goldsmiths and thread-of-gold pullers of Lyons were still, successfully, litigating against this edict well into the seventeenth century. See Archives Municipales de Lyon (AML), FF 612 and HH 111. These were the two edicts for which de la Tourette had been lobbying in 1552! On the background and implementation of these edicts, see Baudouin-Matuszek, "Un tour de France."

settled these in a manner generally favorable to the court, confirming its rank among the sovereign bodies.[59]

The Moneys Day to Day

By the 1560s, the only major outstanding issue around the Monnaies' sovereign status was a dispute with the Parlement of Paris that had emerged out of the debris of the Pinatel affair. In 1558, Jehan Chantal, who had been master of the mint at Villeneuve at the end of its run of spectacular fraud, presented to the Monnaies letters of remission he had somehow obtained from the king pardoning him for his role in that affair. While examining the facts surrounding those letters, as they were legally required to do, the generals discovered (if they had not known it all along) that the royal orders he had presented to the court back in 1551 authorizing him to mint small change had been forged, together with the royal seal imposed on them. This was both a serious capital offense and a good occasion for the court to demonstrate a break with its dubious past, and it was with patent eagerness that the Monnaies sentenced him to be hanged in the Place du Grève, outside the Paris city hall, with his body to be publicly burned afterward.[60]

That should have been the end of Jehan Chantal and a fine amusement for the Parisian crowd, but matters were often not so simple in the old regime. The Parlement of Paris had never accepted its loss of appellate jurisdiction over the Cour des Monnaies, particularly in criminal matters (the Monnaies' civil jurisdiction was limited anyway), complaining to the king in 1552 that leaving the cases the Monnaies heard in the first

---

59. *Edict du Roy Henry II. du mois d'avril M.D. LVII sur les rangs & seances des Cours Souveraines, entre lesquelles est comprise la Cour des Monnoyes* (n.p., n.d.), 1: "en tous actes & assemblées publiques qui seront cy-apres faites en nostredite ville de Paris & hors d'icelles, ou lesdites assemblées se feront par nostredite ordonnance & commandement, nostredite Cour de Parlement ira & marchera la premiere, & apres elle immediatement ira & marchera nostre Chambre dees Comptes, & apres ladite Chambre des Comptes, nostre Cour des Aydes, & apres la Chambre de nos Monnoyes, & apres elle le Prevost de paris & officiers du Chastelet, & apres eux le Prevost des Marchands, Eschevins & officiers de nostredite ville de Paris." Not that such matters were ever truly settled: on 10 January 1577, the Monnaies informed absent members that, on arriving at a memorial service for the late emperor, it had been told by the master of ceremonies "nous dict quil ny avoit poinct de place pour nous & que nous navoit point este samondz ny appelez ains seullement la cour de parlement la chambre des comptes la cour des aides et lhostel de la ville." AN, Z[1B] 376, piece of that date, minute. One major source on the ascribed hierarchy of officers is of no use to us: for some reason, the generals of the moneys were omitted from the *droit de marc d'or*, a tax on offices created in 1578, while the presidents of the court were taxed at an obviously discounted rate. See the 1583 tarif reproduced in Jean Nagle, *Le droit de marc d'or des offices: Tarifs de 1583, 1704, 1748* (Geneva: Droz, 1992), 107–23.

60. Se AN, Z[1B] 487, piece dated 28 May 1558 (arrêt of that date).

instance without a possibility of appeal would run a grave risk of unjusti-
fied executions and other miscarriages of justice.[61] Since this was a period
in which the Parlement exercised a strong, probably increasing, supervision over criminal justice in its jurisdiction, those objections may have had
roots beyond the court's knee-jerk defensiveness about its own standing.[62]
Anyway, only after considerable royal bullying and with explicit, though
unpublished, reservations did the Parlement accept the edict of sovereignty
at all. Then, in early 1558, a dispute came to a head between the Parlement
and the generals' erstwhile superiors in the Chambre des Comptes, also
concerning criminal jurisdiction: the Parlement had been forced to accept
a royal edict somewhat strengthening the Comptes' role in the joint commissions that heard criminal cases arising from the Chambre.[63] Thus when
Chantal appealed to the Parlement, neither side was in a compromising
mood and a battle royal broke out. In particular, the Parlement cited the
recommendations of the Grand Conseil for the abolition of the Monnaies,
in addition to claiming that the generals did not include enough trained
lawyers.[64] What happened to Chantal is unclear, but the Monnaies did not
emerge victorious from its struggle with the Parlement: a royal decision
of 1559 gave the Parlement the right to hear appeals of criminal cases
from the Monnaies, though only after a final sentence had been rendered.[65]
Another edict, in 1570, reversed that decision and revoked the right of
appeal (probably as a sweetener to the simultaneous creation of new officers
in the court); after some struggle, the Parlement was left with the right
to hear appeals of death sentences and orders for torture.[66] In the seventeenth century it was still the case that the Monnaies "admits no appeal,
except in the case of criminal penalties as specified by the restrictions and

---

61. Maugis, *Histoire* 1:411–12, citing AN X[1A] 1572, fols. 86 ff.

62. The classic study here is Alfred Soman, "The Parlement of Paris and the Great Witch Hunt
(1565–1640)," *Sixteenth-Century Journal* 9 (1978): 30–44.

63. Maugis, *Histoire* 1:394–95. I have examined a slightly later restatement of this settlement: *Edit
du Roy, portant reglement entre le Parlement & la Chambre, concernant la Jurisdiction criminelle. A Moulins
au mois de Février 1566* (Paris: Imprimerie Royale, 1726).

64. AN, Z[1B] 65, fols. 98v–100v ("Remonstrance de la court de ceans contre la court de parlement," 7 July 1558). See also another set of remonstrances, AN, Z[1B] 487, piece dated 2 June 1558.

65. See Maugis, *Histoire* 1:415–16. It is not clear that the Monnaies ever actually registered the
1559 decision, which appears in AN, X[1A] 8622, fol. 254. The restriction of appeals to death sentences
may have taken place very early on—there is a reference in some remonstrances to a decision of the
Conseil Privé to that effect of 24 May 1560. See AN, Z[1B] 65, fol. 284r.

66. See Sylvie Daubresse, *Le Parlement de Paris, ou la voix de la raison (1559–1589)* (Geneva: Droz,
2005), 301–2. That particular settlement seems to date to a decision of the Conseil Privé of February 1572, though it is not clear that either the Monnaies or the Parlement ever officially accepted
it. See AN, Z[1B] 374, piece dated 16 February 1572 (letter from Thomas Turquam to the court of
that date, orig.).

modifications made on that subject by the Royal Council and the Court of Parlement, which alone has cognizance of such appeals."[67] By the late 1500s, though, relations between the two sovereign courts had improved, and the appeal process became quick and painless.[68]

In 1560, with this question on its way to being settled and with the new regime of Henri II's widow, Catherine de Médicis, and her sons, the formative period of the Cour des Monnaies could fairly be said to be over and its period of regular functioning to have begun. This is not to say that there were no changes for the remainder of our period: in particular, the Crown's ongoing desperation for funds led to the periodic creation of new offices, which gradually brought the court up to a complement of four presidents and twenty-two generals under Henri IV.[69] Like all officers, the generals of the moneys opposed and sometimes blocked these creations, which diluted the value of their own offices and eventually left the court with more personnel than it really needed, even after it increased their vacation time in 1577.[70] Still, this was preferable to the situation in most of the late 1560s, when the court had no active presidents at all and often no more than eight generals. That in turn was due in part to the chronic absenteeism of Jehan le Lieur, appointed first president when Claude Bourgeois moved on to bigger and better things in 1558, but who,

67. Jacques du Breul, *Le Theatre des antiquitez de Paris, où est traicté de la fondation des eglises & chapelles de la cité, Université, ville, & diocese de Paris: comme aussi de l'institution du Parlement, fondation de l'Université & colleges, & autres choses remarquables* (Paris: Par la Societé des Imprimeurs, 1639): "ne defere à l'appel, sinon en cas des peines criminelles portees par les restrictions & modifications sur ce faites par le Consiel du Roy, & la Cour de Parlement, lequel Parlement cognoist seul desdites appellations." This is from an account of the Monnaies contributed by the former general Nicolas Roland du Plessis around 1614.

68. Documents of the early seventeenth century show the Monnaies' death sentences routinely upheld by the Parlement, generally with a delay of four to six months: see, e.g., AN, Z[1B] 682, piece dated 3 December 1604 (procès-verbal of the service of a death sentence "de la cour de parlement du xxix novembre . . . confirmatif de celluy de ladicte cour des monnoyes du xxie jour de may"); and AN, Z[1B] 500, pieces dated 23 September 1608 (death sentence of Gabriel de Grimonville and others) and 29 January 1609 (confirmation by the Parlement). In 1611 the Parlement attempted to restrict the Monnaies' right to bring criminal charges *proprie motu*, an initiative that the Monnaies bypassed with a direct appeal to the chancellor (see AN, Z[1B] 684, piece dated 13 August 1611 [procès-verbal of Coquerel]), but then one finds two generals of the moneys actually urging a suspect in the case where this issue arose, whom they had ordered tortured, to appeal to the Parlement (see AN, Z[1B] 501, dossier dated 28 January 1611).

69. The final two generals were added as a result of double appointments to two posts while the court was split between Paris and Tours: predictably, promises to suppress the supernumerary offices were never kept.

70. See AN, Z[1B] 70, fol. 147 (3 May 1577). This was instead of moving to a system of serving in alternating years, imposed by an edict of September 1570 but seemingly never actually adopted. Janet Girvan Espiner-Scott, *Claude Fauchet: Sa vie, son œuvre* (Paris: Droz, 1938), 36–38, discusses some of these maneuvers in detail.

by February 1563, had already racked up "a long absence," from which he seems not to have returned for another four or five years.[71] By 1566, de la Tourette, too, was "notoriously absent" in the process of having his office reimbursed and suppressed for a probably involuntary retirement; despite some pro forma objections, the court must have been quite relieved when that office was revived in 1569.[72]

This long interruption of leadership had no great effect on the functioning and status of the court, which is testimony to the stability it had already achieved. The court's work was monotonous and exhausting, though not always both at once.[73] A manuscript handbook for its officers distinguishes between "ordinary" and "extraordinary" service, defining the former as "showing up daily in the court," usually at about eight in the morning,

> to give justice in all issues presented, as, judging the pyxes and work of the mints, regulating the individual officers of those mints, ruling on motions filed by various individuals, drawing up the accounts of mint masters, punishing those who violate the ordinances on the value and validity of coins as well as on matters of goldsmithing and other crafts that fall under your jurisdiction, and punishing counterfeiters.[74]

All of this took place in the court's chambers in the Palais de Justice, on the Île de la Cité at the center of Paris. The court occupied several rooms just above

---

71. AN, Z[1B] 372, piece dated 26 February 1562 (resolution to summons le Lieur for his absence); he was still absent in 1566 but had returned by 1568.

72. AN, Z[1B] 65, fol. 237r (9 August 1566): resolution that "attendu labsence notoire de Me Jehan le Lieur et alexandre la tourette presidens," there will be only two groups of magistrates for the Chambre des Vacations. Though the Edict of Orleans of 1561 had expressed a pious intention to carry out such suppressions, they were in fact almost unheard of, and since de la Tourette could probably have sold his office for more than he would have received as a reimbursement, it is very likely that this represented an involuntary termination.

73. There is a good survey of the working life of late medieval and early sixteenth-century Parisian officers in Bernard Quilliet, "Les corps d'officiers de la prévôté et vicomté de Paris et de l'Ile-de-France, de la fin de la Guerre de cent ans au début des Guerres de religion: Etude social" (doctoral diss., University of Paris IV, 1977), 771–92, who points out that the number of days that courts actually sat, and that individual members attended sittings, could vary a good deal.

74. Bibliothèque Nationale de France (BN), ms. fr. 18500, fol. 46r: "se trouver journellement en la court de ceans pour y faire justice en toutes les occasions qui se presentent comme juger les boestes et ouvraiges des monnayes reigler les officiers particuliers desdites monnoyes ordonner sur les requestes presentees par plusieurs particuliers dresser les estatz des maistres chastier les contrevenans aulx ordonnances tant sur le pris cours que sur le faict de lorfaiverie et mestiers qui dependent de vostre juridiction et chastier les faulx monnoyeurs." The owner is identified as "Robineau," probably Jacques Robineau, who joined the court in 1594. Internal evidence dates the manuscript to between 1599 and 1602. It may have formed a set with the "memoire concernant linstitution des recepveurs des monnoyes de france" inventoried in the papers of the recepveur des boites Robert Robineau, who died in 1597. AN, Z[1B] 388, piece dated 23 April 1597 (procès-verbal of Simon Biseul), fol. 2v.

the Chambre des Comptes.[75] Its main office seems to have been crammed full of armoires of various sizes, and at least after 1604 its walls were painted deep blue, decorated with gold fleurs-de-lis and offset with other gilding: the effect must have been quite impressive.[76] Or at least it must have been impressive when in a decent state of repair: as late as 1609, the court had to undertake substantial renovations "to make the *parquet*," where the solicitor and attorney general worked, "habitable."[77]

The tasks listed in fact covered most of the court's day-to-day business, divided roughly between regulatory and judicial functions. These included auditing the mints, processing leases and appointments to offices in them, confirming the status of hereditary moneyers (who benefited from tax exemptions and thus had to be carefully vetted), and adjudicating more or less picayune disputes among that personnel. One problem was that, given not only the instability of the years of civil war but also the general inadequacy of early modern transportation, communication with the mints was easily interrupted. Consider "Jehan Doeffe, messenger from Avignon, who had brought and deposited with the clerk the pyxes of the mint of Villeneuve." They were found to have already been opened, and he explained that this was because, while on the Rhône "there was such a strong wind that, try- ing to save himself and having his purse in his shirt, his purse fell out and he lost it, so that, being without money, and having been ordered to deliver the packet he was carrying to M. Tulle, without knowing what it was, and needing something to help him get to Paris, and since the packet had got- ten soaked, he opened it."[78] Even assuming the best will in the world, it was a chancy thing to move precious metal and documentation about it around the kingdom; that this method of control had even such modest success as it did is somewhat surprising.

---

75. Espiner-Scott, *Claude Fauchet*, citing AN, Z[1B] 123, 7 August 1776, an inventory prior to repairs following the fire that destroyed the Chambre des Comptes. It is not certain, however, that the Monnaies in the sixteenth century already occupied all the space mentioned in this document.

76. This from a contract with Pierre de Hansy, master painter, for repainting the *grande salle* of the court (there seem to have been a couple of attached offices as well). AN, Z[1B] 394, piece dated 7 April 1604, which is the only document I have found that sheds much light on the physical setting of the court. The room, which abutted "la court du premier huissier de la chambre des comptes," also contained a painting and a gilded "gros roy," presumably a statue.

77. AN, Z[1B] 75, fol. 113v (arrêt of 13 October 1609): "rendre ledict parquet habitable."

78. AN, Z[1B] 387, piece dated 3 October 1596 (extrait des registres): "il fist un sy grand vent que desirant se sauver aiant la bourse dans sa chemise sa bourse tombast & la perdist au moien dequoy estant denue dargent luy aiant este donne charge de bailler le pacquet quil portoit a Monsieur tulle sans scavoir que cestoit ce voiant en necessite pou luy ayder a venir jusques a paris aiant este ledict pacquet bagnie ouvrist icelluy."

This did mean that much work had to be done on the ground in the provinces, which was the key element of the generals' extraordinary duties, "undertaking criminal investigations, visiting changers, carrying out royal and court commissions, and giving advice or delivering remonstrances to the king."[79] Of these tasks the commissions, generically termed *chevauchées,* were by far the most arduous and time-consuming. In theory, each general was supposed to go on chevauchée every other year, and all regions of the country were to be covered every year. In practice there was no such regularity, with generals more often sent out in response to some kind of problem than on any routine schedule. Even leaving aside travel, the procedures for a visit on chevauchée were exhausting. According to another handbook, the general on chevauchée must

> hasten into the countryside and provinces to inform to inform himself on [alleged] abuses and prepare the trials of whoever they find at fault, undertaking visitations of all the houses of mint workers, changers, refiners, and goldsmiths, making a record of whatever they may find, and holding court for them throughout their commission. . . . And they must . . . first of all go into the mint without any delay with their clerks and assistants, seizing receipts and registers of purchase of materials . . . all of which they will take away and deposit with other [officials], to make sure that everything purchased has been coined into money. . . . They will inform themselves from the inhabitants of the city of the state of the mint where they are . . . of all of which things they will make complete written records.[80]

The entire process could easily take a month, sometimes much more, and it would be repeated for perhaps three or four different mints on the course of a chevauchée, with stops in towns and cities along the way to check on royal treasurers, goldsmiths, and changers, and an inevitable collection of legislative enactments to be communicated to and jurisdictional disputes to be fought out with local authorities. Such an expedition was not for the faint of heart, but it

---

79. BN, ms. fr. 18500, fol. 46r: "linstruction des procez criminelz visitation des changeurs execution des commisions du roy et de ladicte court et donner advis au roy luy dresser remonstrances."

80. Bibliothèque de l'Arsenal (BA), ms. 4071, 303–4 (from an anonymous "Bref discours de ce en quoy consiste la pratique du fait des monnoyes"): "courir aux pais et provinces pour informer desdits abus et faire le proces de celuy quils trouvent en faute faisant visitation par touttes les maisons desdits monnoyeurs changeurs affineurs et orfevres et faisant proces verbal de tout ce quil se trouveront et fairoit en iceluy lit pendant leurs commision. . . . Et faut que . . . premierement avec les commis et greffiers se transportent en ladicte monnoye sans sejourner saissant les pacuetz des delivrances registres dachats des matieres . . . tous lesquels il enleveront et confereront les uns aux autres pour voir si tout ce qui a eté achapté a esté converti en monnoye. . . . Sinformeront de ceux de la ville de lestat de ladicte monnoye ou ils seront . . . de touttes lesquelles choses fairont bons procez verbaux."

served an extremely valuable role not only in establishing the Monnaies' authority but as one of the mechanisms whereby the court and the royal government in general gathered information about the state of opinion in the provinces and the infinite adjustments that local conditions imposed on centralized policies.[81]

The activities of the court and its officers, then, were somewhat miscellaneous. Most of them, however, consisted of sometimes frenetic, and perhaps sometimes poorly focused, but generally dedicated attempts to tame with the authority of the state the chaotic and inherently, dishonestly, self-interested world of precious metals. In a mildly paradoxical way, the isolation of chevauchées, attendance on the royal court, and other such expeditions may have served to reinforce the Monnaies' esprit de corps, since out in the field the generals (if they were honest) would have felt themselves isolated, with nothing but the authority and the culture of the court to support them against the chaos all around. The letters exchanged between the court and members on mission testify to this, showing (with occasional significant exceptions) a level of warmth and mutual respect not common in official correspondence. Thus, one finds Thomas Turquam, stranded in Lyons in 1575, saying that "if I have the opportunity to perform some service for the company in the meantime, either for the affairs of the king and the public or for the members of the court, I will esteem myself very happy to employ myself thus to give testimony of the prompt obedience that I owe and will render to you all my life."[82] When Claude de Montperlier, who had served in the court for more than thirty years, died while on mission in the South of France, the court wrote back to President Fauchet, who had sent the news, with a touching expression of "the grief that it has received from the loss of such a man."[83] In 1599, when

---

81. Baudouin-Matuszek, "Un tour de France," is an excellent, exhaustive account of one major campaign of chevauchées. The process of gathering local information on the moneys, which was extremely well developed, will be discussed further in chapter 3, below.

82. AN Z[1B] 375, piece dated 23 September 1575 (letter to the court, orig.): "si jay moien de faire ce pendant quelque bon service a la compagnee soit pour les affaires du roy et du public ou pour les particulliers de la cour je mestimeray bien heureux dy estre emploié pour vous rendre tesmoignage de la prompte obeissance que je vous doy et rendray toute ma vye."

83. AN, Z[1B] 388, piece dated 16 July 1597, published in Janet Girvan Espiner-Scott, ed., Documents concernant la vie et les œuvres de Claude Fauchet. Documents—inédits—bibliothèque de Fauchet—extraits de poèmes—copiés d'après des manuscrits perdus (Paris: E. Droz, 1938), 117. The tribute deserves to be quoted in full: "La triste nouvelle de la mort de feu M. de Montperlier, nostre confrere, que nous avons apprise par voz lettres ne nous a esté moins fascheuse que ses vertueulx labeurs pour le service du public nous donnent subject de le regretter. Ceste compaignie a faict assez paroistre le deuil qu'elle recoit de la perte d'un tel personnage, la memoire duquel y vivra perpetuellement avec aultant de louanges que ses merites l'en ont rendu recommendable; dont elle rendra a l'endroit des siens tout le tesmoignage qu'ilz scauroient desirer, comme elle fera au vostre de toute l'assistance qu'elle pourra pour la conservation de vostre authorité, et pour le service particulier qu'elle desire de vous rendre en tout ce qui vous concernera."

the court wanted to recall Jean Favier from chasing wild geese in the south for reasons perhaps more personal than official, it mixed reassurance and threat. "The reputation you have acquired by your merits in this company will always keep us from believing anything about you except what we have recognized from long experience. Whatever rumors the ill-intentioned might sow, they will never hold our belief against the proof we have of your laudable behavior. This should be a sufficient recompense for the service you have given for so many years; but you should also be extremely careful to preserve that reputation and avoid not only guilt but even suspicion."[84] The court believed that Favier's psychological investment in its solidarity and in his standing with his colleagues was sufficiently great to bring him to heel. Favier was soon back in Paris and happily reintegrated with the court.

A more prosaic basis for the court's solidarity was that its members faced together the chronic arrears of wages and reimbursements that plagued sixteenth-century French officials. Much of the court's political energy in the 1560s, in particular, seems to have been expended in simple attempts to get paid, and the problem of arrears cropped up again periodically thereafter. As early as April 1559, shortly before Henri II's death, the court complained in a circular letter to anyone who was anyone in the royal council that "we have not received any payment for two and a half years . . . so that several of us, having paid large sums to the king for their offices, find themselves so embarrassed by the long delay in their wages that they no longer know how or with what to maintain themselves in continuing the service of the said lord."[85] In January 1560, in a sign of their junior status among the sovereign courts, the members instructed their representative to the king to attempt to make arrangements for payment "like the gentlemen of the Parlement, if possible, and at least like the generals of the Aides," though they soon thought better of that wording.[86] The problem was that such royal payments

---

84. AN, Z^{1B} 74, fol. 123r (letter of 12 October 1599 to Favier in Avignon): "la reputation que vous avez acquise en ceste compagnee par voz merites nous empechera tousjours de croire aucunement de vous que ce que nous avons recognu de longue main par quelques bruictz que les malveillans puissent semer Ilz ne seront jamais arreste nostre croiance contre la preuve que nous avons de voz louables deportmens Ce vous doibt estre une digne recompence pour le service qu'avez rendu tant d'annees Mais aussy debvez estre grandement soigneux de conserver ceste reputation & desviter non le blasme simplement mais le soubcon."

85. AN, Z^{1B} 370, piece dated 20 April 1559 (letter of that date to the Constable [Anne de Montmorency], [Charles] Cardinal de Lorraine, M. d'Ammeson, and others, minute): "nous navons receu aucuns payemens depuys deux ans et demy . . . de sorte que plusieurs entre nous ayans donne grande finance au Roy pour leurs offices se trouvent tant en areir pour la si longue retention de leursdictes gaiges, quilz ne scavent plus comment ny de quoy sentretenir a continuer le service dudict sieur."

86. AN, Z^{1B} 371, piece dated 2 January 1559 (letter to unnamed members of the court, minute): "comme messieurs de la court de parlement de paris si possible est A tout le moins comme les generaulx des aydes." This phrase is struck through in the minute.

proceeded in two steps: first, the financial officers had to "assign" them to a treasurer, account receivable, or some other source of funds, and then the person so assigned had to actually pay up. Some officials were much more able or willing to do so than others, corruption abounded—the plot of an exactly contemporary comedy revolved around an army officer's payment of kickbacks to a treasurer in return for payment of overdue wages—and the claimant's status and political influence weighed heavily in receiving prompt service.[87] Ultimately, the officers of the court were given first claim on the mint receipts for their wages, which seems to have improved matters, although arrears still occurred.[88] Certainly, having an in-house paymaster was an unusual convenience (related to the unique role of the court), a mark of its gradual maturation, and was likely to increase the court's internal solidarity.[89]

It is possible to be somewhat more precise about the Monnaies' financial conditions. Under the reform regulations issued in the wake of the Pinatel scandal, the receiver of the pyxes was supposed to file reports of his income and expenses quarterly and annually; one of each survives, and they give some idea of the court's financial position in time of peace. In 1582, the receiver was owed just over 18,202 écus (54,606 livres) from twenty mints (Rennes, Bordeaux, and Angers made the largest contributions), with only 624 écus listed as still due.[90] Sixty-five percent of expenses, 11,465 écus, went toward the wages of the court officers, though this covered at least five quarters, presumably bringing them up to date.[91] Another 1,523 écus went to operational expenses of the court, though many of those were almost certainly covered by funds from fines and confiscations, handled by the receiver of

87. See Jacques Grévin, *La trésorière, Les esbahis: Comédies,* ed. Elisabeth Lapeyre (Paris: Honoré Champion, 1980).

88. Charles IX instituted this system by letters patent of 13 January 1572. He revoked it the next year but quickly reinstated it. See AN, Z^{1B} 70, fols. 66v–69r: "Remonstrances treshumbles que font au roy nostre sire les gens tenans sa court des monnoyes" (9 March 1573), and fols. 109v–110r.

89. In 1605, when First President Guillaume le Clerc obtained letters patent assigning a 1,200-livre annual pension on the funds used for the *gaiges* of the court, his colleagues issued a decision that "memoratifve des services que rend continuellement ledict le Clerc en lexercise de sa charge pour bien & advancement des affaires dicelle Court consent & concede l'enterinement desdictes lettres." AN, Z^{1B} 394, piece dated 3 March 1605 (arrêt of that date).

90. AN, Z^{1B} 379, piece dated 6 January 1582 ("Estat de la recepte & despence des deniers des boittes & esmolumens des monnaies de france"). The sums for both the receipts and the expenses do not add up to the totals given, and I suspect that this account is in error (which may be why it is in the court's archives, rather than having been sent to be audited by the Comptes). For the receipts, which are hard to read, I accept the receiver's totals; for the expenses, I use my calculation of the total.

91. The receivers of the city of Paris get 1,333 écus "pour les gaiges," probably reimbursing them for an earlier payment. The "normal" annual wages would have come to about 8,105 écus, or 45 percent of annual receipts.

fines (*receveur des amendes*). Another 2,524 écus reimbursed various officers for unspecified expenses, while 1,492 écus were handed over to royal treasurers, leaving a cash balance of 574 écus. In a good year, then, receipts from the mints substantially exceeded the costs of administering them—by anywhere from 15 to 30 percent, depending on what one makes of receivables, charges from previous years, and likely cross-subsidies with the court's criminal jurisdiction.[92] The 5,000 écus or so that the receiver of the pyxes might clear in a year was certainly just a drop in the bucket of the royal budget, not even enough to pay the salary of one of the great officers of the Crown, and political or economic disturbances could easily erase such a margin. It also seems that the French mints were less profitable than their more centralized English counterparts.[93] Nevertheless, this income did provide a certain level of stability to the Monnaies and insulated it from the vagaries of the royal finances.

Which is not to say, however, that the officers of the court individually were free from financial worries. One councillor had his office seized by creditors when he tried to resign it; a clerk and a receiver of the pyxes had their offices seized by the Crown, apparently for unpaid debts.[94] Various documents show retired officers and their heirs collecting, or seeking to collect, sums many years overdue from the court.[95] Alexandre de la Tourette was particularly given to complex and somewhat suspicious financial maneuvers. In 1558 he accepted, as settlement of a debt, a claim by the widow of a receiver of the pyxes for 2,219 livres against the master of the mint of Bayonne, which was being litigated against the king of Navarre in his capacity as admiral of France, a deal bad enough on its face

---

92. Another account survives for the first quarter of 1586: AN, Z[1B] 381, piece dated 29 April 1586. Receipts were 4,441 écus (17,764 annualized); expenses were 2,899 écus (11,596 annualized). Taking account of the extra quarter of gaiges paid in 1581, this is generally similar to what appears in the other document. While the surplus of nearly 35 percent here is doubtless unrealistic for a full year, it may suggest that profits were on the higher end of what one might gather from the 1581 account. A third account, from the Chambre des Monnaies of Tours during the Wars of the League (AN, Z[1B] 383, piece dated 27 April 1592), says very little about the normal operations of the court.

93. Challis, *New History*, offers no figures for the period of Elizabeth's reign after the recoinage, but the seventeenth-century figures he gives in table 39 (p. 332) show average annual payments to the treasury of over £2,000 on a much smaller operation.

94. G. Baudry, 1592; J. Bobusse, 1580; A. de Varade, 1601. Baudry's woes came, admittedly, in the midst of the crisis of the Wars of the League.

95. See, e. g., AN, Z[1B] 436, piece dated 22 September 1593 (petition by "Marye le Picart veufve de feu Me Germain Longuet vivant conseiller & general en ladite court" for payment of his back wages).

that some more complex reality must underlie it.[96] In late 1562 the councillor Hilaire Dain, who had stood pledge for de la Tourette for a debt to the city of Paris, had his goods seized and had to flee town when de la Tourette defaulted.[97] It is not surprising to find the court saying in 1570 (after he had left office) that de la Tourette was "burdened with several large debts, including to some mint masters."[98] In 1565 the general Jehan Bourgoing was placed under house arrest and then imprisoned in Fort l'Evêque for a debt of 1,578 livres owed to the receiver Hochet; ultimately he had to sell his office to repay it.[99] Once the wages of the court's officers began to be paid more regularly, such misadventures became rarer. Still, the officers of the moneys did not necessarily possess the monetary stability their positions might have demanded.

Overall, one can say of the Cour des Monnaies what Jonathan Dewald said of the parlement of Rouen in his pioneering study of that body: "What emerges from this examination, in the first place, is the seriousness of the magistrates' professional commitment and of its effects on them."[100] All the evidence suggests that whether in the pathological case of extreme corruption or in the apparently much more common one of honest and dedicated public service, the officers of the Monnaies were thoroughly acculturated to their unique and complex institution. Indeed, the technical nature of their work may have marked them even more deeply than it did their Rouennais colleagues. This characteristic of the Monnaies was important for French monetary administration, for the development of monetary theory and policy in France, and also for the activities and fortunes of the court itself as it faced the tumultuous political conditions of the last third of the sixteenth century.

---

96. See AN, Z[1B] 434, piece dated 25 October 1560 (notarial act of 17 October 1558). If, as the document claims, this receivable was taken in exchange for a debt of "pareille somme," given the likely cost and dubious success of collecting it, de la Tourette was losing his shirt. From a dossier in ibid. dated 27 March 1564 it appears that de la Tourette had also bought up from the same widow obligations on the master of the Monnaie des Etuves.

97. Ibid., piece dated 31 January 1562 (petition from Dain).

98. AN, Z[1B] 374, piece dated 14 December 1571 (proces-verbal of the delivery of remonstrances): "chargez de plusieurs grandz debtes & mesmes envers aucuns maistres des monnoies."

99. Ibid., pieces dated 6 July, 1 August, and 16 November 1565 and 30 March 1565 après pâques.

100. Jonathan Dewald, The Formation of a Provincial Nobility: The Magistrates of the Parlement of Rouen, 1499–1610 (Princeton: Princeton University Press, 1980), 66; he expands on this insight in Dewald, "The 'Perfect Magistrate': Parlementaires and Crime in Sixteenth-Century Rouen," Archiv für Reformationsgeschichte 67 (1976): 284–300.

The Personnel

Like any relatively small and initially unsettled institution, the Cour des Monnaies depended crucially on its personnel, for good or ill. A proper prosopographical study of the Monnaies would be extremely interesting and could answer many questions about the court's, and the currency's, connection to other elements of the economy and the royal service, about the evolution of the court over time, and about its exact place in the brutal and fluid status hierarchy of the old regime.[101] Unfortunately, such a monumental task is beyond our scope here. We will have to be satisfied with an incomplete and impressionistic picture, which should nevertheless give some preliminary answers to the questions just raised. The task is made easier by the fortuitous prominence of a few members of the court and by the survival of a few valuable and accessible sets of records.

At least at its origins in the 1550s, the personnel of the Monnaies was both somewhat inbred and closely tied to the Chambre des Comptes and, to a lesser extent, to the other Parisian sovereign courts. To begin with our criminals, Loys Vachot (he preferred the aristocratic "de Vachot," which said more about the ambition that got him into trouble than about his pedigree) must have been related to Anthoine Vachot, an auditor in the Comptes.[102] His wife, as we know from the records of his trial, was one Marguerite Ribier, no doubt a relative of Louis Ribier, who joined the court in 1564. The wife of his codefendant Lauthier was Phillippes de Mestayer, presumably related to Jehan le Mestayer, already his colleague on the court. We know very little about Jacques Pinatel's family; the final convict, Simon Radin, had a brother named Jean who was a barrister practicing before the Parlement of Paris.[103] This combination of endogamy, provincial outsiders, and connections both to people more or less highly placed in the Parisian courts and to the world of mint masters was entirely typical of the developing upper robe nobility (that is, those given noble status for their service in the royal administration) who were then at the center of French state building.[104] A bit less typical, and thus more indicative of what was unique in

---

101. A fine example of such a study, for a similar group in an only slightly later period, is Martine Bennini, *Les conseillers à la Cour des aides (1604–1697): Etude sociale* (Paris : Honoré Champion, 2010).

102. Mentioned in Hamon, *L'argent*, 289.

103. See Florence Greffe and Valérie Brousselle, eds., *Documents du Minutier central des notaires de Paris: Inventaires après décès*, vol. 2, *1547–1560* (Paris: Archives Nationales, 1997), no. 60 (inventaire après décès de Jean Radin. Minutier Centrale des Notaires de Paris [MC] LXXXVI, 93: 30 August 1547). This collection allows us to trace the family connections of many early members of the Cour des Monnaies.

104. Another cluster of relations, much less definitively documented, might tie together Jehan Bourgoing, who joined the court early in Henri II's reign; Philippe le Clerc, who appeared as the widow of the councillor in Parlement Guillaume (II) Bourgoing in 1562; and Guillaume le Clerc, a president of the Monnaies from 1581, See Maugis, *Histoire*, 3:167 (s. v. "Guillaume II Bourgoing").

the Monnaies, was Sébastien de Riberolles. The son of a petty country merchant who had risen to become master of the Paris mint, he had been one of Pinatel and Vachot's victims and thus may have avoided otherwise obvious questions of conflict of interest (he replaced Alexandre Faucon, who had been accused and acquitted but was perhaps eased out anyway as insufficiently vindicated). Honestly or not, de Riberolles did manage to die a rich man.[105]

But connections to higher social strata were more common. This can be seen in the case of Loys Hennequin, solicitor general in the court at the same time. The Hennequin clan, originally from Champagne, had its tentacles through the entire robe nobility of northern France. Loys was married to Anne Alligret, sister of his colleague from September 1553, Pierre Alligret (who in turn had brothers who were a barrister and a councillor in the Parlement of Paris).[106] In that capacity, on 28 February 1553, he witnessed the inventory of the goods of the recently deceased Charlotte Briçonnet, whose first husband had formerly been married to Hennequin's wife's uncle, Pierre Legendre, seigneur d'Hallaincourt, a treasurer of France.[107] Charlotte was the niece of the great reforming bishop of Meaux, Guillaume Briçonnet, and had a cousin, Anne Briçonnet, married to the treasurer and famous bibliophile Jean Grolier, whose work had often brought him into contact with the Monnaies.[108] She was also the sister of another Anne Briçonnet, married to Robert Dauvet de Rieux, a president in the Comptes: one of their daughters, Charlotte Dauvet (perhaps named after her aunt) married a Protestant nobleman named François de Béthune, baron de Rosny. Among that couple's children would be Maximilien de Béthune, duc de Sully.[109] Nor did that exhaust Hennequin's illustrious connections. One of his brothers-in-law, married to Anne Alligret's sister Renée, was Guillaume de Marillac, a *valet de chambre* to the king and the entrepreneur who

---

105. See Greffe and Brouselle, *Documents*, no. 1799 (his inventaire après décès. MC LIV, 226 quinquies: 7 March 1559). Quilliet, "Les corps d'officiers," 177, 696, briefly discusses his career, which he describes as "un cas pratiquement unique dans le monde des officiers."

106. For the Alligret brothers, see Greffe and Brouselle, *Documents*, no. 2035 (inventaire après décès de Jean Alligret. MC LIV, 226 quinquies: 13 November 1560). Note that the executors of Jean Alligret and of Sébastien de Riberolles used the same notary.

107. Greffe and Brouselle, *Documents*, no. 773 (inventaire après décès de Charlotte Briçonnet. MC LXXXVI, 95: 28 February 1553).

108. On the Briçonnet, see Quilliet, "Les corps d'officiers," 665–66. Charlotte's father had also been a president in the Comptes. For Grolier's involvement with the Monnaies, see, e.g., a procès verbal of an assay of foreign coin in 1559, by "Jean l'Huiller Sr. de Boulancourt president en la chambre des comptes, et Jean Groslier d'Aquis Tresorier de France appellez avec nous Mr Alexandre de la Tourette president en la cour des monnoyes, Guillaume Marilliac maistre ordinaire en la chambre des comptes, Claude Marcel essayeur general desdites monnoyes et Guillaume le gras marchand bourgeois de Paris," Bibliothèque de l'Arsenal ms. 4071, fol. 307.

109. On Sully's maternal genealogy, see Bernard Barbiche, "Les deux familles de Sully," *XVIIe siècle* 174 (1992): 21–32.

had installed the engines of the Monnaie des Etuves to make the Henriques d'or. Guillaume in fact joined the court the next month; when he left three years later, he joined the Chambre des Comptes, and in the reign of Charles IX he took a leading place in the inner councils of the royal finances. His son Michel later rose to head that administration as superintendent of finances, ultimately becoming *garde des sceaux* (acting chancellor).[110]

Indeed, to some extent it was all downhill from there for the Cour des Monnaies, for there are relatively few similarly influential connections or illustrious careers after the reign of Henri II. The corruption scandal probably did not help, but other factors must have been more important. The Monnaies was in some sense a pet project of Henri II's, and though he saw it through to a reasonably firm foundation, no future king gave it as important a role in his scheme of government. Nor was the chaos of the civil and religious wars that broke out after Henri II's death and lasted until after 1595 conducive to smooth and productive career paths for civil servants. The Protestant associations of so many of the most prominent early members of the Cour des Monnaies may well have served in the medium term to weaken the connections of the Monnaies to the power centers of the robe nobility, since Huguenots were gradually frozen out of such positions. Most important, probably, was the gradual displacement of royal officers generally from the inner councils of the French kings, to be replaced by more tractable temporary commissioners and the clans of *grands serviteurs d'état*.[111] In the new dispensation, the Monnaies was simply too junior a group to maintain its share of the diminishing supply of close links to the court.

This is not to say, however, that the Monnaies lacked for accomplished and prominent members, though many owed their appointment to the court to their relative prominence, not the other way around. This was particularly true of presidents. Alexandre de la Tourette's replacement (with a gap of a year after his office was suppressed) was Claude Fauchet, who received the post as a reward for his pioneering work on the history of the monarchy and its ceremonial life.[112] In 1580 Henri III appointed Odet de Turnèbe, son

110. On Guillaume de Marillac's career, see Antoine, *Cœur de l'état*, 58–64, 66–69, 179n. The family was already well placed in the royal councils in the reign of François I.

111. See Roland Mousnier, "Sully et le Conseil d'état et des finances," *Revue historique* 192 (1941): 68–86, cautiously endorsed in Mark Greengrass, *France in the Age of Henri IV: The Struggle for Stability*, 2nd ed. (London: Longman, 1994), 149–55.

112. See Espiner-Scott, *Claude Fauchet*, 31–33. Espiner-Scott repeatedly and correctly stresses the dedication with which Fauchet performed his duties in the court, even though it was something of an afterthought in his career. Fauchet paid (or at least got a receipt for) nine thousand livres for his office, which may have represented a discount even if he actually paid the full sum.

of a major classical scholar and himself a promising poet, as first president; when Turnèbe promptly dropped dead, Fauchet received the position.[113] Pierre des Jardins, who replaced Louis Ribier (the Protestant who was related to Vachot's wife) in 1569, was the son of a professor of medicine; Jerosme de Varade, who joined the court in 1577, was the son of a royal physician. Jacques Colas, whose theories will concern us later, seems to have worked his way first into the Paris mint and then into court by peppering the royal council with interesting works on the nature and control of the currency, annoying his future colleagues in the process.[114] Such rewards for intellectual endeavor were reasonably common under the later Valois kings.

Most newly appointed members of the court, however, had no such accomplishments to their name. Typically they gave their profession as "barrister in the Parlement," the traditional first step in a career in royal office, when new university graduates, in the words of a Rouen magistrate quoted by Jonathan Dewald, "can have some experience of practice so that one can, in part, digest what one has learned of theory."[115] It is possible to undertake a crude sociological analysis of the background of these officers based on their own statements, character witnesses they offered at the time of their confirmation, scattered genealogical information, and comparison of family names with lists of officers in other courts. We can make a rough guess at the social origins of 78 out of 146 officers (53%) who served in the Monnaies in our period. Of those, 29 (37%, including almost all of the receivers and most of the clerks) show signs of coming from the world of the bourgeoisie or the lesser financial officials; 33 from the world of lesser legal officials or the learned professions (42%); and only 16 (20%, including most of the presidents) from established families of the emerging robe nobility. It is worth bearing in mind that the unknowns are probably nearly entirely

---

113. The only source for Turnèbe's appointment, which does not appear in the records of the Monnaies, is François Grudé de la Croix du Maine, *Les bibliothèques françoises de La Croix du Maine et de du Verdier sieur de Vauprivas*, ed. Rigoley de Juvigny, 4 vols. (Paris: Saillant et Nyon et Michel Lambert, 1772–73), 2:203 (s.v. "Odet de Turnèbe"): "Il fut premièrement avocat en la Cour de Parlement, et enfin il fut pourvû de l'etat de premier Président en la Cour des Monnoyes à Paris, a la poursuite duquel état il mourut d'une fièvre chaude l'an 1581, âgé de vingt-huit ans." La Croix du Maine's source appears to have been the inscription on Turnèbe's funerary monument.

114. According to remonstrances the court presented to Henri III in 1588, Charles IX "en consideration de sa service & experience au faict des monnoies se seroit voulu servir par luy [et] auroit donne partye de la finance dudict estat." AN, Z[1B] 72, fol. 243r. According to the same document, the prices of offices of general of the moneys had fallen from 2,000–3,000 écus in the 1560s to no more than 1,500 at that time.

115. Dewald, *Formation*, 27n, citing Bibliothèque Municipale de Rouen, ms. Y214, v, 27. I have translated the term *la pratique*, which had a specific connotation of legal procedure.

divided between the bourgeois/finance category and that of lesser officials and professionals. If the same ratio obtained for them as for those at whom we can guess, the ratio of origins would be 40 percent from the bourgeoisie and finances, 48 percent from officers and learned professions, and 11 percent from the robe nobility.[116] The court thus appears to have been a socially intermediate body, where the various elements of the sixteenth-century urban elites met in relatively equal proportions.[117]

One reason that that the court could draw qualified candidates from such a broad social spectrum is that the positions were really very attractive, despite the hard work they involved.[118] The broad competence of the Monnaies meant that its judges had to be at least reasonably proficient in accounting, metallurgy, and the details of mint and goldsmiths' work; those with law degrees, who wore the "long robe," had to instruct and judge civil and criminal trials and carry out sometimes complex criminal investigations; at least some members had to be prepared to advise the king on matters of monetary policy and to follow the court in order to present it; and all members had to be ready to travel the country for months on end (with uncertain reimbursement of expenses) in order to oversee the mints. On the other hand, the prestige of and prospects of ennoblement from even the newest and least prestigious sovereign court were great. This, more than relatively modest wages and equally modest prospects for enrichment by other means once corruption had been brought under control, seems to have been the major incentive for joining the court. Some members clearly regarded it as a steppingstone in broader careers, given the large number of relatively brief tenures: a bit more than a quarter of members for whom sufficient information survives from our period (twenty-three

---

116. Just for councillors and *avocats du roi*, we have ten robe noble, twenty-six law and professions, nineteen bourgeois and finance, forty-one unknown, or by the same procedure of splitting up the unknowns, ten (11%) robe noble, fifty-one (55%) law and professions, and thirty-three (35%) bourgeois and finance. This analysis is based essentially on the surviving minutes of the *provisions d'office*, AN, Z^{1B} 548–61.

117. Unsurprisingly, the world of the goldsmiths was very well represented, with more than one in eight officers of the court in our period (20 of 147) sharing a family name with one or more sixteenth-century members of the Paris *compagnie des orfèvres* as listed in Michèle Bimbenet-Privat, *Les orfèvres parisiens de la Renaissance: 1506–1620* (Paris: Commission des travaux historiques de la Ville de Paris, 1992).

118. One late symptom of strong recruitment was the court's decision, in 1609, to formally abandon the distinction between councillorships of the long and short robe, indicating a confidence that they would never lack for trained legal specialists. AN, Z^{1B} 561, piece dated 13 April 1609. This had been far from clear to them as recently as 1588, admittedly a year of great political turmoil. See AN, Z^{1B} 72, fols. 242v–243r and 246r.

of eighty-nine) stayed on the court for less than five years. It is hard to say what happened to them when they left: one former royal attorney became a judge in the presidial court of Troyes, while one general took the less prestigious but probably more lucrative position of royal treasurer for Champagne.[119] On the other hand, long tenures were substantially more common. At any given time there were likely to be several generals with twenty or thirty years' service on the court, which gave it the high level of continuity and institutional memory necessary for performing its complex and technical functions.[120]

The officers of the moneys also maintained strong links to the world of learning and erudition. A few owed their appointments to such links. Others published more or less prolifically in fields related to their professional expertise. Some had more complex ties, among them Denys Godefroy, royal solicitor in the court for an astonishing thirty-eight years (1570–1609) who published a brief pamphlet of his own.[121] He was also was the first cousin of an important legal scholar who bore the same name (a Protestant and a refugee from France), whose son Théodore, in his turn, was one of the great erudites of the early seventeenth century. To make matters even more complex, the mother of Denis the jurisconsult (the solicitor's aunt by marriage) was the daughter of one Geneviève Andry (daughter of a master of accounts and of a member of the great robe and erudite family of the de Thou); Geneviève's second marriage was to Nicolas Fauchet, and in that marriage she was the mother of Claude Fauchet![122] More straightforwardly, Jean Hotman, clerk in the 1550s and 1560s, was a first cousin of François and Antoine Hotman, who were important legal scholars and, in François's case, a writer on numismatics, while de la Tourette dabbled in alchemy after his forced retirement from the court and became embroiled in a small public controversy concerning that science with the royal historiographer, occultist, translator of Machiavelli, and brother of the clerk of the Monnaies, Jacques

---

119. Chérubin Favier and François Garrault.

120. The average tenure for the officers for whom sufficient information survives (89 of 147, with a strong bias toward the middle of the period studied) was twelve years, with a standard deviation of nine years.

121. Denys Godefroy, *Advis présenté à la Royne pour reduire les Monnoies à leur juste prix & valeur, empescher le surhaussement & empirance d'icelles* (Paris: Pierre Chevalier, 1611).

122. See Denis Charles de Godefroy-Ménilglaise, *Les savants Godefroy: Mémoires d'une famille pendant les XVIe, XVIIe et XVIIIe siècles* (Paris: Didier, 1873), 14–17. This is a marvelous work, apparently written by a character from Proust. Our Godefroy's wife was one Nicole Turquant, related to a family of councillors in the Parlement and the Aides, and possibly to Thomas Turquam, general of the moneys from 1557 to 1577.

Gohory.[123] In an age when the French sovereign courts were noted for their intellectual brilliance, the Cour des Monnaies could hold its own, especially in highly technical and even tedious subjects.[124] This was an important element of its success, since the discourse of monetary policy quickly evolved to require a combination of erudition and technical proficiency.

The Wars of Religion and Beyond

Like the rest of the kingdom, the Cour des Monnaies was profoundly affected by the civil wars that broke out shortly after the death of Henri II and continued, with longer and shorter interruptions, until 1598.[125] These wars fed off of two intertwining and mutually reinforcing struggles: one between Catholics and Calvinists ("Huguenots," as they were nicknamed, or the "So-Called Reformed Religion" [la religion prétendue réformée], as it was officially known) over the religious character of the nation and one among aristocratic factions and, increasingly, popular movements for control of the apparatus of governance with its revenues and instruments of coercion. Both of these tendencies had a profound impact on the Cour des Monnaies itself and on its functioning since, on the one hand, the officers of the court had to choose privately and publicly between the religious alternatives, and on the other, the mints and the currency were an obvious target for local or factional forces attempting to take over the apparatus of the state. Also, the fighting and the general breakdown of public order that became more and

---

123. On the genealogy of the Hotmans, see Ralph E. Giesey, *François Hotman: A Revolutionary's Ordeal* (Princeton: Princeton University Press, 1973), 335, which does not include the *greffier* Jean Hotman; and Etienne Patou, "Famille Hotman" (family tree), 2004, p. 3, http://racineshistoire.free. fr/LGN/PDF/Hotman.pdf. For de la Tourette, see Alexandre de la Tourette, *Bref discours des admirables vertus de l'or potable . . . avec une apologie de la tresutile science d'Alchimie* (Paris: Jean de l'Astre, 1575), published with Jacques Gohory, *Discours responsif à celuy d'Alexandre de la Tourette, sur les secrets de l'art chymique, faict en la defense de la philosophie & medecine antique, contre la nouvelle Paracelsique.* De la Tourette's two tracts were first published together at Lyons. On Jacques Gohory's relationship with François Gohory, greffier of the Monnaies from 1570 to 1572, see M. E.-T. Hamy, "Un précurseur de Guy de la Brosse: Jacques Gohory et le Lycium philosophal de Saint-Marceau-lès-Paris (1571–1576)," *Nouvelles archives du Muséum,* 4th ser., no. 1 (1899): 5n, quoting d'Hozier dossier no. 318. Jacques Gohory was also on friendly terms with Fauchet and the general Simon de Cressé. Ibid, 19, 22.

124. Claude Fauchet was renowned for both his technical skill and his tediousness. While there were no mathematicians in the Monnaies in our period, Bernard Frenicle de Bussy, whose father of the same name joined the court in 1595, succeeded to that office and was an important number theorist. See Charles Gillespie, ed., *Dictionary of Scientific Biography,* 16 vols. (New York: Scribner, 1970), 5:158–60.

125. For a survey of these conflicts, see Mack Holt, *The French Wars of Religion, 1562–1629,* 2nd ed. (Cambridge: Cambridge University Press, 2005), chap. 5.

more a feature of French life as the Wars of Religion went on interfered with and sometimes entirely shut down the Monnaies' ability to supervise the far-flung network of mints.

Unfortunately, on the most central problem of those conflicts—namely, the religious and political opinions of the officers of the court themselves— there is almost no information. One index we do possess suggests that the Monnaies was, if not unique, at least an extreme case among the sovereign courts of Paris. As the religious wars reached their height in 1588, King Henri III fled Paris, which fell under the control of the Catholic League. At the beginning of 1589, when it became clear that this situation would last for some time, he formally dissolved the sovereign courts of Paris and ordered their members to report to new versions set up in the city of Tours, which he controlled. While most magistrates chose to remain in Paris, non-trivial rumps of the Parlement, the Chambre des Comptes, the Grand Conseil, and the Cour des Aides were soon operating, staffed by officers who had been absent from Paris when the League took over or who subsequently slipped away. From the Cour des Monnaies, however, precisely one general reported to Tours: Nicolas Coquerel, a man congenitally incapable of getting along with anyone.[126] None of his colleagues followed, unless one counts Augustin de Varade, one of the receivers of the pyxes, as well as one retired general (François Garrault) and three retired presidents (Fauchet, le Clerc, and du Lyon, though there is no evidence that the last actually served), who agreed to resume their old duties.[127] Such solidarity was unheard of among the other sovereign courts—by way of contrast, the parlement at Tours began with about fifteen members and received about fifty refugees from Paris over the course of its existence—and indicated an unusual degree of commitment to the Catholic cause.[128] But where did that commitment originate?

In its early years, the Cour des Monnaies had a number of Protestants among its officers and ties to some of the major Protestant families of

---

126. Not only did Coquerel have a number of run-ins with the Monnaies subsequent to his service at Tours, which might have been expected, but he managed to annoy his fellow royalists there. On 19 August 1590, for example, the Chambre des Comptes of Tours stopped his wages for leaving duty without permission. AN Z^{1B} 19, fol. 87r, also 109r–110v.

127. Two new generals were also admitted at Tours. One of them, Simon Bizeul, obtained the office from one Pierre Pigeart, who seems never to have actually served but presumably obtained it from Claude Pigeart, who in turn had bought his office from Garrault when he left the court. See AN, Z^{1B} 556, piece dated 20 September 1592 (provision d'office of Bizeul). Pigeart might then be counted as a kind of "virtual" royalist general, since he is linked to royalists on either side.

128. On the Parlement of Paris transferred to Tours (its official name), see Maugis, *Histoire*, 2:136–78; there was also a sort of satellite of the Parlement in Châlons-sur-Marne.

the robe nobility. We have already noted the links that bound Hennequin, Alligret, and Marillac to the Protestant establishment of Paris. When religious warfare broke out in 1562, a police report named Alligret, Marillac, and Faucon (of whom only the first was still in the court) as Protestants while in the Parlement the Dauvet clan revealed itself as overwhelmingly Protestant.[129] In 1568, when another round of fighting broke out, the generals Jehan le Mestayer and Louis Ribier were deprived of their offices as Protestants, while Loys Hennequin resigned as royal solicitor after dodging an order to affirm his Catholic faith by oath.[130] While the deprived generals should have been entitled to return to their offices after the conclusion of the fighting, in fact, both decided or were convinced to sell their offices (to Guillaume Baudry and Pierre des Jardins, respectively). At this point the Protestant presence on the court ended, with one possible exception. The first president, Jehan le Lieur, did take the oath in 1568, but the fact that he had vanished for a considerable period as soon as fighting broke out in 1562—along with his likely relation to Roberte le Lieur (wife of the great classical scholar and monetary historian Guillaume Budé), who ultimately emigrated to Geneva—suggests at least a temporary adherence to the Reform; he too was replaced not long afterward.[131] Protestants did not reappear until the reign of Henri IV (Simon Bizeul at Tours in 1592 and Jean de Layre in 1603).[132]

One peculiar data set throws some more light on the process of the court's confessionalization. Men taking up posts as royal officers were supposed to provide testimonials as to their good life and morals, to which

---

129. See Linda L. Taber, "Religious Dissent within the Parlement of Paris in the Mid-Sixteenth Century: A Reassessment," *French Historical Studies* 16 (1990): 684–99, especially the appendix on the last page.

130. See AN, Z^{1B} 373, piece dated 23 October 1568 (procès-verbal of the administration of the oath). Ribier, le Mestayer, and Hennequin all made themselves scarce when the oath was administered; Claude de Montperlier was absent but only because he was accompanying his sister back to the convent of Val-de-Grace, where she was a nun—he happily took the oath when he returned. Thomas Turquam seems never to have taken the oath but apparently because he was ill rather than because he was a Huguenot.

131. Roberte's sister Isabeau married one Jean Ruzé, who was a general of the moneys in the first years of the sixteenth century (and famous as a cuckold). See R. Fromage, "Clément Marot— Son premier emprisonnement, identification d'Isabeau et d'Anne," *Bulletin de la société de l'histoire du protestantisme français*, 5th ser., 8 (1910): 65.

132. For Bizeul's reception, see AN, Z^{1B} 556, piece dated 20 November 1592. The information on his religion comes from Pierre de l'Estoile, who in 1609 referred to him as "de la Religion." *Mémoires-journaux*, ed. Gustave Brunet et al., 12 vols. (Paris : A. Lemerre, 1881–1896), 10:4. For de Layre, see AN, Z^{1B} 74, fol. 438: "Lettre de jussion par laquelle est commande de recevoir ledict de layre audict estat [de general] nonobstant quil soit de la religion pretendue reformee" (Paris, 9 August 1602).

Henri II added Catholic religion.[133] These dossiers survive in considerable numbers for the Cour des Monnaies and have an interesting pattern, as the plot in figure 1 shows. For many years, the standard number of witnesses was four: the first time more appeared was in 1569, when Baudry and des Jardins took up the offices of the expelled Protestant councillors. With one exception, the old pattern returned until the final collapse of religious détente in 1585: from then on, as civil war and radicalization took hold, there was a rapid escalation in the number of witnesses, until by 1593 ten became a common tally.[134] As religious conflict intensified, new recruits to the court felt pressure to demonstrate their own loyalty to the Catholic cause ever more intensely.

The Monnaies also participated more directly in the process of religious polarization. The Paris "Sixteen," named after the number of administrative divisions in the city, was a secret and radical offshoot of the Catholic League, which in turn was a movement, guided by the powerful Guise family, dedicated to preventing Henri de Bourbon, king of Navarre, cousin of Henri III, and leader of the Protestant cause from acceding to the throne of France.[135] There are two major accounts of the early days of the Sixteen; the more authoritative ascribes its foundation, in 1584 or 1585, to Charles Hotman, receiver for the bishop of Paris and brother of Jean Hotman, clerk of the Monnaies from 1552 to 1563.[136] Among the earliest members was a general of the Monnaies, Nicolas Roland du Plessis, and the other main source for the period (the report of a royal spy named Nicolas Poulain) portrays him as one of its most active leaders and probably the person with

---

133. For some thoughts on the significance of these inquiries, see Mark Greengrass, *Governing Passions: Peace and Reform in the French Kingdom, 1576–1585* (Oxford: Oxford University Press, 2007), 281.

134. The first to produce this many was René Macquegnon. AN, Z[1B] 557, dossier dated 13 March 1593. Macquegnon replaced Baudry and was apparently a pious man, since a resolution dispensing him from judgment in cases involving corporal punishment (AN, Z[1B] 558, piece dated 18 December 1597) must have been prompted by his taking holy orders.

135. On the rules of dynastic succession, which were not entirely straightforward, see Ralph Giesey, *The Juristic Basis of Dynastic Right to the French Throne* (Philadelphia: American Philosophical Society, 1961).

136. See Nicolas Poulain, "Le procez-verbal d'un nommé Nicolas Poulain," in *Archives curieuses de l'histoire de France depuis Louis XI jusqu'à Louis XVIII*, ed. M. L. Cimber and F. d'Anjou, vol. 11 (Paris: Beauvais, 1836); and Giesey, *François Hotman*, 300–301. Jean Hotman was married to a Catherine Boucher, possibly related to the ultraradical curate Jean Boucher, "le pape des Halles." See Pattou, "Famille Hotman," 3. Charles Hotman's son of the same name was also involved in the leadership of the Sixteen, while Antoine Hotman, Jean's cousin, was active in the League from an early date. It is possible that Nicolas Poulain was related to Henri Poulain, who joined the Monnaies immediately after the religious wars.

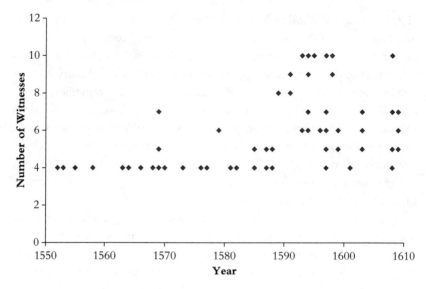

FIGURE 1.   Witnesses produced by year.
Source: AN, Z¹ᴮ 548–561: Cour des Monnaies, minutes des provisions d'office, 1550–1610.

the highest social standing within that active group.[137] To some extent, then, the Monnaies' strong adhesion to the party of the Catholic League was an accident of personnel. Though Hotman was dead by the 1580s, and Roland left the court in 1588 to become a full-time revolutionary, the ties they had epitomized remained active. The general Jehan de Riberolles (nephew of Sébastien) was active in the Sixteen at least through 1589.[138] And when Pierre Longuet replaced his father, Germain, in the court in Paris in January 1593, he offered as one of his character witnesses Ambroise de Varade, S.J., rector of the Jesuit college, who was to be vehemently accused of complicity in Pierre Barrière's attempt that August to assassinate Henri IV.[139] Ambroise was the brother of two long-standing members of the court: the councillor

---

137. See Poulain, "Procez-verbal," 292–93 ; and Robert Descimon, *Qui étaient les seize?* (Paris: Kinksiek, 1983), 212–13.

138. See Descimon, *Qui étaient les seize?*, 211, basing this judgment on Riberolles's role in a municipal election of August 1589 and mention therein of his service in the militia. Roland and Riberolles were probably linked, in that the former sold his office to Amelot Robineau, while Riberolles sold his (in 1594, not long after the fall of Paris) to Jacques Robineau.

139. AN, Z¹ᴮ 556, piece dated 29 January 1593 (provision d'office of Pierre Longuet). On Abroise Varade, see Eric Nelson, *The Jesuits and the Monarchy: Catholic Reform and Political Authority in France (1590–1615)* (Aldershot, UK, and Rome: Ashgate and Institutum Historicum Societatis Iesu, 2005), 13, 24; and Etienne Pasquier, "Bref discours du proces criminel fait à Pierre Barrière, dit la Barre, natif d'Orléans," in Cimber and Anjou, *Archives curieuses*, vol. 13 (Paris: Beauvais, 1837), 368. Henri IV seems not to have given much credence to these accusations, which were indeed less than entirely convincing, but they at least suggest a plausible link between Varade and the more radical element of the League.

Jerosme and Augustin, the receiver who defected to Tours in late 1593, perhaps to plead Ambroise's case before the king.

Such personal connections, however, do not suffice to explain the institutional behavior of the Monnaies. The Chambre de Comptes also counted
many adherents of the Sixteen among its members and their kin, yet it split
after 1589. Nor was there any obvious affinity between the position or
activities of the Monnaies and the ideology of the League, which roughly
centered on a profound, rather traditionalist piety and a strong defense of
the legitimate role of nobles, civic bodies, and the Estates General in resist-
ing royal actions that violated religious or political norms.[140] One significant
factor is the very striking similarity of the Monnaies' social composition to
that of adherents of the Paris Sixteen, which must have contributed to the
court's comfort with the radical movement.[141] Another is a lack of royalist
leadership in the court. It was among the presidents of sovereign courts,
who generally owed their appointment to the king or his ministers and who
were chosen in part for loyalty and reliability, that such leadership would
have been expected, and indeed President le Clerc and First President Fauchet both rallied to Tours in due course. Fauchet, in particular, was a man of
great stature, a fierce royalist and ferocious Gallican, and he might well have
been able to lead a royalist party in the court. As it turned out, though, when
the Sixteen rose against Henri III in 1588, le Clerc had apparently already
begun the process of retirement, and Fauchet had certainly done so, resign-
ing his office to Robert Becquet.[142] Clearly, even given what were probably
already-planned retirements, neither man, at least in the short run, had the
stomach to fight for Henri III's rights (it was not until December 1588, that
Fauchet completed his transaction with Becquet), but for whatever reason,
any potential royalist group on the Monnaies was left to its own devices by
its natural leaders.

Finally, one may speculate that the character of the Cour des Monnaies
itself—its relatively small size, technical nature, and history of both struggle and success—created a degree of solidarity not seen in the larger, more
prestigious, but also more amorphous sovereign courts of Paris. The court's

---

140. See Elie Barnavi, *Le Parti de Dieu: Etude sociale et politique des chefs de la Ligue parisienne
1585–1594* (Brussels: Nauwelerts, 1980).

141. According to Descimon's calculations, identifiable adherents of the Sixteen were 12 percent
magistrates (mainly from sovereign courts); 48 percent legal professions; 39 percent merchants and
artisans; compare with our estimate of the Monnaies as 11 percent from backgrounds in the magistracy, 48 percent from the professions, and 40 percent from the bourgeoisie. See Descimon, *Qui
étaient les seize?*, 230–31.

142. See AN, Z[1B] 557, piece dated 1 April 1594 ("Declaration de Monsieur le General Fauchet"). This document has been published in Espiner-Scott, *Documents*, 129.

experience from 1588 to the surrender of Paris to King Henri IV in March 1594 was one of isolation and combat, against royalist or Protestant forces but also against the desperate expedients of the League—whether in the shape of the Paris city council or of the duc de Mayenne (leader of the League after his brother, the duc de Guise, was murdered on Henri III's orders)—and against the rapidly encroaching chaos of a currency collapsing under the weight of war and the dissolution of central authority. Still, mutatis mutandis, it was business as usual for the court, which in its own view perpetually found itself alone against the world fighting for effective government and a solid currency. As a rule, this experience and attitude made the Cour des Monnaies into a highly effective instrument of royal government by the standards of the time, but with the locus of royal authority cast into doubt, it seems that the court preferred to follow its most passionate and activist members en bloc rather than compromise its effectiveness by splitting according to more individualistic criteria.

The Monnaies did not escape entirely unscathed from its exceptional solidarity on the losing side of the civil wars. When Henri IV took possession of Paris and officially reestablished the sovereign courts there, the chancellor presided in person over the opening of all except the Monnaies, where "not esteeming this function to be worthy of his position, he sent two of His Majesty's councillors," who were not men of great standing, to do the job.[143] The king's displeasure showed itself more concretely in a strange and soon-abandoned project to erect new Cours des Monnaies distributed around the kingdom in Toulouse, Lyons, and Poitiers.[144] The Parisians saw Coquerel's hand in this plan, probably correctly; remonstrating against it, they found the opportunity to address their new sovereign on their understanding both of the current situation and of their own role in the state. They stressed their expert status, arguing that creating new officers was unhelpful, "above all in the *fait des monnaies*, which is learned by long experience and should be kept secret and known by few persons, whose worth and probity are well known." They also touted the value of their unity as a guarantee against external pressure, warning that if they were dispersed in multiple courts the king should fear lest "governors might constrain the officers to coin under their name, arms, and figure at whatever title they please, which could not happen if the

---

143. L'Estoile, *Mémoires-journaux*, 6:268: "N'estimant pas cette fonction digne de sa charge, il y envoya deux conseillers de Sa Majesté, Claude Faucon de Ris et Geoffroy Camus de Pontcarré."

144. According to Zeller, *Les institutions*, 243, "Henri IV créa trois nouvelles Cours des Monnaies, à Toulouse, Poitiers et Lyon; mais elles sont supprimées peu après," but in fact it seems that no steps were ever taken to establish them. Toulouse was at that time still controlled by the League.

company of the generals remains whole in one body, as it has been from all time."[145] Whether because he was moved by such arguments or because he had never been serious in the first place, Henri IV did not proceed with the erection of the new courts—though Louis XIV would eventually establish a secondary Cour des Monnaies in Lyons.[146]

Otherwise, in the fifteen years between the collapse of the Catholic League and the death of Henri IV in 1610, the Cour des Monnaies underwent few changes. The reintegration of the Paris and Tours versions of the court went smoothly enough, though an enormous amount of the court's energy was for many years devoted to cleaning up the mess left by the civil wars, which included damage to the currency itself, to the bureaucratic system that the Monnaies oversaw, and to some extent even to the physical plant of the court and its mints. Having traced the outlines of the institutions that produced money and monetary policy between 1550 and 1610, we will turn from the world of things to the world of ideas to see how this bureaucratic reality interacted with the understandings and prejudices of late Renaissance France in matters of commerce, money, and coinage.

---

145. AN, Z[1B] 73 ("Remonstrances treshumbles que font les presidens conseillers et generaulx des monnoyes de france au Roy et a nosseigneurs de son conseil parlement sur ledict du moys de septembre mil cinq cens quatre vingtz et quatorze, portant erection de troys cours des monnoyes es villes de thoulouse poictiers et lyon," 26 September 1594), fol. 77r: "principallement au faict desdictes monnoyes qui saprend par long usage et doibt estre tenu secret et entendu de peu de personnes qui soient gens de bien & dont le probite soit cogneu"; fol. 77v: "les gouverneurs contraignent lesdits officiers dy faire travailler soubz leur nom armes et effigies a tel tiltre quilz voudroit Ce qui ne peut advenir demeurant la compagnie desdictes generaux entiere en ung seul corps comme a este de tout temps."

146. See *Edit du roy portant création d'une Cour des monoyes à Lyon* (Paris: Veuve F. Muguet et H. Muguet, 1704). The Lyons court, created for largely fiscal reasons, was suppressed in 1771.

CHAPTER 2

The Logic of Economic Regulation

> Thus in the beginning all the World was America, and
> more so than that is now; for no such thing as Money
> was any where known. Find out something that hath
> the Use and Value of Money amongst his Neighbors,
> you shall see the same Man will begin presently to
> enlarge his Possessions.

—John Locke

It is a commonplace to say that Europeans initially found the New World all but incomprehensible and proceeded to project onto it models and concerns drawn from their own history and society.[1] One of the things they found most alien, from the very moment of contact, was the absence from American society of money as they understood it. Columbus himself initiated this trope in his description of the initial contact with the Americans, who "brought skeins of cotton thread, parrots, darts, and other small things, . . . and they give all in exchange for anything that may be given to them; . . . they give away all they have got, for whatever may be given to them, down to broken bits of crockery and glass."[2] This quickly developed a strong moral valence, as Bartolomé de las Casas

---

1. See J. H. Elliott, *The Old World and the New, 1492–1650* (Cambridge: Cambridge University Press, 1970), and the more recent work of Anthony Pagden, *European Encounters with the New World: From Renaissance to Romanticism* (New Haven: Yale University Press, 1994).

2. Clements R. Markham, ed., *Journal of Christopher Columbus (during His First Voyage, 1492–93): And Documents Relating to the Voyages of John Cabot and Gaspar Corte Real* (London: Hakluyt Society, 1893), 39–40. For influential readings of this passage, see Tzvetan Todorov, *The Conquest of America: The Question of the Other*, trans. Richard Howard (Norman: University of Oklahoma Press, 1999), 1–50; and Steven Greenblatt, *Marvelous Possessions: The Wonder of the New World* (Chicago: University of Chicago Press, 1991).

contrasted the Indians, "poor people, for they not only possess little but have no desire to possess worldly goods—for that reason they are not arrogant, embittered, or greedy," with their conquerors, whose "ultimate aim . . . is to acquire gold, and to swell themselves with riches in a very brief time and thus rise to a high estate disproportionate to their merits."[3] The New World gave Europeans an opportunity to consider what it might mean to have a world without money and without the moral and political distortions that money could cause. Two centuries after Columbus's voyages, John Locke continued to imagine that situation. But the events recounted by Las Casas and the later exploits of the conquistadors made it abundantly clear that no such world could continue to exist.[4] In practice, Europeans used the New World to help them understand what monetary exchange meant in their own societies and, above all, what was to be done about it. For the elaborate governmental apparatus devoted to the regulation of the moneys did not exist at random or in a vacuum: it responded to what were seen as very deep and very urgent problems in Western society, and it took its place in a much larger institutional and intellectual structure that governed, or attempted to govern, economic life in France.

This chapter will concentrate on the logic that lay behind educated, elite, and public understanding of that regulation. This is, in other words, an intellectual history of economic regulation, a very large subject that has not been particularly well served in the scholarly literature.[5] What work there is on the topic orbits obsessively around a trio of problems belonging properly to a rather later period—the development of "mercantilism," the "quantity theory of money," and the origin of "political economy"—and a trio of interesting but atypical writers, Jean Bodin, Barthélemy de Laffemas, and

---

3. Bartolomé de las Casas, *The Devastation of the Indies: A Brief Account*, trans. Herma Briffault (Baltimore: Johns Hopkins University Press, 1992), 28, 31.

4. One major exception was Sir Walter Raleigh, who in his *Discovery of Guiana* imagined somehow combining English control of Guiana's gold with the protection of native innocence from Spanish perfidy. See Mary C. Fuller, "Ralegh's Fugitive Gold: Reference and Deferral in *The Discoverie of Guiana*," *Representations* 33 (1991): 42–64.

5. John U. Nef, *Industry and Government in France and England, 1540–1640* (Ithaca: Cornell University Press, 1957), is the classic study on economic policy, and on economic ideology. The remarks in Lionel Rothkrug, *Opposition to Louis XIV: The Political and Social Origins of the French Enlightenment* (Princeton: Princeton University Press, 1965), have hardly been superseded. Henry C. Clark, *Compass of Society: Commerce and Absolutism in Old-Regime France* (Lanham, MD: Lexington Books, 2007), includes an interesting but very brief examination of early seventeenth-century thought.

Antoine de Montchrestien.[6] We will take a broader view, examining political theory and rhetoric alongside legislative activity and some texts more traditionally in the domain of political economy. From this perspective a number of organizing principles emerge. While Christian morality and piety are by no means absent from the discourse of economic regulation, Renaissance elites turned more insistently to a set of concepts grounded in classical philosophy: money as a product of the development of social order beyond the household, at once a spur to blind acquisition and a technology of justice, and the passions of ambition and avarice as the chief destructive forces unleashed by money and in desperate need of regulation by royal legislation, royal courts, and royal inspectors. And despite the view that money and monetary exchange were sources of profound danger and instability, there was general and possibly growing stress on their social utility, and indeed on the government's obligation to protect them and to promote the prosperity with which they were intimately associated.

The Aristotelian Heritage

There was no such thing as "economic policy" in early modern Europe. Institutional responsibility and intellectual engagement with the issues we would categorize that way were fragmented. The fiscal system was certainly by far the largest and most influential point of contact between the government and the broader economy. It had both an extensive bureaucracy and its own experts, "financiers," a shadowy and ill-defined group whose members were frequently cast as villainous perpetrators of destruction in a narrative that would survive to the end of the old regime.[7] External trade fell under the

---

6. On mercantilism, see, e.g., Charles Cole, *French Mercantilist Doctrines before Colbert* (New York: Richard R. Smith, 1931); Eli Hecksher, *Mercantilism*, 2 vols. (London: Allen and Unwin, 1955); and Pierre Deyon, *Le mercantilisme* (Paris: Flammarion, 1969), 18–31 and 52–54. More recent, but unchanged in its outlines, is Lars Magnusson, *Mercantilism: The Shaping of an Economic Language* (London: Routledge, 1994), 176–87. On the quantity theory of money, see the classic account of Joseph Schumpeter, *History of Economic Analysis* (New York: Oxford University Press, 1954), 311–17; more recently, e.g., Thomas Guggenheim, *Preclassical Monetary Theories* (London: Pinter, 1989), 19–36. For current thinking on Montchrestien, the supposed father of "political economy," see Alain Guéry, ed., *Montchrestien et Cantillon: Le commerce et l'émergence d'une pensée économique* (Paris: E.N.S. Editions, 2011), and Henry C. Clark, "Commerce, the Virtues, and the Public Sphere in Early-Seventeenth-Century France," *French Historical Studies* 21 (1998): 415–40 (the version of this essay in *Compass of Society* is better). Only the old work of Paul Harsin, *Les doctrines monétaires et financières en France du XVIe au XVIIIe siècle* (Paris: Félix Alcan, 1928), 1–68, extends the body of texts substantially.

7. Our period falls neatly between the two major studies of early modern French financiers, Philippe Hamon, *Messieurs des finances: Les grands officiers de finance dans la France de la renaissance* (Paris: Comité pour l'histoire économique et financière de la France, 1999), and Daniel Dessert, *Argent, pouvoir et société au grand siècle* (Paris: Fayard, 1984).

unsystematic supervision of customs and admiralty organizations; specialized bodies such as the great Spanish Casa de las Indias, quasi-public merchant associations such as the English Cinque Ports and Merchant Adventurers, and joint-stock companies remained almost unknown in France. The idea of creating a specialized organ for commercial policy was occasionally broached in this period and even briefly and imperfectly implemented in France in the reign of Henri IV, but it would be another century before the French Council of Commerce began to operate in earnest.[8] Otherwise, economic affairs were left to the general organs of royal governance, with frequent, often unsolicited input from what the English called "projectors" and the Spanish *arbitristas*.[9] These political entrepreneurs or entrepreneurial politicians were as diverse in background and motivation as they were in the schemes they put forward: occasionally pure cranks, they more usually had commercial or political backgrounds and might promote anything from very specific business plans to major reworkings of the state. They came into their heyday in our period and were certainly numerous in France—we shall meet a number of them in due course. That they did not appear in French as a distinct social category, though, is revealing. As centralized as it was, the French system of governance did not provide a single nexus around which economic discourse could crystallize.

The situation in England provides a useful contrast here. England faced a serious economic crisis at midcentury, provoked by changing markets and the disastrous financial and currency policies instituted by Henry VIII to fund his wars, policies that Edward VI and Mary I were unable to disentangle. These difficulties attracted the attention of a group of well-educated and ambitious Protestants, some with mercantile connections, who had gravitated to the orbit of Protector Somerset—the best-known are Thomas Smith, William Cecil (later Lord Burghley) and, more peripherally, the merchant and financial expert Thomas Gresham. This political and economic conjunction produced an unusually coherent and influential discourse (usually identified with a broader "commonwealth" ideology) that stressed the state's moral duty to foster both prosperity and community through policies friendly to skilled labor, notably including a stable coinage and foreign

---

8. See David Kammerling Smith, "Structuring Politics in Early Eighteenth-Century France: The Political Innovations of the French Council of Commerce," *Journal of Modern History* 74 (2002): 490–537.

9. On projectors, see the classic work of Joan Thirsk, *Economic Policy and Projects: The Development of a Consumer Society in Early Modern England* (Oxford: Clarendon Press, 1978). There is a substantial literature on the *arbitristas* but little in English more recent than J. H. Elliott, "Self-Perception and Decline in Early Seventeenth-Century Spain," *Past & Present* 74 (1977): 41–61.

exchange.[10] This might be described as a semipublic discourse—many of its most important documents circulated solely or mainly in manuscript, within circles close to royal policymaking, and it eventually took root in the memoirs of the projectors.[11] Indeed, thanks largely to Cecil's role in the Elizabethan regime, it was something close to the official ideology of the realm in the later sixteenth century.

In France, the situation was far more diffuse. Neither institutions nor ideologies offered a center for economic policy. Indeed, the closest there was to such a center was the Cour des Monnaies itself, established (according to Henri II's edict of sovereignty) "to counsel us in what it is best to do to give order to the affairs of our moneys, by which all things necessary to men and invented for the facility of commerce with one another are valued, and by which all things receive their sure price and value."[12] That counsel, however, had special characteristics that offer an opening into the particular role of money in what would come to be called political economy. First, it was, or ought to be, removed from the public view and attached to the great mysteries of state.[13] An auditor in the Chambre des Comptes named Vincent Gelée made that point explicitly in a guidebook for public accounting. Speaking of a table he had drawn up to assist himself in auditing mint accounts—"which are the most difficult accounts in the Chambre, since few are knowledgeable in monetary affairs"—he said, "I would willingly have inserted that table here, with a brief commentary, for the understanding of monetary affairs. But I have been prevented from doing this because of the danger that there is in

10. The standard work on this subject, Arthur B. Ferguson, *The Articulate Citizen and the English Renaissance* (Durham, NC: Duke University Press, 1965), is outdated and unsatisfactory in a number of respects, including that it barely touches on Elizabeth's reign. G. R. Elton, "Reform and the 'Commonwealth-men' of Edward VI's reign," in *The English Commonwealth, 1547–1640: Essays in Politics and Society Presented to Joel Hurstfield*, ed. Peter Clark, Alan G. R. Smith, and Nicholas Tyack (New York: Barnes and Noble, 1979), 23–38, was (perhaps unduly) unimpressed by this tendency.

11. The most important of these treatises was written in 1549 but not published until 1581: *A Discourse of the Commonweal of This Realm of England*, ed. Mary Dewar (Charlottesville: University Press of Virginia for the Folger Shakespeare Library, 1969). See also Raymond de Roover, *Gresham on Foreign Exchange: An Essay on Early English Mercantilism with the Text of Sir Thomas Gresham's Memorandum for the Understanding of the Exchange* (Cambridge, MA: Harvard University Press, 1949). On the adoption of this language by projectors, see Thirsk, *Economic Policy*, passim.

12. *Edict du roy pour la souvereineté de la Cour des monnoyes en l'annee 1551*(Paris: Jean Dalier, n.d.), 2: "pour nous conseiller en ce qu'il convient faire pour donner ordre au faict de nosdictes monnoyes, par lesquelles sont estimees toutes choses qui sont necessaire pour l'usage des hommes & inventees pour la facilité du commerce des uns aux autres, & par lesquelles toutes choses recoivent leur certain prix & extimation."

13. See Ernst Kantorowicz, "Mysteries of State: An Absolutist Concept and Its Late Mediaeval Origins," *Harvard Theological Review* 48 (1955): 65–91.

divulging such things, which should be secret and reserved only for those who make a profession of it, and have taken an oath to the king and the public."[14]

That narrative reappears notably in a set of remonstrances presented to the king in 1585, probably the work of the historian and president Claude Fauchet. The later reappearance of their basic narrative in later published work suggests that they (or the notes prepared for them) influenced contemporary erudition.[15] The Monnaies, trying to keep its membership down, leaned hard on the principle of secrecy. "Just as the regulation of the moneys is one of the principal [elements] of the administration of all states and kingdoms," it began, "so the best governed of them have always kept it secret and communicated it to few people, so as to avoid the problems that follow from communication and disagreement on this matter."[16] The models of this wise administration were the Roman *triumviri monetales*, "drawn from the principal and best senatorial families."[17] The French kings had initially followed that model, and Henri II had granted the court sovereignty, "not wishing monetary affairs to be communicated to persons who had not taken an oath to himself in that regard," as would happen when appeal lay to other courts.[18] Only recently had the unhappy circumstances of the religious wars and the Alexandre de la Tourette's machinations caused the number of primary and subsidiary generals to balloon. If the king wished to be well served in monetary affairs, he would try to reverse that trend.

---

14. In a gloss to Jean Hennequin, *Le guidon general des finances. Contenant l'Instruction du maniement de toutes les finances de France . . . Avec les Annotations de Me. Vincent Gelee . . . Le tout nouvellement revue & corrigé* (Paris: Abel l'Angelier, 1596). Fol. 124r–v: "qui sont les comptes les plus difficiles de la Chambre, à cause que peu entendent le faict desdites monnoyes." Fol. 125v: "J'eusse volontiers icy inseré ledit bavouer & une sommaire instruction, pour l'intelligence du fait des monnoies. Mais j'ay esté retenu de ce faire, pour le peril qu'il y a de divulguer telles choses, lesquelles doivent estre secrettes & suelement reservees à ceux qui en font profession, ont serment au Roy & au public."

15. Pierre de Miraulmont, *Les memoires . . . Sur l'origine & institution des Cours souveraines, & Justices Royalles estans dans l'enclos du Palais Royal de Paris* (Paris: Claude de la Tour, 1612), 629–49; and Germain Constans, *Traité de la Cour des monnoyes et de l'estendue de sa jurisdiction divisé en cinq parties* (Paris: Sebastien Cramoisy, 1658), follow the outline sketched in these remonstrances.

16. AN, Z[1B] 380, piece dated 14 November 1585 ("Remonstrances treshumbles que font a sa Majeste les gens tenants la court des monnoyes Sur leedict du moys de septembre mil v^c iii^xx cinq portant restablissement des generaulx des monnoyes cy devant supprimez par mort suyvant les eeditz precedens"), fol. 1r: "Tout ainsy que le reiglement des monnoyes est ung des principaulx de la police de tous estatz et royaumes aussy a il este par les mieulx gouvernez tenu secret et communicque a peu de personnes pour eviter les inconveniens qui suyvent et la communication et la variation en ce faict."

17. Ibid.: "tirez entre les principaulx et des meilleurs maisons du Senat." In fact, the *monetales* were a minor magistracy drawn somewhat peripherally into the *cursus honorum* only in the late republic. See Charles D. Hamilton, "The Tresviri Monetales and the Republican Cursus Honorum," *Transactions and Proceedings of the American Philological Association* 100 (1969): 181–99.

18. AN, Z[1B] 380, piece dated 14 November 1585, fol. 1v: "ne veullant ledict faict des monnoyes estre communicque a gens qui neussent pour ce regard le serment a luy."

This was a tendentious and self-serving argument put forward by men in danger of seeing their investment in their offices diluted. There were in fact many occasions when monetary policy was discussed in public and well-publicized assemblies. Fauchet's was a fairly pure piece of political rhetoric, but it clearly had some resonance beyond the walls of the court itself. Monetary affairs were seen as in some important sense especially dangerous. This was partly because of the often-overwhelming temptations of fraud and malversation, but it is hard to understand how that could be the whole story since one would expect openness and a well-informed public to make dishonesty more, not less, difficult. As it turns out, early modern thinkers believed that those dangers lay deeper than the superficial, if still important, incentives that might push one or another individual or institution toward corruption; money, in their view, was the unavoidable instrument of a general disarrangement of human motivations toward ends that might well prove destructive of the common good.

This outlook, and the frame of reference in which sixteenth-century France generally regarded the articulation of money and political economy, originated with Aristotle. Since the recovery of his corpus in the twelfth and thirteenth centuries, "the Philosopher" had been central to Europe's intellectual life. Far from fading in the sixteenth century, interest in his thought only increased as, thanks to the humanist revolution in classical studies, Aristotle became a better-known and more controversial figure.[19] French scholars could read the new Latin translations of Aristotle's moral works by the royal professors of Greek Denys Lambin and Adrien Turnèbe (father of Odet, the ill-fated would-be first president of the Monnaies).[20] A larger public could follow the deadly controversy between the educational reformer Pierre de la Ramée (Petrus Ramus) and the defenders of Aristotelianism led by Pierre Galland and could read Aristotle's *Politics* in an elegant, heavily annotated new

---

19. There is a good summary of the *fortuna* of Aristotle's *Politics* in the Budé edition: Aristotle, *Politique,*bks. 1 and 2, ed. Jean Aubonnet, 2nd ed. (Paris: Les Belles Lettres, 1968), cxx–cxcvi. On Aristotle in the Renaissance, see Charles B. Schmitt, *Aristotle in the Renaissance* (Cambridge, MA: Harvard University Press for Oberlin College, 1983).

20. Turnèbe's version of the *Ethics* is, in the edition I have consulted, *Aristotelous Ethikon Nikomacheion biblia deka. Aristotelis de moribus ad Nicomachum libri decem. Ita Græcis interpretatione recenti cum Latinis conjunctis* (Heidelberg, 1560); Lambin translated both the *Politics* and the *Ethics*. For the former, I have consulted *Aristotelis de Reip. bene administrandæ ratione, libri octo, a Dionys. Lambino Monstroliensi, litterarum Græcarum Lutetitiæ doctore Regio, olim Latini facti* (Paris: Apud Joannem Bene-natum, 1567); for the latter, *Ethicorum, sive de moribus ad Nicomachum libri decem adiecta ad contextum græcum interpretatione latina Dionysii Lambini, ed. altera* (Frankfurt: apud her. A. Wecheli, C. Marn. & J. Aubr., 1596).

French translation by the political thinker Loys le Roy, successor of Turnèbe and Lambin in the chair of Greek.[21] Almost anyone who progressed to the philosophy course that was the capstone of early modern "undergraduate" education would have spent two years in intensive study of the Stagirite, for most teachers shared the Jesuits' conviction that in the schools "above all one should know how to interpret the Aristotelian texts well."[22] And, as le Roy's case suggests, political theorists continued to develop and adapt Aristotelian concepts to the realities of Renaissance Europe.[23]

Aristotle's centrality is less self-evident than one might suppose, though. In recent decades much of the most influential work on the history of early modern European social and political thought has shied away from him. In some cases it has pursued the interest in Neostoic thought first broadly aroused by Gerhard Oestreich.[24] Quentin Skinner's dismissal of Aristotelian influence on humanist political thought—and his stress instead on the influence of more or less Stoic Roman writers such as Sallust and, above all, Cicero—has been particularly influential.[25] And a revival of interest in Renaissance Platonism has also served to push Aristotle into the background.[26] Certainly no one would now deny the importance of Roman or Platonic models in early modern

---

21. On the Ramus/Galland controversy, which was notorious enough to be lampooned by Rabelais in the preface to his *Quart livre*, see Frank Pierrepont Graves, *Peter Ramus and the Educational Reformation of the Sixteenth Century* (New York: Macmillan, 1912). Galland supposedly arranged Ramus's murder during the St. Bartholomew's Day massacres in Paris. Aristotle, *Les politiques*, trans. Loys le Roy (Paris: A. Drouart, 1599 [1568]) (hereinafter Le Roy, *Politiques*): quotations from the *Politics* below are my translation of le Roy's (generally excellent) translation. The only significant recent study of it is Enzo Sciacca, *Umanesimo e scienza politica nella Francia del XVI secolo: Loys le Roy* (Florence: Leo S. Olschki, 2007), esp. 134–40.

22. Claude Pavur, ed., *The* Ratio Studiorum: *The Official Plan for Jesuit Education* (St. Louis: Institute of Jesuit Sources, 2005), 104: "Summopere conetur aristotelicum textum bene interpretari" (§226), my translation. The *Politics* did not figure in the Jesuit curriculum, but anyone trained in the *ratio* would have been primed to consult it when questions of political theory arose.

23. The most influential study of this process is J. G. A. Pocock, *The Machiavellian Moment: Florentine Political Thought and the Atlantic Republican Tradition* (Princeton: Princeton University Press, 1975), and the depth of my debt to that book should be evident.

24. See Gerhard Oestreich, *Neostoicism and the Early Modern State*, trans. David McKlintock (Cambridge: Cambridge University Press, 1982).

25. The most complete expression of this view is Quentin Skinner, *Visions of Politics*, vol. 2, *Renaissance Virtues* (Cambridge: Cambridge University Press, 2002). Kari Palonen, *Quentin Skinner: History, Politics, Rhetoric* (Cambridge: Polity, 2003), provides a good overview of the development and influence of Skinner's thought.

26. James Hankins, *Plato in the Italian Renaissance*, 2 vols. (Leiden: E.J. Brill, 1990), is the seminal work in this field; Eric Nelson, *The Greek Tradition in Republican Thought* (Cambridge: Cambridge University Press, 2004), is its reductio ad absurdum.

politics, but it would be equally mistaken to ignore the power and persistence of structures of thought stretching back into the Middle Ages. Aristotle was the common heritage of scholastics and humanists, of lawyers and theologians, and indeed of the entire educated public of Europe. Well into the seventeenth century he remained an inextricable part of the way they thought about most aspects of their world, and there is much that can best be understood with at least initial reference to his thought.

That is not to say that early modern thought about political economy was in any strict sense "Aristotelian." Indeed, one of the major problems in reading political thought in terms of schools, influences, and "languages," as is so often done, is that early modern Europeans emphatically did not conceive of their own discourse or, still less, the classical tradition on which they drew as being segmented in that way. This is not the place for a comprehensive critique of the "Cambridge School" and related approaches that have dominated the Anglophone history of political thought for several decades now, though one is probably needed.[27] At the least, that school's initial promise to connect political thought and practice in precise and detailed ways has been only very partially kept. One must resist the persistent temptation to impose philosophical and theoretical categories on historical actors for whom "political thought," of whatever kind, was above all a way of understanding and organizing political and social practice with all its personal, historical, and institutional constraints and in all its messiness. More simply, whether or not sixteenth-century French magistrates were in any strict sense Aristotelians, Aristotle was almost the only theoretician, and almost the only ancient writer about money, ever cited by the Cour des Monnaies, sufficient evidence that his authority remained unparalleled among those involved in monetary policy.[28]

Money enters Aristotle's account of the structure and flourishing of human society at two crucial points.[29] The longer passage is in the first book of his *Politics*. Aristotle begins that treatise (or so the standard sixteenth-

---

27. The current "state of the question" in the field is well represented by George Klosko, ed., *The Oxford Handbook of the History of Political Philosophy* (Oxford: Oxford University Press, 2011); see especially the second chapter: Mark Bevir, "The Contextual Approach," 11–23.

28. As we shall see, Aristotle's one rival in citation was the late antique encyclopedist Cassiodorus.

29. The seminal studies of Aristotle's economic thought are Karl Polanyi, "Aristotle Discovers the Economy," in *Primitive, Archaic and Modern Economies: Essays of Karl Polanyi*, ed. George Dalton (Boston: Beacon Press, 1969), 78–115 (first published in a slightly different form in 1957); and M. I. Finley, "Aristotle and Economic Analysis," *Past and Present* 47 (1970): 3–25. Scott Meikle, *Aristotle's Economic Thought* (Oxford: Clarendon Press, 1995), explicates the relevant texts thoroughly and convincingly.

century interpretation went) with an anatomy of the components of the polis: man, the "political animal"; the household (*oikos*); and larger communities culminating in the polis itself.[30] After treating some questions on the nature of the household, Aristotle turned to the question of how the art of household management (*oikonomikê*; *mesnage* in le Roy's French; *res familiarum administrando* in Lambin's Latin) related to that of acquiring wealth (*chrematistikê*; *acquerir*; *ars pecuniæ quærendo*). He answered the question by distinguishing two types of chrematistic: "the former according to nature, the latter truly not," in Jacques Lefèvre d'Etaples's paraphrase.[31] The "natural" chrematistic consists of obtaining materials for the household either through the direct exploitation of nature (hunting, farming, raiding, and the like) or by barter. The second form of chrematistic was made possible by a technical or artificial innovation, namely, money.[32]

After money was invented for exchange, another form of acquisition inevitably came about, that is, resale [*kapêlikon*], which was probably exercised simply at first, and then through experience became more artificial, as people learned where and how to make great profits from exchange. For this reason, it seems that acquisition consists principally in money, and that its task is to be able to see where one can get a great deal of coin, because such an art produces wealth and coin: for they often believe that riches consist in an abundance of money.[33]

---

30. The starting place for sixteenth-century French readings of the *Politics* is the summary or "formula" of Jacques Lefèvre d'Etaples, which prefaced most school-text editions, e.g., *Contenta politicorum Aristotelis libri Octo. Economicorum eiusdem duo. Haec Aristotelis opera ullis absque commentarijs emissa sunt, quibus in fronte familiaris in Politica introductio, una cum indice vocabulorum*, ed. Franciscus Zampinus (Paris: In Clauso brunello sub Geminarum Cipparum insigni, 1529), sigs. A iii r–A viii r.

31. *Contenta politicorum*, sig. Aiii r: "hae quidem secundum naturam: illae vero non." Aristotle puts it similarly, *Politics* 1257a: "ἔστι δ' ἡ μὲν φύσει ἡ δ' οὐ φύσει αὐτῶν, ἀλλὰ δι' ἐμπειρίας τινὸςα καὶ τέχνης γίνεται μᾶλλον." The distinction between *physin* and *technê* is fundamental to Aristotle's thought.

32. The Monnaies quoted Aristotle's definition of money during an important reform debate: AN, Z¹ᴮ 170, fol. 170v: "A ce propos aristotte parlant de lusaige de la monnoie dict que cest medium quoddam per quod nos omnia metunno que in commercium cadunt" (from a set of "Remonstrances sur ledict du roy du moys de mars an vclxxvii").

33. Le Roy, *Politiques*, 50: "Apres que la monnoye fut inventee pour l'eschange, necessairement survint une autre espece d'acquerir, à sçavoir la revenderie, qu'on exerçoit aussi du commencement paraventure simplement: puis est devenuë par experience plus artificielle, apres avoir cogneu d'où & comment l'on feroit grand gaing par eschanger. Parquoy semble que l'acquisition consiste principalement en la monnoye, & que son office soit, pouvoir veoir d'où l'on recouvrera abondance de pecune, par ce que tel art produit richesse & pecune: car ils cuident souvent richesse estre abondance de monnoye."

While Aristotle admitted the utility of that art (essentially market activity or economy in the modern sense) in supplying the household or polis, he did not fully approve of it.

The reasons for his disapproval are complex. In Aristotle's view, money is almost a contagious disease: in Scott Meikle's words, "the activity of pursuing money has a capacity to attach itself to other activities, to infiltrate its aim" (the *telos* of Aristotelian metaphysics), "into theirs, and to subordinate their ends to its own."[34] It then creates a kind of ethical confusion, so that even "those who desire to live well seek to enjoy physical pleasures; and since those seem to them to consist in riches, they put all their effort into acquiring them." This Aristotle probably and his Renaissance readers certainly saw as the herald of a complete moral collapse, which ends, according to le Roy's gloss, with us "abusing our natural virtues, our understanding, and our faculties, which it renders entirely mercenary and money-grubbing."[35] Aristotelians and Stoics both associated such disordered passions not only with individual vice but with political disorder, and so did the political elites of sixteenth-century France, as Mark Greengrass has shown.[36] Money also encouraged an error that is often supposed to have dominated economic thought in the "mercantilist" era: identifying wealth with the money that was its mere representation. The Cour des Monnaies was paraphrasing Aristotle when it complained to the king that "the common people believe that whoever has the most gold is the richest, even though such riches are more imaginary and a legal fiction than true and natural. The example of Midas, who died of hunger amid so much gold, shows this clearly."[37] Aside from its moral problems, this was an attitude that tended to favor inflation.

But if money's tendency to become an end in itself was one source of its power as a disruptive ethical and political force, the heart of its power

---

34. Meikle, *Economic Thought*, 74.

35. Le Roy, *Politiques*, 51: "mais ceux qui desirent aussi bien vivre, cherchent jouïr des voluptez corporelles. et pourtant que cela leur semble consister és richesses, ils mettent tout leur estude à en acquerir." Page 54: "abusant des vertus naturelles, & des sciences & facultez qu'elle rend toutes mercenaires & pecuniaires."

36. See Mark Greengrass, *Governing Passions: Peace and Reform in the French Kingdom, 1576–1585* (Oxford: Oxford University Press, 2007), 35–65.

37. AN, Z^{1B} 72, fol. 45v: "le commun ayt opinion que celluy qui a le plus dor soit le plus riche Sy est ce que telle richesse est plus tost imaginative et legualle que vraye et naturelle Ce que monstre evidemment lexemple de midas lequel au millieu de tant dor mourroit de faim" (from a set of "Remonstrances faictes au conseil destat du roy nostre sire a sainct Germain en laye le samedi xxviiie jour de janvier an vc iiiixx quatre"). Compare *Politics* 1257b; the court's "plus tost imaginative et legualle que vraye et naturelle" loosely translates "νόμος παντάπασι, φύσει δ᾽ οὐθέν."

was that in *kapêlikon* "money is the beginning and end of such exchanges, and . . . riches that one thus acquires are infinite."[38] The unboundedness of monetary acquisition, divorced from the natural realities of subsistence and raised into the abstract realm of easily stored metal tokens—themselves virtually dematerialized and turned into pure numbers by a public mark denoting a certain quantity—was a source of danger. Aristotle even went so far as to contradict a verse of the sage Solon's that "there is no set limit to the riches of men."[39] From this point of view, there was something inhuman about money: it removed the natural limits of the acquisitive instinct and launched its would-be possessors into the infinite realm of the integers. It was this characteristic of money that John Locke seized on in a key development in his *Second Treatise of Government*, quoted at the head of this chapter. Locke suggests that the originary and purely natural *"Rule of Propriety (viz.)* that every Man should have as much as he could make use of," essentially a version of Aristotelian household management, "would hold still in the World . . . had not the *Invention of Money*, and the tacit Agreement of Men to put a value on it, introduced (by Consent) larger Possessions, and a Right to them."[40] Eighty years earlier, a French commentator had described the early years of Roman power (pregnant with parallels to the Americas) in similar terms: "Money began to circulate then, and gain so tempted men that they invented that pernicious method of lending at interest and usury, so much so that the number one hundred thousand, which was as far as they counted, was multiplied by these means, and mounted so high that they counted by millions."[41] And thus the republic entered its decline.

One abstruse but useful way to understand this kind of seemingly unreasonable anxiety, which money tended to elicit throughout the pre-industrial West, is to analyze it with the tools of post-structuralist philosophy. In particular, as Jean-Joseph Goux has pointed out, there is a

---

38. Le Roy, *Politiques*, 50: "que la monnoye est le commencement & la fin de telle permutation, & la richesse qu'on acquiert ainsi, est infini."

39. *Politics* 1256b: "πλούτου δ' οὐθὲν τέρμα πεφασμένον ἀνδράσι κεῖται." Lambin, *Aristotelis de Reip.*, 17, has "Nulla homini finis certa haæret divitiarum." The unboundedness of money in Greek thought is the paradoxical counterpart of its invisibility: see Marc Shell, "The Ring of Gyges," in *The Economy of Literature* (Baltimore: Johns Hopkins University Press, 1978), 11–62.

40. John Locke, *Two Treatises of Government*, ed. Peter Laslett (Cambridge: Cambridge University Press, 1988), 293 (III.36) (emphasis in original).

41. Isaac de Laffémas, *Histoire du commerce de France. Enrichie des plus notables antiquitez du traffic des païs estranges* (Paris: Toussaincts du Bray, 1606), 148: "La monnoye commençoit à lors d'avoir cours, & le gain allechoit tellement les hommes qu'on inventa ceste pernicieuse façon de prester à interest & usure, si bien que le le [sic] nombre de cent mil jusques auquel on contoit seulement, fust multiplié par ce moyen, & monta si haut que l'on conta par milions," citing Pliny, *Historia naturalis* 33.10.

homology between the development of money and the development of writing as the Greek philosophers understood them.[42] Plato's criticism of writing began with *absence*: writing is a dead and inadequate substitute for a writer who is not present to explicate his or her thoughts or (in the case of writing as memorandum) for what one has thought but forgotten, which is no longer present to the spirit. In a similar way, Aristotle's money comes into being when households cannot present their needs directly to each other because of their dispersion from each other either in space or in time (you may need my apples now, but you will need my assistance in rebuilding a barn only at some future date after the apples have already rotted or been consumed).[43] This might, as Derrida contends is the case with language, echo a deeper, metaphysical absence—perhaps the failure of "value" to inhere in the objects of exchange—but that is of no immediate importance to us.[44] What is important is that once established, money in Aristotle's system seems to follow what Derrida calls a logic of the "supplement": something "inessential and nevertheless damaging to the essence, . . . a surplus that *ought not* to have come and added itself to the unopened plenitude of the interior" of, in this case, the act of exchange.[45] Having supposedly come into being to repair a specific gap in the process of exchange, as writing does for communication, money shows a strong tendency to take over all aspects of that process. Just as writing reveals a tendency in language and narrative to obey an entirely internal logic, escaping the control of both authorial intent and external referents, so money installs its own logic of exchange that aims only at itself, imposes its own technology, and erases the human aims toward which exchange was to be directed. This is a dismaying enough prospect for an age inured

---

42. See Jean-Joseph Goux, *Freud, Marx: Economie et symbolique* (Paris: Editions du Seuil, 1973), esp. 125–48; a combination of Marxian dogma and lack of historical grounding leads Goux astray in the details of the analogy. For Derrida's theories, see, e.g., Jacques Derrida, "La pharmacie de Platon," in *La dissémination* (Paris: Editions du Seuil, 1972), 69–197; and Derrida, *De la grammatologie* (Paris: Editions du minuit, 1967). Derrida discusses money explicitly in *Donner le temps 1: La fausse monnaie* (Paris: Editions Galilée, 1991), 95–138.

43. At *Nicomachean Ethics* 1233b14. This phenomenon also underlies Aristotle's discussion of market cornering at *Politics* 1259a.

44. Mielke sees Aristotle's economic thought as largely driven by an unsuccessful attempt to understand how exchange value could inhere in the objects of exchange, but no one familiar with marketing can be very sanguine about the inherent nature of use value either.

45. Derrida, *La dissémination*, 147: "La pureté du dedans ne peut dès lors être restaurée qu'en *accusant* l'extériorité sous la catégorie d'un supplément, inessentiel et néanmoins nuisible à l'essence, d'un surplus qui *aurait dû* ne pas venir s'ajouter à la plénitude inentamée du dedans" (my translation, emphasis in original). See also Derrida, *Grammatologie*, 207–18.

to the enlightened despotism of the invisible hand: in ancient Greece, or in Renaissance France, it was terrifying.

While there were no deconstructionists on the Cour des Monnaies, the idea that money and language functioned in similar ways was certainly not foreign to the Renaissance. One frequently quoted dictum of the Roman rhetorical theorist Quintilian, for example, had it that "custom is indeed the surest guide to speaking, and language is to be used like money that bears the public stamp."[46] And this parallel was not neutral. Terence Cave has described in detail both the anxieties aroused in sixteenth-century France by rhetorical *copia*—the abundant flow of words that showed off rhetorical skill but might be driven as much by citation, wordplay, and general sophistry as by the requirements of truth—and the ways in which they interacted with the desire for and fear of material abundance.[47] In a culture so deeply impregnated with rhetoric, rhetorical theory, and rhetorical education, the power of words seemed very real. The fact that money could be understood in some of the same terms was perhaps more significant then than it is now; anxiety over verbal power and deception flowed easily into economic fears in the reverse of the process we would now be more inclined to expect.

The question remains, however, how exactly the problem of monetary accumulation became a *political* problem. This becomes clearer in Aristotle's *Nicomachean Ethics*. In the fifth book of that work, in the course of his discussion of justice in society, he argued that distributive justice required there to be a common measure of the value of all goods exchanged. To translate Turnèbe's Latin, "This thing is in fact use [*chreia*], which holds all things together. . . . But by common consent coinage has been substituted for use, and for that reason it is called *numus* [*nomisma*], because it exists not by nature but by decree [*nomos*], and it is in our power to change it and

---

46. Quintilian, *Institutio oratoria* 1.6.3: "consuetudo vero certissima loquendi magistra, utendumque plane sermone, ut nummo, cui publica forma est." One finds an allusion to this passage, for example, in a philosophical work by our friend Loys le Roy, *De la vicissitude ou variété des choses en l'univers* (Paris: Fayard, 1988 [1577]), 80. Montaigne made parallel comments regarding the humanities generally, particularly in the "Apologie de Raymond Sebond." See Edward J. Benson, "Guerrier or Glossateur? Montaigne's Monetary Metaphors," *Renaissance and Reformation/ Renaissance et réforme* 16 (1992): 58–59.

47. Terence Cave, *The Cornucopian Text: Problems of Writing in the French Renaissance* (Oxford: Clarendon Press, 1979); Rebecca Zorach, *Blood, Milk, Ink, Gold: Abundance and Excess in the French Renaissance* (Chicago: University of Chicago Press, 2005), suggests that a similar dynamic was at work in the visual culture of the day.

to make it worthless."[48] Money appears again as a supplement, an artificial addition to the natural force, *chreia*, that holds economic exchange together, needed because chreia is not quantitative: for "the just," Aristotle held, "is a proportion of things being compared; proportion belongs not to individual numbers, but to numbers in general."[49] More specifically, though, money is a creation of the political community: its creation seems less spontaneous than in the *Politics*.[50] And money in this account is a technology of justice, which (as everyone agreed) was the foundation of any worthwhile community. When discussing distributive justice—the apportionment of public rewards and goods among those eligible to receive them—Aristotle treated this as essentially a metaphor: distributive justice is "geometrical," greater or less as the giver and receiver are greater or less, by whatever criteria (birth, wealth, virtue) may be appropriate. For retributive justice—essentially, the legal enforcement of contracts—however, "all that of which there is exchange must in some way be comparable, which is where money comes in," with a precision suitable for legal judgment.[51]

This justice-based account of the function of money had two important consequences. One was an immediate appeal to jurists, and in fact Aristotle's language was incorporated wholesale into the Roman law and thence into the mental world of educated Europeans from the twelfth century onward. Money, according to the *Digest*, was "a material of which the public and perpetual valuation supplies by the equality of quantities the difficulties

48. Turnèbe, *Aristotelous Ethikon*, 251: "at id est re veræ quidem usus, qui omnia consociat. . . . nimirum in usus vicem nummus ex pacto substituitur: & idcirco numus appellatur, quod non natura sit, sed instituto: in nobisque sit, eum mutare, atque inutilem reddere" (1133a19ff.). Lambin, *Ethicorum*, 313, has "Hoc autem re quidem vera usus, seu indigentia est: quæ omnia continet. Nam si nulla egerent homines, aut si non similiter egerent: vel nulla, vel non eadem esset permutatio. Sed in indigentiæ locum ex hominum quasi compacto & convento quodammodo successit nummus: atque ob hanc causam, *nomisma* vocatur a Graecis, *apo tô nomô*, id est, a lege: quia non natura, sed lege valeat, sitque in nobis situm eum immutare, inutilemque reddere."

49. Turnèbe, *Aristotelous Ethikon*, 238–39: "Jus igitur quiddam est proportione comparatum. Proportio enim non tantum numeri solitarii est, sed numeri in totum" (1131a29). Lambin, *Ethicorum*, 293, has "Ius igitur proportione & comparatione quadam constat. Non enim solum eius numeri, quo aliquid numeramus, proprium esse, proportione constare: sed etiam ejus, qui universe & omnino numerus est." Lambin probably represents the way this passage was read at the time.

50. On the relation of Aristotle's account to contemporary Greek monetary practice, see Olivier Picard, "Aristote et la monnaie," *Ktema* 5 (1980): 267–76, who comes close to describing Aristotle as a chartalist *avant la lettre*.

51. Turnèbe, *Aristotelous Ethikon*, 250: "Idcirco omnia ea quorum est commutatio, comparabilia esse quodam modo debent, quamobrem nummus accessit." Lambin, *Ethicorum*, 312: "Quapropter quarum rerum sit permutatio, eas res oportet esse ejusmodi, ut inter se quodammodo comparari possint. Atque ad hanc rem, nummus quæsitus & comparatus est."

of exchange . . . stamped with a public form."[52] And it remained closely bound up with the overall concept that underlay the entire edifice of the Roman law, that "justice is a constant and perpetual inclination to give to each his own right [*jus*]."[53] This tended to lead people to identify coinage with law more and more completely, so that for Jean Bodin, for example, it was "of the same nature as the law, and only he who has the power to make law may give law to the moneys."[54] He amplified this identification in his *Response aux paradoxes de M. de Malestroict*, where he asserted that "the king of the Indies, having seen that the Romans observed the same proportion of gold to silver that was kept in his country, according to the report of the ambassador, praised their justice. For coinage is a law, properly speaking: thus, the Greeks used the same word for money and law, as we say law and alloy." A sixteenth-century reader of one copy added (in Latin) in the margin, "νόμος, 'law' [or] 'institute' and 'coin' in the Doric tongue: whence the Latin's *numus*."[55] Money became an integral part of political science, in particular as part of the science of legislation—for Bodin, the power to legislate in itself constituted sovereignty.[56] For this reason, for example, François le Begue began his 1600 monetary treatise with a long preface on laws and legislation. In 1608, to take another example, Nicolas de Coquerel started a similar work with the statement that "in establishing empires, kingdoms,

---

52. *Digest* 18.1.1: "materia . . . cujus publica ac perpetua æstimatio difficultatibus permutationem æqualitate quantitatis subveniet. Eaque materia forma publica percussa usum dominiumque non tam ex substantia præbet quam ex quantitate nec ultra merx utrumque, sed alterum pretium vocatur." On the classical discussion of money and price and its debt to Aristotle, see Claude Nicolet, "Prix, monnaies, échanges: Les variations des prix et la 'théorie quantitative de la monnaie' à Rome, de Cicéron à Pline l'Ancien," *Annales ESC* 26 (1971): 1203–7.

53. *Digest* 1.1.10: "Iustitia est constans et perpetua voluntas ius suum cuique tribuendi." The account in Nelson, *Greek Tradition*, 9–15, of Roman-law justice as a system opposed to both Platonism and Aristotelianism seems to me incorrect and would have seemed to sixteenth-century thinkers simply insane.

54. Jean Bodin, *Les six livres de la republique* (Paris: Jacques du Puis, 1583), 242: "Quant au droit de moneage, il est de la mesme nature de la loy, & n'y a que celuy qui a puissance de faire la loy, qui puisse donner la loy aux monnoyes."

55. Jean Bodin, *La vie chère au XVIe siècle: La response de Jean Bodin à M. de Malestroict, 1568*, ed. Henri Hauser (Paris: Armand Colin, 1932), 52–53 and note: "le Roy des Indes, ayant veu la mesme proportion de l'or à l'argent qui estoit en son pays estre gardee par les Romains, au rapport qu'en faisoit l'ambassadeur, loua leur justice. Car la monnoye est une loy à bien parler: aussi les Gregeois apellent la monnoye et la loy d'un mesme nom, comme nous disons loy et aloy." "νόμος, lex, institutum et numisma, lingua dorica, unde Latinis numus." This is an edition of the BN's copy of the 1568 edition (Rés. Lf 77.20b), with marginalia.

56. See, e.g., Bodin, *Six livres*, 223: "Sous ceste mesme puissance de donner & casser la loy sont compris tous les autres droits & marques de souveraineté: de sorte qu'à parler proprement on peut dire qu'il n'y a que ceste seule marque de souveraineté." On legislation in Renaissance political thought, see also Pocock, *Machiavellian Moment*.

and republics, the first legislators, guided by a divine grace," saw first to religion, next to defense, and then to money.[57] As we shall see in chapter 4, this association between money and law had a profound impact on the way money itself was theorized in early modern France.

Ambition and Avarice

The other consequence of the link between money and justice was that it suggested a detailed account of how money posed a danger to the political order. Money, in the view of most sixteenth-century theorists, opened the way to the systematic corruption of the citizens and hence to the decay or ultimate collapse of the polity. For once the spread of money and trade had opened up the possibility of the unlimited accumulation of wealth, it presented a temptation that would almost inevitably turn those charged with directing the polity away from the common good to the satisfaction of their own disordered passions. As Guicciardini put it in an early discourse, there was a limit to the perfection of a modern republic, "because if we wished to take it to a higher level, we would have to get to the root of the fragility and softness of our spirits . . . ; it would be necessary to eliminate the enormous esteem and reputation in which riches are held, the immoderate appetite for which destroys the desire for true glory, and turns our spirits away from the quest for virtue [virtù] while leading it into a thousand usurpations and dishonesties." The Spartan legislator Lycurgus, "who in a single day uprooted all riches and display from Lacedæmon, gathering together all the necessities of life from everyone and then dividing them up equally, banning money, removing all customs because of which riches are desired, like display, banquets, excess of servitors, [and] beautiful clothing and household goods," had been in a position to do so, but Guicciardini knew of no later examples.[58] His readers would

---

57. François le Begue, *Traicté et advis sur les desordres des monnoyes, & diversité des moyen d'y remedier* (Paris, 1600), 1–7; Nicolas Coquerel, *Discours de la perte que les François reçoivent en la permission d'exposer les Monnoyes estrangeres* (Paris: François Jaquin, 1608), 1r.: "En l'establissment des Empires, Royaumes & Republiques, les premiers Legislateurs conduits d'une grace divine, avant tout autre establissement de police ont consideré l'honneur due au Souverain pour l'establissement de la Religion."

58. Francesco Guicciardini, "Discorso di Logrogno" (1511), in *Opere*, ed. Emanuella Lugnani Scarano, 3 vols. (Turin: Unione Tipografico-Editrice Torninense, 1970–81), 1:293–94: "perché a volerla condurre in maggiore grado bisognerebbe venire alla radice delle delicatezze e mollizie delli animi nostri . . . ; bisognerebbe tagliare el tanto prezio, la tanta riputazione in che sono le ricchezze, lo appetito immoderato delle quali leva el desiderio della vera gloria, aliena li animi dal cercare le virtù e li introduce in mille usurpazaione e in mille disonestà. . . . El quale estirpò in uno dì da Lacedemone tutte le ricchezze e suntuosità, accumulando insieme le facultà di tutti, dividendole di poi per equali parte, vietando e' danari, levando tutti li usi perché le ricchezze si desiderano, di suntuosità, di conviti, di copi di servi, di bellezza di veste e masserizie." I quote this passage less because of its influence in sixteenth-century France, though it may have had some, than because Pocock, *Machiavellian Moment*, 135–38, identifies it as lying at the origin of important elements in early modern Aristotelian republicanism.

have remembered that in the very recent past the Florentine prophet and reformer Girolamo Savonarola had discovered the futility of reforming a modern republic through a bonfire of the vanities and had paid for his presumption with his life.

Though Gucciardini passed quickly over the role of money in this process, no one familiar with Aristotle would have missed it, and other authors recognized that building a genuinely ideal republic would have to begin by somehow fighting off the institution of money. This appears in a particularly dramatic form in Thomas More's *Utopia*.[59] There, the Utopians use trade in a distinctly Aristotelian fashion. They supply their neighbors with useful commodities, and in exchange "they bring back to the fatherland not goods that are lacking at home (for other than iron there are practically none), but above all a great store of gold and silver," which they then have to find something to do with. The very perfection of their Aristotelian autarky threatened to set the Utopians on the road to a corrupting chrematistic. The usual premodern modes of immobilizing wealth were of no help here: if the precious metals were stockpiled in public treasuries, maintained as a mystery of the state, the people would suspect them of being siphoned off for private use, while "if they made goblets or other fine work of that sort out of them, then should the occasion arise where they had to be melted down again . . . taking away what the people had already begun to delight in would be tolerated only mutinously." Avarice was so powerful and so ingrained in human nature (partaking of Augustinian cupidity and original sin) that the very presence of accumulating gold or silver was enough to awaken it and break down even the most perfect social harmony.

The Utopians therefore resorted to a kind of anti-coining. "They make chamber pots and other small and sordid containers from gold and silver indiscriminately not just for public places but even for private dwellings. And the chains and weighty fetters that bind slaves are wrought of the same metals."[60] More repeatedly stressed how hard this would be for modern

---

59. The classic study of the political and social thinking behind *Utopia* is J. H. Hexter, *The Vision of Politics on the Eve of the Reformation: More, Machiavelli and Seyssel* (New York: Basic Books, 1973). For a recent defense of Hexter's general approach, see Skinner, *Visions of Politics*, 2:213–44. Richard Halpern, *The Poetics of Primitive Accumulation: English Renaissance Culture and the Genealogy of Capital* (Ithaca, NY: Cornell University Press, 1991), 136–75, has a fine Marxist reading of the economic themes of the *Utopia*.

60. Thomas More, *The Complete Works*, ed. Edward Surtz and J. H. Hexter, vol. 4 (New Haven: Yale University Press, 1965), 148: "non . . . merces, quibus domi egent (nam id fere nihil est praeter ferrum) sed argenti atque auri praeterea, magnam vim in patriam reportant." Page 150: "si phylas inde aliaque id genus opera fabre excusa conficerent, si quando incidisset occasio, ut conflanda sint rursus . . . vident nimirum fore, ut aegre patiantur avelli quae semel in delitiis havere coepissent." Page 152: "ex auro, atque argento non in communibus aulis modo, sed in privatis etiam domibus, matellas passim, ac sordidissima, quaeque vasa conficiunt. Ad haec catenas & crassas compedes, quibus coherent servos: iisdem ex metallis operantur." The translation is mine. Note how closely this tracks Guicciardini's description of Lycurgus's achievement.

Europeans to believe, and indeed the density and ductility of gold and silver would make them highly unsuitable for fetters, while, because of its excellent heat conduction, using a gold chamber pot on a cold morning would be an almost unimaginably unpleasant experience. The Utopians went through literally incredible contortions to arrest the progression Aristotle had identified leading to the creation of money and the corruption of the polity, using public authority to stamp on precious metals not the forms of coin or plate, suitable to their shiny and malleable nature, but rather signs of degradation and especially of *stasis*, opposing the social mobility and circulation associated with the monetary metals. Such a procedure was, of course, impossible in real life, but since the dilemma to which it responded emerged from the basic nature of exchange, the only other solution would have been the elimination of such exchange, not just "internationally" but probably among households as well.

And almost everyone at the time considered reducing the world to a series of autarkic and (in both senses of the word) Spartan households not just impossible but also highly undesirable. As Lionel Rothkrug pointed out many years ago, there was in early modern France a strong strain of ethical argument in favor of trade as a means of and encouragement to mutual fraternity and charity.[61] Less theoretically, as Henri IV claimed in the preamble to an edict on the grain trade, "experience teaches us that free trade that the population and subjects of kingdoms conduct with their neighbors and foreigners is one of the principal means of making them wealthy, rich, and opulent."[62] Loys le Roy, once again, held that "now all men may communicate one to another their commodities, and supply their mutual wants; as inhabiting all the selfe same citie and common wealth of the world."[63] At the same time, within generally undefined limits, the abundance of material goods enabled by monetary exchange was considered good in itself. As Pierre de Ronsard pointed out in his 1555 "Hymn to Gold,"

---

61. Rothkrug, *Opposition*, 69–80. Rothkrug identifies such views as "humanist sources of opposition to mercantilism," a characterization with which I would tend to disagree on a number of grounds, but he is surely correct about the importance of the overall view, which had its origins in the Middle Ages.

62. *Lettres patentes du Roy, portant defenses a tous marchands & autres, de transporter hors de ce Royaume aucuns Bleds, Grains, & legumes, n'y d'en faire aucunes traictes, sur peine de confiscation desdicts grains & crime de leze majesté* (Bourges: Pierre Bouchier, 1595), 2: "l'experience nous enseigne que la liberte du traffic que les peuples & subjects des Royaumes font avec leurs voisins & estrangers, est un des principaux moyens de les rendre aysez, riches, & opulens." As the title suggests, this edict chose to derogate from that general lesson.

63. Loys le Roy, *Of the Interchangeable Course or Variety of Things in the Whole World*, trans. Robert Ashley (London: Charles Yetsweirt, 1594), quoted in Rothkrug, *Opposition*, 73n. This "modern" situation had implications for the understanding and management of money to which we must return in due course.

Aristotle placed [wealth] among the virtues,
not as a virtue, but as the instrument
whereby virtue shines out clearly.
Whoever lacks it is on his own, and will never
appear in the light if he does not find gold as his guide.[64]

Aristotle had in mind the kind of "natural" household wealth that he contrasted to the limitless accumulation of money, but as Ronsard's invocation of
gold made clear, such a distinction was hard to maintain in an economy as
monetized as that of Renaissance France.

The basic distinction whereby Renaissance thinkers attempted to resolve
that tension was between an honest wealth on the one hand and, on the other,
prodigality and avarice. This was how Ronsard structured his hymn, following his encomium on gold with a satirical attack on "those who do nothing /
But mortgage their property and eat up their goods," and "Those who, with a
thousand pains, pile up gold, / Then starve to death beside their hoard."[65] The
latter, in particular, is close to Aristotle's vision of the misuse of chrematistic, and
Ronsard illustrates it (forcing the texts) with images of political failure drawn
from Homer: the abasement of Priam before Hector and the humble retirement of Laertes, father of Odysseus. But in fact, these two pathological states
could very easily coexist or even merge. Thus, a Catholic League pamphleteer
named Nicolas Roland (not the general of the moneys Nicolas Roland du
Plessis) criticized Henri III's "tax and spend" policies by saying that while
prodigality and avarice were usually contraries, "it is not thus with respect to
princes and kings, whose avarice, joined with prodigality, is even more pernicious for their subjects than avarice for the sake of saving."[66] Money was by its
nature limitless, and hence so was the desire either to have or to spend it; royal
power could link these two excesses together, with even more disastrous results.

Poets are unsystematic in their discussions of political economy, so for a
more detailed understanding of how avarice was supposed to undermine the
republic, it would be useful to turn to a work of political theory; and if we want

---

64. Pierre de Ronsard, Œuvres complètes, ed. Gustave Cohen, 2 vols. (Paris: N.R.F./Gallimard,
1950) 2:265: "entre les vertus Aristote l'a mise / Non pas comme vertu, mais comme l'instrument /
Par lequel la vertu se monstre clairement, / Qui manque est de soy-mesme, et jamais ne se montre /
En lumiere, si l'Or pour guide ne rencontre."

65. Ibid., 2:271–72: "ceux-là qui ne font rien, / Sinon vendre leur rente, et gourmander leur
bien"; "Ceux qui par mille soins amorcellent un Or, / Puis, languissent de faim aupres de leur tresor."

66. Nicolas Roland, Remonstrances tres-humbles au roy de France & de Pologne Henry troisiesme de ce
nom, par un sien fidele officier & subject, sur les desordres & miseres de ce Royaume, causes d'icelles, & moyens d'y
pourveoir à la gloire de Dieu & repos universel de cet estat (n.p., 1588), 59: "Mais il n'est pas ainsy au regard des
Princes & des Rois, desquels l'avarice jointe à la prodigalité, est plus pernitieuse aux subjets, que l'avarice
qui se faict pour l'espargne." This work was successful enough to go immediately into a second edition.

to understand the conventional wisdom on such matters, a mediocre work of political theory would be best. One good example, exploited in Foucault's essay on "governmentality" but otherwise almost unstudied, is the *Political Mirror* of Guillaume de la Perrière, a Toulousan man of letters.[67] Probably written in the decade or so leading up to the author's death in 1553, this work was published posthumously in 1555 and was fairly successful, being printed four times in French and twice in English. The structure of the *Mirror* was Aristotelian (one can detect traces of Lefèvre d'Etaples's epitome in la Perrière's text), with the usual admixture of Ciceronian/Stoic and other miscellaneous elements and some peculiarities of its own. One of those, of particular interest given the way Aristotle had connected money to the household economy, was (as Enzo Sciacca has pointed out) that it highlights the household as both the basis and, in a sense, the ideal form of the republic.[68] For the most part, however, la Perrière contented himself with arranging the classic concepts and questions of early modern political science in convenient engraved and commentated "trees."

Thus he inevitably came to list the causes by which "republics change or are ruined." The first of these was "gain and avarice: . . . but what gain? It is when the common people . . . perceive that the governors of the city are avaricious and covetous, striving to make great gains and acquire great riches, and imposing great exactions on the community." And la Perrière made it clear that the fault here lay with the rulers, not with the rebels: "Aristotle, in his moral works, detests avarice in all sorts of people, but it is more execrable in princes or magistrates than in all others."[69] This was, as it were, the same

_____

67. I have consulted one of the later Paris editions: Guillaume de la Perrière, *Le miroir politique, contenant les diverses manieres de gouverner & policer les Republiques, qui sont, & ont esté par cy devant: Œuvre, non moins utile que necessaire à tous Monarches, Rois, Princes, Seigneurs, Magistrats & autres qui ont charge du gouvernment ou administration d'icelles* (Paris: Robert le Mangnier, 1567); for details of publication and of de la Perrière's biography, see Greta Dexter, "Guillaume de la Perrière," *Bibliothèque d'humanisme et renaissance* 17 (1955): 56–73. The *Miroir* is the starting point for Michel Foucault, "Governmentality," in *The Foucault Effect: Studies in Governmentality*, ed. Graham Burchell, Colin Gordon, and Peter Miller (Chicago: University of Chicago Press, 1991), 87–104.

68. See Enzo Sciacca, "Forme di governo e forma della società nel'Miroire politique' di Guillaume de la Perrière," *Pensiero politico* 22 (1989): 183: "È questo l'aspetto forse più rilevante della concezione societaria di La Perrière, quella che sembra riflettere con maggiore immediatezza le immagini e le convizioni dei *milieux* intelletuali del tempo, ed in cui potremmo trovare interessanti anticipazioni del più maturo pensiero politico della seconda metà del secolo e primo fra tutti quello di Jean Bodin." On Bodin's parallel theories of the household, see Vittor Ivo Comparato, "Note su Bodin e Aristotele: Famiglia, sovranità e proprietà nella definizione dello stato," *Annali della Facoltà di Scienze Politiche: Materiali di Storia* 18 (1981): 7–13.

69. La Perrière, *Miroir*, fol. 30v: "Les Republiques se changent ou ruinent par." Fol. 31r: "gain et avarice . . . mais quel gain? C'est quand le populaire . . . apperçoit que les gouverneurs de la cité sont avares & convoiteux taschans de faire grans gains, & acquerir grandes richesses, & imposent sur le commun grandes exactions." Fol. 32v: "Aristote en ses livres moraux, deteste avarice en toute sorte de gens: mais en Princes ou magistrats, elle est plus execrable qu'en tous autres."

language Roland would be speaking in 1588. "The second cause that changes and ruins republics" was "ambition or covetousness of honor: for from those great troubles and perturbations arise among the citizens, which happens when those who are not honored with offices and public administration envy those who do administer them." Contemporaries would have thought of the bitter contest between the Montmorency and Guise clans, whose role in the outbreak of the religious wars a decade later would make these words prophetic.

This was an old chestnut of Italian political theory (Machiavelli and Guicciardini had both stressed it),[70] but one of la Perrière's later points suggested that ambition was in fact organically related to avarice: "The seventh cause that ruins republics is the too great augmentation of one part of it more than another, beyond their due and requisite proportions. This happens when one group of citizens enriches itself more than the others, or has the advantage in honors and profits."[71] Both of these defects, in Aristotelian terms, involved a violation of the geometrical harmonies of distributive justice. Either honors and rewards were not (seen to be) correctly distributed according to the ascribed merit of the members of the polity, or the ratios themselves changed, perhaps illicitly, without a corresponding change in the arrangement of the republic. But, as the reference to citizens "enriching themselves" suggests, avarice and the kapêlikon that was both its tool and the ground from which it sprang were the most likely causes of that derangement. As Loys le Roy said, "It is something natural for those who have an appetite for great things to covet goods and honors: and that covetousness has no term or limit."[72]

70. On ambition in Machiavelli, see Russell Price, "*Ambizione* in Machiavelli's Thought," *History of Political Thought* 3 (1982): 383–445; and Price, "Self-love, 'Egoism' and *Ambizione* in Machiavelli's Thought," *History of Political Thought* 9 (1998): 237–61. Skinner, *Visions of Politics*, 2:166–69, describes how Machiavelli articulates ambition and avarice. On ambition in Guicciardini, see Pocock, *Machiavellian Moment*, 145–47 and 252–53.

71. La Perrière, *Miroir*, fol. 35r: "La seconde cause qui fait changer & ruiner les Republiques, est ambition ou convoitise d'honneur: car pour icelles s'esmeuvent grands troubles & perturbations entre les citadins: ce qui advient quand ceux qui ne sont honnorez des offices & administrations publiques, portent envie à ceux qui les administrent."Fol. 38v: "La septiesme cause qui fait ruiner les Republiques, est trop d'augmentement en une partie plus qu'en l'autre d'icelle, outre deue & requise propotion. Cecy advient quand une partie des citoyens s'enrichit plus que l'autre, ou a advantage en honneur & prouffit."

72. Le Roy, *Politique*, 310: "c'est une chose naturelle a ceux qui appetent les grandes choses, d'estre convoiteux de biens et d'honneurs: laquelle convoitise n'a point de fin ne de terme," glossing a description of Dionysus of Syracuse's seizure of power.

Indeed, ambition and avarice went together in the Renaissance mind like the proverbial horse and carriage.[73] Specifically, ambition and avarice, as a pair, shared two key characteristics with the Aristotelian conception of monetary exchange. First, in spite of their danger, ambition and avarice could be productive, even necessary, in constructing a functioning social order. In the 1580s, Michel de Montaigne was already advancing a backhanded argument for the social value of self-interest that at least dimly prefigured Mandeville's *Fable of the Bees*. "What avarice, ambition, quarrels, lawsuits do for others who, like me, have no particular occupation, love would do more suitably: it would give me back vigilance, sobriety, grace, care for my person, . . . by which I could make myself more esteemed and beloved."[74] More definitely, and more significantly, ambition and avarice, like kapêlikon, were characterized specifically by their unboundedness. Thus, in the same essay, Montaigne remarked that "if there is no goal [*bout*: both a stopping place and a final cause] to avarice and ambition, no more is there one to lustfulness. It lives on after being satisfied, and can be given neither a constant satisfaction nor an end. It always goes beyond its own possession."[75] This was a rather doubtful claim from an Aristotelian perspective (though perhaps not from an Augustinian one), given that lust was an essentially natural passion that had its own natural bounds, but the point is that ambition and avarice provided the model of how a passion could feed on itself, detached from any actual satisfaction. Another of Montaigne's dicta summed up the problematic inevitability of these vices: "In truth, it is not ~~neediness~~ shortage, but rather abundance that

---

73. A search of the ARTFL database for the period 1525–1625 produces eighteen examples of those two terms within three words of each other, mostly from the most influential moralists of the era, Michel de Montaigne and his follower Pierre Charron; significantly, the same database shows that the two terms overwhelmingly appeared together rather than separately (though not always within three words) in those two authors.

74. Michel de Montaigne, *Les essais*, ed. Pierre Villey (Paris: Presses Universitaires de France, 1992), 893: "Ce que l'avarice, l'ambition, les querelles, les procés, font à l'endroit des autres qui, comme moy, n'ont point de vacation assignée, l'amour le feroit plus commodéement: il me rendroit la vigilance, la sobrieté, la grace, le soing de ma personne . . . ; par où je me peusse randre plus estimé et plus aymé." Albert O. Hirschman, *The Passions and the Interests: Political Arguments for Capitalism before Its Triumph* (Princeton: Princeton University Press, 1996 [1976]), 7–66, makes the claim that arguments for the social utility of certain passions, notably avarice, or of some form of self-interest played a key role in the ideological prehistory of the modern political economy.

75. Montaigne, *Essais*, 885: "si on ne trouve point de bout en l'avarice et en l'ambition, il n'y en a non plus en la paillardise. Elle vit encore apres la satieté; et ne luy peut on prescrire ny satisfaction constante ny fin: elle va tousjours outre sa possession." Both of these passages are from bk. 3, chap. 5, "Sur des vers de Virgile." There is a very similar statement in bk. 2, chap. 33, "L'Histoire de Spurina," 729: "les passions qui sont toutes en l'ame, comme l'ambition, l'avarice et autres, donnent bien plus à faire à la raison: car elle n'y peut estre secourue que de ses propres moyens, ny ne sont ces appetits-là capables de satieté, voire ils s'esguisent et augmentent par la jouyssance."

produces avarice."[76] Abundance is not something one would want to do without, and one would suspect that as abundance produces avarice, so avarice could produce more abundance in something like the circle, vicious or virtuous, of kapêlikon.

But still, ambition and avarice appeared to theorists above all as dangers. In sixteenth-century France they were of course familiar as deadly sins—ambition as a subspecies of pride and avarice in its own right. Through most of the Middle Ages, those had successively been considered the greatest of sins, and the necessity of reconciling that fact with a growing commercial economy had given rise to an immense and fruitful theological literature around economic issues.[77] By our period, however, the Ten Commandments had largely displaced the Seven Deadly Sins as an organizing principle of Western Christian morality, leaving ambition and avarice in a much more subordinate position.[78] And while scholastic economic thought remained vital in the Iberian Peninsula, it largely withered in sixteenth-century France.[79] No French moralist followed the elevation of the Decalogue and the denigration of the scholastic tradition more thoroughly, or more influentially, than Calvin. In his *Institutes*, ambition and avarice have a cursory and purely negative role, as the human negative of the complete surrender to God on which his theology rests. In his view, when we look at the worldly, "we see how restless they are in mind, how many plans they try, to what fatigues they submit, in order that they may gain what avarice or ambition desires, or, on the other hand, escape poverty and meanness. To avoid similar entanglements, the course which Christian men must follow is this: first, they must not long for, or hope for, or think of any kind of prosperity apart from the blessing of God; on it they must cast themselves, and there safely and confidently recline."[80] Outside the purest realms of theology, this doctrine offered no analysis of or remedy for the sins in question.

---

76. Ibid., 62. "De vray, ce n'est pas la necessité disette, c'est plustost l'abondance qui produict l'avarice." This is from bk. 1, chap. 14, "Que le Goust des Biens et des Maux Depend en Bonne Partie de l'Opinion que Nous en Avons." The emendation to the 1588 text, made silently in most modern editions, is from Montaigne's corrected "exemplaire de Bordeaux," 21. A Derridean might amuse himself by pointing out how *chreia* continues to operate in Montaigne's text, if only *sous rature*.

77. On the cardinal sins, see Lester K. Little, "Pride Goes before Avarice: Social Change and the Vices in Latin Christendom," *American Historical Review* 76 (1971): 16–49.

78. See John Bossy, "Moral Arithmetic: Seven Sins into Ten Commandments," in *Conscience and Casuistry in Early Modern Europe*, ed. Edmund Leiters (Cambridge: Cambridge University Press, 1988), 214–34.

79. On the Iberian writings of most interest to us, see Marjorie Grice-Hutchinson, ed., *The School of Salamanca: Readings in Spanish Monetary Theory, 1544–1605* (Oxford: Oxford University Press, 1952).

80. John Calvin, *Institutes of the Christian Religion*, trans. Henry Beveridge, 2 vols. (London: James Clarke, 1953), 2:13.

Calvin's remained a minority opinion in France, but Catholic writers, if anything, offered even less useful insight into the workings of these vices. During the Wars of Religion, French Catholic moral theology was at low ebb, but even as those conflicts receded, it was some time before that discipline had much to offer. The only Catholic figure appearing on the public stage before 1610 with a stature even remotely comparable to Calvin's was Jean-Pierre Camus, bishop of Bellay, the first in a line of great moralists of the "century of saints."[81] His 1609 collection of moral essays touches on both ambition and avarice, but it does so purely in the terms of classical pagan moral philosophy, terms fundamentally similar to Montaigne's, though firmly negative. "Ambition is insatiable . . . and all the more pernicious for that," while avarice "is infinite and insatiable: any abundance whatsoever diminishes it not at all."[82] As with Calvin, the only remedy offered was a complete conversion to God and (for Camus) to a Christianized Stoic virtue. This situation would change; by the middle third of the seventeenth century a changing social and ideological context (which will be touched on in the final chapter), as well as the wholesale importation of an Ibero-Italian approach to moral theology structured substantially around socioeconomic relations, would bring money, avarice, and ambition back to the foreground of French Catholic thought.[83] Until that time, however, those issues remained subject to only the most general theological influences.

To understand how our subjects understood the threat of ambition and avarice, then, and the ways that threat might be controlled, we must return to the secular side of social and political thought and in particular to the substantial genre of treatises on political theory. Ideas very like la Perrière's can be found in a 1566 treatise by a Calvinist lawyer named Roland Pietre, who emphasized the economic aspects of governance even more than la Perrière did. Thus the "political art or discipline" was a gift from God, who desired "that possessions and goods should be distributed so that each possesses his own in all security, and all things circulate and are exchanged for one another by legitimate contracts for the support of life in common." Pietre too believed that avarice and ambition

81. On his career, see Thomas Worcester, *Seventeenth Century Cultural Discourse: France and the Preaching of Bishop Camus* (Berlin: Mouton de Gruyter, 1997).

82. Jean-Pierre Camus, *Les diversitez*, 2 vols. (Paris: Claude chappellet, 1609), 1:fol. 41v: "L'Ambition est insatiable . . . & pour cela d'autant plus pernicieuse." Fol. 85r: "est infinie et insatiable, quelque abondance que ce soit ne la diminuë en rien," citing Sallust, *Cataline* 11. Ambition and avarice account for only two out of well over a hundred essays in this collection, though the fact that they appear in the first two books (1.5 and 2.2) suggests a certain prominence.

83. On the importation of moral theology, see Jean-Pascal Gay, "Les paradoxes d'un réseau institutionnalisé: Les jésuites français et la théologie morale ibérique et italienne au XVIIe siècle," *SOURCE(S): Cahiers de l'équipe de recherche Arts, Civilisation et Histoire de l'Europe* 1 (2012): 31–44.

were the greatest dangers to the stability of the republic. Lawyers, his main concern, needed to be taught ethics, for "if their tongue, their pen, and their learning are led with excessive license by the two vices that are most dangerous in all persons, ambition and avarice, then we will see them praise [virtues and vices] like slaves to the will of the richest and most powerful."[84] And those magnates would presumably be no less corrupted by the potential of unlimited gain.

When Pietre wrote, his country was already mired in an increasingly desperate civil war, and as the crisis deepened through the early 1590s, France approached the brink of dissolution. In the circumstances, there could hardly be a more vitally immediate question than the causes of and remedies for civil discord and the fall of republics. To continue with the views of obscure but typical lawyers, a barrister in the parlement of Brittany reflecting on the past troubles in the tranquillity of Henri IV's later reign attributed them to a neglect of piety and justice on the part of the kings and, on the part of the subjects, to disobedience, from which "come civil wars, and from the desire that some have to increase and enrich themselves from the ruin of others. *Thence war, hungry for interest and greedy for the profit of time, and faith destroyed, and useful to many.*" In particular, he blamed ambition, which "is never without some specious pretext, and is always followed by avarice, as these verses from Claudian's *De laudibus Stiliconis*, book 1, testify: *You drive out avarice, whose filthy nurse is ambition.* If the ambitious man's word has no faith, that of the avaricious man and him who desires to enrich himself from the goods of others has no more: *avarice subverts all faith and probity,* as Sallust said, speaking of an ambitious man."[85] Belordeau's somewhat tired rhetoric and probably borrowed erudition obscure but do not

---

84. Roland Pietre, *Le premier livre des considerations politiques* (Paris: Robert Estienne, 1566), sig Aiii v: "Art ou discipline Politique." Sig. Bi r: "Que les possessions & biens soyent partis, à ce que chascun possede le sien en toute seureté, & que toutes choses se communiquent & baillent de l'un à l'autre par contracts legitimes pour l'entretement de la vie commune." Sig Hiii v: "si leur langue, leur plume, leur scavoir se conduit par trop licentieusement par ces deux vices, qui sont le plus dangereux en toutes personnes, ambition & avarice, voyla les uns & les autres louez comme serfs à la volonté des plus riches & puissans." I have not found a single reference to this work in the secondary literature: admittedly, it is not very good, but it deserves better than that.

85. Pierre Belordeau de la Grée, *Polyarchie, ou, de la domination tyrannique et de l'auctorité de commander, usurpee par plusieurs pendant les troubles,* 2nd ed. (Paris: Nicolas Buon, 1617), 21–22: "viennent des guerres civiles, & du desire que plusieurs ont de s'accroistre, & de s'enrichir de la ruine des autres. *Hinc usura vorax avidúmque in foenore tempus,/Et concussa fides, & multis utile bellum,*" quoting Lucan, *Bel. civ.* 1:181–82. Page 24: "n'est jamais sans quelque specieux pretexte, & est tousjours suivie d'avarice, comme tesmoigne ce vers de Claudian *de laudib. Stiliconis lib. 1: Trudis avaritiam cuius foedissima nutrix/Ambitio.* Si l'ambitieux n'a ny foy ny parole, l'avaritieux & celuy qui desire s'enrichir du bien d'autruy, n'en a non plus, *omnem fidem & probitatem subvertit avaritia,* disoit Saluste, parlant d'un ambitieux," paraphrasing Sallust, *Cataline* 10: "Namque avaritia fidem probitatem ceterasque artis bonas subvertit."

erase the real trauma that the ambition and avarice of thousands of subjects great and small had inflicted on France for the past generation.

Sumptuary Legislation

But what could be done about the dangers of avarice? One possibility that Pietre raised, and indeed one of the great themes of sixteenth-century French reform, was the limitation or abolition of the venality of office.[86] Less direct responses were also available, though, and more likely to succeed. Probably the most widely canvassed was some form of sumptuary legislation. Pietre, for example, believed that strict control of the display of precious metals was vital to the state's cohesion: "Recently several edicts and ordinances have been published, most beneficial to the republic, on the regulation of justice and on luxury both in clothing and food, and regulating the use of fabrics, tissues, ornaments, and gold, silver, and silk embroidery, in which it seems that one has intended to see the sumptuary laws of the ancients reborn."[87]

Sumptuary laws were a prominent phenomenon throughout late medieval and early modern Europe, though with significant regional variations. In England, for example, a 1533 act of Parliament (which appears in the statute books immediately after the Act in Restraint of Appeals) attempted to promote "good and politick order in knowledge and distinction of people according to their estates preeminences dignities and degrees" by a minute enumeration of permitted apparel up and down the social scale.[88] Under Elizabeth, sumptuary matters came under the sway of Cecil and the Protestant "commonwealth" ideology of his cohort, with its focus on prosperity and Christian virtue. This found narrower support: the only act that made it through Parliament was a ridiculously technocratic measure banning contracts to sell imported apparel to persons worth less than £3,000 on more than twenty-eight days' credit.[89] Instead, Elizabeth legislated by proclamation,

---

86. The classic study is Roland Mousnier, *La vénalité des offices sous Henri IV et Louis XIII*, 2nd ed. (Paris: Presses Universitaires de France, 1971); more recently, Jean Nagle, *Un orgueil français: La vénalité des offices sous l'Ancien Régime* (Paris: Odile Jacob, 2008). On the rhetoric and politics of anti-venality in this period, see Greengrass, *Governing Passions*, 274–85.

87. Pietre, *Considerations*, sig. Diii r–v: "Depuis peu de temps l'on a publié quelques Edicts & Ordonnances fort salutaires à la Republique sur le reiglement de la Justice, sur le luxe tant des habits que des viandes, & reiglement des usaiges de draps, toilles, passemens, broderies d'or, dargent & soye: en quoy il semble qu'on a voulu faire renaistre les Loix somptuaires des anciens: mais que lon nomme un lieu ou deux en France où ils s'observent."

88. *The Statutes of the Realm: Printed by Command of His Majesty King George the Third*, 9 vols. in 10 (London: George Eyre and Andrew Strahan, 1810–22), vol. 3, pt. 1: 430.

89. Ibid., 3.2: 428.

aiming to regulate "vain devices of so great cost for the quantity thereof as of necessity the moneys and treasure of the realm is and must be yearly conveyed out of the same to answer the said excess"—though enforcement and, perhaps, public support for such a program were already collapsing when the proclamation was issued in 1574.[90]

The French trajectory, though more complex, was basically similar. It ran a few years behind England, starting in 1543, during the same crisis of François I's later years that eventually led to the reformation of the Cour des Monnaies. Henri II took up his father's project with his usual vigor, reissuing the 1543 edict on his accession in 1547, and putting forward a new one in 1549 that undertook a slightly less elaborate version of the English social taxonomy. Confronted, like the 1533 Parliament, with extreme political and religious turmoil, the 1561 Estates of Orléans proposed sumptuary legislation, to which Pietre was alluding. Henri III, too, issued edicts in 1576 (on the recommendation of the Estates of Blois) and in 1583; finally, Henri IV introduced yet another new form of edict in 1601, reissued in 1606.[91] Unlike laws in England and Italy, where elaborate enforcement mechanisms had at least an intermittent effect, all this French legislation was, by popular consensus, a dead letter; Pietre pointedly asked, "Can anyone name even one or two places in France where they are observed?"[92] They seem to have approached closely to what Alan Hunt, in the only comprehensive study of sumptuary laws, called "'hegemonic legislation,' legislation from above forming a component of a project of governance," but largely indifferent to results as opposed to rhetoric.[93]

---

90. Paul L. Hughes and James F. Larkin, eds., *Tudor Royal Proclamations*, 3 vols. (New Haven: Yale University Press, 1967–69), 2:381. For the context, see Frederic A. Youngs, Jr., *The Proclamations of the Tudor Queens* (Cambridge: Cambridge University Press, 1976), 161–70.

91. Pascal Bastien, "'Aux tresors dissipez on cognoist le malfaict': Hiérarchie sociale et transgression des ordonnances somptuaires en France, 1549–1606," *Renaissance and Reformation/Renaissance et réforme* 4 (1999): 23–43, surveys legislation from exactly our period from the point of view of relations between the monarchy and the nobility and provides an excellent overview of the ordinances themselves, as well as the text of the ordinance of 1549. All the relevant edicts may be found in Antoine Fontanon, *Les edicts et ordonnances des rois de France, depuis Louys VI. dit le Gros, jusques a present: Avec les verifications, modifications, & declarations sur iceux . . . de nouveau reveuz, corrigez et augmentez de plusieurs belles ordonnances, anciennes & nouvelles. Par Gabriel Michel*, 4 vols. (Paris, 1611), 1:980–97.

92. Pietre, *Considerations*, sig. Diii v: "mais que lon nomme un lieu ou deux en France où ils s'observent." On Italy, see Catherine Kovesi Killerby, "Practical Problems in the Enforcement of Italian Sumptuary Law, 1200–1500," in *Crime, Society and the Law in Renaissance Italy*, ed. Trevor Dean and K. J. P. Lowe (Cambridge: Cambridge University Press, 1994), 99–120.

93. Alan Hunt, *Governance of the Consuming Passions: A History of Sumptuary Law* (New York: St. Martin's, 1996), 356.

The question remains, though, whose hegemony and what project for governance they represented. The earliest and most durable explanation for this legislation, judging from the preambles, was one that might be termed "mercantilist": to save the "great sums of money" that "are drawn out of this our realm" to pay for imported materials.[94] It is important, however, not merely to take this mercantilism at its face value. After all, as Pascal Bastien has pointed out, François I and (to a lesser degree) his son and grandsons, strongly encouraged the domestic production of luxury cloths even while the laws strictly limited their consumption.[95] And only under Henri IV did this reasoning (as it had long done in England) substantially displace the older goal of creating transparency in a society where "it is not easy today to recognize the quality and condition of persons, because of how little difference there is in the material, value, and sumptuousness of their clothing."[96] Thus, for example, those below the status of a duke "may no longer dress and accoutre themselves in any drapery or cloth of gold or silver, make use of gold thread, embroidery, ornaments, fringes, decorated ribbons, metal wire, rich taffetas, [or] velour or silk barred with gold or silver."[97]

But why was this social transparency so important? The laws themselves do not elaborate; Hunt postulates a generalized urban anxiety brought about by the transformations of early capitalism, while Bastien sees a slightly narrower but similar dynamic of noble anxiety over the rise of bourgeois and robe elites at work.[98] And they are probably both right, though in the Estates

---

94. M. François André Isambert and Athanase Jean Léger Jourdan, eds., *Recueil général des anciennes lois françaises, depuis l'an 420 jusqu'à la revolution de 1789*, 29 vols. (Paris: Belin-Leprieur, 1826–33), 12.:834: "grandes sommes de deniers se tirent de cestuy nostre royaume."

95. See Bastien, "'Aux tresors,'" 36: "Il était déjà paradoxal qu'on enregistrât des ordonnances visant à restreindre le port de la soie alors que les manufactures de Lyon et de Tours étaient encouragées par la politique royale; il aurait donc été encore plus insensé de vouloir les appliquer." A contemporary history of Lyons dates royal support of the silk industry there to 1536, when the city fathers received a proposal for its introduction: "A quoy lesdicts Eschevins prestarent volontiers l'oreille, & de faict, le Roy estant de retour de son voyage de Provence, d'où il avoit chassé l'Empereur & ses forces: ils en firent la requeste à sa Majesté, qui leur fut accordée, & leur en furent expediées lettres en bonne forme." Claude de Rubys, *Histoire veritable de la ville de Lyon* (Lyons: Bonaventure Nugo, 1604), 369–70.

96. *Ordonnance du Roy pour le Reglement & reformation de la dissolution & superfluité qui est és habillmens, & ornemens d'iceux: & de la punition de ceux qui contreviendront à ladicte ordonnance. Publié en Parlement le vingtneufiesme iour de Mars, l'an mil cinq cens quatre vingts trois* (Paris: Federic Morel, 1583), fol. 2v: "Malaisement peult on recognoistre aujourd'huy les qualitez & conditions des personnes, pour le peu de difference qui est és estoffes, valeur, & sumptuosité de leurs vestemens."

97. *Edict et Ordonnance du Roy, pour l'usage des draps de Soye, & superfluitez des habitz: & les arrests de la Court de Parlement intervenuz sur iceluy* (Paris: Guillaume de Niverd, 1563), fol. 4r: "ne pourront doresnavant se vestir & habiller d'aucun drap & toille d'or ou d'argent, user de pourfileurs, broderies, passemens, franges, tortilz, canetilles, recamures, veloux ou soyes barrées d'or ou d'argent." As one might expect, Charles IX's edicts were slightly more elaborated than that of 1549.

98. See Hunt, *Governance*, 108-41, and Bastien, "'Aux tresors,'" 36.

of Orléans, the Third Estate was just as vocal in its support of sumptuary legislation as the Second. The way they justified that support was revealing. "In this kingdom," they said, "the people of the Third Estate, merchants, artisans, and workers, their wives and children spend so much on habits and clothing that, in order to keep up that superfluity of clothing, they are compelled to misuse their professions and their merchandise, and to overcharge for [*survendre*] their handiwork."[99] There is a good deal to unpack in this statement, which was echoed in subsequent legislation, as in 1576: "The commoners and the popular masses spend so much on their clothing, that they are constrained to overcharge for their merchandise: from which in part proceeds the great dearness of food and other merchandise necessary for human use."[100] It suggests an almost inextricable relationship between ambition and avarice, as the desire for advancement in the society of orders leads both to the ostentatious display of wealth and to a lawless mania for the accumulation of money that short-circuits the ability of commerce to actually satisfy the needs for which exchange should exist. Thus fraud begets fraud, and, in the absence of government intervention, economic and social dislocation feed on each other.

Fear of commercial fraud was pervasive throughout early modern Europe, but in this case it was tied unusually tightly to the function of money, since the end result was supposed to be systemic overcharging: in a word, inflation.[101] The link was semantically evident in French, for when ambition and avarice led the merchants to *survendre* their goods, it was only a short step for them to *surhausser* the currency, the term for the phenomenon (which we shall explore in the next two chapters) of the inflation of the money of account. This argument even has some superficial plausibility from the viewpoint of modern economics. A systematic and surreptitious reduction

---

99. Bastien, "'Aux tresors,'" 27, citing *Recueil des cahiers généraux des trois ordres aux Etats-Généraux* (Paris: Barrois l'aîné, 1789), 1:400: "En ce royaume, les gens du tiers-état et les marchands artisans et mécaniques, leurs femmes et enfans font telles dépenses superflues en habits et vestemens qu'ils sont contrains, pour entretenir ladite superfluité d'habits, mal user en leurs états et marchandises et survendre leur manufactures."

100. *Declaration du Roy sur le faict et reformation des habits: Avec defense aux non nobles d'usurper le tiltre de noblesse, & à leurs femmes de porter l'habit de Damoiselle, sur les peines y contenues. Ensemble l'Ordonnance du Roy Henry second, par laquelle toutes personnes, tant Nobles que non Nobles & Roturiers, sont reglez de leurs habits & accoustremens qu'ils doivent porter: sur les mesmes peines aux contrevenans* (Paris: Federic Morel, 1577), 5: "les Roturiers & commun populaire font telle despense de leurs habits, qu'ils sont contraincts de survendre leurs marchandises: dont procede en partie la grande cherté des vivres & autres marchandises necessaires à l'usage de l'homme." As we shall see, this edict came at a key moment in the royal monetary policy.

101. On the obsession with controlling fraud in Italy, see Evelyn Welch, *Shopping in the Renaissance: Consumer Culture in Italy, 1400–1600* (New Haven: Yale University Press, 2005), 63–94.

in the quality of goods would in fact be inflationary, but though we would say that this is because it would shrink the economy relative to the monetary stock, early modern Europeans would have concentrated on the way it allowed merchants to produce money out of nothing, with reminders of the unbounded nature of the medium of exchange. That this nexus of ambition, ostentation, and avarice would appear particularly threatening in a period of actual inflation is more or less self-evident.

But more important for our immediate purposes is that, in the minds of contemporaries, this was a problem that required the intervention of the royal legislative power, even if the resulting legislation lacked any chance of having a noticeable effect.[102] Here we return to money as *nomos* and to the identification of justice with the structure of both commerce and social stratification. Thomas More could not imagine the social structures even of his perfectly instituted society withstanding the assault of foreign trade and precious metals unless the authorities specifically banned ostentation while legislating the form and (negative) value that specie should take. In the same way, it seems, the Estates of France could not imagine their social order withstanding that same assault without homologous royal intervention. And that intervention would (in a much less utopian form) have as a major objective the fixing of the value of circulating specie. The most thorough though perhaps not the most typical formulation of that particular program came from Jean Bodin, who was not only the most brilliant political thinker of the day but also a leading figure in the Estates General held at Blois in 1576–1577. His *Responses à Malestroict*, on which we have already touched, was framed as an investigation of the problem of inflation, and one of the major causes it diagnosed for that problem was an inadequate system of sumptuary legislation.

In Bodin's account, the link between sumptuary extravagance and inflation was not so much fraud (though he did include that among his explanatory factors) as waste. Excessive use of luxury products, especially in the form of slashed and lined sleeves and other accretions of "silk on silk" (a frequent target of the sumptuary edicts) led directly to artificial shortages and inflated prices. This very direct inflationary mechanism, no less than its more complex cousin, raised the old threat of boundless accumulation. "At this point,

---

102. Michèle Fogel, "Modèle d'Etat et modèle sociale de dépense: Les lois somptuaires en France de 1485 à 1660," in *Genèse de l'état moderne: Prélèvement et redistribution. Actes du colloque de Fontevraud 1984*, ed. Jean Philippe Genet and M. le Mené (Paris: Editions du C.N.R.S., 1987), 226–35, very plausibly reads the entire history of French sumptuary legislation as a chapter in the centralization of symbolic power in the French monarchy.

someone will say that if the prices of things increase partly because of waste and partly also because of the abundance of gold and silver, then ~~we would finally be all made of gold and~~ no one would be able to live because of the expense." The evocation of Midas (struck out in the second edition) may, in fact, have come directly from the *Politics*. "But," Bodin continues, "wars and disasters that afflict republics arrest the course of things." His example is a classic account of the decline and fall of the Roman Empire, born in austerity and fabulously enriched by plunder but whose "extravagances and luxuries did not last forever, for in less than three hundred years . . . cruel nations trampled the Romans under their feet. . . . This is what happens to all republics . . . as I have shown . . . in my *Method of History*."[103] The line from monetary exchange unmoored from actual needs through moral decay to the collapse of the state could not be expressed any more clearly.

What was left was the challenge of arresting that process. "Good edicts have been issued" to do so, "but they have no effect, for, since what is forbidden is worn at court, it is worn everywhere."[104] But for Bodin, this was no cause for despair. Unsurprisingly, given his reputation as the great champion of royal sovereignty, he thought that stronger royal leadership could turn the situation around. Indeed, mere royal whim had accounted for a substantial part of the inflation: "It comes from the pleasure of princes, who give all things their prices." There was no reason this could not work equally well in the opposite direction; and the king's own example would presumably be powerful in promoting reasonable clothing, "for cunning courtiers always counterfeit princes, even in the most ridiculous things."[105] Bodin combined at least implicit recommendations for direct royal action and example with (substantially less practical) technical suggestions regarding monetary policy, to which we shall have occasion to return in subsequent chapters.

---

103. Bodin, *Vie chère*, 22: "Icy, me dira quelqu'un: Si les choses alloyent en encherissant en partie pour le degast, en partie aussi pour l'abondance d'or et d'argent, nous serions enfin tous d'or et personne en pouroit vivre pour la charté. Il est vray: mais les guerres et calamitez qui adviennent aux républiques, arrestent bien le cours de la fortune." Page 25: "Mais ses excès et braveries ne durèrent pas toujours: car en moins de trois cens ans, . . . cruelles nations fouragèrent aux pieds les Romains . . . . Ainsi advient il à toutes républiques . . . comme j'ay monstré . . . en la Méthode des histoires." For the changes to the second edition, see Jean Bodin, *Response to the Paradoxes of Malestroit*, ed. Henry Tudor and R. W. Dyson (Bristol, UK: Thoemmes Press, 1997), 74.

104. Bodin, *Vie chère*, 20: "On a fait de beaux editz, mais ils ne servent de rien: car pource qu'on porte à la cour ce qui est defendu, on en portera partout."

105. Ibid., 17: "elle provient du plaisir des princes, qui donnent le pris aux choses." Page 81: "Car les fins courtizans contrefont tousjours les princes, et mesmes ès choses les plus ridicules," this in the context of a suggestion for fighting the inflation of agricultural goods by promoting the consumption of fish.

In this way, "sovereign princes and those who have the power to make laws, along with those who give them counsel, will be . . . more resolute in what needs to be ordained for the growth and honor of the republic."[106] Bodin's conviction that a more vigorous and concentrated attention by the central government at the intersection of moral and economic (conceived of in monetary and mathetical if not mathematical terms) concerns eventually led him, in his *Six Books of the Republic*, to an enthusiasm for resurrecting the Roman censorship, which in his vision could carry out both a control of mores and a program of demographic and econometric surveys.[107] This was something of a dead end in the history of political thought, but it is interesting to note how Bodin interwove the censorship, sumptuary control, and monetary policy as acts of a strong, tightly centralized, and technically sophisticated monarchy seeking to control powerful forces working toward the instability and decline of republics. The censors and the *triumviri monetales* were at opposite ends of the *cursus honorum*, the greatest and most minor regular offices of the Roman Republic, respectively, but both could readily be incorporated into similar visions of the danger that money, ambition, and avarice posed to the state, and of the potential for an authoritative royal response to that danger.

Virtue, Commerce, and Regulation

Sumptuary legislation, however, for all its ideological interest, was in the larger scheme of things a minor part of early modern governmental intervention in the economy. One can get a broader perspective on the logic of early modern French economic regulation by looking at the theory and practice of regulation in the broader economy: of agriculture, industry, and trade. Alongside sumptuary legislation and much else, this made up part of the rather ill-defined category that contemporaries called "police"—roughly, the ordering of daily civil life. It was a basic part of early modern governance at all levels throughout Europe. While it always carried a strong moral element and became closely associated in the seventeenth and eighteenth centuries with the various Protestant and Catholic reforms and perhaps with the

---

106. Ibid., 53–54: "les princes souverains, qui ont puissance de donner la loy, avec ceux qui leur donnent conseil, seront . . . plus résolus en ce qu'il faut ordonner pour l'honneur & accroisement de la république."

107. Bodin, *Six livres*, bk. 6, chap. 1: "De la censure, et s'il est expedient de lever le nombre des subjects, les contraindre de bailler par declaration les biens qu'ils ont." On this project see Jotham Parsons, "The Roman Censors in the Renaissance Political Imagination," *History of Political Thought* 22 (2001): 565–86: 578–80.

"social discipline" they encouraged, in sixteenth-century France its focus was clearly economic.[108] An edict of Charles IX glossed "police affairs" as "food, merchandise, works, handicrafts, and similar things."[109] Its status, in other words, was another sign of the central place economic exchange held in the sixteenth-century French political understanding of political life. Though it is worthwhile once again to note that this was not the kind of central, even obsessive concern in France that it was for other governments, notably the English, whose statutes and proclamations return continually to the textile industry, in particular. For just this reason, though, France may provide a more subtle case of how such concerns were interwoven with larger programs of governance.

Such an articulation, in an exaggerated form suitable to a humanist writing for the municipal authorities in a commercial city, may be represented once again by Guillaume de la Perrière. He certainly believed that material prosperity ranked prominently among the ends of any civil society, which he defined along Aristotelian lines as an "assembly and affective union of many into one, tending toward the acquisition of some good that is useful, delightful, honorable, or apparently so"; it was, indeed, like "that of several merchants who place themselves into a mercantile company, which concerns at once their private utility and the universal utility of the republic."[110] As central as wealth was to a republic, though, the aims of the magistrates in controlling it were surprisingly narrow: "The magistrates' main concern and care toward the artisans should be such as to not let them be unemployed through idleness or doze by negligence, and still less to engage in fraud in

---

108. The concept of "police" (or "*polizei*") is best studied for the German-speaking lands, with the classics being Gerhard Oestreich, "'Police' and 'Prudentia civilis' in the Seventeenth Century," in *Neostoicism*, 155–65; and Marc Raeff, *The Well-Ordered Police State: Social and Institutional Change through Law in the Germanies and Russia, 1600–1800* (New Haven: Yale University Press, 1983). For France in our period there is essentially nothing besides a short overview by Thomas Brennan, "Public and Private and *la Police* in the Old Regime," *Proceedings of the Western Society for French History* 18 (1991): 582–91.

109. Fontanon, *Edicts*, 1:805 (edict of Paris, 4 February 1567): "toutes choses qui dependent du fait de la police: comme vivres, marchandises, œuvres, ouvrages, & autres semblables." Brennan, "Public and Private," 583, supplies this and other equivalent definitions running into the early seventeenth century.

110. Perrière, *Miroir politique*, fol. 57r: "assemblee & consentement de plusieurs en un, tendans à aquerir aucun bien utile, delectable, honneste, ou ayant apparence de l'estre"; fol. 58r: "celle de plusieurs marchans qui se mettent en une compagnie de marchandise, le tout concernant tant leur privee utilité, que l'universelle utilité de la Republique." Perrière was somewhat radical in his sixfold division of the orders of society, which placed the robe in second place, behind the clergy but before the sword, while dividing the rest of society into merchants, artisans, and agriculturalists.

their arts."[111] This concern with combating laziness was a humanist obsession, and Margo Todd has demonstrated how it made its way into the legislation of a number of (mainly Protestant) states—it was certainly an important element of the "commonwealth" ideology in England.[112] La Perrière, however, places it in the larger context of the struggle against fraud, which we have already seen as a motivating force behind sumptuary legislation.

Turning from abstract theorizing to public justifications of economic regulation in the preambles of royal edicts, one finds the same general outlook.[113] Wealth, commerce, and industry are all positive goods, both for the kingdom and for individual subjects. An unusually cheerful measure in the summer of 1564 removed all restrictions on the grain trade in anticipation of a bumper crop, "desiring that those of our subjects to whom they belong may more easily draw profit and utility from them, seeing moreover that, thank God, we are currently at peace with all our neighbors."[114] Usury, on the other hand, might be condemned not only for its offenses against Christian charity but "for the good and public utility of our kingdom, and the succor of our subjects, so that they may live, engage in commerce, and buy and sell in all security, without being oppressed by abuses, pillage, and usuries . . . to the prejudice of commerce and public utility."[115] Indeed, an edict regulating the textile industry could aim at once "to repress all luxury, sumptuousness, and superfluous expenditures, to which our subjects have licentiously given themselves, so that most of them consume themselves daily in both food and

---

111. Ibid., fol. 117v: "le principal soing & cure des magistrats doit estre telle envers les artisans, de ne les laisser chommer par paresse ou negligence assoupir: & moins encore faire fraude en leurs artifices." Like Bodin, Perrière suggested a kind of census to carry out this task.

112. See Margo Todd, *Christian Humanism and the Puritan Social Order* (Cambridge: Cambridge University Press, 1987), esp. 122–58.

113. I base this discussion on an examination of the following groups of edicts, which it would perhaps be going too far to call a "sample" but which should provide a fairly comprehensive window on royal economic legislation in our period: (1) all edicts on monetary affairs; (2) edicts included in Fontanon, *Edicts*, vol. 1, bk. 5, "traittant generalement & particulierement de la police de France, & du reglement des artisans & arts mechaniques"; (3) edicts in the microfilmed Goldsmiths'/Kress collection of economic literature; and (4) edicts in the Gustave Gimon Collection on French political economy at Stanford University. The Fontanon collection gives an idea of what contemporaries considered significant, while the Goldsmiths'/Kress and Gimon collections are effectively random.

114. *Lettres patentes du roy pour la traicte generalle de toutes sortes de bledz par tout le Royaume de France, tant par mer que par terre* (Paris: Jean Dallier, 1564), sig. Aii v: "desirans que noz subjectz à qui ilz appartiennent en puissent plus aysement tirer proffit & utilité, attendu mesme que graces à Dieu, nous sommes à present en paix avec tous noz voisins."

115. *Lettres patentes et commission du roy pour la recherche, perquisition & poursuyte des usuriers* (Paris: Robert Estienne, 1567), sig. Aii r–v: "pour le bien & utilité public de nostre Royaume, & soulagement de nos subjects, à ce qu'ils puissent vivre, commercer & negotier en toute seureté, sans estre oppressez des abus, pilleries & usures . . . au prejudice du commerce & utilité public."

dress" and "to see to it that they can profit and enrich themselves from the ease, fertility, and abundance with which it has pleased God to endow and bless our kingdom."[116] One could multiply such examples.

The threats to such prosperity, though, and by extension the actions required to combat them, were less obvious, but by this point they should be familiar. The principal such threat, both a cause and a consequence of more general disorders in the realm, was avarice and the fraud that avarice engendered. The public order was subverted, for example, "by the extreme avarice and cupidity of the innkeepers, tavern keepers, and wine shop owners, who have only their own profit in view," which has led them "to so greatly increase the price of all things year after year, whatever abundance of food God in his bounty has since granted to this kingdom, that there is no longer anyone who has to travel through the country either in our service, for their private affairs, to traffic in merchandise, or for any other cause or occasion, can live while supporting such a heavy and great expense as that which they face daily." Dealing with this would help solve "also the excessive dearness of all sorts of foodstuffs, which has proceeded principally from the luxury and superfluity that has little by little crept into the lives of our subjects."[117] Exactly how innkeepers got this kind of pricing power was a bit unclear (though in remote parts of the country regional monopolies were probably not rare), but it certainly involved dishonesty and flouting royal legislation.

Henri III was particularly insistent on this phenomenon, which fit both the extreme crisis of his reign and the simultaneously moralistic and technocratic tendencies of his response. Thus, an edict regulating leather goods

---

116. Fontanon, *Edicts*, 1:901 (edict of Amboise, January 1572): "reprimer tous luxes, somptuositez, & despenses superfluës, en quoy nosdits sujets se sont licencieusement addonez, & la pluspart se consument tous les jours, tant en vivres qu'habilements. Pour pourvoir aussi à ce qu'ils puissent profiter & s'enrichir de la commodité, fertilité & abondance dont il a pleu à Dieu doüer & benir nostre Royaume." Evidently there is a distinction between a true and a false form of wealth here, probably parallel to Aristotle's distinction between proper and improper chrematistic.

117. Fontanon, *Edicts*, 1:939 (edict of Paris, 20 January 1563): "par l'extreme avarice & cupidité desdits hosteliers, taverniers & cabaretiers, qui n'ont que leur profit devant les yeux, tant s'en faut que lesdits Edicts & ordonnances ayent servy à diminuer quelque chose de l'exessivité dudit prix, qu'au contraire lesdits hosteliers, taverniers & cabaretiers, pour frauder l'intention de nosdits predecesseurs, n'ont cessé depuis l'expedition desdits Edicts & ordonnances, de tellement accroistre d'annee en annee le prix de toutes choses, quelque abondance de vivres, que Dieu ait par sa bonté depuis envoyee en ce Royaume, qu'il n'y a plus personne qui ayant à aller par les champs, soit pour nostre service, affaires particuliers, commerce de marchandise, ou pour quelque autre cause ou occasion que ce soit, puisse vivre & supporter une si lourde & grande despense, que celle qu'il faut qu'il face journellement . . . aussi à l'excessive cherté de toutes sortes de vivres, procedee principalement du luxe & superfluité qui s'est peu à peu introduit au vivre de nos sujets."

(which seem to have been a source of perennial difficulties), "in particular because of the excessive price of those products, which increases daily," complains that

> tanners . . . commit such great fraud and abuse in working these that the public suffers a great loss, in that a pair of shoes or other piece of leatherwork lasts only half the time it ought to . . . , and our subjects would not generally be given the runaround and cheated when buying them, as they now are, not knowing the interior vice of the leather that is so well hidden by the artfulness and malice of the tanners that only they, and the most expert shoemakers, can judge and know it . . . . But . . . to enrich themselves quickly and move their inventory, they leave it [in the tanning vats] not even half the time specified by the ordinances, nor do they apply the working and finishing that they should, enriching themselves by these illicit means in a short time from the loss and incommodity of the public.[118]

Fundamentally, these edicts differ little from the sumptuary laws of the same period: they seek to contain the ambition and avarice of particular economic groups and to cause them to sell their merchandise honestly, thus keeping price levels down, increasing general prosperity, and protecting public order and royal authority.

But from the point of view of the contemporary understanding of money, a few other things stand out. One relatively obvious one is the pervasive concern with inflation, which is certainly not surprising during the "great inflation" of the second half of the sixteenth century. More subtle is the way in which the economic results of avarice and ambition could be assimilated to the counterfeiting of coins and precious metals. This was metaphorical and perhaps unconscious in the case of sumptuary regulation: an overdressed commoner

---

118. *Edict du Roy sur le retranchement des grans abus qui se commettent en l'appareil, traffic & commerce des Cuirs qui se vendent & distribuent en son Royaume contenant erection en tiltre d'office d'un controlleur, visiteur & marqueur desdits Cuirs, avec le reglement que sa majesté veult & entend estre sur ce observé* (Paris: Vefve Nicolas Rosset, 1586), 4: "mesmes pour le prix excessif desdits ouvrages, qui de jour en jour s'augmente." Pages 5–6: "Les tanneurs & megissiers commettent de si grandes fraudes & abus, en l'appareil d'iceluy que le public en souffre grand detriment en ce qu'une paire de soulliers ou autre ouvrage de cuir ne dure moytie, de ce qu'elle feroit si elle estoit de cuir bien & deuëment tanné, & appareillé d'ou encores l'on en auroit plus d'abondance & à meilleur compte & ne seroient nos subjets ordinairement circonvenus & deceus en l'achapt d'iceux, comme ils sont ne cognoissans le vice interieur du cuir qui est si bien caché par l'artifice & malice desdits tanneurs qu'il ny a qu'eux, & les plus experts cordonniers qui le puissent juger & cognoistre. . . . Mais . . . pour promptement s'enrichir en se deschargeant de leur marchandise, ils ne l'y laissent pas la moitié du temps porté par les ordonnances ny ne baillent l'appareil & façons qu'ils devroient s'enrichissans par ces illicites moyens en peu de temps du dommage & incommodité publicque."

was effectively a counterfeit noble—gold on the outside but base on the inside. In the humbler case of leather, though, it becomes much more explicit. Through their art the tanners can give their product a specious appearance of quality, which only experts can unmask, so that the government must step in (by affixing official stamps) to enforce honesty. We will see, when we turn to the problems of counterfeiting and criminality, that this particular nexus strongly influenced the ways in which the coinage was violated and defended in the Monnaies' jurisdiction. It had a more immediate effect too, though, in that the Cour des Monnaies' regulation of the coinage and the precious-metal trades seems to have served as a model for commercial regulation in general.

On occasion, the use of monetary regulation as a model appeared more or less explicitly. A general set of economic regulations issued immediately after a very important set of monetary reforms opened with these words:

> The king, having issued his edict and ordinance on the regulation of the moneys (which he judged to be most necessary in order to avoid the disorder and great diminution of the wealth of his subjects that the inflation [*surhaussement*] the people had taken the license to give the gold and silver coinage brought with it—by which the sales price of all sorts of goods, merchandise, and handiworks are notoriously raised, and like-wise the wages of persons who work in mechanical trades), has deemed it necessary to make some good provision for that, as also for several other disorders that have come about on occasion of the troubles.[119]

This manages to combine in a remarkably small space almost all the elements in the French Renaissance logic of economic regulation: the ambiguous but definite defense of wealth; the license of citizens impelled, no doubt, by ambition and avarice to upset the legislated order; the close association between such behavior and civil disorder; and the need for royal action to set all to rights. But more particularly, this preamble makes concrete the implications of the sumptuary laws. The great problem that regulation of the trades, at least, had to solve was the tendency of the people to abandon their proper places in

---

119. Fontanon, *Edicts*, 1:832 (edict of Paris, 21 November 1577): "Le Roy ayant fait son Edict & ordonnance sur le reglement des monnoyes, comme il a jugé estre tres-necessaire, à fin d'obvier au desordre & grande diminution de la richesse de ses subjects, qu'apportoit avec soy le surhaussement de pris que le peuple s'est licensié de donner aux especes d'or & d'argent: Par lequel il est notoire que la vente de toutes sortes de denrees, marchandises & ouvrages a esté aussi rehaussee: & semblablement augmenté le salaire des personnes qui travaillent aux œuvres mechaniques. A estimé estre requis d'y donner quelque bonne provision: comme semblablement à plusieurs autres desreglemens advenus à l'occasion des troubles." The monetary reforms of 1577 are discussed in detail below; see also Jotham Parsons, "Governing Sixteenth-Century France: The Monetary Reforms of 1577," *French Historical Studies* 26 (2003): 1–30.

the social order and overcharge for their work. The king had to prevent ambition from making the accumulation of money (of account) an end in itself.

The broader pattern of premodern economic regulation confirms that view. A good example is an edict generally considered to have defined the French approach to such matters for the entire old regime: a 1581 ordinance on *métiers jurés*, or craft guilds.[120] It postulated a uniform system of sworn economic associations based on those of Paris and overseen by royal courts, down to the level of small towns. This was needed because, "since there is nothing so good and holy in its institution . . . that avarice does not corrupt it, most of the artisans of our kingdom, particularly in the towns and places where there is no instituted mastership, or *jurés* to inspect their manufactures, have so far emancipated themselves that most of them are not of half the goodness and integrity they should be."[121] This was the general form of the problem with leather workers dealt with four years later, as avarice leads to fraud on inexpert consumers and generally inflated prices, so that justice and expertise must cooperate to remedy the ill; indeed, there is reason to think that the parallel was understood explicitly at some level of the royal government.[122] And this was the system that had already been applied, this time with some vigor, to the precious-metal trades under the supervision of the Cour des Monnaies.

The most important phase of that project, at least, began in 1554, forming part of Henri II's general policy in the regulation of the moneys. An edict of that year had been motivated, according to its preamble, mainly by concern over the "great loss and damages because of the lack and defect of alloy" discovered when plate had been brought to the mints for coining to meet war expenses, "proceeding from the bad faith of the goldsmiths."[123] In order to prevent abuses in this key area,

---

120. On this initiative, which formed the basis of further legislation under Louis XIV, see Hecksher, *Mercantilism* 1:145, 179.

121. Fontanon, *Edicts*, 1:1091 (edict of December 1581): "comme il n'est chose si bien & sainctement ordonnee, ou coustume si vertueuse, que l'avarice ne corrompe: la pluspart des artisans de nostre Royaume, mesmes des villes, bourgs & lieux où il n'y a Maistrise instituee, ny jurez pour visiter leur manufacture: se sont tellement emancipez, que la pluspart d'icelles ne sont à moitié pres de la bonté & integrité qu'elles doivent estre."

122. Although the testimony is somewhat later: I. de Laffémas, *Histoire*, 75–78: "Je pense avoir leu dans les memoires de mon pere, qui parlent des abuz generalement de toutes sortes de marchandises & manufactures, que les cuirs ont esté tellement alterez de leur bonté que ceux qui s'en souloient fournir en France, ont esté contraints d'en chercher ailleurs. . . . C'est donc la fidelité qu'il faut aujourd'huy garder, si nous ne voulons perdre les ouvrages qu'on met tant de peine de restablir, & la vaiselle d'argent de vostre ville de Paris, qu'on recherche par tout le monde pour s'estre conservée en son titre, nous en donne tesmoignage."

123. *Edict faict par le Roy sur la reformation, reduction, & reiglement des Orfevres, Joyauliers, Affineurs, Departeurs, Batteurs, & Tireurs d'or, & d'argent se don Royaulme, pays, terres, & seigneuries de son obeissance* (Paris: Jean Dallier, 1555), sig. Aii r: "grand perte & interest, pour la faulte & tare de loy . . . procedant

goldsmiths were to be organized into sworn corporations on the Parisian model, to practice only in towns with royal courts, to mark their work (once it had been duly inspected) with individual, registered punches like those used to track the output of mints, and to be supervised throughout the kingdom by the Cour des Monnaies and local mint officials. The generals of the moneys on their chevau-chées in succeeding years carried commissions "to have the goldsmiths swear [association] . . . so that they do not henceforth work gold or silver that is not of the alloy it ought to be and as it is worked by those of Paris, to avoid the abuses and counterfeits [*faulses*] committed therein."[124] Admittedly, they were still litigat-ing for this authority against the goldsmiths of Lyons, with little success, a century later, but the very persistence of the controversy testifies that this was taken more seriously than most economic regulation and suggests its unusual importance.[125] It was also, naturally, directly related to the institutional structure of the Monnaies; in England, for example, the Tudors placed the kingdom's precious-metal workers under the semiprivate regulation of the London Goldsmiths' Company.[126]

Was the Cour des Monnaies' regulatory activity the explicit model for French royal economic regulation? It seems quite possible, though the evidence is not definitive. At least the terrain covered by the Monnaies—creating money, of course, but also using technical expertise for the public benefit, combating fraud, and exercising royal power uniformly throughout France—was central to the way the government understood economic regulation as a whole. Money was vital to the operations of the state, of course, but it was also the form that economic transactions took in general, and insofar as the characteristic crime of the ambitious and avaricious economic actor was to divorce the money price

---

de la mauvaise foy des Orfevres." Moves in this direction went back as far as 1543, but the 1554 edict was the most detailed and seems to have been the first to be pursued with any vigor (for the major edicts of that period, see Fontanon, *Edicts*, 1:1112–20). On regulation of Parisian goldsmithing in this period, see Michèle Bimbenet-Privat, *Les orfèvres parisiens de la renaissance (1506–1620)* (Paris: Com-mission des travaux historiques de la Ville de Paris, 1992).

124. AML, BB 78, fol. 250v (registers of the Bureau de ville, 8 June 1556): "de faire jurer les orfevres. . . . A ce que par cy apres ils nayent a mectre en oeuvre ny argent qui ne soit de la loy qui doit estre et comme besoignent ceulx de paris pour obvier aux faulses et abus qui se font." This was the procès-verbal of Jamet Metayer and Pierre Alligret's report: unsurprisingly, the goldsmiths and the city fathers saw little reason to accept the Monnaies' authority, though they agreed with its general goals. Ibid., fol. 253r.

125. See AML, HH 111 (dossier concerning that litigation, mostly before the Parlement of Paris, to 1660). The Monnaies does seem to have had more luck asserting its authority in other towns. For an example of (ultimately) successful enforcement in Bordeaux, see AN, Z[1B] 682, pieces dated 21, 22, 23, and 30 October 1603 (information by Simon Biseul, on chevauchée).

126. This system went back to 1462 and continued through the seventeenth century: see C. E. Challis, "Controlling the Standard: York and the London Company of Goldsmiths in Later-Tudor and Early-Stuart England," *Northern History* 31 (1995): 123–37.

from the actual value of the object being exchanged, it was the technology of economic disorder. Policing counterfeiting, preventing the inflation of the currency, blocking illegitimate social climbing, and enforcing regulations against almost any form of commercial fraud, usury, or sharp dealing were thus fundamentally comparable activities, subject to the same logic, the same rhetoric, and the same or similar administration. It is thus no wonder that the administration of the moneys might be thought of as a crucial nexus of government activity: the source of the king's justice in economic affairs but also a place of danger where the unscrupulous could and would work to counteract the king's (artful) efforts to keep exchange natural and the social order stable. No wonder some thought it advisable to conceal the details of the process from impious eyes!

The Autonomous Economy

Essentially all the sources we have looked at so far date from or describe the period before the close of the Wars of Religion and Henri IV's consolidation of power around 1595. This is not coincidental, for the rhetoric and the logic of economic regulation underwent some quite noticeable changes as the house of Bourbon replaced that of Valois on the throne. The reasons for such a change are hard to discern: one might suspect that the rise of Protestant advisers in the ex-Huguenot king's court played a role, as well as a generation of economic change while France's attention had been focused elsewhere—the united Netherlands had become a major economic power, for example, and North Atlantic colonization projects were getting seriously underway. And the very experience of pacification may indeed have convinced the government "that nothing is left to perfect this great work" other than to fill France "with as much or more wealth and goods as their predecessors were once seen to abound in."[127] Whatever the reason, there was a new tone and a new emphasis to French economic policy under the new dynasty, one that, despite an interruption after 1610, continued in many ways up to the Revolution.

A little bit of both the old and the new can be seen in a 1601 edict banning the use of indigo dye, a New World product that was displacing a French

---

127. Fontanon, *Edicts*, 1:1046 (edict of Paris, Jan. 1599): "qu'il ne reste plus pour la perfection d'un si grand ouvrage, qu'à . . . les remplir d'autant, ou plus de richesses & de commoditez, que l'on aye veu leurs devanciers abonder par le passé." This edict was part of Henri's program for promoting luxury cloth manufactures. A speech from the 1614 Estates General gives a feel for how this blended with the old rhetoric: Louis XIII, like his father, hoped to revive France "ainsi qu'elle estoit, en la fleur de ses prosperitez, puis qu'elle estoit gastée & infectée par l'avarice des financiers, par l'ambition des plus petits, par l'oppresion des plus grands, par le sale commerce qui se fait en la Justice à cause de la venalité des offices." Marmiesse, *Remonstrances*, 39–40.

product, pastel. The initial concern, that "among the things that most maintain commerce in our kingdom, both with our subjects and with foreign peoples, is the goodness and loyalty of the goods that are made in it," is certainly not unfamiliar. But there seems to be a somewhat different perspective than had prevailed in the previous century. The king is not quite as directly concerned as before with damage to the public or the republic: that is certainly in view, but internal and external "commerce," abstractly conceived, is the immediate victim. The ideally transparent market of classical political economy, requiring protection from the state only against fraud and violence, seems not too far away. And perhaps it is not, but the next phrase of the edict reminds us that much of the old regulatory logic remains, for commercial goods, "good and loyal" or otherwise, are still spoken of in the vocabulary of the currency: "The abuse daily committed . . . hinders sales and little by little cries down the said goods."[128] Bad products, like bad money, will drive good ones out. Poor workmanship is still described as counterfeiting—and even as lèse majesté, since only the king had the right to cry down circulating coinage.

The broader concept of the "economy" as an autonomous object, regulated by the kind of internal logic we now associate with it, appears intermittently under Henri IV. At times, the illusion of modernity can be striking, as when an edict criticized the high rates of interest on perpetual rents that had prevailed for the past forty years and more and had "hindered the traffic and commerce of merchandise, which formerly was more popular in our kingdom than in any other in Europe, and caused agriculture and manufacturing to be neglected, since some of our subjects prefer, by the ease of a gain that is illusory in the end, to live idly from their rents in the towns, rather than working with some effort at the liberal arts, or cultivating and improving their lands."[129] Alongside the humanist moralizing distaste for laziness is a sense of the economy's technical complexity and even of the more subtle tools that

---

128. *Edict du Roy, contenant prohibition et defence de l'usage de l'Inde & Anil, & entree dans le Royaume* (Paris: Jamet Mettayer and Pierre l'Huillier, 1601), 3–4: "entre les choses qui maintiennent le plus le commerce en nostre Royaume, tant à l'endroit de nos subjets, que les peuples estrangers, c'est la bonté & loyauté des marchandises qui se façonnent en iceluy, & l'abus que l'on y commet journellement, qui empesche le debit & descrie peu à peu lesdites marchandises." The term *décrier* is used again a few pages later to refer to the same phenomenon.

129. *Edict du Roy, sur la reduction des Rentes qui se constitueront d'ores-navant à prix d'argent au denier quatozre [sic]* (Rouen: Martin Mesgissier, 1610), sig. A iiii r.: "empsché le trafic & commerce de la marchandise, qui auparavant avoit plus de vogue en nostre Royaume qu'en aucun de l'Europe, & fait negliger l'agriculture & manufacture, aymans mieux plusieurs de nos subjects sous la facilité d'un gaing à la fin trompeur, vivre de leurs Rentes en oisivité parmy les Villes, qu'employer leur industrie avec quelque peine aux arts liberaux, où à cultiver & approprier leurs heritages." The edict actually dated to July 1601; lowering interest rates was a pet cause of Sully's.

governments have available to manipulate it. And famously, if not particularly influentially, the titles of two notable books prescriptive or descriptive of early Bourbon economic policies—Antoine de Montchrestien's *Treatise of Political Economy* and the duc de Sully's *Memoirs on the Wise and Royal Economies of State*—associated the Aristotelian *oikonomia* with Bourbon public administration in a way that prefigured (though they did not directly influence) the modern concept of political economy.[130]

Beyond these works, Henri IV's reign saw a small renaissance of economic thought at the hands of a number of very energetic and original economic thinkers and projectors. The most prominent member of this group was Barthélemy de Laffemas, a man of modest background with great energy, considerable charisma, and a talent for losing money. He collaborated with Louis de Mayerne Turquet, a Lyonnais merchant who had fled to Geneva before joining Henri's cause, and Pierre de Béringhen, a Flemish armorer who had become a favorite of Henri's.[131] Laffemas invented the office of "contrôleur général du commerce de France" for himself, while Béringhen became "grand maître surintendant et général réformateur des mines" (not a new office).[132] Their writing and activities were fairly disjointed and not, in the short run, particularly influential. They were striking, though, and they found some resonance beyond the usual boundaries of French economic discourse. When an English pamphleteer writing in the Netherlands opined that "there is nothing in the world so ordinarie, and naturall unto men, as to contract, truck, merchandise, and traffike one with another, so that it is almost unpossible for three persons to converse together two

---

130. Sully's memoirs appeared under that title in 1638. Isaac de Laffémas used an equivalent term, assuring Henri IV that commercial bureaus "rendront une police œconomique en vostre Royaume." *Histoire*, 104.

131. On Theodore de Mayerne, see H. R. Trevor-Roper, *Europe's Physician: The Various Life of Sir Theodore de Mayerne* (New Haven: Yale University Press, 2006). On Isaac—whose wife, Charlotte Bécquet, was the daughter of a Robert Bécquet who was apparently not the general of the moneys of that name but was almost certainly related to him—see Georges Mongrédien, *Le bourreau du Cardinal de Richelieu: Isaac de Laffemas (documents inédits)* (Paris: Editions Bossard, 1929), 48; this book is also the only significant biographical study of Barthélemy. On the Béringhen family, which deserves a more thorough study, see Joseph and Gabriel Michaud, *Biographie universelle, ancienne et moderne: Ou, Histoire, par ordre alphabétique, de la vie publique et privée de tous les hommes qui se sont fait remarquer par leurs écrits, leurs actions, leurs talents, leurs vertus ou leurs crimes*, vol. 4 (Paris: A. T. Desplaces, 1843), s.v. "Béringhen." On the collaboration between Mayerne and Béringhen, see Roland Mousnier, "L'opposition politique bourgeoise à la fin du XVIe siècle: l'œuvre de Louis Turquet de Mayerne," *Revue historique* 79 (1955): 4, citing a letter of Théodore's, BN, fr.17934, fol. 115r.

132. For the latter title, see AN, Z[1B] 74, fols. 217v–223r (letters patent, Grenoble, 28 September 1600, making that appointment).

houres, but they wil fal into talk of one bargaine or another, chopping, changing, or some other kinde of contract."[133] This dictum, with its air of Adam Smith, was an unacknowledged translation of Mayerne Turquet.[134] It was not necessarily a contraction of the traditional Aristotelian view on exchange, which after all had a strong natural component, but it certainly suggested a different emphasis from the one that had dominated the French sixteenth century. If followed through it would suggest a reevaluation of the dangers and potential of chrematistic and of the monetary technology that enabled it.

To pursue the ideas of these thinkers further would draw us away from the specific issues of concern here, but what is clear is that, for this small group of thinkers at least, money and commerce seemed far less threatening and far more healthy in the body politic than would have been conceivable a generation before. There was now some confidence, or at least the possibility of confidence, that fostering money, and indeed encouraging its multiplication, would not necessarily lead to an inflationary dislocation of social and political norms; indeed, a due measure of wealth would satisfy the legitimate material expectations of all orders of society and reduce the tendency toward illegal and disorderly behavior. This was by no means a definitive victory for a "modern" vision of political economy that would embrace commerce as strengthening and stabilizing and reject the Aristotelian models of the ancient world: the Laffemas school was scattered after Henri IV was assassinated and Sully disgraced. Montchrestien's *Treatise*, the most significant attempt to restate the Huguenot theses to the new regime, fell on deaf ears, and its author died a rebel on the field of battle a few years later. But the very existence of this relatively radical vision of commercial society suggests that major changes were afoot in the intellectual underpinnings of political economy. As we will see in the next chapter, a more detailed investigation of the *nummus/nomos*, of the nexus of government and money, in French political discourse confirms that impression.

---

133. John Wheeler, *A Treatise of Commerce Wherein Are Shewed the Commodities Arising by a Well Ordered Trade, Such as That of the Societie of Merchant Adventurers Is Proved to Be* (London: John Harison, 1601), 6.

134. Compare Louis de Mayerne Turquet, *Traicté des negoces et traffiques, ou contracts qui se font en choses meubles. Reiglement, & Administration du Bureau, ou Chambre politique des marchans. Prins de memoires de L.D.M. dediez & pieça præsentez au Roy de France Henry IIII* ([Geneva]: Pour Jaques Chouet, 1599), 7–9. It was also paraphrased by I. de Laffemas, *Histoire*, 14–15: "chacun se mesle de la Marchandise, non seulement d'aujourd'huy, mais de touttemps, & semble que nous y soyons naturellement portez."

CHAPTER 3

The Inflationary Crisis and the Reforms of 1577

> It will be found from all times and all antiquity that any time anyone has tried to interfere however little with the faict des monnoyes, either by changing the price, the alloy, or the character, they have ruined everything to the great loss of all the people, for the faict des monnoyes is so vital a limb that if one touches it ever so lightly it causes great spasms [in the body politic].
>
> —Merchants of Paris, 1565

Given how central money was to the sixteenth-century understanding of the economy and economic regulation and how closely tied it was to the sense of danger surrounding economic affairs, the suspicions expressed by the wealthy merchants of Paris in 1565 are not surprising.[1] Maintaining the currency required intense activity at the best of times, and the second half of the sixteenth century was very far from being the best of times. Economic and political circumstances twice led to the near collapse of the French currency; this chapter and the next will examine the ways that governing authorities sought, with considerable success, to meet those challenges. This story provides a series of detailed, concrete case studies on the relationship between money and governance at the highest levels. Control of the currency was at the same time an important source of legitimacy for the French monarchy and a site of unusually intense engagement with the broader society—public and specialized opinion, the market, and so on.

---

1. Paul Guérin et al., eds., *Registres des délibérations du Bureau de ville de Paris*, vol. 5, *1558–1567* (Paris: Imprimerie Nationale, 1896), 544 (remonstrances of the drapers, grocers, mercers, and wine merchants of Paris): "Il se trouverra que de tout temps et ancienneté, lorsque l'on a voullu toucher tant et si peu que rien au faict des monnoyes, soit pour la mutation du pris, alloy ou carractere, l'on a ruiné toutes choses au grand dommaige de tout le people, comme estant le faict des monnoyes ung member si precieulx que l'on [n']y peult si peu toucher qu'il n'en advienne ung grand remuement." (Transcribing AN, H, 1784, fol. 389.)

It was also an area where practice and theory, the institutional structures of the state and society, and the conceptual structures that circulated broadly or among decision makers acted intensively and visibly upon each other.

Following these stories involves many details of policymaking, but it also illuminates monetary theory as it existed at the time. Connected only loosely to the more general economic thinking discussed in the previous chapter, this little-studied literature, produced by royal advisers both inside and outside (but generally orbiting around) the Cour des Monnaies, was dominated by both a deep classical-humanist culture and immersion in the realities of the "modern" system of sovereign states and a monetized, commercial economy.[2] It was a technical literature, but it dealt in innovative ways with the most important issues of the early modern state. Beginning in the mid-1560s, the government began to seek expert advice from outside the circles of merchants and moneychangers on how to deal with the disorder and inflation of the period. It was able to draw on the monetary bureaucracy that Henri II had reshaped and also on the humanist culture that by then pervaded the French political classes. The public discourse thus engendered continued well into the seventeenth century. At least the embryo of a scientific political economy emerges out of these writings, the original response of a developing political culture to novel and urgent problems. Though these royal advisers never did achieve the control over economic forces that they sought, their efforts played a significant part in producing the culture that made modern economic thought possible.

Challenges and Policies

The difficulties confronting French monetary policy in our period can be summed up in one word: inflation. But in practice that tells us very little, since inflation can vary enormously in its causes and characteristics. We have already seen that the French government began to be concerned with at least some inflationary phenomena as early as the later years of François I's reign. The disorder in the mints that Henri II's reforms eventually, and indirectly, brought under control may well have been a contributing factor to that inflation: by increasing the money supply, at least locally, uncontrolled

---

2. Aside from my own work, the only recent study of this literature is Mark Greengrass, "Money, Majesty, and Virtue: The Rhetoric of Monetary Reform in Later Sixteenth-Century France." *French History* 21 (2007): 165–86. Two old articles remain useful: Germain Martin, "La monnaie et le crédit privé en France aux XVIe et XVIIe siècles; les faits et les théories (1550–1664)," *Revue d'histoire des doctrines économiques et sociales* 2 (1909): 1–40; and Emil Sczlechter, "La monnaie en France au XVI siècle," pt. 1, *Revue historique du droit français et étranger* 19 (1951): 501–21.

minting of even small change could be expected to raise price levels, while at the same time the bad money, by driving out the good, would raise its price for those who needed it. This would in turn tend to raise the nominal price mints would need to pay to attract precious metal—it was the precious metal content, after all, that made good coins good. Other things besides fraud at the mints could lead to the same effect as well: large-scale counterfeiting, for example, or the uncontrolled import of overvalued coin from abroad (counterfeiting of copper *vellón*, for example, seems to have been behind the collapse of the Spanish currency in the first half of the seventeenth century).[3] In all these cases, inflation would result when actors other than the state that controlled the currency in question sought more or less illicit profit for themselves.

That was a game a state could play for its own benefit, too, by means of a devaluation of the currency. By increasing the nominal value of existing coins in money of account or reducing the specie content of those coins—perhaps secretly, though it was not a secret that could be kept for long—while maintaining their nominal value, the state could profit in two ways. First, the attractive new prices would for a time draw specie to the mints, and the government could then collect seigniorage on its coining. Second, the domestic government debts were generally contracted in money of account, and thus could be paid off in inflated currency, or "monetized," to use the modern term. Such behavior had been common in France in the fifteenth century, and Henry VIII of England had resorted to it on a massive scale.[4] In this case, of course, inflation was not necessarily an undesired effect of currency manipulation and might indeed be the main point of it.

Other factors could lead to inflation without any conscious attempt by anyone to profit from it. One was the wear and tear that coins suffered in circulation. If worn coin continued to circulate at par, this would result in a gradual appreciation of the money of account against specie. Governments could try to prevent this by forbidding worn coin from circulating at all, requiring that it circulate by weight rather than at par, or paying for it at par at the mint and coining

---

3. See Akira Motomura, "The Best and Worst of Currencies: Seigniorage and Currency Policy in Spain, 1597–1650," *Journal of Economic History* 54 (1994): 104–27. Cross-border arbitrage, which could approach outright counterfeiting, was an ongoing preoccupation of early modern monetary authorities. For some particularly striking examples, see Edoardo Grendi, "Falsa monetazione e strutture monetarie degli scambi nella Repubblica de Genova fra cinque e seicento," *Quaderni storici* 66 (1987): 803–37.

4. See Harry A. Miskimin, *Money and Power in Fifteenth-Century France* (New Haven: Yale University Press, 1984). The English debasement will be discussed below.

it at a loss. The first two expedients, however, were likely to be ineffective given the relative weakness of early modern governance, and the last was, of course, expensive. Thus there was a strong tendency for governments to simply accept the inflation resulting from wear and tear, periodically raising the mint price of specie to draw in worn coin.[5] A subtler but probably more powerful inflationary ratchet resulted from the perpetual shortage of small change, which was expensive to coin as long as it contained anything like its par value in silver.[6] Thomas Sargent and François Velde have argued on the basis of econometric calculations that this was the main driver of inflation in preindustrial Europe, though since it operated more or less constantly, it is an insufficient explanation for variations in the intensity of inflation.

Another complication was that both gold and silver were monetary, but their relative value (the "bimetallic ratio") fluctuated on the open market, both over time and across space. Arbitrage against the prices assigned by the government to the two metals might easily draw one of them almost entirely out of circulation, something that would certainly be perceived as inflationary by anyone in need of the missing metal (for example, to make payments to especially picky counterparties like foreign mercenaries). Finally, direct changes in the money supply could be inflationary. These might occur either through the creation of "book money" of one kind or another—increasing use of letters of exchange, book transfer payments, and so on—or through an influx of specie, particularly from mining, which would in theory inflate prices both in specie and in the money of account and might not concern authorities targeting only specie prices against the money of account. Both new monetary instruments and New World specie entered the European economy on a large scale in the sixteenth century, but it is unclear how much their impact was offset by increased levels of economic activity in general and by increased specie flows to south and east Asia and thus how much they affected price levels.[7] It is a fact, however, that price levels rose rapidly throughout Europe in the second half of the century, as expressed both in specie and to an even greater extent in

5. See Debra Glassman and Angela Redish, "Currency Depreciation in Early Modern England and France," *Explorations in Economic History* 25 (1988): 75–97.

6. See Thomas J. Sargent and François R. Velde, *The Big Problem of Small Change* (Princeton: Princeton University Press, 2002).

7. For metallurgical evidence of the inflow of American silver, see Bruno Collin, "L'argent de Potosí (Pérou) et les emissions monétaires franaises," *Histoire et mesure* 17 (2002): 217–25; for a good introduction to global bullion flows in this period, see Dennis O. Flynn, "Comparing the Tokagawa Shogunate with Hapsburg Spain: Two Silver-Based Empires in a Global Setting," in *The Political Economy of Merchant Empires: State Power and World Trade, 1350–1750*, ed. James D. Tracy (Cambridge: Cambridge University Press, 1991), 332–59.

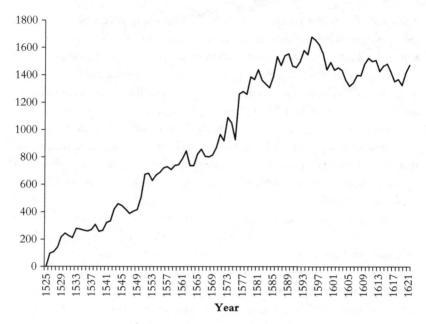

FIGURE 2.   Cost of living: composite index, 1525 = 1.

Source: Two indexes (for France and Alscace) from E. H. Phelps-Brown and Sheila Hopkins, "Wage Rates and Prices: Evidence for Price Pressure in the Sixteenth Century," *Economica,* n.s., 24 (1957): 289–306, tables 2 and 3, summed with a renormed index for Poitou generated from R. Raveau, "La crise des prix au XVIe siècle en Poitou," *Revue historique* 162 (1929): 1–44 and 268–93, table 1.

money of account.[8] The chart above, showing a composite cost-of-living index (in money of account) for the general area of northern France, gives an idea of the inflationary pressures at work.

As the graph makes clear, these pressures were unrelenting up through the end of the civil wars. Not only were general price levels rising throughout the latter half of the sixteenth century, and not only did the money of account continue its secular inflation against specie without any noticeable letup, but from the 1560s on, the value of the money of account (particularly against gold) kept threatening to collapse catastrophically.[9] And in the 1560s, monetary authorities lost control over the value of foreign coin circulating

---

8. The literature on the sixteenth-century "price revolution" is vast and, from our point of view, almost entirely irrelevant. For a relatively recent overview, see Michael D. Bordo, "Explorations in Monetary History: A Survey of the Literature," *Explorations in Economic History* 23 (1986): 339–415.

9. For a reasonably good general account of this monetary crisis, see Louis Monnier, "Causes et conséquences économiques de la Saint-Barthélemy: Etude sur le système monétaire en France de 1568 à 1578," in *Actes du colloque l'Amiral de Coligny et son temps (Paris, 24–28 octobre 1972)* (Paris: Société de l'histoire du protestantisme français, 1974), 651–701.

in France. Where previously they had set it at its intrinsic specie value and thus below the value of equivalent French coins, it began to command a market premium and thus to fuel domestic inflation.[10] In short, the challenges to which the new class of French monetary experts responded were real, novel, and intractable.

Henri II and Charles IX: From Police to Policy

Henri II tackled inflationary pressures by improving the police functions of the monetary and judicial administration. And during his reign inflation remained under control despite the disastrous condition of the royal finances, while the mints seem to have been brought into much better order. He had no difficulty making technical adjustments to the coinage: the 1549 monetary edict changed the bimetallic ratio slightly, "so as to equilibrate silver and billon with gold, and so that the values of our moneys will correspond in the red and the white [metal]," while also increasing the allowance for manufacturing costs in coins, which would in principle encourage mint activity.[11] Unfortunately, no sources survive to shed light on the reasoning or debates behind this edict, so it tells us relatively little about the way monetary policy functioned at that point. There is not even any real indication of who most of the important players in monetary policy were, though it is suggestive that when Alexandre de la Tourette found the *garde des sceaux* unhelpful in moving forward the edict on goldsmiths' regulation, he told the court that "I have decided to speak about this to the Constable"—the king's right-hand man, Anne de Montmorency—"and ask him for another audience in the council to make the necessity of the matter . . . clearer."[12]

One policy initiative on which we are well informed, and that had important consequences for the future of the coinage throughout Europe, was the creation of the mechanized mint at the Etuves under the supervision of

---

10. On the details of this process see Denis Richet, "Le cours officiel des monnaies étrangères circulant en France au XVIe siècle," *Revue historique* 225 (1961): 367–72.

11. *Edict et ordonnance sur le faict des monoyes & nouvelle fabrication poids alloy & prix, ouverture & jugement des boettes d'icelles*, etc. (Paris: Pierre Haultin and Jean Dallier, 1550), sig. A2 r: "a fin de equipoler, largent & billon avecques lor, & que les valeurs de nos monoyes se correspondent tant du rouge que du blanc." See articles 1, 2, and 6.

12. AN, Z[1B] 368, piece dated 13 September 1552 "peu avant minuit" (Alexandre de la Tourette to the court, orig.): "je suys delibere den parler demain a monseigneur le connestable & luy demander encore une audiance au conseil pour fere plus a plain entendre la necessite de laffaire dont aussi jay dresse quelques articles."

Guillaume de Marillac.[13] Correspondence survives between Montmorency and Charles de Marillac, Guillaume's brother, who, as ambassador in Augsburg, located and purchased the minting machinery that Michel then oversaw at the Mint of the Etuves.[14] It shows that Henri's government took the coinage very seriously, devoting to it not only the time and effort of top advisers but also money. Indeed, Montmorency was willing to pay *more* money than the inventor ultimately demanded (four thousand as opposed to three thousand écus; the expenses of sending experts back and forth and building test equipment must have come to at least as much again). Compared with the costs of a military campaign this was not much, but it was more than was usually devoted to the currency, and it was paid in cash up front.

Henri's government seems to have understood this initiative in terms of foreign as much as economic policy. On 16 September 1550 Charles de Marillac warned the king that "the Emperor, too, has pretensions to taking advantage of this invention, and for that reason has had their first master in the affairs of the moneys brought from Spain to learn what he [the inventor, Schwab] knows how to do."[15] Not long after the machinery went into operation in Paris, Henri arranged for another set of machines to be installed at the small mint his client, King Henri of Navarre, operated at Pau. In the 1560s the English government made a serious attempt to steal the technology through the agency of a renegade employee of the Etuves, Eloi Mestrelle, who wound up being executed for counterfeiting.[16] This was a quest for prestige as much as a practical undertaking. That is not to deny, however, that there was a strong technocratic element to this project. The king and his advisers were evidently impressed by the sheer ingenuity of the process. The edict organizing the Etuves, for example, described it as the invention

---

13. On the Marillac family, see the biographical appendix to Michel Antoine, *Le cœur de l'état: Surintendance, contrôle général et intendance des finances 1552–1791* (Paris: Fayard, 2003); and Nicolas Lefèvre de Lezeau, *La vie de Michel de Marillac (1560–1632), Garde des Sceaux de France sous Louis XIII,* ed. Donald A. Bailey (Quebec City: Presses de l'Université Laval, 2007).

14. The correspondence is in BN, ms. de Brienne, 89; the relevant portions were published by Pierre de Vaissière, *La découverte à Augsbourg des instruments mécaniques de monnayage moderne et leur importation en France en 1550 d'après les dépêches de Charles de Marillac, ambassadeur de France* (Montpellier: Imprimerie Ricard Frères, 1892).

15. Ibid., 25–26: "l'Empereur aussy pretend se valloir de cest artifice, ayant à cest effect faict venir d'Espagne leur premier Maistre en faict de monnoye pour apprendre ce que ledict Chevalier sçait faire."

16. On Mestrelle's machinery, see C. E. Challis, "Presidential Address Part II: The Introduction of Coinage Machinery by Eloy Mestrell," *British Numismatic Journal* 59 (1990): 256–62; this is based on account books of the construction of test machinery under Mestrelle's direction, which are by far our best source on the details of this family of engines. The best overview of the spread of coining machinery is still W. J. Hocking, "Simon's Dies in the Royal Mint Museum, with some Notes on the Early History of Coinage Machinery," *Numismatic Chronicle*, 4th ser., 9 (1909): 56–118.

of "some of our good and loyal servants, experienced in the matter of the said moneys, who have succeeded so well in this task that with time and results they have shown us the excellent workmanship of that money, which, because it is perfectly round, cannot be clipped without it being clearly and immediately apparent."[17] This wonder (especially with the role of Germans conveniently elided) was itself not unrelated to issues of national pride and identity.

The idea that technical improvements leading to a more consistent and uniform coinage would improve the state of the currency was neither new nor silly. One of Henri II's first actions on coming to the throne was to create the new office of Engraver-General of the Moneys of France, which partially centralized the production of punches used in making coining dies. The justification was familiar: it is "most requisite and necessary, in order to more easily know and discern the true and good money, in which the art of sculpting has been guarded and observed, from the false and adulterated, made evident and known by the lack of skill in the said art," to appoint a single skilled individual to produce images.[18] The ongoing appeal of such centralization projects, as well as new methods of mechanized minting—a project of one Nicolas Briot was seriously canvassed in France under the regency of Marie de Médicis and then in England when that came to nothing, while the French mints were definitively mechanized after 1645—testify to the power of this outlook.[19] But while the reasoning that justified these projects was fairly sound, they were not unideological exercises in pure practicality. The Cour des Monnaies and the mint officers consistently opposed this kind of initiative, and while much of their opposition was no doubt (as scholars have generally assumed) driven by innate conservatism and a fear of seeing their authority, or the value of their offices, eroded, they also made

---

17. *Edict de la creation et establissement de la monnoye des estuves du Roy à Paris, & des officiers en icelle* (Paris: Jean Dallier and Vincent Certenas, 1554), sig. Aii r–v: "certaine invention nouvelle de forger monnoye, par aulcuns de noz bons & loyaulx serviteurs experimentez au faict desdictes monnoyes. Lesquelz ont faict en ce tel debvoir que leur travail & industrie avecques le temps & l'effect, nous ont tesmoingé l'excellence de l'ouvraige de ladicte monnoye: qui pour estre en perfection de rotundité, ne peult estre rongnée sans manifeste & claire apparence."

18. AN, Z^{1B} 63, fol. 286r (edict of August 1547). This is published, along with almost all archival documents relating to the mint of the Etuves and the engravers of the moneys, in Fernand Mazerolle, *Les médailleurs français du XVe siècle au milieu du XVIIe*, vol. 1, *Introduction et documents* (Paris: Imprimerie Nationale, 1902), 38: "soyt très requis et neccessaire, pour plus facilement dicerner et congnoistre la vraye et bonne monnoye, en laquelle l'art de sculpture a esté gardée et observée, avec la faulse et adulterine, manifeste et congneue, par le deffault de sçavoir dudict art."

19. On those mechanization projects, see Hocking, "Simon's Dies," 82–85. All the documents surrounding Briot's French project are published in Mazerolle, *Médailleurs*, 1:298–485.

some good points. When the Monnaies objected to Claude Hery's appointment as engraver-general in 1557, it was quite correct in pointing out that
since the office was created, "the engravings on the coinage have not and
will not cease to be as different as before, or almost so; nor are the moneys
less counterfeited," and that transporting the punches under high security
all over France (while paying the engraver three hundred livres a year) was a
substantial expense.[20]

The Schwab machinery, too, even as it was modified by the French engi-
neer Aubin Olivier, remained less than ideal. It consisted of three sets of
machines.[21] The first was a rolling mill that produced uniform sheets of the
alloy to be coined. The second was an instrument that punched out blanks
from those sheets, apparently in a two-stage process. The third was a screw-
press that struck the blanks between a pair of dies. This set of equipment
was capital-intensive: it cost 750 livres to build less than full-size prototypes
in Augsburg, and outfitting the mint of the Etuves must have cost several
times that amount; by way of comparison, a contemporary inventory of the
old Paris mint valued its entire contents at less than 400 livres.[22] Even so, the
machines were finicky, as the frequent references to repairs in the records of
the Monnaies and Olivier's apparently indispensable role in running the mint
show. They were also expensive to operate. The Monnaies petitioned the
king in 1553 that "given that the Etuves mint produces a great deal of scrap
and refounding, which leads to loss of materials and losses that other mints
in this kingdom are not accustomed to and turn to the loss of the master, the
brassage of this one should be increased by four sols per mark of gold . . .
and as for [silver] testons, the brassage can be increased by twelve deniers

---

20. AN, Z[1B] 65, fol. 83v (remonstrances of 13 December 1557), in Mazerolle, *Médailleurs*, 1:61:
"N'ont delaissé et ne delaissent les tailles des monnoyes estre autant differantes ou à peu près que au
precedent et ne sont les monnoyes moings falcifiées."

21. These details can be inferred from the Marillac correspondence, the documentation of
Mestrelle's English project, and the inventory of the Etuves.

22. AN, Z[1B] 369, piece dated 4 May 1555 (procès-verbal of B. de Riberolles and Bergeron). The
major items were the furnaces and precision equipment, which were of course needed at the Etuves
as well—the rolling mill was horse-powered, and the Etuves used a horse mill already installed for
an earlier gem-polishing operation. The only detailed description of the equipment of the Etuves
comes from an inventory made by the Monnaies after Aubin Olivier's death. AN, Z[1B] 378, piece
dated 10 April 1581 (procès-verbal of Dain and Desjardins); Mazerolle, *Médailleurs*, 1:90–95. This
lists five large presses, plus a spare—all with framing that the heirs carefully noted had been reinforced at Aubin's own expense—five cutting machines, and two large rolling mills, "plus, ung autre
moien engin à rolleux desmonté, que lesdicts Ollivier et Corbie nous ont dict avoir esté faict en
Allemaigne." Ibid., 94. It is hard to imagine this equipment costing any less than five times what the
prototypes had cost.

[one sol] per mark of material."[23] The organizational edict issued two months later followed this advice, decreasing the king's seigniorage to accommodate the increased production costs.[24]

Even so, projects based on this set of ideas continued into the reign of Charles IX. One was a plan mooted in 1565 to centralize the production not just of some punches but of dies for the obverse of all coins. They were to be the work of one Guillaume Martin, a goldsmith styling himself "engraver-general of the moneys of the queen of Navarre."[25] His letters patent specified that he was being appointed "to keep our moneys from being falsified and deal with the diversity and difference of their cutting and engraving."[26] The Monnaies was dubious, questioning how these dies would match the reverses that would still be produced locally, how they would be distributed, and whether there would be bottlenecks in production.[27] In the end, nothing came of it. This was just the tail end, though, of a more elaborate scheme or set of schemes to consolidate the farm of the mints, which excited even more widespread (and probably well-founded) opposition.

The first version of this proposal had emerged in 1563, when the king issued letters patent to Pierre Assézat of Toulouse and Abel Foulon to mechanize the production of coinage in the Southwest with machinery of their invention. This was a curious affair in many ways: Foulon, a royal *valet de chambre* who had in 1555 received what is generally considered the first French inventor's patent, for a holographic machine designed to engrave hard metals, died shortly after this plan was submitted—"not without suspicion," according to the bibliographer la Croix du Maine, "of having been poisoned out of jealousy for his fine inventions."[28] Assézat was presumably

---

23. AN, Z[1B] 368, piece dated 22 April 1553 (arrêt): "attendu que ladicte monnoye des estuves est subiecte a grande quantite de sizaillees et refontes dont proviennent plusieurs dechets de matieres & plus de fraiz qui nont acoustume destre faictz es aultres monnoyes de ce royaulme et qui tournent a la perte du maistre que le brassaige dicelluy peult estre augmente de quattre soulz tourn. pour marc dor . . . et quant aux testons le brassaige peult estre augemente de douze deniers tourn pour marc doeuvre." Mazerolle does not reproduce this document, which is important because it shows the hostile Monnaies agreeing with the probably self-interested operators' request to increase their brassage.

24. See *Edict de la creation et establissement*, sig. Bi r–v. The problem was most likely with the blank-cutting machines, which may not have been needed for the medals and counting tokens that the Etuves mainly produced from the 1560s, and exclusively from 1584.

25. See AN, Z[1B] 372, piece dated 13 February 1565 (petition of Martin); Mazerolle, *Médailleurs*, 1:46–47.

26. AN, Z[1B] 372, piece dated 1 June 1565; Mazerolles, *Médailleurs*, 1:48: "pour eviter que noz monnoies ne soient falciffiés et pourveoir à la diversité et difference de la taille et graveure d'icelles."

27. See an interrogatory of Martin, attached to the letters patent; Mazerolles, *Médailleurs*, 1:49.

28. François Grudé de la Croix du Maine, *Les bibliothèques françoises de La Croix du Maine et de du Verdier sieur de Vauprivas*, ed. Rigoley de Juvigny, 4 vols. (Paris: Saillant et Nyon et Michel Lambert,

the exceptionally wealthy Toulousan merchant and financier who had led a failed Protestant coup in the city the previous year, suggesting that this project may have been related to efforts at pacification following the First War of Religion.[29] Despite these overtones of high politics, though, the project was advanced under the sign of the fight against inflation and civil disorder, an answer to the pressing question of

> what order and means we could observe to stop the unbridled and inflated prices that the common will has given to the moneys for the past twelve years . . . and come to a means for reducing and returning our said moneys from weak to strong as soon as it pleases God to continue for us the peace that He has brought to fruition after the wars, conflicts, and seditions that have occurred in our kingdom.[30]

The event did not live up to the king's hopes. Ten months later he told the Monnaies that though "Assézat and his associates had boldly claimed to have several machines in hand for making the coins so perfectly that they could not be clipped or counterfeited," "since then, having heard from your commissioners and deputies that Assézat and his associates have not complied with the lease or even produced diagrams of their products and machinery," he had to put the project on hold.[31]

1772–73), 1:2: "non sans soupçon d'avoir été empoisonné pour la jalousie de ses belles inventions." Foulon was also the brother-in-law of the portraitist and *controlleur des éfigies* François Clouet. He died in Orléans, where according to Théodore de Bèze, *Histoire ecclésiastique des églises réformées de France*, ed. P. Vesson, 2 vols. (Toulouse: Société des livres religieuses, 1882), 1:509, he had installed and operated a mint for the Huguenots.

29. See Francis Brumont, "Politique, religion et affaires: Pierre Assézat (vers 1515–1581)," *Annales de Bretagne et des Pays de l'Ouest* 112 (2005): 147–56. The mint project seems to have escaped the attention of Assézat's biographers.

30. AN, Z[1B] 537, piece dated 23 December 1563 (letters patent), fol. 1r: "quel ordre et moien pourrions observer pour arrester le cours et haulsement effrené qui par volonté populaire sest donné depuis les douze derniers ans aux monnoies . . . et acheminer ung moyen pour reduire et remener du foible au fort nosdictes monnoyes lors quil aura pleu a dieu nous continuer la paix De laquelle apres plusieurs geurres emotions et seditions advenues en nostredict royaume Il nous a donné la fruition." Assézat and Foulon were given the farm of the Lyons, Toulouse, Bordeaux, and Bayonne mints for two years, and two thousand livres from the seigniorage to offset their startup expenses. As we have seen, this was almost certainly far too little to build an effective mechanized mint.

31. AN, Z[1B] 372, piece dated 5 October 1564 (letters patent): "assezat et ses associez sestoient faictz fort davoir en main quelques engins pour faire lesdictes especes de telle perfection quelles ne se pourroient rongner ny contrefaire . . . depuis ayans entendu par voz commis et depputez que lesdicts assezat & associez nont satisfaict audict bail a ferme ny mesmes exhibe les patrons figurez desdicts ouvraiges et leurs engins." The letters were registered on 22 November 1564. This incident helps clarify why the Marillacs took such careful precautions against fraud and double-dealing in Augsburg.

It resurfaced immediately, though, in a less mechanical but otherwise more ambitious form. This time Martin Malus, master of the Bordeaux mint, proposed to pay the king one hundred thousand livres for the farm of all the mints in the kingdom for the next six years, paying not only their officers and employees but also those of the Cour des Monnaies. Even without interest costs and a profit margin for Malus, this would have represented an optimistic estimate of how much the moneys might clear over that period, which should immediately have aroused suspicion.[32] Despite their knowledge of the mint system and dislike of potential challenges to their authority, half of the generals of the moneys supported Malus, who promised not only to pay their wages promptly but to pay off their massive arrears and buy out the offices supposedly suppressed by the Edict of Orléans.[33] Malus proposed two new and dubious sources of revenue to pay for all these expenses: an increase of one grain in the remèdes, the legal margin of error for the specie content of coins (which would have amounted to a slight devaluation of the coinage); and a license to appoint denunciators throughout the kingdom who would prosecute violations of the monetary edicts in return for a third of the fines and forfeitures. Given that he would have been paying the salaries of those charged with supervising his operations, there is no reason to believe that he would have exploited these and more traditional privileges with particularly strict probity.[34]

More opposition came from the influential wholesale merchants of Paris. The remonstrance they presented to the Paris city council, quoted at the head of this chapter, is interesting, and not only for the clear connection it drew between currency policy and the broader health of the body politic. They clearly recognized the potential for corruption inherent in Malus's plan and objected to the process by which it had been moved forward "because monetary policy should be changed only after many public bodies have deliberated on it, . . . as has been done since time out of mind, and not as in the past few days after having heard a few of the gentlemen of the

---

32. On this project, see AN, Z[1B] 372, dossier dated 17 March 1564 (o.s.), esp. piece no. 3, Malus's petition to the Monnaies.

33. See AN, Z[1B] 372, piece dated 20 October 1564. Alexandre de la Tourette, Jehan le Mestayer, Hilaire Dain, Jehan Bourgoing, Jacques Roullie, and Thomas Turquam were in favor; Charles de Valles, Gerard des Valles, Germain Longuet, Guillaume Desmoulins, Charles Vinot, and Olivier Emery were against. The conclusions of the procureur général Hennequin, included in the dossier noted above, were negative.

34. Over the next year Malus was fined 140 livres for tardiness in submitting the pyxes from the Bordeaux mint and failure to keep his registers in order: see AN, Z[1B] 372, pieces dated 2 May 1565 and 10 July 1565 (arrêts).

Monnaies, who for all we know have now gone into business with some of those who drew up the memoirs on the [consolidated] farm." They were greatly exercised by the proposed increase of the *remèdes*, which raised the specter of a fiscal devaluation of the coinage, still remembered even if it had not been practiced in France for almost a century. More generally, they objected to the Malus scheme as ineffective and even damaging in the fight against inflation, which they self-servingly blamed on the decay of French trade. In the end, because of "the calamities of recent times, the current dearness of foodstuffs and the great distress of the poor people, and the inflation of gold and silver that arises more from the high politics of this kingdom than from anything else," they could not accept the general farm.[35] This was a series of objections that much better plans would also have to meet. By the time they were made, though, a group of advisers loosely affiliated with the Paris sovereign courts had begun to develop a much more sophisticated set of theories about the nature of inflation and of money itself.

Jacques Colas and the New Monetary Thought

Beginning around 1560, commentators put forward if not full theories, at least a few characteristic principles. First, they held that the ratio of the value of gold to silver essentially controlled the market value of coin. Second, many of them believed that this ratio had to be absolutely consistent in all coins. If that were done, then (to take the example of the most commonly preferred ratio of silver to gold, 12:1) any combination of silver coins adding up to a given value would weigh exactly twelve times as much as any combination of gold coins adding up to the same value. By acting in this way, commentators claimed, the government could maintain public faith in the value of its coinage, protect it from foreign speculators, and prevent its devaluation. Finally, they generally believed that foreign coins should simply be forbidden to circulate in France. They advanced a variety of arguments to support this proposition, but they agreed that the gap in legislative power that the circulation of foreign coins opened could destroy governmental control over the currency. Slightly later,

---

35. Guérin et al., *Registres* 5:544: "parce que l'on ne doibt toucher aulcunement au faict des monnoyes, si ce n'est avec deliberation de beaucoup de compaignées, . . . tout ainsi qu'il a esté faict de tout temps et ancienneté, et non pas faicte, comme il a esté cy devant ces derniers jours, après avoyr oy quelques ungs des Messieurs des Monnoyes, qui peult estre sont maintenant accompaignez d'alcuns qui ont faict les memoires des fermiers." Page 547: "la calamité du temps qui a esté, et la charté des vivres qui est de present, la grande necessité en laquelle est le pauvre peuple, et que le surhaulsement des especes d'or et d'argent vient plus par les grandz affaires qui ont esté en ce royaulme que pour aultres occasions."

a fourth item joined this list, though it never achieved the general acceptance of the other three. Many theorists proposed that the money of account be simply abolished, at least in name. The legislative activity of the prince could be placed on a firm footing by naturalizing it: by identifying the unit of value with an actual, circulating coin, and setting the value of all other coins as parts thereof, in proportion to their relative precious-metal content. In this way, there would be no possibility for confusion or for defiance of the royal will.

This cluster of ideas originated in part with the late fourteenth-century bishop, theologian, and royal counselor Nicole Oresme. His widely circulated treatise *On Money* was influential among the nominalists of the fifteenth century, creating a tradition focused on maintaining a true correspondence between the form or name of a coin and its intrinsic value. Thus, according to the important fifteenth-century theologian Gabriel Biel, "the form of money is a testament to its genuineness and legality, namely that it is of genuine substance and weight."[36] For this reason, any attempt by either the authorities or private persons to change or circumvent the correspondence between the value, form, and substance of a coin (by devaluation, for example) was simply perjury. Oresme, moreover, had worried that foreign powers might undermine this correspondence. "It should," he claimed, "be prohibited and punishable for a foreign prince or any other to coin money of like design [to an existing one] but of lower weight, so that the common people could not distinguish one from the other. This should be a crime; . . . and it is just cause for war."[37] These medieval tracts, however, were works of moral theology, not of political economy, coming from the church, not from the world of economic or monetary experts or of the royal bureaucracy. They sought above all to dissuade princes, on both practical and moral grounds, from manipulating their currency, rather than attempting to understand and control the fact of money on a theoretical level.

The pioneer of this effort was an obscure but enterprising man named Jacques Colas, who was a part, but a peripheral part, of the new monetary

---

36. Gabriel Biel, *Treatise on the Power and Utility of Money*, trans. Robert Belle Burke (Philadelphia: University of Pennsylvania Press, 1930), 23. The work was reprinted fairly frequently in the sixteenth century: e.g., *Tractatus de potestate & utilitate monetarum* (Oppenheim: J. Köbel, 1516); and in Marquard Freher, ed., *De re monetaria veterum Romanorum et hodierni apud Germanos Imperii, libri duo* (Leiden: Apud Gothardum Vœgelinum, 1605).

37. Nicole Oresme, *The De moneta*, ed. Charles Johnson (London: Thomas Nelson, 1956), 10: "Debet eciam prohiberi sub pena, ne aliquis aut extraneus princeps vel alter favicaret monetam similem in figura et minoris valoris, ita quod vulgus nesciret distinguere inter estam et illam. Hoc esset malefactum . . . et est causa juste bellandi contra talem extraneum." I have altered Johnson's translation slightly.

apparatus that Henri II had constructed. Probably originally from the milieu of lesser Parisian barristers and solicitors, he became comptroller of the Monnaie des Etuves in the late 1550s.[38] He was also something of a go-getter: in 1562, he tried to have himself appointed "comptroller of the moneys of France," covering the entire kingdom, but the Monnaies remonstrated vigorously and the idea was dropped.[39] Instead, he got his office united with that of the guard of the regular Paris mint, taking the unique title of "comptroller in the mints of Paris."[40] At the same time, starting at least as early as the fall of 1560 (probably as part of the preparations for the Estates General to be held at Orléans) he began to present the royal councils with his opinions on monetary policy and the theory that should govern it. The memoirs he prepared on this occasion do not survive, which makes it hard to reconstruct his reasoning, but the reply drawn up by the Cour des Monnaies does. From this, it appears that Colas had already embraced the equivalence of gold and silver worked and unworked, and that he advocated, if not a ban on all foreign coinage, at least a policy of allowing it to circulate only at the value of the specie contained, without any seigniorage.

From what we know of him, Colas seems to have been a classic projector, similar to (if slightly less nakedly self-interested than) the advocates of new machines and national farms. The royal council took him seriously enough to send his proposals to the Monnaies for its opinion, and the court in turn took him seriously enough to appoint Pierre Alligret and Thomas Turquam (who would later emerge as one of the court's own experts in monetary theory) to examine his proposals. Only on receiving their report and "after having heard the said Colas several times at the bureau of the said court on the contents of the said request and memoirs presented by him, and the matter being duly deliberated," did the Monnaies point out that Colas's second point was already official policy, while indicating the practical difficulties of his first: that it "has never been implemented, as has been verified by the old registers of the said court. And it cannot be done without burdening the said marc of worked gold with a great and excessive

---

38. It seems likely that he was, or was a close relation of, the "Jacques Colas, avocat au Châtelet" who witnessed the *inventaire après décès* of his mother-in-law, the wife of one *procureur* in the Châtelet and widow of another, in 1557. Florence Greffe and Valérie Brousselle, eds., *Documents du Minutier central des notaires de Paris: Inventaires après décès*, vol. 2, *1547–1560* (Paris: Archives Nationales, 1997), no. 1450 (*inventaire après décès* of Nicole Esyenne, MC IX, 138: 16 August 1557).

39. See AN, Z[1B] 65, fol. 188r (remonstrances of 9 December 1562).

40. "Contrerolleur ès monnaies de Paris." On these transactions, see AN, Z[1B] 435, piece dated 2 June 1573 (pleas on a case arising out of Colas's promotion), which also reveals that at that point he still owed 1,900 livres for the purchase of his original office as *contrerolleur*.

charge . . . and consequently weaken the said gold coinage to the loss of the people, or unless the [king] bears the part of the costs necessary for making silver and billon coins."[41] That is, it cost no more to manufacture a coin of greater than of smaller value, and by the same token, it was cheaper to make a given value (in money of account) of gold than of silver coins.[42] If Colas's suggestion were followed, either high-denomination coins would have to be disproportionately taxed, or the government could not recover the costs of producing lower-denomination coins. Thus, maintaining a consistent ratio throughout the coinage and between coined and uncoined metal, was likely to be an expensive proposition. Instead, the Monnaies recommended that the young king concentrate on beginning coinage under his own name and portrait—all in all, the court's approach remained practical and empirical.

Events soon rendered that advice moot: a bit more than a month later, François II died, his brother Charles IX, a child of ten, took the throne, and France began its descent into civil war. Not surprisingly, issues of monetary policy and theory retreated for some time from the public stage. Not until 1566 did they again come to the royal attention, and Colas was ready. The first surviving work in which he himself set out his theory—and the theory's culminating statement—was an extravagant manuscript presented to the king on 10 April 1566. It was never printed and appears to have been forgotten since the seventeenth century.[43] This was a text designed to display its author's command of a wide range of cultural forms. The presentation manuscript was in a fine, professional, italic book hand, rubricated and illuminated, clearly much more extensive, impressive, and well-thought-out than the "sheet and a half-page of paper written and signed with his own hand" that he had produced in 1560.[44] Its rhetoric was a reasonable facsimile of the

---

41. AN, Z[1B] 371, dossier dated 24 October 1560, item no. 1 (arrêt of that date): "apres avoir oy ledict colas par diverses foys au bureau de ladicte court sur le contenu en ladicte requeste et memoires par luy presentes [et] la matiere mise en deliberation"; "ne fust jamais faict comme a este veriffie par les registres anciens de ladicte court Et ne se peult faire sans surcharger ledict marc dor en oeuvre dune trop grande et excessive traict ~~qui revient a la perte et foulle des subgectz dudict sieur & qui seroit ung affoiblissment desdictes monnoies dor revenant a~~ et par consequence affoiblir lesdictes monnoies dor a la foulle du peuple Ou que ledict sieur portast partie des frais necessaires pour la fabrication de ses monnoies dargent et billon." (Strikeout in original.)

42. This was one of the basic facts that drove the inflationary ratchet identified by Sargent and Velde, *Big Problem*; Colas had identified a real problem, though not in a way he was in any position to understand.

43. "Secret des monnoyes par Jaques Colas controrolleur dicelles es monnoyes de Paris," in BN, n. a. fr. 5064, fols. 235–41.

44. AN, Z[1B] 371, dossier dated 24 October 1560, item no. 1 (arrêt of that date): "ung feuillet & demy page de papier escript & signe de sa main."

fashionable Pléiade style, constructed around the exegesis of emblems and of scriptural passages. The entire enterprise was clearly part of Colas's ongoing and successful campaign to obtain a higher position in the monetary bureaucracy.[45] He believed, with reason, that technical expertise in money and in contemporary humanist culture could combine to promote his ambitions.

Colas's "Secret of the Moneys" was a response to a much better-remembered contribution to monetary theory, the *Paradoxes on Monetary Affairs* of Jehan Cherruyl de Malestroict, presented a month earlier. Malestroict, though a specialist in finances rather than in currency and a member of the Chambre des Comptes rather than the Cour des Monnaies, was part of the same milieu from which the Monnaies drew its officers. Before taking up his charge in the Comptes he had been a receiver of the city of Paris, a position that involved frequent contact with the Monnaies (one finds him refusing to pay it members' wages in 1560, for example).[46] Like François Gohory he had also been a *notaire et sécretaire du roi*, and like François Garrault, he later left his court to take up a position as a provincial general of the finances, in his case in his home province of Brittany.[47] It is thus not surprising to find that Malestroict's analysis drew attention, as Colas had, to the relationship between prices measured in specie and those measured in money of account; he had argued that the rampant inflation of the day was purely nominal and that in specie terms prices had not changed since the Middle Ages. The nature of this inflation "must necessarily be drawn from the source and depths of the said moneys, and demonstrated by most paradoxical reasoning, that is, very far from the opinion of the vulgar."[48] That is, it was susceptible only to sophisticated, theoretical, expert analysis—it called for an entire science, centered on the details of the coinage. Malestroict did not quite produce one, but others were willing to try.

If this science revealed that a monetary disorder was the root cause of one of the great problems of the day, then it was also vitally important to understand

---

45. Colas was later given the office of general in the Cour des Monnaies: see above, chapter 1.

46. See AN, Z[1B] 371, piece dated 23 August 1560; remember that Charles Hotman, the Catholic League leader, later worked as receiver of the city of Paris.

47. See Jean-Michel Servet, "Malestroit. Eléments pour une biographie," in *Pratiques et pensées monétaires*, Monnaie et financement 15 (Lyons: University of Lyon 2, 1985), 98–100.

48. *Les paradoxes du seigneur de Malestroict conseiller du Roy, & maistre ordinaire de ses comptes, sur le faict des Monnoyes, presentez à sa Majesté, au mois de Mars, M. D. LXVI. Avec la response de Jean Bodin ausdicts Paradoxes* (Paris: Jacques du Puys, 1578 [1566]), fol. 2ii v: "peu de gens peuvent gouster la source & origine de ce mal, lequel faut necessairement tirer du fons & abysme desdictes monnoyes, & icelle demonstrer par raisons grandement paradoxes, c'est à dire, fort esloingnees de l'opinion du vulgaire." This statement in itself was classical in its form and authority, being a near quotation of Cicero, *Paradoxa stoicorum*, proœmium: "Quæ quia sunt admirabilia contraque opinionem omniun—ab ipsis [Stoicis] παραδοξα appellantur."

how the nominal value of gold and silver could be controlled. This was all the more the case because the officials in charge of monetary policy were clearly no longer willing to accept the view that deliberate and immoral manipulation by a ruling prince (the basic evil against which Oresme and his followers had written and, more recently, the target of a sizable section of the first book of Thomas More's *Utopia*) was the essential cause of any devaluation of the nominal currency.[49] For this reason, as Colas told the king, "I have, according to your command, told your *maître des comptes* M. de Malestroict the cause which has made [gold and silver] rise in price in your kingdom for a century and more."[50] In the next year, the two men collaborated on a memoir for the royal council, which further developed their thought.[51]

Colas continued and deepened Malestroict's move to make the knowledge of monetary affairs specialized, even arcane, and systematically precise. His tract began with an explanation of two mathematical emblems. The first was "a zero in the middle of the nine figures of arithmetic," the other "a square in the corners of which are numbers by which the manner of equivocating gold to silver is known." Throughout the work, Colas continually returned to how deeply he had "considered the saying of Solomon in the eleventh chapter of *Wisdom*, that all things have been ordered by God in Measure, Number, and weight."[52] This verse was much cited at the time by those who wished to justify a mathematical approach to the study of the natural world.[53] It was a particular favorite of the English mathematician, scientist,

---

49. On the basically moralistic nature of early-sixteenth century economic and monetary thought, see Arthur B. Ferguson, *The Articulate Citizen and the English Renaissance* (Durham, NC: Duke University Press, 1965).

50. BN, n. a. fr. 5064, fol. 238r: "lon peult clairement juger par mes supputacions (que j'ay faict entendre a Monsieur de malestroict maistre de voz comptes suivant vostre mandement) la cause qui les a faict encherir en vostre Royaume depuis cent ans & plus."

51. "Memoires sur le faict des monnoyes," in *Paradoxes inédits du Seigneur de Malestroit touchant les monnoyes*, ed. Luigi Einaudi (Turin: Giulio Einaudi, 1937), 99–130. This memoir, dated 16 May 1567, is edited from BN, ms. fr. 4534; BN, fr. 4600; and a manuscript in the collection of the editor. Malestroict's memoir is in large part merely a restatement of Colas's treatises. Note the following sentence (p. 106, my emphasis): "j'ay mis peine de voir les registres anciens & nouveauls estant tant en la chambre des comptes que Cour des monnoyes, dont j'ay faict plusieurs grands extraicts de ce qui concerne le faict des dittes monnoyes, que j'ay *avec l'aide du controlleur des monnoyes de Paris qui est icy present* exactement supputez."

52. BN, n. a. fr. 5064, fols. 234r–v; 241r: "un 0 au millieu des neuf figures d'Arithemetique"; "un quarré aux coings duquel y'a des nombres par lequelz est cogneu la maniere d'équipoler l'or à l'argent"; "Apres avoir longtemps ratiocine pour empescher ce malheur, & considere la sentence de Salomon a l'unziesme de Sapience que toutes choses ont esté disposees de Dieu par Mesure, Nombre & poiz."

53. See Allen G. Debus, "Mathematics and Nature in the Chemical Texts of the Renaissance," *Ambix* 15 (1968): 1–28; and Deborah Harkness, *The Jewel House: Elizabethan London and the Scientific Revolution* (New Haven: Yale University Press, 2007), 103.

and occultist John Dee, whose *Monas hieroglyphica*, published two years earlier, was constructed around a similar exegesis of geometrical forms invented for that purpose.[54] Colas thus linked his own project to the idea of quantification that extended from occult Neoplatonism to the science of Galileo. Besides emblems, mathematics, and biblical exegesis, Colas backed up his argument with apposite classical quotations, duly identified in the margins. The overall effect was to carve out a domain of expertise legitimated by the king, by intellectual accomplishment and by technical experience with the coinage.

More substantively, Colas complained that previous policy had "subjected number (which is the proportion between gold and silver) to the number called 'price,' and the said price to weight, which is to reverse the order which there should be." To summarize his argument in modern terms, he believed that whenever France's bimetallic ratio departed by more than 1/24 from the natural universal ratio of 1:12, one metal was underpriced on the world market. Foreigners exploited the price difference by buying one metal cheap in France and selling it dear at home, thus depleting French specie stocks. In particular, if certain silver coins were overvalued with respect to gold (which tended to happen, since more of them had to be manufactured to create coinage of a given value), then

> the foreigner will draw the gold out of France with his silver, which will make it rare. This rarity will increase it[s price] at least by the excess value of silver. Thus, for this reason it will be impossible to prevent the foreigner from drawing out one of the said metals thus to make all things in France dearer.
>
> Thus, France must not regulate itself by the proportion which is used abroad: for today only the said proportion of twelve marks of pure silver for one of pure gold is observed, and if it is held higher, this is only because of the advantage which they have gained in France by the course given to their coins. . . . If it is held lower . . . it is after having raised the price of silver in France by rarity in order to draw gold from France more cheaply than the price set in the [royal] ordinance. By such tricks they can draw goods and merchandise from France at a better price than its inhabitants, which is the ruin of this kingdom.

Since disorder in the French price structure was purely an import, the way to prevent it was for the king "to buy from your people all the gold and silver foreign coins which are in your kingdom, and order everyone to take them to

---

54. Dee had spent some time in Paris in 1551, and it is just conceivable that he could have come into contact with Colas or someone known to him.

the nearest of your mints . . . to be restruck with your dies."[55] If the government also proceeded to faithfully maintain the duodecimal (1:12) ratio, there would be no further opportunity for disorder.

Besides adopting and expanding Malestroict's call for an expert science of money and generally accepting his diagnosis of the inflationary crisis, Colas definitively located the vulnerability of the price system at the intersection of the coinage and the French border. With the partial exception of Guillaume Budé's 1514 work on the Roman coinage, *On the As and Its Parts*, which Colas repeatedly cited as his own inspiration, previous writers had not considered money a specifically *national*, as opposed to a political or legal, phenomenon, nor had they placed it in the context of an international economic system.[56] Casuists and moralists such as Oresme and More had simply assumed that public authorities could set the price of their coinage—the question was whether they *should*—while classical scholars had naturally focused on the Roman Empire, which had no acknowledged peers. For Colas, the prince's freedom of action was severely constrained by actors abroad. Even his true desire to "to keep the well-being of his subjects in a good state of tranquillity and peace of mind" could easily be undermined if he did not properly understand the secret of moneys.[57]

When one examines Colas's theory a bit more closely, though, one quickly realizes that something besides a pure understanding of economic reality contributed to his thought. Though numerical, precise, and universal,

---

55. BN, n. a. fr. 5064, fols. 235r–236v, 290r: "Autrement si une portion d'or fin vault plus en France que douze d'Argent fin, l'estranger qui est Seigneur des Mynes tirera largent de France par son or, le rendant rare, laquelle rarité l'encherira a cause de son utilite, tellement que ladicte quantité d'argent pour valloir l'or, augmentera de la plus valeur de l'or pour le moins. Ou bien si une portion d'or fin vault moins que douze portion d'argent le Roy, L'estranger tirera l'or de France par son argent qui le rendra rare, Laquelle rarité laugmentera de la plus valeur de largent pour le moins Dont par ce moyen ne sera possible d'empescher l'estranger de tirer l'un desdicts metaulx pour tousjours faire encherir toutes choses en France. Parquoy ne se fault reigler en France à la proportion que tient l'estranger : car s'il n'observe pour le jourdhuy la susdicte proportion de douze marcs d'argent fin pour un d'or fin et qu'il la tienne plus haulte cest a cause de l'avantage quil a gaignee en france par le cours donné à ses monnoyes, et par les faultes commises aux ordonnances du passé, ce qu'il luy donne moyen d'encherir son or, Et par iceluy tirer l'argent de france à meilleur marché que les pris porté par l'ordonnance. Si la tient plus basse que Douze d'argent le Roy, c'est apres avoir faict encherir ledict argent en france par rarité affin de tirer l'or de France a meilleur marché que le pris porte par lordonnance Par telles menées il peult tirer de france les mannes et marchandises a meilleur marché que les regnicoles qui est la Ruyne de ce Royaume." "acheptant de vostre peuple toutes les monnoyes d'or & d'argent estrangeres qui sont en vostre Royaume & enjoindre a tous les porter a la plus prochaine de voz monnoyes durant ledict temps pour les reduire a voz coings."

56. Guillaume Budé, *De asse et partibus ejus libri quinque* (Paris: Josse Badius, 1514).

57. BN, n. a. fr. 5064, fol. 238r: "L'une des plus grandes choses qu'un Roy peult cognoistre, apres Dieu, Cest de scavoir entretenir en bon estat la bien de ses subjectz en toute tranquilité & repos desprit."

the duodecimal ratio was entirely arbitrary: it in fact came from Colas's classical erudition alone, since he justified it solely with a reference to the pseudo-Platonic *Hipparchus*.[58] Any deviation from this ideal abroad he dismissed as the effect of a fraud perpetrated on France by foreigners. Colas was not truly writing from a detached, apolitical perspective. Rather, his foreigner served as a kind of malevolent god from a machine, not commensurate with France herself. Such an attitude was in no way unusual, and in fact it probably became more common as the French, riven by civil war, could less and less plausibly blame outsiders for their woes.[59] Foreign coinage was the tool used by this mysterious force to attack the French economy, and it needed to be banned to prevent that mischief. Overall, a sense of mystification and xenophobia clings to this text and to its many successors.

Still, much of Colas's analysis seems to have become the received wisdom very quickly—though he may have had precursors whose works do not survive. Bodin's *Response* (which seems to have responded in fact to Malestroict and Colas's 1567 joint memoir) disagreed with details of how inflation was caused and could be cured. But Bodin accepted the essential elements of his opponents' analysis. To solve the nation's monetary problems, one had to control the influx of foreign coinage, maintain a duodecimal ratio between the precious metals, and prevent distortions due to the production costs of certain coins. As far as later commentators were concerned, his main innovation was to propose that this be done by making coins out of very pure (23/24) metal. This would eliminate any possible opacity between the metallic and monetary value of a coin, so that each coin would "make its value known even to little children."[60] In other words, the government could make the coinage tractable by imposing on it a mathematical and logical purity. This was impractical: most metal available to the mints, and particularly the Iberian and Ibero-American coinage in which most precious metal arrived in France, was of a far lower title and

---

58. He refers to *Hipparchus*, 231D. Colas quoted Ficino's translation, obviously from memory. This suggests that his familiarity with the text was more than merely borrowed or cursory.

59. For one perspective on this issue, see Charlotte Wells, "Leeches on the Body Politic: Xenophobia and Witchcraft in Early Modern French Political Thought," *French Historical Studies* 22 (1999): 351–77.

60. Jean Bodin, *La vie chère au XVIe siècle: La response de Jean Bodin à M. de Malestroict, 1568*, ed. Henri Hauser (Paris: Armand Colin, 1932), 46: "laquelle estant forgée comme j'ay dit, fera cognoistre son titre jusques aux petits enfans." In the 1578 edition and the *Republic* (VI.3), Bodin added the stipulation that gold coins should weigh the same as silver ones, to further increase the transparency and interchangeability of the system.

would have had to have been refined at great expense in order reach the purity this plan demanded. Still, Bodin's fame as a political and historical theorist and the rhetorical skill of his *Response* gave Colas's and Malestroict's views a larger audience. By contrast, Bodin's most celebrated theory, the addition to the second (1578) edition of the *Response* that partially attributed French inflation to the influx of precious metal from the New World, seems to have made a remarkably small impression on his fellow countrymen, who seldom mentioned and never discussed it.[61] It may well have been subsumed into the general view that inflation came, one way or another, from foreign coin.

Facing Crisis: 1572–1577

At any rate, in the 1570s, amid ever greater paroxysms in the monetary system, the new experts (including Bodin) were called on to apply their theories. In 1576 the Cour des Monnaies advised the Estates General on a proposed reform of the coinage. While it passed over the bimetallic ratio in silence, it did claim that an overvaluation of gold had caused the inflation ravaging France. This resulted from the operation of Gresham's law "and from the ignorance of those who, against your ordinances receive cried-down coins and expose at too high a price those in circulation . . . always giving the advantage to foreign currency over that forged with your stamps and arms, which alone they should know." They, like Colas, first proposed that the king forbid the circulation of any foreign coin, "their official placement in circulation having been the source and first origin of the said inflation . . . which has come about above all from the cunning of the foreigner, who has always tried to pay for the sums which he takes from your kingdom as much as possible with the currency which he brings in."[62] Such things, they

---

61. Foreigners, particularly the English, seem to have been more impressed. One might recall here J. H. M. Salmon's thesis that Bodin rapidly disappeared even from French discourse on political theory: "The Legacy of Jean Bodin: Absolutism, Populism or Constitutionalism?" *History of Political Thought* 17 (1996): 500–522. Hauser, in his introduction to Bodin, *Vie chère*, liv–lxxvii, gives a fairly complete account of its *fortuna*.

62. François le Blanc, *Traité historique des monnoyes de France* (Paris: Pierre Ribon, 1703), 343, 344–45: "Or la source du-dit surhaussement procede . . . de l'ignorance & temerité des autres, lesquels contre vos Ordonnances reçoivent les Monnoyes décriées & exposent à plus haut prix celles qui on cours . . . donnant toûjours l'avantage aux especes étrangeres sur celles qui sont forgées à vos coins & armes qu'ils doivent seulement connoistre." "La première, décrier toutes especes étrangeres . . . étant le cours que on leur a donné la source & premiere origine du-dit surhaussement . . . ce qui est advenu principalement par la finesse de l'etranger, qui s'est toujours efforcé au payment des deniers qu'il tire de vôtre Royaume exposer les especes qu'il nous apporte le plus qu'il peut."

assured the king, had not happened in better-regulated eras of French history. Already, experts were presenting the threat of foreign coin more strongly and more politically than had Colas.

Here again, the experts did not explain in any detail the mechanism whereby foreign coins caused domestic inflation. Instead, they stated more strongly than before the importance of national coinage to the functioning of royal political authority:

> Thus it belongs only to the prince to give money to his subjects, because the effigy and arms which are there engraved give them a witness of the superiority which God has given him over them . . . and is the surest means of preserving your name and arms in all countries, and conserving them forever for posterity for, as an Ancient said, the coins of princes are so many statues raised to them by all; and in fact, for all that the Greeks and Romans could do to conserve their memory forever, no monument is left more whole to us than their coinage.[63]

This kind of argument had deep cultural roots to which we will return, but here it was mainly the expression of a vague sense of threat. Like Colas's invocation of Plato or Bodin's of the Indies, though, it substituted classical erudition for a worked-out economic theory.

The ensuing edict of 1577 did not institute a consistent duodecimal ratio, but it did eliminate the livre as a money of account. In its place was a new écu, worth three old livres and fixed at parity with the gold coin of the same name. This, like Colas's and Bodin's projects, gave the appearance of simplicity, universality, and philosophical clarity. It seemed to make obedience to the king's legislation natural and even automatic. The government hoped that this would not only discourage official devaluations but also prevent the common and ignorant people from being "defrauded" by French subjects or foreigners who sought to buy one or another type of coin cheaply.[64] As the "real" écu replaced the "imaginary" livre, words and things would coincide, and the French people would immediately understand the government's

---

63. Ibid., 345: "Aussi il n'appartient qu'au Prince donner Monnoye à ses sujets, parce que l'effegie & armes qui y son gravées leur donne témoignage de la superiorité que Dieu luy a donné sur eux . . . & est le moyen seur de perpetuer vostre nom & armes par tout pays, & les conserver à jamais à la posterité; car, comme disoit un Antien, les Monnoyes des Princes sont autant de Statuës, qui leur son dressées par tout le monde; et de fait de tout ce que les Grecs & Romains ont pû faire pour conserver leur memoire à jamais, il ne nous est demeuré monument plus entier que leurs Monnoyes."

64. See, for example, the preamble to the edict, ibid., 351–53.

monetary policy and the law.[65] This was the same goal that the promoters of a careful attention to the bimetallic ratio had in mind.

According to the general of the moneys, François Garrault, the government intended the measure to remedy the collapse of the official valuation of the coinage, which

> increases from day to day to the great disrespect and contempt of the Royal authority, a much greater crime than striking [private] money: for one finds records of several princes having permitted their subjects to have money made, but always retaining the authority to circulate it and set its value . . . . And today, everyone licentiously wishes to play the king, setting the price of currency after his own pleasure and will.[66]

The abolition of the livre would guarantee that "the Ordinance which will be made should be inviolable and preserved, taking away from the people the ability and even, if possible, the desire to transgress and infringe [the monetary ordinances] anymore."[67] Of course, in a sense, this was actually a surrender of legislative power, a renunciation of any claim that such power could be *absolute* (in the sense in which the term was then used). Some experts objected that "one must not subject the value of the coinage to the weight and alloy alone, if one does not wish to infringe on the authority of the Prince, to whom by law is given the power of imposing a price on money, and transfer and give it into the hands of private persons."[68] In its

---

65. These terms were immediately and universally adopted by supporters of this reform: see, for example, "Memoires presentez au Roy estant en sa ville de poictiers ou moys de Juillet m v^c lxxvii pour reduire toutes comptes en france en especes descuz ou valleur diceulx par proportions correspondantes en supprimant le compte de livre comme incertaine & imaginaire qui seroit a vray dire tacitement remetre la forte monnoye," BN, ms. fr. 18503, fols. 113–15. These are obviously the memoirs referred to in the title of Garrault's work, below.

66. François Garrault, *Recueil des principaux advis donnez es assemblees faictes par commandement du Roy . . . sur le contenu des memoires, presentez à sa majesté estant en la ville de Poictiers, portans l'establissement du compte par escuz, & suppression de celuy par solz & livres* (Paris: Jacques du Puys, 1578), fol. Aiv v: "Lequel surhaussement est tellement venu en usage entre le peuple qu'il croist de jour en jour au grand mespris & contenemment de l'auctorité Royale, crime trop plus grand que de battre monnoye: car il se trouve par escript plusiurs princes avoir permis a leur subjectz de faire forger monnoye, se reservans neantmoings l'auctorité de donner cours & estimation. . . . Et pour le jour d'huy licentieusement ung chacun veult faire le roy imposant prix aus especes à son plaisr & volonté."

67. Le Blanc, *Traité*, 343: "l'Ordonnance qui sera faite soit inviolable & gardée ôtant au peuple le pouvoir ; & même s'il est possible le vouloir de plus les transgresser & enfraindre" (from the remonstrance of the Cour des Monnaies).

68. Garrault, *Recueil*, fols. Ci v–Cii r: "ne faut restraindre la valleur de la monnoye soubz les poyds & loy seullement, qui ne veu entreprendre sur l'auctorité du Prince, auquel de droict est concedee la puissance d'imposer prix à la monnoye, pour la deferer & mettre entre les mains de personnes privees."

attempt to control the coinage, the French monarchy faced a challenge that clearly would admit of no easy solutions. Under the dire conditions of 1577, the "gold standard" of the écu seemed the lesser of two evils.

Confronting the Great Inflation

The disaster that these measures addressed had been a long time coming. Henri II's untimely death had been a disaster for the currency, as it was for all of France. His sickly son François II died less than a year afterward, and the heroic attempts of his widow, Catherine de Médicis, to hold the kingdom together in the face of ever-deepening factional and religious divisions proved unsuccessful. By 1563, France was in a full-fledged state of civil war that would continue intermittently into the late 1590s. Amid chaos and desperation, however, the currency still received its share of attention. The largely futile effort to reform the kingdom at the Estates of Orléans, as we have already seen, included an entirely futile call for the dissolution of the Cour des Monnaies. More constructively, a 1561 edict attempted to bring order to the moneys, mainly by devaluing the livre (the écu coin went from forty-six sols to fifty) and crying down some coins that were judged too unreliable. The preamble to the edict was revealing both in its traditional rhetoric and in its concern with inflation.

> One of the things we have most eagerly desired since we came to the crown is to provide for the matter of our moneys—in which consist principally the wealth of our kingdom . . .—and in so doing to bar the way of the avarice of certain persons who have hazarded to counterfeit or clip those moneys . . . . Besides which, many have taken the liberty of passing and receiving all foreign gold and silver coins indifferently, whether clipped or whole, and at whatever price seems good to them, even so high and excessive that all things needful for the life of mankind have become more expensive and continue to do so immoderately from day to day.[69]

69. AN, Z^{1B} 537, piece dated 17 August 1561 (edict), fol. 1r: "Lune des choses que nous avons plus affectueusement desire depuis nostre advenement a la couronne Cest de pourveoir au faict de noz monnoyes Esquelles consistent les principalles richesses de nostre Royaume. . . . Et en ce faisant coupper chemyn a lavarice de plusieurs personnes qui se sont hazardez les ungs a contrefaire, et les autres a roigner Icelles monoyes. . . . Oultre ce que plusieurs ont prins cest liberte dexposer et recevoir Indiferement toutes especes dor et dargent estangeres soient roignees ou entieres et pour tel pris que bon leur a semblé si haul et excessif que toutes choses necessaires a la vie des hommes en sont encheries et encherissent par chacun jour oultre mesure." Some sort of currency-reform plan had been floated under François II—see the Monnaies' remonstrances against it, AN, Z^{1B} 371, piece dated 8 March 1559—but its details and provenance are obscure.

Both the edict itself and its enforcement were distinctly half-hearted, and little was accomplished.

It was not until the spring of 1566, after the collapse of the plans for a general farm of the mint, that the government began to take action on the emerging theoretical debate about the nature of currency and inflation. By midsummer of that year, Charles IX began to put some of Jacques Colas's ideas into practice, issuing an edict forbidding the circulation of many foreign coins.[70] To enforce the edict the king sent one of the most able generals of the Cour des Monnaies, Thomas Turquam, on chevauchée into the southwest, where a great deal of now-banned English coin circulated. Turquam tried gamely for several months to bring the situation under control but without noticeable success.[71] Within five years, many of the coins banned in 1566 were allowed to circulate again, while the value of the livre suffered new downward pressures. Faced with the failure of this initiative, the royal council turned to the kind of large-scale consultation that the merchants had called for a few years earlier. It brought together "several assemblies of notable persons, including some from our court of Parlement, the Chambre des Comptes of Paris, generals of the moneys, as well as others instructed and experienced" in monetary affairs.[72] Urgency was lacking, though: a month after the assemblies, representatives of the Monnaies were at court complaining of a lack of communications, only to be informed by the clerk of the royal council that the king had personally decided not to proceed further for the time being.[73]

As figure 3 shows, though, the main policy response was a series of belated surrenders to the inflationary pressures, as the value of coins in money of account was repeatedly raised. In January 1569 the écu was at fifty-six sols, brought down to fifty-four in September 1570. Charles IX struggled to reduce it or even keep it stable. In October 1571, he decreed that the écu would be reduced to fifty-two sols the following April 1 and to fifty sols in June. That date of the first proposed devaluation proved prophetic, and the écu remained at fifty-four sols. The inadequate nature of these interventions was underscored when a member of the royal council opined to the representatives of the Monnaies "that enough monetary ordinances had been made, and they only needed to be obeyed."[74]

---

70. *Ordonnance du Roy sur le descry de certaines especes d'or & d'argent estrangieres* (Paris: Jean Dallier, 1566), edict of 15 June 1566.

71. The procès-verbal of his chevauchée is AN, Z^{1B} 276, with a more legible copy in AN, Z^{1B} 277.

72. *Ordonnance du Roy pour le reiglement general de ses monoies. Publiée à Paris en sa Court de Parlement le Vendredy vingt & troisiesme jour de May, 1572* (Paris: Jean Dallier, 1572), fols. 4r, 15r.

73. See AN, Z^{1B} 373, piece dated 21 July 1568 (procès-verbal of Dain and Turquam).

74. AN, Z^{1B} 374, piece dated 5 April 1571 (procès-verbal of Dain and Turquam): "quil y avoit assez de ordonnances faictes pour le fait des monnoyes et quil nestoit besongne que de les faire garder."

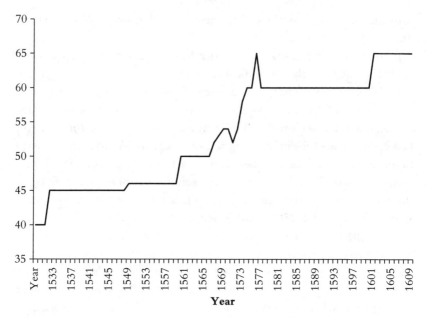

FIGURE 3. Official course of the ecu in sols. *Revue historique* 152 (1929): 9–10 (table 3). This slightly simplifies the official record, AN, Z¹ᴮ 54, fols. 62–65.

How this might be done remained unclear. Finally, in 1572, after much badgering from Thomas Turquam, Charles issued a fairly comprehensive new edict.[75] "In order to contain our people in the observation of our said ordinance, since the obedience they owe to us and to our edicts has not been able to suffice up to now," the king outlawed the private ownership of smelting furnaces—a measure that would have affected mainly counterfeiters and alchemical adepts. More significantly, he required all officers of justice to take an oath to uphold the edict, specified that all fines and seizures falling under the edict would be employed toward its further enforcement, and, finally, allowed parties to draw up contracts in écus rather than livres. In that way, they could avoid the effects of any future inflation. The Monnaies geared up for an unusually vigorous effort to enforce it, agreeing to patrol the city by quarters and preparing for a series of chevauchées around the kingdom, overseen by Marillac.[76] Then, on 24 August,

---

75. For more details on the consultations leading up to this edict, see Greengrass, "Money, Majesty," 178–79.

76. See AN, Z¹ᴮ 374, pieces dated 9 July 1527 (arrêt) and 30 August 1572 (procès-verbaux of the revocation of commissions for the chevauchées). The patrol by quarters had first been decreed by letters patent in 1571 (see AN, Z¹ᴮ 537, piece dated 25 October 1571), though it is not clear that it was implemented at that time.

eve of the Feast of St. Bartholemew, Admiral Coligny, leader of the Protestant party, was assassinated, and in the ensuing weeks anti-Huguenot massacres swept over France, followed by a new outbreak of religious war. Monetary policy would never again figure among Charles IX's priorities. He died in May of 1574, having signally failed to stabilize his realm politically or economically; in Champagne, at least, an edict he issued just before his death reducing the écu to fifty-four sols "was not kept . . . for [even] six full weeks."[77]

This situation was on Henri III's docket when he returned from Poland to take the throne, and Turquam met him in Lyons to discuss it with the newly reorganized council. Unsure of its footing, the council decided to call an assembly of experts in Paris to advise on the matter.[78] This assembly finally met in January 1575, and in April the king issued an edict, based on the assembly's recommendations, which raised the écu to a round sixty sols.[79] It also attempted to align the coinage and the money of account more closely by (re)introducing a one-livre silver piece, the franc. The edict cannot be said to have been a success. The franc never really circulated—apparently, given how heavy and thick it was, the Monnaies feared that it would be a magnet for counterfeiters—and the price level was stabilized for a year at best.[80] In 1576, as Henri III called a meeting of the Estates General and laid the groundwork for a new offensive against the Huguenots, the livre truly began to collapse. The écu neared seventy sols on the unofficial market. More worryingly still, foreign coin circulated freely despite all prohibitions and had begun to command a substantial and increasing premium over French coin.[81] In remonstrances drawn up on the occasion of the summoning of the

---

77. Claude Haton, *Memoires*, ed. Félix Bouquelot (Paris: Imprimerie Impériale, 1857), 750: "Cest édict ne fut gardé en ce pays l'espace de six sepmaines."

78. AN, Z[1B] 538, pieces dated October 1574 : "Extraict des Resultatz du conseil prive du Roy viii[e] octobre v[c] lxxiiii": "Apres avoir ouy le general Turquam sur aucunes expeditions concernant la refformation des monnoies par le moien de surhaussement du marc dor & dargent et la commutation des especes estrangieres a semble que le Roy doibt escripre a Messieurs levesque et premier president de Paris sassembler et deliberer sur ce faict avec ceulx des generaulx des finances et des monnoies et aultres quils adviserons Pour ce faict envoier leurs advis a sa majeste." As early as May 1571 Alexandre de la Tourette had suggested raising the mint price in order to produce more coin: "Advis pour le faict des monoyes estrangieres courans es pays de Champaigne, Bourgogne," BN, ms. fr. 18497, fols. 11–18.

79. AN, Z[1B] 538, piece dated 4 January 1575 (letter of Henri III to the Monnaies, confirming the summoning of the consultative assembly); piece dated 5 May 1575 (ordinance).

80. Among other things, the Swiss refused to accept the new coins: see AN, Z[1B] 70, fols. 105v–107r (letters patent of Paris, 7 May 1576).

81. See Denis Richet, "Le cours officiel des monnaies étrangères circulant en France au XVIe siècle," *Revue historique* 225 (1961): 359–96.

Estates, the Cour des Monnaies suggested a remedy: an even firmer ban on foreign coin combined with the abandonment of the livre as the money of account.[82] The Cour des Monnaies might have been correct in believing that a policy promulgated "in a company so notable" as an Estates General would be "better received, more respected and upheld," but it did not live up to those hopes.[83] Jean Bodin, who considered himself the éminence grise of the assembly, put forward a proposal that combined his own theoretical concerns with already-discredited projects for a machined coinage and centralized minting.[84] It was not adopted, and in the end the Estates achieved very little in monetary affairs.[85] The royal council took action on its own in late May of 1577, issuing an edict that did ban most foreign coin but left the livre in place, merely repeating the permission first granted in 1572 to contract in écus.[86] It also raised the écu rather drastically, to sixty-five sols. The council made up for the relatively conservative provisions of this edict with extremely strenuous efforts to ensure its enforcement. In the short term, though, "neither the king, nor the court [of Parlement], nor the generals of the moneys, nor any others of the king's officers gave any order or remedy, but the people acted at their own discretion in this matter. Thus, these ordinances were not observed or kept."[87] Indeed, by the summer, the French currency appeared to be in the process of utter collapse.

---

82. BN, ms. fr. 18503, fols. 67–71, dated 20 October 1576. Though the remonstrances were signed by du Lyons and the *procureur du roi* Dain, the style is recognizably Turquam's, and as we shall see, he was strongly associated with the policies recommended. It was copied into the registers of the Monnaies, AN, Z[1B] 70, fols. 132–38; there is another copy in AN, J 971, no. 16, and it was published in le Blanc, *Traité historique*, 338–51.

83. BN, ms. fr. 18503, fol. 67r: "lesperance quilz [viz. les gens tenants la cour des monnaies] ont que ce qui aura esté arresté en une compaignie si notable sera mieulx receu plus respecté & entretenu."

84. See Greengrass, "Money, Majesty," 182; the proposal is preserved in BN, ms. fr. 16250, fols. 139ff.

85. On 16 February 1577 the Third Estate resolved "que le Roy seroit supplié . . . que ses monnoyes seroyent receues en ses receptes, au pris qu'elles avoyent cours en ce Royaume," which was granted: [Jean Bodin], *Recueil de tout ce qui s'est negotié en la compagnie du tiers Estat de France, en l'asemblee general des trois Estats, assignez par le Roy en la ville de Bloys aux xv. Novembre 1576* (n.p., 1577), 89.

86. Though it did not adopt all of the Cour des Monnaies' suggestions, this edict was drawn up with the advice and consent of presidents Turquam and du Lyons: "Advis pour le faict des monnoyes," 27 May 1577, BN, ms. fr. 18503, fols. 143–46.

87. Pierre de l'Estoile, *Registre-journal du règne d'Henri III*, ed. Madeleine Lazard and Gilbert Schrenck, vol. 2, *1576–1578* (Geneva : Droz, 1996), 115: "Et neantmoins n'y donnoient, ne le Roy, ne la Cour, ne les generaux des Monnoies, ni tous les autres officiers du Roy, aucun ordre ni remede, ains vivoit le peuple à sa discretion pour ce regard. Aussi ne furent lesdites ordonnances observées, ne gardées." L'Estoile quotes the same rate of seventy-five sols per écu that Briet encountered.

An anecdote from the Monnaies' archives illustrates this. In July of 1577 Sebastien Briet, comptroller of the artillery at Calais, came to Paris on business. He brought with him a letter of exchange for one thousand livres drawn on Menault de Caussart, a Bordeaux merchant, and addressed to his factor, Jehan de Brocart. When Briet went to collect on it, though, he had an unpleasant shock. He had paid for the note with a bit over 308 écus, but Brocart offered him only about 266 écus back, or, if he preferred, about 154 English angels with a gold content equivalent to 240 écus![88] Brocart's offer was flatly illegal. According to an ordinance of the previous month, the écu was worth three and one-third livres, the value at which Briet had exchanged his cash for his letter of exchange, while Brocart was offering him 13 percent less. Angels were not supposed to circulate at all, let alone at such a ridiculously inflated value.[89] Briet knew his rights: he went and got a pair of notaries and asked Brocart to repeat his offer in front of them. Confronted, Brocart "accepted that he would pay the said sum of one thousand livres, without wishing to declare in what coins." A week and more went by, and still Brocart would not pay what Briet thought he owed. At last, the comptroller decided to take his problem to the top. He had some connections with mint officers, and he used them.[90] He went to the house of First President François du Lyons and swore out a complaint demanding "prompt and summary justice, since it was to be feared that if the said Brocart heard something about the said complaint he would leave without paying him."[91] Du Lyons scheduled a hearing for the next day and instructed Briet to bring witnesses. There is no sign in the records, though, that the hearing ever occurred or that the court took any action. Perhaps the intervention of these high magistrates convinced Brocart to pay up, but more likely, as Briet had feared, it caused him to skip town.

---

88. These conversions are based on the table of specie content of sixteenth-century coins in Marie-Thérèse Boyer-Xambeu et al., *Private Money and Public Currencies: The Sixteenth-Century Challenge*, trans. Azizeh Azodi (Armonk, NY: M. E. Sharpe, 1994), 144.

89. *Ordonnance du Roy sur le faict de ses Monnoyes. Publiée à Paris le xv jour de Juing, 1577* (Paris: Veufve Jehan Dallier, 1577).

90. Such connections are implied by the fact that two years later Pierre de Seignant, comptroller of the artillery of Guyenne, obtained the recently renewed office of *prevôt-royal* in the mint of Bayonne by resignation of its original purchaser. AN, Z^{1B} 553, piece dated 30 July 1579 (*provision d'office* of Seignant).

91. AN, Z^{1B} 435, piece dated 22 July 1567 [*recte* 1577] (procès-verbal of Briet's complaint), fol. 1r–v: "il [Brocart] auroit accepter payer ladicte somme de mil livres sans voulloir declarer en quelles especes." "nous requerant faire prompte & sommaire justice parce quil estoit a craindre que si ledict brocart entendoit quelque chose de ladicte plaincte il sen allast sans le payer."

The man who stepped forward to deal with this catastrophe was one of the king's oldest and most trusted advisers: Jean de Morvilliers. He had held high offices in both the church (as bishop of Orléans) and the state (as *garde des sceaux*), and was best known for having abandoned both them and the opportunity for higher ones.[92] He was also a financial specialist and in the well-informed opinion of Nicolas Roland (who had been sent by the Monnaies to push the *faict des monnaies* at the Council in Poitiers), "a grave man, the greatest statesman France has ever known, and just as all know him to be."[93] It was he who reported the affair in July and pushed for the abolition of the livre, even working out the technical details of how that might be arranged. It seems that the decision to abolish the livre had been reached at that point, but "because the matter concerned the general public of our realm," Henri called a new consultative assembly like that held in 1574, to be chaired by his closest loyal relative, the Cardinal de Bourbon.[94] The assembly convened in the first week of September. Turquam, representing his court, strongly defended the abolition of the livre, but after vigorous debate a slight majority of those present opposed it; they did, however, agree on the other points of the proposal laid before them, notably a substantial deflation to sixty sols per écu from the following January 1.[95]

---

92. There is one old biography of him: Gustave Baguenault de Puchesse, *Jean de Morvillier, évêque d'Orléans, garde des sceaux de France, 1506–1577: Etude sur la politique française au XVIe siècle, d'après des documents inédits*, 2nd ed. (Paris: Didier, 1870). He was also Bellièvre's early sponsor in the royal councils. See Olivier Poncet, *Pomponne de Bellièvre (1529–1607): Un homme d'état au temps des Guerres de religion* (Paris: Editions de l'Ecole des Chartes, 1998), passim.

93. AN, Z[1B] 376, piece dated 24 July 1577 (Nicolas Roland to the Monnaies of that date, orig.): "homme grave le plus grand pollitique que jamais la france veit et tel que chacun le congnoist."

94. Guérin et al., *Registres* 8:127 (Henri III to the *Prevôt des marchands* and *échevins* of Paris, 6 August 1577, transcribing AN, H 1788, fol. 144r): "d'autant que ce faict concerne le general de nostredicte Royaulme, nous desirons avoir l'advis d'une bonne et notable assemblée." The text of the proposals put to this assembly is preserved in AN, J 971, no. 19.

95. François Garrault, *Recueil des principaux advis donnez es assemblees faictes par commandement du Roy, en l'Abbaye saint Germain des prez au mois dAoust* [sic] *dernier, sur le contenu des memoires, presentez à sa majesté estant en la ville de Poictiers, portans l'establissement du compte par escuz, & suppression de celuy par solz & livres.* (Paris: Jacques du Puys, 1578). Garrault may not even have been present. His major source was the official procès-verbal of the assembly, preserved in BN, ms. fr. 18503, fols. 125–33, which gives the date as 6 September. This may not be correct either: the presence register of the Cour des Monnaies (AN, Z[1B] 192) notes that on 3 September "monsieur le general turquam excuse pour estre en lassemblee." Turquam printed his speech in favor of the reforms. *Advis de M. Thomas Turquam, General des monnoyes, donné en une assemblee faicte à Paris, au moys de Septembre 1577. par devant Monseigneur le Reverendissime Cardinal de Bourbon, pour deliberer sur les memoires presentez au Roy, afin d'abolir le compte à sols, & à livres, & d'oresenavant faire tous contracts & obligacions à escus* (Paris: Veufve Jehan Dallier, 1578).

The assembly, however, had largely been for show, an exercise in royal rhetoric and propaganda rather than a genuine consultation.[96] A month later a new ordinance appeared that essentially adopted the policy put forward by the Monnaies and Morvilliers: abolishing the livre and replacing it with the écu; setting the écu at sixty-six sols for the present, to drop to sixty at the New Year; maintaining the ban on all non-Iberian foreign coin; and instituting various new enforcement provisions that mainly strengthened the powers of lower courts. The Parlement of Paris objected and drew up remonstrances, but on 13 November, after *lettres de jussion* and the intervention of the bishop of Paris, it registered the ordinance with a few modifications.[97] One important element of this new policy, which required separate action, was a concerted attempt to coin and distribute new small change "to comfort the lower classes [and] avoid greater tumult."[98] A new mint was opened at Amiens, and a special edict banned foreign billon in the northeast, where it had always been a particular plague. Henri also borrowed substantial sums at Lyons and perhaps elsewhere in order to produce the new coins quickly and have them ready when people brought old coin to the mints.[99] Two more edicts revived the institution of provincial generals of the moneys and first-instance judges in the mints, extensions of the Cour des Monnaies' arm that had been abolished by Henri II twenty-five years before.[100] The Cour des Monnaies itself and the Parlement registered them promptly, though with some reservations.[101]

----

96. Roland reported on the assembly to the council "avec les depputez de lyon gens honnorables mes ils sont Italiens cest a dire bons mesnaigers et qui ne viennent icy pour le proffict dautruy mais pour le leur toutesfois il [sic] semblent avoir grande raison en ce quils remonstrent." AN, Z^{1B} 376, piece dated 19 September 1577 (Nicolas Roland to the Monnaies of that date, orig.).

97. *Ordonnance du Roy, sur le faict & Reglement de ses Monnoyes* (Paris: Veufve Jehan Dallier, 1577).

98. L'Estoile, *Registre-journal*, 148: "pour soulager le bas peuple et leur changer leurs pieces au prix de l'ordonnance pour eviter à plus grande tumulte."

99. The Amiens mint was instituted by article III of the September ordinance. The billon in Champaign and Burgundy was cried down by the September *Ordonnance du Roy sur le descry des Monnoyes de billon estrangeres* (Paris: Veufve Jehan Dalier & Nicolas Rosset, 1577). On the sixty thousand-livre loan from Lyons, see Pierre Champion and Michel François, eds., *Lettres de Henri III, Roi de France*, vol. 3 (Paris, 1972), 370 (Henri III to de Mandelot, 3 September 1577, transcribed from BN, ms. fr. 2704, fol. 182v). On the long-standing problems of foreign coin in Champaign and Burgundy, see, e.g., la Tourette's 1571 "Advis" (BN, ms. fr. 18497, fols. 11–18); and Haton, *Mémoires*, 748–51.

100. *Deux Edicts du Roy, pour le restablissement des Generaulx des Monnoyes, qui resideront és douze principales provinces de ce Royaume: Et d'un Prevost Juge Royal, un Procureur du Roy, un Greffier, & deux Sergens pour la Justice en chacune Monnoye de cedict Royaume, pays, terres, & Seigneuries de sa Majesté* (Paris: Federic Morel, 1577).

101. The Monnaies' remonstrances are preserved: AN, J 971, nos. 24 and 28. The Monnaies, Comptes, and Parlement all added restrictions to their registrations.

Where all else had failed, the legislative and administrative activity of the autumn of 1577 succeeded. Both domestic and foreign coins stabilized in price, and by 31 December, Henri III could issue an edict congratulating himself on the obedience the September program enjoyed.[102] The devaluation of the écu to sixty sols went through with few hitches. François Garrault summed up what quickly became the conventional wisdom. "The people, having long been tormented by the uncertainty of the price of currency and its continual inflation, received this edict with such great contentment and willingness that, forgetting all personal profit, they submitted themselves voluntarily and without any difficulty to its execution."[103] Although tensions within the currency system did not disappear, they ceased to be acute: the most important ongoing one was the chronic shortage of small change.[104] Since the settlement endured through the remainder of the civil wars while metal flowed more freely than ever through the royal mints, one can only conclude that 1577 ended on a distinctly positive note for the French monarchy.[105]

Explaining the 1577 Reforms

The magistrate and erudite historian Jacques-Auguste de Thou explained the success of the monetary reforms in terms that contain no less truth for being couched in the language of classical republicanism: "As everyone sought a remedy for the common disaster, what was offered was freely embraced, so that one agreed with equanimity to sacrifice private interests to the public utility."[106] It is worth probing a bit beyond that comforting narrative, though, because this is a moment at which it is possible to see much about how early

---

102. *Declaration du Roy, sur l'edict faict par sa Majesté de Septembre dernier, pour le Reglement general des Monnoyes* (Paris: Veufve Jehan Dallier, 1578).

103. Garrault, *Recueil des principaux advis*, sig. C iv r: "Toutesfois le peuple ayant esté par long temps travaillé de l'incertitude du prix des especes & continuelle augmentation d'icelles, receut cest edict avec un si grand contentement & elegresse, que posposant tout proffit particulier, se rangea de luy mesme, & sans aucune difficulté soubz l'execution d'iceluy."

104. See, for example, a 1579 set of "Remonstrances treshumbles au Roy par les gens tenans sa Cour des monnoyes sur la plainte . . . de la rarite & necessite de monnoyes de billon," BN, ms. fr. 18504, fol. 47.

105. On the revival of mint activity (a crude indicator of the health of the currency) after 1577, see Frank C. Spooner, *L'Economie mondiale et les frappes monétaires en France, 1493–1680* (Paris: Armand Colin, 1956), 525.

106. Jacques-Auguste de Thou, *Historiarum sui temporis*, vol. 6 (London: Samuel Barclay, 1733), 511: "dum quisque communi calamitati remedium quærit, et oblatum libentissime complexus, quod privatis commodis ex eo decedebat, publicæ utilitati condonari æquissimo animo patitur."

modern governance in economic affairs worked. First, there is the question of what exactly had gone wrong. Even within the general inflationary trend, the collapse of the livre in 1574–1577 stood out as anomalous: suddenly and with increasing vehemence, the French developed a distaste for holding abstract livres and even actual French coins. Since rational expectation theory came to prominence in the 1970s, economists have generally acknowledged that public expectations about future government policy play a large role in determining price-level movements, and there is no reason to believe that matters were different in the sixteenth century.[107] With that in mind, one explanation for the particularly severe crisis of the mid-1570s is that a widespread fear had arisen that the livre and the French coinage would soon lose their value, while specie and above all foreign coin would not. This is what would have happened had the French government undertaken a fiscal devaluation of the currency. This would have netted the government substantial seigniorage and reduced the real burden of its debts. At the same time, it would have imposed huge costs on holders of livre-denominated debts and substantial costs on holders of livre-denominated coins. Thus, expectation of such a move in a country already unnerved by two generations of inflation could easily explain the observed reluctance to hold exactly those instruments.

The evident intractability of the civil wars, Henri III's early reputation as an anti-Protestant crusader, his disastrous inability to pay off the Elector Palatine's mercenary troops, and the revival of the wars in 1576, together with the subsequent refusal of the Estates to fund them, must all have raised fears that Henri would soon turn to extraordinary expedients.[108] The reports of the English ambassador to France in 1576–1577 are full of pitiful accounts of the government's penury, "forced in their greatest matters and sometimes to their great loss to deal uncertainly, because they have no money, being driven to such shifts for matters of trifles that it is marvelous to see it."[109] Under such circumstances, it would be difficult to resist the temptation to put one's wealth beyond the reach of the royal prerogative. Once confidence

---

107. For an overview of economic thought on the issue, see Thomas J. Sargent, *Rational Expectations and Inflation*, 2nd ed. (New York: Harper and Row, 1993).

108. On the humiliating episode of the *reîtres*, in which the superintendent of finances Bellièvre had to pledge his personal credit for the king and was then held hostage in Germany until September 1576 when his pledge could not be redeemed, see Poncet, *Pomponne de Bellièvre*, 87–88 and 137–38, and Edmund H. Dickermann and Anita M. Walker, "Missions Impossible: Pomponne de Bellièvre and the Policies of Henry III," *Canadian Journal of History/Annales canadiennes d'histoire* 35 (2000): 425–28.

109. *Calendar of State Papers, Foreign Series*, 23 vols. (London: Longman, 1861–1950), 11:1368 (Sir Amias Paulet to Lord Burgheley, 2 May 1577).

in the government's willingness and ability to support the currency began to slip, it was difficult to retrieve. Moreover, the expectation of inflation easily breeds new inflation. A priest from Provins, Claude Haton, describes such a spiral in his memoirs. "The evil," he says, "was such that a week after receiving an écu for 62 s., you hoped to pass it on for 63, and a week later for 64. And when someone got an écu, pistole, teston or other silver coin from his debtor, he did not wish to take it at the same rate that he had paid out to others."[110] Reversing this cycle would require both a restoration of confidence in the government's future policy and a psychological change—central bankers today talk of "anchoring expectations"—among the population.

The Cour des Monnaies' understanding of the situation was of course not identical to the modern perspective. The court's primary villain was not an impersonal force but the malice or ignorance of the people, "whose nature is to know nothing" as Turquam liked to say (in Latin).[111] The royal council publicly shared this view: turning to the familiar language of ambition and avarice, the September 1577 ordinance blamed the dire situation on "the extreme avarice of some of our subjects and foreigners trading here as well as the ignorance and simplicity of others."[112] Those who stressed the importance of the ratio of the prices of gold and silver put the blame more specifically on the malice of (probably foreign) arbitrageurs. Others, particularly Turquam, looked instead to the debtors who benefited from inflation, finding therein "a means of frustrating the creditor of a part of his due."[113] Whether it was a case of simple ignorance or some form of self-interested malice, though, the important point was that, as with all aspects of economic regulation, the king must find a way, by persuasion or compulsion, to change the behavior of his individual subjects.

The hard question was how to accomplish that in practice. "The kings," complained Turquam, "by too great a softness and goodness have wished to

---

110. Haton, *Mémoires*, 870: "Le mal estoit que, huict jours après qu'on avoit receu ung escu pour 62 s., on le vouloit bailler pour 63, et huict jours après pour 64 ; et que, quand quelqu'un recepvoit ung escu, pistolet, teston ou aultre pièce d'argent de ceux qui luy debvoient, ne les vouloit prendre pour pareil pris qu'il avoit mis à ceux qu'il avoit baillé a aultruy."

111. Turquam, *Advis*, 12: "cuius proprium est nihil sapere."

112. *Ordonnance sur le faict & Reglement des Monnoyes*, fol. 2r: "Le tout par l'extreme avarice, tant d'aucuns noz subjects & estrangers y traffiqans que par l'ignorance & simplicité des autres." Compare the 1576 *doléances* of the Monnaies, Le Blanc, *Traité historique*, 343: "Or la source dudict surhaussement procede de la malice d'aucuns qui billonnent les meilleures de vos Monnoyes . . . & de l'ignorance & temerité des autres, lesquels contre vos Ordonnances recoivent les Monnoyes descriees & exposent à plus haut prix celles qui ont cours."

113. Turquam, *Advis*, 12: "un moyen pour frustrer le creancier, de partie de son deu."

accommodate themselves to the course given to coins by the people against his ordinances, arming the license and temerity of their subjects with a public act rather than punishing and chastising them as they deserve."[114] Despite such tough rhetoric, though, the Cour des Monnaies preferred not to rely too heavily on coercion. The great benefit of suppressing the livre was that doing so would remove the mechanism and incentive of the inflation, effectively enforcing itself. "One must . . . find means by which the ordinance which is to be made may be inviolably kept, taking from the people the power, and even the desire any longer to transgress and infringe it. Thus (said Plato) the wise Legislator should not be as careful to see to it that delinquents are punished, as to find the means whereby one may no longer wish or be able to commit a fault."[115] This technocratic ideal fit in well with the distinctive strengths of the court.

Switching the money of account to the écu would act in this way in part by preventing malicious or ignorant subjects from fooling themselves or others about the "real" specie value of the currency. And, as Turquam said, it "will bring us this benefit, that if the king for some necessity raises the price of the mark of gold and silver [i. e., the mint price], the écu remaining in the same state, that is, of the same fineness, that increase will cause no damage in payments: for the creditor will always receive the number of écus he has stipulated."[116] As the context makes clear, this rather obscure statement actually revealed a quite profound understanding of the problem at hand. First, it suggested that the new system would insulate the currency from the effects of devaluing the small change, a frequent way of combating shortages.[117] Moreover, as the discussion of the

---

114. From a draft of the *Advis*: "Advis du General Turquam sur les memoires apportez de la court par Mr nicolas Roland aussi general des monnoies." BN, ms. fr. 18503, fol. 110: "Voila ce que nous a apporte que les roys par une trop grande doulceur & bonte se sont voullu accomoder au cours donne aux especes par le peuple contre ses ordonnances armant dune acte publicque la licence & temerite de leurs subiectz au lieu de la punir & chastier comme elle meritoit." Turquam apparently drew up this document thinking that his health would not permit him to attend the assembly in person: the published version tones down the rhetoric slightly.

115. From the 1576 *doléance* of the Monnaies, BN, ms. fr. 18503, fol. 69v: "il faut travailler . . . de trouver les moyens que l'Ordonnance qui sera faite soit inviolable & gardée, ostant au peuple le pouvoir, & mesme s'il est possible le vouloir de plus les transgresser & enfraindre. Aussi le sage Legislateur (disoit Platon) ne doit pas estre si soigneux de faire que les delinquants soient punis, comme de trouver les moyens que l'on ne puisse plus ou veuille plus faire faute." Turquam's *Advis* echoes this reasoning.

116. Turquam, *Advis*, 14: "nous apportera ce bien, que si le Roy pour quelque necessité haulse le marc d'or & d'argent, l'escu demeurant en estat, c'est à dire de pareille bonté, ce surhaulsement n'apportera aucune tare aux paiemens: parceque le creancier aura tousjours le nombre d'escus qu'il a stipulez."

117. In the draft version, Turquam had said that "si le roy pour quelque occasion voulloit empirer ses monnoies de billon cest empirance napporteroit aucune tarrre ny diminution aux payemens." BN, ms. fr. 18503, fol. 109r.

fifteenth-century devaluations that preceded this passage suggested, Turquam was pointing out that the new system would make fiscal manipulations more difficult for the king and more transparent to the market. It could thus function as a signal that the government intended to avoid such manipulations in the foreseeable future. To that extent, the Cour des Monnaies based its prescription on a reasonably precise understanding of the economic nature of the crisis.

There was, however, a competing explanation for the collapse of the currency and a corresponding prescription for its cure. On this view, the basic issue was that royal magistrates lacked either the will or the means to enforce the king's edicts. If those could be reinforced and, above all, more closely supervised, one might expect some progress toward the restoration of order. This was merely a specific case of a much more general political philosophy, the implications of which can be grasped quite clearly from a memoir on administrative reform that the new superintendent of finances, Pomponne de Bellièvre—a rising star in the royal administration—prepared for Charles IX in 1573. He began with the common sentiment that new laws by themselves were not needed. Indeed, "their multiplicity and the diligence which we devote to them is damaging almost as often as it is useful, since it serves as good evidence of the corruption of the state . . . . If it were a question of actual success, it would be enough to bring back the old laws without working to make new ones, which could only have too little authority." In particular, Bellièvre thought that injustice and incompetence were rife among the "lieutenants general of the *baillis*, who are the most necessary officers of your justice, presidial councillors, *élus, prévôts des mareschaux*," and other lower judicial officers.[118] This belief that the health of a republic depended on ensuring virtuous and diligent lower magistrates had very deep roots in Renaissance thought, and Bellièvre and many of his associates were profoundly devoted to it.[119] It also complemented the enormous emphasis on the rhetorical power of virtuous leadership that came to the fore at the beginning of Henri III's reign.[120]

---

118. From a memoir "Au roy touchant lordre a tenir pour le r[oyaume?] apres la paix faite a la Rochelle 1573," BN, ms. fr. 15890, fols. 388–89: "Pour le regard des loix la multiplicite et diligence qu'on y mect est presque aussi souvent dommageable qui utile, quoy que soit on prend par la un grand argument de la corruption de lestat . . . et s'il estoit question de s'en prevaloir, suffiroit de remectre sus les loix ancyennes, sans se travailler a en faire des nouvelles, qui ne peuvent avoir que trop moins d'auctorité." "L'ignorance, l'incapacité l'injustice est si avant descouverte en plusieurs lieutenants generaux des Bailliz qui sont les plus necessaires officiers de vostre justice conseillers presidiaux esleuz prevosts des marechaux et aultres."

119. On the intellectual roots of this position, see Jotham Parsons, "The Roman Censors in the Renaissance Political Imagination," *History of Political Thought* 22 (2001): 565–86.

120. See Mark Greengrass, *Governing Passions: Peace and Reform in the French Kingdom, 1576–1585* (Oxford: Oxford University Press, 2007).

When the Parlement of Paris remonstrated against the edict of September 1577, it did so on the grounds that it failed to follow lines like those set out in Bellièvre's memoir. The *parlementaires* were not fully convinced of the competence of "those who have the charge and oversight of the moneys." They believed that the "fashion of accounting by livres, being so long approved by custom which has the force of nature . . . should not be subject to easy change."[121] Above all, though, they thought that "the corruption of the age, disobedience to justice, that impunity which is the nursing mother of all vices, disrespect for magistrates who are the protectors of the laws have engendered this evil in monetary affairs. So that both in this matter and others which we see that the calamity of these times has brought about it is necessary to bring back the power and authority of justice."[122] Not surprisingly, they stressed the disobedience of the people rather than that of the judicial officers. Still, their starting point for the reestablishment of the kingdom was not some technical intervention in the mechanisms of commerce and avarice but rather, taking steps to make the people obey the magistrates as a body and repairing the machinery of justice.

The project of creating provincial generals of the moneys resident in each town possessing a parlement, as well as royal provosts who would act as first-instance judges at the mints, might have been one way of following that strategy. It was a pet scheme of Alexandre de la Tourette, who had advanced it already in the previous reign.[123] In theory it should have substantially increased both the personnel devoted to enforcing monetary laws and the oversight of low-level officials. In practice, it never got off the ground. The Cour des Monnaies maintained its initial hostility to the

---

121. "Remonstrances treshumbles qui font les gens tenans le parlement au Roy leur souverain sur ledict contenant la reformation generalle des monnoyes de ce royaulme donnees [sic] a Poictiers au mois de septembre mil v^e lxxvii," BN, ms. fr. 18497, fols. 31v: "ceulx qui ont la charge & superintendance des monnoies"; 33r: "ceste facon de compter a livres estant de si longtemps appreuvee par coustume qui a force de nature confirme par tant deictz de vos predeceseurs ne doibt estre subjectz a facile mutation."

122. BN, ms. fr. 18497, fol. 34r: "la corruption du siecle la desobeissance a la justice limpunite qui est la mere nourrice de toutes vices le mespris des magistrats qui sont les protectuers des loix ont engendre ce mal au faict desdictes monnoyes. Tellement que tant pour ce faict que autres que nous voions apporte la calamite du temps il est besoing de remettre la puissance & auctorite de la Justice." The Parlement also complained that the July edict was being flouted in the king's own entourage, a fact mentioned by other sources as well, which recalls the discourse surrounding sumptuary laws.

123. See "Remonstrances treshumbles que faict au roy Alexandre de la Tourette nagueres president en sa court des monnoies Touchant le desordre qui est a present sur tout le faict desdictes monnoyes Avec les moyens pour y pourveoir," BN, ms. Duchesne 89, fols. 51–73, particularly fols. 67ff. Large sections of this remonstrance were incorporated verbatim into the edicts of September 1577 establishing the new officers.

project. Three years later, when de la Tourette tried to take up the position of general for Dauphiné himself, the Monnaies remonstrated "that the said de la Tourette not only was the inventor of the creation and erection of the said Generals, but also was a party with the Queen of Navarre for the said offices, which have not taken effect because no one has been found who has wished to take the said offices except for the office of general for the country of Normandy: which makes it clear that the said offices are useless."[124] If creating new officers to improve enforcement did not work, the obvious alternative was to strengthen the powers or the supervision of existing magistrates. Projects as far back as the single-farm schemes had included such elements. Yet another edict mooted in September 1577 would have drastically tightened regulations on the goldsmiths—accused of contributing to the monetary disorder by promoting luxury and removing specie from circulation—while increasing the powers of the generals of the moneys to police them. The goldsmiths complained bitterly, accusing the proposals of having been put forward "to cover the failure of those who have the charge of the said moneys, by whom the public notoriously finds many faults committed in the matter."[125] When the Parlement weighed in on their side, the measure died.

The most important efforts along these lines, though, had accompanied the earlier July edict. Not only had that edict included numerous provisions designed to ensure its vigorous enforcement—provisions that were extended in September—but it had also been the subject of a concerted campaign on the part of the royal council and the Parlement of Paris to goad lower magistrates into prompt and enthusiastic compliance. The cornerstone of that effort was a set of measures designed to ensure the most effective possible *publication* of the edict. This cut to the heart of the question of the regime's effectiveness, for the first prerequisite in enforcing the king's will was making

---

124. AN, Z[1B] 554, piece dated 17 December 1580 (letters of provision of Alexandre de la Tourette to the post of provincial general of Dauphiné), 2: "Je requiers remonstrances estre faict au Roy & a nosseigneurs de son conseil Que ledict de la tourette non seulement a este inventeur de la Creation & erection desdictes Generaulx Mais aussy a faict party avec la Royne de Navarre pour lesdicts offices Lequel na sorty effect our ne sestre trouve aucun qui ait voullu prendre lesdicts offices excepte loffice de general au pais de normandie Ce qui faict cognoistre que lesdicts offices sont inutilz." Only one of the offices of provosts-royal (for Paris) had been filled by this time, and the holder, the euphoniously named Galloys Raoul, had great difficulty getting paid. AN, Z[1B] 554, passim. In two other mints (Lyons and Bayonne), provosts still holding their offices from an abortive creation twenty years earlier took advantage of the situation to sell them on. See AN, J 971, no. 28.1, art. 2.

125. See the goldsmiths' dossier on the affair, AN, K 1036, nos. 63, 64, 67, and 68. The quote is from the last of these (remonstrances of the *corps des orfèvres* of Paris), 2.

sure that it was known, and that was by no means a straightforward matter. There was a standard process for publicizing legislative acts, of course, one that depended almost entirely on the ordinary hierarchy of law courts. Generally, the parlements would register new laws and then send them to midlevel royal courts—the presidial courts, *bailliages*, and *sénéchaussées*. These would send them in turn to local royal and seigniorial magistrates. At every stage, the edicts would be read in court, recorded in registers, and, if appropriate, posted and cried in the towns where judges sat.[126] Things were slightly more complex for the Monnaies, since its jurisdiction covered the entire kingdom, including mints as well as royal courts. Moreover, major edicts had to be printed up in complex editions that included woodcut depictions of all the current coins, designed by the engraver general and approved by the court, which would also be sold as reference works to the general public. The job of royal printer for the moneys was thus a complex as well as a potentially lucrative one, but it, and the system it rested on, changed little through the sixteenth century.[127]

Nevertheless, in the context of the 1570s the royal council lacked confidence in this system, apparently with good reason. One of the main tasks of generals of the moneys on chevauchée was to hector local courts into properly registering and publicizing recent ordinances. This was a particular specialty of Turquam's. In Bordeaux in 1566 he had to enlist the aid of Jean de Monluc, bishop of Valence, member of the Council of State and brother of the lieutenant general of Guyenne, to get the edict removing English angels from circulation published.[128] In 1571, passing through the region of Chartres, he found one small town where "the latest edict was not kept at all, since no one had seen it, and the judges of Chartres had completely failed to send it

---

126. On the details of the system of publication in the later sixteenth century, see Hélène Michaud, *La grande chancellerie et les écritures royales au XVIe siècle, 1515–1589* (Paris: Presses universitaires de France, 1967), 351–92. There is a copy of the form letter the Monnaies sent along to lower courts with royal ordinances in AN, Z^{1B} 368, piece dated 15 April 1553, which includes a request for a reply "nous certiffiant de la reception de ces presentes Ensemble de la publication que aurez faicte de ladicte ordonnance le plustost que pourrez."

127. See AN, Z^{1B} 375, piece dated 22 June 1575 (arrêt requesting the *tailleur général* to furnish woodcuts); and AN, Z^{1B} 373, piece dated 2 July 1566 (proof sheet of "portraictz & figures des especes" signed by le Mestayer and Dain). AN, Z^{1B} 369, dossier dated 28 September 1556, preserves a sheaf of receipts to the printer Jehan Dallier for copies of edicts from the preceding summer, for a total of a bit over sixteen livres.

128. See AN, Z^{1B} 277, fols. 45–53. Since 1562, Blaise de Monluc, famous as a soldier, memoirist, and Catholic bigot, had been lieutenant general and military commander in Guyenne. On his political influence in this period, see *Commentaires et lettres de Blaise de Monluc*, ed. Alphonse de Ruble, 6 vols. (Paris: Veuve J. Renouard, 1864–72), 3:65–90.

to them." In Vendôme, on the other hand, he found that the judges possessed the edict but had simply failed to publish it.[129] In 1573, Turquam was sent to Dijon to persuade the parlement there to register an edict removing foreign billon from circulation.[130] Henri III continued this tradition in a slightly altered form by sending the retired Alexandre de la Tourette on chevauchée in October 1577 to the northeast, with a "very ample" commission.[131] In the summer, though, the generals of the moneys had confined their efforts to the Paris region while the attorney and solicitor general of the Parlement of Paris undertook the main effort to get the June edict properly implemented.

That edict contained draconian provisions regarding publication and enforcement. "So that the present ordinance might not be infringed like the previous ones, to the great contempt of our authority and inestimable damage to us and our subjects, which seems to have come about principally by the fault and negligence of the said ordinary judges of our provinces, who do not pay attention to having our edicts and ordinances on monetary matters published and observed,"[132] the local judges were to renew publication monthly on market days. They were to go to the markets themselves to police payments made there. They were to maintain procès-verbaux of these actions for eventual presentation to the council. In less important cases they should administer summary justice. Any failure in carrying out or accounting for these provisions would be punished with suspension of wages. In effect, the

---

129. AN, Z^{1B} 280, fol. 10: "Quand au cours des Especes quon ne guardoict point ledict dernier mesmes quilz ne lavoient point veu et les juges de Chartres ne leur avoyent point envoye." He names this town "Bonnend": it was almost certainly Bonneval, a dependency of the bailliage of Chartres on the road south. See Gustave Dupont-Ferrier, *Les officiers des bailliages et sénéchaussées et les institutions monarchiques locales en France à la fin du moyen âge* (Paris: E. Bouillon, 1902), map 1. I thank Ted Margadant for this suggestion. On Vendôme, see fol. 12.

130. See Thomas Turquam, *Remonstrances faites au Parlement de Dijon le x. jour de Septembre, 1573. par M. Thomas Turquam General des Monnoyes, Commissaire deputé par sa Majesté, pour l'execution du descry des especes de Billon entrangeres qui s'exposent au Duché de Bourgogne* (Paris: Jean Dallier, 1573).

131. AN, Z^{1B} 17, fols. 34v–38v (letters of commission to Alexandre de la Tourette, copies). The clerk who compiled this register noted in the margin that the first letter was a "Commission . . . fort ample tant pour aller aux provinces que de toutes affaires deppendant de la charge de ladicte court et de son pouvoir." Despite the king's claim in the first letter that "nous avons advise que pour icelle [ordonnance] faire garder & entretenir il estoit requis & necessaire denvoyer en toutes les principalles provinces de nostre roayaulme . . . Commisse expres avec ample pouvoir" (fol. 34v), there is no sign that any further commissioners were dispatched.

132. AN, X^{1A} 8633, fols. 374v–375r: "Et a ce que la presente ordonnance ne soit violee et enfraincte comme les precedentes au grand mespris de nostre autorite et domaige inestimable de nous et de noz subjectz ce qui seroit principallement advenu par la faulte de negligence desdits juges ordinaires de noz provinces qui ne tennent compte de faire publier et observer noz eedictz et ordonnances sur le faict de noz monnoies."

edict was to be an experiment in the control of the lower magistrates. And when the Parlement registered the edict, it added another administrative layer to the provisions designed to ensure its execution. The solicitor-general, Jacques de la Guesle, demanded that each court report back to him immediately with a detailed account of its publication. Many of their replies are conserved in a dossier collected perhaps for the chancellor, René de Birague (like Morvilliers, his predecessor in the seals, and Bellièvre, his successor in the superintendence, he was a financial specialist), which provides unique insight into how royal economic legislation was received on the local level.[133]

In the communications from the local courts one finds almost none of the theoretical and philosophical speculation so characteristic of the sovereign courts. The judges and *gens du roi* who wrote back to Paris confined their personal observation on the royal edict to vague hand waving toward the "public good" and much more practical doubts about its enforceability. The laconic comment of the royal solicitor at Chartres was typical: "While I foresee great difficulty in the observation of this edict, still, sir, we will truly do our full duty to put into effect his Majesty's will as much as we are able."[134] Indeed, these lower magistrates encountered intense pressure from the inhabitants of their jurisdictions, who were clearly well informed and well organized. A few officials raised the specter of insurrection. One from Laon warned that "if one thought to execute the edict by force, there would be a danger of seeing a popular uprising, and hearing the cry of 'famine,' which in fact the people have already begun murmuring loudly."[135] More commonly, though, they reacted to and passed on the polite but firm objections of civic elites: merchants, municipal governments, and the Third Estate generally. In Riom, the town consul, "with the express charge and commission" of the

---

133. AN, J 971. The documents formed a single unit in the Trésor des chartes by at latest 1614, as is shown by systematic labeling in the hand of Pierre Dupuy, who reorganized the Trésor in that year. On that reorganization and the general state of the archive, see Mathieu Molé, *Mémoires*, ed. Aimé Champollion-Figeac, 4 vols. (Paris: J. Renouard, 1855–57) 1:1–5 and 58–62. On its earlier history, see E. A. R. Brown, "Jean du Tillet et les archives de France," *Histoire et Archives* 2 (1997): 29–63.

134. AN, J 971, no. 12 (Nicolas Goulet to Jacques de la Guesle, 3 July 1577, orig.): "combien que je prevoy beaucoup de dificultez sur lobservation dudict edict sy estce Monseigneur que de vraye nous y ferons nostre entier debvoir pour effectuer lintention de sa maieste en tout ce que nous sera possible." The *présidial* of Orléans assured de la Guesle that "si nostre labeur ny peult apporter le fruict et le remedde tel comme pour le service de sa Majeste nous le desirons, nous supplions treshumblement la court et vous monseigneur vous asseurer, que la faulte nen proviendra aucument de nostre part." No. 4: Lobmeau, F. Chenu, and Choppin to de la Guesle, 9 July 1577, orig.

135. AN, J 971 no. 7 (unidentified official from Laon to de la Guesle, 7 July 1577, orig.), fol. 1v: "si lon pensoit executer ledict par force ce seroit en danger de veoir une emotion populaire et ouyr crier famyne comme de faict le peuple commence ja a en murmurer bien fort."

Third Estate of Lower Auvergne, intervened with the first president of the presidial court. He brought with him not only a delegation of local merchants but even officials of the local mint, all of whom testified that there was no French money to be found in the area and no prospect of providing any in the immediate future. In response, the court suspended registration of the edict while the Third Estate sent remonstrances to the king and his council.[136]

The lesser magistrates were in the uncomfortable position of acting as intermediaries between local populations and the organs of the central government. They were royal officers of course and obliged (as they themselves constantly repeated) to carry out the king's will. However necessary it was to stay on the good side of the Parisian authorities, though, the local magistrates were caught up in an even more intense relationship with the constant clamor of their neighbors, whom they saw every day and whose circumstances they shared. They clearly believed that it was part of their job to accommodate the will of the king and Parlement to those circumstances by getting the edict changed, silently adapting it, or suspending it entirely—and despite their theoretical programs, the central authorities in practice accepted that interpretation. This did not imply corruption or rebellion on the part of either the local magistrates or what it would not be too misleading to call their constituents. Of course such things existed, in unusual profusion in the later sixteenth century, and the government was concerned to repress them. Commissions from Paris were one way the central government could and did impose its authority on unreliable officers, for example, whether through the gradually fading institution of the chevauchées of the generals of the moneys and *maîtres des requêtes* or the newborn one of the intendants.[137] However, to concentrate on the need for such extraordinary supervision is to miss the essence of the local magistrates' intermediary function.

As a *coercive* force they may not have lived up to the king's expectations, but they were a very effective conduit of *information*, and as such they were the backbone of a very real government power. This is particularly evident

---

136. AN, J 971, no. 18.1 ("Conclusions et arreté du President et tiers Etats de la province d'Auvergne portant que la publication de ledit concernant la cours des monnoyes sera differée," 20 July 1577): "comme ayant charge et mandement expres." These maneuvers were doubtless related to the long-running three-cornered dispute between the présidial of Riom, the city of Clermont, and the Estates of Basse-Auvergne over who best represented that province. See J. Russell Major, *From Renaissance Monarchy to Absolute Monarchy: French Kings, Nobles, and Estates* (Baltimore: Johns Hopkins University Press, 1994), 284.

137. See Michel Antoine, "Genèse de l'institution des intendants," *Journal des savants*, 1982, 283–317. The *chevauchées* of the generals of moneys disappear from the records early in the reign of Louis XIII; those of the maîtres des requêtes probably ended somewhat earlier. Still, there was a continuity of *function* between these practices and the *intendants de justice et finances*.

in the area of monetary policy, where information and confidence were overwhelmingly important. The central authorities placed great store by the prompt and thorough publication of monetary edicts, which tended to feature extremely long and elaborate preambles explaining the background of royal policy. When Turquam at least went on chevauchée, he took care everywhere he stopped to assemble the local magistrates and lecture them in pedantic detail on the mysteries of monetary thought. In turn, by their own account, the local magistrates explained these matters to the inhabitants of their jurisdictions. At the same time, the sovereign courts and the royal council relied on the local magistrates to inform them on local conditions and public opinion. In this particular case, the voice of the provinces was remarkably uniform. Everywhere the people complained above all that there was no royal money that they could use and that recoining their foreign pieces all at once would be an unbearable hardship. The summary from Sens was completely representative, though all crammed into a single sentence:

> Since the common people offered innumerable complaints and griev-ances during the said publication, solely in regard to the acceptance of . . . such small coins which have been indifferently received—and not about the increase in [real] value of the coins which pass current by the said edict and decision—and as we are informed that there is little other money in the hands of the common people, which will thus continue its clamors, we have not wished to fail to advise you of this in sending the procès-verbal of what we have done, so that you can provide as you think best for the inconveniences which might occur through lack of public officials established at Sens to receive such small coins from the common people, send them to be melted down, and give them what they are owed.[138]

The striking thing is that the central authorities seem to have paid close attention to such analyses, for the next attempt to resolve the monetary crisis took them into account rather precisely. The king delayed the ban on small

---

138. AN, J 971, no. 3.2: "pour ce que en lacte de ladicte publication se sont offertes plainctes et doleances inumerables du commun peuple pour le regard seullement de lexposition des . . . menues pieces qui ont este indifferement receues non pour le surhaulsement de la valeur des especes qui ont cours par leedict et arrest, que sommes informez quil y a peu daultre monnoye entre les mains dudict peuple commun Lequel continuera ses clameurs Navons voulu faillir vous en advertir en envoyant le proces verbal de ce qui a par nous este faict a fin de faire pourveoir ainsi que mieulx il vous plaira aux inconveniens qui pouroient avenir a faulte avoir personnes publiques establiz audict sens pour recevoir telle menue espece de monnoye du commun peuple, les mettre au billon et leur en bailler ce quilz en doibvent recevoir."

foreign coins in Burgundy, where they were most widespread, and took steps to provide French coin ahead of time so that people could change small sums without the long delay usually required for reminting. In late 1577 and 1578 the Cour des Monnaies created many provisional changers in smaller towns precisely in order to provide those "public officials" for which the presidial court of Sens had asked.[139] The mints were even instructed to issue some small-denomination copper currency, one of Europe's first real fiat moneys, where the value in money of account explicitly bore no real relation to the commodity value of the coin. Not only were these steps calculated to win over public support, but by effectively cutting the seigniorage on small change, they relieved a significant source of inflationary pressure.[140] At the same time, the council became much less cautious in its assault on the inflated value of the écu. These provisions must have contributed substantially to the eventual success of the September edict. The technical interventions into commercial practice favored by the Monnaies and the theorists of economic regulation were clearly more effective than the pure reliance on royal authority favored by Bellièvre and the Parlement—but in practice the exercise of that royal authority provided mechanisms that enabled effective technocratic governance.

The Great Debasement and Recoinage

The crisis and reforms of Henri III's reign were unique in their context and details but not in their general outline. Periodic crises and more or less successful public attempts to deal with them are, it seems, characteristic of all systems of currency and presumably inherent in their nature as complex systems of confidence and coercion. In 1577, someone in France looking for a relevant and recent model of such a crisis would probably have thought first of England; by that time, as we have seen, English coins were bywords for reliability, but when Elizabeth had taken the throne, her coinage was still feeling the effects of severe disruptions in the 1540s. While those disruptions were clearly much more the result of government policy than of market or

---

139. See AN, Z^{1B} 553, passim. A document dated 5 February 1578 suggests that the Cour des Monnaies also tried to send out changers from Paris to help in the provinces but that the Parisians refused to go, with the (possibly true but probably not honest) excuse that they were shorthanded in Paris as it was.

140. For the rather complex mechanism whereby this worked, see Sargent and Velde, *Big Problem*, 15–36. While these steps almost certainly soothed public opinion, they do not seem to have significantly alleviated the chronic shortage of small change in the long run. As early as 1579, the Monnaies was again issuing "Remonstrances treshumbles au Roy . . . sur la plainte . . . de la rarite & necessite de monnoyes de billon." BN, fr. 18504, fol. 47.

other outside forces, Elizabeth's successful recoinage showed some of the same characteristics of Henri III's reforms.[141]

The roots of England's monetary disarray lay in the combination of excessively ambitious foreign policy and chronically weak fiscal policy that characterized the reign of Henry VIII and (to a somewhat lesser extent) Edward VI and Mary I. Faced with expensive, and usually unsuccessful, wars against France and lacking many of the resources their opponents had developed over the previous century—broad-based land taxes, venal offices, the ability to draw on domestic, urban credit networks through expedients like the *rentes* on the Hôtel de Ville of Paris or the (admittedly catastrophic) consortium of bankers known as the Grand parti de Lyon—those monarchs turned to the mints.[142] The process, which had been extensively used in France in the fourteenth and fifteenth centuries, was fairly crude. Coinage in circulation would be declared no longer current, with orders to return it to the mints for recoining. New coins would then be issued in exchange for the old, with a favorable nominal value but a lower precious-metal content The difference was usually made up by diminishing the alloy rather than the weight—the precise loss of title was considered a state secret, and it required significantly more effort and expertise to analyze the alloy than the weight of a new coin. Even after paying the not-inconsiderable costs of this transaction, the Crown could then pocket a substantial quantity of precious metal. This process might then be repeated as needed, at least until the specie content of the coinage dropped to insignificant levels. Indeed, from 1542 to 1551, successive debasements dropped the fineness of English silver from 11/12 to 3/12, beyond which it would have been entering into the territory of fiat currency.

This process did have its advantage as a source of revenue. Notably, market forces did all the heavy lifting: appropriate mint prices and rates of seigniorage could make it highly profitable to recoin existing currency, thus avoiding problems of enforcement and ensuring some level of support from the wealthy. The biggest problem was that, though such policies were self-evidently inflationary, the English government's major expenses (military expenditures and

---

141. The basic works on this episode are J. D. Gould, *The Great Debasement: Currency and the Economy in Mid-Tudor England* (Oxford: Clarendon Press, 1970); C. E. Challis, *The Tudor Coinage* (Manchester, UK: Manchester University Press, 1978), 81–134; and Challis, ed., *A New History of the Royal Mint* (Cambridge: Cambridge University Press, 1992), 228–51.

142. In a fine reversal of fortune, Louis XIV, at war with the fiscally and financially more sophisticated Dutch and English, would in turn exploit his mints in the later decades of his reign. For details, see Guy Rowlands, *The Financial Decline of a Great Power: War, Influence, and Money in Louis XIV's France* (Oxford: Oxford University Press, 2012), 53–130.

debt service) had to be paid overseas, in good coin.[143] Such policies were also still broadly viewed as immoral, and commentators under Queen Mary were still using arguments that went back to medieval sources. In England as in France they were still current, though in this case more obviously apt to the situation at hand, as appears in a 1553 memoir by a lawyer with the apt name of John Price:

> There is [*sic*] two ways of abasing the coin one by mixture of base metal with fine . . . which is the deceit that is imputed to these alchemists. The other is by giving less weight of good metal in the coin, than the nature, name and credit of that coin doth require, which is much like as if the clerk of the market, would put the King's seal to a less bushel . . . than that which was used and allowed beforetime.[144]

The debasement also left a number of very similar coins of radically different fineness in circulation, with attendant confusion. Otherwise, however, unlike ongoing debasement, the debased coins themselves once set by law at their proper relative values probably did not do England any particular harm.

Nevertheless, as soon as she had settled the outstanding religious and foreign-policy issues that directly threatened her reign, Elizabeth implemented a radical policy of revaluation and near-complete recoinage, which turned out to be something of a triumph. Not only did the recoinage go through successfully on a technical level (with the help of some imported German refiners), but it actually turned a substantial profit for the Crown. By crying down the debased coin below its intrinsic value and ultimately forbidding it to circulate at all, Elizabeth effectively taxed its holders for the cost of reminting it, and by doing so very efficiently she kept much of that tax for herself. This may, among other things, help explain the Elizabethan regime's decreasingly productive obsession with metallurgical and even alchemical projects through the end of the century.[145] That this went over without significant resistance indicates that a broad public, as in France, shared her concern with a stable currency and accepted her authority over it. And like the 1577 reforms, though in a happier context, Elizabeth's recoinage became enshrined as a major political achievement.

---

143. Gould, *Great Debasement*, 83, estimates that the money supply rose from £850,000 in 1542 to £2,170,000 in 1551. It is almost impossible to imagine economic activity rising by more than 25 percent over this period.

144. W. A. J. Archbold, "A Manuscript Treatise on the Coinage by John Pryse, 1553," *English Historical Review* 13 (1898): 710. Compare in particular with Oresme, *De moneta*, but also with the papal bull *Spondent* (1317), which will be discussed below.

145. See Harkness, *Jewel House*, 169–80.

Thus, in language parallel to his contemporary de Thou, the erudite historian William Camden explained that "(which turned to her greater, yea greatest glory) she began by little and little to take away the brasse money, and restore good money of cleane silver, for the repairing of the glory of the Kingdome, and to prevent the fraud of those few which embased monies both at home and abroad, exchanged the best commodities of the Land for base monyes, and exported the currant money into foraine Countries, and also for the abating of the prices of things vendible, which were very much raised to the great damage of the Common-wealth."[146] He was in turn echoing the government's explanation in the preamble to the proclamation launching the recoinage:

By the long sufferance of the said base and copper moneys, not only her crown, nobility, and subjects of this her realm [are] daily more and more impoverished, the ancient and singular honor and estimation which this realm of England had beyond all other by plenty of moneys of gold and silver, only fine and not base, is hereby decayed and vanished away, but also by reason of these said base moneys great quantity of forged and counterfeits have been and are daily made and brought from beyond the seas. . . . And finally hereby all manner of prices of things in this realm necessary for sustentation of the people grow daily excessive.[147]

On the one hand, Elizabeth and her advisers were undoubtedly sincere in their contention that the debasement was largely responsible for inflationary trends. This view had appeared in the previous reign, as in Price's tract, but it had been the central theme of Sir Thomas Smith's *Discourse of the Commonweal*, written under Edward VI, the classic expression of the "Commonwealth" thought that inspired Cecil and others in Elizabeth's inner circle. Such concerns, differently phrased, were of course a major motivation for all the different reforms mooted in France.

The other element of Camden's and the preamble's account was far more abstract: an appeal to the "glory" and "honor" of the realm and to a semimetaphorical purity and luster that the body politic derived from the literal purity and luster of the ancient coinage. In that sense, it seems likely that

---

146. William Camden, *Annales rerum gestarum Angliae et Hiberniae regnante Elizabetha (1615 and 1625) with the annotations of Sir Francis Bacon*, ed. Dana F. Sutton (Birmingham, UK: Philological Museum, 2001), http://www.philological.bham.ac.uk/camden/1560e.html#goodmon.

147. Paul F. Hughes and James F. Larkin, eds., *Tudor Royal Proclamations*, 3 vols. (New Haven: Yale University Press, 1964–67) 2:150–51 (proclamation of 27 September 1560).

Elizabeth's recoinage was designed fairly explicitly as a display of sovereign power. Like the military and diplomatic reckonings with Scotland and France and the Protestant religious settlement that marked the first two years of her reign, Elizabeth's recoinage was an act of majesty designed as much to publicly solidify what might be expected to be a weak government as to solve admittedly pressing problems. This in turn depended for its effect not only on probably modest economic benefits but on a broadly understood connection, both practical and symbolic, between coinage and the dignity of royal governance. This connection certainly included both the administrative practicalities and the broader issues of economic policy discussed so far, but it went beyond them. In France, it became increasingly important as the deteriorating civil wars called royal sovereignty into question and then as that sovereignty was rebuilt along new lines under the Bourbon kings.

CHAPTER 4

Money and Sovereignty

> Everyone . . . must above all seek integrity in the
> moneys, on which our features are imprinted and on
> which the general good depends. For what would be
> safe if our image were offended, and if that which a
> subject ought to venerate in his heart were immedi-
> ately violated by a sacrilegious hand?
>
> —Cassiodorus

When an anonymous French writer set out in
the early seventeenth century to compile the best monetary thought of his
time, he summed up his project in a double epigraph. Alongside the fifth-
century Roman chancery formula above,[1] he placed a brief, inelegant, and
incorrect Latin poem presumably of his own composition. It went as follows:

A single faith should be a single weight, measure, and money,
And the state of all the world will be healthy.
The right to coin money resides in the bones of princes.
Spurn foreign customs: they have a thousand faces.
He ordered that the mass that was to be formed by fire into his features
Be melted down.[2]

---

1. Cassiodorus, Variæ 7.32 ("Formula qua moneta comittitur"): "Omnis . . . omnino monetae debet
integritas quaeri, ubi et vultus noster imprimitur et generalis utilitas invenitur. Nam quid erit tutum,
si in nostra peccetur effigie, et quam subiectus corde venerari debet, manus sacrilega violare festinet?"

2. BN, ms. fr. 18499, fol. 1r: "Vetus est et elegans dictum hoc disticho sic redditum: Una fides
pondus mensura moneta sit una / Et status illaesus totius orbis erit. / Principum ossibus inhaeret jus
cudenda moneta / Sperne mores peregrinos mille habent effigias. / Jussit ut in vultus igni formanda
liquescat / Massa suos." This and the quotation from Cassiodorus form the epigraph to "Recueil
concernant les monnaies" (fols. 1–85 of the ms.). The Latin is dreadful: in the second couplet, in
particular, the author seems to hesitate between altering the rules of Latin syntax to make his scan-
sion work and altering the rules of Latin prosody to make his grammar work. My thanks to Sylvia
Parsons for her help with the translation.

None of this was particularly original. The Cassiodoran *locus* had been exceptionally popular at least since the 1580s.[3] The poetic outburst codified the thought of Colas and his peers, which had been current for at least as long. That very codification, continued in more detail in the (unpublished and indeed unfinished) collection itself, does, however, testify to a rather different status and practice of the *fait des monnaies* than in the period before 1577. More integrated than ever into the humanist erudition of the robe elites and continuing its reflections on the nature of nationality and sovereignty, monetary thought had matured into a coherent and broadly recognized if increasingly diverse body of expertise with a significant place in the process of French governance. Despite the somewhat shoddy antique trappings on display in this manuscript, it was strikingly modern in its reliance on methodical expertise and its attachment to a calculus of national interest; indeed, it even generated some explicit reflection on the modernity of the emerging European state system.

But that maturity did not come easily. If the inflationary crisis and the reforms of 1577 illustrate some of the strengths of sixteenth-century French governance and the ways the currency could mobilize them, in the two succeeding decades the currency became a victim of the state's near-total collapse. It is indicative, however, of the importance that both the elites and the general population placed on control of the currency and of the intimate relationship that had developed between that control and royal sovereignty that bringing order to the moneys was one of the first priorities as Henri IV sought to stabilize the kingdom. That stabilization, if slow to arrive, was ultimately successful, and from the later 1590s until Henri's death in 1610 both monetary policy and the discourse around it could proceed more systematically than at any time in the previous half century. The resulting debates, which were highly sophisticated and attracted wide interest, showed that money was already well on its way toward its status as the single most important tool not just for effecting but for conceptualizing the ordering and regulation of society.

---

3. It appeared in François Hotman, *De re numaria populi Romani liber* (n.p., 1585), and by the seventeenth century it was common coin. See, e. g., François le Begue, *Traicté et advis sur les desordres des monnoyes & diversité de moyens d'y remedier* (Paris, 1600), 16. The second of his ways of avoiding forgery "seroit forger & tailler coings difficiles à contrefaire par la face du Prince qui y seroit emprainte, pour luy estre autant de statues erigees à son honneur, qui les rendroit plus sacrees & inviolables. *Omnino debet integritas quæri* (dit Cassiodore) *ubi vultus regius imprimitur. Et comme dit cest Empereur. Quidnam erit tutum si in noster peccetur effigie?* ce qui defaut à nos escus, quarts, & demy quarts d'escu."

The Wars of the Three Henries

Though the 1577 reforms were relatively successful, there is no way to tell how well they would have worked in the long run, for within a decade they had fallen victim to the same forces that destroyed Henri III's reign and ultimately the king himself. In 1584, Henri's feckless and sickly younger brother, François d'Anjou, died. Henri had no children and no one thought it likely that he would father any, which made his cousin Henri of Navarre the presumptive heir to the throne. Since Navarre was a Protestant and the leader of the Huguenot faction, he was flatly unacceptable to a very wide spectrum of French opinion; to make a bad situation worse, he too had no legitimate children and since he was estranged from his wife, Henri III's sister Marguerite, no immediate way of producing any—and the next heir in line, the Cardinal de Bourbon, was equally childless, in orders, and quite elderly. With no credible path forward, the already shaky edifice of royal legitimacy began to collapse, and within two years the civil wars had reached a new paroxysm. Henri III threw in his lot first with the Catholic Guise faction against Navarre; he then switched sides and in 1588 was driven out of Paris for his trouble, leaving the Cour des Monnaies behind. He responded by having the duc de Guise assassinated, and the next year he himself was assassinated in turn. This left Navarre and the senior surviving Guise, Henri, duc de Mayenne, to fight it out. Over the next four years Navarre's superior claims to legitimacy, greater political and military skills, and ultimate conversion to Catholicism turned the tide in his favor and finally allowed him to begin the process of restoring order to the kingdom.

Between 1577 and 1588, the French currency remained fairly stable, though there were still complaints. In 1579, the Cour des Monnaies remonstrated that coin was still critically scarce in France because of the "monetary manipulations of neighboring princes who notoriously have melted and do melt down the said coins . . . which they draw out with their weaker ones, and convert them to their stamps and arms, with which they have filled the frontiers and provinces of this kingdom."[4] But the deteriorating political situation soon overwhelmed such relatively petty issues. Even before the

---

4. "Remonstrances treshumbles au Roy par les gens tenans sa Cour des monnoyes sur la plainte . . . de la rarite & necessite de monnoyes de billon," BN, ms. fr. 18504, fols. 47–49. This rarity had two causes, the first being the export of coin by French merchants. "La seconde cause est venue du billonage des princes boysins qui nottoirement ont fondu & fondent encores lesdites monnoyes . . . quilz tirent par les leurs foibles & [illeg.] & les convertissent a leur coings & armes dont ils ont remply les frontieres & provinces de ce royaume." Fol. 47r.

crisis that followed d'Anjou's death, it is very easy to find examples of severe disruptions in the coinage brought about by the civil wars. Mints in cities that fell into Protestant hands were out of the Monnaies' control for the duration. This could result in a situation like that of Grenoble in the first round of the wars, where the master of the mint fled and reported on his return that "the mint and the house of [the master] had been sacked and the coffers and tools therein smashed and broken."[5] In Saintes, the mint's engraver buried all his materials before fleeing the conflicts that followed the St. Bartholomew's Day massacres and unsurprisingly found them in an unusable condition when he returned.[6] Even in the much less chaotic Protestant stronghold of La Rochelle, that same round of wars left the estate of the deceased mint master bankrupt, and the remaining mint officers reported nervously that "it happened that last January the mayor and his council decided to constrain us to coin money from a small amount of gold jewelry and silver bullion, and though we read out several remonstrances, nevertheless, due to acts of constraint, the mint had to operate."[7] This kind of coining without royal authorization was in fact routine during the wars, so the edicts of pacification issued to end each phase almost always included an article to the effect that rebels would "remain quit and not liable for all acts of hostility, the levy and conduct of troops, the fabrication and evaluation of money made according to the ordinances of the . . . leaders."[8]

While such breakdowns in mint function and supervision were certainly not helpful, they were likely to do severe damage to the French currency and economy only if they led to the large-scale issue of genuinely bad coin. To some extent, this may have happened as a result of sheer chaos. The officers

---

5. AN, Z[1B] 372, piece dated 2 August 1564 (petition of Pierre de Luan): "auroit ladicte monnoie & maison dudict suppliant este sagagee & les coffres & ustancilles dicelle rompuz & brisez."

6. See AN, Z[1B] 375, dossier dated 12 July 1575.

7. Ibid., piece dated 17 July 1573 (letter of the officers of the mint of La Rochelle of that date): "est advenu que audit moys de janviers dernier Monsieur le Maire et conseil estably pres sa personne sadviserent de nous contraindre de faire travaille de la monnoye pour quelque peu de bagues dor et marcs dargent combien que nous leusismes plusieurs remonstrances et neantmoins par les voyes de contraincte il falluest que ladicte monnoye travaillast." They must have done a creditable job of coining to the legal standards, since they volunteered to send in the pyx they had prepared in that incident.

8. Richard L. Goodbar, ed., *The Edict of Nantes: Five Essays and a New Translation* (Bloomington, MN: National Huguenot Society, 1998), 55 (art. 76 of the edict). Similar language appeared in the Edict of Amboise (1563), art. 7; the Peace of Longjumeau (1568), art. 6; the Edict of St. Germain-en-Laye (1570), art. 19, where that exact wording first appeared; the Peace of La Rochelle (1573), art. 11; the Peace of Monsieur (1576), art. 53, which specifically indemnified Montmorency-Damville and the city of La Rochelle; and the Peace of Bergerac (1577), art. 55. See Bernard Barbiche and Isabelle Chiavassa, eds., *L'édit de Nantes et ses antécédents (1562–1598)* (Paris: Editions en ligne de l'Ecole des Chartes, n.d.), http://elec.enc.sorbonne.fr/editsdepacification/.

of the mint of Montpellier, under cover of the civil wars, carried out massive fraud in the silver coinage.[9] A small-town judge complained to Turquam "that the said city and surrounding area were filled with counterfeit money . . . which it was absolutely necessary to deal with, and to do so to have force, because it was said that those counterfeiters took refuge in castles and strong places."[10] The president of the presidial court of Lyons, commissioned to carry out an investigation, uncovered evidence of systematic corruption among the guards charged with preventing specie from being smuggled out of that city. The lieutenant of the Master of the Gates would only outline the ongoing corruption, "not daring at present to openly declare what he knows and still less correct it as would be needful and expedient for the due of his charge, given the obstruction, menaces, and intimidation which [the corrupt guards] make toward him."[11] Even the president Nicolas de Langes, an extremely prominent and well-connected man, did not feel up to continuing with the case. "If there is a need to go further to investigate more thoroughly," he told his kinsman Bellièvre, "I would greatly appreciate it if the commission were not addressed principally to me, for some may be found guilty whom I would not wish to displease."[12]

Producing bad coin in the mints on a truly large scale, though, required actors more substantial than poorly constrained petty criminals. The first to take that step was Henri de Montmorency de Damville, nicknamed not without reason the "King of Languedoc." From his family he had inherited a deadly feud with the Guise lineage, which ruled out his adherence to the Catholic League rebellion, but he also was deeply and justifiably suspicious of the last Valois kings and their mother, Catherine de Medicis, who would happily have sold him down the river as they did his cousin, the assassinated

---

9. See AN, J 971, piece no. 17 (remonstrance of the Cour des Monnaies, 12 December 1576).

10. AN, Z^{1B} 280, fol. 10r: "que ladicte ville et pais circonvoisins estoient rempliz de faulse monnoye . . . auquel il estoit plus que necessaire pourvoir et pour ce faire avoir main forte par ce qu'on disoit que lesdictz faux monnoiers se retiroient en chasteux et places fortes."

11. BN, ms. fr. 18497, fol. 27v ("Proces verbal fait par monsieur le lieutenant de langes sur les lettres patentes a luy envoyees touchant le transport des monnoyes et billon hors le royaulme de france," April 1577): "Nosant pour le present appertement declarer ce quil en sait & moings y donner ordre comme il seroit besoing et expedient pour le deue de son charge, actendu les empeschemens menasses & intimidations que lesdicts Merle et ses adherans luy font."

12. BN, ms. fr. 18497, fol. 21r (Nicolas de Langes to Pomponne de Bellièvre, 28 April 1577, orig.): "Sil est besoing passer oultre a informer plus amplement je desirerois bien que la commission ne fust dresse a moy principallement parce que aulcuns se peuvent trouver coupables ausquelz je ne vouldroit deplaisir." On the relationship between Langes and Bellièvre, who had preceded his cousin at the présidial of Lyons, see Olivier Poncet, *Pomponne de Bellièvre (1529–1607): Un homme d'état au temps des Guerres de religion* (Paris: Editions de l'Ecole des Chartes, 1998), 15, 52, 351.

Admiral de Coligny. Caught between the two parties and equipped with resources that, while considerable, were no match for either, he fortified himself in Languedoc, sometimes allied with the Huguenot rebels who were strong in his region and sometimes in uneasy peace with the monarchy, while trying to attract a following of Catholic malcontents. And given his desperate situation, he had no hesitation in attacking the currency. As early as 1574, he had issued a debased coinage, leading the Monnaies to complain of "the damage and injury to the reputation of this kingdom for the opinion which foreigners might have that these coins had been made by order of his majesty, and that the recent troubles had reduced him to so extreme a necessity that he would debase the coinage to that extent."[13] This probably caused a small diplomatic crisis in 1576, when three of France's key military allies, the Swiss cities of Berne, Friburg, and Solothurn, complained about an influx of drastically underweight French sols. Soothing allies was one of the major challenges of monetary policy, and the Monnaies launched a hurried but thorough investigation, even canvassing Swiss troops in Paris for similar coins. The results were inconclusive, with no unambiguously French bad coins found, but Damville's coinage was the obvious culprit.[14] By that time, Montmorency had patched up relations with Henri III and ceased these activities, but starting almost immediately after François d'Anjou's death, he began systematically flooding the Midi with heavily debased coinage. He opened and operated mints under his own authority in Beaucaire and Béziers, set new, lower standards for the silver content of the coinage (standards that his mints never actually met), legislated on the circulation and price of coins, and generally did everything a king would do short of coining under his own name and arms.[15] His motives were entirely mercenary—indeed, the reports of Philip II's agents suggest that raising money in this way was

---

13. AN, J 971, piece no. 17, fol. 1r: "le tort et injure faict a la reputation de ce royaulme pour lopinion que les estrangers pourroient avoir que ces pieces aient este faictes par ordonnance de sa maieste et que les troubles passez layt reducicte a ceste extremite quelle ait este contraict empirer ses monnoies jusques a ce poinct."

14. See AN, Z[1B] 376, pieces dated 19 March, 29 April, 12 May, and 7 June 1576 (respectively, complaint of the cantons; reply of the French ambassador, Haultefort; arrêt of the Conseil d'Etat; procès-verbal of the Monnaies' investigation; and arrêt reporting on the investigation). The Monnaies found no coins in the Swiss sample that were both identifiably French and seriously underweight. The Swiss Cantons complained again in 1582, this time about an influx of bad testons and francs: the Monnaies, which had always considered the franc excessively vulnerable to fraud, blamed the depredations of coiners. AN, Z[1B] 379, piece dated 14 January 1583 (memoir of the court).

15. The story is told exhaustively by J. Bailhache, "Le monnayage de Montmorency pendant la Ligue à Montpellier, Beaucaire, Béziers et Villeneuve d'Avignon (1585–1592), d'après des documents inédits," Revue numismatique, 4th ser., 25 (1932): 37–91.

an important part of Montmorency's political strategy—but the effect was a comprehensive and pioneering usurpation of monetary authority, and a real degradation of the coinage.[16]

As the wars progressed, Montmorency-Damville's tactics proved contagious. One good place to observe that process is in the city of Lyons, which was for most of the sixteenth century France's main financial center. That position was already eroding well before the Catholic League rebelled against Henri III in 1588, but it did give the city the expertise and connections it needed to manage its own currency with some confidence. Unlike the situation in Languedoc, the decision to coin money under the city's authority was not taken immediately. As late as January 1590, the officers of the Lyons mint wrote to the Monnaies, complaining that

> for some time people have taken the liberty of accepting and exposing . . . [small coins] forged and made in the mints of Montpellier, Béziers, Beaucaire, and other places, which are defective . . . and there is such a quantity of them that one sees no other payments among the people, and by this means all or most of the good coins of France which were in this area have been taken to the places where those coins are made and melted down and converted into them, so that the best merchants of this city, and even the best banks have found themselves unable to promptly furnish from their funds one or two hundred écus in cash in the good coins of France. And what is worse, this evil grows worse every day.[17]

This lament could, mutatis mutandis, have been repeated almost anywhere in France, and the authorities in Paris had no immediate guidance to offer.

By the following September the situation had deteriorated enough that the treasurer general of Lyons, Jacques Daveyne, proposed coining money like that of Montpellier "in order to provide for the urgent necessity of affairs, that is for funds for the expenses the war and notably to receive the

---

16. See Joan Davies, "Neither Politique nor Patriot? Henri, Duc de Montmorency, and Philip II, 1582.–1589," *Historical Journal* 34 (1991): 556.

17. AN, Z[1B] 383, piece dated 16 January 1590: "depuys quelque temps en ca lon cest tellement licensie de recepvoir et exposer . . . les pieces de six blancz forgees et fabricquees es monnoyes de monpelier beziers beaucaire et autres lieulx lesquelles sont deffectueuses . . . et y en a bien telle quantite que lon ne voit autre payement entre le peuple et par ce moyen toutes les bonnes monnoyes de france qui estoyent en ses quartiers ou la plus grand part ont estes transportees es lieulx ou on se fabriquent lesdites pieces de six blancz et ilec fondues et converties en la fabrication dicelles tellement que des meilleurs marchantz de ceste ville ny voyre mesmes des meilleurs banques ce treuveroyent empesches de fournir promptement de leur propre cent ou deux cents escuz comptant de bonne monnoye de france. Et qui pis est le mal croit tous les jours."

troops the Duke of Savoy is sending to aid this city." When the master of the Lyons mint responded that he could not and did not wish "to work on the said coinage without the express permission of the generals of the moneys in Paris," he and his fellow officers were threatened with immediate imprisonment.[18] They submitted, and the city council proceeded to collect the seigniorage of its mint for the rest of the war. In many ways this only made a bad situation worse, and it led the city council into new conflicts. The duc de Nemours, governor of Dauphiné and the local League magnate, seems to have posed as a champion of strong money, instituting draconian regulations in 1590 to keep heavily debased coin out of Lyons and banning it outright in the fall of 1592—a ban that the city authorities felt compelled to override, "wishing to address the discontent of the people . . . arising . . . from the fact that there circulate among them no other small coins by which they might be assisted and purchase their necessities."[19]

More important, the authorities felt that the coinage and circulation of debased money was a significant obstacle to reintegration into the monarchy. Once that became the city's policy as the League crumbled in early 1594, repairing the currency suddenly became an immediate preoccupation. On 3 February the city councillors arranged with the master of the mint to accept most debased coins for five livres per mark of weight in good coin; on the weekend of the seventh to the tenth, they turned the city over to the forces of Henri IV; and on 18 February, acting under the authority of an edict issued by the duc de Nemours a year earlier, the councillors, "by the aid and succor of certain notables who are friends of the public good," raised a fund to carry out the reminting.[20] This was not an entirely new project: three months earlier, the Lyons mint had petitioned Mayenne's council to fund such a buyback.[21] The willingness of the city elites to do this out of their own pockets, however, testifies to an entirely new urgency. By 1 March, a royal maître des

---

18. AML, BB 125, fols. 177v, 199v ("Assemblee pour la fabrique des Nesles," 13 September 1590): "pour survenir a lurgente necessite des affaires, mesmes pour fondz pour les fraiz de la guerre notamment pour recepvoir les troupes que Monseigneur de Savoye envoye au secours de ladite ville." "il ne peult ne doibt & ne veult faire travailler a ladicte fabrique sans permission expresse de Messieurs les genereaulx des monnoyes a paris."

19. AML, AA 139, piece no. 17 (remonstrances to Nemours, undated minute); BB 129, fol. 104r (assembly of 3 September 1592): "desirans pourvoir au mescontentement du peuple . . . , provenant . . . de ce quil ne se court parmy le peuple aultre menue monnoye dont il peult estre soulage & avoir ses necessitez."

20. AML, BB 130, fol. 15, fols. 18v–21r: "par laid & secours de quelques notables & affectionnez au bien public."

21. AN, Z^{1B} 384, piece dated 22 December 1593.

requêtes was in Lyons formally reestablishing royal control over the mint, and the city council's oversight of the currency was reduced to the modest proportions of receiving letters from the neighboring town of Clermont en Auvergne (longtime royalists) asking the Lyons mint officers to review an unfavorable assay of some of the Auvergnat coinage.[22]

Little about this story was unique. After 1589, France was flooded with a dizzying array of debased coins ranging in quality from bad to atrocious, known generically as *nesles* (as they appear in Lyons) or as *pinatelles*, after a long-obsolete Provençal coin and, quite likely, after the corrupt general of the moneys who had done so much to promote bad coinage at midcentury. Navarre and Mayenne, at least, also coined large amounts of copper, which may have contributed in the long run to the relative failure of France's precocious and promising experiment with fiat-value small change. The rump Chambre des Monnaies at Tours seems to have had very little influence, but the court in Paris was determined to remain the champion of the traditional *fait des monnaies* no matter what the external circumstances might be. On 1 October 1590, when a Spanish relief force had just lifted the terrible siege by Henri IV's troops that had nearly brought the capital to its knees, an assembly of representatives from the Parlement, the Comptes, the Monnaies, and the bourgeoisie (summoned by Nicolas Roland, on behalf of Mayenne) gave dramatic evidence of this, vehemently opposing a plan to set a favorable exchange rate for the Flemish coins with which the Spaniards were paid. This was above all because if implemented as proposed, "the ordinance on the moneys made in the year 1577 . . . as well as the accounting by écus introduced in that ordinance, by means of which everyone's revenue is certain and assured, . . . would be entirely undermined and annulled." Precious metal would leave the kingdom and inflation would surge "and cause us more loss and damage than all the ransomings, robberies, and sackings of those soldiers."[23] Even as the kingdom fell apart around it, the Monnaies, with considerable public support, clung to its hard-won model of a stable currency.

---

22. AML, BB 131, fols. 142v–143r; AA 66, letters dated 20 March 1594. The comte de Clermont, the local royalist military commander (and a client of Montmorency-Damville), had seized the mint of Clermont as early as November 1590: see AN, Z^{1B} 383, piece dated 3 November 1590 (notarized act of Armand, master of the Clermont mint, copy).

23. Sylvie Daubresse and Bertrand Haan, eds., *Actes du parlement de Paris et documents du temps de la Ligue (1588–1594): Le recueil de Pierre Pithou* (Paris: Honoré Champion, 2012), 214–15: "l'ordonnance des monnoies faicte en l'année Vc soixante-dix-sept . . . comme aussy le compte à escuz introduict par lad. ordonnance, par le moyen duquel le revenu d'un chascun est certain et asseuré . . . seroient du tout pervertiz et annullés." "et nous faire souffrir plus de pertes et dommaiges que n'avons faict par les ransonnementz, volleries et saccagementz desd. gens de guerre."

This attitude continued through the war. In the winter of 1592–1593, the Paris city fathers noticed that the main arch of the Pont au Change (linking the Palais de Justice on the Île de la Cité to the Right Bank) was on the point of collapse. Not only did this jeopardize the many structures on the bridge itself, but if the bridge fell it also threatened to bring down the neighboring Pont aux Meuniers, which in turn, combined with winter ice, might create a dam that would flood much of central Paris. Unfortunately, there seemed to be no good way to make the urgently needed repairs, "the laborers not wishing to work without some advance payment, and (because of the misery of our times) the city being reduced to such poverty that there was nothing in the ordinary or extraordinary treasury."[24] The result was an ungainly mess. Members of the city council, following a standard if unwelcome procedure, guaranteed an advance to the workers in their private names.[25] Then, in hopes of having their credit validated, they approached Mayenne for an emergency infusion of royal funds. He authorized a complex transaction whereby two obsolete brass artillery pieces stored in the Paris Arsenal would be coined into copper pennies, which would then be lent to the city council for repair work. As a way of debasing the currency, this at least had the virtue of being ingenious. The Monnaies, however, remained thoroughly opposed to all such expedients. It had already waged a long and fruitless action against Jehan de la Haye, the master of the Paris mint supported by Mayenne and the city council, whose financial participation was a major component of the artillery-for-bridges deal.[26] In that case, too, the Monnaies acted as a spoiler, raising both technical objections (that the cannon might not be of the requisite alloy) and financial ones (that the money coined might not find takers and that de la Haye might be paying his share in bad money) and sending a delegation to remonstrate unsuccessfully with Mayenne.[27] Probably as part of a political horse trade, though, the Monnaies fended off a simultaneous

---

24. AN, Z[1B] 73, fol. 5v (1 February 1593): "les ouvriers ne voullant travailler sans quelque advance Et pour la misere du temps la ville estant reduite en telle pauvreté quil n'y avoict au leurs deniers ordinaires ny extraordinaires."

25. There is frequent mention of this procedure in Roger Doucet, *Finances municipales et crédit public à Lyon au XVIe siècle* (Geneva: Mégariotis, 1980).

26. See, e.g., AN, Z[1B] 383, dossier dated 8 January 1591, which consists mainly of de la Haye's (successful) appeals to Mayenne. By the time the matter of the bridge arose, de la Haye had, over the objections of the Monnaies but supported by Mayenne, coined copper and debased silver to a nominal value of at least twenty-two thousand écus.

27. That the cannon were in fact coined is proved by a receipt in the archives of the Bureau de Ville de Paris, *Registres des délibérations du bureau de la ville de Paris,* ed. Paul Guérin et al., vol. 10 (Paris: Imprimerie Nationale, 1900), 399.

request to officially approve the debased coinage brought to the city by Burgundian delegates to the upcoming meeting of the Estates General—even at this late date, its concerns remained extraordinarily consistent.

The Cour des Monnaies had effectively become just one of many agents in an intensely localized monetary landscape. Combating such particularism had been the court's raison d'être, and even when it was no longer reduced to being part of the problem, the Monnaies found for some time that the civil wars had made its task much harder. This is well illustrated by events that occurred in late 1597, when Henri IV's victory was in theory all but complete. In an attempt to draw business away from the mint operated at Dinan by the duc de Mercoeur, the still-rebellious governor of Brittany, the Monnaies persuaded the king to open a satellite office of the Rennes mint in St. Malo. The officer sent to oversee this venture reported that

> I encountered resistance, to the point that the inhabitants, knowing that the mint master [of Rennes] had rented a building and that I had put him in possession of it, had held a meeting of the city council on the previous day and resolved therein not to allow the said master to work at making money. . . . And following that resolution . . . they sent two of the inhabitants to me, who came to see me saying that the city council had charged them to declare to me that they did not at all wish to have a money office in their city and that if the master set up work there, they would prevent it most effectively.[28]

And in the end, the Rennes mint master "was chased so quickly from the said city of St. Malo that he was not able to get his papers out."[29]

This, however, was the end game of the monetary disturbances. Even Montmorency-Damville had by then decided, like the city of Lyons, that his usurpation of the moneys had to be sacrificed to his rapprochement with Henri IV. As early as mid-1592, he began shutting down his minting operations and trying to control the bad coinage he had loosed on the Midi but

---

28. AN, Z^{1B} 388, dossier dated 4 December 1597, piece no. 2 (letter of Simon Bizeul to the Cour des Monnaies, 22 November 1597, orig.): "jay tant trouve de resistance que les habitans scachant que ledict maistre [de Rennes] avoit loue un logis et que je lavoit mis en pocession dicelluy Ont le jour dhier tenu leur conseil de ville et en icelluy resolu ne laisser travailler ledit maistre en la fabrication de la monnoie . . . et sur ceste resolution . . . Menvoierent deux des habitans qui mestoient venuz veoir que le corps de la ville les avoit chargez me declarer quilz ne voulloient point de tablier de monnoie en leur ville et que sy le maistre siegeroit travailler ilz len empescheroient fort bien."

29. AN, Z^{1B} 389, piece dated 8 January 1598 (petition by Guillaume Pasnages, master of the mint of Rennes): "fut chasse sy promptement de ladicte ville de st malo quil neust le moien den retirer ses pappiers."

no longer controlled. He (theoretically) returned the official mint at Montpellier to the standards specified in royal legislation, accepted a royal edict crying down the debased pinatelles entirely, and, most dramatically, accepted the oversight of a royal envoy: Nicolas Coquerel, the only member of the Monnaies who had defied the League in 1589 and by now Henri IV's principal troubleshooter in the field. He arrived in Montpellier on 4 July 1593 and quickly set about reasserting royal sovereignty. He put the farm of the Montpellier mint out to bid according to the forms, though without success, since any recoinage was bound to be expensive rather than profitable. He continued to sign off on dubious transactions designed to fund the royalist armies, but at least he put them under the king's aegis (and they mostly benefited the duc d'Epernon, not Montmorency). His activities were not free from conflict: most important, Montmorency-Damville and the Estates of Bas-Languedoc were attached to a plan to reopen the mint at Béziers, but Coquerel was able to put a stop to it, primarily by threatening to make life miserable for any mint workers who went to work there. Ultimately, neither Montmorency nor the Estates nor the Parlement sitting at Béziers (royalist counterpart to the League court at Toulouse) had the stomach to overrule him. On 27 August, he remonstrated to the Estates "that it was not the place of Monsieur the Constable [Montmorency] or of the Parlement nor of the Estates to establish mints, but that of the king alone." Even when, "notwithstanding all these remonstrances, we were commanded by the First President of the Court to proceed with opening the mint of Beziers, . . . the president having offered to indemnify us with respect to the king, and to sign the discharge even with his blood," Coquerel persisted in his refusal, and in the end he had his way.[30]

Magnate warlords were at least able to negotiate more favorable terms for abandoning their debased currency than "recoin it at your own expense." The government of Lyons was completely overhauled and stripped of much of its authority immediately after the wars ended; by contrast, not only did Henri IV confirm all the actions of Mayenne's government (which had, after all, pretensions to legitimacy), but he gave Montmorency much the same deal, confirming in particular (and over the Cour des Monnaies' objections) his oversight of the mints he had seized or created. The man who had run the Toulouse mint for most of the Montmorency regime was rehabilitated to the point of being

---

30. AN, Z[1B] 383, piece dated 22 March 1593 (procès-verbal of Nicolas Coquerel), fol. 24v: "que ce n'estoit a monsieur le connestable comme au parlement ny aux estatz establir monnoyes mais seullement au roy seul. . . . . Nonobstant toutes lesquelles remonstrances par le premier presidant de la Cour nous auroit este commandé de proceder a louverture de la monnoye de Beziers, . . . lequel ledit president nous offert nous indempniser envers le roy et signer nostre descharge voire de son sang."

allowed to take up the lease on it again. But even the warlords had limited ability to extract concessions from the king. The duc d'Epernon, Montmorency's neighbor and sometimes ally in Provence, saw similar letters patent stalled for years by the Cour des Monnaies, and his pet mint master wound up having letters of remission canceled and being pursued across the South of France by an avenging general of the moneys.[31] When Mercoeur finally surrendered Brittany, the Dinan mint had to have all its activities reviewed by the court.

Reconstruction

Regaining control of the currency was an important part of Henri IV's project of regaining control of France as a whole. For the most part, this took the tedious form of reestablishing control over the mints and accounting, if only symbolically, for their irregular operations during the troubles. Aside from its practical benefits, this had the advantage that, in conformance with the traditions of economic regulation, it could lay the blame for France's dire straits on "certain masters, officers, workers, and moneyers in [the mints] and others . . . desiring to enrich themselves from the ruin of the people by the weakness and devaluation of the moneys," rather than on the leaders, factions, and structural factors that had enabled their behavior.[32] One such act, suggestive of the continuing importance of coining as display, was an order to return to Paris, at the expense of the master of the Etuves, "a number of machines and presses for making silver jetons and other pieces for the king's service" that Navarre had set up in his strongholds at Compiègne and Châlons-sur-Marne to do the work traditionally assigned to the mechanized mint.[33] This machinery had apparently become something of a mark of sovereignty in its own right, and bringing it back to the Île de la Cité was part of normalizing Henri's exercise of that sovereignty. The damage done to the money of account was harder to repair than that done to the coinage; the flood of bad money had caused renewed inflation, while the continuing influx of American silver meant that the French bimetallic ratio was slipping ever further out of date. And once the pinatelles vanished, small change appeared to be scarcer than ever.

31. AN, Z[1B] 390, dossier dated 31 July 1599, piece no. 7 (letter from Jean Favier in Avignon to the court, 5 November 1599).

32. *Lettres patentes du roy, sur l'ouverture des monnoyes, jugement des boettes & reglement d'icelles* (Paris: Veufve Jean Dalier, & Nicolas Rosset, 1594), 3–4: "aucuns Maistres Officiers, ouvriers, & monnoyers d'icelles & autres, . . . desirans s'enrichir de la ruine du peuple, par un affoiblissement & empirance desdictes monnoyes."

33. AN, Z[1B] 386, piece dated 26 May 1595 (arrêt): "plusieurs engins et presses pour faire gettons dargent et aultres pieces pour le service du roy." In fact, though, the machines from Châlons were still there in 1603: see AN, Z[1B] 393, piece dated 17 July 1603 (arrêt).

In the medium term, Henri's response was entirely traditional. He had no stomach for an Estates General to deal with this and the other disorders facing the realm, but he summoned a more manageable Assembly of Notables to meet at Rouen in 1596–1597.[34] Its remit was the finances rather than the equally disastrous currency, but the Monnaies, apparently of its own accord, drew up a cahier on that subject as a pendant to the assembly. It was an unusually significant rhetorical exercise, the first major occasion on which the court could address the new king, whom most of its members had long opposed, on the subject of its expertise. The court managed to almost entirely avoid mentioning the civil wars (going so far as to strike out the word "troubles" in its draft and replace it with *remuements*—"disorders"). Blame was shifted from the mint workers, who were at least theoretically back under the Monnaies' supervision, to "the foreign bankers spread through all the best cities and commercial centers of France, merchants, native and otherwise, billoneurs, and certain financiers." More abstractly, the problem was not the system of 1577, which "if it were kept inviolably could justly be called the honor of all the others ever issued on the matter, and even perhaps of those that could ever be put forward in the future," but that very lack of observance. Bellièvre, by then chancellor, was then at the height of his influence, having been the moving spirit behind the relatively successful Assembly of Notables, and the Monnaies took care to speak his language.[35] Thus, "if the evil is great and palpable, it also brings with it the opportunity for even greater and more assured glory for those who will take up its correction, since the fact is that we live in a time when no one has due reverence for the laws anymore if they are not accompanied by punishment in case of contravention."[36]

---

34. The most detailed study of this event is J. Russell Major, "Bellièvre, Sully, and the Assembly of Notables of 1596," *Transactions of the American Philosophical Society*, n.s., 64, pt. 2 (1974): 3–34. The assembly concluded on 26 January 1596; the Monnaies prepared its recommendations three days later, presumably on receiving confirmation of that conclusion.

35. One suggestive example of good relations between the chancellor and the Monnaies: in 1596 he agreed not to seal royal letters assigning some funds from the mints until their remonstrances had been heard. See AN, Z[1B] 387, piece dated 18 October 1596 (letter of Jacques Parfait to the court of that date, Rouen, orig.).

36. AN, Z[1B] 388, piece dated 29 January 1597 (remonstrances), fol. 2r: "les bancquiers des nations estrangeres espanduz par toutes les meillieures villes et places plus propres pour le commerce de la france marchandz tant regnicolles qu'autres billoneurs et quelques financiers." Fol. 1v: "si elle estoit inviolablement gardee se peult a juste tiltre appeler l'honneur de toutes las autres qui soient sur ce auparavant intervenues ny que possible lon puisse oncques mectre sus a l'advenir." "Que sy [le] mal est grand et palpable aussy apportera il une occasion de gloire plus grande et asseurée a ceux qui apporteront la main a la correction d'iceluy puisque tant est que nous vivons en ung siecle auquel lon ne porte plus la reverence deu aux loix si elles ne sont accompaignees de chastiment en cas de contravention."

Substantively, however, the Monnaies had almost nothing to offer. Aside from a mercantilist aside suggesting higher import duties on luxury manufactured goods (also very much of the moment politically), it recommended only a series of impractical measures aimed at stopping the export of precious metals and reducing the circulation of foreign coin.[37] There is some reason to believe that this program, limited as it was, gained a certain amount of traction. The records of the Monnaies show a noticeable increase in the number and scope of investigations for trafficking specie at the turn of the century.[38] And the royal council demonstrated a greater tendency to intervene in jurisdictional questions surrounding the moneys, often to the Cour des Monnaies' benefit.[39] This did nothing, however, for the course of the écu, which remained around sixty-five sols on the market.[40] More concrete action came slowly. There seems to have been a general consultation in Paris in mid-1600 and a report to the royal council, but the Monnaies' fear that "because of the multitude of affairs the council is usually burdened with (especially given the recently concluded war with Savoy) it may remain entirely ignored" proved to be well founded.[41] An ordinance of May 1601, which did almost nothing but confirm the 1577 edict in terms that echoed the Monnaies' rhetoric,

---

37. The court had made similar mercantilist arguments at slightly greater length on 18 November 1595 in a set of "Remonstrances . . . sur le triage refonte & transport qui se faict impugnement a la veue d'ung chacun Contre les eeditz & ordonnances de toutes especes & matieres dor & dargent hors la france qui sera en brief du tout espuizee sil ny est remedye." AN, Z^{1B} 73, fols. 216v–217v.

38. See, e.g., AN, Z^{1B} 388, piece dated 15 February 1597 (commission of Fauchet and Montperlier to investigate transport on their mission in the Midi); AN, Z^{1B} 499, piece dated 19 November 1600 (procès-verbal of the customs of la Rochelle); AN, Z^{1B} 498, piece dated 14 August 1601 (denunciation of Martin Noue and Hendrick Stirman, horse merchants); ibid., piece dated 25 September 1601 (commission of Thomas Villars to investigate transport of specie in the Lyonnais—he did bring a few cases based on that commission); ibid., piece dated 15 March 1602 (letter of Germain de la Tourette, subsidiary general of Dauphiné, to the court, orig., complaining of failures in prosecuting transport). None of this was remotely on a scale that would have had a measurable macroeconomic impact.

39. See, e.g., AN, Z^{1B} 74, fols. 84r–85r (arrêt of the Conseil privé, 2 October 1598, quashing a decision of the parlement of Rouen); ibid., fol. 264 ("Arrest du conseil destat contre les arrests donnez aux parlemens de Tholoze bordeaulx & grenoble sur le cours des especes," 10 July 1600); ibid., fol. 271 (arrêt of the Conseil d'état, 25 August 1601, quashing an attempt by the parlement of Rouen to interfere with a general of the moneys policing a local fair).

40. A 1602 letter to the court from the clerk Godefroy in Rouen gives a figure of sixty-five sols per écu, exactly the value at which the king would set it later that year. AN Z^{1B} 392, piece dated 13 April 1602.

41. AN, Z^{1B} 391, piece dated 12 August 1600 (arrêt): "pour la multitude daffaires dont est charge dordinaire ledict conseil ~~(attendu mesme la guerre de Savoye resolue depuis peu)~~ quil ne demeurera de tout delaisse." (Strikethrough in original.) At this point the Monnaies was still primarily concerned with securing obedience to its jurisdiction: see the letters sent with Biseul, AN, Z^{1B} 74, fols. 179r–180r (30 August 1600).

began with a royal admission that "we have tried all means to remove the confusion that the license of civil war had introduced into every aspect of the governance of our kingdom, and in most we see some progress on the road to the reestablishment of the necessary and requisite order—except in the matter of our moneys, the disturbance in which continues and even grows from day to day."[42]

Finally, a year later, a much more comprehensive edict raised the écu to sixty-five sols, returned the livre as the money of account, legalized the circulation of a number of foreign coins, and generally restored the pre-1577 dispensation. The preamble to the new edict took perhaps malicious care in detailing the ways that the king had vigorously tried all the Cour des Monnaies' suggestions, only to have "recognized by experience that all these means were made useless both by the universal disposition of the minds of the peoples of our kingdom and by the confusion to which our neighbors had reduced their coinages."[43] Maybe because other methods had patently failed to work, though, the new edict excited surprisingly little opposition from either the courts or the people. The Parlement of Paris objected briefly, and at the instance of a group of merchants, the city council of Paris requested to the king "to please not allow the reflation of the moneys, which could bring no commodity or utility to your majesty, but rather will cause loss, ruin, and damage to your subjects." He replied, leavening his customary political skill with substantial economic sophistication, that an overvalued currency actually hurt trade and "that the best means to keep foreigners from having France's gold and silver was to price it very high, so that there was no gain to be had on it."[44]

42. *Ordonnance du Roy sur le faict & reglement de ses Monnoyes* (Paris: Vefve Nicolas Rosset, 1601), 3–4: "Nous avons tasché par tous moyens d'oster la confusion que la licence des guerres civiles avoit introduite en toutes sortes de polices en cestuy nostre Royaume, & en la plus part nous voyons quelque progrez & acheminement au restablissement de l'ordre requis & necessaire, sinon au fait de nos Monnoyes. Le desreglement desquelles continue, voire augemente de jour à autre." The edict did confirm the legality of Florentine ducats, which had had course in France since Henri's marriage to Marie de Médicis—another reminder, if one is needed, of the close association of coinage and the sovereign person.

43. *Edict du roy sur le faict et Reglement general de ses Monnoyes. Contenant l'augmentation du cours des especes & interdiction d'aucunes estrangeres* (Paris: Veufve Nicolas Rosset, 1602), 6: "recogneu par experience que tous ces moyens estoient rendus inutiles, tant pour la disposition universelle des esprits des peuples de nostredit Royaume, que par la confusion en quoy noz voysins ont reduit leurs Monnoyes."

44. Guérin et al., *Registres*, 13:18 (transcribing AN, H 1793, fol. 19v): "de ne voulloir permettre le rehaulsement des monnoyes, qui ne peult apporter aulcune commodité et utilité à Vostredicte Majesté, ains causer toute perte, ruyne et dommaige à vos subjectz"; "que les vrais moyens d'empescher que l'estranger n'eust l'or et l'argent de France estoit de le tenir fort hault, affin qu'il n'y peust rien gaigner." On the Parlement's resistance, which was promptly vanquished by the king's personal intervention, see the note at the same page, quoting AN, X[1B] 800, piece dated 16 September 1602 (minutes of the conseil of the Parlement of Paris).

Such arguments must have come from his Protestant economic advisers—Laffémas, Turquet de Mayerne, Behringen, and of course Sully.[45] The last had by this time effectively taken charge of monetary policy in the council, and his influence is everywhere visible in the 1602 edict. He had been calling for a devaluation since 1596; he appears in the records of the Monnaies as the chief authority on monetary affairs at least from 1600; and in the subtle and polite damnation of rivals that we have seen in the preamble, one recognizes the man who would bring this to a fine art as the inventor of the political memoir.[46] Sully in turn was able to take advantage not only of those economic specialists but also of an increasingly broad array of experts and pamphleteers; indeed, he almost certainly played an important role in encouraging their proliferation. This made him far less reliant than he would otherwise have been on the Cour des Monnaies or any other institutional source of monetary expertise, an independence that was furthered by his personal qualities. He had come up through the military as an expert on logistics, fortifications, and ballistics (as Henri's minister he took as his main office grand master of the artillery and lived in the Paris Arsenal), and he had a well-justified pride in his ability to master highly technical and quantitative issues. He had no hesitation in turning this skill to the currency—remember, too, that he had family connections to the Monnaies on his mother's side. One of the most fascinating documents in the archives concerning monetary affairs is the "Forme de dresser un pied de monnaie," that is, an explanation of how to calculate the composition and value of the different coins given a mint price and bimetallic ratio, addressed to Sully by Henri Poullain. It is followed by six sheets of calculations in Sully's own hand working out both the composition of foreign currencies and the implications of possible reforms of the French currency according to Poullain's system.[47] This represented a fundamental reconfiguration of the traditional system of expertise and consultation.

What made this so important was that between 1600 and 1605 Sully rose to a definitive position of power in Henri's government; after defeating Bellièvre

---

45. Specifically, they are broadly similar to those advanced in an anonymous memoir preserved in Sully's papers, AN, 120 AP 37, fol. 138.

46. On his 1596 call for devaluation, see Major, "Bellièvre, Sully," 16, citing BN, ms. fr. 18510, fol. 105.

47. See AN, 120 AP 37, fols. 126–133. The memoir is undated but seems to be from 1601 or 1602, since its opening sentence, "Il semble que le faict des Monnoyes, qui estoit comme negligé durant vostre absence de cette ville, se reanime maintenant par vostre presence en icelle," would apply most naturally to the period following the war in Savoy.

in a series of conflicts that culminated with the dispute over the so-called *pau-
lette* tax on venal royal offices in 1605, he was effectively the first prime minister of France.[48] Politically, the Monnaies had backed the wrong horse. And
that was the key background to the final drama in the monetary policy of our
period, the ultimately abortive edict of 1609. What is most interesting about it
is its politics, for it seems that it was here that the sovereign courts determined
to take their stand against Sully and his policies, reviving the struggle in which
Bellièvre had been defeated.[49] It also attracted the interest of the aging but very
well-connected memoirist Pierre de l'Estoile, who leaves us exceptionally well
informed on the details of how the Parisian robe reacted to this particular incident. It is also indicative of the suddenly central place that monetary policy had
taken in French politics. L'Estoile had been as concerned as everyone else by
the crisis of 1577, and he noted in passing events such as the Parlement's opposition to the 1602 edict, "verified rather unwillingly . . . having been strongly
urged and importuned by his majesty," but before 1609 currency policy had
not otherwise been of pressing concern to him.[50] Now it was.

L'Estoile certainly had no doubt that the edict was Sully's personal project,
"the publication of which he greatly promoted and desired." His report of
the minister's reaction to its initial rejection by the Parlement is interesting:
he "said that 'they're masters of arts, and understand not a single thing about
the matter!'"[51] Sully's confidence in his own expertise shines through, but he
was also (no doubt deliberately) ignoring the fact that this rejection was very
publicly a joint effort of the Parlement and the Cour des Monnaies, which
were typically competitive if not actively hostile to each other.[52] The Monnaies carefully preserved a copy of the register of the Parlement describing
how its deputies "had spoken with their heads covered and seated at the first

48. On those conflicts see Roland Mousnier, "Sully et le Conseil d'Etat et des finances: La lutte
entre Bellièvre et Sully," *Revue historique* 192 (1942): 68–85; Bernard Barbiche, "De l'Etat de justice à
l'Etat des finances: Le tournant de l'année 1605," in *Henri IV, le roi et la reconstruction du royaume: Actes
du colloque, Pau-Nérac, 14–17 septembre 1989* (Pau: Association Henri IV, 1990), 95–109; Raymond
F. Kierstead, *Pomponne de Bellièvre: A Study of the King's Men in the Age of Henry IV* (Evanston, IL.:
Northwestern University Press, 1968), 104–36; Major, "Bellièvre, Sully," 26–30; and Poncet, *Pomponne de Bellièvre,* 218–26.

49. On this context, see Vincent J. Pitts, *Henri IV of France: His Reign and Age* (Baltimore: Johns
Hopkins University Press, 2009), 260–61.

50. Pierre de l'Estoile, *Mémoires-journaux,* ed. Gustave Brunet et al., 12 vols. (Paris : A. Lemerre,
1881–96), 8:43: "verifié, comme à regret . . . en ayant esté fort pressée et importunée de Sa Majesté."

51. Ibid., 10:4: "duquel il pressoit et affectoit for la publication"; "dit que 'c'estoit des maistre-ès-
arts, et qu'ils n'y entendoient trestous rien!'"

52. They collected the records of their opposition carefully in one place in their registers: see
AN, Z[1B] 76, fols. 154v–178r.

bar beside the [nominally] clerical counselors," being treated ceremonially as full members of the Parlement.[53] L'Estoile reported the scene, noting the Protestantism of Bizeul, one of the Monnaies' representatives, which helped to underscore the notion that there was no religious or factional motive to the opposition to Sully. More generally, l'Estoile placed it in the context of accounts of civic virtue in opposition to the tyrannical ambitions of an evil adviser. He followed the rejection of the monetary edict with stories of a friend pointing out to him a passage in Dante in which Philip Augustus was condemned as a counterfeiter for weakening the coinage; of a Parisian judge, condemned for malversation at Sully's instance, who complained to the king that "the ones who told you this about me take, not *pots de vin* [modest bribes] but pots of gold"; and of the Marshal d'Ornano, governor of Guyenne, who was thanked by his master after delivering a damning report of the discontent that the government's exactions were arousing in his province.[54]

Next came a letter from a friend in the parlement of Rouen, divided between articulating opposition to the monetary edict and reporting that "we are told . . . that president Richardot is at court to assure the king that the archduke [of Austria] will not interfere in the Cleves affair," the nominal casus belli for the anti-Habsburg war that Sully was assumed to be promoting, "and that this has wrong-footed M. de Sully." Finally, he returned to his principal topic, with an unproductive meeting of the chancellor (Nicholas Brûlart de Sillery—Bellièvre had died two years before), Sully, and representatives of the Parlement. It failed, l'Estoile thought, because of

> M. de Sully's pride and hauteur not being able to accept deferring or abandoning anything to anybody, and the gravity and authority of a court not being able to endure being mastered and despised . . . by a *mignon* like Sully, . . . a very dangerous and consequential thing in a state, as Polybius noted . . . in these words: *there is nothing in princes' courts more dangerous to great and prominent men than calumniators of the good.* And (the court could now say) if his majesty had followed another

---

53. AN, Z[1B] 397, piece dated 5 September 1609 (extract from the registers of the Parlement): "ont parlé couvers et assis au premier barreau du costé des conseillers clercs." To give just one example of the continuing conflict between the courts, they had a dispute then pending in the royal council about jurisdiction over the goldsmiths of Paris, which was still not resolved at the end of the year. See AN, Z[1B] 76, fols. 126r–132v (arrêt of the Conseil d'état, 3 December 1609).

54. L'Estoile, *Mémoires-journaux* 10:5: "ceux qui vous ont rapporté cela de moy ne prennent pas des pots de vin, mais des pots d'or."

172 **MAKING MONEY IN SIXTEENTH-CENTURY FRANCE**

passage of Polybius . . . which follows that one, where he says: *the prudent prince will beware of great men, courtiers, and the ambitious, nor give them
much, or allow them to accumulate, even though they appear the king's friends,*
his affairs and his state would be in better shape than they are.

That lengthy passage could hardly make his interpretation clearer: in pushing the monetary edict, Sully was being a classic tyrannical favorite, promoting his own interests at the expense of the king's and the nation's—moved
by the standard combination of ambition and avarice, "which (as Sallust
says in his *Catilina*) teaches us to put everything up for sale, overthrowing
all fidelity and virtue, which are the instruments of good counsel"—and
pulling France into the cycle of political decay of which Polybius was the
great theorist.[55]

As the conflict went on, l'Estoile continued to react in the same vein
while noting, as was his custom, the pamphlet literature that appeared
around it. Some of that literature, particularly an odd burlesque pamphlet
entitled *Further Encounters of Maître Guillaume in the Other World*, had affini-
ties with l'Estoile's views, but otherwise it is hard to say how typical he
was of the opinions of the French elites.[56] In one sense, the point was
moot, since first preparations for war and then, more definitively, the king's
untimely death stalled the edict more effectively than its opponents ever
could have. In another sense, though, it serves as a reminder of several
important things. First, the Paris merchants were by no means alone in
their contention that the fait des monnaies was so vital to the state that any
intervention in it could touch on the most vital issues. Specifically, it shows
how the issues of the nature of sovereignty and high political theory that

55. Ibid.,10:7: "on nous dit . . . que le président Richardot est en Cour, pour asseurer le Roy que
l'Archiduc ne se meslera point de l'affaire de Clèves, et que cela a fait contremander M. de Sully."
Pages 8–9: "la superbe et hautesse de M. de Sully ne pouvant souffrir d'en rien céder ni quitter à
personne, et la gravité et auctorité d'une Cour ne pouvant endurer d'estre maistrisée et mesprisée . . .
d'un tel mignon que Sully; . . . chose très dangereuse et de conséquence en un Estat, comme l'a noté
Polybe . . . en ces mots: *Nihil in aula principum periculosius est magnatibus et proceribus regni quam sunt
calumniatores bonorum.* Que si Sa Majesté (peult dire la Cour aujourd'hui) eust prattiqué l'autre traict
qui est dans ledit Polybe . . . consécutif d'icelui, où il dit: *Princeps prudens sibi a quovis aulico, magnate,
ambitioso, caveat, neve illi multum tribuat, aut eum crescere sinat, quantumvis appareat regis amans,* les affaires
du Roy et de son Estat se porteroient mieux qu'elles ne font." Page 19: "laquelle (comme dit Saluste
en son *Catilina*) apprend à mettre toutes choses en vente, renversant toute fidélité et preud'hommie,
qui sont les instrumens d'un bon conseil."
56. *Suitte des rencontres de M. Guillaume en l'autre monde* (Paris: Pierre Ramier, 1609). If this was
in fact a sequel, the work it follows no longer survives.

we have examined in their more abstract dimensions were present in real political negotiations, at least to acute and impassioned observers. Finally it confirms that the moneys were one of the sites of contention in the creation of the new style of government traditionally labeled "Bourbon absolutism." Indeed, some years later, Richelieu's government would take up a project based closely on the 1609 edict and see it through against the opposition of the courts, instituting the basic monetary scheme that would endure to the Revolution.[57]

A Science of Maxims

The relatively deliberate policy activity of the post–civil war period was informed by theoretical reflections and public discourse that showed distinct signs of settling into a defined, if still contentious, body of expert knowledge. In 1586 the indefatigable Colas, pushing forward the ideal of a systematic science, had reduced monetary policy to "six maxims." The last conveys the flavor of the project well enough: that "the public faith resides in the coinage, and for this reason gold and silver coins should be related in alloy, weight, and price, so that one can [always] buy the other with no loss."[58] This project of codification was taken up again after the wars by a new generation of writers but one that was explicit in its debts to its predecessors from the 1560s and 1570s. According to Henri Poulain, the most subtle and intelligent of the group, one author "found . . . a part of this proposition and excised the other from certain recent authors, like Colas, Malestroict, and Garrault." Bodin's work, moreover, "has served and still serves today as a charm to ground all those who wish to become wise in the matter of moneys: and has given birth in their infancy, adolescence and maturity not only to our Advice-givers [today] . . . but also to almost all those who have written on the matter of moneys since the printing of the

---

57. See Erik M. Thomson, "Chancellor Oxenstierna, Cardinal Richelieu, and Commerce: The Problems and Possibilities of Governance in Early-Seventeenth-Century France and Sweden (PhD diss., Johns Hopkins University, 2004), 681–767.

58. BN, fr. 18503, fol. 50r: "Quen la monnoye gist la foy publicque, & pour ce les monnoyes dor & dargent se doivent raporter en loy, poix, & prix, afin que l'une soyt acheptee par laultre, sans aucun perte." This is followed by a calculation of the bimetallic ratio in every royal ordinance since 1540. Later in the same manuscript is "Memoire faict par le commandement du roy a la cause qui faict encherir lor et largent par dessus son ordinance, et du moien dempescher ledict encherissment" (fols. 103–4), which shares some text with the maxims and is doubtlessly also by Colas. It blames foreign merchants for selling specie at 35 percent above the legal price, thus destroying the entire monetary system.

above-mentioned *Response*."[59] More crudely and spectacularly, another pamphlet from 1609 took the form of a dialogue of the dead between the folkloric "maistre Guillaume" and Thomas Turquam, "a general whom I knew in the other world, who was the honor of his time in monetary affairs."[60] A 1612 work on the Paris sovereign courts directed those less technically inclined to

> infinite fine and curious research to which several learned persons of
> our day have given much time and effort; among others those learned
> men Budé and du Moulin, Bodin in his discourse on the paradoxes of
> a maître des comptes and in book six of his *Republic*, chapter 3, Hotman, . . . the *avocat* Grimaudet, . . . the sieur du Choul, . . . by reading
> whom the curious mind will be contented with all it might desire in
> the knowledge and understanding of moneys.[61]

Clearly, the French tradition of monetary thought had by this time developed its own canon and continuity.

There was general agreement that the fait de la monnaie was complex and difficult, requiring expert and intelligent explanation and a clearly reasoned, well-grounded theoretical apparatus. Once more, only the discovery and application of "true propositions, made clear and discussed by the force and rules of reason," which would thus supplement human with natural law,

---

59. [Henri Poulain], *Refutation de l'erreur cy devant publié en un livret imprimé, Que le Traite proposee par l'autheur d'iceluy n'excede se qui se souloit lever, & se leve de present* (n.p., 1609), 14 (responding to Nicolas de Coquerel; the attribution to Poulain is mine, based on thematic and stylistic considerations): "Ayant trouvé ledit autheur une partie de ceste proposition, & tronqué l'autre partie de quelques autheurs recens, comme Colas, Malestroit, & Garrault." Poulain, *Traictés des monnoyes, pour un Conseiller d'Estat* (Paris, 1621), 81–82 (responding to Denys Godefroy): "a servy, & sert encores à present de charme, pour enraciner tous ceux qui sans maistre se veulent rendre sçavans au faict des monnoyes: & a engendré en son enfance, adolescence & aage de maturité, non seulement nos donneurs d'Advis qui ont paru en l'année six cens neuf; mais aussi presque tous ceux qui ont escrit du faict des monnoyes, depuis l'impression de la susdite Response" (the "conseiller d'état" in question was Sully). No work by Colas had ever been printed, so there must have been a strong manuscript tradition among students of monetary affairs. A copy of Colas's treatise by the erudite jurist Pierre Pithou seems to have survived: see L. de Rosanbo, "Pierre Pithou érudit," *Revue du XVIe siècle* 16 (1929): 311–12.

60. *Suitte des rencontres*, 9–10: "un general que j'avois cogneu en l'autre monde, qui estoit l'honneur de son temps, au faict des Monnoyes."

61. Pierre de Miraulmont, *Les memoires de Pierre de Miraulmont . . . Sur l'origine & institution des Cours souveraines, & Justices Royalles estans dans l'enclos du Palais Royal de Paris* (Paris: Claude de la Tour, 1612), 647: "infinies belles, & curieuses recerches [*sic*], à quoy plusieurs doctes personnages de nostre temps ont donné bonne partie de leur temps & labeur; entr'autres ces doctes Budé, & du Molin, Bodin en son discours aux paradoxes d'un Maistre des Comptes, & au livre sixiesme de sa Republique, cap. 3. Hotman . . . Grimaudet Avocat, . . . le sieur du Choul, . . . par la lecture desquels, l'esprit curieux recevra contentement, ce de qu'il pourroit desirer de la science & cognoissance des monoies."

could solve these problems.[62] The meaning of such phrases, however, seemed to shift somewhat from the pre-1577 era. Appeals to a generalized concept of the power of number in creation, scriptural exegesis, and love of "paradoxes" not apparent to the vulgar that had characterized monetary thought in the era of Malestroict, Colas, Bodin, Garrault (and even, in a cameo appearance, the mystic Guillaume Postel) were replaced by still arcane but slightly less hermetic sources of authority.[63]

Particularly after 1600, the notion that monetary knowledge could be reduced to method and maxims or axioms gained in popularity. There are numerous examples of this tendency in the early seventeenth-century literature. One pamphleteer rather backhandedly complimented his opponent for "the good order which he follows, and the method which he observes in the deduction of all the points of which he treats" and for the fact that he "remains in accord precisely with most of the good, true, and necessary maxims of the *fait des monnoyes*."[64] Another said that the "science of moneys, as difficult as it may be, is, when treated in order and without confusion, in itself certain and true, and like every other science has its solid and immutable principles, which are entirely distinct and different from erroneous and merely seeming principles, which are simple and easy to destroy and refute." [65] More

---

62. Le Begue, *Traicté*, 5: "propositions veritables, esclaircies & discutées par la force & regles de la raison"; "lequel n'a peu toutesfois avoir effet jusques icy, faute paravanture de n'estre ce subject assez esclaircy à ceux qu'il se pouvoit."

63. In addition to the works discussed above, one should note two further works by Garrault. The first was *Les recherches des monnoyes, poix et maniere de nombrer, des premieres & plus renommees nations du monde . . . livres trois* (Paris: Martin le Jeune, 1576). This work combined Colas's emphasis on number and scripture with erudite history in the school of Budé and Bodin and a claim of personal, experiential expertise. It also featured a liminal poem by Postel, defending the duodecimal ratio on numerological grounds. The title was clearly meant to echo that of Etienne Pasquier's then-recent historical work, the *Recherches de la France*. The second, a *Paradoxe sur le faict des monnoyes* (Paris: Jacques du Puys, 1578) was an emulation of Malestroict.

64. Nicolas Roland du Plessis, *Advertissement pour servir de response au discours nagueres publié sur le faict des Monnoyes* (Paris: Nicolas Buon, 1609), 7: "le bon ordre qu'il suit, & la methode qu'il observe, en la deduction de tous les points desquels il traict . . . . Ledit autheur par son discours demeure d'accord precisement, de la pluspart des bonnes, veritables, & necessaires maximes du fait des monnoyes." The unnamed opponent was Loys de Chabans, with whom du Plessis engaged in an extended controversy.

65. Poulain, *Refutation*, 4: " la science des Monnoyes difficile qu'elle soit, estant traitee par ordre & sans confusion est en soy certaine & veritable, & a comme toute autre science, ses principes solides & immuables entierement distincts & differens des propositions simplement apparentes & erronnees, faciles de destruire & refuter." Compare the anonymous "Maximes sur le faict des monnoyes," in BN, ms. fr. 18503, fols. 173–76, which begins, "Il est tout certain, que toutte science ou art, soit liberal ou mecanique, doit avoir ses fondements, et maximes, certaines, fermes, et resolues que lon appelle en latin, *Principia*, sur lesquelles, tout ce qui se faict, dict, et propose, concernant la science ou lart, doit estre fondé."

important, commentators presented a sophisticated understanding of money as an indispensable part of political knowledge. According to Poulain again, the "first maxim" of moneys was "that the faict de la monnoye is a matter of state, and that knowledge of them is necessary for him who has the conduct of the state and government of his prince."[66] Du Plessis held that "among the parts of political administration (after the matter of arms) that of moneys is the first."[67] Monetary thought had achieved the status of a discipline, with its own place in the universe of studies, canon, maxims, method, and set of problems; the possibility of an economic science had begun to appear on the horizon.

The subjects of disagreement in the first decades of the seventeenth century were correspondingly narrow. Everyone agreed that foreign coin should be banned as strictly as possible, and everyone agreed that foreign trade was the key to understanding France's monetary difficulties. Along with the role of iconography in the coinage, to which we shall return, controversy arose over familiar issues. Analysts disagreed over the bimetallic ratio, the relationship between nominal and specie value in different coins, and the name of the money of account and its relationship to actual circulating coins. Two schools of thought emerged. One operated generally outside the established structures of the royal council and the Cour des Monnaies. It insisted upon a strict and invariable bimetallic ratio and favored ambitious iconographic programs. This group would include Coquerel (who broke with the Monnaies in theory as in politics), Chabans, Rascas de Bagarris, Montchrestien, and to some extent the attorney general in the Monnaies, François le Begue (who nevertheless supported the court in the dispute of 1609). The other was much more official and pragmatic. Its members advocated more flexibility in the bimetallic ratio and, frequently, the retention of the livre as the money of account. In this group one may count Guillaume de Herail, Henri Poulain, Nicolas Roland du Plessis, and Guillaume le Clerc. Denys Godefroy and le Begue might be placed into a centrist group of their own, generally in favor of the écu but against strictness in the bimetallic ratio, and strongly supporting the court of

---

66. Poulain, "De la science & cognoissance que doibt avoir un Conseiller d'Estat, au faict des Monnoyes," in *Traictés*, 1: "Maxime premiere: Que le faict des Monnoyes, est un faict d'Estat: & le cognoissance d'icelles, necessaire à celuy qui a la conduitte de l'Estat & gouvernement de son Prince." The title alone is significant, and the counselor to whom this tract is addressed is (in a victory for the conventional wisdom) Sully, which dates it to before 1611. Nicolas Coquerel began his *Discours de la perte que les François reçoivent en la permission d'exposer les Monnoyes estrangeres* (Paris: François Jaquin, 1608), fols. 1–4, with a complete history of human society in order to demonstrate the centrality of money and monetary policy to the state.

67. Du Plessis, *Advertissement*, 81: "entre les parties de la police (apres le faict des armes) celle des monnoyes est la principalle." Coquerel had said much the same thing.

which they were members. The two groups clashed openly at hearings organized by the royal council in 1609 while preparing the new monetary edict.[68]

This indecisive debate continued to use not only the issues but also the conceptual framework of the previous century. While the ambition to make the
monetary system transparent to the common people by abolishing the "imaginary" livre and reforming the coinage continued, the idea that confusion and
misunderstanding caused monetary disorder developed broader resonances. Du
Plessis worried that a new coin to be named the Henrique d'or (after Henri IV)
would, in later reigns, mean that the people "would find themselves, from a single
coin, having several of different names and figures, which would make everyone
doubtful of their equal worth and value."[69] Coquerel believed that much the
same thing had precipitated the crisis of 1577 and that abolishing the livre again
would cause even greater confusion and distress in the public. Whether this was
true or not is impossible to say, but the fact that such varied factors were raised
in what had begun as a highly ideological and aprioristic debate shows that,
by the early seventeenth century, French monetary discourse had reached a
stage of maturity.

Coquerel was the champion of an exceptionally cautious and pragmatic
monetary policy, and his pragmatism and hard experience lent him a greater
insight than his peers into the character of the contemporary monetary
scene. He realized, for instance, that there could be no single "best" bimetallic
ratio but that the ratio had to be readjusted constantly to maintain a median
between the areas to the south of France, where silver was cheap, and those
to the north, where it was dear. This was probably as close as anyone at the
time came to a true understanding of the bimetallic problem, which (at least
according to the exhaustive researches of Frank Spooner) contemporaries
were right to see at the root of early modern monetary disturbances.[70] The

68. The text of the edict now survives only in a single manuscript copy, BN, ms. fr. 18503, fols.
177–80: "Projet d'Edict du Roy Henry le Grand l'an 1609 au mois d'Aoust touchant les monnoyes,"
published in Bernard Barbiche, "Une tentative de réforme monétaire à la fin du règne d'Henri IV:
L'édit d'août 1609," XVIIe siècle 61 (1963): 3–17.

69. Du Plessis, Advertissement, 75: "se trouveroit d'une mesme espece en avoir plusieurs de divers
noms & figures, ce qui rendroit un chacun douteux de leur egalle bonté & valeur." Though Louis
XIII did eventually begin coining a louis d'or, this particular issue never arose, as all subsequent
French kings bore the same name.

70. See Frank C. Spooner, L'Economie mondiale et les frappes monétaires en France, 1493–1680
(Paris: Armand Colin, 1956), 330: "A côté de la Péninsule, prête à réagir aux changements métal-
liques, la France, pays divers et complexe, aura joué le rôle d'un réservoir métallque opportun; on
pourrait dire d'une éponge capable d'équilibrer les nécessités et revendications de sa voisine trop
puissant, l'Espagne." The chronological limits of this book are almost exactly those of Spooner's
"silver phase" in French monetary history.

French monetary theorists' concern with royal authority in an international context at least pointed them in the right direction. It also allowed the theorists to develop devastating critiques of monetary projects that ignored or misrepresented the nature of royal sovereignty and international politics.

At the same time, though, monetary policy was being placed ever more firmly in the orbit of foreign policy—this development doubtless contributed to contemporary espousal of an active and protectionist trading policy.[71] While some disorders, according to François Le Begue, were the result of the recent civil wars, "this one which we see taking its course and growing under the peace,"—that is, the devaluation of the currency—"seems to be planned by the foreigner in order to destroy and weaken this State by cunning, since it could not be made to fail and succumb through violence."[72] According to Loys de Chabans, foreign coin "is a principle of sedition among the population, which, seeing a great deal of foreign coin, easily imagines that the princes who strike it must be much greater and more powerful than their own."[73] The implications of this ever-stronger nationalism were not necessarily paranoid or bellicose. Denys Godefroy claimed that "moneys have been compared to a boundary wall, to the construction of which neighbors should contribute equally."[74] The idea of an international concord on monetary affairs was not yet dead; this, after all, was the milieu that gave rise to Sully's famous (if poorly dated) "Grand Design" for an international confederation of collective security and religious coexistence.[75] Such philosophical reflections on the nature of the state and the state system, it turns out, had a deeper impact on the understanding of money than the long-standing links between coinage and the funding of foreign wars had ever had.

---

71. Antoine de Montchrestien in fact included the control of foreign coinage (and Bodin's pure-metal program) in his recipe for the economic defense of the realm. See *Traicté de l'œconomie politique*, ed. François Billacois (Geneva: Droz, 1999), 317–23.

72. Le Begue, *Traicté*, 19: "Les maux que nous venons de traicter sont restes & effects de noz troubles, mais celuy-cy que nous voyons prendre cours & s'accroistre par la paix semble estre excogité par l'estranger pour perdre & saper cest Estat par astuce, lequel n'a peu fair choir & succomber par la violence."

73. Loys de Chabans, *Raisons pour montrer que l'edit nouvellement faict sur les monnoyes est juste, est qu'il est au soulagement du peuple* (Paris: Chez la veufve Nicolas Rosset, 1609), 55: "c'est un principe de sedition parmy les peuples qui voyans beaucoup de monnoye étrangere s'imaginent aisement que les princes qui les font fabriquer doibvent estre beaucoup plus grands & puissants que le leur."

74. Denys Godefroy, *Advis presenté à la Royne pour reduire les Monnoies à leur juste prix & valeur, empescher le surhaussement & empirance d'icelles* (Paris: Pierre Chevalier, 1611), 17: "Pour ceste cause les monnoyes auroient esté comparees à un mur mitoyen; à la construction duquel les voisins doivent egallement contribuer."

75. See Maximilien de Béthune, duc de Sully, *Sages et royales œconomies d'estat*, ed. Michaud and Poujoulat, 2 vols. (Paris: Chez l'éditeur du commentaire analytique du code civil, 1837), 2:418–36.

Money and the Modern State

The claim of scientific expertise, the identification of monetary policy with royal legislative sovereignty, and the location of threats to that sovereignty in foreign coin and in the linguistic and mathematical valuation of the coinage were all major achievements. They contributed to the development of a political culture in which the practice of government was technical, economic, and autonomous with respect to external (particularly theological) conditions. Joyce Appleby has pointed out the importance, during the English monetary debates of the 1690s, of the way in which John Locke invoked "the dogma of natural, universal, inexorable laws working outside the purview and power of human legislators."[76] It was the French monetary theorists who made such a dogma available to European thinkers. On the other hand, currency values were never reliably stabilized. It was impossible to insulate France from foreign coin or the influence of international markets.[77] Major reforms in the form and valuation of the coinage had to be introduced slowly as technology developed. A systematic, quantified understanding of economic operations was still at least a century and a half away. The development of a sound historical numismatics had more negative than positive value: the duodecimal ratio on which Colas and Bodin leaned so heavily, for example, was proved to have been variable over time.[78] Historical scholarship shed light on the operation of monetary phenomena but did not by itself explain them.

And to a considerable degree, despite such progress and despite the rationalizing tendency already noted, the post-1577 monetary discourse remained trapped within the classical erudition and symbolic modes of analysis that its pioneers had favored. On the other hand, the international system of sovereign states; the quickly growing importance of commerce; the discovery of the New World (which, as Bodin at least recognized, had had an immediate and profound impact on Europe's monetary system); and of course a vast cultural gulf all separated the early modern from the classical world.

---

76. Joyce Appleby, "Locke, Liberalism and the Natural Law of Money," *Past and Present* 71 (1976): 55–56. The relationship between sixteenth-century French and seventeenth-century English monetary debate would be an interesting subject for examination in itself.

77. The work of Marie-Thérèse Boyer-Xambeu, Ghislain Deleplace, and Lucien Gillard, *Private Money and Public Currencies: The Sixteenth-Century Challenge*, trans. Azizeh Azodi (Armonk, NY: M.E. Sharpe, 1994), demonstrates that the international financial system of sixteenth-century Europe was far more complex than the French government and its advisers ever conceived.

78. This was done more or less immediately, by Garrault, *Recherches*, 16–18. See also Hotman, *De re numaria*, 348–55. Hotman concludes his discussion, "Auri ad argentum, cujusvis denique metalli aut aliud metallum, nullam esse proportionem, nisi quæ Regis aut Principum imperio arbitrioque varie pro temporum varietate constituitur" (p. 354).

To fully appreciate the nature, accomplishment, and historical place of the French monetary literature, we must investigate in greater depth the manner in which it came to grips with this difference. And indeed, if we take a very slightly broader view of the French Renaissance monetary discourse, we will see that it did give rise to a series of important reflections on the historical specificity of the contemporary world.[79] This broader view also opens up the question of the symbolic role of money in the Renaissance political imagination, a question that will concern us increasingly for the remainder of this book.

After his king's death and his disgrace, so his secretaries inform us, "Sully, piously preserving the memory of the monarch who had showered him with benefits, always wore on his breast a great gold medal stamped with the image of Henri IV."[80] The image of the king's face was a vital symbol of early modern princely authority and charisma, as it had been in imperial Rome, and its appearance on the coinage could not help but be significant.[81] The ubiquity and, in some sense, public character of money made it almost irresistible as a vehicle of propaganda and the royal mystique. The idea that the royal visage rendered the coin almost sacred dated back to the Roman Empire, as Cassiodorus implied. In another passage that early modern commentators were fond of quoting, Cassiodorus had the emperor say, "Truly, you ornament this, our liberality with another obedience, in that the figure of our features is imprinted in the customary metals, and you make money remind future ages concerning our times. Oh great invention of the wise! Oh praiseworthy institution of our forebears: that even the image of princes seems to feed their subjects through commerce, while their counsel does not cease to oversee the well-being of all!"[82] The royal portrait on a coin became, as Chabans said, "the true essential

---

79. The developing realization that modern European politics must be based on a commercial system radically different from that of its classical antique models has been the major theme of J. G. A. Pocock's work, most recently in *Barbarism and Religion*, vol. 1, *The Enlightenments of Edward Gibbon, 1737–1764* (Cambridge: Cambridge University Press, 1999).

80. Sully, *Sages et royales œconomies*, 2:417: "Sully, conservant religieusement la mémoire du monarque qui l'avoit comblé de bienfaits, portoit toujours sur sa poitrine une grande médaille d'or où étoit empreinte la figure de Henri IV."

81. The classic study of the royal image in French political discourse is Louis Marin, *Le portrait du roi* (Paris: Minuit, 1981), esp. 147–206.

82. Cassiodorus, *Variae* 6.7 ("Formula comitivæ sacrarum largitionum"): "Verum hanc liberalitatem nostram alio decoras obsequio, ut figura vultus nostri metallis usualibus inprimatur, monetamque facis de nostris temporibus futura sæcula commonere. O magna inventa prudentium! O laudabilia instituta majorum! Ut et imago principum subjectos videretur pascere per commercium, quorum consilia invigilare non desinunt pro salute cunctorum." This is quoted, for example, in Hotman, *De re numari*, 30, and Miraulmont, *Memoires*, 623–24. Godefroy had a characteristic take on this sentiment, making it an *international* matter. See also le Begue, *Traicté*, 119: "Un prince est estimé nourir son peuple, luy donnant facilité de faire & exercer le commerce avec les peuples voisins."

form of money, which is the public mark."[83] The very popular and influential
mid-sixteenth-century classicist Guillaume du Choul interpreted it as giving
coins a sacred power: "To guard from the sacrilegious hands of counterfeiters,
the emperors had their faces engraved on their coins, to arouse in them, when
they looked at it, a fear of falsifying it." On the one hand, the ubiquity and
durability of the coinage was the perfect expression of imperial or royal power.
On the other, this movement of princely authority into the public domain
involved a potential loss of control. If the money was defaced or devalued, so
was the prince himself or herself: "and that which fire, nor the injury of time,
nor the earth can do, is done by those who undertake to falsify it."[84]

The Roman-style portrait bust, which appears on the obverse of most
modern coins, fell out of use in the Middle Ages but was revived in fifteenth-
century Italy. When Charles VIII of France conquered the Duchy of Milan,
he adapted this tradition for the largest French silver coins, and Henri II
introduced the gold Henrique d'or bearing his portrait as part of the 1550
monetary reforms. With the failure of that coin, the écu (bearing the arms
of France on the obverse—hence its name) regained its position as the flagship coin and, of course, the unit of currency from 1577 to 1602, though
the silver teston continued in use. The process of integrating the royal image
into the coinage was clearly incomplete and remained so until the introduction of the *louis d'or* and associated coins in 1641. The Italian and French
Renaissances also saw a revival of the medal, another imperial Roman device
designed to commemorate individuals or events. Clearly, in both form and
function there was some overlap between medal and money. In the debate
over the 1609 edict, Loys de Chabans proposed "to change the marks and
inscriptions of the coins, and in their place to put, on one side, the true image
of the king with a cross and the French arms . . . and as for the reverse, to fill
it with the most important parts of the history of his Majesty, represented in
images, inscriptions, figures, and emblems in the manner of the ancients."[85]

---

83. Loys de Chabans, *Apologie de l'edict des monnoyes, ou refutation des Erreurs de Maistre Guillaume
et de ses adherents* (Paris: veuve Nicolas Rosset, 1610), 31: "la vray forme essentiel de la Monnoye qui
est la marque publique."

84. Guillaume du Choul, *Discours de la religion des anciens romains* (Lyons: Guillaume Rouille,
1556), 115–16: "Pour garder les mains sacrileges des faulx monnoyeurs, firent insculper leurs visaiges
les Empereurs par leurs monnoyes, pour leur donner, en le regardant, crainte de la falsifier . . . & ce
que le feu, ne l'injure du temps, ny la terre ne peuvent faire, font ceux qui se meslent de la falsifier."
The (unacknowledged) paraphrase of Cassiodorus glosses a coin of Diocletian with the inscription
"sacra moneta Aug. et Cæs. nostr."

85. Chabans, *Raisons*, 24: "De changer les Marques & inscriptions des Monnoyes, & au lieu
d'icelles mettre d'un costé l'image au vray du Roy, avecques la croix & l'escu de France selon le
modelle qu'il presenta, & pour le revers le remplir des princiapaux articles de l'histoire de sa Majesté,
representez par images, inscriptions, figure, & emblesmes à la façon des Antiques."

The real source of this proposal was probably not Chabans, though, but Pierre-Antoine de Rascas de Bagarris. Rascas, an ardent collector, was the keeper of Henri IV's cabinet of antiquities. From that position, he agitated for a reformation of the coinage according to his idea of ancient practice.

In 1608, Rascas proposed that the government introduce a series of large copper coins to circulate as currency, with the physical form of historical medals glorifying the French monarchy.[86] Though the idea sounds eccentric, it was neither outside the scholarly mainstream nor even particularly original. Rascas may have been influenced by Guillaume du Choul, who did not distinguish between coins and medals, but he was almost certainly directly inspired by the Italian scholar Enea Vico, whose contention that ancient medals were circulating coins had excited a scholarly debate in the mid-sixteenth century.[87] According to Rascas, the "glory" and the "memory" of princes—which he identified with their physical image and their historical actions—could be correctly preserved only if they were joined together, presented both in picture and in text, and widely and authoritatively published. Only monetized medals could fulfill these criteria. In them, countenance and action were joined as obverse and reverse; text and image were both present on each side; and, most important, the wide circulation and the legal imposition of public authority that characterized money would also perfect the historical monument.[88] Clearly, Cassiodorus directly influenced this project with his union

---

86. Pierre-Antoine de Rascas, sieur de Bagarris, *La nécessité de l'usage des medailles dans les monnoyes* (Paris: Jean Berjon, 1611). This was a slightly augmented version of *Discours qui montre la necessité de retablir le tres-ancien et auguste usage public des vrayes et parfaites medailles* (1608: sometimes erroneously dated 1602, probably because Rascas printed the date as "MDCIIX"), which I have not examined.

87. See du Choul, *Discours*; Enea Vico, *Discorsi . . . sopra le medaglie degli antichi. Divisi in due libri, ove si Dimonstrano notabili errori di Scrittori Antichi, e Moderni, intorno alle Historie Romane* (Paris: Maceo Ruette, 1619); and Sebastiano Erizzo, *Discorso . . . sopra le medaglie de gli antichi: con la particolar dichiaratione di esse medaglie : nellaquale oltre all'istoria de gli imperßdori romani, si contengono le imagini delle deità de i gentili, con le loro allegorie: & insieme vna varia & piena cognitione delle antichità* (Venice: Giovani Varisco et compagni, 1568). The major Francophone contribution to this debate was Antoine le Pois, *Discours sur les medailles & graveurs antiques, principallement romains* (Paris: Mamert Patisson, 1579), which took a nuanced and, as far as I know, essentially correct position on the matter. As we will see in chapter 6, Rascas was not the only early seventeenth-century French writer to take up this issue—but the copy of le Pois's work at Harvard University (call no. Typ 515.79.517) bears the ex libris of one of the titans of the French republic of letters of that period, Jacques-Auguste de Thou.

88. See, for instance, the (unpaginated) "advis au lecteur" of *La neccessité*: "la Vraye Raison de la Medaille . . . Consiste A Establir . . . Tant par Pourtraicture, que par Inscription, sur la Modelle des Antiques, . . . La Gloire, & la Memoire, Desquelles, comme le Public demeure Eternellement Oblige, De Recompenser toute Personne Illustre, & sur tout le Grand Prince: Ainsi, pour ceste effect, il ne les luy sçauroit, ny ailleurs, ny mieux Consacrer, Qu'en Representant ensemble, aux yeux de l'Univers, d'un Costé, l'image au vif d'iceluy, De laquelle Provient Sa Particuliere Memoire ; Et de l'autre, les Œuvres, Vertus, &, sur tout, Actions Heroiques du meme. D'où Principalement Procede sa Gloire. Afin de les Publier par tout, & de les Eternizer à la Posterite La plus Eloigniee: Soubs l'Authorite, la Foy, La Marque & le Tesmoignage Publiques; Et partant Irreprochables à jamais."

of portraiture, memory, posterity, and circulation. What was new, or at least post-classical, was the consistent stress on the legislative authority of the state in creating both money and history. All other historical monuments, and particularly books, might be questioned as to both their authority and their authenticity. They suffered "above all from their lack of certain faith and assured proof."[89] It is not an accident that the word "faith" (*foi, fides*) recurred here and in our epigraph, echoing the great French constitutional formula "one faith, one law, one king." The faith that the people put in their king and that was made both immediate and eternal by his coined image was produced by, and depended on, his legislative action and the faith it in turn inspired. Augustus (Rascas claimed) had first applied this insight to Roman medals "by having applied to them the public authority of their most sovereign magistrate, which was the Roman Senate: and that not lightly, but with a full knowledge of the case [*connoissance de cause*], ripe deliberation, and finally an *arrest* or rather an *ordonnance* of the said Senate, with its mark."[90] The antiquity of Rascas's exemplars should not distract us from the modernity of his vocabulary. After due judicial process, his Augustus obtained from the senate either an *arrêt* like those issued by the French sovereign courts or an *ordonnance* like those the king himself promulgated. The essential fact about coinage was that its circulating value incarnated this modern legislative power. The moneys themselves became the instrument whereby the state could be protected against the assaults not only of ignorance or of internal and external enemies but of time itself.

These ideas bring to mind what the Cour des Monnaies had said in its consultation on the edict of 1577. Chabans's and Rascas's projects were taken seriously at the time, and they had a real hold on contemporary imaginations. The abortive edict of 1609 went as far as to specify that "on one side of all gold and silver pieces . . . our effigy should be imprinted and our name engraved around it," proceeding beyond even Henri II's innovations.[91] Rascas's ideas were controversial, though, and prominent government advisers prepared two formal refutations of the plan. One of the first things critics noted about it was that since it involved a large issue of copper coinage (something

---

89. *La necessité*, 13: "surtout A manquer de foy certaine, & preuve assuree, touchant ladite verite du Sujet qu'ils contiennent." The word *foi* was multivalent: Rascas had just concluded a discussion on how the inalterability of medals would aid in settling "les Doutes, Contrarietez, ou Disputes (mesmement aux Controverses de Religion) des choses qui consistent en faict, ou en histoire" (p. 7).

90. Ibid., 14–15: "Et en dernier lieu de leur avoir encore applique l'Authorite Publique de leur plus Souverain Magistrat qui estoit le Senat Romain: & ce non legerement; ains avec plaine connoissance de cause; meure Deliberation; & en fin Arrest, ou bien Ordonnance dudit Senat; avec la marque d'iceluy."

91. BN, ms. fr. 18503, fol. 179r: "dung Costé de toutes pieces dor & dargent . . . nostre effigie soit imprinte & nostre nom engravé a lentour."

the Monnaies had long opposed), it was likely to be inflationary.[92] According to Henri Poulain, many examples of copper coinage could be found in French history. "But instead of going in search of them in such distant centuries," he suggested, "let us glance at the current disorder in the Spanish moneys" as a result of its infamous copper *vellón*.[93] With the same problem in mind, Poulain distinguished two types of commerce: "The first is that which is carried out abroad. . . . The other . . . is that which occurs within a State by the residents themselves . . . in which no transport of specie takes place, but one is rather obliged to take those [coins] which are legal tender, however good or bad they may be."[94] Any large supply of non–precious-metal currency in circulation would cause foreign merchants to move from the second to the first type of commerce. They would buy up and export gold and thus necessarily cause an increase in the nominal price of gold in the home country, with all the consequences only too familiar to the French authorities.

This, however, was only the beginning of Rascas's difficulties, as a striking reconsideration of his central argument in 1611 by the first president of the Monnaies, Guillaume du Clerc, made clear. Poulain had admitted that it was necessary to preserve princely glory but argued that there was "nothing more natural, for the French above all, than to perpetuate the memory of their princes by history."[95] Royal historiographers, among others, were already doing this very well, and a series of medals would produce only obscurity.[96] Le Clerc agreed, but he proceeded to attack the very notion that a state such as France could or should imitate classical commemorative practices.

---

92. The Monnaies saw a place for copper coins but thought they needed to be produced with great caution. For a colorful example of this argument, see AN, Z1^B 73, fols. 5v–7v: "Remonstrances faictes a la Court pour les reparations du pont au change pour quoy il convient faire fondre deux pieces dartillerie pour faire doubles" (1 February 1593).

93. Henri Poulain, "Advertissement sur le placet presenté au Roy, par Pierre Antoine de Rascas, sieur de Bagarras," in Poulain, *Traictés*, 56: "Mais sans les aller chercher en les siecles si esloignez, jettons l'oeil sur le desordre qui est à present aux monnoyes d'Espagne." In 1599, Philip III had begun issuing vellón with reckless abandon, leading to its massive devaluation. In 1608 the *cortes* of Castile forced him to cease this practice, but he and Phillip IV later resumed it, largely contributing to the collapse of Castilian finances during the Thirty Years' War. See Earl J. Hamilton, *American Treasure and the Price Revolution in Spain, 1501–1650* (Cambridge, MA: Harvard University Press, 1934), 75–103.

94. Poulain, *Traictés*, 41: "L'un et premier, est celuy qui se fait chez l'estranger. . . . L'autre sorte de traffic est celuy qui se fait dans l'Estat, par les regnicoles mesmes . . . pour lequel, il ne se fait aucun transport d'especes, ains l'on est obligé recevoir celles qui sont ordonées y avoir cours, pour bonnes ou mauvaises qu'elles soient."

95. Ibid., 57: "Y a-il rien de plus naturel, principalement aux François, que perpétuer la memoire de leurs Princes par histoire?" This was a contemporary commonplace.

96. On the royal historiographers of the period and their place in royalist ideology, see Orest Ranum, *Artisans of Glory: Writers and Historical Thought in Seventeenth-Century France* (Chapel Hill: University of North Carolina Press, 1980). A few of them come into our story: Jaques Gohory had held that position for a while as, later, would Charles Sorel.

As for the devices of the most memorable actions of our kings, which these people wish to have engraved on the copper half-sols, after the example of the Romans (to whom they wish to compare us): they will excuse me if I say that they do not understand how to make comparisons, which should be between not dissimilar things. For to compare a fly to an elephant is foolishness. . . . So to compare this small, weak, and narrow realm to the Roman Empire, which was strong, spacious, and of great extent . . . is most impertinent. The Romans, victorious and triumphant over all peoples could . . . have the marks of their victories engraved on their coins without any fear, and totally to the shame of their enemies. But our kings, who are Christians and have dealings with other great and powerful Christian princes with whom, after wars, it is necessary to be reconciled and to efface all memories of hostility on both sides—what will become of your moneys, on which you have engraved the defeats of such enemies, or other advantages and actions of the times? . . . Other spirits must see further than these people in considerations of state.[97]

While medals, presented and circulated purely in private, were suitable for the commemoration of conflict, coins emphatically were not.

It is extraordinary to find a high government official and a humanist—le Clerc scribbled a number of Latin notes on historical commemoration in ancient currency in the bottom margin of his draft of this memorandum—actively *rejecting* the identification of the French state with the Roman Empire. This move called attention to the way contemporary monetary policy not only existed in but was essentially determined by a social system incommensurable with the classical framework within which it was understood. Even the vestigial Roman Empire of Cassiodorus's day was a universal state.

---

97. Guillaume du Clerc, "Contre l'invention qui est donnee de faire des demys sols de cuivre et sur iceulx y faire graver les actions les plus memorables de nos roys," BN, ms. Dupuy 51, fols. 46–47: "Quant aux devises que ces gens icy entendent faire graver sur ces demysolz de cuivre des actions plus memorables de nos roys a lexemple des Romains auxquels ils nous veulent comparer quils mexcusent si je dis quils entendent mal a adjouster les comparaisons qui doibvent estre faictes de choses non dissemblables. Car de comparer une mousche a un elephant cest simplesse et riser [?] tout ensemble. Aussy de comparer ce royaume foible petit et estroit a lempire Romain qui estoit fort, spacieux et de longue estendue voire que mettoit sa pied rome sur les trois parties du monde cest trop impertinent. Les Romains victorieux et triomphans de tous les peuples pouvoient apres les deffaictes posez des Illyrians Macedoniens Parthes et autres quils avoient subjugez ou menez en triomphe faire graver sans aucune crainte les marques de leurs victoires en leurs monnoyes et par tout alliener au mespris de leurs ennemys. Mays noz Roys qui sont chrestiens et qui ont affair avec dautres chrestiens grans et puissans princes avec lesquels apres les guerres il est besoing de se reconcillier et effacer touttes memoires dhostilite de part et dautre Que deviendroient voz monnoies sur lesquelles vous auroit grave quelques deffaictes de tels ennemys ou autres advantages et actions [illeg.] du temps? . . . Il est besoing que dautres esprits penetrent plus avant que ces gens icy aux considerations de lestat." This manuscript was a working draft, and the readings are sometimes dubious.

Within a multinational system, though, reasons of state had to determine which aspects of royal power could and could not be publicly circulated. The economic constraints on copper currency and the political constraints on triumphalist coinage were in fact the same. Each overstepped the bounds of natural political authority; each violated the maxims of prudent statecraft by inviting incursions from across the border. Separately, money and medals might be able to preserve the authority of the prince even against the ravages of time, but when combined, they could confound memory and law so that the past continually disrupted the present.

The New Marvels

How widespread was the awareness that forces alien to the ancient world governed modern money? We can see its traces at least in the later sixteenth century, in the very question of New World metal that Bodin made classic to the history of economic thought. Unlike the technicalities of monetary policy, this was an issue with some degree of mass appeal. "Among all the books of spiritual and honest pleasure," said Jacques Gohory (whose ties to the Cour de Monnaies have already been noted), "I find none more recreative to contemplate than those that treat the history of the new lands, and the conquests of faraway and foreign countries." In a preface to his 1545 translation of a Spanish account of the conquest of Peru, Gohory argued that such histories could be read on two levels.

> Now if by chance this book . . . falls into the hands of the common man . . . there is no need to ask if he will find it pleasant and delectable given the matter that it treats, which one may call the most rich and precious that the earth bears: it is gold, that gold toward which everyone tends, everyone aims, for which, night and day, this miserable world lives in continual torment of body and soul. . . . Now, I can show it to whoever loves it, knowing that it is placed in common circulation, and there is lacking only the way to get it.[98]

---

98. *L'histoire de la terre neuve du Perú en l'Inde Occidentale, qui est la principale mine d'or du monde, naguères descouverte, & conquise, & nommée la nouvelle Castille, traduitte d'Italien en Francoys* (Paris: Vincent Sertenas, 1545), sig. A iiii v: "Or si d'avanture ce livre . . . tumbe es mains du commun . . . Il ne convient demander s'il se trouvera plaisant & delectable veu la matiere qu'il traitte qu'on peult reclamer la plus riche & plus prcieuse que la terre porte. C'est l'or, cest or auquel chacun tend, chacun vise, pour lequel nuyt & jour ce miserable monde vit en continuelle tourment de corps & d'ame. . . . Or qui l'ayme si le monstre sachant qu'il est exposé en commun, & n'y à [*sic*] que maniere de l'avoir." On Gohory's authorship of this translation, see W. H. Bowen, "L'Histoire de la Terre Neuve du Peru: A Translation by Jacques Gohory," *Isis* 28 (1938): 330–40.

As Gohory helpfully pointed out, however, merely reading about gold was unlikely to do much practical good. On the other hand,

> perfect spirits will contemplate what rude and savage human nature is, without laws or polity . . . and how much those who have settled in cities and towns ruled and governed by order and civil learning surpass them: such, as you will see here, are the Indians about whom this history is written. Still, they do not have their minds styled and fashioned by as many exercises and diverse customs as ours, but rather have a kind of middle position between men and beasts.

The ease of the European conquest shows this gap in development but at the same time raises some troubling questions. It shows how little our human nature, even our soul, profits us by itself, apart from the culture in which we live. It also tends to "reduce the heroic and superhuman marvels of Alexander the Great, Pompey, and other ancient emperors, who, using their arms against peoples who were not people but beasts, gained victories more brave and glorious than virtuous."[99] This at least suggested that the moderns significantly surpassed the ancients, but if Gohory saw any connection between that achievement and the pursuit of coin, he did not mention it.

Gohory, however, was not the only person at midcentury to juxtapose gold and money, the ancient and the modern, and the Old World and the New.[100] Guillaume Budé's difficult and unwieldy treatise on ancient coinage was translated and condensed numerous times over the course of the century. A man named Charles Fontaine published the most drastic summary in 1554, as half of a book entitled *The New and Ancient Marvels.*[101] The "new

---

99. Ibid., sig. A iii v: "les esperitz parfaitz contempleront que cest qu de l'humaine nature rude & sauvage sans loix ne police. . . . Et de combien la passent ceux qui sont reduitz es villes & bourgades regies & gouvernées par ordre & institution civile, telz que verrez estre icy les Indoys dont ceste histoire est escritte. Lesquelz toutesffois n'ont les esperitz stilez & faconnez en tant d'exercises & usages divers que les nostres: ains tiennent quasi une moyenne nature entre les hommes & les bestes." Sig. A iv r: "abbatre les merveilles heroiques & plus que humaines d'Alexandre le grand, de Pompée & des autres anciens empereurs, lesquelz employans leurs armes sur gens, non gens mais bestes, en rapporterent victoires plus glorieuses, & braves que vertueuses."

100. See J. H. Elliott, *The Old World and the New 1492–1650* (Cambridge: Cambridge University Press, 1970); and Anthony Grafton, *New Worlds, Ancient Texts: The Power of Tradition and the Shock of Discovery* (Cambridge, MA: Belknap Press, 1992).

101. Charles Fontaine, *Les nouvelles, & antiques merveilles. Plus, un traicté des douze Caesars, Premiers Empereurs de Romme, nouvellement traduit d'Italien en François. En fin y a une Ode pour Dieu gard à la ville de Paris, faite en Juin 1554* (Paris: Guillaume le Noir, 1554). A second edition (leaving out the Caesars and the ode) was published under the title *La description des terres trouvees de nostre temps. Avec le Sommaire de plusieurs belles antiquitez, contenant une partie de l'excellence & magnificence des richesses, triomphes, & largesses des anciens* (Lyons: Benoit Rigaud, 1559).

marvels" were Columbus's discovery of the Americas. In this rendering, Budé's painstaking scholarly detective work on the relative values of ancient and modern monetary units was reduced to a catalog of wildly expensive objects and events, mainly from Augustan Rome, encouraging the gold-loving reader to marvel at the power and glory of the ancients. The New World was starkly different. There the inhabitants "brought much gold to the ships, which gold they exchanged for a piece of earthenware or of glass; and for a pin, a whistle, or a mirror, they would give whatever weight of gold one asked."[102] Their gold was not money. Thus it failed to serve as the sign of a real, political, legislative power and, by the same token, failed to operate as a real measure of value. As Stephen Greenblatt has argued, Europeans could use this kind of contrast between Europe and America to justify their appropriation of the Americas.[103] On the other hand, it could serve as a starting point to explore the difficulty both of recapturing the world of the ancients and of maintaining national integrity in a world of international exchange.

In the short run, it did no such thing. In the second half of the sixteenth century, French readers interested in the New World were more likely to read André Thevet's accounts of their own colonial misadventures than translations of the Spanish conquistadors. Gohory's and Fontaine's potboilers would have remained culturally sterile, despite the former's pious hopes to the contrary, had they not, as it seems, happened to inspire a genius of an entirely different order. In his essay "On Coaches," written in the mid-1580s, Michel de Montaigne wove together the narratives, which Fontaine had placed side by side, of classical pomp and the conquest of the Indies. Near the beginning, he expressed a "fantasy" of his: "that it is a species of cowardice, and a sign of not understanding nearly well enough what they are, for monarchs to struggle to improve their appearance and reputation by excessive spending. This might be excusable in a foreign country; but among his own subjects, where he is all-powerful, he draws from his dignity the greatest honor he can possibly

---

102. Fontaine, *Nouvelles & antiques merveilles,* sig. A6 v: "Les habitans . . . incontinent accouru-rent à flote aux navires . . . & nageans apportoient force or aux navires, lequel or ilz changerent avec une piece de pot de terre ou de verre: & pour une aguilette, sonnette, ou miroir, bailloient tant pesant d'or que lon demandoit." One might reasonably ask how the natives, who did not value gold themselves and did not share a language with the explorers, divined that gold would be a welcome item of exchange.

103. Stephen Greenblatt, *Marvelous Possessions: The Wonder of the New World* (Chicago: University of Chicago Press, 1991).

have."[104] In other words, as the rest of the essay made clear, economic resources generally, and precious metals in particular, should obey different rules when deployed within or outside the jurisdiction of a prince. In Rome, where "it was no novelty for a simple citizen . . . to dispose of kingdoms,"[105] where total power had abolished the distinction between the domestic and the foreign, this was irrelevant. The same was true for the pre-Columbian emperors of Mexico and Peru, lords of all they surveyed. For them, as for the Romans but not for modern European monarchs, the display of treasure demonstrated magnificence and cultural fertility—Montezuma made this clearest, with gold models of the entire flora and fauna of his land—rather than moral degeneracy.[106] "Equity was shown by the ancients," said Guillaume du Choul in his numismatically based work on Roman religion, "with a scale and a cornucopia, and similarly the image of the holy and sacred goddess Money."[107] In this view, the marvels of Rome and the Indies alike, whether or not they take the form of coins, are in fact displays of power, magnificence, and justice: indeed, of virtue. The questions are, how is modernity different, why has it prevailed across time and space, and what are the moral implications of that triumph?

Montaigne's answer circles outward from its title ("On Coaches") through the related concepts of gold, power, travel, and circulation.[108] Modern money summed up all of these in a single historical force. When the Mexican and Peruvian empires encountered an expansionist and commercial Europe, the absence of money proved their undoing. In the New World, "the use of money was entirely unknown, and consequently their gold was all collected together, being used only for show and display, like furnishings passed down

---

104. Michel de Montaigne, *Les Essais*, ed. Pierre Villey (Paris: Presses universitaires de France, 1992), 902 (3.9): "L'Estrangeté de ces inventions me met en teste cett' autre fantaisie: que c'est une espece de pusillanimité aux monarques, et un tesmoignage de ne sentir point assez ce qu'ils sont, de travailler à se faire valloir et paroistre par despences excessives. Ce seroit chose excusable en pays estranger; mais, parmy ses subjects, où il peut tout, il tire de sa dignité le plus extreme degré d'honneur où il puisse arriver."

105. Ibid., 686 (from 2.24, "De la grandeur romaine"): "Il n'estoit pas nouveau à un simple citoyen Romain, comme estoit lors Cæsar, de disposer des Royaumes."

106. While most critics read this essay as stressing the similarities between the ancient and the new worlds, it is possible to discern a level of contrast between the two. See Dain Trafton, "Ancients and Indians in Montaigne's 'Des coches,'" *Symposium* 27 (1973): 76–90.

107. Du Choul, *Discours*, 114: "L'Equité fut paincte des Anciens . . . avecques des balances, & un cor d'abondance: & semblablement le simulacre de la Monnoye Deesse saincte & sacrée."

108. On Montaigne's obsession with the instability of the political realm, see Dan Engster, "The Montaignian Moment," *Journal of the History of Ideas* 59 (1998): 625–50; le Pois, *Discours*, fol. 18, discusses the pervasive image of chariots and other conveyances on Roman medals, which may have influenced Montaigne.

from father to son among their most powerful kings, who constantly emp-
tied their mines to create this great pile of vases and statues to decorate
their palaces and their temples, where our gold is entirely in circulation and
commerce." "Where the Spanish did not find the goods which they desired,
they neither stopped nor meddled." On the other hand, the static Inca and
Aztec accumulations of gold for political display—the precise opposite of the
European system of monetary circulation and international trade—excited
the uncontrollable avarice of the conquistadors. Alexander and his fellow
ancients conquered new worlds, it seems, out of virtue. The Spanish did so
for money, "for the traffic in pearls and pepper."[109] For Montaigne, this was
the root of the gap that Gohory had observed between the Old World and
the New in destructive power but also between the ancient and modern
worlds in virtue—though he inverted Gohory's valuations of the two.

The last king of Peru, Atahualpa, carried in a gold litter by subjects so virtuous that they would die to the last man before they let it fall—"who, in their
obstinate devotion (oh barbarous fidelity!), when their arms were cut off, still
lent their shoulders to that miserable burden," as Gohory put it—but finally
pulled down by a European on a Spanish horse, became an emblem of modernity.[110] The litter echoed the chariot of Marcus Antonius, "who was the first
to have himself drawn into Rome" in triumph "by lions";[111] it may remind
us of the golden triumphs that "the Romans victorious and triumphant over
all peoples . . . engraved on their coins without any fear." Time, however, had
overthrown them all, and any attempt to imitate them in the present could
lead only to confusion and disaster. The inaccessibility of the classical world
as a political and cultural model is a recurring theme in the *Essais*. In this
case, though, it clearly intersects with a broader stream of reflection on the

109. Montaigne, *Essais*, 913, 911, 910: "l'usage de la monnoye estoit entierement inconneu,
et que par consequent leur or se trouva tout assemblé, n'estant en autre service que de montre et
de parade, comme un meuble reservé de pere en fils par plusieurs puissants Roys, qui espuisoient
toujours leurs mines pour faire ce grand monceau de vases et statues à l'ornement de leurs palais et
de leurs temples, au lieu que nostre or est tout en emploite et en commerce." "où les Espagnols ne
trouverent les marchandises qu'ils cerchoient, ils ne feirent arrest ny entreprise"; "pour la negotiation
des perles et du poivre."

110. *L'histoire de la terre neuve*, sig. G i r: "lesquelz par une devotion obstinée (ô fidelité barbare)
ayans les bras couppez subrogerent encores les espaulles à ce miserable faiz." For a rather different
reading of "Des coches" as an attempt to articulate the specificity of the modern within history, see
Timothy Hampton, "The Subject of America: History and Alterity in Montaigne's 'Des coches,'" in
The Project of Prose in Early Modern Europe and the New World, ed. Elizabeth Fowler and Roland Greene
(Cambridge: Cambridge University Press, 1997), 80–103.

111. Montaigne, *Essais*, 901: "Marc Antoine fut le premier qui se fit mener à Romme; et une
garse mestriere quand et luy, par des lyons attelez à un coche."

relationship among political structures, statecraft, the symbolic and economic role of precious metals, and modernity. In short, while some commentators saw the revival of classical practices of sovereign display as a real possibility in the context of contemporary monetary circulation, another—and, it would appear, a more influential group—objected that the system of mutually hostile states carrying on large-scale trade made this impossible in the modern world.

All the literature we have considered was concerned above all with the question of how political authority might survive the challenge of economic encroachment from without. When Montaigne published the final version of his essay, the presence of Spanish troops and Spanish gold in France made this a desperately pressing issue, and Marshal Biron's 1601 conspiracy to betray French arms to the Spanish and the Savoyards, which left the French political class in shock for over a year, made clear that it would not go away any time soon. It was certainly still on people's minds toward the end of Henri IV's reign when Chabans warned that the circulation of foreign coin meant that French subjects would "receive much more easily the pensions and presents of neighboring princes, since they can pass their coins in the state where they are, and in this way they sell their wills and their souls to foreigners, to the great prejudice of the state." The struggles for commerce and colony of the emerging mercantilist age only underlined what was already known.[112] But it is hard to escape the impression that this also represented a form of projection, since experience had so clearly shown that the greatest dangers to the French currency came from internal strife and governmental weakness. True, internal weakness did genuinely open the way to foreign interference, which in turn could exacerbate internecine strife, but the rhetorical disconnect is real nonetheless.

What seems to have been happening, as one surveys how the theory and practice of commerce and currency developed over our period, is that this kind of protomercantilist discourse was a way of expressing the vital but extremely complex relationship between state power and the control of commerce and currency. These tasks exposed the most basic challenges to national institution building, in their technical difficulty and their exposure to interest and corruption. They opened up very starkly the balance that governments had to strike between coercion and cooperation when regulating economic behavior, while opening up new methods of conducting both. In the second half of the sixteenth century, the commercial and price revolutions made abstract,

---

112. Chabans, *Raisons*, 55: "puis il en reçoivent bien plus facilement les pentions & les presents des princes voisins, pouvans esposer leurs monnoies dans l'estat ou ils sont, & vendent par ce moyen leurs volontez & leurs ames aux étrangers au grand prejudice de l'estat."

external, and largely uncontrollable economic forces evident to all those who considered the matter carefully; these might be figured as "foreign" (and such a figuration might be largely correct), but few theorists stopped there, and almost all wrestled seriously with possible technical understandings of those forces. The currency might either promote or fall victim to the ambition and avarice of the great, and it was certainly no illusion to believe that that was a problem that needed to be understood and addressed in an international context. And of course the coinage was at once the most ubiquitous symbolic representation of state power and the most ubiquitous test of how well that power functioned for the benefit of the population at large.

Money, in other words, was the perfect indicator, at once a metaphor and a direct measurement, of social power and social control in the age of the emerging nation-state. As such, it was of constant concern to the governing elites and those who spoke to or for them, and it is at that level that we have so far examined it. But it is important to keep in mind that administrative and political matters were the direct concern of a small and sometimes even a tiny minority. As broad as their impact could be, except at moment of crisis (and sometimes even then), they existed very much in the background of everyday life. The actual circulating coinage, however, was part of the very fabric of that life, in its economic aspects, of course, but also in the way it was understood and imagined. It is notoriously difficult to discern the history of this kind of everyday life, despite a large literature devoted to such quotidian reality, both for lack of sources and because it can be conceptually very slippery.[113] We will attempt to approach it somewhat indirectly in two very different ways that should prove complementary. One way is through the imaginary ideals that appeared in literature, where the nature and impact of money, in Renaissance France as today, were important recurring themes. Another, to which we will now turn, is the pathologies of monetary circulation exemplified by those who violated the laws concerning the currency. In doing so, they indicated something about the boundaries of what money meant to the population at large; at the same time, if caught, they left extensive though involuntary traces in the archives.

---

113. It is sufficient to cite the classic of this genre, Phillipe Ariès and Georges Duby, eds., *Histoire de la vie privée*, 5 vols. (Paris: Editions du Seuil, 1985–87).

CHAPTER 5

Crimes against the Currency

> [Charles IX] wanted to know how to do everything, to
> the point of making écus, double ducats, testons, and
> other coins, some true and of good alloy, others falsified
> and tampered with. And he took pleasure in show-
> ing them off; so that one day I saw him showing one
> of them to the Cardinal de Lorraine. "See here," he
> said, "what I've made. This one is true, and the other is
> deceptive, but show it to whoever you please, try it by
> cupellation or by fire, and it will be found good." The
> cardinal did not know how to reply, except to say "By
> God, Sire, you can do as you please in this, for you carry
> your pardon with you; justice has nothing to do, or to
> reproach you with, as it would do with someone else."
>
> —Brantôme

The courtier and memoirist Pierre de Bourde-
ille, abbé de Brantôme, professed to admire King Charles IX and placed a
long tribute to him in his collection of the lives of great French captains.[1] The
passage quoted above seems to undermine that tribute, even more so when
read in its context. It comes immediately after a description of the young
king's eagerness for arms and his impressive performance—especially compared
with that of his younger brother, the future Henri III—at a tournament organized to celebrate his coronation. "Thenceforth, everyone judged that the king
appeared beautifully at arms." That should certainly have been a good thing,
recalling the mythical days of chivalry that still, despite Henri II's gory death

---

1. Pierre de Bourdeille de Brantôme, *Œuvres complètes*, ed. Ludovic Lalanne, 11 vols. (Paris:
Renouard, 1865–82), 5:278: "Il vouloit tout sçavoir et faire, jusqu'à faire l'escu, le double ducat, le
teston et autre monnoye, ores bonne et de bon alloy, ores falcifiée et sophistiquée, et prenoit plaisir à la
monstrer; voire qu'un jour je le vis qu'il en monstra à M. le cardinal de Lorraine: 'Voylà, disoit-il, M.
le cardinal, que j'ay faict: celle-là est bonne, celle-là ne vaut rien; mais monstrez-la à qui vous voudrez;
esprouvez-la à la couppelle ou au foeu, elle se trouvera bonne.' M. le cardinal ne luy sceut que respondre, sinon luy dire: 'Ah Dieu! sire, vous pouvez en cela faire ce qu'il vous plaira, car vous portez vostre
grâce avec vous; la justice n'y a rien à voir ny que vous reprendre, comm' elle fairoit sur un autre.'"

in a jousting accident, helped underpin the ideology of royal authority. But in Brantôme's narrative, Charles's martial, physical vigor then took a strange turn. The king made a hobby of blacksmithing, crafting not only cannons but even horseshoes, "with as much strength as the most robust farrier or smith working at the forge." From this honest if plebeian activity he moved on to counterfeiting and thence to a Faginesque scheme of presiding over a group of cutpurses and pickpockets, "highly skilled and so smooth you could gild them," whom he invited to ply their trade at his court for their profit (to the tune of "three thousand écus in purses and money, gems, pearls, and jewelry") and his amusement.[2]

It is hard to know exactly what to make of this collection of stories. They might even be true, at least in part: Charles IX showed some interest in technological development as a matter of policy, and some of his contemporaries, such as Duke Emmanuel Philibert of Savoy, engaged in hands-on experimentation in fields like alchemy.[3] To the extent that we accept this narrative, it reveals a distinctly casual attitude toward the currency that might partially explain Charles IX's notable lack of success in monetary policy. It would also make him by far the most highly placed counterfeiter of his day, if certainly not the most typical. But even if one is inclined to doubt Brantôme's reliability, the fact that he considered this story worth telling challenges us to imagine how it might have made social and political sense, which in turn sheds some light on the political and cultural position of counterfeiting in sixteenth-century France.

Specifically, Brantôme's narrative plays off of three important aspects of the relationship between counterfeiting and early modern culture. The first is the intimate connection between counterfeiting and state sovereignty. Counterfeiting highlights some of the more troubled and troubling elements of that nexus. It is hard to avoid hearing in Brantôme an echo of the last Valois kings' fall from grace, as through the civil wars they gradually lost not only much of their concrete authority but also much of their popular support and their sacred aura. A political theorist (which Brantôme emphatically was not) might have seen this narrative as an allegory, or simply an example, of the

---

2. Ibid., 278: "Du despuis, on jugea tousjours les armes belles entre les mains du roy"; "aussi fortement que les plus robustes mareschaux et forgerons qui fussent aux forges." Page 279: "desliez et fins à dorer"; "trois mill' escus, ou en bources et argent, ou en pierreries, perles et joyaux." On this passage, see Ludovic Lalanne, *Brantôme, sa vie et ses écrits* (Paris: Renouard, 1896), 189–97.

3. On Charles IX's technological policy, see Henry Heller, *Labour, Science, and Technology in France, 1500–1620* (Cambridge: Cambridge University Press, 1996), 97–118 (though many of his examples apply more to the reign of Henri II); on Emmanuel Philibert's alchemical experiments, which were reported by the usually reliable Venetian envoys, see PierPaolo Merlin, *Emanuele Filiberto* (Turin: SEI, 1995), 183. Brantôme himself claimed to have seen Emmanuel Philibert operating a forge: see *Œuvres*, 2:151. My thanks to Matthew Vester for his assistance on this point.

king's abandoning justice, the "fixed disposition to give to each his due."[4] We have already seen the strategic role that money as a technology played in justice and thus the role that the sovereign's protection of the integrity of the money played in his duty toward justice. When Charles undermined that integrity, merely for his own amusement, it was deeply ironic to reply that "justice has nothing . . . to reproach you with"; in fact, the king was on a slippery slope toward arbitrarily assigning other people's property to those who had no just claim on it and ultimately toward undermining the very foundations of the monarchy and losing control over his kingdom. Looked at from this angle, Brantôme's story confirms the centrality not just of monetary policy but of counterfeiting in particular to the basic integrity of royal sovereignty.

A second relationship, more explicit here, is the close association between counterfeiting and skill, at arms, at the forge, or at theft—counterfeiting involved the kind of ability that could arouse wonder and give its possessor both wealth and standing in society. In this respect, it was akin to alchemy, in a relationship to which we will have occasion to return. At the same time, as the brilliant but straight-laced cardinal de Lorraine's nonplussed reaction to Charles's display suggests, counterfeiting was considered thoroughly antisocial, a crime on whose repression royal justice and the broader society could easily agree. And as the way Brantôme placed a literal irruption of a gang of *picarós* immediately after the story of Charles's counterfeiting illustrates, the place of that crime in early modern society can fruitfully be understood through the lens of the picaresque, a genre that dealt explicitly with the intersection of skillful and antisocial behavior in the treacherous world of early modern class mobility.[5]

The most striking thing about the way Brantôme arranged his narrative is the slide it enacts from the heights of nobility to petty criminality—a descent, however, with complex layers of meaning. There is in fact a way of reading Brantôme that reflects positively on Charles IX—it is even ostensibly the reading the author intended. In his mastery of all arts, honest or otherwise, the king was not only displaying the almost superhuman force of his character (Ronsard, in his semiofficial eulogy for the king, spoke of "his strength like Mars, / His mind, a storehouse of all kinds of arts") but also his sovereignty over the class structure of French society.[6] Actions that would be derogating

---

4. Besides what has been discussed in previous chapters, see Jacques Krynen, *L'idéologie de la magistrature ancienne* (Paris: N.R.F./Gallimard, 2009), esp. 17–38.

5. Any attempt to interpret the narrative structures of early modern French criminal records depends heavily on Natalie Zemon Davis, *Fiction in the Archives: Pardon Tales and Their Tellers in Sixteenth-Century France* (Stanford: Stanford University Press, 1987).

6. Pierre de Ronsard, *Œuvres complètes*, ed. Gustave Cohen, 2 vols. (Paris: N.R.F./Gallimard, 1950), 2:475: "sa force de Mars, / Son esprit, magazin de toutes sortes d'arts."

or criminal for a mere noble, whose status depended ideologically on his force of arms, became virtuosity, if not actually virtue, in the king, and the public exhibition of his ability to bend law and social norms to his will reinforced his supreme position in the society. In doing this, the king conducted a microcosmic tour of French society as his contemporaries imagined it, governed as it was by military prowess, skill in the arts, royal favor, and, most problematically, money. Charles's promotion of the gang of cutpurses to the appearance and social standing of courtiers (they must have been dressed up for the occasion) echoes his creation of a notionally undetectable counterfeit coin. And at the end of the story he reified this still further, not only giving the thieves the noble trappings they had stolen but sending them to practice his own noble profession of arms under the direction of the "Captain la Chambre" who had stage-managed the whole affair.[7] And when the king confronted the cardinal de Lorraine and extorted a confession of his sovereignty over the moneys, he was confronting one of his most potentially overmighty subjects and reminding him that royal power, like money itself, potentially knew no bounds.

For in the end, counterfeiting, like money in general, was closely connected to other ways of manipulating social power. Protecting the coinage was at the core of the royal duty to provide justice, but at the same time manipulating the coinage, for good reasons or bad, remained an essential royal prerogative—one whose boundaries could be especially fuzzy in the context of civil war. At the same time counterfeiting, a highly skilled endeavor, functioned as a shadow version of the system whereby mechanical and intellectual skills could bring their possessors wealth and prestige. The world of counterfeiting paralleled many aspects of "legitimate" French society. It had its own family economy, its engagement in the process of upward and (especially) downward socioeconomic mobility, and, of course, in worked in intimate though antagonistic involvement with royal governance. The fight against counterfeiting was thus a fight for social regulation, while counterfeiters themselves sought, out of desperation or opportunism, to remake unsatisfactory social situations for themselves in a way that not only broke the king's laws but directly challenged his and the broader society's ability to set the basic rules of social relations and socioeconomic status. Brantôme's Charles IX, in a somewhat twisted way, actually captured the spirit of the laws protecting the coinage, for what they amounted to was the exercise of royal power to control, however partially, not just the economic but the social structure of France.

---

7. Brantôme, *Oeuvres* 5:280: "Le roy leur rendit tout le butin avec commandement et deffence . . . de ne faire plus ceste vie, . . . et qu'ils s'en prendroit au capitaine La Chambre, et qu'ilz l'allassent servir à la guerre."

Crimes and Enforcement

The range of crimes against the currency was considerable, extending well beyond straightforward counterfeiting. Anything that undermined the king's right to set the price and specie content of coins was illegal. Thus an entire class of crimes revolved around removing precious metal from legitimate coins, most often by clipping the edges: this was in fact almost certainly the most common type of "coining," as the English called such criminality. Someone with access to a large number of coins could exploit variations in their weight, "triaging" those that were slightly heavy and melting them down or exporting them. Knowingly passing false or clipped coins was obviously a crime; using coin that had been cried down or exporting French coin was in a different category, but such acts also fell under the Monnaies' jurisdiction. This was a diverse set of practices with an equally diverse set of practitioners, but one thing that all these prohibitions had in common was that they were difficult to enforce: wearing the "long robe" of a criminal magistrate on the Cour des Monnaies was not an easy job.

Triage was perhaps the most challenging crime to investigate. Sorting and weighing coins was usually done in private, and it was not in itself illegal. Furthermore, anyone with a large enough stack of coins to make the exercise worthwhile was either very rich or an important public treasurer, which notoriously came to much the same thing.[8] It seems likely that it was only the sheer scale of such operations that ever brought them to the authorities' attention, as in the case of a barrel stuffed with twenty-six sacks of triaged coins, probably destined for export, that the Monnaies intercepted in 1576.[9] It made much more sense, as contemporaries realized, to concentrate on minimizing the variability in the weight of the coinage and thus the incentive to triage it. Of course, the French authorities had no control over foreign mints, which could cause problems, as when the master of the mint of Toulouse was accused of having bought Spanish *reals* at above the official price and triaged them, recirculating the weak ones and converting the strong ones into French money.[10] At any rate, like the often related crimes of exporting French and circulating foreign coin, this was a secondary and often undetectable crime and does not seem to have placed much of a call on the Monnaies' law-enforcement (as opposed to policymaking) efforts.

---

8. That is, for example, the theme of Jacques Grévin's 1559 comedy *La trésorière*.

9. AN, Z^{1B} 491, piece dated 14 July 1576 (arrêt).

10. AN, Z^{1B} 485, piece dated 13 April 1554 (conclusions of the procureur général). This case was part of the process of cleaning up the mess left behind by the Pinatel affair.

Most of the serious criminality that the Monnaies dealt with, then, involved various kinds of clipping and counterfeiting. Those crimes have been somewhat neglected in the large literature on early modern European criminality and law enforcement; most of the specialized studies there are focus on the very different world of eighteenth-century England.[11] Coining was certainly not among the crimes most commonly confronted by general criminal jurisdictions: Malcolm Greenshields's study of the *maréchaussée* (rural police) in the Auvergne region shows counterfeiting making up fewer than 1 percent of their arrests, for example, while a similar proportion of the criminal dossiers indexed from the Parlement of Paris in the period 1556–1623 involves coiners.[12] The latter figure might have been depressed by the nature of the Cour des Monnaies' jurisdiction, though.[13] It was "preventive," meaning that (barring the royal council's not-infrequent transfers of individual cases from one court to another) the Monnaies could investigate and judge any coining case of which it initially took cognizance. Given its location, essentially sedentary nature, and the nature of criminal enforcement as generally a secondary priority for the Monnaies, this meant that its criminal caseload came overwhelmingly from Paris and its immediate vicinity, siphoned off from the other criminal courts of the Paris region.

This fact about the Monnaies' caseload makes it unrepresentative in one very important way. It seems clear that a very substantial proportion of early modern coining took place in rural areas, for the simple and practical reason that the relatively large-scale industrial operations that high-quality, profitable coining required were much easier to hide from prying eyes in more

---

11. See especially John Styles, "'Our Traitorous Money Makers:' The Yorkshire Coiners and the Law, 1760–83," in *An Ungovernable People: The English and Their Law in the Seventeenth and Eighteenth Centuries*, ed. John Brewer and John Styles (New Brunswick, NJ: Rutgers University Press, 1980), 172–249; Malcolm Gaskill, *Crime and Mentalities in Early Modern England* (Cambridge: Cambridge University Press, 2000), 123–99; and most recently Thomas Levenson, *Newton and the Counterfeiter: The Unknown Detective Career of the World's Greatest Scientist* (Boston: Houghton Mifflin Harcourt, 2009). Aside from differences in legal and monetary institutions, the main difference between eighteenth-century England and sixteenth-century France is that there seems to have been much greater social tolerance for coiners in the former.

12. See Malcolm Greenshields, *An Economy of Violence: Crime and Justice in the Haute Auvergne, 1587–1664* (State College: Pennsylvania State University Press, 1994), 68; and the index of AN, X[2B] 1174–1184, prepared by Y. Bézard and P. de Vaissière, 1927–33, at the Centre d'accueil et recherche des Archives nationales (CARAN).

13. In a sample of three hundred cases in the Parlement between 1380 and 1422, before the jurisdiction of the Chambre des Monnaies had developed, 4 percent concerned counterfeiting. See Claude Gauvard, *"De grace especial:" Crime, état et société en France à la fin du moyen âge*, 2 vols. (Paris: Publications de la Sorbonne, 1991), 1:29. There are some reasons to think that counterfeiting was under better control in the second half of the sixteenth century than it had been in the later Middle Ages.

remote places.[14] Thus, when the (admittedly rather sketchy) Villefranche-de-Rouergue mint moved to a country house to escape an outbreak of the plague in 1521, the neighbors quickly decided that it must have been a counterfeiting operation.[15] Indeed, on those occasions when the Cour des Monnaies went looking for coining in the countryside, it had no difficulty finding it, whether in the Île de France or in Normandy, which seems to have been a hotbed of such crimes. For the most part, though, what the Monnaies dealt with was the subset of coining that took place in relatively small-scale urban or suburban operations. This meant that the criminal enterprises appearing in the Monnaies' archives, besides being smaller and probably on the whole less sophisticated and successful than average, involved the specifically urban elements of sixteenth-century French society. This was by no means an absolute in an era when large proportions of the urban population were more or less recent migrants from the countryside and when urban-rural contacts were generally very intense, but it is something that has to be kept in mind while analyzing these kinds of data.[16]

Another thing that emerges strongly from the secondary literature and that the Monnaies' records generally confirm is that coining, and especially counterfeiting, was something of an elite crime; those prosecuted for it were unlikely to be truly marginal or members of an "underclass" or professional criminal milieu. While the evidence is difficult to interpret, this seems to have differentiated them from the perpetrators of much early modern property crime.[17]

---

14. In addition to the works on England cited above, see Laurent Feller, *Faux-monnayeurs et fausses monnaies en France à la fin du moyen âge (seconde moitié du XVe siècle)* (Paris: Le léopard d'or, 1986); and Bernard Lloansi, "La répression du faux-monnayage en Roussillon aux XVIIe–XVIIIe siècles," in *Les faux en numismatique* (Perpignan: Musée Numismatique Joseph Puig, 1997), 37–70. William Challoner, the counterfeiter pursued by Isaac Newton, usually did his actual coining in the countryside but based himself mainly in London: this kind of hybrid operation was probably not uncommon.

15. Urbain Cabrol, *Histoire de l'atelier monétaire royal de Villefranche-de-Rouergue* (Villefranche: Société Anonyme d'Imprimerie, 1913), 146.

16. Gauvard, "*De grace especial*," 1:264–81, generally plays down the differences between urban and rural crime in the later Middle Ages, though he suggests that Paris did see a disproportionate level of organized criminality and crimes against strangers. These differences are likely to have been accentuated by the urban boom of the late fifteenth and sixteenth centuries.

17. Thus, according to Ulinka Rublack, "it was predominantly the lower classes and marginal groups that were prosecuted" for such crimes in southwestern Germany. *The Crimes of Women in Early Modern Germany* (Oxford: Clarendon Press, 2001), 93. Thompson reached similar conclusions about serious property crime in Spain in "A Map of Crime in Sixteenth-Century Spain," *Economic History Review*, 2nd ser., 21 (1968): 244–76 (he also suggests that such crime was a predominantly urban phenomenon). And Florike Egmond, *Underworlds: Organized Crime in the Netherlands, 1650–1800* (Cambridge: Polity Press, 1993), concludes that much Dutch crime was the work of professionals, often poor and from marginalized groups such as Jewish immigrants, Gypsies, and demobilized soldiers. Violence, on the other hand, was endemic in early modern society, and indeed probably especially virulent in the aristocracy in our period. For an overview of that phenomenon, see Stuart Carroll, *Blood and Violence in Early Modern France* (Oxford: Oxford University Press, 2006).

Not only did making a convincing counterfeit require considerable technical skill, especially in engraving and metallurgy, but collecting coin for clipping or triage and passing clipped or counterfeit coin could be a complex operation. One consequence of this fact is that the social origins of coiners were very diverse, running from the bottom rungs of society well into the lesser nobility, with an especially strong representation of skilled craftsmen from the metal-working trades. It also meant that coining was almost never a solitary crime: it was carried out by groups and very often, as we shall see, by households or collections of households. In that respect, it had much in common with the legitimate economy in which it was embedded.

Given that its practitioners were relatively skilled and socially integrated, that it could be and was practiced in seclusion, and that its victims were as much as possible kept at arm's length from the crime itself, coining presented some obvious problems to would-be enforcers. The most important factor working in the authorities' favor, at least in the Parisian setting, was what seems to have been an almost total lack of popular toleration for coiners. At times, the magistrates may have wished that this was not quite so true: at least, that was probably how Simon Bizeul felt on 30 December 1608 when, at five in the morning, "while I was still asleep in bed a young man came banging on the door of my house. When my servant opened the door, he asked to speak to me; when I heard that, I had him brought to my room," where he denounced his master, a goldsmith, for clipping and persuaded the magistrate to launch a pre-breakfast raid to seize the incriminating evidence.[18] This was not an isolated incident. Men denouncing a fellow lodger for counterfeiting had awakened Bizeul's colleague Jean Moreau at five-thirty just a few months earlier. (In that case, the denouncers were police sergeants—the lodging in question was in the jurisdiction of St. Germain, but the complainants walked a kilometer and a half through Paris at the crack of dawn to turn the case over to an expert rather than to their own less specialized court.)[19] It was routine for generals of the moneys to be accosted in the street and presented with evidence of coining by random passersby. The infamy of coining could

---

18. See AN, Z^{1B} 683, dossier dated 30 December 1608, cover (procès-verbal of Bizeul): "estant encores au lict couché seroit venu heurter a la porte de nostre loges un jeune homme Auquel la porte aiant este ouverte par nostre serviteur luy auroit demande le faire parler a nous Ce que nous aiant este rapporté laurions faict venir en nostre chambre."

19. Ibid., dossier dated 19 August 1608, piece dated 9 August 1608 (procès-verbal of Moreau). The lodging was in the rue du Four, while Moreau's *hôtel* was on the rue des Bernardins, at the other end of the Left Bank. The uselessness of the bailliage of St. Germain-des-Près (for which one of the sergeants worked—the other was with the *prévôté* of Issy, six kilometers to the west) was sufficiently notorious to serve as a principal theme of Antoine Furetière's great comic novel *Le roman bourgeois*, discussed in the next chapter.

occasionally even impede investigations, as in a 1599 incident in which magistrates investigating the provenance of a bag of clippings from gold coins went to a printer's shop. They found "several neighbors; when we gave them to understand the consequence and importance of the crime of clipping coins, . . . Estienne Vallet said, with threats and furious words, that he would strangle and put to death all those who might think that he had done such a thing, which immediately caused several bystanders to complain noisily about us, saying that their neighbor was a good man." Faced with this hostility, they felt compelled to withdraw after issuing summonses (which were, however, duly obeyed).[20]

For coining, then, the presumption of early modern criminal law that the community would largely police itself and bring cases to the courts proved quite viable, and tensions between "community law" and "state law" were minimal.[21] Getting from a denunciation to a conviction was less straightforward. Passing counterfeit or clipped coin was illegal, but mens rea was easy to deny, and the Monnaies seems to have exercised considerable caution about inflicting punishment without clear evidence of malicious intent. And while it was easy to find people who would denounce suspicious conduct, the actual actions of coining were relatively easy to conceal, and thus direct eyewitnesses to criminal conduct were rare. This meant that the Monnaies was often faced with difficult and complex investigations requiring considerable dedication, expertise, and expense. The specialized knowledge that the generals had of the precious-metal trades clearly stood them in good stead in this work. One goldsmith, arrested for counterfeiting in 1594, "confessed to having begged those who took him prisoner to take him to the Châtelet [the main Paris criminal court] and not before Messieurs of the Monnaies"; the vigor with which the Monnaies pursued discrepancies in his supposedly professional tools more than justified his fears.[22]

---

20. AN, Z[1B] 499, dossier dated 16 March 1599, piece 10 (procès-verbal of Robert Becquet and Jacques Cartays): "plusieurs voysins ausquelz ayans fait entendre la consequence & combien importayt le crime de rognement de pieces ledict estienne vallet auroyt avec menasses et parolles furieuses dict quil estrangleroyt et feroyt mourir tout ceulx quil pensoyt quil eust fait ledict faict ce qui auroyt occasionne aussi tost a plusieurs de murmurer contre nous deisant que leur voysin estoyt homme de bien." The case remained unsolved, though.

21. The distinction is from Bruce Lenman and Geoffrey Parker, "The State, the Community, and the Criminal Law in Early Modern Europe," in *Crime and the Law: The Social History of Crime in Western Europe since 1500*, ed. V. A. C. Gatrell, Bruce Lenman, and Geoffrey Parker (London: Europa Publications, 1980), 11–48. Subsequent scholarship has greatly tempered though not quite eliminated this dichotomy.

22. AN, Z[1B] 497, piece dated 13 June 1594 (interrogatory of Jehan Levesque, fair copy), fol. 27v: "A confesse avoir prie ceulx qui le menerent prisonnier de le mener au Chastellet et non par devant messieurs des monnoies."

Otherwise, the basic techniques it used would be familiar to any law enforcement organization today: searching suspect premises, turning low-level participants into witnesses, arranging stakeouts and sting operations, and collecting and analyzing physical evidence, among other things. The court did not, however, conform to the at least nominal ideals of early modern criminal law, to which witness testimony and confession were central.[23] Examples are plentiful, but consider the case of Jehan Abelly, arrested in a sting at the church of St. Séverin on 10 June 1590 after a master engraver denounced him for having ordered punches to make double pistoles. He was eventually released because he was able to ditch the incriminating evidence before he could be seized.[24] The Cour des Monnaies also relied routinely on the testimony of expert witnesses: most often the assayer-general, who analyzed samples of suspect metals, but also handwriting experts and others.[25] At one point, one of the generals even organized a full-dress lineup in hopes of identifying a suspect![26]

Although the records suggest that the generals of the moneys showed due caution in convicting suspects, once they reached a conviction they did not hesitate to hand out harsh punishments.[27] Those they judged major participants

---

23. There is some reason to think that even beyond coining cases, physical evidence in the sixteenth and seventeenth centuries was already beginning the journey to its modern status as the gold standard for conviction. See Christiane Plessix-Buisset, *Le criminel devant ses juges en Bretagne aux 16e et 17e siècles* (Paris: Editeur Maloine, 1988), 232–33 and 260–63. For a particularly dramatic example, see James R. Farr, *A Tale of Two Murders: Passion and Power in Seventeenth-Century France* (Durham, NC: Duke University Press, 2005), esp. 150–60.

24. For his arrest, see AN, Z[1B] 681, dossier dated 1 June 1590 (procès-verbal of Gosseau); for his release into the custody of his father, AN, Z[1B] 496, piece dated 9 August 1590 (arrêt). Jehan claimed to be a light horseman in the service of the Duc de Nemours. While the documentation is confusing, he may have been the brother of Pierre Abelly, alias Abelier, son of a doctor regent in the faculty of medicine, who was arrested a few months earlier for forging an ingot suitable for use in counterfeiting. Ibid., pieces dated 2 March and 22 June 1590.

25. The most spectacular example was the case of the forged letters of remission in the Pinatel affair, where the Monnaies made use of the "deposition dudict du thiet conseiller du Roy et secretaire de ses commandements et finances . . . sur la recognoissance du seing appose esdictes lettres et falsification dicelluy rapport des maitres escripvains expers jures pardevant monsieur le garde des sceaulx de france et aultres procedures et rapportz faictz en ladicte court par maitres escripvains et parcheminiers jures en ladicte ville de paris sur la pretendue faulsete desdictes lettres." AN, Z[1B] 487, piece dated 28 May 1558, fol. 1r–v.

26. See AN, Z[1B] 489, piece dated 13 March 1570 (information of Hilaire Dain).

27. The generals' approach had become somewhat harsher since the late medieval period studied by Claudine Bloch, "Les peines appliquées aux faux monnayeurs en France par la Chambre des monnaies (fin du xve siècle)," *Tijdschrift voor Rechtsgeschiedenis/Legal History Review* 58 (1990): 73–94, with a larger role for corporal punishments; but this was in part a function of the gradual expansion of the range of criminal activities they prosecuted.

in counterfeiting or large-scale clipping were generally condemned to death—by hanging for most, by beheading for those with some claim to nobility, and by the traditional, almost folkloric punishment of boiling for one unlucky soul. Those more peripherally involved in counterfeiting, passers of counterfeit coin, and clippers on a smaller scale were generally banished from the Paris region or the kingdom or in the most serious cases sent to the galleys, usually with heavy fines or confiscation of goods and often with a public whipping. Very small-scale clipping, passing invalid but reasonably honest coin, and other such offenses brought fines of a few tens of écus. As was usually the case with premodern criminal justice, the imprisonment that suspects routinely faced was sufficiently traumatic to serve as a serious punishment in itself. In an extreme case, one Pierre Granges was released after two years in the basement cells of the Fort L'Evêque prison because he suffered from a severe hernia and was on the point of death.[28] Unlike many contemporary jurisdictions, the court does not seem to have resorted on a large scale to convictions in absentia and punishments in effigy; perhaps it felt too busy for such often-futile maneuvers; also, such convictions were used to advance settlements through royal letters of remission, which were not available for coining.

There is one important qualification to this account of the Monnaies' law enforcement. By far the greatest part of its criminal cases, in number if not in importance, arose from its regulation of the precious-metal trades in and around Paris.[29] These infractions were carried out by often well-established businesspeople and incurred little if any social opprobrium (though some goldsmiths disciplined for such infractions did petition the court for formal assurance that the fines imposed on them carried no note of infamy and did not impugn their honor).[30] Most of the cases were based on complaints brought by the *jurés et gardes* of the relevant craft, with the court only occasionally pursuing its own investigations. The issues it encountered centered on the sale of work below the legally specified alloy but included a number of other miscellaneous infractions, especially working in a specialty inappropriately or without proper authorization. The case of Mathurin Bruneau illustrates what this meant in practice. He was the goldsmith of the three

28. AN, Z^{1B} 488, piece dated 5 April 1562 (arrêt on report of the physician Pierre Collier).

29. On regulation of Parisian goldsmithing in this period, see Michèle Bimbinet-Privat, *Les orfèvres parisiens de la renaissance (1506–1620)* (Paris: Commission des travaux historiques de la Ville de Paris, 1992).

30. See, e.g., AN Z^{1B} 489, piece dated 10 March 1570, and AN, Z^{1B} 491, piece dated 21 November 1576. (arrêts on petition). These requests, routinely granted, may have had to do with marriage negotiations.

youngest sons of Henri II. He got into trouble in 1559 while reworking for his masters the plate of the dauphin, who had just become King François II. The guards of the Paris goldsmiths found his apprentice working in an attic rather than "in a shop and in the view of all and sundry," removing not only the coats of arms but also the original goldsmith's marks and guild countermarks from the vessels.[31] Suspecting that either the solder used to fill in the arms or the vessels themselves were being tampered with, the Monnaies ordered those pieces on which the marks were already effaced melted down, with the others to be worked on only under close guild supervision.

No one objected to this intervention in the functioning of the royal court. Even when the generals of the moneys arrested a valet of the royal wardrobe for operating as a jeweler or goldsmith without the permission of either guild and on suspicion of selling counterfeit gemstones, the only person who complained was the famous historian Jean du Tillet.[32] Du Tillet had left some items to be repaired by the accused, and since he was also clerk of the Parlement of Paris, a man with whom the Monnaies had to deal every day, it returned the pieces to him promptly. Even the English resident at the court of Henri IV had to go through channels to retrieve jewelry seized under similar conditions.[33] And the system seems to have worked. There was a fairly careful high-level inquiry in 1580, for example, led by the then attorney general (later first president) of the Parlement of Paris, Barnabé Brisson. It found the gold- and silver-workers of Paris working well above the minimum standards set by law.[34] On the whole, given its basic aims of ensuring standards of quality and protecting consumers, encouraging national uniformity, and enhancing the power of royal officers, the regulation of precious metals appears to have been a considerable success.

The Criminals: Elites and Upward Mobility

It is much harder to judge the overall effectiveness of the campaign against coining, since it was a far more diffuse battle in which the Cour des Monnaies

---

31. AN, Z[1B] 487, piece dated 2 October 1559 (arrêt), fol. 1v: "en bouticque & en la veue dun chascun."

32. AN, Z[1B] 491, pieces dated 16 March 1576 (interrogatories of Claude Denenet); 3 April 1576 (information against same); and 22 May 1576 (arrêt on petition from du Tillet).

33. See AN, Z[1B] 499, dossier dated 26 September 1598. Thomas Edmund had obtained a letter from the king asking for the return of his property on grounds of diplomatic immunity.

34. See AN, Z[1B] 492, pieces dated 10 and 13 May 1580 (procès-verbaux). Thirty-three pieces were sampled; notably, the silver was all between seven and eleven grains over the minimum.

played a much smaller role. What is possible is to make some judgments about the role of coining in society by looking more closely at the coiners, their associates, and their interactions with the broader society as they appeared in the court's records. The coiners were a motley crew, so it is neither particularly easy nor entirely safe to generalize about them, even from the rather broad cross section that appears in the criminal dockets. Still, while it is hard to talk with much confidence about the typical *social profile* of suspected coiners, there are some interesting themes that emerge from their *stories*—that is, from their dynamic relationship to the broader society. This makes sense because the coinage was not the tool of any particular social group, being common (with only quantitative differences) to all regardless of age, gender, class, profession, or estate. Instead, the coinage was a tool of social interaction, and those who manipulated it illicitly, or were suspected of doing so, shared above all a combination of a profound discontent with their current social position and limited but not nonexistent means to change that position. In that way (and only in that way), Charles IX was typical of contemporary coiners.

Royalty aside, it was far from unheard-of to find people of considerable social and economic status among the ranks of coiners. The priests and students who show up with some regularity may often have been somewhat marginal characters—though someone like Esme Despartes, "scholar studying medicine," banished in 1554, sounds respectable enough—but substantial merchants also made occasional appearances in these cases.[35] Thus, a clipping ring broken up in 1548 was run by Charles Eustace, an extremely wealthy "grocer, wood and wine merchant, dealer in cloth, grocery, iron, and other merchandise."[36] Another grocer, arrested in Lyons in 1555, was able to post a thousand-livre bond.[37] Successful merchants' natural habitat, however, was in crimes such as the transport of specie out of the country and large-scale violation of official exchange rates—though these practices probably appeared to those who engaged in them as the normal course of business. They also have left few traces in the records, in part because they clustered close to the frontiers but also because they involved men wealthy and powerful enough

---

35. AN, Z^{1B} 38, fols. 186v–187r (arrêt of 6 July 1554): "escollier estudiant en medecine." Despartes was convicted of possessing counterfeiting tools and complicity in counterfeiting.

36. AN, Z^{1B} 483, piece dated 30 August 1548, fol. 4v (interrogatory): "marchand espicier marchand de bois de vins de draps mercerye fer et aultres marchandises." The investigating magistrates found several hundred livres in cash when they searched Eustache's house, which itself must have been very large, since he let out one "grand corps de logis" for the substantial sum of eighty livres a year.

37. See AN, Z^{1B} 678, piece dated 21 January 1554 o.s. (procès-verbal of de la Tourette).

to more or less thoroughly legitimize their activities. To give one striking example, a 1601 investigation into activities of this sort by German merchants engaged in the lucrative and strategically vital trade of importing cavalry horses went nowhere, despite producing some solid evidence.[38] As the subsidiary general Germain de la Tourette wrote to the court concerning the failure of his parallel investigations in Grenoble, "Every effort is made useless by the authority of those who have power who, not content to do whatever they please on their own account, interpose their authority to allow everyone to carry out *as they wish the traffic* of coinage."[39] The fact was that successful merchants almost by definition were able to command the coinage to their own satisfaction, if not necessarily to the monetary authorities'.[40]

On the other hand, one of the surprising things about counterfeiting cases is how often they included members of the nobility. While great nobles and magnates engaged in such expedients only wholesale, as Montmorency-Damville did so spectacularly, their households and clienteles were by no means immune to coining. An abortive counterfeiting operation in 1549 involved Jehan Eude, sieur de Vimes, son of a *marchand bourgeois* of Honfleur, who was a member of the Constable de Montmorency's household.[41] Andrea Tranchetti, a "self-styled gentleman . . . of the city of Ferrara" arrested for counterfeiting in 1569, was in the train of the papal legate.[42] An especially bizarre case in the same year featured Charles Guynet, alias Captain la Chambre—probably not the same man who stage-managed Charles IX's gang of pickpockets. He claimed to have served in the infantry under "Captain Strosse," probably the colonel-general of the infantry Philippo di Piero Strozzi, of the great Florentine patrician family. Guynet's father, Mathieu, "Captain la Chambre the Elder," was merchant-provisioner to the household of the king's cousin Jean de Bourbon, duc d'Enghien, and had previously worked for such luminaries as the prince de

---

38. See AN, Z[1B] 498, pieces dated 14 (act of Loys du Port) and 17 August 1601 (procès-verbal) and AN, Z[1B] 391, undated piece labeled "1601" (anonymous memoir). On the centrality of cavalry to Henri IV's military undertakings, see Ronald S. Love, "'All the King's Horsemen': The Equestrian Army of Henri IV, 1585–1598," *Sixteenth Century Journal* 22 (1991): 511–33.

39. AN, Z[1B] 498, piece dated 15 March 1602 (letter of that date, autog.): "on rend tout innutille par lautorité de ceulx qui ont du pouvoir et lesquelz ne se contentent de faire pour leur particullier ce qui leur plaist, interposent leur authorité pour laisser faire chacun a *sa volonte le trafficq des* monnoies" (emphasis, apparently added by a reader in the Monnaies, in original).

40. For another example along the same lines, involving Italian merchants, see AN, Z[1B] 680, a group of pieces dated from "dernier fevrier 1576."

41. See AN, Z[1B] 483, piece dated 18 February 1548 o.s. (deposition of Jehan de Villiers) and 6 and 8 March 1548 o.s. (procès-verbaux of Eude's arrest and of a commission sent to his hometown).

42. AN, Z[1B] 678, no. 22 (interrogatory of Philippes Domet), fol. 1r: "soy disant gentilhomme . . . de la ville de ferrare."

Condé, the cardinal de Châtillon, and the duke of Ferrara.[43] And a 1608 case involved, peripherally, a translator for the Spanish ambassador, and centrally, one Charles de la Ville, esquire, sieur de St. Bréart de Molle, maître d'hôtel to Henri II's daughter (and Henri IV's ex-wife) Marguerite de Valois.[44] These nobles were not infrequently foreigners, such as Tranchetti and the half-brothers Pedro and Diego de Miño, who worked with the sieur de St. Breart, while others— such as a family of Breton nobles, the de la Minaudière, whose patriarch had supposedly come to Paris originally "to seek health and treatment"—may have felt foreign enough.[45]

Norman nobles made up another geographically distinct group. As the case of the sieur de Vimes illustrates, they seem to have been particularly susceptible to the lure of false money, perhaps because provincial liberties and a relatively high level of class solidarity helped them to avoid prosecution. In 1550, the Monnaies, investigating a case that had begun with a Parisian draper passing some counterfeit coin, had difficulty arresting one Jehan Hue. Though Hue's counterfeiting operations were locally notorious, he had to be seized quickly before he could "go back to his home in the town of Nonancourt, which is in Normandy, where it will later be difficult to remove him, because of the liberties of that country." Moreover, Hue had to be heavily guarded, because word was "that the relatives and other friends of Jehan Hue, together with other gentlemen of the country, had determined to recover him, some of them having even boasted that this was liable to cost ten men their lives." Finally, the key witness, a brother of the draper first arrested, who had received the original counterfeit coins as a payment from Hue, was reluctant to testify because "a certain Jehan Hue, brother of the said Jehan Hue, and Charles Castelogne seigneur de Rondeville, were threatening to kill him, and indeed had already attempted to do so, [so that] he was forced not to budge from his house, and to give up the traffic of his merchandise."[46]

---

43. See AN, Z^{1B} 489, dossier dated 14 September 1569.

44. See AN, Z^{1B} 683, dossier dated August 1608.

45. AN, Z^{1B} 678, piece dated 15 March 1560 o.s. (interrogatory of Françoise de Terne): "pour cercher sante & guerisson."

46. AN, Z^{1B} 484, piece dated 6 June 1550 (procès-verbal of Simon Radin), fols. 2r–4r: "se retirer en son domicille ou bourg de Nounancourt qui est pays de Normandie [dept. Eure] Auquel lieu seroit difficille cy apres luy retirer & distraire A moyen des libertez pretendues par ceulx dudict pays"; "que les parens & autres amys dudict Jehan Hue ensemble autres gentilhommes du pays estoient deli-berez de le recouvrir Mesmes que aucuns sestoient ventez quil leur cousteroit plustost la vie de dix hommes"; "ung nomme messire Jehan Hue frere dudict Jehan Hue & charles castelogne seigneur de Rondeville le menassoient de le tuer Et de faict sen estoient ja mis en leur effort et estoit contrainct ne bouger de sa maison & laisser la trafficque de sa marchandise." To make matters simpler, both the draper and his brother were named Jehan Desfebues.

Even that pales in comparison with the career of another Norman, Fédéric Godet, sieur de St. Amand, and his family, who supposedly covered up their own coin clipping for years by framing an innocent man.[47]

On their home turf, these Normans operated in the patterns of mafia-style organized crime and were thus quite unlike most other counterfeiters, except perhaps for their marginal position in the Parisian world.[48] The robber barons who infested the countryside during the chaos of the civil wars could also easily have turned to counterfeiting on a broader scale. Still, the geographic logic of France did tend to funnel such people and their crimes toward Paris. For one thing, it was a good place to pass bad coin: this is probably what was going on with Jehan Symon Solay, esquire, an Angevin arrested for possession of a substantial sum of counterfeit silver in 1577. Whether he had, as he claimed, got it from a Captain de Lalande in payment for a draft horse or whether he had made it himself, the anonymity and vast markets of Paris would have made it a convenient place for him to profit from his counterfeits.[49] And political and legal forces brought the activities of important and influential counterfeiters to the attention of the Parisian authorities. In 1556 and 1557, for example, a group operating out of Dieppe but circulating its products in England drew complaints from the English ambassador to France and the dispatch of a judge from Cour des Monnaies to clear the matter up.[50] The tendency of all French life to orbit around Paris in one way or another was already present for sixteenth-century coiners.

To return to our main point, though, what foreign nobles in Paris and hangers-on of the great aristocratic households had in common was their liminal status, and this extended to the majority of coiners, whether noble or common—or, of course, somewhere in between. Like Eude and Guynet, several of the notionally gentle counterfeiters were the sons of

---

47. The source here is a suit brought by the heirs of the innocent man, Phillipes Cavalier, to recover his inheritance and clear his name. See AN, Z^{1B} 433, piece dated 7 June 1555 (case file), and AN Z^{1B} 487, piece dated 23 Aug. 1557 (letters patent).

48. By "mafia-style" I mean a form of organized crime dependent on local and family solidarity and with some participation of local elites. Aside from banditry, early modern organized crime remains understudied. The main work is Egmond, *Underworlds*, which concentrates on rural property crime, apparently not including coining.

49. See AN, Z^{1B} 492, dossier dated 1 February 1577.

50. See *Calendar of State Papers, Foreign Series, of the reign of Mary, 1553-1558* (London: Longman, 1861), 243–45 (no. 523: Dr. Wooton to the Queen, 4 August 1556); and AN, Z^{1B} 487, piece dated 12 June 1557 (letters patent assigning the case to Joseph Dumaignet).

merchants. The sixteenth-century nobility was dynamic and relatively permeable, but ensconcing oneself in it, becoming one of the "bourgeois gentlemen" George Huppert has studied, required cash money.[51] The case of Laurent le Conte, *élu* of Coutances (in Normandy), accused by a member of the queen's household of the relatively minor crime of overvaluing foreign coin when paying for letters of nobility, dramatizes this dynamic. Le Conte attempted to push responsibility back onto the would-be nobles for whom he had been acting, who were presumably hard-pressed to fund their social ambition.[52] According to some contemporary theories, these men's newly minted nobility was already itself a counterfeit of truly virtuous blood.[53]

Even those whose status was less open to question might be tempted by criminality. Jehan Chaussay, tried for counterfeiting at Châtellerault in 1550, was well aware of this, as appears from the testimony of a pantler in the households of the king and the dauphin named René du Puys, sieur de Basneulx. A few years before, Chaussay had come to his door, saying "that he had heard that he was looking for money to go to the king's service, and that if he would lease him one of his lands and houses, he would raise him good money for it. To which the deponent replied that he did in fact need to raise some money to go to the king's service . . . and that he would gladly give him the farm of one of his lands and would give him good terms, provided that he had the money to put up and advance." Chaussay admitted that he had no cash on hand,

> but that if it would please him to give him one of his houses in the area, he knew of a way to manage it to raise money so that the deponent would be free and clear in all his business. To which the deponent replied that he would very much like to know that means, enjoining Chaussay to explain it to him. He told him that he had a cousin who

---

51. See George Huppert, *Les Bourgeois gentilshommes: An Essay on the Definition of Elites in Renaissance France* (Chicago: University of Chicago Press, 1977).

52. See AN, Z^{1B} 485, piece dated 22 July 1553 (formula for an interrogatory of Michel du Jardin and Raoul Table).

53. On contemporary theories of old nobility, which may have been becoming stricter in reaction to an actual or perceived sixteenth-century inflation of noble status, see, besides Huppert, *Bourgeois gentilshommes*, Ellery Schalk, *From Valor to Pedigree: Ideas of Nobility in France in the Sixteenth and Seventeenth Centuries* (Princeton: Princeton University Press, 1986); and Jay Smith, *The Culture of Merit: Nobility, Royal Service, and the Making of Absolute Monarchy in France, 1600–1789* (Ann Arbor: University of Michigan Press, 1996).

knew how to augment gold [alchemically], from which they made reals, and that if he would lease them one of his houses, he would very soon furnish a large sum of them, without fail.[54]

De Basneulx claimed that he drove Chaussay away after determining that this trick was to be carried off without royal permission, but the esquire's temptation is palpable in his account.

The Criminals: Artisans and Downward Mobility

In important ways, though, these men who more or less plausibly sought upward mobility were atypical of coining suspects. If nobles were overrepresented among their number, they were still a distinct minority, and even the nobles among them were generally pretty sad cases. In fact, the dominant elements of coiner's life stories as they appeared in evidence were insecurity, downward mobility, and personal catastrophe. There were exceptions, but in general the turn to coining seems to have been the result not of a cold economic calculation or of logical progression in a criminal career but rather of desperate attempts to achieve a new social position or, more often, to retrieve one that was slipping away. Etienne Butel, who came to the Monnaies' attention in 1587, was initially described as "one of the richest" merchants of Beaumont-sur-Oise, a substantial village halfway between Paris and Beauvais. When the court interrogated his wife of eighteen years, Marie Deanebonne, though, a rather different picture emerged. She was the widow of the royal provost of Beaumont and claimed that at the time they married, Butel "had a good reputation and many relatives in the city of Beauvais, where she often went, and among Butel's other relatives was someone named Boisleau, comptroller of the salt depot." Butel had worked in this world of minor but solid royal officers, but "for the past four years, seeing that her husband no longer

---

54. AN, Z^{1B} 484, piece dated September 1550 (information against Chaussay), fols. XXIXv–XXXv: "quil avoyt entendu quil cherchoit de largent pour aller au service du Roy et sil luy bailloyt affermer lune de ses terres et maisons Il luy en feroit bien recouvrer A quoy ledict depposant dist que veritablement il en avoyt bien affaire de recouvrer de largent pour aller audict service du Roy . . . et quil affermeroy voullontiers une de ses terres et luy en feroyt bien la raison pourveu quil eust argent a bailler et avancer"; "mays que sil luy plaisoyt luy offrir lune de ses maisons qui feust es environs quil scavoyt les moyens pour len faire avec le [illeg.] recouvrert pour argent de sorte que ledict depposant se metroyt de hors de touts ses affaires A quoy icelluy depposant feit response que vouldroyt fort bien scavoir le moyen interpellant ledict chaussay de luy dire lequel luy dist que avoyt cousin germain qui scavoyt augmenter largent dont on faisoyt les realles et que sil luy plaisoyt leur bailler lune de ses maisons il en fournyroit tantost de assez dargent et ne avoyt faulte."

earned anything from his position . . . she has taken to selling wine and lodging travelers in her house from time to time, whenever some showed up who
wanted to lodge there," and despite their denials, it is clear that the couple
also turned to making counterfeit douzains.[55] An even more dramatic family
drama is the case we have already mentioned of the Italian Andrea Tranchetti.
He lived with a merchant's widow named Barbe (alias Michelle) Croumet,

> with whom he fell in love, and thereafter, seeing their love progress, the
> said Michelle several times requested money from him. And since the
> confessant saw that she importuned him so often for money, he replied
> one time among other things that at some point they would make so
> much of it that they would have plenty. Wherefor the said Michelle
> several times importuned him to say how he thought they would make
> the said money, to which the confessant replied that they would need
> to make punches

for use in creating coining dies.[56] Croumet confirmed the outlines of this
story; in their desire to make a new life together in a city new to Tranchetti,
they turned to making money in the literal sense.

Such stories appeared further down the social scale than dubious nobles
and merchants' widows. If one were to pick a typical counterfeiter, it would
probably be someone like Antoine Lacanie, called Sagon. According to his
own testimony, he had once been a master goldsmith in Rouen, but now he
"worked in his room for the master goldsmiths on small chains and other
small minor pieces. . . . He had no forge or furnace, but an iron pot in which
he melted his materials." He had left "the city of Rouen because of a misfortune that befell him in the form of a servant who robbed him of five or

55. AN, Z^{1B} 681, piece dated 13 September 1587 (procès-verbal of Jacques le Grand), fol. 5r;
piece dated 17 September 1587 (interrogatory of Deanebonne), fol. 1r: "avoit bonne renomme et
plusieurs parens en la ville de beauvays ou elle frequentoit souvent et entre aultres parens dudict butel
sont ung nomme boisleau controlleur de grenier a sel." "depuis quatre ans elle voyant que son mary
ne gaingoit plus rien en son estat . . . elle sest mesle de vendre vin et loger les passans en sa maison
par foys quant il sen presentoit qui y voulloient loger."

56. AN, Z^{1B} 679, dossier dated 6 November 1569, no. 24 (interrogatory of Tranchetti), fol. 1r:
"de laquelle il sest rendu amoureux Et depuys voyant continuer leur amour ladicte michelle luy a par
plusieurs fois demande de largent Et voyant ledict confessant quelle limportunoyt sy souvent pour
avoir de largent luy feist response une fois entre autres que quelquefois ilz en feroient tant quilz en
aouroient assez. Amoyen de quoy ladicte michelle le par plusieurs foix importunant de declarer le
moyen quil entendoit pour faire ledict argent A quoy ledict confessant luy feist response quil falloyt
faire des fers."

six hundred livres of merchandise."[57] So in 1559 he found himself in Paris with his family, committing the capital crime of forging coining blanks for eighteen pence apiece. The legitimate goldsmiths of Paris must have paid him truly miserably, and he had fallen indeed from whatever prosperity he had enjoyed at home. A similar tale from 1600, another step down the social ladder, involved a master sword polisher named Michel Pasté; his wife, Foy; his sister, Jehanne; and his brother-in-law, Helye, "a domestic servant of sieur Captain Belon." Huguenots from various parts of northwestern France, they had come together, presumably as refugees, in the Protestant stronghold of La Rochelle. What brought Michel to Paris is unclear, but according to Jehanne, her aunt (with whom she had been living) "and her husband had lost everything in a fire that had burned down their house, and since they only had a very little, her brother's wife . . . had brought her to this city to help with a small business she had." Like Sagon, Michel Pasté earned a meager living doing piecework for Parisian masters while his wife and sister, more honest counterfeiters, made wax-flower bouquets.[58]

In both these cases, catastrophes had left skilled metalworkers who were probably already in difficult circumstances essentially destitute, tempting them to turn their skills toward the illicit creation of money they could not obtain by selling their labor. More banal and everyday forces could have a similar effect. The young man who woke Bizeul up at five in the morning in 1608, for example, was denouncing his master, a goldsmith named Loys Doner, who had been clipping silver coins. He had been doing it for the past three months, and under interrogation he broke down and admitted "that finding himself needing to pay out two livres that he owed for rent on his house and having no money, he had taken to clipping to try to hustle up and earn a few sous." He had a new baby and a young wife, and she clarified that

57. AN, Z^{1B} 678, piece dated 8 April 1559 (interrogatory of Antoine Lacanie), fol. 1r–v: "Enquis de quoy il sest mesle depuys ledict temps [qu'il habite Paris]. Dict quil cest mesle tousjours de lestat dorfaiverye & besongne en chambre pour les maistres orfevres en petitz filletz et aultres petitz menuz ouvraiges. Enquis ou il fondeoit & sil tenoyt forges & fourneaulx en chambre. Dict quil ne tenoyt aulcune forge ny fourneaulx Ains avoit ung pot de fer ou il faisoit fondre ses matieres Et a dict quil ya trente ans quil est maistre orfevre audict Rouen depuis lequel temps il a tousjours excerce son estat audict Rouen & en ceste ville et . . . depuis ledict temps de huict a neuf ans & quil partit de ladicte ville de Rouen pour une fortune qui luy advient par ung sien serviteur qui le desrobyt pour cinq ou six cens livres de besongnes." Compare ibid., piece dated 10 April 1559 (interrogatory of Lucques Sagon), where his wife puts their loss in Rouen at £4,000.

58. AN, Z^{1B} 499, dossier dated 12 February 1600, piece 6 (interrogatories), fol. 6r: "serviteur domesticque du sr capitaine Belon"; fol. 1r: "& son mary ayant tout perdu par le feu qui a bruslé leur maison & nayant que bien peu de moyens l'a femme de son frere nommee foy fleury l'a fist venir avec elle en ceste ville pour tenir ung petite affaire quelle a."

the couple still owed rent on their previous lodging as well as their current one. This was not, however, a case of utter desperation, as the sleepy and angry Bizeul pointed out: "We remonstrated with him that he was moved by great avarice to commit such dishonesty . . . given that he was not in such great need as he says, seeing that he has so much goldsmith's work in his house." And his wife, at least, concurred in this moral interpretation, pleading that "her husband had told her that he did not want to be involved in this forever, and that he wanted to go to the penitencer to receive absolution for his sin, since the respondent . . . had it on her conscience."[59] Doner, it seems, actualized the entire complex of anxieties about money, ambition, avarice, and artisanal fraud examined in chapter 2.

Such situations of actual or threatened downward mobility were always common in premodern Europe given how subject the economy was to the vagaries of nature and how threadbare the safety net was at the best of times. From the second half of the sixteenth century, though, the chaos and destruction of the Wars of Religion would have made them even more prevalent. And there was a deeper secular trend at work. Skilled urban artisans, especially those who lacked (or lost) substantial capital, found themselves increasingly squeezed by an oversupply of labor, rising food prices, and the concentration of power in the hands of wealthier, existing masters; in particular, it became increasingly difficult for journeymen to obtain the credentials and capital needed to set up as masters with their own shops. The result was a kind of creeping proletarianization that swelled the ranks of potential counterfeiters in cities such as Paris.[60] As an illustration of this phenomenon, one can take the case of Nicolas les Dalles, who despite being the son of a Parisian master goldsmith found himself constrained to work as a journeyman in Orleans and after returning to Paris confessed that he illegally "works for no master, but for gentlemen and merchants who give

---

59. AN, Z[1B] 683, dossier dated 30 December 1608, pieces dated 31 December 1608 (procès-verbal of Bizeul): "que se voyant charge de payer deux livres quil devroient de louaige de maison et nayant poinct dargent il sestoit mis a rongner pour tascher de praticquer et gaigner quelques sols." "Luy avons remonstré quil estoit pousse de grand avarice de commectre une telle meschancette . . . attendu quil nestoit poinct en telle necessite comme il dict veu quil a grande quantite douvraige dorfeverie en sa maison." (Interrogatory of the wife): that "sondit mary luy avoict dict quil ne sen vouloit pas tousiours mesler Et que il vouloict aller au penitencier pour avoir pardon de sa faulte daultant quelle respondante . . . auroict cela sur la conscience." Besides the clipped coin, Doner had about £55 in cash on hand, making his claims of illiquidity somewhat less convincing.

60. The best account of this process in contemporary France is James R. Farr, *Hands of Honor: Artisans and their World in Dijon, 1550–1650* (Ithaca, NY: Cornell University Press, 1988), esp. 76–121; on the broader European context, see, e.g., Robert S. Duplessis, *Transitions to Capitalism in Early Modern Europe* (Cambridge: Cambridge University Press, 1997), 88–140 and 190–302.

him rings and earrings to work on, and only works in his chamber." While he was at it, he clipped coin. "Asked . . . what he intended to do with the silver clippings found on him, he said that he would have melted them down and sold them to help him pass master."[61] The irony of this situation is that the Monnaies' collaboration with the guilds of the precious-metal trades in strengthening their organization and policing probably led artisans to turn to more serious violations of the laws.

Naturally, representatives of the marginal groups more traditionally associated with property crime were present in the ranks of counterfeiters, though even they tended to be a cut above ordinary vagrants. Some were deracinated soldiers, or ex-soldiers, though probably not in proportion to their representation in the general population of ne'er-do-wells in the chaotic and war-torn sixteenth century. Indeed, it was possible to be something like a skilled artisan of war. Such was the case, for example, of Claude Charpentier, arrested in 1604 in possession of mercury and unmarked coining blanks. He was, he said, the son of a *laboureur et fermier*, that is, a substantial peasant, from Milleray in Brie.[62] Since his father's death, he had been a professional soldier mainly in the Dutch armies of Maurice of Nassau, one of the great commanders of the age and a pioneer in the technical aspects of war.[63] In particular, he had served under a sapper, the sieur de la Roche, and "when he was under the said la Roche he had learned to produce the fireworks [*artiffices de feu*] that are used in warfare." Apparently, that was not the limit of his technical competence, since his traveling companion, Louis le Brun, who claimed to be "sieur" de Brissac, had told a Parisian acquaintance "that the said soldier knew many things: among others, he made half-pistoles very well."[64] Le Brun (who was perhaps trying to trade on the prestige of the

---

61. AN, Z[1B] 680, piece dated 26 January 1580 (interrogatory), fol. 1r: "ne travaille pour aucun maistre Ains pour des gentilzhommes & marchans qui luy baillent a faire des anneaulx & pendans doreille & ne travaille quen chambre"; fol. 4r: "Remonstre que puys quil ne travaille que en or quil voulloit faire des rongnemens dargent sur luy saisyes. A dict quil les eust fondues & puys apres vendues pour ayder a se faire passer maistre."

62. This appears to have been a village in the current *département* of the Marne, near Châlons, though as far as I can tell it no longer exists.

63. On Maurice of Nassau, see, e.g., Geoffrey Parker, *The Military Revolution: Military Innovation and the Rise of the West, 1500–1800*, 2nd ed. (Cambridge: Cambridge University Press, 1996), 18–23.

64. AN, Z[1B] 682, dossier dated 18 and 19 May 1604 (interrogatory of Charpentier): "estant soubz ledict la Roche il a appris a faire des artiffices de feu servans a la guerre"; (deposition of Jehan Gardera): "que ledict soldat scavoit beaucoup de choses & entre autres faiste fort bien de demis pistolletz." From their line of questioning, it is clear that the generals of the moneys had some outside source of information about Charpentier. Gardera was "chevaucheur de l'écurie ordinaire du roi" and on friendly terms with the long-standing master of the Bordeaux mint Jehan Malins.

Marshal de Brissac, governor of Bordeaux in the 1580s) was the son of the jailer of Bordeaux, and the man to whom he boasted of his friend's skill was a fellow Bordelais. In fact, this friend later turned him in to the Monnaies, through the intermediary of the master of the Bordeaux mint, who was in Paris at the time. In other words, Charpentier and le Brun were not antisocial outcasts but men of solid background with ongoing connections to an influential Bordeaux network and considerable technical skills. Whether they really hoped to "rise above their station," as le Brun's flirtation with a fictitious lordship suggests, or whether they were merely trying to stay afloat amid the stress of war and family disintegration, their turn to counterfeiting was an attempt to mobilize that social capital. For Charpentier, at least, it was a dismal failure, leading him to the hangman's noose.

That is not to say that destitution, subsistence crises, and marginality are entirely absent from the archives. Pierre le Sourd, "a poor mason's assistant" arrested in 1593, had learned how to counterfeit from his fellow laborers (casting the coins in plaster, a material his humble trade would have familiarized him with) and by his own admission had done so for about a year, "and passed the said coins wherever he could to buy food." By that time, Paris had been under intermittent siege from royalist forces for nearly five years, and such food was not easy to come by; indeed, le Sourd said that he had taken up coining consistently only "since the times became dear."[65] Alain Rouget, a tailor arrested in a village near Poissy on suspicion of involvement with the Tranchetti affair (and who had a previous arrest on suspicion of counterfeiting), seems to have fit the profile of the marginalized semiprofessional criminal: according to a local official, he had moved there a couple of years ago and "had a reputation for haunting taverns and making good cheer even though he was very poor, and he often changed his lodgings for unknown reasons."[66] Even Antoine Lacanie and his wife, presented above as type specimens of coiners, seem at the end to have fallen into real marginality: his poverty was real enough, but more significantly a former landlord testified that "because of the bad reputation the wife of the said Lacanie

---

65. AN, Z[1B] 496, dossier dated 8 June 1593 (procès-verbal of Jerosme de Varade): "ung pauvre ayde a Macon"; (interrogatory of le Sourd, 9 June), fol. 2r: "et exposoit lesdites especes par tout ou il pouvoit a achepter vivres"; (14 June): "depuis le cher temps."

66. AN, Z[1B] 489, piece dated 19–21 November 1569 (procès-verbal of Hilaire Dain) ; fol. 2r: "avoit le bruit de hanter les tavernes & fere bonne chere encores quil fut bien pauvre et quil changeoit souvent de demeure ne saichant les occasions." This was in the commune of Alluets-le-Roi (Yvelines). There is more detail on this suspect's marginal existence in ibid., dossier dated 24 February 1569 o.s. His associates, who included charcoal burners, are all described as very poor.

had as a procuress, he dismissed and evicted them from the house," while two other witnesses suggested that she had tried to lure a niece into prostitution.[67] Such cases, however, were exceptional, representing, respectively, extreme economic conditions, a distinctive rural milieu, and the end point of a long decline. The bulk of coiners remained much more firmly implanted in the social and economic life of their communities, which they hoped to manipulate, not spurn.

The Criminals: Women and Households

In short, when the Cour des Monnaies confronted the world of coining, it confronted a reverse image of the society it was charged to uphold, with its urban-rural links, its social mobility, its noble patrons, its sharp-dealing merchants and masters, and its increasingly disenfranchised workforce. One of the most interesting aspects of this phenomenon, and an instance in which the criminal records give us an unusual level of detail, is the role of women and family structures. In the cases discussed above, it was almost always families or households, rather than individuals, that confronted or desired socioeconomic mobility. And it is rare to find any counterfeiting enterprise that did not involve women as active or passive participants. Even the most marginal coiners were usually married. Le Sourd had a wife twenty years his senior; Rouget's wife was keeping his shop open in his absence when Hilaire Dain came looking for him. It was Lacanie's wife, Lucques Sagon, who was actually caught with the incriminating coins, and on his account, he both received his raw materials from and delivered his finished products to the wives of associates. Coining in sixteenth-century France remained very much a part of a "household economy," even as increasingly centralized, capitalized, and politicized forms of production eroded that economy and created pressures that drove some into coining in the first place.[68] And

---

67. AN, Z[1B] 678, piece dated 22 September 1560 (inquest by Hilaire Dain), fol. 1r: "au moyen de la mauvaise reputation que la femme dudict Lacanye avoyt destre macquerelle il leur donnat conge & desloiquence de ladicte maison."

68. In an influential analysis, Jan de Vries has suggested that the migration of production and consumption out of the household from the seventeenth century on was largely constitutive of economic modernity. See *The Industrious Revolution: Consumer Behavior and the Household Economy, 1650 to the Present* (Cambridge: Cambridge University Press, 2008). It is worth noting that the later English coining operations mentioned above seem to have been substantially less embedded in household economies.

women's roles in coining were shaped by the responsibilities, opportunities, and limitations of the early modern household.[69]

Women hardly ever performed actual manual labor in counterfeiting operations, though they sometimes did clip coin—perhaps a contested role, as one clipper confessed that when his associates were at work, "the wife of [his housemate] was present, and that her husband did not want her to clip and try her hand at it because she stole from it, and he always found problems with the accounting when she meddled in it."[70] However, they did appear frequently among the aristocratic patrons and sponsors of such groups, generally for reasons closely related to their vulnerabilities as women. After being turned away by the law-abiding sieur de Basneulx, Jehan Chaussay took up "two or three rooms" in the home of the Demoiselle de la Harderaye, apparently a widow, "which the lady lent or rented to him in order to avoid the crowd and oppression of armed men who roamed the area."[71] Having taken him in, she was unable to get rid of him and ended up abandoning her house and living with friends. This was an entirely involuntary household, but it is noteworthy that Chaussay felt it worth his while to extort it, feeling that some form of household was a necessary component of his operation.

Generally, the domestic lives of counterfeiters seem to have been like their economic lives: of the same form as the legitimate world but in an illegal and even pathological variant.[72] We have already seen a good example of this

---

69. On women in the (eroding) household economy of sixteenth-century urban northern Europe, see Natalie Zemon Davis, "Women and the Crafts in Sixteenth-Century Lyon," and Martha C. Howell, "Women, the Family Economy, and the Structures of Market Production in the Cities of Northern Europe during the Late Middle Ages," in *Women and Work in Preindustrial Europe*, ed. Barbara Hanawalt (Bloomington: Indiana University Press, 1986), 167–97 and 198–222, respectively.

70. AN, Z[1B] 483, piece dated 20 October 1548 *bis* (interrogatory of Denis Laurens), fol. 3r–v: "la femme dudict Bastien y estoit presente & que son mary ne vouloit pas quelle rongnast et esquisast Parce quelle en desroboyt et quil trouuvoit tousjours faulte a son compte quant elle y touchoit." In the Comporion case discussed below, the women seem to have done most of the actual clipping, but an abortive move into counterfeiting was a purely male endeavor.

71. AN, Z[1B] 484, piece dated September 1550, fol. XXIIv: "ledict chaussay salla tenir en deux ou troys chambres dudict lieu de la harderaye que ladicte demoiselle luy avoit prestees ou louees pour obvier a la foulle et oppression des gensdarmes qui passoient pars." The exact nature of Chaussay's protection racket is unclear: were the armed men his confederates or an unrelated nuisance?

72. The existing literature on early modern nonclerical concubinage deals almost exclusively with Italy. See, e.g., Seidel Menchi and Diego Quagliioni, *Trasgressioni: Seduzione, concubinato, adulterio, bigamia (xiv–xviii secolo)* (Bologna: Il Mulino, 2004); and Jana Byars, "The Long and Varied Relationship of Andrea Mora and Anzola Davide: Concubinage, Marriage and the Authorities in the Early Modern Veneto," *Journal of Social History* 41 (2008): 667–90. According to Jacques Depauw, "Amour illégitime et société à Nantes au XVIIIe siècle," *Annales E.S.C.* 27 (1972): 1155–82, this kind of concubinage was quite rare in Nantes, especially before the late eighteenth century.

kind of often-unsatisfactory relationship in the case of Andrea Tranchetti and Barbe Croumet. We even have her account of their relationship, which suggests both her level of dissatisfaction with her life and the importance of her gendered identity in their crime. Asked "if sieur André kept her and they slept together," she initially "said no, and that he lodged in her apartment as a stranger." But after a night in prison she broke down, recanted, and "after having given a long speech on the poor treatment she had received from Messire André," gave an account of her role in the genesis of the counterfeiting plot. One day,

> while they were living on the Rue de Seine, Messire André told her that the grand vicar, the cardinal of Ferrara, had promised to give him a pension or something of three hundred livres with which, along with other things that he knew well, they would be able to live together. And afterwards he told her that he had great need of a locksmith who knew how to do good work. Later on, she needed some money, and to raise it she went to a woman called la Prunelle, . . . who introduced her to the wife of a certain goldsmith named d'Homet, who could arrange to get her a loan. After that, while visiting la Prunelle on her business, she heard la Prunelle speak of a close friend of hers who was a locksmith, and the deponent . . . asked if he did good work.[73]

These characters were her fellow conspirators in the counterfeiting ring. In her quest to convert her irregular and apparently unsatisfactory liaison into something more stable, or even to maintain it in its current condition, she turned to the kind of female credit networks that Julie Hardwick has described as a frequent last resort of stressed households.[74] Only then, and

---

73. AN, Z^{1B} 679, dossier dated 6 November 1569, no. 20 (information against Tranchetti), fol. 5r: "Si ledict sieur andre lentretenoit & couscherent ensemble. A dict que non & quil loge seullement en son logis comme ung estranger." Fols. 9v–10r: "depuys quilz sont demourans en ladicte rue de seine ledict messire andre luy dist que monsieur le grand vicaire du cardinal de ferrare luy avoyt promis luy bailler pension ou quelque chose et est de troys cens livres avec lesquelz & autres choses quil scavoyt bien Ilz avoient moyen de vivre ensemble Et que depuys luy dist quil avoyt grandement affair dun serurrier qui sceust bien faire quelque chose de bien. Que depuys ce temps elle a eu affaire dargent & pour en recouvrir elle saddressa a une femme nommee la prunelle demourante en la tour de nesle Laquelle luy enseigna a la femme dung nomme dhomet orfevre quelle disoyt avoir moyen de luy en faire prester Que depuys ce temps allant chez ladicte prunelle pour sesdicts affaires elle entendit que ladicte prunelle parloyt dun sien complis serurier & ladicte conffesant se soubvenant de ce quelle avoyt oy dire audict messire Andre dece quil disoyt avoir affaire dun serurier senquist sil estoyt bon ouvrier." Croumet was evidently not in a particularly coherent condition when she made this statement, and it was copied down in a truly vile hand, so it is a bit difficult to interpret.

74. See Julie Hardwick, *Family Business: Litigation and the Political Economies of Daily Life in Early Modern France* (Oxford: Oxford University Press, 2009), 142–52.

utilizing that network, did she and Tranchetti launch their half-baked scheme to counterfeit the money they needed.

Croumet's remorse here signals recognition that her entire way of life went against contemporary social norms. Others took this to more psychopathic lengths. The limiting case was Captain la Chambre. He lived with a thirty-one-year-old woman named Mathurine Gallopin, widow of a gilder named Pierre Bertyn. There can be little doubt that la Chambre was in fact Gallopin's lover: workers assumed her to be his wife, he took charge of her children's education, and he paid well above market rent for his rooms in her house. She had actually met la Chambre's father, the provisioner, through her late husband—presumably, great lords needed many items gilded. Monsieur Bertyn's friendship with the la Chambres may have been good for business, but it proved bad for his health. Four years earlier, "returning . . . from supper at the home of Captain la Chambre the elder, he was stabbed from behind with a dagger, on the Rue Simon le Franc."[75] The murderer was never caught, but given the circumstances it is hard to escape the conclusion that the younger la Chambre knew more than he was saying.

There were of course degrees of legitimacy in such relationships. More toward the other end was the case of the Spanish nobleman Diego de Miño, who met the sieur de St. Biart's sister and "having fallen in love with her he accosted him one day perhaps a year ago while hunting and proposed his plan to settle in France." Saint Biart made some perfunctory investigations into de Miño's background and arranged a contract of marriage "by which [de Miño] promised to bring in four or five thousand écus . . . so that he could not be reproached for having married his sister off badly," but that very disclaimer suggests that the couple had already taken matters into their own hands.[76] And it might well have been to get his hands on the promised money that de Miño turned to crime. The striking thing about such relationships, confirming one of the major themes of coiners' narratives, is the determination they reveal to create lives and social identities in the face of laws, mores, and practical exigencies. The move to counterfeiting appears here to be the culminating point of a potentially pathological but profound

75. AN, Z^{1B} 489, *liasse* dated December 1569, piece C (interrogatories of Gallopin, 13–19 Dec.), fol. xxiv v: "revenant de soupper . . . du logis du Cappitaine la chambre laisne fut frappe par derrier dung coup de dague comme elle estime en la rue simon le franc."

76. AN, Z^{1B} 683, dossier dated August 1608, "second interrogatoire des accuzes," fol. 4r: "estant venu amoreux delle il laborda un jour estant a la chasse il y peult avoir ung an et luy proposa son desseing de sarrester en france." Fols. 1v–2r: "par lequel il promectroict apporter quatre ou cinq mil escuz . . . a ce que lon [ne] luy peust reprocher avoir mal emparante sa soeur."

process of "self-fashioning."[77] Given the absolutely central role of household formation in the early modern world, it is not surprising to find it at the heart of identity-forming activities.

Women were important players in enforcing the monetary laws as well. There was nothing anomalous about this, since the institutions of the early modern French state relied heavily on women and female social networks to supplement their limited enforcement powers.[78] Women could even partially bypass the state. A herb seller in the Halles, when passed a false coin, consulted with all her neighbors as to its status and then together with "a fat woman unknown to her" tracked down the guilty party. Not only did they berate him and identify him to a passing magistrate, but they "took off his hat and a leather covering . . . that he was wearing," keeping them as compensation for her loss![79] This was all the more true in the case of coining because handling cash was very distinctly a woman's job.[80] In the records of the Monnaies, it is almost unheard-of to find a man giving or receiving cash except in an official capacity or when he has no available female household members.

Women thus tended to be on both sides of transactions involving bad money. To take one example, a woman from Beaumont who sold bread reported that one time "when the deponent could not accept the said six-blanc coins" that another woman had offered in payment, saying that they had come originally from Etienne Butel's wife Marie Deanebonne, "she and the said woman . . . brought them back to Butel's wife, who freely took them back and gave them different ones."[81] Women were expected to know and recognize bad coins, helping each other to do so. As a rule, women coiners

---

77. On this concept, the classic work is Stephen Greenblatt, *Renaissance Self-Fashioning: From More to Shakespeare* (Chicago: University of Chicago Press, 1980).

78. See, e.g., Jacob Melish, "Women and the Courts in the Control of Violence between Men: Evidence from a Parisian Neighborhood under Louis XIV," *French Historical Studies* 33 (2010): 1–31; and Georg'ann Cattelona, "Control and Collaboration: The Role of Women in Regulating Female Sexual Behavior in Early Modern Marseille," *French Historical Studies* 18 (1993): 13–33.

79. AN, Z^{1B} 491, piece dated 18 November 1575 (information against Jehan Besne), fol. 1v: "Toutesfoys ladicte depposant . . . ne le lascha poinct . . . et ladicte depposant & ladicte grosse femme luy ostaient sa cappe & une housse de cuyre . . . quil portoyt." The exercise in summary judgment was at least approved if not initiated by a councillor in the Cour des Aides and his father-in-law, a retired notary. Ibid., fol. 2v.

80. See Jacob Melish, "The Power of Wives: Managing Money and Men in the Family Businesses of Old Regime Paris," in *Enterprising Women: Gender, Agency and Work in Eighteenth-Century France* (Baton Rouge: Louisiana State University Press, forthcoming).

81. AN, Z^{1B} 681, piece dated 21 December 1587 (information against Butel), fol. 3r: "quand elle qui depose ne pouvoyt allouer lesdictes pieces de six blancs elle et ladicte femme . . . les reportoyent a la femme dudict butel laquelle les reprenoyt librement et leurs en bailloyt dautres."

seem to have been more likely than men to handle the transfer and storage of precious metals and actual coins. In the clipping ring of which the merchant Charles Eustace was the nominal head, his wife, Claude Girard, did all the actual work. She collected the bits of metal clipped by the confederates, often on her expeditions to hear daily mass. One subcontractor delivered the clippings to her home but "never gave them to the woman in the presence of her husband, and he sometimes gave them to her by herself in an upper room and in her shop room." This particular artisan received the coins he clipped from one Catherine, the sister or sister-in-law of a housemate, "and he thinks that she got half the profit."[82] Such examples could be multiplied almost indefinitely. Whether working as or against coiners, it was women who most often made concrete the social power of coins by actually passing them in transactions.

The affair of the Comporion gang, convicted of clipping in 1584, well illustrates the gender and family dynamics of coining.[83] The core members of this group were the brothers François and Jehan Comporion; the latter's wife, Noelle Guerin; their eighteen-year-old son, also named Jehan; and their former roommate, with whom the younger Jehan still lived, a widow named Jehanne Bourrien. Bourrien's recently dismissed servant, Pierrette Vallement, admitted to having helped circulate the clipped coin—to the tune of perhaps 1,400 écus: this was a large-scale operation. The Comporions were originally from Sens; the Jehans had apparently been in Paris for some time, but François had joined them only recently when Sens got too hot for him. He left behind a failed marriage: he was separated from his wife, Olive Barbes, supposedly on account of her "bad life." In fact, though, such separations were given on the wife's petition and required a demonstration of the husband's mistreatment of her or mismanagement of her property.[84] He did, however, have a concubine, a servant named Françoise Javelier, who was pregnant and passed in his neighborhood as his wife and who also participated in the coining. For the sake of

---

82. AN, Z[1B] 483, piece dated 20 October 1548 (confession under torture of Denis Laurent), fols. 6v, 3v: "nen a poinct baille a la femme en la presence de son mary et quil la bailloit a elle seulle aulcunes fois en une chambre haulte et en son chambre bouticque"; "et pense quelle y avoit la moictye du profict." It is interesting that illegal activity very often did occur in "chambres haultes" and other marginal commercial locations. The regulations that sought to confine business to open shops were not confronting an imaginary problem.

83. See AN, Z[1B] 680, *liasse* dated 1584 (case file), and AN, Z[1B] 494, piece dated 22 March 1584 (sentence).

84. On marital separation in early modern France see Hardwick, *Family Business.*

symmetry Bourrien also had a lover, an apothecary named Pierre Berger who was arrested and interrogated but released. This was clearly very much a family concern, but the families in question had a jury-rigged character. Concubinage, domestic service, and the ad hoc household formation dictated by the cramped, often transient housing of early modern Paris all operated alongside blood and marriage in bringing the coiners together.[85] Women were essential to the public face of coining, and they had considerable freedom of action and initiative, even if it would be out of the question for them to act alone, and servants such as Vallement and Javelier presented themselves as harassed and constrained—though the former was also able to extract herself successfully from the situation. And the desire to construct a social identity otherwise out of reach shines through in all the participants.

There is one important nuance to women's involvement in the family business of coining. While male coiners (Tranchetti, for example) did occasionally imply that their partners had driven them into criminality, the narrative of female temptation was far from common. Tranchetti actually drew a rebuke from his interrogators when he used it: "It was remonstrated to him that those are not true words, to say that he had the punches and écu-coining dies made only to please a woman."[86] Rather, women tended to be presented as innocent bystanders—as when the mason's assistant le Sourd "said that his wife saw him casting [his counterfeit coins] but she did not know what it was; he concealed it from her saying that he was casting bullets, [and] never used her to pass them"[87]—or as forces for lawfulness and morality, such as Loys Doner's wife, who had his crimes "on her conscience." They could be portrayed, indeed, as capable of far more assertive action. When the generals questioned Tranchetti's goldsmith accomplice, Philippes Domet, about

---

85. One gets a sense of how these housing arrangements could work from Bourrien's roommate at the time of her arrest, one Simonne du Boys: "Laquelle nous auroit dict se tenir en ladicte chambre avecques une femme nomme Jehanne dont elle ne scavoyt le surnom Et la congnoissoit pour avoir este sa voysine lors que ladicte Jehanne demeuroit aux faulxbourges st victor Et a sa priere estoit venue demourer avec icelle pour luy aider a garder son enfant & faire son mesnaige attendant quelle eust une servante." AN, Z^{1B} 680, piece dated 7 January 1584, fol. 1r.

86. AN, Z^{1B} 679, piece dated 3 February 1570 (interrogatory): "Luy a este remonstre que ce ne sont parolles veritables de dire quil avoyt faict faire les fers et coings a forger escuz seullement pour contenter une femme."

87. AN, Z^{1B} 496, dossier dated 8 June 1593 (interrogatory of le Sourd, 9 June), fol. 2r: "a dit que sa femme la veu fonder mays elle ne scavoit que cestoit se cachoit delle disant quil faisoit des boullez ne la jamays employe pour en exposer." She gave the same story in her interrogation, but his admission that she may have picked up some of his counterfeits unwittingly casts doubt on the denial that he used her to pass them.

whether he had ever counterfeited before, "he said not, and that his wife is too quarrelsome, and that she would never have suffered it, and would sooner have cut his throat!" Her version of the story left her more passive and him guiltier while maintaining the basic structure of the narrative. Though the chemicals he had bought could have been used for legitimate goldsmithing work, she said, "still, suspecting something, she asked him one day what he wanted with those drugs and whether he wanted to undertake some wickedness with counterfeit money; to which the said Domet replied 'that damned stuff will keep busting my head, bitch,' and the confessant was not able to get any other explanation." The court believed her version, releasing her without charges while her husband was put to the question.[88] The Monnaies' general policy of moderate leniency toward women certainly fit in with this overall picture. Important as they were to the operation of coining, women were constructed as mitigating forces against the evils unleashed by the money economy. Perhaps they had to be, given their key roles both in using money and in influencing the family status that men and women alike most often wanted money to buy.

Alchemy

The practice of coining, then, was fundamentally anchored in and shaped by the society in which it occurred. Not all relevant aspects of that society, though, were as concrete or as readily comprehensible to us as socioeconomic and gender relations. Coining was a technical process that aimed to manipulate the natural world in ways that would deceive and (as Charles IX hoped, for example) astonish observers.[89] As such, it overlapped with other contemporary practices that sought at least some of the same ends using at least some of the same materials. Chief among them was alchemy, as contemporaries were quick to notice. According to Bernard Palissy, a

---

88. AN, Z^{1B} 679, dossier dated 6 November 1569, no. 20 (interrogatory of Domet), fol. 12v: "A dict que non & que sa femme est trop fascheuse & quelle ne leust jamais souffrir & luy eust eu plustost couppe la gorge." No. 33, fol. 1r (interrogatory of Guillemette de la Valée): "Toutesfoys se doubtant bien de quelque chose luy demanda ung jour quest ce quil vouylloyt desdicts drogues et qil en voulloyt faire quelque meschancete de faulce monnoye a quoy ledict domet feist response ceste meschante mastiere villaine me rompra tousjours la teste et ne sceust ladicte confessant avoyr autre raison." For sentences see AN, Z^{1B} 489, piece dated 9 December 1569 (conclusions of the procureur général)—I have been able to locate only the actual sentences for Tranchetti and Croumet, but they followed these recommendations.

89. This should be understood in the context of the central role of "wonder" in Renaissance culture, as discussed, for example, by Carolyn Walker Bynum, "Presidential Address: Wonder," *American Historical Review* 102 (1997): 1–26.

Huguenot potter and naturalist and one of the more significant Renaissance critics of alchemy, "All the additions and sophistications that [alchemists] know how to perform have created a thousand counterfeiters, for they cannot pass off their merchandise except as coins, since if they sell it in ingots its falsity will be discovered when it is melted down; but they pour out their coins easily to all and sundry. This is why, when they have worked a long time and cannot recover from their losses, they are forced to fall upon the moneys."[90] This was not a very original sentiment: ironically, and perhaps unwittingly, the very Protestant Palissy was paraphrasing Pope John XXII, whose bull *Spondent* (1317) outlawed alchemy on the grounds that its practitioners' "damned and damnable temerity goes so far that they strike the characters of public money of true metal for trusting eyes, for otherwise the alchemical fires of their furnaces cannot escape the notice even of the inexpert common people."[91] Allowing for differences of style, this common narrative is strangely familiar: skilled men whose dreams of mastery and social advancement lead them to ruin and to the desperate, antisocial expedient of counterfeiting. The pope's understanding of crime against the currency at least broadly matched what appears in the archives; the archives, in turn, suggest that while the relationship between counterfeiting and alchemy was not as mechanical as he suggests, it was nonetheless significant.

Besides broadening our understanding of the nature of coining, this fact highlights something important about the role of alchemy in early modern Europe. Recent studies have tended to emphasize its position as a respectable mode of inquiry into nature and the control of nature and its integration into the social, political, and intellectual structures of the era. Whether we think of alchemy in the context of the history of medicine, of the scientific

---

90. Bernard Palissy, *Œuvres complètes*, ed. Paul-Antoine Cap (Paris: J. J. Dubochet, 1844), 199: "toute les additions et sophistiqueries, qu'ils sçavent faire, ont causé un millier de faux monnoyeurs: par ce qu'ils ne se peuvent deffaire de leur marchandise sinon en monnoye, car si'ls la vendoyent en lingots la fausseté se trouveroit à la fonte. Mais ils se desfont aisément de monnoye à toutes gens. C'est pourquoy quand ils ont bien travaillé et ne se peuvent relever de leurs pertes, ils sont contraints se jetter sur la monnoye." The quote is from the second of his *Discours admirables*, probably composed in the mid-1570s. The basic study of Palissy's relation to alchemy remains Wallace Kirsop, "The Legend of Bernard Palissy," *Ambix* 9 (1961): 136–54.

91. Emil Richter and Emil Friedberg, eds., *Corpus juris canonici, pars secunda: Decretalium collectiones* (Graz: Akademische Druck und Verlaganstalt, 1955), col. 1296 (10.5.6): "Eoque interdum eorum temeritas damnata et damnanda progreditur, ut fidis metallis cudant publicæ monetæ characteres fidis oculis, et non alias alchimitum fornacis ignem vulgum ingorantem eludant." The title under which this bull was inserted into the *Extravagantes communes* of the canon law was "De crimine falsi," after the title of the Justinianic Code that dealt with counterfeiting.

revolution, of technological and economic policy, or of Renaissance culture, we now tend to see it, despite its somewhat controversial nature, as part of the "mainstream" rather than a relic of barbarous superstition or a preserve of a hermeticist subculture.[92] And this undoubtedly represents an advance in our understanding of the phenomenon. But it is not the entire story, for it is also the case that alchemy in its various forms was never entirely respectable and that this contributed almost as much as the fact that it was pure nonsense to alchemy's ultimate failure as a way of understanding nature.

Some reasons for this sulfurous reputation have been relatively well explored: the frequent conflicts that Paracelsian devotees encountered or even sought out with academic medicine, for example, or of course alchemy's incapacity to deliver on almost any of its promises. But alchemy's association with fraud and criminality was at least equally important in the minds of contemporaries. This applied especially to the world of empirical and demotic alchemy, which has figured less prominently in our own imagination than the work of erudite theorists and large-scale operatives. The link in popular culture between the alchemist and the counterfeiter or gallows bird was strong, and this depressed the status of the enterprise as a whole. And there is evidence that this link did not exist merely in the eyes of observers. The records of investigations into counterfeiting cases show the occasional but consistent presence of people who practiced the alchemical arts alongside their criminality or claimed them as a cloak for their more illicit activities. Finally, there is one case in France in which people closely associated with the enforcement of monetary regulation engaged in alchemical controversy: a few details of that controversy suggest how the erudite alchemy of the elites was subtly tinged by the example of the grifters on the streets.

We can begin by returning to a counterfeiter we have already met, Michel Pasté, the Huguenot sword polisher. Before his arrest, other than doing odd jobs for established masters and sharing whatever profits his wife and sister made from their wax-flower business, Pasté had apparently been surviving

---

92. I am thinking of studies such as Allen G. Debus, *The English Paracelsians* (New York: F. Watts, 1966); William Newman, *Gehennical Fire: The Lives of George Starkey, an Alchemist in the Scientific Revolution* (Chicago: University of Chicago Press, 2003); Lawrence Principe, *The Aspiring Adept: Robert Boyle and His Alchemical Quest* (Princeton: Princeton University Press, 1998); Pamela H. Smith, *The Business of Alchemy: Science and Culture in the Holy Roman Empire* (Princeton: Princeton University Press, 1994); Tara Nummedal, *Alchemy and Authority in the Holy Roman Empire* (Chicago: University of Chicago Press, 2007); and Didier Kahn, *Alchimie et paracelsisme en France à la fin de la renaissance (1567–1625)* (Geneva: Droz, 2007). The list is not exhaustive, and I do not mean to imply that the authors on it form any kind of coherent "school"—merely that they share a commitment to seeing alchemical inquiry as normal within early modern society.

by sponging off the household of a noble, M. de Chaumalles, to whom he had been introduced by "a tall man named the sieur Croyer from the city of Meaux, who is involved in philosophy."[93] Pasté, it seems, had a recipe for turning silver into gold that he had received from a Fleming back in la Rochelle, and he was taken on to brew it up it for M. de Chaumalles. We learn little more—it would be interesting to know what Croyer and Chaumalles (if the former even existed) had to say for themselves—but in one sense the point of this story is simple. True or not, it was meant to explain the incriminating presence of various acids and other "drugs" in Pasté's chamber. In this case, the judges of the Monnaies probably felt no obligation to take it very seriously, since Pasté had been caught red-handed. Nevertheless, they did interrogate him about the details of the supposed process and whether he had ever been able to make it work. (The answer was equivocal: "He had seen the said Fleming do it in the city of la Rochelle and other places and the gold produced by [the process], which he had been told was good; as for him, he had made some powders and found grains of good gold.")[94]

In another case, tried in Caen in 1578, Jacques de St.-Hilaire attempted to explain away an entire workshop of "several furnaces, crucibles, . . . and other earthen and glass vessels, acids, saltpeter, sulfur, arsenic . . . several different salts, quicksilver, and a plaque of cast bullion, lime for liming gold and silver, and other materials and drugs," as tools for experiments in medical alchemy, to make "several compositions, liquids, powders, and oils, suitable for healing and curing wounds, catarrhs, gouts, and other maladies."[95] This seems to have succeeded no better than Pasté's excuses, but it underlines the technical kinship between counterfeiting and alchemy. And the younger Jehan Comporion had a long, elaborate story about his supposed unsuccessful alchemical

---

93. AN, Z¹ᴮ 499, dossier dated 12 February 1600 (interrogatory of Michel Pasté), fol. 3v: "ung grand homme nommé le sr. Croyer de la ville de Meaux qui se mesle de la philosophie." There was in fact a prominent Reformed family named Croyer in Meaux. See John Foxe, *The Acts and Monuments of the Church Containing the History and Sufferings of the Martyrs*, pt. 2 (London: Kessinger, 2005), 1002.

94. AN, Z¹ᴮ 499, same piece, fol. 4v: "l'avoir veu faire audict flamant, en la ville de la rochelle & autres lieux et l'or que en estoit produict qui estoit bon ainsy quil estoit dict quand a luy en a faict des poudres & trouvé de grains de bon or."

95. AN, Z¹ᴮ 492, piece dated 9 January 1578 (arrêt of Claude de Montperlier, authenticated copy): "plusieurs fourneaulx creusetz matelatz et autres vaisseaulx tant de terre que de verre Eaulx fortes salpestres souffre arsenic . . . sels de plusieurs sortes vifargent une placque de buillon fondue une lime a lymer or et argent et aultres matieres et drogues"; "plusieurs compostions tant deaulx pouldres cendres que dhuilles propres pour la guarison et cures des playes ulsaires cateres gouttes et autres maladies." This document, from a general of the Monnaies acting on commission in Normandy, merely takes under advisement the accused's petition to be released from prison because of his advanced state of venereal disease, which his unguents had apparently not cured.

experiments, beginning with how one day "walking through the streets he had seen a piece of paper fall from a man's hand written in Italic script (though in French), containing the word 'to make the solar gold'. . . . He had wanted to try this, and in order to do so he bought the following drugs. . . . He bought them from a wholesale grocer on the Rue St. Denis, and to try he got an alembic" and various other instruments.[96] The transparent purpose of this tale was to explain away his chemicals and equipment, but its almost novelistic level of detail, which vaguely echoes contemporary alchemical treatises, suggests a certain level of comfort and familiarity with the world of alchemy.

In other cases, the reality of a suspect's engagement with alchemy appears more clearly. In 1573, a judge of the Monnaies visiting Châlons-sur-Marne searched the lodgings of a local schoolteacher named Hector Marcquemont, who was strongly suspected of clipping coins. He found metalworking equipment, various chemicals useful for counterfeiters, and "notebooks . . . in the hand of the said Marcquemont . . . some . . . making mention of the quintessence of gold and silver and other metals, some of natural magic and chiromancy, and some of the names of the spirits that govern the regions of the world, together with formulas for invoking and conversing with them."[97] It is worth pausing to note how thoroughly entwined alchemy, natural magic, and demonology seem to have been in the life of this well-educated man, who was clearly as fascinated with the frontiers of the natural as he was dishonest. In other cases, the line between alchemy and counterfeiting could blur to the point of invisibility. Martin Cordier, who had a reputation in the Beauvaisis as the region's "most cunning and notorious counterfeiter," had in his house in the village of Francastel some counterfeiting equipment and a copy of a sentence of banishment for that crime. With these were "three other papers containing recipes for making drugs and other materials that are used in the fabrication of counterfeit money," which seem to have been

---

96. AN, Z^{1B} 680, piece dated 17 March 1585 (interrogatories): "allant par les rues il veit tomber des mains dung homme ung papier escript en lectre Italique (toutesfoys en francoys) contentant ces motz 'Pour faire or sol' . . . a voullu esprouver icelle pour quoy faire il a achepte les drogues qui ensuyvent . . . il achepta chez ung marchant grossier demourant rue st denys et que pour esprouver ce faict il prenoit ung allambic." His interrogator wondered how he had been able to afford all these things given his poverty, a question he evaded. Etienne Butel, the *practicien* of Beaumont-sur-Oise, told a similar story for similar reasons, though in his case the failed alchemist was a deceased brother. See AN, Z^{1B} 681, piece dated 17 September 1587 (interrogatory of Butel), fols. viii v–ix r.

97. AN, Z^{1B} 490, piece dated 13 April 1573 (procès-verbal of Pierre Longuet), fol. 1v: "cayiers . . . de la main dudict marquemont . . . aucuns desdicts cayiers faisans mention [de la] quinte essance de lor et de largent et autres metaulx, aucuns de la magie naturelle et de la chiromancie et les aucuns des noms des esperitz qui gouvernent les regions du monde ensemble la forme de linvocation et conversation diceulx."

very much like alchemical recipes: one is described as "beginning with these words, 'For the sun, take' and ending 'and everything proven.'"[98]

These cases suggest not merely isolated malefactors but entire networks of people involved in questionable practices related to alchemy—a dark side of the networks of knowledge so beloved of recent historians of early modern science and intellectual life generally but at the same time redolent of coiners' high level of social implantation. These networks could well be transnational (remember Pasté's Fleming), and they seem to have flourished in the chaos and warfare that marked the last two decades of the sixteenth century. An itinerant *arquebusier* (apparently more of a gunsmith than a soldier, though he seems to have practiced both trades) "who had seen a lot by following the wars in Flanders" and went by the nom de guerre of la Montaigne, was convicted in 1588 for working as an engraver for a counterfeiting ring. Put to the question before his execution, he told his interrogators "that if the king and the Cour des Monnaies knew the exquisite and rare things that he knows, which he got not from the French, but from the Germans he has known, the king and the said court would have pity on him and spare his life," later admitting that it was in Germany that he had learned the counterfeiter's trade.[99] If they existed at all, the mysterious "choses exquises" may not have been alchemical, though they were surely designed to sound that way, and the court paid them little attention. Or take the case of Gallias Viger, an Italian from the duchy of Urbino, who was arrested for counterfeiting while renting a room in the house of the widow of an officer in the Monnaies. The former almoner of Cardinal René de Birague, now down on his luck, Viger seems to have been an all-around dabbler in the occult: he was found in possession of manuscripts on astrology, necromancy, and alchemy, in Italian and French, and had apparently performed some voodoo-like love magic on behalf of the daughter of the household in which he lodged.[100] He

---

98. AN, Z^{1B} 681, dossier dated 13 September 1587, piece A, fol. ii v: "le plus rusé & signalé faulx monnoieur"; fol. iii v: "trois autres pappiers contenans receptes pour composer drogues & matieres servans a fabriquer faulce monnoye"; "commencant par ces mots Pour le soleil prenez et finissant et toutte esprouvée."

99. AN, Z^{1B} 495, piece dated 21 January 1588 (interrogatory of Jacques de Pais), fol. 1v: "qui avoict beaucoup veu pour avoir frequente les gueres de flandres"; piece dated 28 January 1588 (testament of la Montaigne), fol. 1v: "que sy le roy et la court des monnoyes scavoit choses exquises et rares quil scet lesquelles il ne tient des francoys ains des allemands avec lesquelz il a hante, le roy et ladite court auroit pitie de luy et luy suaveroient la vye." The mere threat of torture was sufficient to elicit this testimony. This can be compared to the case of Claude Charpentier, the soldier and sapper discussed above, who also promised important (and, he later admitted, nonexistent) technical secrets if he were spared.

100. See AN, Z^{1B} 681, a group of pieces dated from 15 February 1590.

combined Marcquemont's educated and eclectic occultism with la Montaigne's international flair and Pasté's picaresque lifestyle. And he illustrated how this whole unsavory complex could come uncomfortably close to the magistrates of the moneys themselves.

There is thus good evidence that actual counterfeiters did associate themselves with alchemy, either to provide some kind of alibi, out of genuine interest in the science, or in the course of learning the practical skills needed to produce fake coins. What remains to be explored—in a very preliminary way—is the effect of this real and widely understood connection on the standing and understanding of alchemy in the broader culture. The attitude toward alchemy of the authorities specifically charged with regulating the coinage can provide at least one opening into the question, since they were simultaneously professionally interested in any legitimate investigation into the precious metals and all too familiar with the possible misuses of alchemy. In practice, given its close involvement with the supply and trade in precious metals, alchemy was surprisingly lightly regulated, at least in France; indeed, in France as elsewhere, attempts to control or suppress alchemical activity were most likely to come from faculties of medicine. While the Cour des Monnaies had some theoretical jurisdiction over alchemists, as it did over anyone else who worked in precious metals, it seems never to have exercised it in any kind of systematic way. Even the (very brief) section on alchemy in an eighteenth-century manuscript collection of regulations drawn up for the court has been ripped out.[101]

Still, the court was no stranger to alchemy. The most obvious index of that interest was the involvement of its personnel in alchemical experimentation and controversy. If any sitting members engaged in such activities, the sources do not record it, but as we saw in the first chapter, there was an important exchange of pamphlets closely associated with the court. This took place in 1575, between Alexandre de la Tourette, the former second president of the Monnaies, whose office had been suppressed a few years before, and Jacques Gohory, an important if rather bizarre figure in the Parisian intellectual community and brother of the court's clerk. The participants recognized the importance of these questions of status, as de la Tourette was careful to note in the preface to his pamphlet that it was only after having quit his office of president and "all other public offices however honorable they might be, to return to my country home as a private man" that he took up "the threads of my old studies, and above all that of Philosophy," which, he stressed, was concerned

101. AN, U* 686.

with promoting happiness and specifically health rather than wealth, as worthy as the latter could be in the right hands.[102] The implication is that alchemical investigations were not really compatible with the dignity of a magistrate of the moneys, unlike, for instance, the historical scholarship of de la Tourette's successor—and Gohory's friend—Claude Fauchet. De la Tourette was more specifically aware of the problems alchemy's reputation posed, especially for a man in his position. The second of his two tracts, an "apology for the very useful science of alchemy, against both those who criticize it and the frauds, thieves, and tricksters who abuse it," closes with remarks strikingly similar to Palissy's roughly contemporary attack on the relationship between alchemy and counterfeiting. "Also, such seducers end on the gallows, as by a just judgment of God. For after they have forged and formed a fake alloy, finding no mint master or goldsmith who will buy it, they use it for counterfeiting; and thus, because of some malefactors, so noble a science is vilified."[103] The difference was that Palissy had relied on "a provost at Saintes named Grimaut" for his knowledge of the criminal underworld, while de la Tourette had ample personal experience.[104] But that personal experience actually tended to undercut de la Tourette's authority as a defender of alchemy.

Gohory's reply is probably best understood as a symptom of that problem. For in fact the disagreements between the two men were minimal, as Didier Kahn has shown.[105] Despite the ferocity of his attack, Gohory had to resort to nitpicking and outright bad faith to draw contrasts with his opponent. And Kahn is also almost certainly correct in believing that Gohory's motivations were essentially ad hominem. But the roots of this personal animus most likely lay in the internal politics of the Cour des Monnaies. For de la Tourette was a very controversial figure, given to sharp practice if not outright corruption. To the affairs mentioned in chapter 1 above we can add the fact that in 1571 his former colleagues accused him of having faced "several complaints . . . namely,

102. Alexandre de la Tourette, *Bref discours sur les admirables vertus de l'or potable* (Paris: Jean de l'Astre, 1575), sig. Aii r–v: "toutes autres charges publicques tant honorables qu'elles puissent estre, pour retourner à mon petit champestre comme homme privé"; "les erres de mes anciens estudes, & principallement sur la Philosophie."

103. Alexandre de la Tourette, *Apologie de la tresutile science d'alchimie, tant contre ceux qui la blasment, qu'aussi contre les faulsaires, larrons et trompeurs qui en abusent* (Paris: Jean de l'Astre, 1575), 36–37: "Aussi la fin de tels seducteurs, c'est le gibet: comme par un juste jugement de Dieu. Car apres qu'ils ont prou soufflé & formé de faux billon, ne trouvans maistre de monnoye, ny orfevre qui leur en baille argent: ils les employent à forger de faulse monnoye. Et voyla pourquoy à l'occasion des meschans une si noble science a esté vilipendée." De la Tourette's two treatises, though printed together, were separately paginated.

104. Palissy, *Œuvres*, 200: "un prevost à Xaintes, nommé Grimaut,"

105. See Kahn, *Alchimie*, 218–32.

in his positions of general and later president . . . concerning the familiarity and closeness that he had with various masters and lessors of the mints," which even resulted in some kind of proceeding in the Grand Conseil "for crimes committed in his office, of which he is not yet cleared."[106] The conflict was still going strong in 1577, when de la Tourette helped revive the offices of the subsidiary general, which the court wanted to stay suppressed, giving one to his son.[107] Given Gohory's closeness to the Monnaies, it is hard to believe that he was not in some sense acting on their behalf in his attack on de la Tourette. For aside from the obvious desire not to be confused with those they prosecuted, the officers of the Monnaies had real reasons to fear being tarred with alchemy's unsavory reputation. Their integrity was intermittently called into question, sometimes with good reason. And this threatened not just their status but their effectiveness in law enforcement and indeed their fitness for their role in the entire profoundly interconnected project of the control of the currency.

Politics of Enforcement

That interconnection appears throughout the records of enforcement activity but particularly in the administrative and spectacular elements of the Monnaies' criminal jurisdiction. The line between control of the mints and the suppression of coining was not always a clear one, as the Pinatel affair made dramatically clear. While much of the coining of pinatelles by Montmorency-Damville and others during the civil wars was accepted as a political devaluation rather than counterfeiting and eventually covered under the Edicts of Pacification, it still could be and sometimes was equated with criminal counterfeiting. In a letter that gives a good idea both of how that worked and how frustrating the life of a general of the moneys could be, Jean Favier wrote from Avignon in 1599 relating that the previous year he had

> received letters from the king by which I was commanded to retry [the duc d'Epernon's former mint master] Maurice for the false money he made at Sisteron and Toulon, notwithstanding the abolition he had. Thus my duty required me to work on this, and seeing himself pursued,

---

106. AN, Z[1B] 374, pieces dated 19 May 1571 (procès-verbal of a démarche to the royal court): "plusieurs plainctes . . . savoir en ses estatz de general et depuys de president . . . touschant les familiaritez et habitudes quil avoit avec aucuns maistres et fermiers des monnoyes"; and 14 December 1570 (procès-verbal of the delivery of remonstrances): "pour faultes commises en son estat desquelles il nest encores purge." The accusations against de la Tourette do not appear in the actual 1571 remonstrances as recorded in the court's official registers. See AN, Z[1B] 67, fols. 91v–94r.

107. See chapter 3.

the said Maurice reached a composition around last Christmas to pay 1,500 écus to M. [illegible], but since I did not get news of this until five months later I meanwhile tried him in Tarascon, where he was condemned to death by default; then, I waited a long time for him to surrender in order to justify himself, which he did only on 15 February last, and then he escaped from the said prison with the connivance of the jailer, . . . who is also a fugitive.[108]

Even in more ordinary times it was not always easy to tell if a bad coin was the result of freelance criminality or of fraud or incompetence at the mints. This probably explains, for example, an odd incident in 1580, when the court found three bad écus in the possession of Bernardin Salvi, chaplain to the archbishop of Aix. They had the mark of the Bayonne mint for 1578 and (along with six identical ones located in the next few days) were found to be about 2 percent under the legal alloy. This was not enough to be especially profitable to a counterfeiter, but anyone who could skim off that proportion of the gold flowing through a mint would do quite well. The master of the Bayonne mint happened to be in town, presumably for the judgment of his pyxes, and though he formally disavowed the suspect pieces, the court obviously wondered if they were the result of his malversation.[109]

Such cases are a reminder that suppressing crimes against the currency was an irreducibly political activity. It was continuous and synergetic with currency policy more generally, if only because (as the Spanish and English both discovered in the seventeenth century) unrestrained counterfeiting could render all other attempts to control the currency impotent.[110] It impinged on diplomacy, as we saw with the English démarches mentioned above, the Swiss

---

108. AN, Z[1B] 390, dossier dated 31 July 1599, piece no. 7 (letter from Jean Favier in Avignon to the court, 5 November 1599): "je receu lettres du roy par lesquelles il m'estoit mandé de faire le proces de nouveau a Maurice pour la faulce monnoye par luy fabricquee au paravant quil feust maistre des monnoyes de Sisteron et Tholon et non obstant son abolition a quoy pour mon service il ma fallu vacquer et se voyant ledict Maurice poursuivy il entra environ la feste de Noel dernier en composition de fournir xvc ecus a monsieur [illeg.] et n'en ayant eu nouvelles que cinq moys apres je juge cependant le proces a Tarascon ou il fut condampné a mort par contumace depuis mayant entretenu ung long temps quil se vouloit rendre prisonnier pour se justiffier il me l'auroit faict que le xve Fevrier dernier et dicelle prison esvadé par intelligence de geollier le dimanche viiie aoust ensuivant, le quel geollier s'est aussy rendu fugitif." Obviously Maurice had plenty of money; for an example of his rather horrible work, see Stéphan Sombart, "De nouvelles précisions sur les liards d'Henri IV," *Bulletin de la Société Française de numismatique* 52 (November 1997), http://www.inumis.com/ressources/france/articles/sisteron/sisteron-fr.html.

109. See AN, Z[1B] 492, piece dated 6 February 1580 (procès-verbal of Nicolas Roland).

110. On the Spanish case, where counterfeiting of copper coinage led to rampant inflation of the money of account, see Akira Motomura, "The Best and Worst of Currencies: Seigniorage and Currency Policy in Spain, 1597–1650," *Journal of Economic History* 54 (1994): 104–27; for England, see the ample literature on the recoinage, which is competently summarized in Levenson, *Newton*.

imbroglio discussed in the previous chapter, and a case in 1551 in which the court resolved "that remonstrances will be made to the king or his council" about a case of counterfeiting "that is publicly committed in the Emperor's lands, to inform the ambassador or otherwise deal with it as he sees fit."[111] And the Monnaies and other jurisdictions that tried coiners were happy to employ the kind of theater of punishment that played such an important and well-known role in early modern governance.[112] Criminals (especially clippers) were periodically sentenced to public whippings, to be carried out around Paris, in the case of the Comporion gang "with a placard on their back where these words will be written: 'clippers and exposers of clipped écus and other coins.'"[113] The most spectacular performance available for the punishment of counterfeiting was the traditional penalty for that crime, boiling the perpetrator alive in a giant cauldron, which all jurisdictions of high justice were theoretically required to maintain for that purpose. While this had already fallen into desuetude by the fifteenth century, it remained possible to revive it strategically. The Cour des Monnaies did this once, in January 1587, at a time when royal authority in Paris was becoming seriously threatened. It apparently had an impact, if not necessarily the intended one, since a week and a half later the solicitor general reported that "under the pretext of the exemplary punishment given to Jehan Daulmont and . . . Jehan Thierry, convicted and condemned to death for making counterfeit six-blanc coins, the people indifferently refuse all six-blanc pieces that are presented to them, which greatly impedes commerce."[114] The parlement of Rennes seems to have adopted

111. AN, Z[1B] 38, fol. 34r (10 June 1551): "que remonstrance sera fete au roy ou a son conseil prive du crime et delit dont est question en ce proces que se commet publicquement ou pays de lempereur pour en advertir lembassadeur ou autrement y faire pourvoir comme de raison."

112. The literature on this is huge, originating largely from Michel Foucault, *Surveiller et punir: Naissance de la prison* (Paris: Gallimard, 1975). See, e.g., Richard J. Evans, *Rituals of Retribution: Capital Punishment in Germany, 1600–1987* (Oxford: Oxford University Press, 1996); and for the French case, James R. Farr, "The Death of a Judge: Performance, Honor, and Legitimacy in Seventeenth-Century France," *Journal of Modern History* 75 (2003): 1–22.

113. AN, Z[1B] 494, piece dated 22 March 1584 (sentence of Jehan Comporion and others): "ayant ung escripture sur le doz ou sera escript ces mots, Rongneures & expositeurs descuz & aultres especes rongnees." The women involved in the case were also to wear shears around their necks. See also, e.g., AN, Z[1B] 492, piece dated "dernier fev. 1580" (sentence of Jehan Dalle), where the whippings are to occur at the Palais de Justice and the four principal crossroads of Paris.

114. AN, Z[1B] 72, fol. 205r (12 February 1587): "soubs pretexte de la punition exemplaire faicte de Jehan daulmont et . . . jehan thierry convaincus et condampnes a mort pour la fabrication de pieces de six blancs faulces Le peuple reffuze indiferement toutes les pices de six blancs qui leur sont presentees ce qui incommode grandement le commerce." See AN, Z[1B] 495, piece dated 31 January 1587 (sentence of Jehan Thierry); the court had obtained letters patent specifically confirming its final jurisdiction over this case, suggesting that policy was coordinated with the royal council. See AN, Z[1B] 72, fol. 201 (27 January 1587).

boiling somewhat systematically for a few years after 1600, probably to reinforce Brittany's belated return to royal control after the Wars of Religion.[115]

Certainly, it is only to be expected that the concrete implementation of
royal control over the moneys would be equally important and would have
the same kind prominence in the practice of government. More broadly,
though, the entire experience of the Monnaies' criminal jurisdiction underlines the ways in which controlling the currency was a political enterprise.
Since the very existence of money, and a fortiori its misuse or misappropria-
tion, posed a perceived threat to the order of the polity, policing the moneys
was an essential way of organizing and protecting the body politic. The self-
fashioning, social counterfeiting, and even the desperation of coiners would
have appeared to contemporaries as expressions of the ambition, avarice, and
danger of unlimited, disordered, arbitrary expansion discussed by the theoreti-
cians. The courts controlled them less bizarrely, and probably more effectively,
than did Charles IX's supposed appropriation of lawless money making. But
the fact that such sovereign exercises could shade so easily into the literary is
important. A perfectly historical case from England, where a similar culture
but a different organization of government and different surviving records
allow a different perspective on the same phenomena, helps clarify that point.

On 26 January 1592, the port of Flushing (Vliesing) in the United Provinces of the Netherlands was under the control of an English expeditionary
force engaged in an increasingly desultory fight with the forces of Philip
II. Its governor was Sir Robert Sidney, future earl of Leicester and younger
brother of the poet. That day he sent a group of prisoners to the charge of
the Lord Treasurer Burgheley in London. The group included, in the words
of his covering letter,

> one named Christofer Marly, by his profession a scholer, and the other
> Gifford Gilbert a goldsmith taken heer for coining. . . . The matter was
> revealed unto me the day after it was done, by one Ri: Baines. . . . He
> was theyr chamber fellow and fearing the succes, made me acquainted
> with all. The men being examined apart never denied anything, onely
> protesting that what was done was onely to see the Goldsmiths con-
> ning. . . . And indeed they do one accuse another to have bin the
> inducers of him, and to have intended to practice yt heerafter. . . . But
> howsoever it hapned a dutch shilling was uttred, and els not any peece:
> and indeed I do not thinck that they wold have uttred many of them:
> for the mettal is plain peuter and with half an ay to be discovered.[116]

115. See Plessix-Buisset, *Le criminel*, 163–65.

116. R. B. Wernham, "Christopher Marlowe at Flushing in 1592," *English Historical Review* 91
(1976): 344–45, transcribing Public Records Office SP 84/44, fol. 60.

We have no indication of what became of Gilbert, but Marly and Baines were soon released. Within six months the former had turned to presenting plays on the London stage. In those circles, his last name was usually spelled "Marlowe."

It is very hard to guess exactly what Marlowe, Baines, and Gifford were up to in Flushing. It was not unheard-of for English counterfeiters to set up shop in the port cities across the Channel, as in the 1557 case mentioned above. On the other hand, Marlowe and Baines were both involved in the bizarre underworld of Elizabethan spying, and their prompt release suggests that their counterfeiting might somehow have been in the line of duty. Perhaps they were carrying out some kind of sting operation designed to forestall diplomatic complications between England and her sensitive Dutch allies. They also clearly hated each other, accusing each other not only of counterfeiting but "of intent to goe to the Ennemy or to Rome, both as they say of malice one to another."[117] A year and a half later Baines was testifying to the Privy Council that Marlowe was an atheistic traitor who, among other things, claimed "that he had as good Right to Coine as the Queen of England, and that he was aquainted with one Poole a prisoner in Newgate who hath greate Skill in mixture of mettals and having learned some thinges of him he ment through the help of a Cunninge stamp maker to Coin ffrench Crownes pistoletes and English shillinges."[118] This accusation in turn was very likely related to Marlowe's murder days later at the hands of fellow drinkers and fellow spies, which suggests that Baines's accusations were, if not exactly credible, at least in some way what the Privy Council wanted to hear.[119]

And although Marlow, Baines, and Gilbert remain mysterious characters, we might be able to infer a bit more about what Sidney, Burghley, Queen Elizabeth, and Walsingham (who ran her spy network) were doing. Besides being ridiculously colorful, this little episode shows the control of counterfeiting operating at the very highest levels of early modern governance, alongside war, diplomacy, religious and cultural policy, espionage, and

---

117. Ibid., 345.

118. C. F. Tucker Brooke, *The Life of Marlowe and the Tragedy of Dido Queen of Carthage* (New York: Gordian Press, 1966), 99 (app. 9, "Richard Baines on Marlowe," transcribing British Library Harleian ms. 6848, fols. 185–86). One strongly suspects that the English shillings appear only because coining French écus would have been mere misprision of treason and not a capital crime, while counterfeiting the English currency was the real deal. After all, why counterfeit French gold but English silver?

119. The best though by no means the least speculative account of Marlowe's murder is Charles Nicholls, *The Reckoning: The Murder of Christopher Marlowe* (Chicago: University of Chicago Press, 1995). This passage is the starting point for one of the classics of the New Historicism: Steven Greenblatt, "Invisible Bullets," in *Shakespearean Negotiations* (Berkeley: University of California Press, 1988), 21–65.

the kind of extrajudicial killing that epitomized *raison d'état*. Charles IX, according to Brantôme, played with counterfeiting in order to dramatize his sovereignty and in the same context of factional rivalry among Guise, Montmorency, and Valois that led him to order the assassination of Coligny and Henri III to order that of the cardinal de Lorraine's cousins, the duke and cardinal de Guise.[120] For Elizabeth I, counterfeiting formed a part, though an emblematic part, of the dangerous and chaotic world her government sought to control by any means necessary—including, quite possibly, by sponsoring or tolerating counterfeiters and by fabricating accusations of counterfeiting when convenient. Remember that Elizabeth's ability to stabilize the English coinage had been a major factor in her consolidation of power early in her reign. She surely understood as well as anyone how central the control of the coinage was to the exercise of sovereignty. Whatever game she and her council were playing with it in Marlowe's case, they seem to have won—but in losing England's second-best playwright, they paid a substantial price.

Like any significant author, Marlowe played an important role in his society, among other things by helping to articulate its structures and the various strategies that individuals could use (or should avoid) in navigating those structures. Structures of money and economic activity certainly figured prominently in that work—one thinks immediately of *The Jew of Malta* in Marlowe's case. With significant differences of timing and emphasis, one finds similar phenomena in France. Having seen some of the ways in which the nature, power, and control of money played out not just in theory and policy but in individual lives, we will now turn to narratives that were purely constructed rather than more or less genuinely lived. The former can help to shed light on the latter: the stories of many coiners already seem so dramatic that placing them in a literary context can go far toward making them make sense. Even more important, if perhaps paradoxical, literature is the best available window into the lived experience of the social operation of money. For authors were concerned not, or not primarily, with scoring political points, enforcing laws, avoiding punishments, and so on but precisely with illuminating forms of experience that their audience might find meaningful. In that sense, sources like Marlowe's plays are fundamentally more valuable than his arrest records, and not just for artistic reasons.

---

120. On the theory of the coup d'état and its history, see Gabriel Naudé, *Considérations politiques sur les coups d'état*, ed. Louis Marin (Paris: Editions de Paris, 1989). For Naudé, those assassinations were the paradigmatic cases of the coup d'état.

CHAPTER 6

The Monetary Imaginary
of Renaissance France

> I saw [Diane de Poitiers,] the duchesse de Valentinois
> at the age of seventy as beautiful of face, as fresh and
> lovable as at the age of thirty; and she was loved and
> served by one of the world's greatest and most valor-
> ous kings. I can honestly say that, without insulting
> this lady's beauty, for when any lady is loved by a great
> king it is a sign that perfection abounds and dwells in
> her and makes her beloved—and the heavens' gift of
> beauty should not be spared for demigods. I saw this
> lady six months before her death still so beautiful that
> I know no heart so hard that it would not have been
> stirred, . . . for her beauty, grace, and majesty, her fine
> appearance, were still as they had always been. And
> above all she had very pale skin, with no makeup at all
> (though they say that every morning she partook of
> some broth made up of potable gold and other drugs,
> which I do not understand as a good physician or
> subtle apothecary would). I believe that if this lady had
> lived another hundred years she would not have aged
> either in her face, so well-composed it was, or in her
> body, hidden and covered, so well-tempered and habit-
> uated. Alas that earth covers these beautiful bodies!
>
> —Brantôme

Part I: Gods

This passage, reversing all the gendered polarities of the one with which we
began the previous chapter, is from Brantôme's *Galllant Ladies*.[1] His distress
was premature, for earth did not do a terribly consistent job of covering
Henri II's mistress. Revolutionaries disinterred her from the church at Anet
in 1795, and more recently archeologists have recovered her remains from the
mass grave in the town cemetery where they had been deposited. And the

---

1. Pierre de Bourdeille de Brantôme, Œuvres complètes, 10 vols. (Paris: Renouard, 1886) 9:
356–57: "J'ay veu madame la duchesse de Valentinois, en l'aage de soixante-dix ans, aussi belle de
face, aussi fraische et aussi aymable comme en l'aage de trente ans: aussi fut-elle aymée et servie d'un

analysis of those remains has confirmed a detail of Brantôme's account: she had in fact been consuming potable gold, in quantities large enough to kill her.[2] Unlike Brantôme's account of Charles IX's counterfeiting, this story can be taken more or less at face value; but as in that other story, there is much to unpack in the tale of Diane, who, no less than her royal lover's family, was thoroughly enmeshed in what one might call the "monetary imaginary" of contemporary France.[3]

As factual as it may be, this is a very literary narrative: the final line shows its debt to the genre of ubi sunt, the laments for the beauties and virtues of the dead exemplified in the French vernacular tradition by François Villon's "Ballade des femmes du temps jadis."[4] Brantôme subverts that genre, though, for while it typically focused on the decay of physical beauty, Brantôme initially stresses its preservation; only in death is it subject to the ravages of time. Diane's preservation seems to be both a cause and a consequence of Henri II's love for her. His love signals that "perfection" (which in Aristotelian physics is not subject to corruption) "abounds in her" and at the same time places her among the demigods on whom beauty is lavished. Indeed, contemporary propaganda identified Diane with the goddess Diana in what Françoise Bardon describes as "an astonishing conjunction—the first in France and the most perfect of all time—of history and mythology."[5] Diane partakes of Henri's sacred sovereignty, which places them above ordinary

---

des grands rois et valeureux du monde. Je le peut dire franchement, sans faire tort à la beauté de cette dame, car toute dame aymée d'un grand roy, c'est signe que perfection abonde et habite en elle qui la fait aymer: aussi la beauté donnée des cieux ne doit estre espargnée aux demy-dieux. Je vis cette dame, six mois avant qu'elle mourust, si belle encor, que je ne sçache cœur de rocher qui ne s'en fust esmeu, . . . car sa beauté, sa grâce, sa majesté, sa belle apparence, estoyent toutes pareilles qu'elle avoit tousjours eu. Et surtout elle avoit une très-grande blancheur, et sans se farder aucunement; mais on dit bien que tous les matins elle usoit de quelques bouillons composez d'or potable et autres drogues, que je ne sçay pas comme les bons médecins et subtils apoticaires. Je croy que si cette dame eust encor vescu cent ans, qu'elle n'eust jamais vieilly, fust de visage, tant il estoit bien composé, fust de corps, caché et couvert, tant il estoit de bonne trempe et belle habitude. C'est dommage que la terre couvre ces beaux corps!"

2. See Philippe Charlier et al., "Fatal Alchemy: Did Gold Kill a 16th Century French Courtesan?," *British Medical Journal*, 19–26 December 2009, 339–40.

3. I adapt this term from Phillippe Desan, *L'imaginaire économique de la renaissance* (Mont-de-Marsan: Editions Inter-Universitaires, 1993). For an overview of the secondary literature on economic and monetary tropes in early modern French literature, see Jotham Parsons, "Etat Présent: Socio-economic Approaches to French Literature, c. 1540–1630," *French Studies* 65 (2011): 74–81.

4. For a useful summary of some relevant aspects of this topos, see Lionel J. Friedman, "The Ubi Sunt, the Regrets, and Efficitio," *Modern Language Notes* 72 (1957): 499–505.

5. Françoise Bardon, *Diane de Poitiers et le mythe de Diane* (Paris: Presses universitaires de France, 1963), 3: "une conjonction étonnante—la première en France et la plus parfaite qui fût jamais—, celle de l'histoire et de la mythologie."

mortals while absolving their sexual relationship of any dishonor (Brantôme can speak of it frankly, without wronging her). For adultery, as for coining, the king carries his pardon with him and does so ostentatiously that all may know he is legibus solutus. In this context, the role of Alexandre de la Tourette's beloved potable gold is unclear. If Diane's perfect composition of face and body was enough to preserve her from corruption while the king's love raised her to the level of an incorruptible demigod, why would she have to have recourse to perfection and incorruptibility of the noble metal? In part, this seems to be a case of reality intruding into Brantôme's rhetorical confection, but it plays on a set of associations among gold, permanence, and royal sovereignty that tied into the more specific associations of money and sovereignty.

The gold uncomfortably present in Brantôme's narrative and fatally present in Diane's body reveals a hidden insecurity, a lack of confidence in natural beauty, nobility, and power, but for just that reason it functions as a symbol of those very qualities and of their ability to hold society together. The role of a royal mistress was a fraught one, frequently seen as destabilizing, but while the potable gold may distantly recall the illegitimate means by which wealth, or sexual beauty, could confer rank and status, it much more immediately echoes Brantôme's confidence in the naturalness, stability, and success of this particular relationship.[6] That double movement whereby money and the precious metals could represent the noble or the upstart faces of social power is our subject in this chapter. While both were always structural possibilities within French culture and literature, wealth and gold as noble, stabilizing, and magnificent tended to predominate through much of the sixteenth century. In the seventeenth century, a somewhat different set of ideas came to the fore, and money was portrayed more commonly as counterfeit, destabilizing, and even subhuman. In each case, though, authors had to come to terms with both sides of the coin, exploring how money could subvert the order it symbolized and how it could be foundational of the order it subverted. And in each case, the monarchy was called upon to address the socially destabilizing elements of monetary exchange, both symbolically and practically. But persistent doubts recurred as to its capacity to do that, and one increasingly sees calls for at least a supplemental autonomous system of the production of social value, a literary economy of merit corresponding to the emerging, equally semiautonomous political economy of money.

---

6. On the critique of Henri IV's mistresses, for example, see Katherine Crawford, "The Politics of Promiscuity: Masculinity and Heroic Representation at the Court of Henry IV," French Historical Studies 26 (2003): 225–52.

The Alchemical Narrative

In 1610 a young Toulousan going under the name Antoine Domayron published a book entitled *The History of the Seat of the Muses*.[7] Even by the standards of the time it was rather a generic monstrosity, combining elements of oriental, pastoral, and allegorical romance and moral and philosophical essay—it bears some resemblance to the contemporary work of Béroalde de Verville, though without the master's involuted brio.[8] While Domayron had next to no impact as a writer, he had clearly devoted extensive study to the cultural valences of a constellation of issues—alchemy, treasure, medals, and (surprisingly) cosmetics—that both outline the sixteenth-century French literary engagement with money, power, and value and, as we shall see, link back with a rather eerie precision to the world of Diane de Poitiers. In this vision, royal majesty, virtue, and social order consistently tame the disruptive influence of money while precious metal, monetized or not, both shares in and enhances the sacred dignity of the sovereign.

The book is set in Dalmatia, where, in the course of his postuniversity travels, the author encounters a bizarre little commune of mainly French nobles-turned-amateur shepherds. Their dwelling—the "seat of the muses" of the title—is just over the border into the Ottoman Empire, where their founder had risen from slavery to the sultan's favor. They now spend most of their time in various artistic and intellectual pursuits and discussions, and most of the book is taken up with accounts of those amusements. More specifically, after setting the initial pastoral-romantic scene, Domayron devotes more than half of his book to a series of essayistic dialogues with his hosts on politely erudite topics. The first of these is on the subject of alchemy, which, predictably, raises serious questions about control over both nature and society.

Practically the first thing our hero does after entering the muses' abode is to contemplate a series of eight paintings that depict the four seasons and the four elements. His hosts inform him that these are Bassanos and draw his attention to the allegory of fire in particular.[9] Unlike surviving paintings

7. Antoine Domayron, *Histoire du siege des muses, ou parmi le chaste amour, est traicté de plusieurs belles & curieuses sciences, divine moralle & naturelle, architecture, alchimie, piencture & autres* (Lyons: Simon Rigaud, 1610). There is no further trace of the author and no easy way to tell if he was writing under a pseudonym. The only discussion of this work is a characteristically inconclusive survey by François Secret, "Littérature et alchimie à la fin du XVIe et au début du XVIIe siècle," *Bibliothèque d'humanisme et renaissance* 35 (1973): 106–12.

8. Verville's *L'histoire véritable, ou le voyage des princes fortunés*, published a few months after the *Siege des muses*, is particularly close to it in structure. The *Voyage* would be well worth discussing here except that I can make no sense of it whatsoever.

9. The Venetian workshop of the da Ponte Bassano family specialized in such paintings in the 1570s. There are at least three nearly identical surviving Bassano allegories of fire depicting Vulcan at

from that workshop with that subject, it depicts a group of miserable and impoverished alchemists "living in a smoky fog to make themselves famous in the obscurity of poverty."[10] Domayron's contemporaries did of course associate alchemy with ignobility, dishonesty, and economic failure, but this was only part of a much broader discourse. The century or so after 1550 was a golden age of alchemy, in terms of the number of practitioners, the diversity and popularity of treatises, and impact on the broader culture.[11] Alchemy promised a technological mastery over gold and silver, along with (especially in the Paracelsan variant so popular at this time) a similar mastery of the human body. This meant that alchemy and the alchemical literature touched on many of the major issues surrounding money. And in France at least, a coherent understanding or narrative about the nature of alchemy developed early on and continued well into the classical era. The condemnation of alchemy as wasteful and fraudulent to which the fictitious painting referred was one of the oldest elements of that discourse; its roots stretched back into the fourteenth century, at least to the papal bull *Spondent*. It was already well established when it made what remains its most important appearance in literature, in the "Canon's Yeoman's Tale" of Chaucer's *Canterbury Tales*, written around 1400.[12]

The yeoman in question was the lab assistant and general dogsbody to the canon, an alchemical experimenter. "With this chanoun," he explains,

I dwelt have seven yeer
And of his science am I never the neer.
Al that I hadde, I have lost therby—
And god woot so hath many mo than I.[13]

---

his forge (one at the Ringling Museum of Art, Sarasota, Florida; one at the Prado; one at the Louvre) that do not, however, fit Domayron's description, as well as a number of other seasons and elements that do roughly fit Domayron's text. It seems most likely to me that Domayron had seen a cycle like the one he describes, probably in Venice, but reinvented the allegory of fire for his own purposes.

10. Domayron, *Histoire du siege*, 39: "logés dedans d'un nuage fumeux, pour se rendre fameux en l'obscurité de la misere." The painting, in fact, sounds very much like the elder Breughel's well-known depiction of the alchemist's workshop.

11. Besides the literature cited in chapter 5 above, see William R. Newman, *Promethean Ambitions: Alchemy and the Quest to Perfect Nature* (Chicago: University of Chicago Press, 2004).

12. On the sources for this story, which evidently included both *Spondent* and the wider alchemical literature, see Edgar H. Duncan, "The Literature of Alchemy and Chaucer's Canon's Yeoman's Tale: Framework, Theme, and Characters," *Speculum* 43 (1968): 633–56.

13. Geoffrey Chaucer, *The Canterbury Tales*, ed. N. F. Blake (London: Arnold, 1980), 675–76. Blake, like a number of modern scholars, rejects Chaucer's authorship of *CYT*. This makes no real difference to my argument, since the poem was put out and accepted under Chaucer's name from the first. It does seem clear that this tale dates from the years just before or just after Chaucer's death in 1400.

He goes on to detail how the expenses of alchemy had consumed his, his master's, and his master's friends' substance, while producing neither understanding nor concrete results. This is followed by the story of another, different canon, who was an outright con man, performing a fraudulent transmutation through sleight of hand and, on the strength of that, selling a worthless recipe to an innocent if avaricious priest for forty pounds. The moral of these stories is simply that alchemy produces poverty, dishonesty, and loss of social standing.

This was an important point. First of all, as *Spondent* made clear, one of alchemy's original sins was its attempt to remove precious metals and their circulation from the state's authority. Since public authority was uniquely positioned to control ambition and avarice, those who embarked on the alchemical project for those reasons were naturally destined for either disappointment or criminality. But this was apparently true even of those who pursued alchemy out of a disinterested thirst for knowledge: less surprising in view of the well-known Augustinian model according to which the *libido sciendi* was merely one form of worldly desire alongside the *libido dominandi* (ambition) and the *libido sentiendi* (concupiscence, of which avarice is a subspecies).[14] Chaucer particularly stressed the lure and vanity of alchemical knowledge:

> Whan we been ther as we shul exercyse
> Oure elvysshe craft we semen wonder wyse,
> Oure termes been so clergial and so queynte.

Chaucer himself had risen from humble birth to social and political prominence and intermittent affluence through his study and command of language. Alchemy, which turned away from the public realm in which men like Chaucer lived, was a mirror image of this kind of effort and skill and produced precisely opposite effects.

Certainly, none of this had been forgotten in the first decade of the seventeenth century. Domayron was perfectly ready to admit that "most (not to say all)" alchemists "come to grief because, as they bay after gain, the greedy desire for wealth makes them rush the matter . . . by which they spoil everything. . . . They have already been condemned with their smoke and puffery by one learned in the true science, later sovereign in the church,

---

14. On the fortune of this moral theory (which was destined for a great future among the Jansenists) in Renaissance France, see Gérard Defaux, *Le curieux, le glorieux, et la sagesse du monde dans la première moitié du XVIe siècle: L'exemple de Panurge (Ulysse, Démosthène, Empédocle)* (Lexington, KY: French Forum Publishers, 1982).

who said that being poor themselves they promise to enrich everyone." The hint that John XXII was himself an adept is rather bold, but it also suggests what was by then the standard exception to alchemy's futility, namely, that the Work "cannot come to conclusion except by a special grace of God given to those who make themselves worthy, sometimes by revelation."[15] But once the possibility of a legitimate and worthy alchemy was open, a well-defined set of values immediately crystallized around it. Besides the key element of religious devotion, "whoever wants to practice this Art must have two inseparable qualities, namely, doctrine, so that he is ignorant of none of the qualities and nature of that on which he operates, and also that he have great means and wealth so that he can spend without hope of gain, contenting himself with the pleasure that comes from such exercises."[16] Alchemy was not an instrument for upward social mobility—indeed, it should remain the province of those who were already opulent—and it produced the opposite of the economic plenty that was depicted in the rest of the Bassano cycle. The only road to successful alchemy began with a complete divorce from worldly motives or results, that is, from the domain of the monetary. Only in a second, subsidiary movement did it become economically and politically fructifying.

That was perhaps the single most prominent theme of French alchemical literature in the second half of the sixteenth century. Indeed, in its fully developed form, the alchemical narrative consisted of two parts. The first recapitulated Chaucer's themes, with the adept suffering from failure and fraudulent colleagues. Authors not entirely unsympathetic to the art could continue to a second part, in which the adept sought and received divine guidance, reconfiguring alchemy as a religious devotion and succeeding in it where human means had failed. Examples are numerous, but one of the clearest is the "Autobiography of Denis Zachaire," probably written in the late 1550s or early 1560s

---

15. Domayron, *Histoire du siege*, 43–44: "la plus part (pour ne dire tous) donnent du nez à terre: à cause que beans apres le guain: le goulu desire de richesse leur faict precipiter tout l'affaire . . . par lequel ils gastent tout. . . . Ayants esté jadis condamnez, & leur fumeur soufflement, par un docte au vray sçavoir, par apres Souverain en l'Eglise: disant d'eux que pauvres ils promettent d'enrichir un chacun." Page 44: "ne peut estre ne venir à effet, que par une grace speciale de Dieu, qui donne ce bien à qui s'en rend digne, quelque-fois par revelation." The quotation is the opening sentence of *Spondent*; for his final claim he gives as his source Gerber's *Summa perfectionis*.

16. Ibid., 42–43: "qui veut faire cest Art, faut qu'il aye deux choses inseparables, à sçavoir: la doctrine telle qu'il n'ignore rien des qualitez, & nature de ce, surquoy il veut operer. Et l'autre qu'il aye de grands moyens, & richesses, pour despendre, sans avoir sa visée au gain: se contentant du plaisir qui se prend à tel exercise." There is a good discussion of this aspect of alchemical thought in Deborah Harkness, *John Dee's Conversations with Angels: Cabala, Alchemy, and the End of Nature* (Cambridge: Cambridge University Press, 1999), 196–201.

and thus contemporaneous with Diane de Poitier's career as a gold drinker.[17] Its protagonist fit Domayron's criteria well. He was learned in the humanistic disciplines, having pursued studies at the college in Bordeaux and the University of Toulouse. His alchemical studies were those of a good Catholic. He started out with sheaves of recipes whose dubious authenticity was shored up by the names in some cases "of the late Cardinal of Lorraine, [in] others of the Cardinal of Tournon." As he headed deeper into the gold maker's labyrinth, his guide was an abbot from near Toulouse "who said that he had the duplicate of a recipe . . . which a friend of his who followed the Cardinal of Armagnac had sent him from Rome." When this failed, Zachaire went to Paris, where he joined the alchemical aficionados who met at "the great church of Notre Dame," though at that point the only result was a train of failure and poverty.[18]

At last, returning to his native region, he fell in with a less showy but godlier Catholic, "a religious Doctor who was reputed, and with good reason, learned in natural philosophy." This paragon suggested that Zachaire withdraw from the crowd of sophists and dedicate himself to God, solitude, and the study of the ancient philosophers. Zachaire returned to Paris and, working from Easter to Easter, brought the magnum opus to completion. "After having rendered thanks to our good God who had shown me such favor and grace, and after having prayed that he would illuminate me by his holy spirit to enable me to use it for his honor and praise, I went away the next day to find the abbot at his monastery. . . . But I found that he had died six months previously—at which I was greatly grieved. So it was with the death of the good doctor, of which I was informed while passing near to his convent."[19] Freed from all worldly ties, Zachaire gave his goods to charity and left France for the German-speaking lands, where he became an early model of the adept as wandering "cosmopolite." As such, he unmoored himself entirely from both the socioeconomic order his early masters had tried to manipulate and the political order that his early activities had troubled.

The Zachaire story was popular and influential both in France and in the wider European world, where it circulated in Latin and German translations. And new versions of the same basic narrative continued to be produced through the period of the Wars of Religion. One of the most striking, which

---

17. Denis Zacaire, *Opuscule tres-excellent, de la vraye philosophie naturelle des Metaux* (Lyons: Pierre Rigaud, 1612 [Antwerp, 1563]). I will quote from the easily accessible English translation of the first half of this treatise by T. L. Davis, "The Autobiography of Denis Zachaire," *Isis* 8 (1926): 265–99.

18. Ibid., 268, 290, 291.

19. Ibid., 293, 297.

survives only in manuscript, is the "Discourse by an Unknown Author on the Philosophers' Stone," written (according to a colophon of dubious reliability) "the year of grace 1590, between the first day of June and the last of August, during the memorable siege of this city of Paris."[20] Its (French) protagonist is drawn to alchemy through discussions with an international group of learned and pious men in the "beautiful and pleasant garden of M. [the duc] de Nevers," who had a reputation as a patron of alchemy. In due course, falling asleep while meditating on Genesis, he had a symbolic alchemical dream. He told it to "a monk of the order of St. Augustine, a very learned man who believed this art to be true, and to another who was general of the Capuchins," but they could throw no light upon it. It was only after he had thrown himself upon the grace of the Holy Spirit and the practical work of the furnace that his prayers "that God give me the grace to discover the secret of this art, and my eyes be opened and my understanding illuminated" were answered. Having accomplished the Work, he retired to the country to practice agriculture and study "various books of Holy Scripture, chronicles, and the heroic deeds of men of former times."[21] Another example among many is a "Short Treatise of the Voyage of Frederic Gallus to the Hermitage of St. Michel" (of uncertain date but set in 1602–1611), which, as its title suggests, is structured around the repeated visits of its chivalrous hero to a holy and mystical 150-year-old monk who possesses the secret of transmutation.[22]

---

20. I quote from a fine professional copy, "Discours d'autheur incertain sur la pierre des philosophes," BN, ms. fr. 19957, fol. 23r: "Le discours fut faict et compose lan de grace mil cinq cens quatre vingt dix, depuis le premier jour de Juing jusques au dernier jour daoust, durant le memorable siege de ceste ville de Paris, lequel a interdit la poursuitte de mon oeuvre." There is also at least one copy in the Bibliothèque de l'Arsenal, ms. 3031, which includes some additional material, and another at Harvard University, ms. fr. 114.

21. BN, ms. fr. 19957, fol. 1r: "le beau et plaisant jardin de Monsieur de Nevers." Fol. 4v: "un Religieux de lordre de sainct Augustin, et homme tresdocte lequel approuvoit cest Art estre veritable. Et ung autre qui estoit general des Capuchins." Fol. 5r: "Que Dieu me feist la grace de descouvrir le secret de cest Art, et mes yeux furent ouvers et mon entendement Illuminé"; "divers livres de la saincte Escriture, Chroniques et faictz heröicques des hommes illustres du temps passe." On Nevers's alchemy, see, e.g., an unsigned letter from Venice, dated 30 December 1589, testifying that one "sr. Pragadino" (presumably the well-known alchemical con man Bragadin) had indeed performed a transmutation. BN, ms. fr. 3471, fol. 137. The highest-ranking Capuchin in Paris at the time was Jean-Baptiste Bruslart, brother of Nicolas Bruslart de Sillery, president in the Parlement of Paris and future chancellor. An eighteenth-century note in the Arsenal ms. of the "Discours" claims that the writer has another copy in which "mon grand pere a escrit en marge que le P. R. B. Prieur des Augustins du Grand convent en est l'auteur," which if true would make this an oddly self-referential statement.

22. "Petit traitte du voyage de Frederic Gallus vers l'Hermitage de St. Michel," Bibliothèque de l'Arsenal, ms. 3022, which is in an eighteenth-century hand but seems stylistically early seventeenth century. Both the pieces in this manuscript are probably influenced by Verville's *Voyage des princes fortunés*.

But the most revealing figure of the alchemical imaginary as it developed into the reign of Henri IV is also the one who has proved most reso-
nant even in popular culture. Nicolas Flamel's legend had been cultivated in
the 1560s and 1570s by a number of enthusiasts, notably including Jacques
Gohory.[23] It was crowned in 1612 by the "Book of Hieroglyphic Figures."
This work begins with a version of the hero's sufficient means and doctrine:
"Though . . . I learned only a little Latin because of my parents' limited
means (though they were nevertheless considered well-to-do by my enviers),
still . . . I have not neglected to understand the books of the philosophers at
length." His entry to alchemy is a book (purchased for the already substantial
sum of two florins from one who "who did not know what it was worth")
written by "Abraham the Jew, prince, Levite priest . . . to help his captive
nation pay their tribute to the Roman emperors." After many digressions and
a pilgrimage to St. James of Compostella on which he enlisted the help of
"a physician of Jewish nationality, now Christian . . . who was very learned
in the sublime sciences," he achieved the Work.[24] The proceeds went to a
massive campaign of charitable donations, including the real murals in the
Cemetery of the Innocents that were the foundation of the Flamel legend.

Flamel's alchemy is pious, serious, learned, discreet, and entirely removed
from suspicions of ambition or avarice (note the neat device of the expensive
yet unvalued book of secrets, which demonstrates Flamel's wealth while not
allowing him to simply buy the Great Work). While both are played down
in favor of divine inspiration, the author is careful to note the protagonist's
sufficient means and sufficient doctrine—though in a more bourgeois register
than Domayron would have favored—and the Jewish connection is structured so as to provide not only a whiff of the exotic but also an association
with political sovereignty, both Jewish and Roman. And indeed, this kind
of political subtext often underlies the explicit religiosity of the alchemical
narrative; to take one subtle example, the setting of the "Discourse by an
Unknown Author" parallels, very precisely and almost certainly deliberately,
one of the classics of neo-Stoicism, Guillaume du Vair's *Treatise on Constancy*

---

23. See the comments in Didier Kahn, ed., *Nicolas Flamel: Ecrits alchimiques* (Paris: Les Belles
Lettres, 1993), 105–6. The "Livre des figures," sometimes attributed to Béroalde de Verville, was
published in *Trois traictez de la philosophie naturelle* (Paris: Veuve Guillemot, 1612).

24. *Nicolas Flamel*, 15: "encore . . . que je n'aie appris qu'un peu de latin, pour le peu de moyen
de mes parents, qui néanmoins étaient par mes envieux mêmes estimés gens de bien: si est-ce que . . .
je n'ai pas laissé d'entendre au long les livres des philosophes." Page 17: "ne savait pas ce qu'il valait";
"Abraham le juif, prince, prêtre lévite . . . pour aider sa captive nation à payer les tributs aux empereurs romains." Page 22: "un médecin juif de nation, et lors chrétien . . . lequel était fort savant en
sciences sublimes."

and Consolation amid Public Calamities.[25] As becomes increasingly clear through Domayron's book, the precious metals could never be far removed, for good or ill, from the ideals of governance.

The Noble Metal

Domayron continues his investigation of the relations among social status, precious metal, and the supernatural in his second chapter, largely devoted to the subject of treasure hunting.[26] The narrator recounts a number of treasure-hunting expeditions he has been on or heard of, all conducted by well-to-do Italians and all ending in either failure or an illusory success produced by fraud or demonic magic.[27] In his account, treasure hunters appear structurally almost identical to fraudulent alchemists, down to their use of advance-fee cons ("the subtle inventions of making blades or branches of gold or silver, with assurances that they are all needed to discover the treasure") and gilded props. The moral of the stories, according to Domayron, is explicitly socioeconomic: "Everyone must be content with the fortune that the Lord has placed in his hands, which he should increase by diligent work in his profession, making that his true treasure, and not hope to find a chewed-up morsel of wealth underground, spending sure things in one's possession for something assuredly very uncertain."[28]

This could apply just as well to alchemy, and indeed one finds just such an application in a play published in 1572 by Pierre le Loyer, whose work

---

25. See Guillaume du Vair, *Traité de la constance et consolation ès calamitez publiques*, ed. Jacques Flach and Frantz Funck-Brentano (Paris: L. Tenin, 1915). My thanks to Michael Wolfe for pointing this out to me.

26. The best introduction to the subject of seventeenth-century European treasure hunting is Johannes Dillinger and Petra Feld, "Treasure Hunting: A Magical Motif in Law, Folklore, and Mentality, Württemberg, 1606–1770," *German History* 20 (2002): 161–84.

27. Domayron devotes a great deal of attention to the distinction between the two forms of magic famously described by D. P. Walker, *Spiritual and Demonic Magic from Ficino to Campanella* (University Park: Pennsylvania State University, 2000). The problem of demonic magic had been raised to prominence in French intellectual circles toward the end of the sixteenth century by works like Jean Bodin's *De la démonomanie des sorciers* and, perhaps more immediately relevant, Pierre le Loyer, *Discours des spectres, ou visions et apparitions d'esprits, comme anges, demons, et ames, se monstrans visibles aux hommes*, 2nd ed. (Paris: Nicolas Buon, 1608), on which Domayron seems to have drawn.

28. Domayron, *Histoire du siege*, 101–2: "les subtiles inventions de faire lames, verges d'or ou d'argent; asseurant que le tout est necessaire, pour descouvrir le thresor"; 102: "il faut qu'un chascun se contente de la fortune que le Souverain luy a faict cheoir és mains, laquelle il doit faire valoir par un soigneux travail à sa profession, faisant qu'icelle luy soit le vray thresor: & ne s'attendre à trouver le morceau masché des richesses sous terre, despendant le certain, qui est en possession, pour le treasseuré incertain."

Domayron probably knew. A pastiche of Aristophanes' *Clouds*, it includes an alchemist in the parade of parasites who appear while the cloud-city is being built. The protagonist sends him away to bother instead those inclined

> to seduce themselves
> By a false good that thoroughly destroys their goods,
> And, waiting and falsely hoping for which
> Makes them take the uncertain for the certain.[29]

One sees something similar in Bernard Palissy's *True Formula by Which All the Men of France May Learn to Multiply and Augment Their Treasures*, which is in fact not the alchemical treatise that the title seems to promise but rather a collection of essays on scientific agriculture.[30] This contrast of specious and real wealth was destined for a very long history, but what is more striking in the context of Domayron's book is the way that treasure hunting, as opposed to honest toil, threatened the social hierarchy. Through it, those who have much and are not content give way to avarice and to literally diabolic temptation and end up poorer and less able to fulfill their appointed role in society. They are implicitly contrasted to the residents of the Seat of the Muses, whose Christian and humanist virtue, tried in adversity, has been rewarded with great landed wealth and with a position of sociocultural exemplarity.

But these condemnations of foolishness and ambition toward princely wealth should be seen in the context of a positive and, indeed, sacred conception of treasure that went beyond the alchemist's artificial gold. This was the hidden converse of Domayron's devilish treasure hunting—though it was not without its own ambiguities. We have already seen a few examples of this, notably in the encomiums of Roman magnificence that Montaigne so effectively contrasted to that of the Inca; not surprisingly, though, it went further back than the 1580s. While its roots were ancient, the Pléiade school, which dominated French literature for a generation from the middle of the sixteenth century, brought it to new prominence. The writers of the

---

29. Pierre le Loyer, *Les œuvres et meslanges poetiques de Pierre le Loyer Angevin ensemble la comedie Nephelococugie, ou La nuée des cocus, non moins docte que facetieuse* (Paris: Jean Poupy, 1579), fol. 210r: "soymesme seduire / Par un faux bien qui leur bien faict destruire, / Et dont l'attente & le trompeux espoir / Fait l'incertain pour le certain avoir." There is very likely a common source here, though le Loyer's modern editors make no suggestions. See Pierre le Loyer, *La nephelococugie ou la nuée des cocus*, ed. Miriam Doe and Keith Cameron (Geneva: Droz, 2004), 207–8. The play seems to have been written sometime in the early 1560s; its only appearance was in this edition, where it has a separate title page dated 1578.

30. Bernard Palissy, *Recepte veritable, par laquelle tous les hommes de la France pourront apprendre à multiplier et augmenter leurs thresors. Item, ceux qui n'ont jamais eu cognoissance des lettres, pourront apprendre une Philosophie necessaire à tous les habitans de la terre*, etc. (La Rochelle: Barthelemy Berton, 1563).

Pléiade were self-consciously dedicated to promoting the glory of the French language, the French people, and the French monarchy. "They associated themselves with the pomp of the Valois court," as Timothy Hampton says, "and sought to shine within a courtly context they saw as defining a glorious future for all of France." It is not surprising that they found royal treasure a suitable subject for their lyres.[31]

More specifically, they emerged around the court of Henri II (and Diane de Poitiers) just at the time that the Cour des Monnaies took its place as a sovereign court, and it is not unreasonable to take them as representative of some important cultural trends in that context. Their obsession with glory, nation, and king appears most strongly in the work of Joachim du Bellay, who took as his theme the grandeur and decadence of Rome and its relationship to France and French culture, and of Pierre de Ronsard, the "prince of French poets," who aspired with his Franciade to do for the Valois dynasty what the Æneid had done for Augustus. Budé had already popularized Rome's astounding wealth, "her conquered spoils, acquired over so many years from the entire world," as du Bellay put it.[32] This wealth of empire lent itself (as du Bellay's phrase implied) to the themes of the translatio imperii and the ubi sunt; seized from Rome's predecessors, it had been left to her successors as a mark of their temporary but eternally recurring supremacy.

Ronsard took this up in one of his most philosophical poems, entitled (when it was first published in 1569) "Discourse for Maître Julian Chauveau," or (in a 1584 edition) "Discourse on the Alteration of Human Affairs." Maître Chauveau was a solicitor at the Parlement of Paris, and Ronsard presented his poem to its addressee as an alternative or antidote to the quotidian and ignoble concern for money and property that dominated his practice:

Chauveau, you have beaten your head enough

. . . .

Against movables, goods, money, and inheritances,
A will, a vicious contract.[33]

---

31. Timothy Hampton, Literature and Nation in the Sixteenth Century: Inventing Renaissance France (Ithaca, NY: Cornell University Press, 2001), 150–51.

32. Joachim du Bellay, Antiquitez, 22, ll. 6–7, in Les Regrets et autres œuvres poëtiques suivis des Antiquitez de Rome, plus un Songe ou Vision sur le mesme subject, ed. J. Jolliffe and M. A. Screech (Geneva: Droz, 1966), 293: "sa despouille conquise / Qu'il avoit par tant d'ans sur tout le monde acquise." On economic themes in du Bellay, see François Paré, "L'écriture et l'échange économique dans Les Regrets de du Bellay," Renaissance and Reformation/Rénaissance et réforme 9 (1985): 255–62.

33. Pierre de Ronsard, Œuvres complètes, ed. Gustave Cohen, 2 vols. (Paris: N.R.F./Gallimard, 1950) 2:376: "Tu as, Chauveau, la teste assez rompue / . . . / De meubles, biens, d'argent ou d'heritage, / D'un testament, d'un contrat vicieux." Chauveau was a fine example of the successful legal professional,

Instead, he proposed a reflection on mutability, not an unrelated issue—Ronsard stressed Chauveau's involvement in the circulation and transfer (*mutation* in French) of property—but a nobler one.[34] It was also a politically charged subject, since the outbreak of the Wars of Religion invited speculation about the decay and possible collapse of France itself. One sign of this national decline, a contrast with Brantôme's portrait of Diane de Poitiers, is seen

> When a women desires too much
> To array herself and make herself beautiful,
> Ruining her natural face with paints

and, as Ronsard continues,

> When you see the pompous clothing
> Of a noble, forbidden to the bourgeois,
> Decorating a merchant.

Such mutations, prompted by ambition, fueled by avarice, perverting the natural order and violating the sumptuary laws, resembled both the ignoble transactions that plagued Chauveau's daily life and the destructive monetary logic explored in chapter 2. But gold, considered in itself, had a contrasting role in the cycle of decay and rebirth. Ronsard took the silkworm—not coincidentally the foundation of a growing and royally sponsored French industry—as the symbol of that cycle; before its metamorphosis, the caterpillar will have

> vomited all its silk,
> Which the artisan, drawing it ever more finely,
> Should join with gold for a king's garments.[35]

Like Diane's golden countenance, and unlike the usurped trappings purchased with the merchant's silver, the king's silk and cloth-of-gold combined the cyclical and the incorruptible to produce real majesty.

---

with a busy practice and a brother who wore the long robe in the bailliage of Mélun, an office Julien's son inherited. See Pierre Champion, *Ronsard et son temps* (Paris: E. Champion, 1925), 192n and 420n.

34. On this theme, see Michel Jeanneret, *Perpetual Motion: Transforming Shapes in the Renaissance from de Vinci to Montaigne*, trans. Nidra Poller (Baltimore: Johns Hopkins University Press, 2001), esp. 34–46.

35. Ronsard, *Œuvres*, 2:379: "Quand une femme a trop de volonté / de s'attifer et de se faire belle, / Gastant par fard sa face naturelle, / Quand tu verras que le pompeux habit / D'un gentilhomme, au bourgeois interdit, / Pare un marchant." Page 377: "vomi toute sa soye / Que l'artizan par mainte estroite voye / Doit joindre a l'or pour les habits d'un Roy."

Behind this lay another trope central to Renaissance depictions of monarchy, that of the Golden Age, governed by justice and plenty rather than conflict, toil, and commerce, which could be reborn through the practice of royal justice.[36] Ronsard tackled this theme as well, in his 1555 "Hymn to Justice" addressed to the young cardinal de Lorraine. Justice reigned in the days "when mariners did not yet sail / On Tethys's back to amass gold"—an age of gold detached from money and commerce. When she returned from her long exile to the court of Henri II, Justice carried "a golden scale in her left hand," a tool that could be used to help produce a sound coinage but that was at least one step removed from monetary exchange.[37] On its own, the Reign of Saturn paralleled the ideal of alchemy in its embrace of the sacred at the expense of the economic. But encomiasts of royal sovereignty did not stop at that comfortable point. Ronsard was willing to engage directly with the relationship between commerce and the incorruptible and ennobling principal that gold incarnated, and he did so in a poem we have already had occasion to consider, the "Hymn to Gold" that formed a counterpart to the "Hymn to Justice" in the second book of his hymns.[38]

Ronsard dedicated it to a much less noble personage than the cardinal de Lorraine but a much more intimate friend: his appropriately named former teacher Jean Dorat. Ronsard begins that hymn by explicitly thematizing the link between gold and avarice, "the use / Of ambitious gold," pleading his own poverty as evidence of his bona fides.[39] What is left to praise is in the first place gold's association with royal majesty, which Ronsard illustrates with reference to the Roman gods, from Jupiter's self-transformation into a

36. See above all Frances Yates, *Astraea: The Imperial Theme in the Sixteenth Century* (London: Routledge and Keegan Paul, 1975).

37. Ronsard, *Œuvres* 2:155: "quand les Mariniers ne pallissoyent encor' / Sur le dos de Tethys pour ammaser de l'or"; 163: "Une balance d'or dedans la main senestre." On the multiple valences of the symbol of the balance, see Marie-Luce Demonet, *"A plaisir": Sémiotique et scepticisme chez Montaigne* (Orléans: Paradigme, 2002), 58–63.

38. On the structural correspondence between the "Hymne de la Justice" and the "Hymne de l'or," see Philip Ford, *Ronsard's Hymns: A Literary and Iconographical Study* (Tempe, AZ: Medieval and Renaissance Texts and Studies, 1997), 153–63. The "Hymne de l'or" itself is the subject of a substantial literature: see, for example, the remarks of Terence Cave, *The Cornucopian Text: Problems of Writing in the French Renaissance* (Oxford: Clarendon Press, 1979), 233–52; and J.-C. Margolin, "L'Hymne de l'or' et son ambigüité," *Bibliothèque d'humanisme et renaissance* 28 (1966): 271–93.

39. Ronsard, *Œuvres* 2:260: "l'usage / De l'or ambitieux." Impecuniousness was a frequent and rather nakedly self-interested theme among the Pléiade. On this see Simone Perrier, "La Transaction poétique chez Ronsard," in *Or, monnaie, échange dans la culture de la Renaissance: Actes du 9ᵉ Colloque international de l'Association Renaissance, humanisme, réforme, Lyon, 1991*, ed. André Tournon and G.-A. Pérouse (Saint-Etienne: Publications de l'Université de Saint-Etienne, 1994), 199–211.

shower of gold to a myth, invented for the occasion, in which Earth reveals the as-yet-unseen gold within herself to best the gods in a display of symbols of power and then magnanimously allows her progeny to gild the heavens and their own regalia with it.

> And even Justice, with her scowling eye,
> Disdained it no more than Jupiter,
> But immediately, knowing the excellence of this gold,
> Used it to embroider her robe and make her balance.

The reference to the earlier poem could hardly be more explicit. But in making gold an object of transcendent majesty, this line of argument risked undermining the poet's own expertise on the matter.

> Whoever wishes to properly sing your grace,
> Your virtue, your honors, must make himself
> Bursar, general [of the Moneys?], or treasurer to a king,
> Always having his fingers yellow from your alloy,
> And not a poor scholar who, of your great power,
> (Because he sees you seldom) has little experience![40]

But as the increasingly official encomiast of French royal majesty, Ronsard was not unprepared to face such difficulties.

For gold was not simply a tool of royal majesty. It was a tool of social relations, and the bulk of Ronsard's poem concentrates on its utility in promoting the general good of society. The essence of gold's dignity is its power to fulfill the legitimate needs of every order and above all to promote cooperation within society. This applies to princes as well as commoners: money is the nerve of war, but also the instrument of patronage, which Ronsard knew very well was one of the key roots of royal power. Indeed, as Ronsard asked (with potentially troubling implications), "Why do we bend down before great lords? / Why do our knees pay so many honors, / If not for their wealth?" Money provided the tools and training needed by both artisans and intellectuals. In one of the poem's most striking images, Ronsard shows money doing the work even of the strongest ties of family and friendship:

---

40. Ronsard, *Œuvres* 2:267: "Et mesme la Justice, à l'œil si renfrongné, / Ne plus que Jupiter ne l'a pas dédaigné, / Mais soudain, congnoissant de cest Or l'excellance, / En fist broder sa robe, et faire sa Balance." Vol. 2:274: "Celuy qui dignement voudra chanter ta grace, / Ta vertu, tes honneurs, il faudra qu'il se face / Argentier, general, ou tresorier d'un Roy, / Ayant tousjours les doigts jaunes de ton aloy, / Et non pas escolier qui de ta grand' puissance / (Pour te voir rarement) a peu d'experience!" Charles VII's legendarily rich financier Jacques Cœur had held the title "argentier du roi": he was also reputed to have been an alchemist.

Very often a family member, out of enmity
Or for fear of harm, or overcome by emotion,
Does not dare to go help even a sister or a brother,
And leaves him in bed in his misery with no assistance;
But gold serves as a relative, who immediately sends
To find a doctor who, tempted by gain,
Succors the patient, bleeds him, and consoles him,
And with his drugs restrains the soul that was about to depart.[41]

Gold acts, indirectly, as a life-preserving drug, as it does directly in Brantôme's anecdote. More generally, Ronsard's portrayal of money as the glue of society bears a striking similarity to François Rabelais's famous "elegy of debts," which made up chapters 2–5 of his 1551 *Third Book of Gargantua and Pantagruel*.[42] Ronsard, however, drains the theme of Rabelais's anarchic and somewhat ambiguous satire, leaving it subject to the (partial) certainty of hard cash and the magnificence of royal sovereignty. In a sense he reenacts the logic of contemporary economic regulation, a dangerous technological supplement to the ties of human society that can nevertheless be tamed and made beneficial if royal power restrains the forces of ambition and avarice while of course maintaining a sound currency.

The House of the Goddess

Ronsard's depiction of monetary relations was rather deeper and more complex than the alchemists', but the fundamental structure he envisioned for it was basically similar: the tendency of avarice to disrupt and impoverish society is countered by a sacred and mythologized power, in his case identified very explicitly with the French court. But he left unclear how this kind of literary or mythological construct could become sufficiently concrete to serve as a technology of governance. The encomiastic poetry of the Pléiade

---

41. Ibid., 2:261: "Pourquoy nous courbons-nous devant les grands Seigneurs? / Pourquoy leur faisons-nous du genouil tant d'honneurs, / Sinon pour leur Richesse?" Vol. 2:265: "Bien souvent un parent, ou par inimitié / Ou par crainte du mal, ou par grande pitié, / N'ose aller secourir ny sa sœur, ny son frere, / Et sans ayde le laisse au lict en sa misere; / Mais l'Or sert de parent, qui envoye soudain / Chercher le Medecin, lequel tenté de gain, / Secourt le patient, le panse et le console, / Et par drogues retient son ame qui s'en-vole."

42. For surveys of the large literature on this passage, see Gérard Defaux, "Panurge, le pouvoir et les dettes: Sagesse et folie dans Le Tiers Livre," *Op. cit.: Revue de littératures française et comparée* 5 (1995) : 47–59; "L'Eloge Panurgien des dettes: Table ronde préparée et dirigée par Guy Demerson," in Tournon and Pérouse, *Or, monnaie*, 119–28; and Terence Cave, *Pré-histoires II: Langues étrangères et troubles économiques au XVIe siècle* (Geneva: Droz, 2001), 149–56.

itself could to some extent serve that purpose—more so, anyway, than the illusory procedures of the alchemists—but it was scarcely sufficient for the comprehensive cultural programs of a Renaissance monarchy. The visual arts were one way to promote or even instantiate this kind of ideology, but to say that is not to say anything very specific. For at least a sample of such specifics, we can turn, once again, to Domayron. His sixth book is devoted to a discourse on medals and the seventh to one on the history of feminine makeup and allied topics; both, it turns out, were ways that metallurgy could enact and display the sovereignty of the court over the world of avarice and commerce.

Domayron's discussion of medals is attached to a well-established literature we have already encountered more than once: Domayron argues against the view that medals circulated as money, setting himself explicitly against Enea Vico and implicitly against du Choul and Rascas de Bagarris.[43] Domayron's motives in divorcing money and medals appear to be a mirror image of Rascas's motives for joining them together: rather than hoping to infuse commerce with royal majesty, Domayron wants to preserve royal majesty and even his own identity from the pollution of commerce. When the subject is first introduced, the narrator says that "nothing in the world pleases me as much" as medals, "and I care nothing for gold or silver compared with the least of them." The ancients felt similarly, depositing medals in temples and protecting them with other imperial images under the Roman law of treason: "If medals were the same as money, . . . one would have had to put aside one's purse every time one wanted to perform even the slightest servile or abject action." Domayron even turns Rascas's arguments back against him, saying that Pliny's claim that effigies were made only of men "who merited perpetual memory . . . shows well that medals were made for something other than to serve as money."[44]

Medals were highly valuable articles of commerce themselves, but Domayron found ways to acknowledge this reality while preserving their inherent nobility that recall Ronsard's treatment of gold.[45] The high market value of medals could itself be a sign of their nobility: "Whoever wants to undertake

---

43. On this dispute, see above, chapter 3.

44. Domayron, *Histoire du siege*, 270: "Il n'y a chose qui me plaise tant en ce monde" as medals, "& ne me soucie d'or ne d'argent, à l'esgal de la moindre d'icelles." Page 297: "si la medaille estoit la mesme que monnoye, . . . il eusse esté besoin de laisser la bource à tous coups que l'homme eust voulu faire la moindre action servile ou abjecte." Pages 295–96: "qui meritat perpetuelle memoire . . . montre bien que la medaille a esté faicte pour autre chose que pour servir de monnoye."

45. Though John Cunally, "Ancient Coins as Gifts and Tokens of Friendship during the Renaissance," *Journal of the History of Collections* 6 (1994): 129–43, argues that coins were as much circulating tokens in a gift economy among amateurs as they were objects of commerce, which would help explain the Renaissance reluctance to conceive of them as "real money."

this quest and is not a king or prince must put some bounds on his desire."
Beyond that, the "specious broadcasters of ignorance" who "dismiss as mad
those who spend *honorably* on medals" provoked Domaryon into an exposi-
tion of the demand theory of value. "Most of the things that are held in
esteem in the world today are valued by the fancy and humor of mortals,
without the things being valuable in themselves." He has something not
entirely coherent to add to this analysis, though. Medals "have I know not
what else beyond the pleasure [they engender] in those who understand the
matter; for they must necessarily be intelligent and sufficiently well read to
understand the meaning of the reverses, on which we can see the pleasure
there is in remembering the admirable deeds of him whom the medal represents."[46] The antiquity and obscurity of medals obviously marked their
aficionados as cultivated and educated, playing into the culture of collecting
that had such an important role in creating the early modern system of status.[47] But there was a supplement to this socially and economically arbitrary
source of value: the nobility and exemplarity of the medals' subjects, both
antiquity in general and the individual personages depicted. In this way medals, though not money themselves, came to embody the sociopolitical worth
attached to gold and money.

Domayron separates the medal from the coin in the same way that he separates true and fraudulent alchemy. Learning and nobility attach to the former,
but so does actual prosperity: like Chaucer's alchemists, those in Domayron's
allegorical painting were emaciated and clad in rags, and alchemical experimentation, like medal collecting but unlike the diabolical sport of treasure
hunting, is an appropriate pursuit for wealthy elites. His disquisition on
makeup continues that pattern, especially when read in light of Brantôme's
discussion of Diane de Poitiers. Domayron segues from medals to makeup
via a medal of the Empress Faustina (probably the younger—daughter of
Antoninus Pius, wife of Marcus Aurelius, mother of Commodus, and in

---

46. Domayron, *Histoire du siege*, 305: "qui se veut adonner à telle recherche, & n'est pas Roy ou
Prince, faut qu'il pose borne à son desir." Page 303: "ces beaux causeurs d'ignorances depeschent
pour fols ceux qui despendent *honorablement* l'argent aux medailles . . . ne s'advisant pas que la plus
part des choses qui sont à ce jour en estime au monde, sont prisees par fantasie, & humeur des Mortels,
sans que la chose soit prisable de soy" (my emphasis). Page 305: "toutes-fois ont ne sçay quoy de
plus, que le plaisir en ceux qui s'y entendent; que necessairement faut qu'ils soient capables & d'assez
de lecture, pour pouvoir cognoistre la signification des revers, ausquels se peut voir le plaisir qu'il ya
[a] se souvenir des faicts admirables de celuy, que la medaille represente." The fact that Domayron's
syntax collapses entirely in the last sentence quoted suggests its aporistic character.

47. See Lisa Jardine, *Worldly Goods: A New History of the Renaissance* (New York: Norton, 1996),
especially her discussions of Francesco Cardinal Gonzaga's collections, which are scattered through
the book.

general one of the most royal women imaginable) sacrificing to Venus. He seems to be describing not an actual medal but a combination of two common types: coins of Faustina with Venus on the reverse and a rather common forgery, by the Paduan medalist Giovanni Cavino, with a reverse of Faustian participating in a vestal sacrifice.[48] Domayron's interlocutors credited Faustina (who was portrayed by ancient historians as exceptionally lascivious) with the invention of cosmetics; as the narrator pointed out, this was implausible, but it did underline the link between makeup and misgovernment.

The bulk of his treatment, though, is devoted to a contrast between natural and unnatural beauty and a corresponding contrast between medicine and cosmetics.[49] This dichotomy was relatively complex in ways that help illuminate the overall unity of Domayron's project. Sixteenth-century cosmetics had a close relationship with alchemy, even beyond the potable gold. In part this was because white foundations and rouges were commonly made from compounds of lead, mercury, or other heavy metals (with predictably devastating health effects that Domayron and other contemporaries noted); in part, it had to do with the transmission of cosmetic formulas, which were frequently incorporated into alchemical or iatrochemical works.[50] Early modern cosmetics were also ways of performing or counterfeiting social status, if we accept their historian's claim that "from the Renaissance on, a white complexion imposes itself on the elites as a coercive esthetic norm, because it constitutes the irrefutable testimony of *otium* and the noble estate."[51] When

---

48. For Cavino, see Richard Hoe Lawrence, *The Paduans: Medals by Giovanni Cavino* (Hewitt, NJ: Hellenic-Roman Coins, n.d.), no. 59. According to William Henry Smyth, *Descriptive Catalog of a Cabinet of Roman-Imperial Large Brass Medals* (Bedford, UK: James Webb, 1834), 142, "The medals of Faustina Junior are exceedingly common in all metals, and are therefore selected with particular attention to their state of preservation. In this abundance, it is curious that a large-brass forgery should have been foisted in among them,—it is of admirable workmanship, and represents a sacrifice to Vesta, somewhat like that of Julia Domna; and it is found in such numbers that I have had eight or ten: the fraud has been ascribed to Benvenuto Cellini, but its Patavinity rather assigns it to the noted Lewis Lee [*sic*]." The *Siege* includes a long disquisition on the cult of Vesta, so it is unlikely that Domayron would actually have mistaken the vestal sacrifice for one to Venus.

49. For a brief overview of the contemporary discourse on cosmetics, into which Domayron's dichotomy fits very neatly, see Annette Drew-Bear, "Cosmetics and Attitudes towards Women in the Seventeenth Century," *Journal of Popular Culture* 9 (1975): 31–37. There is a longer survey, with an art-historical focus, in Patricia Phillippy, *Painting Women: Cosmetics, Canvases, and Early Modern Culture* (Baltimore: Johns Hopkins University Press, 2006).

50. This is covered in some detail in Catherine Lanoë, *La poudre et le fard: Une histoire des cosmétiques de la Renaissance aux Lumières* (Paris: Champ Vallon, 2008), 143–60.

51. Catherine Lanoë, "Images, masques et visages. Production et consommation des cosmétiques à Paris sous l'Ancien Régime," *Revue d'histoire moderne et contemporaine* 35 (2008): 10: "Dès la Renaissance, la blancheur du teint s'impose aux élites telle une norme esthétique coercitive, car elle constitue le témoignage irréfutable de l'*otium* et de l'état noble."

Domayron criticized "those women who fraudulently desire to appear beautiful by art," the overlap with the languages of alchemy and criminality was not fortuitous. He went on to make a moral distinction between onetime treatments that actually corrected some esthetic flaw and temporary measures that merely covered it up. One would already see a parallel to the contrast between true and fraudulent transmutation even without his recommendation of the legendary "oil of talc" for such treatment, but only "the true oil made magisterially, without additives as most do, who consider themselves great operators as soon as they know four words borrowed from Geber or some such chemical classic, and boast of performing transmutations at will." The proper oil must be made by "one who knows its nature so as to make it leave behind the sulfurous production it has within, removing it by the paths of the great work."[52] Producing true beauty, true health, and true nobility, it turns out, is literally a branch of the magnum opus.

"Above all she had very pale skin, with no makeup at all (though they say that every morning she partook of some broth made up of potable gold and other drugs, which I do not understand as a good physician or subtle apothecary would)." Brantôme's offhand comment now appears in its full significance: Diane de Poitiers is an example of true, even perfect nobility and truly natural beauty. She not assisted by those metallic ointments that might be prepared by a false practitioner, someone like Able Drugger in Ben Jonson's play *The Alchemist*, who combined bad cosmetics with his friend Subtle's alchemical frauds to make his dishonest living.[53] Instead she consumes the true potable gold and other drugs prepared by good physicians and subtle apothecaries, truly learned and virtuous operators, which operate on her a true if perhaps superfluous transmutation, indeed a kind of apotheosis. If it was more pagan than Christian, that did not prevent it from participating in the general aura of the sacred that surrounded gold, monarchy, and the alchemical ideal alike. There was something about Diane and her inhumanly perfect blending of beauty, mythology, wealth, and political power that evoked the medal. This appeared very strikingly at the Château d'Anet built for her by Henri II and the architect Philibert de l'Orme.[54]

---

52. Domayron, *Histoire du Siege*, 326: "celles qui frauduleusement veulent paroistre belles par art"; 338: "le vray huile fait Magistralement, sans adjonction, ainsi que la plus part font: qui se croyent estre grands operateurs, dés qu'ils sçavent quatre mots empruntez du Gebber, ou tel autre ancien Chimique, & se vantent faire les trans-mutations à leur volonté"; "un qui cognoisse sa nature pour luy faire laisser la dustion soulfree qui l'a en soy, la luy ostant par les chemins de la grande œuvre."
53. See Ben Jonson, *The Alchemist*, ed. Elizabeth Cook, 2nd ed. (New York: Norton, 1991).
54. On the overall design, see Anthony Blunt, *Philibert de l'Orme* (London: A. Zwemmer, 1958), 28–55.

One of the first large triumphs of French Renaissance architecture, it was literally a monument to its owner. Over the main entrance, de l'Orme placed one of the most famous works of the century's most famous medalist: Benvenuto Cellini's *Nymph of Fontainebleau*, originally made for the entrance to François I's palace but thenceforth indissolubly identified with the duchesse de Valentinois. After going through that gateway, a visitor could see, in a courtyard to the right, another of the major works of midcentury French sculpture, *Diana with a Stag*, which has been plausibly attributed to the future "controller general of the effigies of the moneys of France," Germain Pilon.[55] Notably, this Diana sported an elaborate and exquisite Flavian hairstyle very reminiscent of those to be seen on medals of Faustina. And that erudite association would only have been strengthened if Diane's tame humanist, the Italian Gabriel Symeoni, had in fact carried out his decorative project for the loggia of the château's garden. This consisted of a triptych of *imprese*.

> In the third *impresa* I had a Diana depicted with a golden ball in one hand and a flaming torch in the other, and her chariot was drawn by a hind and a bull, with these words: *Chaste Diana fosters and enriches each of the two* [Henri and Diana] *by her probity*. By the golden ball I wished to signify the wealth and power of Diana, and by the torch the splendor of her name, since the ancients used it in this way on the reverse of their medals, as I recently saw in a bronze of Faustina, on the reverse of which is Diana with the torch in her hand and a crescent moon on her shoulders.[56]

He provides a woodcut of this medal and continues with a long discussion of both Faustina and Diana as they appeared on the Roman coinage. He

---

55. See Anthony Blunt, *Art and Architecture in France 1500 to 1700* (London: Penguin Books, 1953), 76–77 and notes. The marble statue was moved to the Louvre after the Revolution but somehow failed to survive World War II. On Pilon's very substantial career as a medalist, see Fernand Mazerolle, *Les médailleurs français du XVe siècle au milieu du XVIIe*, vol. 1, *Introduction et documents* (Paris: Imprimerie Nationale, 1902), lxx–lxxvii.

56. Gabriel Symeoni, *Illustratione de gli epitafi et medaglie antiche* (Lyons: Jean de Tournes, 1558), 106–7: "nella terza impresa io havevo fatto dipingere una Diana con una palla d'oro in una mano, & nell'altra un torchio acceso, & il suo carro era tirato da una Cerbia & da una Toro, con queste parole: *Casta fovet ditatque utros probitate Diana*. Per la palla d'oro io volevo significare il riccezze & il potere di Diana, & per il torchio lo splendore del su nome, havendo questo gl'antichi cosi usato ne rovesci delle loro medaglie, come io ho veduto nuovamente in una di bronzo di Faustina, nel roveschio della quale è Diana col torchio nelle mani, & una Luna che l'esce di sopra alle spalle." This book was also published in French, by the same printer and with the same illustrations (which seem to be the work of Bernard Salomon): *Les illustres observations antiques du seigneur Gabriel Syméon, florentin, en son dernier voyage d'Italie, l'an 1557* (Lyons: Jean de Tournes, 1558). See Bardon, *Diane*, 58–61.

does neglect to mention that the golden ball—a "golden globe or apple," according to the French translation's helpful gloss—is an attribute not of Diana but of Venus, awarded at the judgment of Paris, so this impresa also encapsulates the duchesse's status as an object of love. Otherwise this passage hardly requires comment: coins and medals, mythological divinity and human beauty, wealth and political authority, and learning and virtue are present here in a nearly perfect combination. Anet, its mistress, and its artists were, perhaps, the symbolic heart of Henri II's monetary policy.

Part II: Monkeys

The reign of Henri II was the high point of this set of tropes, which then declined as civil war and monetary disorder rendered them less convincing. Ronsard, Cellini, Pilon, and for that matter Symeoni far outshine figures like Antoine Domayron or even Rascas de Bagarris. In a fascinating study of the use of gold in late Valois art, Rebecca Zorach has shown how over the second half of the sixteenth century gold became increasingly a symbol of mutability and instability and of the wasteful and unnatural aspects of court culture, and this process seems to have worked more broadly.[57] If such ideas were revived and developed in the reign of Henri IV (as the projected monetary edict of 1609 revived the Henrique d'or), they occupied a more obscure corner of early seventeenth- than of mid-sixteenth-century culture. Of course the more positive set of associations with gold, deeply embedded as they were in Western culture, remained available: if nothing else, they were to play a major role in the iconography of the Sun King. And the association of true alchemy with religious virtue, divine majesty, and sometimes religiously based temporal sovereignty became ever more prominent— but mostly outside France, in places such as the courts of the Palatinate, Denmark, and Rudolf II's Prague.[58]

In France, by contrast, the literary treatment of money and the precious metals took new turns, revealing the anxieties provoked both by money and by the growing complexity of the relationship among money, monarchy, and governance in Bourbon France. Whereas the emblem of the Renaissance

---

57. See Rebecca Zorach, *Blood, Milk, Ink, Gold: Abundance and Excess in the French Renaissance* (Chicago: University of Chicago Press, 2005), 189–236.

58. On Prague, see R. J. W. Evans, *Rudolf II and His World: A Study in Intellectual History, 1676– 1612* (Oxford: Clarendon Press, 1973). For a Danish example, see Michael Sendivogius, *Traicté du soulphre*, trans. F. Guiraud (Paris: Abraham Pacard, 1618), sig. iv. For the Palatinate, see the flawed but still valuable study of Frances Yates, *The Rosicrucian Enlightenment* (New York: Routledge, 1972).

monetary imaginary was the god—a being of more than human purity and power capable of bringing transcendence and magnificence to the disordered world of avarice and waste and thus more than worthy of his or her temporal sovereignty—the equivalent emblem of the classical era was the monkey. Less than human, a purely material counterfeit of the human, the monkey revealed disorder and contingency in the human world and called myths of transcendence into question. The literature of the first half of the seventeenth century pointed to a desire for systems of exchange and value that could authorize themselves without the intervention of an immanent divinity—a tendency less surprising if one remembers that this is the era of the Jansenist Hidden God and of the New Philosophies of naturalism and Cartesian dualism, which equally sought to understand the world in the absence of certain kinds of supernatural presence.[59]

But exploring these developments will take us not only into an entirely different literary world from the one that has concerned us in this chapter so far but also well beyond what are otherwise the chronological limits of this book. At least three factors justify such a digression. First, there was a real continuity between the thematic treatments of money in the two periods under consideration: the closest link is to be found in comic plays, which I have discussed at length elsewhere, but there were a number of others.[60] Second, the two approaches to money under consideration are not really separable, with anxiety and glorification always coexisting, if in different proportions and under different presuppositions. Finally, opening up to the seventeenth century helps clarify the broader historical significance of the phenomena studied throughout this book. As the modern, commercial, increasingly autonomous economy came into sharper focus, the institutions, theories, and tropes that had surrounded the sixteenth-century currency continued to inform and shape the discourse around money, society, and governance.

Comedy, Counterfeit, and the Picaresque

Beginning with the revival of the Hellenistic New Comedy in Henri II's reign and under the aegis of the Pléiade, French playwrights extensively explored

---

59. It is worth confessing my debt here to two studies viewed by specialists with not-unjustified suspicion: Lucien Goldmann, *Le dieu caché; étude sur la vision tragique dans les Pensées de Pascal et dans le théâtre de Racine* (Paris: Gallimard, 1955); and Michel Foucault, *Les mots et les choses: Une archéologie des sciences humaines* (Paris: Gallimard, 1966).

60. See Jotham Parsons, "Money and Merit in French Renaissance Comedy," *Renaissance Quarterly* 60 (2007): 852–82.

the ways in which money troubled noble status and social mobility. Intermittent and increasingly poorly attested as time went on, this discourse culminated in Pierre Corneille's enormously successful first play, *Mélite* (1629), and played an important role in shaping the contours of comedy from that point on. One of the clearest statements of this theme can be found not in the comedies themselves but in an epitaph for one of their writers composed by the Pléiade poet Jean-Antoine de Baïf. We have already met its subject: Odet de Turnèbe, abortive first president of the Monnaies and author of *The Contented*, probably the best regular comedy written in French before *Mélite*. Baïf (who had temporarily abandoned the project of renewing the French language and returned to neo-Latin poetry) apostrophized Turnèbe as follows:

> Do counted coins, not virtue, raise you up?
> Is this how the court of moneys gives law?
> An early death, as judge, settled this suit:
> Your own honor adorns you lest you grow swollen with a purchased one.[61]

This is a very direct and literal expression of money's power over social and intellectual achievement and of the superiority of true learning to wealth. Here, though, the sovereign that regulates the system is Death, which seems undesirable as a general solution.

The comic playwrights naturally avoided such a tragic vision. While they occasionally alluded to the power of royal sovereignty, they generally relied on the code of secular virtue and worldly knowledge that came to be called *honnêteté* to govern the disruptive power of money; Molière's *Bourgeois gentilhomme* (1670) proved the ultimate expression of this sensibility. This was easy enough to do in the narrow confines of the New Comedy, where the machinery of the plot could be relied on to punish bad behavior and reward youthful merit. Less orderly genres that rose to prominence in the seventeenth century could reveal more of the complexity involved in understanding monetary relations. We have already noted how the cases of counterfeiters echoed the picaresque: the process also worked in reverse. The major Spanish works that defined the genre—*Lazarillo de Tormes* (1554), *Guzmán de Alfarache* (1595), *El buscón* (1604), *La pícara Justina* (1605), and *Don Quixote* (1605–1615)—were

---

61. *Othonis Turnebi in suprema curia parisiensi advocati tumulus*, ed. Adrien (II) Turnèbe (Paris: Apud Mamertum Patissonium, in officina Roberti Stephani, 1582), 17: "Non virtus, sed te numerata pecunia tollat? / Sícne monetali reddere jura foro? / Hanc judex litem mors immatura diremit: / Ne tumeas empto te tuus ornat honos." On Baïf's neo-Latin turn, which he gave up soon after this was written, see Mathieu Augé-Chiquet, *La vie, les idées et l'œuvre de Jean-Antoine de Baïf* (Geneva: Slatkine, 1979 [1909]).

popular and widely read in France by the early seventeenth century. Domayron saw some of them, for example, in the pleasure library of the Seat of the
Muses, where "the Spanish *pícara* and *pícaro*" rubbed shoulders with a variety
of romances.[62]

On the other hand, the picaresque was slow to appear in French literature and never really coalesced as a distinct genre, held back by an obsession
with the noble and the honnête.[63] Still, elements of the picaresque—clever,
marginalized, and antisocial heroes; comic, episodic, and deliberately aimless
narratives; low-life settings; and an obsession with fraud, impersonation, and
betrayal—were widespread. Since the picaresque took poverty, dishonesty,
and deracination as its particular themes, it is unsurprising that picaresque
characters had regular run-ins with money and currency, and also with clothing, disguise, and chicanery. Indeed, the first and quite possibly the only
explicitly picaresque hero in seventeenth-century French literature appeared
not in a novel but in a play, Corneille's *Comic Illusion* (1635): in the author's
words a "strange monster" vaguely reminiscent in structure and themes of
The Tempest.[64] Clindor, the protagonist, wandered over much of France after
being expelled from the paternal home, pursuing his fortune in various call-
ings that might not have met the strictest standards of honesty in either sense
of the term: "At last, the Buscón, Lazarillo de Tormes, / Saavedra['s characters, or] Guzmán never took so many forms."

This action takes place offstage, however: a magician named Alcandre nar-
rates it to Clindor's father, Pridamant, just prior to beginning a pair of nested
plays-within-a-play. It turns out that Clindor has become an actor, but we
do not learn this until we have first watched him acting, and dying, in his
current productions. The picaresque background serves, in part, a technical
role: Clindor ends his picaresque career, "worn out by so many jobs neither
honorable nor fruitful," by taking service with a captain (as Guzmán had done
at one point in his adventures). By making this captain the stock boastful-
coward character of the New Comedy, Corneille is able to link the picaresque

---

62. Domayron, *Histoire du Siege*, 145: "La Piccara avec le Piccaro Espagnols." *Lazarillo* appeared
in French translation in 1560; *Guzmán* in 1600 (translated by the historiographer Gabriel Chappuys)
and again in 1619–1620 (by the poet and future Academician Jean Chapelain); *Don Quixote* in 1620;
El buscón in 1633 (by the comic novelist Scarron); *Justina* in 1636.

63. The starting place for the secondary literature on this question is W. M. Frohock, "The
'Picaresque' in France before *Gil Blas*," *Yale French Studies* 38 (1967): 222–29.

64. The critical literature on this play has tended to focus on its metadramatic elements: for
a good introduction, which helps clarify the play's structure, see Robert J. Nelson, "Pierre Corneille's *L'Illusion comique*: The Play as Magic," *Proceedings of the Modern Language Association* 71 (1956):
1127–40.

formally with the stage and segue into his first play-within-a-play. If we want to understand why Corneille should have chosen this particular segue, though, we might turn our attention to yet another framing device. Alcandre introduces the narrative of Clindor's success by revealing a vignette at the back of the stage where the father and the audience see "a display of the actors' most beautiful clothing," with the words "judge your son by such an outfit." Then, at the end of act 5, when father and audience have just seen Clindor killed in the denouement of the tragedy, the same curtain rises again and "we see all the actors dividing their money."[65] But invoking the picaresque sits uncomfortably with Corneille's, or Alcandre's, stated purpose of reassuring Pridamant about his son's socioeconomic standing. For neither actors nor pícaros can safely be judged by their clothing: the audience might think of the starving but proud *hidalgo* with whom Lazarillo took service, who maintained a threadbare noble appearance even in utter destitution, or even more strikingly of the band of con men that Pablo joins in *El buscón*, who patched together fancy clothing from rags in order to dupe the unsuspecting.

Indeed, the Spanish picaresque was largely *about* the deceptive nature of appearances in social relations, the ways in which such deception could be deployed to shore up the position of the desperate, the disenfranchised, and the merely dishonest. It was, in other words, about counterfeiting in a general but precise sense—about the use of art and cunning to make the public take objects, or people, at a value not justified by their intrinsic nature or by the laws and social norms in force. To give one more example, Guzmán at one point earns his living as a beggar by artfully faking wounds and sores, "which I knew how to counterfeit excellently," at least until a sharp-eyed magistrate finds him out. Alemán spends some time playing with the contrasts between his counterfeit cripple and the sound coins he requests, as with "some powerful and rich men pondering deeply how they might give that worthless coin, a *blanca*," manipulating their purses so they appeared to be charitable while hardly being so at all.[66] But actors, as the play itself demonstrates, are the professionals

---

65. Pierre Corneille, *L'Illusion comique. Comédie. Publiée d'après la première édition (1639) avec les variantes*, ed. Robert Garapon (Paris: Nizet, 1985), 3: "En fin jamais Buscon, Lazarille de Tormes/ Sayavedra et Gusman ne prirent tant de formes"; 17: "Las de tant de mestiers sans honneur et sans fruit"; 13: "en parade les plus beaux habits des Comédiens. . . . Jugez de vostre fils par un tel esqui-page"; 118: "on voit tous les Comediens qui partagent leur argent."

66. Mateo Alemán, *Guzmán de Alfarache*, ed. Samuel Gili y Gaya, 4 vols. (Madrid: Espasa-Calpe, 1942), 2:224: "que sabía contrahacer por excelencia"; 230: "Algunos hombres poderosos y ricos con curiosidad se ponían a hacer especulación para dar una desventurada moneda que es una blanca." Compare Chappuy's very literal translation, *Guzman d'Alfarache, divisé en trois livres* (Paris: Nicolas & Pierre Bonfons, 1600), fol. 37v: "car le l'a sçavois bien contrefaire, par excellence"; fol. 40r:

par excellence of such social counterfeiting; perhaps Clindor's transformation from pícaro to *comédien* was nothing more than one more comical illusion.

How then could Alcandre expect Pridamant, and the audience, to believe him when he says that "the theater is a fief whose rents are good," that it provides the same kind of genuine social foundation as rich noble lands, and that "your son finds in this sweet profession / More goods and honor than he would have in your household"?[67] Corneille himself had to face the accusation that the theater conferred only a counterfeit social status in the course of the "quarrel of *The Cid*" a few years later.[68] Through the first half of the seventeenth century the figure of the pícaro could be a negative image of the man of letters—the book-mad Quixote being the classic example—just as the counterfeiter was a negative image of the artisan or alchemical magus and the impostor of the gentleman. This appears with particular clarity in one of the earliest successful comic novels, Charles Sorel's *Comic History of Francion*. Corneille might easily have had it in mind when he wrote the *Comic Illusion*, since its final and most popular edition (the one we will consider here) had appeared in 1633, only two years before the play's probable date of composition.

Francion clearly has a significant relationship to the picaresque, but exactly what that relation is has been a subject of controversy.[69] The controversy is even present in the text: when one of Francion's interlocutors compares the hero's "low actions" to those of "Guzman d'Alfarach and of Lazarillo de Tormes"—Alcandre's comments on Clindor's picaresque transformations may directly echo this passage—it is to *contrast* those "beggars and . . . good-for-nothings" with Francion, a "gentleman scholar."[70] This tension

---

"aucuns hommes riches et opulents, par curiosité se mettoient à contempler, pour donner une pauvre piece de monnoye, qui est une blanque." Guzmán seems to have attracted monetary metaphors: see this from the introduction to Chapelain's translation, *Le gueux, ou Guzman d'Alfarache, image de la vie humaine*, 2 vols. (Rouen: Jean de la Maire, 1633), 1: unpag. intro.: "En effect bien encore qu'il ne soit de tout poinct accomply, tousjours le bien y passe-t'il le mal infiniment, qui est le marque & le coing des bons livres."

67. Corneille, *L'illusion*, 121: "Le Theatre est un fief dont les rentes sont bonnes. . . . Vostre fils rencontre en un mestier si doux / Plus de biens et d'honneur qu'il n'eust trouvé chez vous."

68. Some such attacks are reproduced in Georges Mongrédien, ed., *Receuil des textes et des documents du XVIIe siècle relatifs à Corneille* (Paris: Editions du C.N.R.S., 1972), 63ff.

69. See Wolfgang Leiner, "Regards critiques sur le statut picaresque du *Francion*," in *Création et recréation: Un dialogue entre littérature et histoire. Mélanges offerts à Marie-Odile Sweetser*, ed. Claire Gaudiani and Jacqueline Van Baelen (Tübingen: Narr, 1993), 209–21.

70. Charles Sorel, *Histoire comique de Francion: Edition de 1633*, ed. Fausta Garavini, Anne Schoysman, and Lia Franchetti (Paris: Gallimard, 1996), 183 and note: "actions basses"; "Guzman d'Alfarach et de Lazaril de Tormes"; "gueux et . . . faquins . . . gentilhomme escolier."

pervades the novel and is closely related to another of its structural tensions: its relationship to "libertinism." That rather tenuous movement consisted in its literary dimension of a group of men united by a common attitude of revolt against the dominant ideologies in subjects including but not limited to religion, metaphysics, sexuality, and literary style, and more concretely by a common attachment to the poet Théophile de Viau (who is traditionally supposed to have inspired the character of Francion).[71] In the mid-1620s (between the first and second editions of *Francion*) de Viau was arrested, imprisoned, and ultimately hounded to death by the Parlement of Paris, the Jesuit François Garasse, and Garasse's supporters in the court of Louis XIII. Thenceforth, not only would libertinism be more or less an underground movement, but it would be one that inhibited in its adherents the kind of social advancement, or even stability, to which men of letters traditionally aspired. In those circumstances the appeal of the picaresque, both as a genre and as a model for self-mythologization, is evident.[72] So are the specific models of the counterfeiter and the alchemist, men driven by desperation or enabled by a secret grace to take command of human or natural law and produce by their own efforts the wealth and power that society denies them.

This certainly appears in Francion's career, as he recounted it himself in the course of the novel. After a gilded youth he attended the Collège de Lisieux, where he had a series of adventures that recalled El Buscón's school days, and he would have been sent on to study law had his father's death not intervened. Instead, he returned to Paris to learn "honnêtes exercices"—the accomplishments of a gentleman—and fit himself for life as a courtier. But after losing all

---

71. On the various definitions of the libertine movement, see René Pintard, "Aspects et contours du libertinage: Les problèmes de l'histoire du libertinage, notes et réflexions," *XVIIe siècle* 127 (1980): 131–61. The foundational study of the movement is Pintard, *Le libertinage érudit dans la première moitié du dix-septième siècle* (Paris: Boivin, 1943). On libertinism as a literary movement, still an understudied topic, the best place to start is probably the editorial matter in Jacques Prévot, ed., *Libertins du XVIIe siècle*, 2 vols. (Paris: N.R.F./Gallimard, 1998).

72. For a good discussion of the thematic links between libertinism and the picaresque, see Brigitte Hamon-Porter, "Dassoucy, picaro, libertin et honnête homme des *Aventures*," in *Avez-vous lu Dassoucy? Actes du colloque international de Centre d'Etudes sur les Réformes, l'Humanisme et l'Âge classique, Clermont-Ferrand, 25–26 juin 2004*, ed. Dominique Bertrand (Clermont-Ferrand: Presses Universitaires Blaise Pascal, 2005), 177–88. On the fluid boundaries between life, fiction, autobiography, and legend for the libertines, see Joan DeJean, "Seventeenth-Century Libertine Novels: *Autobiographies romancées?*," *L'Esprit créateur* 19 (1979): 14–25. There is an important nuance here: aside from Théophile, almost all the major libertine writers (who were an extravagantly talented lot) had some level of ultimate success within the "establishment." Sorel settled into a solidly bourgeois existence as a kind of up-market hack; Tristan l'Hermite ended his life as the poorest member of the Académie. Even among the irreducibles, Cyrano de Bergerac became an *écrivain à gages* for Richelieu, and Charles Dassoucy never quite lost his grip on his position as a musician at the royal court. But these successes, won only with the bitterest struggle, never came close to what the authors (not entirely unjustly) thought that they deserved.

his money to fraudsters, he instead became for a while a thoroughgoing pícaro. What plunged him into the abyss was a simple inability to buy new clothes: "I was thus forced to reuse an old gray outfit and a scarlet cape. . . . They suited me so badly that hardly anyone would have had the judgment to recognize in me the son of the brave Captain de la Porte." No longer able to *appear* as his father's son, Francion was the opposite of a counterfeit—it required expert judgment to discern his actual nobility. Sorel contrasts Francion with one of his old schoolmates. Tocarète, a man of no intrinsic worth, was the "son of a low merchant," whom "they . . . had always considered the greatest ass at the University" and (like the worthier Odet de Turnèbe) had obtained the ennobling office of a councillor in one of the sovereign courts "by his good money." This "good money," a throwaway phrase but one that will take on significance later, was enough to buy a false legal judgment on Tocarète's quali-fication to hold his office and thus be a noble. It also bought him the right to have Francion literally pushed around (which no man of his condition should willingly suffer), and it enabled him to parade through Paris in a minutely described "lord's outfit . . . to have a quality that would make him respected and to find women who would make very advantageous matches."[73]

The route out of this picaresque dead end is the hero's pursuit of the beau-tiful and noble and very rich Naïs, whose picture he first sees in the midst of recounting his schoolboy adventures and who took on an increasingly central role in subsequent revisions and expansions of the novel. Uncharacteristically, she is always exactly what she seems, in paint or in person, and thus tends to short-circuit the dynamic of counterfeiting. On the other hand, she draws the plot to Rome, a city notorious to French authors at least since du Bellay for dissimulation, fraud, and hypocrisy. Skipping about two-thirds of the novel, this brings us to book 12, added in the 1633 edition to bring some (mock) epic dignity to Sorel's previous hastily arranged conclusion. The main event of this book is an accusation of counterfeiting lodged against Francion, which at last opens up the thematic functions not only of meta-phorical but of real coining.[74]

---

73. Sorel, *Francion*, 222: "apprendre des honnêtes exercices." Pages 224–25: "je me fus donc contraint de reprendre un vieil habit gris et un manteau de couleur de roi. . . . J'étais si mal accom-modé avec qu'il n'y en avait guère qui eussent tant de jugement qu'ils me pussent prendre pour le fils du brave capitaine de La Porte." Page 227: "fils d'un vil marchand"; "que l'on . . . a toujours estimé le plus grand âne de l'Université"; "par son bon argent." Page 228: "équipage de seigneur . . . pour avoir une qualité qui [le] fît respecter et trouver des femmes qui eussent de grands avantages."

74. On themes of counterfeiting in *Francion* see Martine Debaisieux, *Le procès du roman: Écriture et contrefaçon chez Charles Sorel*, 2nd ed. (Orleans: Paradigme, 2000), to which I am much indebted for this discussion, and Jean Serroy, "Francion et l'argent, ou l'immoraliste et les faux monnayeurs," *XVIIe siècle* 105 (1974): 3–18.

Sorel clearly consulted with an expert about the details of counterfeiting investigations.[75] Francion's detention and interrogation and the search of his home on which much of the plot turns have the precise verisimilitude of an unusually facetious police procedural. Clearly, the author felt that it was important that the intrusion of the criminal justice system *feel real* even while remaining, from a broader perspective, quite ridiculous enough to be at home in a comical history. The reason for this is that Francion's brush with counterfeiting serves precisely and finally to stabilize for the reader the reality and honesty of his social position, which has continuously been called into question by many aspects of the novel, not least its picaresque characteristics. To see how that works, we will have to enter into some of the details of book 12's intricate intrigue, which in some ways resembles a stage comedy as much as *The Comic Illusion* resembles a comic novel. And in fact the book opens with the arrival of "a certain man called seigneur Bergamin" (the homophony with the famous Venetian alchemical con man Bragadin was probably not coincidental) who "had been an actor in his youth and was considered the best in his profession" but who had become a kind of court jester.[76] Bergamin announced that a young woman named Emilie was suing Francion for breach of promise—news of this had also reached Naïs (now Francion's fiancée), who let it be known that she wanted nothing more to do with him. Francion admitted that Emilie's case was not entirely without merit: she was the daughter of a widowed Venetian noblewoman of reduced circumstances, in Rome to pursue "damages and interest" against the murderer of her late husband. Having gained an introduction to the mother on the pretense of aiding her suit, Francion had engaged in what he claimed was a noncommittal flirtation with the daughter. While this situation remained unresolved, Francion was the victim of a reverse pocket picking: when he spent some of the money that had newly appeared in his purse, he was immediately arrested for passing counterfeit coin.

"A man who set himself up as a denunciator" then came forward to testify that Francion was actually a wandering con artist who had engaged in elaborate frauds involving coinage, weights, and measures throughout Italy,

---

75. Since he came from a family of *procureurs*, this would have posed no difficulty for him, provided the experts were willing to take his attacks on the courts in good humor. It is quite conceivable that his source was an officer of the Monnaies, though the Châtelet and even the Parlement of Paris had relevant expertise.

76. Sorel, *Francion*, 595–96: "un certain homme que l'on appellait le seigneur Bergamin . . . avait été comédien en sa jeunesse et était estimé le premier de sa profession." Bragadin is actually invoked later in the chapter (p. 629).

particularly in Genoa.[77] This witness also told a fantastic story of a banquet Francion had given for the French community in Rome, which he concluded by distributing an entire basin of "many gold coins," presumably counterfeit, desiring "in this to act the magnificent lord," just as the impostor Bragadin had done. This is clearly meant to indicate that Francion's entire rich web of social stature and respect, one of the novel's major themes, was itself counterfeit. While Francion remained under arrest, a group of functionaries arrived and searched his home, finding nothing, but his friends caught a ringer among the police, who, under threat of torture, admitted to having been sent to plant evidence on our hero. His testimony unravels the entire plot: Francion was framed for counterfeiting by an Italian named Valere, "a gentleman of a good house" but with "more appearance than reality, and his wealth is not as remarkable as the antiquity of his nobility," who hoped to repair these defects by marrying Naïs.[78]

Valere is an echo of the earlier Francion: a man of true nobility (or so our untrustworthy sources tell us), but without the resources to "appear" in his true role and seeking to stabilize his social identity through marriage.[79] He is also, it turns out, a counterfeiter in earnest: "Since the affairs of his house were often in decline, and he could find no way to pay for his sumptuous lifestyle, he turned to this evil trade." His story certainly recalls the desperate, downwardly mobile men so often found in the criminal dockets of the Monnaies. But here it serves only to increase the extent to which Valere troubles the character of Francion—he illustrates a potential reality behind the hero's picaresque diversions. And even if Francion's money by now is good, readers will certainly sympathize with Naïs's reply when told of the charges lodged against him: "If he has not falsified the moneys, at least he has falsified his affection and corrupted the love that is the sweetest bond of society." Moreover, the situation into which Valere had precipitated Francion is one familiar to pícaros, who frequently see their schemes for advancement or enrichment

---

77. Genoa was noted at the time for its more than dubious currency policies: see Edoardo Grendi, "Falsa monetazione e strutture monetarie degli scambi nella Republica di Genova fra cinque e seicento," *Quaderni storici* 22 (1987): 803–37.

78. Sorel, *Francion*, 626: "Un homme, qui faisoit le dénonciateur"; 629: "quantité de pièces d'or"; "en cela faire le Seigneur magnifique"; 643: "gentilhomme de bonne maison . . . plus d'apparence que d'effet et sa richesse n'est pas si remarquable que l'antiquité de sa noblesse."

79. Some critics read Sorel as seriously calling into question the truth of Francion's claim to nobility: see Nathalie Grande, "Un bourgeois gentilhomme? Noblesse et société selon Francion," *Littératures* 43 (2000): 95–105; and Andrew Suozzo, "La bourgeoisie à la recherche de la noblesse: Le libertinage de l'*Histoire comique de Francion*," *Littératures classiques* 41 (2001): 31–40. Desbaisieux, *Procès du roman*, passim, makes similar but more subtle claims. I am inclined to read the relevant passages as questioning the *stability* of Francion's (or anyone's) noble identity rather than the identity itself.

(like Guzmán's counterfeit wounds) brought up short even by the most corrupt and incompetent justice.[80]

Sorel resolves this farrago of intrigue and ambiguity in Francion's favor through a character otherwise rare in comic literature: an honest judge.[81] Rare, but not unknown, for this incident and some other aspects of the chapter's organization strongly recall Théophile's prose fragment, "The First Day" (called "Fragments of a Comic History" in the posthumous 1632 edition of his works).[82] In that story, the Huguenot narrator fell victim to a mob incited by a companion's conspicuous disrespect for the Host. The victims were arrested but gained refuge in their kind and courteous arresting judge's house, where the hot-headed friend began a new flirtation over dinner. The parallel is striking enough to suggest that Sorel's concluding chapter was in some way a coded confession of libertine faith. Lucio, "the superior judge" in Francion's case, was already aware of Valere's crimes and easily elicited the truth from the witnesses. He was also able to confirm that Francion had been set up in his affair with Emilie, by her mother (hoping for a good match) and by another poor noble, one Ergaste, who was an old lover of Emilie's but wanted to free himself from involvement with her financial difficulties. This state of affairs may not fully satisfy the reader, who might say with Naïs that "you won't get out of that as easily as the counterfeiting," but *legally* it was dispositive, since Emilie, having a prior and better claim to breach of promise against Ergaste, was, as Lucio ruled, estopped from pursuing Francion in the matter.[83] Lucio not only freed Francion and exiled Valere but even arranged a marriage between Ergaste and Emilie and, in a final effort, a reconciliation between Francion and Naïs, who turned out to be his cousin. The novel thus ends, in its definitive version, with a definitive ruling that Francion is "true": that his "good money" is actually good, that it is consonant with the nobility he claims, and that both it and he are acceptable at the highest reaches of the state and the market.

---

80. Sorel, *Francion*, 655: "Pource que les affaires de sa maison allaient souvent en décadence et qu'il ne pouvoit trouver de quoi fournir à ses sumptuosités, il se servait de ce mauvais métier." Page 636: "s'il n'avait falsifié les monnaies, au moins il avoit falsifié ses affections et corrompu l'amour, qui est le plus doux lien de la societé."

81. One need only think of Rabelais's Judge Bridoye or practically any of the judges who appear in farces. Significantly, honest judges in comedy are typically sovereigns taking justice into their own hands to settle the intrigue: this was a favorite device of Shakespeare's.

82. See Théophile de Viau, "La première journée," in Prévot, *Libertins* 1:7–26 and notes. The fragment also begins with a stylistic manifesto echoed by several of Francion's pronouncements over the course of the novel.

83. Sorel, *Francion*, 652: "le juge superieur"; 671: "vous ne vous excuserez pas si facilement de cela que de la fausse monnaie."

In *Francion*, then, counterfeiting is a figure for the troubling elements of the picaresque state, and the hero's acquittal serves to exorcise the specter of the picaresque from the novel and replace it with the comic properly so called: a love affair recovered, a reputation reestablished, and a double marriage. This is the work of a judge who, like the duke in *The Merchant of Venice* (the ideal of a comedy of money), can establish, despite all our doubts, that what is, is right. He represents not so much papal sovereignty, an object of profound suspicion to Gallicans and libertines, as Roman law, the closest approximation to the pure justice of the Golden Age. Of course, our belief that this really does stabilize and authorize Francion as noble and honest depends on our trust in Lucio and ultimately on our trust in Sorel himself and his honesty, in some sense, as a writer. Sorel knew this very well and devoted enormous effort in *Francion* to establishing his (or his author-function's) authenticity, originality, and genuine skill in ways that must remain beyond our scope here.

Corneille, though, provides a relatively straightforward glimpse of how those strategies could work. We left hanging the question of how Corneille expected us to believe that the theater gave Clindor a genuine social position rather than another picaresque counterfeit. The answer lies literally in the coins displayed at the back of the stage. If Corneille had any sense of irony at all, the scene of the actors counting out their take would have used as its prop the actual take for that actual performance of the *Comic Illusion* itself.[84] This was a literal *clin d'or*, winking gold that both grounded the character's claims to social success and unquestionably possessed the intrinsic legitimacy that the picaresque called into question.[85] Unlike everything else in the play, those coins were not counterfeit: they were, in a typically perverse way, the pledge of the truth of Corneille's metafictional *mise en abîme*. The audience that paid the money *must* trust that the coins were genuine, not counterfeit, if they were not to accuse themselves of a crime, just as they must admit that the take was a proper reflection of Corneille's authorial skill if they were not to accuse themselves of a lapse of taste. The take and the applause functioned for Corneille in the same way that the legal judgment and the marriage functioned for Sorel but with much more immediate force, since they inserted the play directly into the social processes for which counterfeiting served as a metaphor.

---

84. See Nina Ekstein, *Corneille's Irony* (Charlottesville, VA: Rookwood Press, 2007).

85. In fact, of course, the take for a play would mainly be in silver or billon, not in gold coin, but that is pure pedantry. To buttress what I admit is a somewhat poorly supported play on words, I offer as a possible association in the minds of the contemporary audience the definition that follows *clin* in Furetière's *Dictionnaire*: "Clinquant. . . . Broderie *d'or ou d'argent* qu'on met sur les habits pour les faire *plus brillants & éclatants*. Il se dit plus particulierement de ces lames d'or ou d'argent qui font le plus brillants des dentelles & des broderies" (my emphasis).

We have already seen how real as well as fictional coining, like the theater, functioned (in its practitioners' hopes) as a kind of social alchemy and how its persistent cultural association with actual alchemy was more than just a matter of technical overlap. Writers of libertine comic novels took advantage of the existing alchemical narrative and its connections to the criminal, the picaresque, and the problematics of ambition, avarice, and social mobility. Indeed, besides the Spanish picaresque and the alchemical literature we have already described, libertine novelists could also allude to the rather picaresque adventures of Brother C.R. and the Rosicrucian Brotherhood, who had burst into prominence in France in the bizarre "Rosicrucian Scare" prank of 1623–1624—an outburst of mysterious posters and pamphlets that formed part of the motive for Thóphile's persecution and provoked a brilliantly sardonic response from the great libertine polymath Gabriel Naudé, and so loomed large in the libertine consciousness.[86] Indeed, Joan Dejean has argued quite persuasively for a comprehensive, if deeply troubled, identification of the libertine novelists (and their protagonists) with the powerful, persecuted, deliberately obfuscating, and potentially fraudulent figure of the sorcerer, alchemist, or magus.[87] So it is no surprise that such themes appear in two of the other major works in this genre: Tristan l'Hermite's *The Disgraced Page* and Cyrano de Bergerac's *The Other World*.

L'Hermite's novel is the slightly autobiographical story of an impoverished young Gascon noble. Hoping, d'Artagnan-like, to make his way in Paris and obtain a position at court consistent with his own views on his family's noble antiquity, he took a position as a page to a prince of the blood. And like d'Artagnan, he soon became involved in dueling, an important and low-cost tool for maintaining social status.[88] As a provincial gentleman named Antoine du Verdier said sometime around the turn of the century, dueling was "a true means whereby the richest and most powerful lord may not offend a minor one, who, being a gentleman like himself by the equality of arms, may demand satisfaction for the offense man-to-man from one who is richer, which he could not do otherwise."[89] It was also illegal, though, which

86. On the Rosicrucian Scare and its relation to libertinism, see Didier Kahn, "The Rosicrucian Hoax in France (1623–24)," in *Secrets of Nature: Astrology and Alchemy in Early Modern Europe*, ed. William R. Newman and Anthony Grafton (Cambridge, MA: M.I.T. Press, 2001), 235–344.

87. See Joan DeJean, *Libertine Strategies: Freedom and the Novel in Seventeenth-Century France* (Columbus: Ohio State University Press, 1981), esp. 101–22.

88. On dueling and feuding as modes of social mobility (or prophylactics against downward mobility), see Stuart Carroll, Blood and Violence in Early Modern France (Oxford: Oxford University Press, 2006), 56–59.

89. *Les diverses lecons d'Antoine du Verdier, sieur de Vauprivas, gentil-homme foresien, & ordinaire de la maison du Roy, suivans celles de Pierre Messie. Contenans plusieurs histoires, discours, & faicts memorables.*

made it especially dangerous for those with less social power. Thus, after seriously wounding a man, the page took flight for England. At an inn on the road between Rouen and le Havre, stripped of his social position and down to his last few coins, he met a mysterious stranger. This old man, we soon discover, was both an alchemist and a coiner, who used a "machine . . . with certain wheels" to turn transmuted iron into "moneyed gold."[90]

This gentleman took an interest in the page, accepting him as an apprentice and making "large promises to give him the means to appear honorably in the world," but as that already suggests, the page and the alchemist had divergent views of their project. For despite his willingness to "fall on the currency" in order to survive, the venerable Artefius was a true adept, wandering not from one disreputable adventure to another but from monastery to monastery, committed to a humble and spiritual life. A genuine Artist, he was able to produce the oil of talc—"it is quite vain, but among the peoples of Earth, who love only vanity, this powder has the price of the most solid riches, and can find credit where gold or diamonds are powerless"—as well as the transmuting powder of projection, which he valued hardly more, and the truly priceless universal medicine. The "disgraced" page, though, lacked the divine grace to learn the master's secrets. He could barely even taste the medicine before falling into a stupor, and when told to go await Artefius in London, he instead tumbled into a doomed love affair with the daughter of a fabulously wealthy marcher lord that left him exiled from London, "the place where all my hopes for imaginary wealth lay," and ultimately from Britain. It becomes clear that the page's hopes of finding wealth and social mobility through artifice were neither feasible nor appropriate. He would have done better to stick to a conventionally noble way of life: "I was not born under a happy enough planet to be prosperous in reality. It would have to suffice to have been so as in a dream; and if the hope of being able to find that man had not misled me for so long, I would have found myself

---

Augmentées par l'autheur en ceste cinquiesme edition de trois discours trouvez apres le decez de l'autheur en ses papiers, du Dueïl, de l'Honneur, & de la Noblesse (Tournon: Claude Michel, 1616), 604: "un vray moyen, que le plus riche & puissant Seigneur n'offence le plus petit, lequel estant Gentil-homme comme luy par l'egalité des armes, d'homme à homme pourra tirer raison de l'offence d'un plus opulent, ce qu'il ne pourroit autrement." On du Verdier's essays and their sociopolitical thinking, see Hervé Campagne, "Savoir, économie et société dans les *Diverses leçons* d'Antoine du Verdier," *Bibliothèque d'humanisme et renaissance* 58 (1995): 623–35.

90. Prévot, *Libertins* 1:417: "machine . . . à certaines roues . . . or monnayé." Such high-tech counterfeiting was not in fact unheard of. In 1583, the generals of the moneys seized an "engine" from a cloth merchant that, according to the testimony of the master engraver of the mint and of the director of the Monnaie des Etuves, could serve only for counterfeiting coins. See AN, Z[1B] 680, dossier dated 6 June 1583.

quite rich enough from my patrimony and the talents it pleased God to give me."[91] L'Hermite's critique of alchemy precisely matches le Loyer and, in his negative aspect, Domayron: it is a diversion, perhaps a satanic one, from the true paths of prosperity and honor. Without the grace that comes from a monarch in this world, or God in the next, gold can only lead the page to the life of the desperate and deracinated pícaro.

It remains unclear where l'Hermite's real solution to the dilemma of social mobility—his ascension to the Académie thanks to his skill as a writer—would fit into this narrative. His less successful admirer Cyrano, however, wrote a kind of model for that process: the narrator of his voyage to the moon appears to turn himself into the quintessence by a literal process of distillation and condensation. His original inspiration was the occultist favorite Girolamo Cardano; his method of travel was the capture of evaporating dew, and when (after a preliminary detour to Quebec) he reached the moon, his first encounter was with the Prophet Elijah, whose ascent to the heavens in a fiery chariot had long been taken as an alchemical allegory and who, under the name of Elias Artista, served as a type of the alchemical adept.[92] This was, in its burlesque register, a portrait of true alchemy, inspired by a love of truth (if not necessarily of God: the narrator, like the author, flirts seriously with atheism over the course of the novel) and rewarded by no worldly success, since the sequel to *The Other World*, the *Journey to the States and Empires of the Sun*, opens with our hero destitute and in prison. The product of Cyrano's alchemy can be only the novel itself and the reputation it gives him his only riches. Considering that Cyrano vies with Villon and Marlowe as the prototype of the writer as bohemian hero, his claims have some plausibility.

Monnaie de Singe

This kind of uncommercial self-transmutation might seem like an ideal of literature as a contrary of money or an act of alienation from the communal

91. Prévot, *Libertins* 1:422: "grandes promesses de [lui] donner le moyen de paraître honorablement selon le monde." Pages 423–24: "Elle est fort vaine, mais parmi les habitants de la Terre, qui n'aiment que la vanité, cette poudre est du prix des plus solides richesses et peut trouver du crédit où l'or et les diamants n'auraient point de force." Page 453: "lieu où reposait l'espérance de mes richesses imaginaires." Page 505: "Mais je n'étais pas né sous une planète assez heureuse, pour avoir des prospérités en effet: il me devait suffire d'en avoir eu comme en songe, et se l'espérance de pouvoir trouver cet homme ne m'eût point longtemps abusé, je me fusse trouvé trop riche du bien de mon patrimoine et des talents qu'il avait plu à Dieu de me donner."

92. See Secret, "Littérature et alchimie," and Paula Hartwig van Ells, "Alchemical Metaphor and Cyrano de Bergerac's Apology of the Imagination," *Cahiers du dix-septième* 7 (2000): 13–22.

social power of the monetary. That is not quite the case, though, in ways that closer attention to Cyrano's legend can clarify. A long-established folk etymology holds that the French phrase *payer en monnaie de singe*, "to pay in monkey money"—meaning to respond abusively or facetiously—derives from a tax exemption. According to Etienne Boileau's thirteenth-century *Book of Trades*, an edict of Louis IX had specified that the owners of trained monkeys could pay the penny toll on the Petit-Pont by having their animals dance for the gatekeeper.[93] More likely the phrase derived from lead tokens marked with pictures of monkeys that seem to have been used on the Seine bridges.[94] One of the better legends surrounding Cyrano de Bergerac, often attributed to his frenemy Charles Dassoucy but first appearing in an anonymous pamphlet from 1704, trades on this story. Sometime around 1650, it seems, the already legendary Cyrano went to see the puppet show performed by M. Brioché on the Pont Neuf. There was a crowd of lackeys in attendance, some of whom insulted our hero, with particular reference to his famously large nose; Cyrano, being Cyrano, drew his sword and put them to flight. Unfortunately, Brioché's monkey had been trained to fence and drew its own sword: Cyrano promptly skewered the animal. Brioché took the impoverished Cyrano to court seeking fifty pistoles in damages. "Bergerac defended himself like Bergerac, that is to say, with facetious writings and grotesque words. He told the judge that he would pay Brioché as a poet, or in monkey money; that coins were a furnishing unknown to Phœbus; he swore that he would apotheosize the dead animal with an Apollonian epitaph. On this plea, Brioché was thrown out of court."[95] "Monnaie de singe," it seems,

---

93. See René Lespinasse and François Bonnardot, eds, *Les métiers et corporations de la ville de Paris: XIIIe siècle. Le livre des métiers d'Etienne Boileau* (Paris: Imprimerie Nationale, 1879), 236: "Li singes au marchant doit iiii d., se il pour vendre le porte. . . . Et se li singes est au joueur, jouer en doit devant le paagier, et pour son jeu doit estre quites de toute la chose qu'il achete a son usage. Et ausi tot li jougleur sunt quite pour 1 ver[s] de chançon." The earliest version of this story I have found dates from 1730—*Bibliothèque raisonnée des ouvrages savans de l'Europe pour les mois de janvier, fevrier, et mars 1730*, vol. 4, pt. 1 (Amsterdam: Wetsteins and Smith, 1730), 28—but it was already being presented as conventional wisdom.

94. A number of these have been dredged up from the river. See Jacques Labrot, *Une histoire économique et populaire du moyen âge: Les jetons et les méreaux* (Paris: Editions Errance, 1989), 90–92.

95. "Combat de Cyrano de Bergerac avec le singe de Brioché, au bout du Pont Neuf," in *Cyrano de Bergerac, Histoire comique des états et empires de la lune et du soleil*, ed. P. L. Jacob (Paris: Adolphe Delahays, 1858), lxxx: "Bergerac se defendit en Bergerac, c'est-à-dire avec des écrits facétieux et des paroles grotesques: il dit au juge, qu'il payerait Brioché en poète, ou en monoye de singe; que les espèces étoient un meuble que Phœbus ne connoissoit point; il jura qu'il apothéoseroit la bête morte, par une épitaphe appollinique. Sur les raisons alléguées, Brioché fut débouté de ses prétentions."

was the facetious author's substitute for hard cash, and it could be conceived as even more effective than its legitimate cousin. And a libertine novelist's works could be not just a refined gold of the spirit but a crude and effective social currency.

Besides recalling the privileges of medieval *jongleurs*, Cyrano's adventure directly recalled his most important literary creation. When the narrator of *The Other World* left Elias the Artist for the society of the moon men, he was initially taken to be a kind of monkey and given to a *bateleur*, who "taught me how to act like a mannequin, to cut capers, to make faces; and in the afternoons he would take money at the door to show me."[96] He was redeemed only by the good offices of that paragon of reason so beloved of the Renaissance, Socrates's demon, who in this story was actually a moon man. After being made into an animal and an object of commerce, the narrator is redeemed by reason—and specifically by a libertine, naturalist reason, given the obvious tribute to Gabriel Naudé's argument in his libertine classic, *Apology for All the Great Persons Who Have Been Falsely Suspected of Magic*, that that "demon" was nothing other than "the good regulation of his life, the wise conduct of his actions, the experience he had of things, and the result of all his virtues."[97] It was, in other words, his reason, the thing that made him a man rather than a monkey. Cyrano's slaughter of Brioché's monkey recapitulated that act of (self-) liberation. By destroying a version of his commoditized fictional self, he dramatized his freedom from vulgar commerce. And in putting the lackeys to flight and treating the monkey as an example to them, Cyrano revealed them (like the lackeys who insulted Francion when he went to court in his shabby clothes) as mere popinjays, well-clothed counterfeits lacking the skill and courage of true nobility. Finally, his defense in court, where his verbal monkey money trumped and paid off the plaintiff's literal monkey money, paralleled his literary production in general. Faced with his satirical eloquence, the judge, like the equivalents written by de Viau and Sorel, gave him his due.

Cyrano was not the only libertine hero to tangle with a monkey. When Francion tells his life story, the first thing we learn is that he had been sent

---

96. Prévot, *Libertins*, 1:927: "m'instruisit à faire le godenot, à passer des culbutes, à figurer des grimaces; et les après-dînées faisait prendre à la porte de l'argent pour me montrer."

97. Gabriel Naudé, "Apologie pour tous les grands personnages qui ont été faussement soupçonnés de magie," in Prévot, *Libertins* 1:260: "la bonne règle de sa vie, la sage conduite de ses actions, l'expérience qu'il avait des choses, et le résultat de toutes ses vertus." Cyrano's immediate inspiration was almost certainly a passage at the beginning of that chapter where Naudé mocks Ptolemy's view that familiar geniuses are the particular lot of those "qui ont la Lune pour dame de leurs actions . . . dans la thème de leur naissance" (1:256).

to a wet nurse, though he assures us that the "thousand idiocies invented by the vulgar" he learned there left no permanent mark on his character. The second is the story of how a monkey broke into his parents' house and, while his nurse was distracted, fed him and dressed him "in the new fashion." The servants immediately concluded that they had been visited by an evil spirit, a view only confirmed when "the wicked monkey came back to our house again the next night and, having spilled a purse full of counting tokens on the hall table as if he had meant to count them . . . he left before daybreak."[98] Francion's indomitable father would have none of it, though. He set a careful watch, which succeeded only in catching a peasant stealing his pears—the marquis let him off with a kick in the pants and an offer of as many pears as he wanted—and finally tracked the monkey down at a neighbor's house. Like Brioché's, this monkey represented a danger to the protagonists' social standing: like the wet-nurse, it took the natural parents' place in raising young Francion, though the father's and son's courage and good sense ultimately disarmed the possibility that Francion might just be a boor dressed up, monkey-like, as a lord.

Francion's monkey is also a purveyor of monkey money. On his second visit, he symbolically takes over the family finances, using their *jetons* (which may, like Montaigne's, have been marked with a family crest or motto) in a parody of accounting, underlining the artificial, imitative nature of money and wealth. It was to counter this, one assumes, that Sorel introduced the scene of Francion's father combining physical domination and lordly magnanimity in his treatment of the pear-stealing peasant. And in case the reader should miss the point, Francion added the anecdote of "that Swiss who, finding a monkey at the front door of a tavern, gave him a *teston* to change, and seeing that he was being repaid only in grimaces, kept saying to him: 'Goshdarnit, little boy, ain't you gonna gimme change of my coin?' And it is perhaps from this that the proverb comes, when we say that grimaces, gambols, and mockery are 'monnaie de singe.'"[99] The incident was designed to inoculate both the character of Francion and Sorel's project against charges of being artificial, worthless, and undeserving. Again, this must be read in the context of Sorel's project of exchanging his own facetious words for cash and social recognition.

---

98. Sorel, *Francion*, 163: "mille niaiseries inventées par le vulgaire"; 164: "à la mode nouvelle"; 165–66: "le méchant singe revint encore chez nous la nuit suivante et, ayant étalé tous les jetons d'une bourse sur la table de la salle comme s'il les eût voulu compter . . . s'en retourna avant le jour."

99. Sorel, *Francion*, 164: "Ce Suisse qui, trouvant un singe sur la porte d'une taverne, lui avait donné un teston à changer, et voyant qu'il ne le payait qu'en grimaces, ne cessait de lui dire: 'Par li petite garçon, volle vous pas donner la monnaie de mon piece?' Et c'est de là possible que vient le proverbe quand l'on dit que les grimaces, les gambades ou les moqueries sont 'monnaie de singe.'"

The disgraced page had an equally striking experience involving monkeys, taverns, and money. Toward the end of the novel we learn that in the household of a prince (traditionally glossed as the duc de Mayenne) where Tristan had once more temporarily found grace, there lived a monkey called Master Robert. The lackeys had trained him to buy wine in taverns, even getting change for the coins he brought. One time, when the prince was on campaign with his troops, "this wicked animal, who only looked for ways to get drunk," broke into the paymaster's lodgings and stole the money intended to pay the soldiers. Climbing up on the roof, he began throwing the gold coins down to the crowd below, which of course grew rapidly. All attempts to restore order were in vain: "That crowd of men knew only Master Robert. . . . The cavalry was ill paid that day, but on the other hand some simple soldiers received thirty-five or forty pistoles from Master Robert's hands."[100] Trained to counterfeit a man in handling coin, Robert became the master indeed, replacing the prince and turning the world and the value of the soldiers' services upside down. Only his still greater monetary resources and standing as a great magnate and a royal officer allowed the prince to restore the situation, making good the losses and restoring his authority. Here it is hard not to see a reflection of Tristan's ultimately realized hopes, that royal grace would transform the monkey money of his comic writing into real social standing and financial security.

Monkey money was thus a lot like real money. It could appear to be an instrument of arbitrary and illegitimate social advancement, but in the right conditions it could also be a legitimate source of wealth, commerce, and social power. What made it "good" were the same things that made money good: talent, hard work, education, genuine noble worth, and of course the stabilizing touch of sovereign power, which could allow its transmutation, just as God's grace could allow the transmutation of base metals by the suitably diligent, studious, and virtuous. There is nothing startling about the claim that literature, facetious or otherwise, can function like currency or that authors have often been well aware of this fact.[101] In the first half of the seventeenth century, French writers continued to understand this issue in generally traditional terms but with an overall effect unlike that which predominated in the Renaissance. It was not only that generic shifts and an

---

100. Prévot, *Libertins*, 1:234–35: "ce méchant animal, qui ne cherchait que le moyen de pouvoir aller s'en enivrer"; 235: "ce foule de gens ne conaissait plus rien que maître Robert. . . . La gendarmerie fut mal payée pour ce jour-là; mais en revanche, il y eut tel simple soldat qui reçut par les mains de maître Robert trente-cinq et quarante pistoles."

101. For an overview of this issue, see the editors' introduction to *The New Economic Criticism: Studies at the Intersection of Literature and Economics*, ed. Martha Woodmansee and Mark Osteen (London: Routledge, 1999), and the work of Marc Shell generally.

unfavorable economic climate had turned their focus to the dangers and uncertainties of money; their positive vision of how money could function in society had changed in important ways. Sovereign power no longer governed it through sheer majesty, magnificence, and arcane or revealed knowledge but through a system of increasingly bureaucratized patronage. And its role was supplemented, perhaps even displaced, by public or market judgments, both of literary skill and of individual merit, or *honnêteté*.

That shared reign of public opinion and enlightened monarchy, with the autonomous market lurking in the wings, would seem to prefigure the eighteenth century. But that sense of familiarity should not lead us to forget either the vertiginous, even alien quality it had for contemporaries— the sheer strangeness of libertine and picaresque literature is testimony to that—or how inseparable it remained from the slowly evolving institutions of French society and government. As one moves into the early phase of Louis XIV's personal reign, no one understood this better than the Academician, lexicographer, and novelist Antoine Furetière. During the 1650s he had served as *procureur fiscal* (the equivalent of a royal solicitor in a seigniorial court) and briefly as judge in the jurisdiction of St.-Germain-des-Près.[102] After a decade of vicious conflict with his fellow officers, the ambitious Furetière abandoned those offices for a career in the church and in letters.[103] He returned to that experience, though, in the second half of his comic novel *The Bourgeois Romance* (1666), which centers on a grotesque romance between Charroselles (a semianagram of Charles Sorel) and Collantine (apparently modeled on one Anne Pintard, Furetière's sometime backer in his struggles in the bailliage), middle-aged bourgeois who share a self-satisfied literary culture, a pathological penchant for litigation, and a grudge against the wildly incompetent judge of St. Germain. Furetière thus reverses the good judge/ young love story found in "The First Day" and *Francion*, already introducing a background of the failure of public power.

And as befits a book about the bourgeoisie, *The Bourgeois Romance* is obsessed with money and monetary relations, which appear repeatedly as metaphors, or replacements, for the romantic and literary endeavors that the novel satirizes. Marriage is the first relation to be so treated: "Since the corruption of our age has led us to start marrying one bag of money to another

---

102. For the details of this litigious and unhappy experience, see Jean Nagle, "Furetière entre la magistrature et les bénéfices: Autour du Second Livre du *Roman bourgeois*," *XVII Siècle* 128 (1980): 293–305.

103. On the role and structure of St. Germain, see Pierre Lemercier, *Les justices seigneuriales de la région parisienne de 1580 à 1789* (Paris: Domat-Montchrestien, 1933), passim.

when we marry a girl and a boy, so, just as a tariff [price list] was drawn up when the money was cried down to value the coins, a tariff was made to value men in order to match up the couples."[104] And Furetière proceeds to produce a tariff matching women's dowries to the estates of husbands they might reasonably expect, essentially drawn (as Madeleine Alcover has shown) from recent official inquiries into the value of venal offices.[105] Furetière satirized as he reified both the reduction of social relations and hierarchies to money and the possibility of controlling that process as money was controlled, by state action. The presence of generals of the moneys on the list of husbands (in a distinctly unexalted position) serves as a reminder that the tariff of the moneys was embedded in the same corrupt system as the tariffs of venal offices.

That disillusioned attitude permeates the novel's second book, which turns from marriage to law and literature. Under the sign of frivolous litigation and judicial corruption and incompetence, the possibility of controlling the ambition and avarice that eat away at society appears even more remote. And much of the latter part of the book is devoted to literary judgment (and we are informed that Charroselles's literary judgment is appalling, though there are hints that Furetière may have more confidence in Charles Sorel). Literary reputation and literary production and the economic and social rewards that come from it are subject to the same distortions and the same satirical remedies as the rest of the social hierarchy. "That money (said Collantine) is not to be found in any edict or tariff that has ever been published, so that if you took it to the market you would just die of hunger there. It is true (replied Charroselles) that it has been thoroughly cried down these days, what with all the light coins that have been ordered to be melted down."[106] The money

104. Antoine Furetière, *Le roman bourgeois*, ed. Jacques Prévot (Paris: Gallimard, 1981), 47: "la corruption du siècle ayant introduit de marier un sac d'argent avec un autre sac d'argent, en mariant une fille avec un garçon, comme il s'était fait un tarif lors du décri des monnaies pour l'évaluation des espèces, aussi, lors du décri du mérite et de la vertu, il fut fait un tarif pour l'évaluation des hommes et pour l'assortissement des partis."

105. See Madeleine Alcover, "Furetière et la stratification sociale: Le 'tariffe des mariages,'" *Papers on French Seventeenth-Century Literature* 8 (1981): 74–93. Generals of the moneys appear on the tariff, at twenty to thirty thousand livres, along with councillors in the Treasury or the Waters and Forests and substitutes in the parquet, but below even barristers in the Parlement. This follows the depressed prices of offices in the Monnaies at the time while ignoring their theoretically higher status as councilors in a sovereign court.

106. Furetière, *Roman bourgeois*, 250: "Cette monnaie (reprit Collantine) ne se trouve point dans aucun édit ou tarif qui ait été publié, de sorte que, si on la portait au marché, on mourrait bien de faim auprès.—Il est vrai (répliqua Charroselles) qu'elle est aujourd'hui fort décriée, avec toutes les espèces légères qu'on a ordonné de porter au billon." Note the allusion to François Villon's famous *ballade*—for which he was supposedly well paid—on the refrain "Je meurs de soif auprès de la fontaine."

these characters are discussing is the currency of credit or reputation circulating as literature, in this case a "letter of exchange of reputation" for a dozen adulatory verses, drawn on the Academia degli Umoristi of Florence by the late author Mythophilacte—traditionally assumed to be Tristan l'Hermite.

By the time this passage was published, in 1666, the personal reign of Louis XIV was well under way, and from a certain point of view the model of currency regulation and the Cour des Monnaies permeated the entire enterprise of French literary culture. The Académie Française had been constituted as a kind of sovereign court for the French language, with the authority to determine the worth of individual authors and to fix the tariff of French words through an official dictionary that would determine which ones could circulate and what their precise semantic content would be. In cooperation with the Académie des Inscriptions, it would also manage a propaganda campaign for the Sun King that would realize the Cassiodoran dream of making his face, name, and deeds present on his terms to all peoples present and to come.[107] A series of bronze medals was to play a major role in that campaign, quite likely inspired, directly or indirectly, by Rascas de Bagarras's project of a half-century earlier. The king seemed well on his way to minting language into elegance and glory as easily as he minted gold and silver into coins. But when one left the world of history, encomium, and lousy epic for the anarchic territory of comedy, satire, and popular narrative, royal control was no more than a mirage.[108]

Furetière was deeply involved in the royal project to regulate the literary, both as a member of the Académie and as its competitor in the production of a dictionary. Naturally he was fascinated by the ways in which it worked or failed to work, and he seems to have been particularly intrigued by the metaphor of currency regulation. It also appears earlier in the same section of the novel when after hearing the remnants of Mythophilacte's "tariff of the moderate taxes on . . . illustrious and semi-illustrious roles" in novels and poems, Charroselles suggested that it should be published but not by the printers of belles-lettres. If he had the full text, he says, "I would give it to Cramoisy, royal printer for the moneys, who would be very happy to print

107. The classic surveys of this campaign are Louis Marin, *Le portrait du roi* (Paris: Les éditions de minuit, 1981), 145–206, and Peter Burke, *The Fabrication of Louis XIV* (New Haven: Yale University Press, 1992).

108. The best place to start on the aporias of mid-seventeenth-century literary control is Marc Fumaroli, *Le poète et le roi: Jean de La Fontaine en son siècle* (Paris: Editions de Fallois, 1997).

it up."[109] To be pedantic, the list sounds more like the kind of sales-tax tariffs that were posted in urban markets than like the illustrated catalogs that the printers for the moneys produced of coins authorized to circulate, or perhaps more precisely, like a tariff of the *droit de marc d'or*, Henri III's tax on venal offices that was roughly calibrated to their prestige, though none of them had yet been printed in Furetière's day.[110] Either way, though, Furetière was linking literary reputation to very concrete governmental methods for the regulation of value.

But one should not be too quick to conclude that this is another case of the literary invocation of sovereignty to order and ennoble the chaos of money. For the effect of Furetière's suggestions for the regulation of monkey money depends on two things. The first is that the suggested measures are familiar and appealing. The second, of course, is that they are utterly ridiculous. The fictionalized libertine novelists sitting around discussing how to control the value of their own works were very much like Corneille's comedians count-ing out the take onstage. They dramatized a world in which monetary, like literary, value would be an explicitly social production, divorced, whether one liked it or not, from the powers of kings and magicians alike. It is not clear, however, that that possibility is meant to be taken too seriously either; Furetière's characters are paying each other and their readers in monkey money. For many years the figure of the sovereign would continue to preside over the moneys as it did over the Cour des Monnaies, and when it ceased to do so it would bring about a crisis in the Western understanding of money and its control that has not yet been entirely resolved.

---

109. Furetière, *Roman bourgeois*, 244: "role des sommes ausquelles ont esté moderement taxées . . . les places illustres et demy-illustres"; 246: "Je le donnerais à Cramoisy, imprimeur du Roi pour les monnaies, qui serait bien aise de l'imprimer." Sébastien Cramoisy dominated official printing in the mid-seventeenth century.

110. See Jean Nagle, *Le droit de marc d'or des offices: Tarifs de 1583, 1704, 1748* (Geneva: Droz, 1992). The 1583 tariff was a manuscript memorandum.

Conclusion

The Court and the Queen

> The life of my king was the guide of this work:
> When his death occurred, that checked its course.
> This too-sudden tragedy stole my courage,
> And ended my plans with the end of his days.
>
> —Béroalde de Verville

The abrupt and tragic end of the *Voyages of the Fortunate Princes* was one that contemporaries could have easily understood.[1] May 16, 1610, was meant to be an exceptional day in the ceremonial history of the French monarchy. And so it was, though not at all as its architects had intended. Queen Marie de Médicis, King Henri IV's wife since 1600, had just been formally crowned in Rheims. She was to enter Paris and be presented to the people not just as the king's wife and the dauphin's mother but as the future regent of the kingdom during Henri's anticipated campaign against the Spanish Netherlands. Coronations and the formal entries associated with them were crucial symbolic supports of Renaissance monarchy, and this one was especially important given the political dangers of foreign campaigns and regencies. The aftermath of the Battle of Pavia (1525), which left François I a Spanish captive and his mother, Louise of Savoy, struggling to hold the kingdom together, was still vivid in the public memory.[2] On the afternoon

---

1. Béroalde de Verville, *L'Histoire veritable ou le voyage des princes fortunés* (Albi: Passage du nord-œust, 2005), 685: "La vie de mon roi conduisait cet ouvrage, / Lorsque sa mort advint, elle en rompit le cours. / Ce trop soudain malheur m'emporta le courage, / Et finit mes desseins à la fin de ses jours."

2. On royal entries, see Lawrence M. Bryant, *The King and the City in the Royal Entrance Ceremony: Politics, Ritual, and Art in the Renaissance* (Geneva: Droz, 1986); on coronations, Richard Jackson, *Vive le Roi!*

of May 13, the Cour des Monnaies had suspended business so that the Palais de Justice could be prepared for the coming ceremonies. Most of its members had assembled in a courtyard before attending a ceremonial dinner at the Hôtel de Ville. As they were waiting, they "were told that a wicked man had appeared in the rue de la Ferronerie, near the [cemetery of the] Holy Innocents, where the king was in his carriage, accompanied by the ducs d'Epernon and Monbasson and some others, and had struck the lord king in the side with a knife; for which reason the court arose, afflicted by hearing such news."[3]

The assassination of Henri IV caused almost as brutal and radical a rupture in French politics as the king's servitors claimed that it did in their emotional lives.[4] In the immediate term, it may have appeared to some in the Cour des Monnaies a kind of reprieve, if not in the form they would have chosen. The new regency government had little interest in pursuing Sully's projects for the currency or supporting his attempted takeover of monetary policy; indeed, the man himself promptly fell from grace and retired to become one of the first statesmen to devote his later years to polishing acerbic memoirs. And in the immediate aftermath of the assassination, the sovereign courts rose to a political and ceremonial prominence they had seldom achieved under the old regime. The boy king Louis XIII and his mother met with the Parlement of Paris in a famous *lit de justice* (at the convent of the Augustins, since the Parlement's chambers in the Palais de Justice were still occupied by the trappings of the abortive royal entry) to install a regency government—the Monnaies carefully noted this incident in its registers. The court itself played no such constitutional role, nor did it have the power of the magnates who quickly met with the king and queen mother to demonstrate their support, but it was called on to join the second rank of shows of support, and "the court deputed two of its presidents accompanied by eight counselor-generals and the solicitor

---

A History of the French Coronation from Charles V to Charles X (Chapel Hill: University of North Carolina Press, 1984); and Elizabeth A. R. Brown, "*Franks, Burgundians, and Aquitanians" and the Royal Coronation Ceremony in France* (Philadelphia: American Philosophical Society, 1992). On the aftermath of Pavia, see R. J. Knecht, *Renaissance Warrior and Patron: The Reign of Francis I* (Cambridge: Cambridge University Press, 1994), 216-48. Louise de Savoye had had particular difficulty with the Parlement of Paris, and thus Henri IV might well have felt a particular need to remind the sovereign courts of their obligations to the queen.

3. AN, Z[1B] 76, fol. 200r, 13 May 1610: "fut adverty que ung meschant homme sestant rencontre en la Rue de la feronnerye pres saint innocens ou estoit le roy dans son Carrosse accompganie de Mn le ducz despernon et Monbasson et quelques autres avoict frappe ledict seignieur Roy dun coup de cousteau au coste qui avoit este cause de ladicte cour se seroict levee affligee douir telles nouvelles."

4. The classic account is Roland Mousnier, *L'assassinat d'Henri IV* (Paris: N.R.F./Gallimard, 1964). Mousnier begins his book with the Parlement's counterpart to the narrative found in the registers of the Cour des Monnaies.

and attorney general to go the next day, Sunday the sixteenth of the month, to greet the queen regent and make the submissions required and customary in such cases."

They were kept waiting only briefly when they arrived at the Louvre, after which "the deputies entered the room and found only the queen (since the king had gone to vespers at the Feuillants) accompanied by several princes and lords," presumably those who had offered their support in the wake of the assassination, "who were standing, and on either side were the Constable [Montmorency-Damville] and the Chancellor [Brûlart de Sillery]." President Regin proceeded to give a brief speech.

> Madam: having heard tell of the cruel and horrible death of that great prince, our king, we knew not what to say. We still had our eyes only to cry, voices to bemoan our lot, and emotions to feel our sorrow. It would have seemed as though misfortune and envy had chosen us to serve as a target for all their effects if we had not lightened the regret we bore from this with the certainty we feel that by means of Your Majesty's discreet and careful regency, capable of supporting the weight of affairs, the state will be conserved in its original splendor; and for that reason the Cour des Monnaies comes now to prostrate itself at your feet and offer you the humility of its good wishes, the respect of its affections, and the fidelity of its service, seeking no other happiness in this world than to remain forever Your Majesty's very humble, faithful, and obedient servants and subjects.
>
> And when they finished, the queen said "stand up," and when they had stood, said these words: "Sirs, I thank you. Be faithful to the king my son, and keep for him the same fidelity that you always bore to the late king my husband, and he will be a good king to you."[5]

This is the only ceremonial occasion from the period recorded in any detail in the court's registers.

The court recorded this ceremony in such unusual detail for at least two reasons, I suspect, both of which say something important about how the

---

5. AN, Z[1B] 76, fol. 200v: "par la cour deppute deux presidens dicelle accompaignez de huict conseillers generaulx et du procureur & advocat general et greffier pour au lendain dimanche seiziesme dudict mois aller salluer le roy et la royne comme regente & faire les submissions en telle cas requises et accoustumees." Fol. 201r–v: "lesdictes depputez entroit dans le cabinet ne trouveroit que la royne, le roy estant a vespres aux feuillans, ladicte royne accompagnee de plusieurs princes, & seigneurs, estant debout et aux deux costez estoient Mons. le Connestable et Chancellier . . . . Madame La cruelle et effroyable mort entendue de ce grand prince nostre roy nous ne scaurions que

governance of the moneys functioned at that particular moment. The first and more evident was the ceremonial intimacy it enacted between the court and the Crown. Hearing of the assassination while assembled to participate in the a royal ceremony long designed to highlight the importance of the sovereign courts—and it is worth remembering that the Monnaies had had to fight to maintain its place with those courts and ahead of the city fathers in royal processions—was a powerful reminder of its place within the state. Certainly, anyone looking back through the court's archives might have felt some satisfaction comparing its honorable treatment in 1610 with that in 1559, when it had been provided with only enough cloth to dress half the court in mourning for Henri II. The Monnaies had been moved to complain to the chancellor that "though our company is great in authority, being sole and sovereign in the realm in its cognizance of something as important as the moneys, it is nevertheless so small in the number of its officers that cutting off half of it could not bring our lord much savings, while the other half would hardly suffice for the honor and service that we ought and wish to do for his majesty in such a public act."[6] And in the 1570s, it was still disputing precedence with the officers of the city of Paris.[7] This solidification of the court's ceremonial position was not something trivial: it indicated the greater role that money and its control now played in French government. In a world

---

dire nous n'avions plus des yeux que pour pleurer des voix que pour nous plaindre et des sentimens que pour ressentir notre doleur [?]. Il sembloit desja que le malheur et lenvie nous eussent esleu pour servir de retraicte a tout ce quilz produissent sy nous neussent allege le regret que nous en portions de lasseurance que nous avons que par le moien de la regence discrette & soigneuse de vostre majeste, cappable de supporter le fais des affaires, lestat se conservera en sa premiere splendeur, et pource la cour des monnoyes ce viennant maintenant prosterner a vos pieds pour vous offrir lhumilite de ses veoux, le respect de ses affections, et la fidellite de son service [?] cherchant point dautre heur en ce monde que demeurer tousjours les treshumbles, tresfidelles, & tresobeissants serviteurs & subjects de vostre Majeste, et ayant finy la royne leur dict levez vous et estant levez leur dict ces parolles: Messieurs je vous remercie soiez fidelles au roy mon filz et conservez luy la mesme fidelite quavez porte tousjours au roy deffunct son pere mon mary et il vous sera bon roy."

6. AN, Z[1B] 370, piece dated 27 July 1559 (Cour des Monnaies to the chancellor, minute): "nostre compagnye bien quelle soyt grande en auctorite comme estant souverayne et seule en son Royaulme pour congoistre dung faict tant important comme est le faict de ses monnoyes, toutesfoys elle est si petite en nombre dofficiers que le retranchement de la moytye ne scauroyt aporter grande espargne audict sieur, et lautre moytye ne seroyt gueres suffisant pour faire lhonneur et service que nous debvons et desirons faire a sa majeste en tel acte publicque." The court considered this letter significant enough to be copied into its registers: AN, Z[1B] 65, fol. 137.

7. See AN, Z[1B] 375, piece dated 14 September 1573 (lettre de cachet), on a round it won; and Z[1B] 376, piece dated 10 January 1577 (letter of the court to absent members, minute), where it was excluded from a ceremony that the other sovereign courts and the Paris Hôtel de Ville attended. It was still nibbling at the dispute in 1584: AN, Z[1B] 380, piece dated 27 August 1584 (petition to the Comptes for relevant documents).

where the ceremonial alternately reflected and constituted the political order, this was of no small importance.[8]

At the same time, though, this series of events and interactions can be understood within a much broader set of affective tropes and structures that played an enormous role in early modern European society. Regin's words to the Queen Mother, for example, with their contrast between the sorrow induced by a sovereign's death and the comfort brought be a successor, were on well-trodden rhetorical ground. Just a few years earlier, an English pamphleteer had greeted the accession of James I in a similar vein:

> The highnesse of his Emperiall place, greatnesse of his blood, mightinesse of his alliance, but most, his constancie in the true profession of Religion, even amid my sorrowes, . . . fill me with joyes: when I consider how a number that gaped for our destruction, have their mouths shut close, yet emptie where they thought to eate the sweetes of our painefull sweate: but God be praised, as I saide before, her Highnesse that ruled us many yeeres in peace, left us, in her death, more secure, by committing us to our lawfull Prince, matcht to a royal fruitfull Lady, that hath borne him such hopefull issue, that the dayes we lately feared, I trust are as farre off, as this instant is, from the end of all earthly times.[9]

Many of the same elements appear: fear of disorder joined with personal sorrow at the death of a prince and the reassurance not only of dynastic continuity but of fecundity and of paternal and maternal care.[10] A transition from a queen to an adult king was different from the transition from an adult king to a regent queen, so some polarities were reversed, but the two men spoke the same language.

---

8. The literature on this phenomenon is vast. For a few important theoretical statements see, in addition to the works cited above, Ernst Kantorwicz, *The King's Two Bodies: A Study in Medieval Political Theology* (Princeton: Princeton University Press, 1957); Ralph Giesey, *The Royal Funeral Ceremony in Renaissance France* (Geneva: Droz, 1960); and Edward Muir, *Civic Ritual in Renaissance Venice* (Princeton: Princeton University Press, 1982).

9. Henry Chettle, *Englands Mourning Garment: Worne Heere by Plaine Shepheards, in Memorie of Their Sacred Mistresse, Elizabeth; Queene of Vertue While She Lived, and Theame of Sorrow Being Dead*, 2nd ed. (London: Thomas Millington, 1603), sig. B4r.

10. There is a plentiful literature on the language and theory of patriarchy in early modern European monarchy. For our purposes, the best starting place is probably the (controversial) article of Sarah Hanley, "Engendering the State: Family Formation and State Building in Early Modern France," *French Historical Studies* 16 (1989): 4–27. If one accepts Hanley's argument for a pact between the monarchy and the French elites, especially the robe, whereby a strengthened, patriarchal state strengthened patriarchal power within families, the comforting solidarity of this encounter between the widowed queen and the fatherless court appears in even stronger relief.

This was not merely a set of linguistic conventions. For men like the officers of the Monnaies, who worked closely with the monarchy and drew much of their own identity from that association—but even for the much larger reading and ceremonial public, and the scholars, artists, and hacks who served it—this was doubtless a site of genuine emotional engagement, and that engagement had real social and political effects. It has been suggested that the outpouring of elegies on Elizabeth like the one quoted above played a significant role in stabilizing the new Stuart regime.[11] Marie expected that a highly personal encounter with her while she was surrounded by the magnates and the great officers of the Crown (one of whom had in the past caused the Monnaies no little trouble but was now dramatically rallied to the cause of stability), would both reassure the court and confirm it in its loyalty, and there is no reason to believe that she was disappointed. While important recent work has shed a good deal of light on early modern affective life, our understanding is still tenuous.[12] Still, we know that early modern politics at all levels depended heavily on this kind of formalized intimacy and on the satisfaction it brought to all parties. And if the cash nexus was indeed on the verge of tearing asunder these motley but powerful ties, there were as yet few signs of this even at the heart of the currency.

True, money was widely understood as highly technical, impersonal, and at least partially autonomous in ways that had roots at least as far back as Aristotle while they foreshadowed the discourses of political economy and modern economics. The Cour des Monnaies, like other actors within and outside the government (if more consistently than any others), derived much of its power and prestige from claims that it had mastered those technical mysteries, or at least had discerned the boundaries of possible mastery more precisely than others. This was the domain of the "rational" as Max Weber understood it, subject to mathematical calculation, bureaucratic routine, long-term institutionalization, and dedication to the welfare of impersonal abstractions: the nation, the state, the firm, and that long run in which we are all dead. Indeed, the experts of the moneys promised to protect their society from some of the evils of passion and self-interest that money might encourage or enable. Proper economic regulation would make money an instrument of public prosperity, even opulence, rather than of private avarice and political dislocation

---

11. See Catherine Loomis, *The Death of Elizabeth I: Remembering and Reconstructing the Virgin Queen* (New York: Palgrave MacMillan, 2012), 47–82.

12. On the current state of this field, see Barbara H. Rosenwein, "Worrying about Emotions in History," *American Historical Review* 107 (2002): 821–45; and Ute Frevert, *Emotions in History: Lost and Found* (New York: Central European University Press, 2011).

or civil war. Monetary policy would guard the coinage from speculators and peculators who threatened its value. Repression of coining, if conducted with due expertise and vigor, would produce more orderly social relations and thwart criminals whose disregard for social norms extended well beyond gold and silver. All of this was the domain of that most modern of institutions, the bureaucratic state, in ways that were broadly accepted through society and that could contribute substantially to the process of legitimizing that state.

And even so, this technocratic ideal, though arguably growing in importance, played a distinctly secondary role in the period. Much more clearly than today, Renaissance Europeans thought of money as a technology of social relations and a tool for the impulses and aspirations that drove them. These impulses did not, for the most part, attach to objects—the consumer revolution was still in its very earliest stages—but (after the necessities of life) to status, rank, and position. That is why money so easily became a model or a metaphor for so many aspects of social life, from adornment to office to marriage to literary reputation. By the same token, to control and regulate money was to control and regulate the necessary but potentially destructive social passions, the ambition and the avarice, of the entire population. So, particularly given the somewhat surprising paucity of religious discourse around money at this time, it is equally natural that so much of the control of currency orbited around the project of infusing it with the awe, respect, and love that ought to emanate from the sovereign persons of the monarch and the royal family.[13] The royal image and arms, the sovereign prerogative of giving law to the moneys, the processes of the courts, and the images that made gold royal and royalty golden all operated in that same direction. The ceremonial compact that bound the boy king and the Cour des Monnaies together in sorrow, love, and filial piety represented the human ties and virtues that should, to the early modern mind, lead to order and stability in the currency, the state, and society. For a moment, in 1610, the moneys fit comfortably into that that cultural place. They had arrived there after a long and difficult journey, though, and their position was radically unstable. It would have to be reconquered time and time again, as it still must be in our own day.

---

13. There was of course a substantial debate around the question of usury, which, however, seems to have been of mainly academic interest. See R. H. Tawney, *Religion and the Rise of Capitalism* (New York: Harcourt, Brace, 1926), and the massive literature derived from it.

Bibliography

Manuscript Sources

Archives Municipales de Lyon

AA (correspondance du consulat) 66, 139
BB (actes consulaires) 72, 74, 78, 86, 94, 97, 99, 101, 125, 127, 129–131
CC (pièces de comptabilité) 1116, 1451
FF 612, HH 111 (dossiers of seventeenth-century law cases by the *orfèvres* and the *tireurs d'or et d'argent*)

Archives Nationales de France

SERIES Z¹ᴮ: COUR DES MONNAIES

Registres civils: 19, 20, 23
Registres criminels: 37–39
Registres des ordonnances: 54, 63–67, 69–76
Registres de présence: 192
Registres des procès-verbaux des chevauchées: 277, 280
Minutes des règlements: 368–397
Minutes civils: 433–438
Minutes criminels: 483–501
Minutes des ordonnances: 537–539
Minutes des provisions d'office: 548–561
Procès-verbaux et instructions: 678–684

OTHER SERIES

120 A P 1, 37 (Fonds Sully)
J 971 (Trésor des Chartes)
K 1036 (Corps de Métiers de Paris: Orfèvres)
U★ 686: "Extraict abregé des registres de la chambre des monnayes"
V⁵ 38, 39 (Minutes du Grand Conseil): minutes for 1554

INVENTORIES

Couperdon, Emile. "Table alphabétique des lettres patentes de provisions d'offices enregistrées à la Cour des Monnaies, 1498–1790." 1886. Inv. 480: Usuel Z1/06.
Bézard, Y. and P. de Vaissière. Index of AN, X²ᴮ 1174–1184. 1927–1933.

Bibliothèque Nationale de France

Mss. Duchesne: 89
Mss. Dupuy: 51, 86, 318, 630
Mss. Français (ms. fr.): 18288, 18497, 18499, 18500, 18503, 18504
Nouvelles acquisitions françaises (n. a. fr.): 5064

Bibliothèque de l'Arsenal

Arsenal mss.: 4071, 4594

Printed Primary Sources

Official Acts (in chronological order)

*Edict et ordonnance sur le faict des monoyes & nouvelle fabrication poids alloy & prix, ouver-
ture & jugement des boettes d'icelles. Sur le reiglement presentation gaiges & charges des
Maistres particuliers Gardes Essayeurs Tailleurs Contregardes & Prevostz, Ouvriers &
Monoyers, & aultres officiers des monoyes. Avec declaration de lestablissement du lieu
d'ouverture dicelles. Et sur le reiglement & charge des Changeurs, Orfevres, (leurs ap-
pretifz) Joyauliers, Affineurs, departeurs & Batteurs d'or & d'argent. Et de la justice &
correction des faultes d'ceulx, & de tous lesdictz Officiers.* Paris: Pierre Haultin and
Jean Dallier, 1550.*

*Ordonnance faicte par le Roy sur le cours & pris des especes d'Or & d'Argent, & descry des
monnoyes rongnées. Publiée a Paris le dernier iour de Janvier, Mil cinq cens quarante
neuf.* Paris: Pierre Haultin and Jean Dallier, [1550].

Edict du Roy pour la souvereineté de la Cour des monnoyes en l'annee 1551. Paris: Jean
Dalier, [1555].

*Edict de la creation et establissement de la monnoye des estuves du Roy à Paris, & des officiers
en icelle.* Paris: Jean Dallier and Vincent Certenas, 1554.

*Edict faict par le Roy sur la reformation, reduction, & reiglement des Orfevres, Joyauliers, Aff-
ineurs, Departeurs, Batteurs, & Tireurs d'or, & d'argent se don Royaulme, pays, terres, &
seigneuries de son obeissance.* Paris: Jean Dallier, 1555 [new style].

*Lettres patentes du Roy, contenans evocation & renvoy en sa Court des Generaulx des monoy-
es pour toutes les causes & matieres estans de ladicte Court, en quelque estat qu'elles
soyent, pendentes & indecises par devant les Cours de Parlement, grand Conseil, &
autres jurisdictions de ce Royaume.* Paris: Jean Dallier, 1556.

*Edict du Roy contenant la creation d'un office du Procureur du Roy & de deux Sergens en
chacune des monnoyes, leur pouvoir, privileges & gages, & de la jurisdiction des Prevosts
desdites monnoyes, tant en matiere Civille que Criminelle.* N.p., n.d.

*Edict du Roy sur la creation des changeurs en tiltre d'offices formez par tout le royaume, pays,
terres, & seigneuries de l'obeissance dudict seigneur. Publié en sa Court des monnoyes le
treziesme jour de Decembre, l'an mil cinq cens cinquantecinq.* Paris: Jean Dallier, 1556.

*Edict du Roy Henry II. du mois d'avril M.D. LVII sur les rangs & seances des Cours Souve-
raines, entre lesquelles est comprise la Cour des Monnoyes.* N.p., n.d.

Edict du Roy, contre tous Billoneurs de monnoyes Royalles, tant d'or que d'argent. Paris: Jean
Dallier, 1559.

Edict et Ordonnance du Roy, pour l'usage des draps de Soye, & superfluitez des habitz: & les arrests de la Court de Parlement intervenuz sur iceluy. Paris: Guillaume de Niverd, 1563.

Lettres patentes du roy pour la traicte generalle de toutes sortes de bledz par tout le Royaume de France, tant par mer que par terre. Paris: Jean Dallier, 1564.

Lettres patentes du Roy pour le payment des officiers des Monnoyes, reduict à la forme des anciennes Ordonnances. Paris: Robert Estienne, 1564.

Edict du Roy pour contenir les serviteurs et servantes en leurs devoirs. Paris: Robert Estienne, 1566.

Ordonnance du Roy, contenant la suppressions des offices de Receveurs, Grenetiers, & Contrerooleurs de son Domaine, aydes & gabelles, Collecteurs de ses Finances, Receveurs generaux du taillon de sa Gendarmerie, Tresorier des parties casuelles, Tresoriers ordinaires de ses guerres, & payeurs des compaignies d'icelles, & plusieurs autres Tresoriers & Officiers comptables. Plus, la suppression de toutes les Chambres des Comptes, fors que celle de Paris: Et aussi la reduction de toutes les Receptes generales de la France, en sept. Paris: Robert Estienne, 1566.

Ordonnance du Roy sur le descry de certaines especes d'or & d'argent estrangieres. Paris: Jean Dallier, 1566.

Decry des florins d'or et dalles d'argent, demis dalles, quars de Dalles, nouvellement forgez éz pais bas de Flandres. Publié à Paris le Samedy deuxiéme jour d'Aoust M.C.LXVII. Paris: Jean Dallier, 1567.

Arrest de la court de Parlement, sur le pris & valleur des Escuz sol. Publié à Paris, le Samedi treziesme jour d'Aoust, mil cinq cens soixante-neuf. Paris: Jean Dallier, 1567.

Lettres patentes du Roy sur le descry de certaines pieces d'argent forgees en Flandres, appellées Phillipes Dalles, & autres pieces d'argent, appellées Dalles de Bourgongne. Paris: Jean Dallier, 1570.

Ordonnance du Roy, sur le pris & valleur des Escuz sol & Pistoletz, pour lequel pris sa Majesté veult & entend que ilz soient receus & changez. Publié à Paris le trentiéme jour d'Aoust 1570. Paris: Guillaume de Nyuerd, [1570].

Lettres patentes & Declaration du Roy sur la prolongation du cours & mise de l'Escu Sol à cinquante quatre solz, & autres especes ayans cours par l'ordonnance derniere à l'equipolent, & Teston de France à douze solz & six deniers tournois jusques au premier jour du moys de Janvier prochain. Paris: Jean Dallier, 1572.

Declaration du Roy sur le cours donné par sa Majesté aux testons de Navarre, Portugal, & Gennes pour douze sols six deniers piece. Paris: Jean Dallier, 1572.

Ordonnance du Roy pour le reiglement general de ses monoies. Publiée à Paris en sa Court de Parlement le Vendredy vingt & troisiesme jour de May, 1572. Paris: Jean Dallier, 1572.

Ordonnance du Roy contenant le cours, poix, & pris, donné par ledit sieur, aux Ecuz sols, Testons, & autres especes, tant de Frace que estrangers: Ensemble les pris donnez aux marcs d'or & d'argent. Publiée à Paris le 9e jour de Juin, 1573. Paris: Jean Dallier, 1573.

Ordonnance du Roy Henry troisiesme, sur le faict de ses Monnoyes. Paris: Jean Dallier, 1574.

Ordonnance du Roy Henry III de ce nom, sur le faict de ses monnoies. Paris: Veufve Jean Dallier, 1575.

Ordonnance du Roy, sur le faict des Monnoyes, contenant le descry de certaines especes y mentionees, avec defenses tresexpresses à toutes personnes de les exposer ny recevoir: & a tous marchands & courtiers de faire amas de douzains ny autres monnoyes de billon, pour en trafiquer, ou les transporter de ville en autre, sur les peines portees par icelle. Paris: Federic Morel, 1576.

Declaration du Roy sur le faict et reformation des habits: Avec defense aux non nobles d'usurper le tiltre de noblesse, & à leurs femmes de porter l'habit de Damoiselle, sur les peines y contenues. Ensemble l'Ordonnance du Roy Henry second, par laquelle toutes personnes, tant Nobles que non Nobles & Roturiers, sont reglez de leurs habits & accoustremens qu'ils doivent porter: Sur les mesmes peines aux contrevenans. Paris: Federic Morel, 1577.

Deux Edicts du Roy, pour le restablissement des Generaulx des Monnoyes, qui resideront és douze principales provinces de ce Royaume: Et d'un Prevost Juge Royal, un Procureur du Roy, un Greffier, & deux Sergens pour la Justice en chacune Monnoye de cedict Royaume, pays, terres, & Seigneuries de sa Majesté. Paris: Federic Morel, 1577.

Ordonnance du Roy sur le faict de ses Monnoyes. Publiée à Paris le xv jour de Juing, 1577. Paris: Veufve Jehan Dallier, 1577.

Ordonnance du Roy sur le descry des Monnoyes de billon estrangeres. Paris: Veufve Jehan Dallier, 1577.

Ordonnance du Roy, sur le faict & Reglement de ses Monnoyes. Paris: Veufve Jehan Dalier & Nicolas Rosset, 1577.

Declaration du Roy, sur l'edict faict par sa Majesté de Septembre dernier, pour le Reglement general des Monnoyes. Paris: Veufve Jehan Dallier, 1578.

Edict du Roy Portant Creation Restablissement Declaration Ampliation Privileges Exemptions des Offices de Changeurs hereditaire en toutes les Villes de ce Royaume. N.p., n.d.

Ordonnance du Roy pour le Reglement & reformation de la dissolution & superfluité qui est és habillmens, & ornemens d'iceux: & de la punition de ceux qui contreviendront à ladicte ordonnance. Publié en Parlement le vingtneufiesme iour de Mars, l'an mil cinq cens quatre vingts trois. 2nd impression. Paris: Federic Morel, 1583.

Articles et propositions, lesquelles le roy a voulu estre desliberees par les Princes & Officiers de la Couronne & autres Seigneurs de son Conseil, qui se sont trouvez en l'assemblee pour ce faicte à S. Germain en Laye, au mois de Novembre, mil cinq cens quatre vingts & trois. Avec les advis de ceux desdicts Princes & Seigneurs qui ont esté departis en la Chambre où presidoit monsieur le Cardinal de Vendosme. N.p., 1584.

Edict du Roy pour le restablissement des juges ordonnez sur les malversations commises au faict des Finances de sa Majesté. Et de la recompense des denonciateurs. Paris: Frederic Morel, 1584.

Edict du Roy sur le retranchement des grans abus qui se commettent en l'appareil, traffic & commerce des Cuirs qui se vendent & distribuent en son Royaume contenant erection en tiltre d'office d'un contrerolleur, visiteur & marqueur desdits Cuirs, avec le regelement que sa majesté veult & entend estre sur ce observé. Paris: Vefve Nicolas Rosset, 1586.

Reglement faict par le Roy sur l'execution et entretenement de son Edict, faict sur le retranchement des grands abus qui se commettent en l'appareil & commerce, des Cuirs qui se vendent en son Royaume. Paris: Vefve Nicolas Rosset, 1586.

Ordonnance et Declaration du Roy sur le faict des Monnoyes. Paris: Vefve Nicolas Rosset, 1585.

Ordonnance du Roy, sur le descry des especes legeres & rongnees. Paris: Vefve Nicolas Rosset, 1586.

Declaration du Roy sur son edict du vingt-troisiesme Septembre dernier, contenant le descry des Monnoyes rongnées. Paris: Vefve Nicolas Rosset, 1586.

Lettres patentes du Roy, pour le restablissement de la Cour des Monnoyes de Paris. Paris: Federic Morel, 1594.

Lettres patentes du roy, sur l'ouverture des monnoyes, jugement des boettes & reglement d'icelles. Paris: Veufve Jean Dalier, & Nicolas Roffet, 1594.

Lettres patentes du Roy, portant defenses a tous marchands & autres, de transporter hors de ce Royaume aucuns Bleds, Grains, & legumes, n'y d'en faire aucunes traictes, sur peine de confiscation desdicts grains & crime de leze majesté. Bourges: Pierre Bouchier, 1595.

Ordonnance du Roy, pour les gens de labeur, portant affranchissement, exemption, & delivrance de toute execution en leurs corps, bestail, biens, & meubles servans au labourage. Bourges: Pierre Bouchier, 1595.

Declaration du Roy, sur la surseance de l'execution des commissions de la recherche des ususres, Francs-fiefs, confirmation des Foires, Marchez, usages, terres vaines & vagues, recherche des monnoyes, vin vendu és maisons & cabarets sans permission dudict seigneur, & ceux qui ont abusé du tiltre de Noblesse. Paris: Jamet Mettayer, 1596.

Lettres Patentes du Roy, pour l'observation de l'ordonnance faicte sur le reiglement general des monnoyes de l'an 1577. Paris: Vefve Nicolas Rosset, [1596].

Edict du Roy, pour la levee des droicts d'entree moderez, qui seront cueillez & perceuz en toutes les Provinces de ce Royaume sur les denrees & marchandises, suyvant l'advis de l'Assemblee tenuë en la ville de Rouen. Angers: Anthoine Hernault, 1597.

Lettres patentes du Roy, contenans l'establissement de la Chambre Royale, pour la cognoissance & jugement des abuz & malversations commises en ses Finances. Bourges: Maurice Levez, 1597.

Edict du Roy contenant reglement sur les exemptions & affranchissemens de la Taille, au soulagement du pauvre peuple. Bourges: Maurice Levez, 1598.

Edict du Roy, contenant prohibition et defence de l'usage de l'Inde & Anil, & entree dans le Royaume. Paris: Jamet Mettayer and Pierre l'Huillier, 1601.

Ordonnance du Roy sur le faict & reglement de ses Monnoyes. Paris: Vefve Nicolas Roffet, 1601.

Edict du roy, portant defenses a toutes personnes, de quelques qualitez qu'ils soyent, de porter en leurs habillemens aucuns draps ny toilles d'or ou d'argent, clinquans & passemens. Paris: Jamet Mettayer & P. l'Huillier, 1601.

Edict du roy sur le faict et Reglement general de ses Monnoyes. Contenant l'augmentation du cours des especes & interdiction d'aucunes estrangeres. Paris: Veufve Nicolas Rosset, 1602.

Declaration du roy, sur son Edict & Reiglement general des Monnoyes, du present mois de Septembre. Paris: Veufve Nicolas Roffet, 1602.

Declaration du Roy, sur son Edict du surhaulsement des Monnoyes du mois de Septembre dernier, contenant permission de recevoir toutes Monnoyes sans poiser. Paris: Veufve Nicolas Roffet, 1602.

Lettres patentes donnees par le Roy, portant privileges donnez par sa Majesté a ses officiers & artisans logez dans sa grande gallerie du Louvre. Paris: Federic Morel, 1609.

Edict du Roy, sur la reduction des Rentes qui se constitueront d'ores-navant à prix d'argent au denier quatozre [sic]. Rouen: Martin Mesgissier, 1610.

Pamphlets

Advis, remonstrances et requestes aux estats generaux tenus à Paris, 1614. Par six paisans. N.p., 1614.

Belordeau de la Grée, Pierre. *Polyarchie ou de la domination tyrannique, et de l'auctorité de commander, usurpée par plusieurs pendant les troubles. En forme de remonstrance au Tres-Chrestien Henry IIII. Roy de France & de Navarre. Où sont representées les miseres de la Province de Bretagne, la cause d'icelles, & le remede que sa Majesté y a apporté par le moyen de la Paix.* 2nd ed. Paris: Nicolas Buon, 1617.

Bodin, Jean. *Les paradoxes du seigneur de Malestroict conseiller du Roy, & maistre ordinaire de ses comptes, sur le faict des Monnoyes, presentez à sa Majesté, au mois de Mars, M.D.LXVI. Avec la response de Jean Bodin ausdicts Paradoxes.* Paris: Jacques du Puys, 1578.

———. *La vie chère au XVIe siècle: La response de Jean Bodin à M. de Malestroict, 1568.* Edited by Henri Hauser. Paris: Armand Colin, 1932.

Chabans, Loys de. *Apologie de l'edict des monnoyes, ou refutation des Erreurs de Maistre Guillaume et de ses adherents.* Paris: Veuve Nicolas Roffet, 1610.

———. *Raisons pour montrer que l'edit nouvellement faict sur les monnoyes est juste, et qu'il est au soulagement du peuple.* Paris: Veufve Nicolas Roffet, 1609.

Coquerel, Nicolas. *Discours de la perte que les François reçoivent en la permission d'exposer les Monnoyes estrangeres.* Paris: François Jaquin, 1608.

Garrault, François. "Des mines d'argent trouvées en France, ouvrage et police d'icelles." In *Archives curieuses de l'histoire de France depuis Louis XI jusqu'à Louis XVIII,* edited by L. Cimber and F. d'Anjou, vol. 8, 421–27. Paris: Beauvais, 1836.

———. *Les recherches des monnoyes, poix et maniere de nombrer, des premieres & plus renommees nations du monde . . . livres trois.* Paris: Martin le Jeune, 1576.

———. *Paradoxe sur le faict des monnoyes.* Paris: Jacques du Puys, 1578.

———. *Recueil des principaux advis donnez es assemblees faictes par commandement du Roy . . . sur le contenu des memoires, presentez à sa majesté estant en la ville de Poictiers, portans l'establissement du compte par esucuz, & suppression de celuy par solz & livres.* Paris: Jacques du Puys, 1578.

Godefroy, Denys. *Advis presenté à la Royne pour reduire les Monnoies à leur juste prix & valeur, empescher le surhaussement & empirance d'icelles.* Paris: Pierre Chevalier, 1611.

Lafférmas, Barthelémy de. *Advertissment sur les divers crimes des banqueroutiers. Suivant les edicts et ordonnances des roys de France.* Paris: Jean Milot, 1609.

Le Begue, François. *Traicté et advis sur les desordres des monnoyes & diversité de moyens d'y remedier.* Paris, 1600.

"Parens." *Tres-humble remonstrance, requeste et advis des ouvriers en draps de Soye, sur le fait de leurs manufactures.* N.p., 1604.

Poullain, Henri. *Refutation de l'erreur cy devant publié en un livret imprimé, Que le Traite proposee par l'autheur d'iceluy n'excede se qui se souloit lever, & se leve de present.* N.p., 1609.

———. *Traictés des monnoyes, pour un Conseiller d'Estat.* Paris, 1621.

Rascas, Pierre-Antoine de, sieur de Bagarris. *La necessité de l'usage des medailles dans les monnoyes.* Paris: Jean Berjon, 1611.

Roland du Plessis, Nicolas. *Advertissement pour servir de response au discours nagueres publié sur le faict des Monnoyes.* Paris: Nicolas Buon, 1609.

——. *Discours veritable de la mort, funerailles et enterement de deffunct Messire André de Brancas, en son vivant Chevalier Seigneur de Vilars, Conseiller au Conseil d'Estat & privé du Roy, Cappitaine de cent homes d'armes de ses ordonnances, Gouverneur & Lieutenant general pour sa Majesté, ès villes & Bailliages de Rouen, Caux, Havre de grace, & Admiral de France. Auqel est traicté succinctement du mespris des choses du / monde, & de l'utilité qui vient de la meditation/de la mort & choses dernieres.* Rouen: Richard l'Allemant, 1595.

Suitte des rencontres de M. Guillaume en l'autre monde. Paris: Pierre Ramier, 1609.

Tres-humble remonstrance, requeste et advis des ouvriers en draps de soye, sur le fait de leurs manufactures. N.p., 1603.

Turquam, Thomas. *Advis de M. Thomas Turquam, General des monnoyes, donné en une assemblee faicte à Paris, au moys de Septembre 1577. par devant Monseigneur le Reverendissime Cardinal de Bourbon, pour deliberer sur les memoires presentez au Roy, afin d'abolir le compte à sols, & à livres, & d'oresenavant faire tous contracts & oblicagions à escus.* Paris: Veufve Jehan Dallier, 1578.

——. *Remonstrances faites au Parlement de Dijon le x. jour de Septembre, 1573. par M. Thomas Turquam General des Monnoyes, Commissaire deputé par sa Majesté, pour l'execution du descry des especes de Billon entrangeres qui s'exposent au Duché de Bourgogne.* Paris: Jean Dallier, 1573.

Collections of Documents

Barbiche, Bernard, and Isabelle Chiavassa, eds. *L'édit de Nantes et ses antécédents (1562–1598).* Paris: Editions en ligne de l'Ecole des Chartes, n.d. http://elec.enc.sorbonne.fr/editsdepacification.

Bouchel, Laurent. *La bibliothèque ou thresor du droict francois. Œuvre auqel non seulement tout ce qui est de de matieres civiles, criminelles, et beneficiales, Ordonnances & Coustumes de la France est sommairement rapporté: Mais aussi les questions plus difficiles & remarquables d'icelles y sont expliquees & resoluës par les Expositions, Traittez & Decisions des plus celebres Jurisconsultes, Practiciens François, & Arrests des Cours Souverains Et encore illustré en plusieurs endroits par la conference & rapport des Loix & coustumes des nations etrangeres.* 2 vols. Paris: Eustache Foucault et al., 1615.

Breul, Jacques. *Le Theatre des antiquitez de Paris, où est traicté de la fondation des eglises & chapelles de la cité, Université, ville, & diocese de Paris: Comme aussi de l'institution du Parlement, fondation de l'Université & colleges, & autres choses remarquables.* Paris: Par la Societé des Imprimeurs, 1639 [1614].

Cabrol, Etienne. *Annales de Villefranche de Rouergue.* 2 vols. Villefranche: Imprimerie de Veuve Cestan, née Moins, 1860.

Calendar of State Papers, Foreign Series. 23 vols. London: Longman, 1861–1950.

Daubresse, Sylvie, and Bertrand Haan, eds. *Actes du parlement de Paris et documents du temps de la Ligue (1588–1594): Le recueil de Pierre Pithou.* Paris: Honoré Champion, 2012.

Espiner-Scott, Janet Girvan, ed. *Documents concernant la vie et les oeuvres de Claude Fauchet. Documents—inédits—bibliothèque de Fauchet—extraits de poèmes—copiés d'après des manuscrits perdus.* Paris: E. Droz, 1938.

Fontanon, Antoine, ed. *Les edicts et ordonnances des rois de France, depuis Louys VI dit le Gros jusques à present. Avec les verifications, modifications, & declarations sur iceux.* 4 vols. Paris, 1611.

Freher, Marquard, ed. *De re monetaria veterum Romanorum et hodierni apud Germanos Imperii, libri duo.* Leiden: Apud Gothardum Vœgelinum, 1605.

Greffe, Florence, and Valérie Brousselle, eds. *Documents du Minutier central des notaires de Paris: Inventaires après décès.* Vol. 2, *1547–1560.* Paris: Archives Nationales, 1997.

Grice-Hutchinson, Marjorie, ed. *The School of Salamanca: Readings in Spanish Monetary Theory, 1544–1605.* Oxford: Oxford University Press, 1952.

Guerin, Paul et al., eds. *Registres des délibérations du bureau de la ville de Paris.* Vols. 5–14. Histoire générale de Paris. Paris: Imprimerie Nationale, 1896–1908.

Henri III (King of France). *Lettres de Henri III, Roi de France.* Edited by Pierre Champion and Michel François. 5 vols. Paris: Klinckseick, 1959–2000.

Hughes, Paul F., and James F. Larkin, eds. *Tudor Royal Proclamations.* 3 vols. New Haven: Yale University Press, 1964–67.

Isambert, François-André et al., eds. *Recueil général des anciennes lois françaises, depuis l'an 420 jusqu'a` la révolution de 1789.* 29 vols. Paris: Plon, 1821–33.

Lespinasse, René de, ed. *Les métiers et corporations de la ville de Paris.* Vol. 2, *XIVe–XVIIe siècle: Orfèvrerie, sculpture, mercerie, ouvriers en métaux, bâtiment et ameublement.* Histoire générale de Paris. Paris: Imprimerie Nationale, 1892.

Markham, Clements R., ed. *Journal of Christopher Columbus (During His First Voyage, 1492–93): And Documents Relating to the Voyages of John Cabot and Gaspar Corte Real.* London: Hakluyt Society, 1893.

Mazerolle, Fernand. *Les médailleurs français du XVe siècle au milieu du XVIIe.* Vol. 1, *Introduction et documents.* Paris: Imprimerie Nationale, 1902.

Mongrédien, Georges, ed. *Recueil des textes et des documents du XVIIe siècle relatifs à Corneille.* Paris: Editions du C.N.R.S., 1972.

Recueil d'aucuns Edicts, Declarations, Lettres Patentes, & Arrests du Conseil d'Estat & Privé de nos Roys touchant la Souveraineté & Jurisdiction privative & cumulative de la Cour des Monnoyes, Juges Gardes, Officiers & Justiciables d'icelle. Paris, 1635.

Richter, Emil, and Emil Friedberg, eds. *Corpus juris canonici, pars secunda: Decretalium collectiones.* Graz, Austria: Akademische Druck und Verlaganstalt, 1955.

The Statutes of the Realm: Printed by Command of His Majesty King George the Third. 9 vols. in 10. London: George Eyre and Andrew Strahan, 1810–22.

Vaissière, Pierre de. *La découverte à Augsbourg des instruments mécaniques de monnayage moderne et leur importation en France in 1550 d'après les dépêches de Charles de Marillac, ambassadeur de France.* Montpellier: Imprimerie Ricard Frères, 1892.

Works of Literature

Alemán, Mateo. *Guzmán de Alfarache.* Edited by Samuel Gili y Gaya. 4 vols. Madrid: Espasa-Calpe, 1942.

———. *Le gueux, ou Guzman d'Alfarache, image de la vie humaine.* Translated by Jean Chapelain. 2 vols. Rouen: Jean de la Maire, 1633.

———. *Guzman d'Alfarache, divisé en trois livres.* Translated by Gabriel Chappuys. Paris: Nicolas et Pierre Bonfons, 1600.

Béroalde de Verville, François. *L'Histoire veritable ou le voyage des princes fortunés.* Albi: Passage du nord-œust, 2005.

Chaucer, Geoffrey. *The Canterbury Tales.* Edited by N. F. Blake. London: Arnold, 1980.

Henry Chettle, *Englands Mourning Garment: Worne Heere by Plaine Shepheards, in Memorie of Their Sacred Mistresse, Elizabeth; Queene of Vertue While She Lived, and Theame of Sorrow Being Dead. To the Which Is Added the True Manner of her Emperiall Funerall. With Many New Additions, Being Now Againe the Second Time Reprinted, Which Was Omitted in the First Impression. After Which Followeth the Shepheards Spring-Song, for Entertainment of King Iames our most Potent Soveraigne.* London: Thomas Millington, 1603.

Corneille, Pierre. *L'Illusion comique. Comédie. Publiée d'après la première édition (1639) avec les variantes.* Edited by Robert Garapon. Paris: Nizet, 1985.

Cyrano de Bergerac, Hector-Savinien de. *Histoire comique des états et empires de la lune et du soleil.* Edited by P. L. Jacob. Paris: Adolphe Delahays, 1858.

Domayron, Antoine. *Histoire du siege des muses, ou parmi le chaste amour, est traicté de plusieurs belles & curieuses sciences, divine moralle & naturelle, architecture, alchimie, piencture & autres.* Lyons: Simon Rigaud, 1610.

du Bellay, Joachim. *Les Regrets et autres œuvres poëtiques suivis des Antiquitez de Rome, plus un Songe ou Vision sur le mesme subject.* Edited by J. Jolliffe and M. A. Screech. Geneva: Droz, 1966.

Furetière, Antoine. *Le roman bourgeois.* Edited by Jacques Prévot. Paris: Gallimard, 1981.

Grévin, Jacques. *La trésorière, Les esbahis: Comédies.* Edited by Elisabeth Lapeyre. Paris: Honoré Champion, 1980.

Jonson, Ben. *The Alchemist.* Edited by Elizabeth Cook. 2nd ed. New York: Norton, 1991.

Kahn, Didier, ed., *Nicolas Flamel: Ecrits alchimiques.* Paris: Les Belles Lettres, 1993.

le Loyer, Pierre. *Discours des spectres, ou visions et apparitions d'esprits, comme anges, demons, et ames, se monstrans visibles aux hommes.* 2nd ed. Paris: Nicolas Buon, 1608 [1605].

———. *La nephelococugie ou la nuée des cocus.* Edited by Miriam Doe and Keith Cameron. Geneva: Droz, 2004.

———. *Les œuvres et meslanges poetiques de Pierre le Loyer angevin. Ensemble la comedie Nephelococugie, ou la nuee des cocus, non moins docte que faceteuse.* Paris: Jean Poupy, 1579.

Prévot, Jacques, ed. *Libertins du XVIIe siècle.* 2 vols. Paris: N.R.F./Gallimard, 1998.

Rabelais, François. *Œuvres complètes.* Paris: Editions du seuil, 1973.

Ronsard, Pierre de. *Œuvres complètes.* Edited by Gustave Cohen. 2 vols. Paris: N.R.F. Gallimard, 1950.

Sorel, Charles. *L'histoire comique de Francion: Edition de 1633.* Edited by Fausta Garavini, Anne Schoysman, and Anna Lia Franchetti. Paris: Gallimard, 1996.

Turnèbe, Adrien (II), ed. *Othonis Turnebi in suprema curia parisiensi advocati tumulus.* Paris: Apud Mamertum Patissonium, in officina Roberti Stephani, 1582.

Turnèbe, Odet de. *Les contens.* Edited by Norman B. Spector. Société des textes français modernes. Paris: Librarie Nizet, 1984.

Other Printed Primary Sources

Aristotle. *Aristotelis de Reip. bene administrandae ratione, libri octo, a Dionys. Lambino Monstroliensi, litterarum Graecarum Lutetitiae doctore Regio, olim Latini facti.* Paris: Apud Joannem Bene-natum, 1567.

———. *Aristotelous Ethikon Nikomacheion biblia deka. Aristotelis de moribus ad Nicomachum libri decem. Ita Graecis interpretatione recenti cum Latninis conjunctis, ut fermè singula singulis respondeant: In eorum gratiam, qui Graeca cum Latinis coparare volum.* Heidelberg, 1560 [1555].

———. *Contenta politicorum Aristotelis libri Octo. Economicorum eiusdem duo. Haec Aristotelis opera ullis absque commentarijs emissa sunt, quibus in fronte familiaris in Politica introductio, una cum indice vocabulorum.* Edited by Franciscus Zampinus. Paris: In Clauso brunello sub Geminarum Cipparum insigni, 1529.

———. *Ethicorum, sive de moribus ad Nicomachum libri decem adiecta ad contextum græcum interpretatione latina Dionysii Lambini.* 2nd ed. Frankfurt: Apud her. A. Wecheli, C. Marn. et J. Aubr, 1596.

———. *The Politics.* Edited by Stephen Everson. Cambridge Texts in the History of Political Thought. Cambridge: Cambridge University Press, 1988.

———. *Politique,* bks. 1 and 2. Edited by Jean Aubonnet. Collection Budé. Paris: Les Belles Lettres, 1968.

———. *Les politiques.* Translated by Loys le Roy. Paris: A. Drouart, 1599 [1568].

Bèze, Théodore de. *Histoire ecclésiastique des églises réformées de France.* Edited by P. Vesson. 2 vols. Toulouse: Société des livres religieuses, 1882.

Biel, Gabriel. *Tractatus de potestate & utilitate monetarum.* Oppenheim, Ger.: J. Köbel, 1516.

———. *Treatise on the Power and Utility of Money.* Translated by Robert Belle Burke. Philadelphia: University of Pennsylvania Press, 1930.

Bodin, Jean. *Recueil de tout ce qui s'est negotié en la compagnie du tiers Estat de France, en l'asemblee general des trois Estats, assignez par le Roy en la ville de Bloys aux xv. Novembre 1576.* N.p., 1577.

———. *Les six livres de la republique.* Paris: Jacques du Puis, 1583.

Boileau, Etienne. *Les métiers et corporations de la ville de Paris: XIIIe siècle. Le livre des métiers d'Etienne Boileau.* Edited by René Lespinasse and François Bonnardot. Paris: Imprimerie Nationale, 1879.

Brantôme, Pierre de Bourdeille de. *Œuvres complètes.* Edited by Ludovic Lalanne. 10 vols. Paris: Renouard, 1886.

Breul, Jacques. *Le Theatre des antiquitez de Paris, où est traicté de la fondation des eglises & chapelles de la cité, Université, ville, & diocese de Paris: comme aussi de l'institution du Parlement, fondation de l'Université & colleges, & autres choses remarquables.* Paris: Par la Societé des Imprimeurs, 1639 [1614].

Budé, Guillaume. *De asse et partibus ejus libri quinque.* Paris: Josse Badius, 1514.

Calvin, John. *Institutes of the Christian Religion.* Translated by Henry Beveridge. 2 vols. London: James Clarke, 1953.

Camden, William. *Annales rerum gestarum Angliae et Hiberniae regnante Elizabetha (1615 and 1625) with the Annotations of Sir Francis Bacon.* Edited by Dana F. Sutton. Birmingham, UK: Philological Museum, 2001. http://www.philo logical.bham.ac.uk/camden.

Camus, Jean-Pierre. *Les diversitez.* 2 vols. Paris: Claude Chappellet, 1609.

Cassander, George. *Supputatio romanorum et grecorum numismatum, collata ad monetam flandricum et gallicam. De mensuris et ponderibus romanis, atticis, grecis, & hebraeorum nonullis De mensuris geometricis. Cum ad olim veterum, tum ad sacrarum litterarum intellectum plurimum conducentia.* Ghent: Iodicus Labertus, 1537.

Colenges, Jean de. *Mémoires.* Rodez, Fr.: Société des lettres, 2011.

Constans, Germain. *Traité de la Cour des monnoyes et de l'estendue de sa jurisdiction divisé en cinq parties.* Paris: Sebastien Cramoisy, 1658.

[Cromé, François.] *Dialogue d'entre le maheustre et le manant: Texte original, avec les variantes de la version royaliste.* Edited Peter M. Ascoli. Geneva: Droz, 1977.

de Roover, Raymond. *Gresham on Foreign Exchange: An Essay on Early English Mercantilism with the Text of Sir Thomas Gresham's Memorandum for the Understanding of the Exchange.* Cambridge, MA: Harvard University Press, 1949.

du Choul, Guillaume. *Discours de la religion des anciens romains.* Lyons: Guillaume Rouille, 1556.

du Moulin, Charles. *Sommaire du livre analytique des contracts, usures, rentes constituées, interests & monnoyes.* Paris: Jean Houzé, 1586.

du Verdier, Antoine. *Les diverses lecons d'Antoine du Verdier, sieur de Vauprivas, gentilhomme foresien, & ordinaire de la maison du Roy, suivans celles de Pierre Messie. Contenans plusieurs histoires, discours, & faict s memorables. Augmentées par l'autheur en ceste cinquiesme edition de trois discours trouvez apres le decez de l'autheur en ses papiers, du Dueil, de l'Honneur, & de la Noblesse.* Tournon: Claude Michel, 1616.

Erizzo, Sebastiano. *Discorso . . . sopra le medaglie de gli antichi: Con la particolar dichiaratione di esse medaglie: Nellaquale oltre all'istoria de gli impersdori romani, si contengono le imagini delle deità de i gentili, con le loro allegorie: & insieme vna varia & piena cognitione delle antichità.* Venice: Giovani Varisco et compagni, 1568.

Fernández de Oviedo y Valdés, Gonzalo. *L'histoire de la terre neuve du Perú en l'Inde Occidentale, qui est la principale mine d'or du monde, naguères descouverte, & conquise, & nommée la nouvelle Castille, traduitte d'Italien en Francoys.* Translated by Jacques Gohory. Paris: Vincent Sertenas, 1545.

Froumenteau, Nicolas. *Le secret des finances de France, Descouvert, & departi en trois livres.* 3 vols. in 1. N.p., 1581.

Gasson, Jules. *Sommaire mémorial (souvenirs) de Jules Gasson, Sécretaire du roi (1555–1623).* Edited by Pierre Champion. Paris: Honoré Champion, 1934.

Guicciardini, Francesco. *Opere.* Edited by Emanuella Lugnani Scarano. 3 vols. Turin: Unione Tipografico-Editrice Torninense, 1970–81.

Haton, Claude. *Mémoires de Claude Haton contenant le récit des événements accomplis de 1553 à 1582, principalement dans la Champagne et la Brie.* Edited by Félix Bouquelot. 2 vols. Collection des documents inédits sur l'histoire de France. Paris: Imprimerie Imperiale, 1857.

Hennequin, Jean. *Le guidon general des finances. Contenant l'Instruction du maniement de toutes les finances de France. . . . Avec les Annotations de Me. Vincent Gelee Conseiller du Roy & Correcteur ordinaire en sa Chambre des comptes. Livre necessaire non seulement aux comptables & autres ayans charge & pouvoir aux finances du Roy, mais aussi aux gens tant Ecclesiastiques nobles que autres, pour cognoistre les torts & exactions que pourroient faire leur Receveurs. Divisé en cinq parties. Le tout nouvellement revue & corrigé.* Paris: Abel l'Angelier, 1596 [1585].

Hotman, François. *De re numaria populi Romani liber.* s. l., 1585.

la Barre, René-Laurent de. *Formulaire des esleuz. Auquel sont contenuës & declarées les functions & devoirs desdits Officiers, & sommairement ce qu'ils sont tenus sçavoir & faire, pour l'acquit/de leur charge. Ensemble quelques recherches, touchant les Tailles, Taillon, subsides, creuës, imposts, tributs & peages; Foires, marchez, sallages, quatriesmes, huictiesmes, & autres deniers qui se levent sur les boires & breuvages, tavernes & taverniers, &c. Avec un Traité des monnoyes, & metaux.* Rouen: Jean Osmont, 1622.

la Croix du Maine, François Grudé de. *Les bibliothèques françoises de La Croix du Maine et de du Verdier sieur de Vauprivas.* Edited by Rigoley de Juvigny. 4 vols. Paris: Saillant et Nyon et Michel Lambert, 1772–1773.

Laffémas, Isaac de. *Histoire du commerce de France. Enrichie des plus notables antiquitez du traffic des païs estranges.* Paris: Toussaincts du Bray, 1606.

la Perrière, Guillaume de. *Le miroir politique, contenant les diverses manieres de gouverner & policer les Republiques, qui sont, & ont esté par cy devant: OEuvre, non moins utile que necessaire à tous Monarches, Rois, Princes, Seigneurs, Magistrats & autres qui ont charge du gouvernment ou administration d'icelles.* Paris: Robert le Mangnier, 1567.

las Casas, Bartolomé de. *The Devastation of the Indies: A Brief Account.* Translated by Herma Briffault. Baltimore: Johns Hopkins University Press, 1992.

le Pois, Antoine. *Discours sur les medailles & graveurs antiques, principallement romains.* Paris: Mamert Patisson, 1579.

Lefèvre de Lezeau, Nicolas. *La vie de Michel de Marillac (1560–1632), Garde des Sceaux de France sous Louis XIII.* Edited by Donald A. Bailey. Quebec City: Presses de l'Université Laval, 2007.

l'Estoile, Pierre de. *Mémoires-journaux.* Edited by Gustave Brunet et al. 12 vols. Paris, A. Lemerre, 1881–96.

——. *Registre-journal du règne d'Henri III.* Edited by Madeleine Lazard and Gilbert Schrenck. Vol. 2 (1576–1578). Geneva: Droz, 1996.

Locke, John. *Two Treatises of Government.* Edited by Peter Laslett. Cambridge Texts in the History of Political Thought. Cambridge: Cambridge University Press, 1988.

Malestroict, Jehan Cherruyl de. *Paradoxes inédits du Seigneur de Malestroit touchant les monnoyes.* Edited by Luigi Einaudi. Turin: Giulio Einaudi, 1937.

Miraulmont, Pierre de. *Les memoires de Pierre de Miraulmont . . . Sur l'origine & institution des Cours souveraines, & Justices Royalles estans dans l'enclos du Palais Royal de Paris.* Paris: Claude de la Tour, 1612.

Molé, Mathieu. *Mémoires.* Edited by Aimé Champollion-Figeac. 4 vols. Paris: J. Renouard, 1855–57.

Monluc, Blaise de. *Commentaires et lettres de Blaise de Monluc.* Edited by Alphonse de Ruble. 6 vols. Paris: Veuve J. Renouard, 1864–72.

Montaigne, Michel de. *Les Essais.* Edited by Pierre Villey. Paris: Presses universitaires de France, 1992. Also, http://www.lib.uchicago.edu/efts/ARTFL/projects/montaigne/.

Montchrestien, Antoine de. *Traicté de l'œconomie politique.* Edited by François Billacois. Geneva: Droz, 1999.

More, Thomas. *Utopia. The Complete Works of St. Thomas More.* Edited by Edward Surtz and J. H. Hexter. Vol. 4. New Haven: Yale University Press, 1965.

Oresme, Nicole. *The De moneta.* Edited by Charles Johnson. London: Thomas Nelson and Sons, 1956.

Palissy, Bernard. *Recepte veritable, par laquelle tous les hommes de la France pourront apprendre à multiplier et augmenter leurs thresors. Item, ceux qui n'ont jamais eu cognoissance des lettres, pourront apprendre une Philosophie necessaire à tous les habitans de la terre,* etc. La Rochelle: Barthelemy Berton, 1563.

Pasquier, Etienne. "Bref discours du proces criminel fait à Pierre Barrière, dit la Barre, natif d'Orléans." In Cimber and d'Anjou, *Archives curieuses,* 1st ser., vol. 13, 359–70. Paris: Beauvais, 1837.

Pavur, Claude, ed. *The* Ratio Studiorum: *The Official Plan for Jesuit Education.* St. Louis: Institute of Jesuit Sources, 2005.

Pietre, Roland. *Le premier livre des Considerations Politiques.* Paris: Robert Estienne, 1566.

Poulain, Nicolas. "Le procez-verbal d'un nommé Nicolas Poulain." In Cimber and d'Anjou, *Archives curieuses,* 1st ser., vol. 11, 289–323. Paris: Beauvais, 1836.

Pugnet, Henri. "Il memoriale di Henry Pugnet." Edited by Mario Abrate. In *Studi in onore di Amintore Fanfani,* vol. 4, 1–38. Evo moderno. Milan: Giuffrè, 1962.

Rolland, Nicolas. *Remonstrances tres-humbles av roy de France & de Pologne Henry troisiesme de ce nom, par un sien fidele officier & subject, sur les desordres & miseres de ce Royaume, causes d'icelles, & moyens d'y pourveoir à la gloire de Dieu & repos uniuersel de cet estat.* N.p., 1588.

Sendivogius, Michael. *Traicté du soulphre.* Translated by F. Guiraud. Paris: Abraham Pacard, 1618.

[Smith, Thomas.] *A Discourse of the Commonweal of This Realm of England.* Edited by Mary Dewar. Charlottesville: University Press of Virginia for the Folger Shakespeare Library, 1969.

Sully, Maximilien de Béthune, duc de. *Sages et royales œconomies d'estat.* Edited by Joseph-François Michaud and Jean-Joseph-François Poujoulat. 2 vols. Nouvelle collection des mémoires pour server à l'histoire de France, 3rd ser., no. 2. Paris: Chez l'éditeur du commentaire analytique du code civil, 1837.

Symeoni, Gabriel. *Illustratione de gli epitafi et medaglie antiche.* Lyons: Jean de Tournes, 1558.

———. *Les illustres observations antiques du seigneur Gabriel Syméon, florentin, en son dernier voyage d'Italie, l'an 1557.* Lyons: Jean de Tournes, 1558

Thou, Jacques-Auguste de. *Historiarum sui temporis.* Vol. 6. London: Samuel Barclay, 1733.

Vergil, Polydore. *De inventoribus rerum libri tres.* Cologne: In officina Mathiæ Schurerii, 1512.

Vico, Enea. *Discorsi . . . sopra le medaglie degli antichi. Divisi in due libri, ove si Dimonstrano notabili errori di Scrittori Antichi, e Moderni, intorno alle Historie Romane.* Edited by Giovanni Battista du Vallio. Paris: Maceo Ruette, 1619.

Wheeler, John. *A Treatise of Commerce Wherein Are Shewed the Commodities Arising by a Well Ordered Trade, Such as That of the Societie of Merchant Adventurers Is Proved to Be.* London: John Harison; Middelburg: Richard Shilders, 1601.

Wolowski, M. L., ed. *Traictie de la premiere invention des monnoies de Nicole Oresme, textes français et latin d'après les manuscrits de la Bibliothèque Impériale et Traité de la monnaie de Copernic texte latin et traducion française.* Paris: Librairie de Gillaumin, 1864.

Secondary Works

Alcover, Madeleine. "Furetière et la stratification sociale: Le 'tariffe des mariages.'" *Papers on French Seventeenth-Century Literature* 8 (1981): 74–93.

Antoine, Michel. *Le cœur de l'état: Surintendance, contrôle général et intendance des finances 1552–1791.* Paris: Fayard, 2003.

——. "Genèse de l'institution des intendants." *Journal des savants,* 1982, 283–317.

Appleby, Joyce. "Locke, Liberalism and the Natural Law of Money." *Past and Present* 71 (1976): 55–56.

Archbold, W. A. J. "A Manuscript Treatise on the Coinage by John Pryse, 1553." *English Historical Review* 13 (1898): 709–10.

Augé-Chiquet, Mathieu. *La vie, les idées et l'œuvre de Jean-Antoine de Baïf.* Geneva: Slatkine, 1979 [1909].

Baguenault de Puchesse, Gustave. *Jean de Morvillier, évêque d'Orléans, garde des sceaux de France, 1506–1577: Etude sur la politique française au XVIe siècle, d'après des documents inédits.* 2nd ed. Paris: Didier, 1870.

Bailhache, J. "Le monnayage de Montmorency pendant la Ligue à Montpellier, Beaucaire, Béziers et Villeneuve d'Avignon (1585–1592), d'après des documents inédits." *Revue numismatique,* 4th ser., 25 (1932): 37–91.

Baldwin, John R. *The Medieval Theories of the Just Price: Romanists, Canonists, and Theologians in the Twelfth and Thirteenth Centuries.* Transactions of the American Philosophical Society. Philadelphia: American Philosophical Society, 1959.

Barbiche, Bernard. "De l'Etat de justice à l'Etat des finances: Le tournant de l'année 1605." In *Henri IV, le roi et la reconstruction du royaume: Actes du colloque, Pau-Nérac, 14–17 septembre 1989,* 95–109. Pau: Association Henri IV, 1990.

——. "Les deux familles de Sully." *XVIIe siècle* 174 (1992): 21–32.

——. "Une révolution administrative: La charge de Grand voyer de France." In *Pouvoir et institutions en Europe au XVIe siècle. Vingt-septième Colloque International d'Etudes Humanistes, Tours,* edited by André Stegmann, 283–96. Paris: Librairie Philosophique J. Vrin, 1987.

——. "Une tentative de réforme monétaire à la fin du règne d'Henri IV: L'édit d'août 1609." *XVIIe siècle* 61 (1963): 3–17.

Barbiche, Bernard, and Ségolène de Dainville-Barbiche. *Sully: l'homme et ses fidèles.* Paris: Fayard, 1997.

Bardon, Françoise. *Diane de Poitiers et le mythe de Diane.* Paris: Presses universitaires de France, 1963.

Barnavi, Elie. *Le parti de Dieu: Etude sociale et politique des chefs de la Ligue parisienne 1585–1594.* Brussels: Editions Nauwelaerts, 1980.

Bastien, Pascal. "'Aux tresors dissipez on cognoist le malfaict': Hiérarchie sociale et transgression des ordonnances somptuaires en France, 1549–1606." *Renaissance and Reformation/Renaissance et réforme* 4 (1999): 23–43.

Baudouin-Matuszek, Marie-Noëlle. "Un tour de France des généraux des monnaies (1556)." In *Etudes sur l'ancienne France offertes en hommage à Michel Antoine,* edited by Bernard Barbiche and Yves-Marie Bercé, 25–46. Paris: Editions de l'Ecole des Chartes, 2003.

Baumgartner, Frederick. *Henry II, King of France*. Durham, NC: Duke University Press, 1988.

Bayard, Françoise. *Le monde des financiers au XVIIe siècle*. Paris: Flammarion, 1988.

Bennini, Martine. *Les conseillers à la Cour des aides (1604–1697): Etude sociale*. Paris: Honoré Champion, 2010.

Benson, Edward J. "Guerrier or Glossateur? Montaigne's Monetary Metaphors." *Renaissance and Reformation/Renaissance et réforme* 16 (1992): 55–72.

Bimbenet-Privat, Michèle. *Les orfèvres parisiens de la Renaissance: 1506–1620*. Paris: Commission des travaux historiques de la Ville de Paris, 1992.

Bisson, Thomas M. *Conservation of Coinage: Monetary Exploitation and Its Restraint in France, Catalonia, and Aragon (c. A.D. 1000—c. 1225)*. Oxford: Oxford University Press, 1979.

Blanchet, Adrien, and Adolphe Dieudonné. *Manuel de numismatique française*. 4 vols. Paris: Picard, 1912–36.

Bloch, Claudine. "Les peines appliquées aux faux monnayeurs en France par la Chambre des monnaies (fin du xve siècle)." *Tijdschrift voor Rechtsgeschiedenis/Legal History Review* 58 (1990): 73–94.

Bluche, François. *Les magistrats de la Cour des monnaies de Paris au XVIIe siècle, 1715–1790*. Paris: Les Belles Lettres, 1966.

Blunt, Anthony. *Art and Architecture in France 1500 to 1700*. London: Penguin Books, 1953.

———. *Philibert de l'Orme*. London: A. Zwemmer, 1958.

Bodon, Giulio. *Enea Vico fra memoria e miraggio della classicità*. Rome: "L'Erma" di Bretschneider, 1997.

Bordo, Michael D. "Explorations in Monetary History: A Survey of the Literature." *Explorations in Economic History* 23 (1986): 339–415.

Bossy, John. "Moral Arithmetic: Seven Sins into Ten Commandments." In *Conscience and Casuistry in Early Modern Europe*, edited by Edmund Leiters, 214–35. Cambridge and Paris: Cambridge University Press and Editions de la Maison des sciences de l'homme, 1988.

Bowen, W. H. "L'Histoire de la Terre Neuve du Peru: A Translation by Jacques Gohory." *Isis* 28 (1938): 330–40.

Boyer-Xambeu, Marie-Thérèse, Ghislain Deleplace, and Lucien Gillard. *Private Money and Public Currencies: The Sixteenth-Century Challenge*. Translated by Azizeh Azodi. Armonk, NY: M. E. Sharpe, 1994.

Braudel, Fernand. *The Mediterranean and the Mediterranean World in the Age of Philip II*. Translated by Siân Reynolds. 2 vols. New York: Harper and Rowe, 1972.

Brennan, Thomas. "Public and Private and *la Police* in the Old Regime." *Proceedings of the Western Society for French History* 18 (1991): 582–91.

Brooke, Tucker. *The Life of Marlowe and The Tragedy of Dido Queen of Carthage*. New York: Gordian Press, 1966.

Brown, E. A. R. "Jean du Tillet et les archives de France." *Histoire et Archives* 2 (1997): 29–63.

Brumont, Francis. "Politique, religion et affaires: Pierre Assézat (vers 1515–1581)." *Annales de Bretagne et des Pays de l'Ouest* 112 (2005): 147–56.

Burke, Peter. *The Fabrication of Louis XIV*. New Haven: Yale University Press, 1992.

Byars, Jana. "The Long and Varied Relationship of Andrea Mora and Anzola Davide: Concubinage, Marriage and the Authorities in the Early Modern Veneto." *Journal of Social History* 41 (2008): 667–90.

Bynum, Carolyn Walker. "Presidential Address: Wonder." *American Historical Review* 102 (1997): 1–26.

Cabrol, Urbain. *Histoire de l'atelier monétaire royal de Villefranche-de-Rouergue*. Villefranche-de-Rouergue: Société Anonyme d'imprimerie, 1913.

Campangne, Hervé. "Savoir, économie et société dans les *Diverses leçons* d'Antoine du Verdier." *Bibliothèque d'humanisme et renaissance* 57 (1995): 623–35.

Carrasco Vazquez, Jesús. "Contrabando, moneda y espionaje (el negocio del vellón: 1606–1620)." *Hispania* 58 (1997): 1081–1105.

Carroll, Stuart. *Blood and Violence in Early Modern France*. Oxford: Oxford University Press, 2006.

Cattelona, Georg'ann. "Control and Collaboration: The Role of Women in Regulating Female Sexual Behavior in Early Modern Marseille." *French Historical Studies* 18 (1993): 13–33.

Cave, Terence. *The Cornucopian Text: Problems of Writing in the French Renaissance*. Oxford: Clarendon Press, 1979.

———. "L'économie de Panurge: 'Moutons à la grande laine.'" *Revue d'humanisme et renaissance* 37 (1993): 7–24.

———. *Pré-histoires II: Langues étrangères et troubles économiques au XVIe siècle*. Geneva: Droz, 2001.

Challis, C. E. "Controlling the Standard: York and the London Company of Goldsmiths in Later-Tudor and Early-Stuart England." *Northern History* 31 (1995): 123–37.

———, ed. *A New History of the Royal Mint*. Cambridge: Cambridge University Press, 1992.

———. "Presidential Address Part II: The Introduction of Coinage Machinery by Eloy Mestrell." *British Numismatic Journal* 59 (1990): 256–62.

———. *The Tudor Coinage*. Manchester, UK: Manchester University Press, 1978.

Chantrel, Laure. "Les notions de richesse et de travail dans la pensée économique française de la seconde moitié du XVIe et au début du XVIIe siècle." *Journal of Medieval and Renaissance Studies* 25 (1995): 129–58.

Charlier, Philippe et al. "Fatal Alchemy: Did Gold Kill a 16th Century French Courtesan?" *British Medical Journal*, 19–26 December 2009, 1402–3.

Clark, Henry C. "Commerce, the Virtues, and the Public Sphere in Early-Seventeenth-Century France." *French Historical Studies* 21 (1998): 415–40.

———. *Compass of Society: Commerce and Absolutism in Old-Regime France*. Lanham, MD: Lexington Books, 2007.

Claustre, Julie. *Dans les geôles du roi: L'emprisonnement pour dette à Paris à la fin du Moyen-Âge*. Paris: Publications de la Sorbonne, 2007.

Cloulas, Ivan. *Henri II*. Paris: Fayard, 1985.

Cole, Charles. *French Mercantilist Doctrines before Colbert*. New York: Richard R. Smith, 1931.

Collin, Bruno. "L'argent du Potosí (Pérou) et les émissions monétaires françaises." *Histoire et mesure* 17 (2002): 217–25.

Comparato, Vittor Ivo. "Note su Bodin e Aristotele: famiglia, sovranità e proprietà nella definizione dello stato." *Annali della Facoltà di Scienze Politiche: Materiali di Storia* 18 (1981): 7–13.

Cowen, Tyler, and Randall Kronzsner. "The Development of the New Monetary Economics." *Journal of Political Economy* 95 (1987): 567–90.

Crawford, Katherine. "The Politics of Promiscuity: Masculinity and Heroic Representation at the Court of Henry IV." *French Historical Studies* 26 (2003): 225–52.

Cunally, John. "Ancient Coins as Gifts and Tokens of Friendship during the Renaissance." *Journal of the History of Collections* 6 (1994): 129–43.

Daubresse, Sylvie. *Le Parlement de Paris, ou la voix de la raison (1559–1589).* Geneva: Droz, 2005.

Davies, Joan. "Neither Politique nor Patriot? Henri, Duc de Montmorency, and Philip II, 1582–1589." *Historical Journal* 34 (1991): 539–66.

Davis, Natalie Zemon. *Fiction in the Archives: Pardon Tales and their Tellers in Sixteenth-Century France.* Stanford, CA: Stanford University Press, 1987.

———. "Sixteenth-Century French Arithmetics on the Business Life." *Journal of the History of Ideas* 21 (1960): 18–48.

Davis, T. L. "The Autobiography of Denis Zachaire." *Isis* 8 (1926): 287–99.

Day, John, ed. *Etudes d'histoire monétaire.* Lille: Presses Universitaires de Lille, 1984.

Debaisieux, Martine. *Le procès du roman: Ecriture et contrefaçon chez Charles Sorel.* 2nd ed. Orleans: Paradigme, 2000.

Debus, Allen G. *The English Paracelsians.* New York: F. Watts, 1966.

———. "Mathematics and Nature in the Chemical Texts of the Renaissance." *Ambix* 15 (1968), 1–28.

Defaux, Gérard. *Le curieux, le glorieux, et la sagesse du monde dans la première moitié du XVIe siècle: L'exemple de Panurge (Ulysse, Démosthène, Empédocle).* Lexington, KY: French Forum Publishers, 1982.

———. "Panurge, le pouvoir et les dettes: Sagesse et folie dans Le Tiers Livre." *Op. cit.: Revue de littératures française et comparée* 5 (1995), 47–59.

DeJean, Joan. *Libertine Strategies: Freedom and the Novel in Seventeenth-Century France.* Columbus: Ohio State University Press, 1981.

———. "Seventeenth-Century Libertine Novels: *Autobiographies romancées?*" *L'Esprit créateur* 19 (1979): 14–25.

Demonet, Marie-Luce. *"A plaisir": Sémiotique et scepticisme chez Montaigne.* Orléans: Paradigme, 2002.

Depauw, Jacques. "Amour illégitime et société à Nantes au XVIIIe siècle." *Annales E.S.C.* 27 (1972): 1155–82.

Derrida, Jacques. *La dissémination.* Paris: Editions du seuil, 1972.

———. *Donner le temps 1: La fausse monnaie.* Paris: Editions Galilée, 1991.

———. *De la grammatologie.* Paris: Editions du minuit, 1967.

Desan, Phillippe. *L'imaginaire économique de la renaissance.* Mont-de-Marsan: Editions Inter-Universitaires, 1993.

Descimon, Robert. *Qui étaient les Seize?* Paris: Klincksiek, 1983.

Dessert, Daniel. *Argent, pouvoir et société au grand siècle.* Paris: Fayard, 1984.

de Vries, Jan. *The Industrious Revolution: Consumer Behaviour and the Household Economy, 1650 to the Present.* Cambridge: Cambridge University Press, 2008.

Dewald, Jonathan. *The Formation of a Provincial Nobility: The Magistrates of the Parlement of Rouen, 1499–1610.* Princeton: Princeton University Press, 1980.

——. "The 'Perfect Magistrate': Parlementaires and Crime in Sixteenth-Century Rouen." *Archiv für Reformationsgeschichte* 67 (1976): 284–300.

Dexter, Greta. "Guillaume de la Perrière." *Bibliothèque d'humanisme et renaissance* 17 (1955): 56–73.

Deyon, Pierre. *Le mercantilisme.* Paris: Flammarion, 1969.

Diefendorf, Barbara B. *Paris City Councilors in the Sixteenth Century: The Politics of Patrimony.* Princeton: Princeton University Press, 1983.

Di Piero, Thomas. *Dangerous Truths & Criminal Passions: The Evolution of the French Novel, 1569–1791.* Stanford, CA: Stanford University Press, 1992.

Dillinger, Johannes, and Petra Feld. "Treasure Hunting: A Magical Motif in Law, Folklore, and Mentality, Württemberg, 1606–1770." *German History* 20 (2002): 161–84.

Doucet, Roger. *Finances municipales et crédit public à Lyon au XVIe siècle.* Geneva: Mégariotis, 1980 [1937].

——. *Les institutions du France au XVIe siècle.* 2 vols. Paris: J. Picard, 1948.

Drew-Bear, Annette. "Cosmetics and Attitudes towards Women in the Seventeenth Century." *Journal of Popular Culture* 9 (1975): 31–37.

Duncan, Edgar H. "The Literature of Alchemy and Chaucer's Canon's Yeoman's Tale: Framework, Theme, and Characters." *Speculum* 43 (1968): 633–56.

Duplessis, Robert S. *Transitions to Capitalism in Early Modern Europe.* Cambridge: Cambridge University Press, 1997.

Dupont-Ferrier, Gustave. *Les officiers des bailliages et sénéchaussées et les institutions monarchiques locales en France à la fin du moyen âge.* Paris : E. Bouillon, 1902

Egmond, Florike. *Underworlds: Organized Crime in the Netherlands, 1650–1800.* Cambridge: Polity Press, 1993.

Elliott, J. H. *The Old World and the New, 1492–1650.* Cambridge: Cambridge University Press, 1970.

——. "Self-Perception and Decline in Early Seventeenth-Century Spain." *Past & Present* 74 (1977): 41–61.

Elton, G. R. "Reform and the 'Commonwealth-Men' of Edward VI's Reign." In *The English Commonwealth, 1547–1640: Essays in Politics and Society Presented to Joel Hurstfield*, edited by Peter Clark, Alan G. R. Smith, and Nicholas Tyack, 23–38. New York: Barnes and Noble, 1979.

Engster, Dan. "The Montaignian Moment." *Journal of the History of Ideas* 59 (1998): 625–50.

Ertman, Thomas. *Birth of the Leviathan: Building States and Regimes in Medieval and Early Modern Europe.* Cambridge: Cambridge University Press, 1997.

Espiner-Scott, Janet Girvan. *Claude Fauchet: Sa vie, son œuvre.* Paris: Droz, 1938.

Evans, Richard J. *Rituals of Retribution: Capital Punishment in Germany, 1600–1987.* Oxford: Oxford University Press, 1996.

Evans, R. J. W. *Rudolf II and His World: A Study in Intellectual History, 1676–1612.* Oxford: Clarendon Press, 1973.

Farr, James R. "The Death of a Judge: Performance, Honor, and Legitimacy in Seventeenth-Century France." *Journal of Modern History* 75 (2003): 1–22.

——. *Hands of Honor: Artisans and Their World in Dijon, 1550–1650.* Ithaca, NY: Cornell University Press, 1988.

——. *A Tale of Two Murders: Passion and Power in Seventeenth-Century France*. Durham, NC: Duke University Press, 2005.

Feller, Laurent. *Faux-monnayeurs et fausses monnaies en France à la fin du moyen âge (seconde moitié du XVe siècle)*. Paris: Le léopard d'or, 1986.

Finkelstein, Andrea. *The Grammar of Profit: The Price Revolution in Intellectual Context*. Leiden: Brill, 2006.

Finley, M. I. "Aristotle and Economic Analysis." *Past and Present* 47 (1970): 3–25.

Fogel, Michèle. *Les cérémonies de l'information dans la France du XVIe au milieu du XVIIIe siècle*. Paris: Fayard, 1989.

——. "Modèle d'Etat et modèle sociale de dépense: Les lois somptuaires en France de 1485 à 1660." In *Genèse de l'état moderne: Prélèvement et redistribution. Actes du colloque de Fontevraud 1984*, 226–35. Paris: Editions du C.N.R.S., 1987.

Fontaine, Laurence. *L'Economie morale. Pauvreté, crédit et confiance dans l'Europe préindustrielle*. Paris: Gallimard, 2008.

Ford, Philip. *Ronsard's* Hymnes: *A Literary and Iconographical Study*. Tempe, AZ: Medieval and Renaissance Texts and Studies, 1997.

Forman, Valerie. "Counterfeit Investments: Economy and Sovereignty in Early Modern Texts." PhD diss., University of California Santa Cruz, 2000.

——. "Marked Angels: Counterfeits, Commodities, and The Roaring Girl." *Renaissance Quarterly* 54 (2001): 1531–60.

Foucault, Michel. "Governmentality." In *The Foucault Effect: Studies in Governmentality*, edited by Graham Burchell, Colin Gordon, and Peter Miller, 87–104. Chicago: University of Chicago Press, 1991.

——. *Les mots et les choses: Une archéologie des sciences humaines*. Paris: Gallimard, 1966.

——. *Surveiller et punir: Naissance de la prison*. Paris: Gallimard, 1975.

Frevert, Ute. *Emotions in History: Lost and Found*. New York: Central European University Press, 2011.

Friedman, Lionel J. "The *Ubi Sunt*, the *Regrets*, and *Efficitio*." *Modern Language Notes* 72 (1957): 499–505.

Friedman, Milton, and Anna Jacobson Schwartz. *A Monetary History of the United States, 1867–1960*. Princeton: Princeton University Press, 1963.

Frohock, W. M. "The 'Picaresque' in France before *Gil Blas*." *Yale French Studies* 38 (1967): 222–29.

Fromage, R. "Clément Marot—Son premier emprisonnement, identification d'Isabeau et d'Anne." *Bulletin de la société de l'histoire du protestantisme français*, 5th ser., 8 (1910): 52–71.

Fuller, Mary C. "Ralegh's Fugitive Gold: Reference and Deferral in *The Discoverie of Guiana*." *Representations* 33 (1991): 42–64.

Fumaroli, Marc. *Le poète et le roi: Jean de La Fontaine en son siècle*. Paris: Editions de Fallois, 1997.

Ferguson, Arthur B. *The Articulate Citizen and the English Renaissance*. Durham, NC: Duke University Press, 1965.

Gambino, Luigi. *Un progetto di Stato perfetto: "La monarchie aristodemocratique" di Turquet de Mayerne (1611)*. Turin: G. Giappichelli Editore, 2000.

Gaskill, Malcolm. *Crime and Mentalities in Early Modern England*. Cambridge Studies in Early Modern British History. Cambridge: Cambridge University Press, 2000.

Gauvard, Claude. *"De grace especial:" Crime, état et société en France à la fin du moyen âge.* 2 vols. Paris: Publications de la Sorbonne, 1991.

Gay, Jean-Pascal. "Les paradoxes d'un réseau institutionnalisé: Les jésuites français et la théologie morale ibérique et italienne au XVIIe siècle." *SOURCE(S): Cahiers de l'équipe de recherche Arts, Civilisation et Histoire de l'Europe* 1 (2012): 31–44. http://ea3400.unistra.fr/fileadmin/upload/DUN/ea_3400/Revue_sources/source-s-2012-1.pdf.

Génaux, Maryvonne. "La corruption avant la lettre: La vocabulaire de la déviance public dans l'ancien droit pénal." *Revue historique de droit français et étranger* 81 (2003): 15–32.

Giesey, Ralph. *The Royal Funeral Ceremony in Renaissance France.* Geneva: Droz, 1960.

Glassman, Debra, and Angela Redish. "Currency Depreciation in Early Modern England and France." *Explorations in Economic History* 25 (1988): 75–97.

——. "New Estimates of the Money Stock in France, 1493–1680." *Journal of Economic History* 45 (1985): 31–46.

Godefroy-Ménilglaise, D. C. *Les savants Godefroy: Mémoires d'une famille pendant les XVIe, XVIIe et XVIIIe siècles.* Paris: Didier, 1873; facs. rpt., Geneva: Slatkine, 1971.

Goldmann, Lucien. *Le dieu caché; étude sur la vision tragique dans les Pensées de Pascal et dans le théâtre de Racine.* Paris: Gallimard, 1955.

Gould, J. D. *The Great Debasement: Currency and the Economy in Mid-Tudor England.* Oxford: Clarendon Press, 1970.

Goux, Jean-Joseph. *Freud, Marx: Economie et symbolique.* Paris: Editions du seuil, 1973.

——. "Language, Money, Father, Phallus in Cyrano de Bergerac's Utopia." *Representations* 23 (1988): 105–17.

Graeber, David. *Debt: The First 5,000 Years.* New York: Melville House, 2011.

Grafton, Anthony. *New Worlds, Ancient Texts: The Power of Tradition and the Shock of Discovery.* Cambridge, MA: Belknap Press, 1992.

Grande, Nathalie. "Un bourgeois gentilhomme? Noblesse et société selon Francion." *Littératures* 43 (2000): 95–105.

Greenblatt, Stephen. *Learning to Curse: Essays in Early Modern Culture.* London: Routledge, 1990.

——. *Marvelous Possessions: The Wonder of the New World.* Chicago: University of Chicago Press, 1991.

——. *Shakespearian Negotiations: The Circulation of Social Energy in Renaissance England.* Berkeley: University of California Press, 1988.

——. *Sir Walter Ralegh: The Renaissance Man and His Roles.* New Haven: Yale University Press, 1973.

Greengrass, Mark. *Governing Passions: Peace and Reform in the French Kingdom, 1576–1585.* Oxford: Oxford University Press, 2007.

——. "Money, Majesty, and Virtue: The Rhetoric of Monetary Reform in Later Sixteenth-Century France." *French History* 21 (2007): 165–86.

——. "The Sixteen, Radical Politics in Paris during the League." *History* 69 (1984): 432–39.

Greenshields, Malcolm. *An Economy of Violence: Crime and Justice in the Haute Auvergne, 1587–1664.* State College: Pennsylvania State University Press, 1994.

Grendi, Edoardo. "Falsa monetazione e strutture monetarie degli scambi nella Repubblica de Genova fra cinque e seicento." *Quaderni storici* 66 (1987): 803–37.

Guéry, Alain, ed. *Montchrestien et Cantillon: Le commerce et l'émergence d'une pensée économique*. Paris: E.N.S. Editions, 2011.

Guggenheim, Thomas. *Preclassical Monetary Theories*. New York: Pinter Publishers, 1989.

Halpern, Richard. *The Poetics of Primitive Accumulation: English Renaissance Culture and the Genealogy of Capital*. Ithaca, NY: Cornell University Press, 1991.

Hamilton, Charles D. "The Tresviri Monetales and the Republican Cursus Honorum." *Transactions and Proceedings of the American Philological Association* 100 (1969): 181–99.

Hamilton, Earl J. *American Treasure and the Price Revolution in Spain, 1501–1650*. Cambridge, MA: Harvard University Press, 1934.

Hamon, Philippe. *L'argent du roi: Les finances sous François Ier*. Paris: Comité pour l'histoire économique et financière de la France, 1994.

Hamon-Porter, Brigitte. "Dassoucy, picaro, libertin et honnête homme des *Aventures*." In *Avez-vous lu Dassoucy? Actes du colloque international de Centre d'Etudes sur les Réformes, l'Humanisme et l'Âge classique, Clermont-Ferrand, 25–26 juin 2004*, edited by Dominique Bertrand, 177–88. Clermont-Ferrand: Presses Universitaires Blaise Pascal, 2005.

Hampton, Timothy. *Literature and Nation in the Sixteenth Century: Inventing Renaissance France*. Ithaca, NY: Cornell University Press, 2001.

———. "The Subject of America: History and Alterity in Montaigne's 'Des coches.'" In *The Project of Prose in Early Modern Europe and the New World*, edited by Elizabeth Fowler and Roland Green, 80–103. Cambridge: Cambridge University Press, 1997.

Hamy, M. E.-T. "Un précurseur de Guy de la Brosse: Jacques Gohory et le Lycium philosophal de Saint-Marceau-lès-Paris (1571–1576)." *Nouvelles archives du Muséum*, 4th ser., 1 (1899): 1–26.

Hanawalt, Barbara, ed. *Women and Work in Preindustrial Europe*. Bloomington: Indiana University Press, 1986.

Hankins, James. *Plato in the Italian Renaissance*. 2 vols. Leiden: E.J. Brill, 1990.

Harding, Robert. *Anatomy of a Power Elite: The Provincial Governors of Early Modern France*. New Haven: Yale University Press, 1978.

Hardwick, Julie. *Family Business: Litigation and the Political Economies of Daily Life in Early Modern France*. Oxford: Oxford University Press, 2009.

Harkness, Deborah. *The Jewel House: Elizabethan London and the Scientific Revolution*. New Haven: Yale University Press, 2007.

———. *John Dee's Conversations with Angels: Cabala, Alchemy, and the End of Nature*. Cambridge: Cambridge University Press, 1999.

Harrison, Helen L. *Pistoles/Paroles: Money and Language in Seventeenth-Century French Comedy*. Chalottesville, VA: Rookwood Press, 1996.

Harsin, Paul. *Les doctrines monétaires et financières en France du XVIe au XVIIIe siècle*. Paris: Félix Alcan, 1928.

Haskell, Francis. *History and Its Images: Art and the Interpretation of the Past*. New Haven: Yale University Press, 1995 [1993].

Hautebert, Joël. "L'affaire Bois Chevalier: Procès d'un magistrat sous le règne de Louis XIV." *Revue historique de droit français et étranger* 77 (1999): 519–31.

Hayden, J. Michael. *France and the Estates General of 1614*. Cambridge: Cambridge University Press, 1974.

Heckscher, Eli. *Mercantilism*. 2 vols. London: Allen and Unwin, 1955.

Heller, Henry. *Labour, Science, and Technology in France, 1500–1620*. Cambridge: Cambridge University Press, 1996.

Hexter, J. H. *The Vision of Politics on the Eve of the Reformation: More, Machiavelli and Seyssel*. New York: Basic Books, 1973.

Hirschman, Albert O. *The Passions and the Interests: Political Arguments for Capitalism before Its Triumph*. Princeton: Princeton University Press, 1996 [1976].

Hocking, W. J. "Simon's Dies in the Royal Mint Museum, with some Notes on the Early History of Coinage Machinery." *Numismatic Chronicle*, 4th ser., 9 (1909): 56–118.

Hoffman, Philip T. *Growth in a Traditional Society: The French Countryside, 1450–1815*. Princeton: Princeton University Press, 1996.

Hoffman, Philip T., Gilles Postel-Vinay, and Jean-Laurent Rosenthal. *Priceless Markets: The Political Economy of Credit in Paris, 1660–1870*. Chicago: University of Chicago Press, 2000.

Holt, Mack. *The French Wars of Religion, 1562–1629*. 2nd ed. Cambridge: Cambridge University Press, 2005.

——, ed. *Renaissance and Reformation France, 1500–1648*. Oxford: Oxford University Press, 2002.

Hooper, Wilfrid. "The Tudor Sumptuary Laws." *English Historical Review* 30 (1915): 433–49.

Hunt, Alan. *Governance of the Consuming Passions: A History of Sumptuary Law*. New York: St. Martin's, 1996.

Huppert, George. *Les Bourgeois gentilshommes: An Essay on the Definition of Elites in Renaissance France*. Chicago: University of Chicago Press, 1977.

Jardine, Lisa. *Worldly Goods: A New History of the Renaissance*. New York: Norton, 1996.

Jardine, Lisa, and Alan Stewart. *Hostage to Fortune: The Troubled Life of Francis Bacon*. New York: Hill and Wang, 1999.

Jeanneret, Michel. *Perpetual Motion: Transforming Shapes in the Renaissance from de Vinci to Montaigne*. Translated by Nidra Poller. Baltimore: Johns Hopkins University Press, 2001.

Jollet, Etienne. *Jean & François Clouet*. Translated by Deke Dusinberre. Paris: Lagune, 1997.

Kahn, Didier. *Alchimie et paracelcisme en France à la fin de la renaissance (1567–1625)*. Geneva: Droz, 2007.

——. "The Rosicrucian Hoax in France (1623–24)." In *Secrets of Nature: Astrology and Alchemy in Early Modern Europe*, edited by William R. Newman and Anthony Grafton, 235–344. Cambridge, MA: M.I.T. Press, 2001.

Kantorowicz, Ernst. *The King's Two Bodies: A Study in Medieval Political Theology*. Princeton: Princeton University Press, 1957.

——. "Mysteries of State: An Absolutist Concept and Its Late Mediaeval Origins." *Harvard Theological Review* 48 (1955): 65–91.

Kaye, Joel. *Economy and Nature in the Fourteenth Century: Money, Market Exchange, and the Emergence of Scientific Thought*. Cambridge: Cambridge University Press, 1998.

Keynes, John Maynard. *A Treatise on Money*. 2 vols. New York: Harcourt, Brace, 1930.

Kierstead, Raymond F. *Pomponne de Bellièvre: A Study of the King's Men in the Age of Henry IV*. Evanston, IL: Northwestern University Press, 1968.

Killerby, Catherine Kovesi. "Practical Problems in the Enforcement of Italian Sumptuary Law, 1200–1500." In *Crime, Society and the Law in Renaissance Italy*, edited by Trevor Dean and K. J. P. Lowe, 99–120. Cambridge: Cambridge University Press, 1994.

Kleinclausz, A. et al. *Histoire de Lyon*. Vol. 1, *Des orgines à 1595*. Lyons: Pierre Masson, 1939.

Klosko, George, ed. *The Oxford Handbook of the History of Political Philosophy*. Oxford: Oxford University Press, 2011.

Knapp, Georg Friedrich. *The State Theory of Money*. Edited by H. M. Lucas and J. Bonar. London: Macmillan, 1924.

Knecht, R. J. *Renaissance Warrior and Patron: The Reign of Francis I*. Cambridge: Cambridge University Press, 1994.

Krynen, Jacques. *L'idéologie de la magistrature ancienne*. Paris: N.R.F. Gallimard, 2009.

Labrot, Jacques. *Une histoire économique et populaire du moyen âge: Les jetons et les méreaux*. Paris: Editions Errance, 1989.

Lalanne, Ludovic. *Brantôme, sa vie et ses écrits*. Paris: Renouard, 1896.

Lanoë, Catherine. "Images, masques et visages. Production et consommation des cosmétiques à Paris sous l'Ancien Régime." *Revue d'histoire moderne et contemporaine* 35 (2008): 7–27.

———. *La poudre et le fard: Une histoire des cosmétiques de la Renaissance aux Lumières*. Paris: Champ Vallon, 2008.

Lawrence, Richard Hoe. *The Paduans: Medals by Giovanni Cavino*. Hewitt, NJ: Hellenic-Roman Coins, n.d.

Le Blanc, François. *Traité historique des monnoyes de France*. Paris: Pierre Ribon, 1703.

Le Goff, Jacques. *La bourse et la vie: Economie et religion au moyen age. Textes du XXe siècle*. Paris: Hachette, 1986.

Leiner, Wolfgang. "Regards critiques sur le statut picaresque du *Francion*." In *Création et recréation: Un dialogue entre littérature et histoire. Mélanges offerts à Marie-Odile Sweetser*, edited by Claire Gaudiani and Jacqueline Van Baelen, 209–21. Tübingen: Narr, 1993.

Lemercier, Pierre. *Les justices seigneuriales de la région parisienne de 1580 à 1789*. Paris: Domat-Montchrestien, 1933.

Lenman, Bruce, and Geoffrey Parker. "The State, the Community, and the Criminal Law in Early Modern Europe." In *Crime and the Law: The Social History of Crime in Western Europe since 1500*, edited by V. A. C. Gatrell, Bruce Lenman, and Geoffrey Parker, 11–48. London: Europa Publications, 1980.

Levenson, Thomas. *Newton and the Counterfeiter: The Unknown Detective Career of the World's Greatest Scientist*. Boston: Houghton Mifflin Harcourt, 2009.

Little, Lester K. "Pride Goes before Avarice: Social Change and the Vices in Latin Christendom." *American Historical Review* 76 (1971): 16–49.

Lloansi, Bernard. "La répression du faux-monnayage en Roussillon aux XVIIe–XVIIIe siècles." In *Les faux en numismatique*, 37–70. Journées d'études numismatiques 12. Perpignan: Musée Numismatique Joseph Puig, 1997.

Loomis, Catherine. *The Death of Elizabeth I: Remembering and Reconstructing the Virgin Queen*. New York: Palgrave MacMillan, 2012.

Magnusson, Lars. *Mercantilism: The Shaping of an Economic Language*. London: Routledge, 1994.

Major, J. Russell. "Bellièvre, Sully, and the Assembly of Notables of 1596." *Transactions of the American Philosophical Society*, n.s., 64, pt. 2 (1974): 3–34.

———. *From Renaissance Monarchy to Absolute Monarchy: French Kings, Nobles, and Estates*. Baltimore: Johns Hopkins University Press, 1994.

Margolin, J.-C. "L'Hymne de l'or' et son ambigüité." *Bibliothèque d'humanisme et renaissance* 28 (1966): 271–93.

Marin, Louis. *Le portrait du roi*. Paris: Editions de minuit, 1981.

Martin, Germain. "La monnaie et le crédit privé en France aux XVIe et XVIIe siècles; les faits et les théories (1550–1664)." *Revue d'histoire des doctrines économiques et sociales* 2 (1909): 1–40.

Maugis, Edouard. *Histoire du Parlement de Paris de l'avènement des rois Valois à la mort d'Henri IV*. 3 vols. Paris: A. Picard, 1913–16.

Marx, Karl. *Capital: A Critique of Political Economy*. 3 vols. New York: International Publishers, 1967.

———. *The Communist Manifesto*. Edited by Frederic Bender. New York: Norton, 1988.

Maza, Sarah. *The Myth of the French Bourgeoisie: An Essay on the Social Imaginary, 1750–1850*. Cambridge, MA: Harvard University Press, 2003.

Meikle, Scott. *Aristotle's Economic Thought*. Oxford: Clarendon Press, 1995.

Melish, Jacob. "The Power of Wives: Managing Money and Men in the Family Businesses of Old Regime Paris." In *Enterprising Women: Gender, Agency and Work in Eighteenth-Century France*. Baton Rouge: Louisiana State University Press, forthcoming.

———. "Women and the Courts in the Control of Violence between Men: Evidence from a Parisian Neighborhood under Louis XIV." *French Historical Studies* 33 (2010): 1–31.

Menchi, Seidel, and Diego Quagliioni. *Trasgressioni: Seduzione, concubinato, adulterio, bigamia (xiv–xviii secolo)*. Bologna: Il Mulino, 2004.

Merlin, Pier Paolo. *Emanuele Filiberto*. Turin: SEI, 1995.

Michaud, Hélène. *La grande chancellerie et les écritures royales au XVIe siècle 1515–1589*. Paris: Presses universitaires de France, 1967.

Minard, Philippe, and Denis Woronoff, eds. *L'Argent des campagnes: Echanges, monnaie, crédit dans la France rurale d'Ancien Régime. Journée d'études tenue à Bercy le 18 décembre 2000*. Paris: Comité pour l'histoire économique et financière de la France, 2003.

Miskimin, Harry A. *Money and Power in Fifteenth-Century France*. New Haven: Yale University Press, 1984.

Mollenauer, Lynn Wood. *Strange Revelations: Magic, Poison, and Sacrilege in Louis XIV's France*. University Park: Pennsylvania State University Press, 2007.

Mongrédien, Georges. *Le bourreau du Cardinal de Richelieu: Isaac de Laffemas (documents inédits)*. Paris: Editions Bossard, 1929.

Monnier, Louis. "Causes et conséquences économiques de la Saint-Barthélemy: Etude sur le système monétaire en France de 1568 à 1578." In *Actes du colloque l'Amiral de Coligny et son temps (Paris, 24–28 octobre 1972)*, 651–701. Paris: Société de l'histoire du protestantisme français, 1974.

Monter, William. *Judging the French Reformation: Heresy Trials by Sixteenth-Century Parlements.* Cambridge, MA: Harvard University Press, 1999.

Motomura, Akira. "The Best and Worst of Currencies: Seigniorage and Currency Policy in Spain, 1597–1650." *Journal of Economic History* 54 (1994): 104–27.

Mousnier, Roland. *L'assassinat d'Henri IV: Le problème de tyrannicide et l'affermissement de la monarchie absolue.* Paris: N.R.F. Gallimard, 1964.

——. "L'opposition politique bourgeoise à la fin du XVIe siècle et au début du XVIIe siècle: L'œuvre de Louis Turquet de Mayerne." *Revue historique* 213 (1955): 1–20.

——. "Sully et le Conseil d'Etat et des finances: La lutte entre Bellièvre et Sully." *Revue historique* 192 (1942): 68–85.

——. *La vénalité des offices sous Henri IV et Louis XIII.* 2nd ed. Paris: Presses universitaires de France, 1971.

Moyes, Craig. "Juste(s) titre(s): L'économie liminaire du *Roman bourgeois.*" *Etudes françaises* 45 (2009): 25–46.

Muir, Edward. *Civic Ritual in Renaissance Venice.* Princeton: Princeton University Press, 1982.

Muldrew, Craig. *The Economy of Obligation: The Culture of Credit and Social Relations in Early Modern England.* London: St. Martin's, 1998.

——. "'Hard Food for Midas': Cash and Its Social Value in Early Modern England." *Past and Present* 170 (2001): 78–120.

Nagle, Jean. *Le droit de marc d'or des offices: Tarifs de 1583, 1704, 1748. Reconnaissance, fidélité, noblesse.* Geneva: Droz, 1992.

——. "Furetière entre la magistrature et les bénéfices: Autour du Second Livre du *Roman bourgeois.*" *XVII Siècle* 128 (1980): 293–305.

——. *Un orgueil français: La vénalité des offices sous l'Ancien Régime.* Paris: Odile Jacob, 2008.

Nef, John U. *Industry and Government in France and England, 1540–1640.* Ithaca, NY: Cornell University Press, 1957.

Nelson, Eric. *The Greek Tradition in Republican Thought.* Ideas in Context 69. Cambridge: Cambridge University Press, 2004.

——. *The Jesuits and the Monarchy: Catholic Reform and Political Authority in France (1590–1615).* Aldershot, UK, and Rome: Ashgate and Institutum Historicum Societatis Iesu, 2005.

Nelson, Robert J. "Pierre Corneille's *L'Illusion comique*: The Play as Magic." *Proceedings of the Modern Language Association* 71 (1956): 1127–40.

Newman, William R. *Gehennical Fire: The Lives of George Starkey, an Alchemist in the Scientific Revolution.* Chicago: University of Chicago Press, 2003.

——. *Promethean Ambitions: Alchemy and the Quest to Perfect Nature.* Chicago: University of Chicago Press, 2004.

Nicholls, Charles. *The Reckoning: The Murder of Christopher Marlowe.* Chicago: University of Chicago Press, 1995.

Nummedal, Tara E. *Alchemy and Authority in the Holy Roman Empire.* Chicago: University of Chicago Press, 2007.

——. "The Problem of Fraud in Early Modern Alchemy." In *Shell Games: Studies in Scams, Frauds, and Deceits (1300–1650),* edited by Mark Crane, Richard

Raiswell, and Margaret Reeves, 37–58. Toronto: Centre for Reformation and Renaissance Studies, 2004.

Oestreich, Gerhard. *Neostoicism and the Early Modern State.* Translated by David Mc-Klintock. Cambridge: Cambridge University Press, 1982.

Pagden, Anthony. *European Encounters with the New World: From Renaissance to Romanticism.* New Haven: Yale University Press, 1994.

Palonen, Kari. *Quentin Skinner: History, Politics, Rhetoric.* Cambridge: Polity Press, 2003.

Paré, François. "L'écriture et l'échange économique dans *Les Regrets* de du Bellay." *Renaissance and Reformation/Rénaissance et réforme* 9 (1985): 255–62.

Parker, Geoffrey. *The Military Revolution: Military Innovation and the Rise of the West, 1500–1800.* 2nd ed. Cambridge: Cambridge University Press, 1996.

Parsons, Jotham. "Etat Présent: Socio-economic Approaches to French Literature, c. 1540–1630." *French Studies* 65 (2011): 74–81.

———. "Governing Sixteenth-Century France: The Monetary Reforms of 1577." *French Historical Studies* 21 (2003): 1–30.

———. "Money and Merit in French Renaissance Comedy." *Renaissance Quarterly* 60 (2007): 852–82.

———. "Money and Sovereignty in Early Modern France." *Journal of the History of Ideas* 62 (2001): 59–79.

Phelps-Brown, E. H., and Sheila Hopkins, "Wage Rates and Prices: Evidence for Price Pressure in the Sixteenth Century." *Economica,* n.s., 24 (1957): 289–306.

Phillippy, Patricia. *Painting Women: Cosmetics, Canvases, and Early Modern Culture.* Baltimore: Johns Hopkins University Press, 2006.

Picard, Olivier. "Aristote et la monnaie." *Ktema* 5 (1980): 267–76.

Pintard, René. "Aspects et contours du libertinage: Les problèmes de l'histoire du libertinage, notes et réflexions." *XVIIe siècle* 127 (1980): 131–61.

———. *Le libertinage érudit dans la première moitié du dix-septième siècle.* Paris: Boivin, 1943.

Pitts, Vincent J. *Henri IV of France: His Reign and Age.* Baltimore: Johns Hopkins University Press, 2009.

Plessix-Buisset, Christiane. *Le criminel devant ses juges en Bretagne aux 16e et 17e siècles.* Paris: Editeur Maloine, 1988.

Pocock, J. G. A. *Barbarism and Religion.* Vol. 1, *The Enlightenments of Edward Gibbon, 1737–1764.* Cambridge: Cambridge University Press, 1999.

———. *The Machiavellian Moment: Florentine Political Thought and the Atlantic Republican Tradition.* Princeton: Princeton University Press, 1975.

Polanyi, Karl. *Primitive, Archaic and Modern Economies: Essays of Karl Polanyi.* Edited by George Dalton. Boston: Beacon Press, 1969.

Poncet, Olivier. *Pomponne de Bellièvre (1529–1607): Un homme d'état au temps des Guerres de religion.* Paris: Editions de l'Ecole des Chartes, 1998.

Potter, David. "A Treason Trial in Sixteenth-Century France: The Fall of Marshal du Biez, 1549–51." *English Historical Review* 105 (1990): 595–623.

Price, Russell. "*Ambizione* in Machiavelli's Thought." *History of Political Thought* 3 (1982): 383–445.

———. "Self-love, 'Egoism,' and *Ambizione* in Machiavelli's Thought." *History of Political Thought* 9 (1998): 237–61.

Principe, Lawrence. *The Aspiring Adept: Robert Boyle and His Alchemical Quest.* Princeton: Princeton University Press, 1998.

Prodi, Paolo. *Settimo non rubare: Furto e mercato nella storia dell'Occidente.* Bologna: Il Mulino, 2009.

Quilliet, Bernard. "Les corps d'officiers de la prévôté et vicomté de Paris et de l'Ile-de-France, de la fin de la Guerre de cent ans au début des Guerres de religion: étude sociale." Doctoral diss., University of Paris 4, 1977.

Raeff, Marc. *The Well-Ordered Police State: Social and Institutional Change through Law in the Germanies and Russia, 1600–1800.* New Haven: Yale University Press, 1983.

Ramsey, Anne W. *Liturgy, Politics, and Salvation: The Catholic League in Paris and the Nature of Catholic Reform, 1540–1630.* Rochester, NY: University of Rochester Press, 1999.

Ramsey, Peter H., ed. *The Price Revolution in Sixteenth-Century England.* London: Methuen, 1971.

Ranum, Orest. *Artisans of Glory: Writers and Historical Thought in Seventeenth-Century France.* Chapel Hill: University of North Carolina Press, 1980.

Raveau, R. "La crise des prix au XVIe siècle en Poitou." *Revue historique* 162 (1929): 1–44 and 268–93.

Richet, Denis. "Le cours officiel des monnaies étrangères circulant en France au XVIe siècle." *Revue historique* 225 (1961): 359–96.

———. *De la réforme à la révolution: Etudes sur la France moderne.* Paris: Aubier, 1991.

Rosanbo, L. de. "Pierre Pithou érudit." *Revue du XVIe siècle* 16 (1929): 301–30.

Rosenwein, Barbara H. "Worrying about Emotions in History." *American Historical Review* 107 (2002): 821–45.

Rothkrug, Lionel. *Opposition to Louis XIV: The Political and Social Origins of the French Enlightenment.* Princeton: Princeton University Press, 1965.

Rowlands, Guy. *The Financial Decline of a Great Power: War, Influence, and Money in Louis XIV's France.* Oxford: Oxford University Press, 2012.

Rublack, Ulinka. *The Crimes of Women in Early Modern Germany.* Oxford: Clarendon Press, 2001.

Salmon, J. H. M. "The Legacy of Jean Bodin: Absolutism, Populism or Constitutionalism?" *History of Political Thought* 17 (1996): 500–522.

———. "The Paris Sixteen: The Social Analysis of a Revolutionary Movement." *Journal of Modern History* 44 (1972): 540–76.

Sargent, Thomas J. *Rational Expectations and Inflation.* 2nd ed. New York: Harper and Row, 1993.

Sargent, Thomas J., and François R. Velde. *The Big Problem of Small Change.* Princeton: Princeton University Press, 2002.

Saulcy, F. de. *Histoire numismatique du règne de François I, roi de France.* Paris: Librairie numismatique C. van Peteghem, 1876.

Sawyer, Jeffrey. "Judicial Corruption and Legal Reform in Early Seventeenth-Century France." *Law and History Review* 6 (1988): 95–117.

Schalk, Ellery. *From Valor to Pedigree: Ideas of Nobility in France in the Sixteenth and Seventeenth Centuries.* Princeton: Princeton University Press, 1986.

Schmitt, Charles B. *Aristotle in the Renaissance.* Cambridge, MA: Harvard University Press for Oberlin College, 1983.

Schnapper, Bernard. *Les peines arbitraires du XIIIe au XVIIIe siècle (doctrines savants et usages français).* Paris: R. Pichon et R. Durand-Auzias, 1974.

Schumpeter, Joseph. *History of Economic Analysis.* New York: Oxford University Press, 1954.

Sciacca, Enzo. "Forme di governo e forma della società nel' 'Miroire politique' di Guillaume de la Perrière." *Pensiero politico* 22 (1989): 174–97.

——. *Umanesimo e scienza politica nella Francia del XVI secolo: Loys le Roy.* Florence: Leo S. Olschki, 2007.

Sczlechter, Emil. "La monnaie en France au XVI siècle," pt. 1. *Revue historique du droit français et étranger* 19 (1951): 501–21.

Secret, François. "Littérature et alchimie à la fin du XVIe et au début du XVIIe siècle." *Bibliothèque d'humanisme et renaissance* 35 (1973): 103–16.

Serroy, Jean. "Francion et l'argent, ou l'immoraliste et les faux monnayeurs." *XVIIe siècle* 105 (1974): 3–18.

Servet, Jean-Michel. "Malestroit. Eléments pour une biographie." In *Pratiques et pensées monétaires*, 97–114. Monnaie et financement 15. Lyons: Université de Lyon 2, 1985.

Shell, Marc. *The Economy of Literature.* Baltimore: Johns Hopkins University Press, 1978.

Simmel, Georg. *The Philosophy of Money.* Translated by Tom Bottomore, David Frisby, and Kaethe Mengelberg. 2nd ed. London: Routledge, 1990.

Simms, Brendan. "The Return of the Primacy of Foreign Policy." *German History* 21 (2003): 275–91.

Skinner, Quentin. *Visions of Politics.* Vol. 2, *Renaissance Virtues.* Cambridge: Cambridge University Press, 2002.

Smith, David Kammerling. "Structuring Politics in Early Eighteenth-Century France: The Political Innovations of the French Council of Commerce." *Journal of Modern History* 74 (2002): 490–537.

Smith, Pamela H. *The Business of Alchemy: Science and Culture in the Holy Roman Empire.* Princeton: Princeton University Press, 1994.

Smith, Pamela H., and Paula Findlen, eds. *Merchants and Marvels: Commerce, Science and Art in Early Modern Europe.* New York: Routledge, 2002.

Smyth, William Henry. *Descriptive Catalog of a Cabinet of Roman-Imperial Large Brass Medals.* Bedford, UK: James Webb, 1834.

Soman, Alfred. "The Parlement of Paris and the Great Witch Hunt (1565–1640)." *Sixteenth-Century Journal* 9 (1978): 30–44.

Sombart, Stéphan. "De nouvelles précisions sur les liards d'Henri IV." *Bulletin de la Société française de numismatique* 52 (November 1997). http://www.inumis.com/ressources/france/articles/sisteron/sisteron-fr.html.

Spang, Rebecca L. "The Ghost of Law: Speculating on Money, Memory and Mississippi in the French Constituent Assembly." *Historical Reflections* 31 (2005): 3–25.

Spooner, Frank C. *L'Economie mondiale et les frappes monétaires en France, 1493–1680.* Paris: Armand Colin, 1956.

Spufford, Peter. *Money and Its Use in Medieval Europe.* Cambridge: Cambridge University Press, 1988.

Styles, John. "'Our Traitorous Money Makers:' The Yorkshire Coiners and the Law, 1760–83." In *An Ungovernable People: The English and Their Law in the*

Seventeenth and Eighteenth Centuries, edited by John Brewer and John Styles, 172–249. New Brunswick, NJ: Rutgers University Press, 1980.

Suozzo, Andrew. "La bourgeoisie à la recherche de la noblesse: Le libertinage de l'*Histoire comique de Francion*." *Littératures classiques* 41 (2001): 31–40.

Taber, Linda L. "Religious Dissent within the Parlement of Paris in the Mid-Sixteenth Century: A Reassessment." *French Historical Studies* 16 (1990): 684–99.

Thirsk, Joan. *Economic Policy and Projects: The Development of a Consumer Society in Early Modern England*. Oxford: Clarendon Press, 1978.

Thompson, A. A. "A Map of Crime in Sixteenth-Century Spain." *Economic History Review*, 2nd ser., 21 (1968): 244–76.

Thomson, Erik M. "Chancellor Oxenstierna, Cardinal Richelieu, and Commerce: The Problems and Possibilities of Governance in Early-Seventeenth-Century France and Sweden." PhD diss., Johns Hopkins University, 2004.

Todd, Margo. *Christian Humanism and the Puritan Social Order*. Cambridge: Cambridge University Press, 1987.

Todeschini, Giacomo. *Franciscan Wealth: From Voluntary Poverty to Market Society*. Translated by Donatella Melucci. St. Bonaventure, NY: Franciscan Institute, St. Bonaventure University, 2009.

Todorov, Tzvetan *The Conquest of America: The Question of the Other*. Translated by Richard Howard. Norman: University of Oklahoma Press, 1999.

Tournon, André, and G.-A. Perouse, eds. *Or, monnaie, échange dans la culture de la Renaissance. Actes du Neuvième Colloque International de l'Association Renaissance, Humanisme, Lyon 1991*. Saint-Etienne: Presses de l'Université de Saint-Etienne, 1994.

Trafton, Dain. "Ancients and Indians in Montaigne's 'Des coches.'" *Symposium* 27 (1973): 76–90.

Trevor-Roper, H. R. *Europe's Physician: The Various Life of Sir Theodore de Mayerne*. New Haven: Yale University Press, 2006.

Tucci, Ugo. *Mercanti, navi, monete nel cinquecento veneziano*. Bologna: Il Mulino, 1981.

Valenze, Deborah. *The Social Life of Money in the English Past*. Cambridge: Cambridge University Press, 2006.

van Ells, Paula Hartwig. "Alchemical Metaphor and Cyrano de Bergerac's Apology of the Imagination." *Cahiers du dix-septième* 7 (2000): 13–22.

Vilar, Pierre. *A History of Gold and Money, 1450–1920*. Translated by Judith White. London: Verso, 1991.

Walker, D. P. *Spiritual and Demonic Magic from Ficino to Campanella*. University Park: Pennsylvania State University, 2000 [1958].

Waquet, Jean-Claude. *Corruption: Ethics and Power in Florence, 1600–1770*. Translated by Linda McCall. University Park: Pennsylvania State University Press, 1992.

Weber, Max. *Economy and Society*. Edited by Guenther Roth and Claus Wittich. 2 vols. Berkeley: University of California Press, 1968.

———. *The Protestant Ethic and the Spirit of Capitalism*. Translated by Talcott Parsons. London: Routledge, 2001 [1930].

Welch, Evelyn. *Shopping in the Renaissance: Consumer Culture in Italy, 1400–1600*. New Haven: Yale University Press, 2005.

Wells, Charlotte. "Leeches on the Body Politic: Xenophobia and Witchcraft in Early Modern French Political Thought." *French Historical Studies* 22 (1999): 351–77.

Wernham, R. B. "Christopher Marlowe at Flushing in 1592." *English Historical Review* 91 (1976): 344–45.

Wolfe, Martin. *The Fiscal System of Renaissance France.* New Haven: Yale University Press, 1972.

Woodmansee, Martha, and Mark Osteen, eds. *The New Economic Criticism: Studies at the Intersection of Literature and Economics.* London: Routledge, 1999.

Worcester, Thomas. *Seventeenth Century Cultural Discourse: France and the Preaching of Bishop Camus.* Berlin: Mouton de Gruyter, 1997.

Wortham, Simon. "Sovereign Counterfeits: The Trial of the Pyx." *Renaissance Quarterly* 49 (1996): 334–59.

Yates, Frances. *Astraea: The Imperial Theme in the Sixteenth Century.* London: Routledge and Keegan Paul, 1975.

——. *The Rosicrucian Enlightenment.* New York: Routledge, 1972.

Youngs, Frederic A., Jr. *The Proclamations of the Tudor Queens.* Cambridge: Cambridge University Press, 1976.

Zeller, Gaston. *Les institutions de la France au XVIe siècle.* Paris: Presses universitaires de France, 1987.

Zelizer, Viviana. *The Social Meaning of Money.* New York: Basic Books, 1994.

Zorach, Rebecca. *Blood, Milk, Ink, Gold: Abundance and Excess in the French Renaissance.* Chicago: University of Chicago Press, 2005.

Index

Académie Française, 265n72, 273, 278, 280
Aides, Cour des. *See* Cour des Aides
alchemy, 9, 51, 130, 150, 194–95, 209–10,
  223–31, 240–48, 251–57, 259, 264–65,
  267, 271–73
Aléman, Mateo. *See* Guzmán de Alfarache
Alligret, Pierre, 47, 54, 99n124, 118
ambition. *See* avarice
Americas, 60–61, 71, 100, 179, 188–90. *See
  also* silver, American
Anet, 237, 257–59
Anjou, François de Valois, duc d', 3,
  155–56, 158
Aristotle, 14, 62–83, 102–3, 238, 287
assemblies, advisory, 131, 134–35, 139n114,
  161, 167; of Rouen, 166
Assézat, Pierre, 113–14
Augustine of Hippo, 77, 82, 242; monastic
  order of, 245
Auvergne, 146, 198
avarice, 15, 62, 76–86, 89–90, 92, 95–98,
  128, 138, 141, 172, 190, 192, 213, 234,
  242, 246, 248, 250–54, 260, 271, 279,
  287–88
Avignon, 20, 39, 42n84, 165n31, 231–32

banking, 107, 133, 149, 159, 166, 179n77
Bassano, da Ponte (family of painters),
  240–41
Baudry, Guillaume, 44n94, 54–55
Bayonne, 23n23, 44, 114n30, 133n90,
  142n124, 232
Becquet, Robert, 57, 102n131, 201n20
Bedant, Guy, 26
Begue, François le, 75–76, 154n3, 175–76,
  178, 180n82
Bellay, Joachim du, 249, 266
Bellièvre, Pomponne de, 134n92, 137n108,
  140–41, 145, 148, 157, 166, 169–71
Belordeau de la Grée, Pierre, 85–86
Béringhen, Pierre, 102–3, 169
Béroalde de Verville, François, 240, 245n22,
  246n23, 282

Béziers, 158–59, 164
Biel, Gabriel, 117
billon, 8, 20, 2–25, 106–9, 119, 135–36,
  139, 144, 148, 148n140, 161, 165, 230,
  270n85. *See also* copper coinage
bimetallic ratio, 75, 107, 109, 116–19,
  122–27, 138, 165, 169, 173n58, 175n63,
  176–77, 179
Birague, René de, 145, 228
Bizeul, Simon, 38n74, 53–54, 99n125,
  163n28, 167n41, 171, 200, 212–13
Bodin, Jean, 61, 75, 80n68, 90–92, 124–26,
  132, 173–75, 178n71, 179, 186, 247n27
boestes. *See* pyxes
Bordeaux, 43, 99n125, 114n30, 115, 133,
  143, 214n64, 215, 244
Bourgeois, Claude, 25–26, 33, 37
bourgeoisie, 1, 49–50, 57n141, 88, 145–46,
  161, 206, 209, 246, 250, 261. *See also*
  Furetière, Antoine; Marx, Karl; mer-
  chants; nobility, robe
Bourgoing, Jehan, 45–46, 115n33
Brantôme, Pierre de Bourdeille, abbé de,
  193–95, 236–39, 250, 253, 255, 257
Briçonnet family, 47
Brisson, Barnabé, 204
Brittany, 27n38, 120, 163, 165, 207, 234
Brûlart de Sillery, Nicolas, 171, 284
Budé, Guillaume, 54, 123, 174–75, 187–88,
  249
Butel, Etienne, 210–11, 220, 227n96

Calvin, John, 83–84
Camden, William, 151
Camus, Jean-Pierre, 84
Cassiodorus, 68n28, 153, 180–82, 185
Catherine de Médicis (queen of France),
  17, 37, 128, 157
Catholic church, 54–55, 83–84, 92, 117,
  134, 143n128, 155, 158, 221, 269, 235,
  242, 244, 278
Catholic League, 56, 59, 79, 120n46, 155,
  157, 159

Cave, Terence, 73, 251n38
Cavino, Giovanni, 256
Cecil, William, Lord Burghley, 63–64, 86, 151
Cellini, Benvenuto, 258–59
Chabans, Loys de, 175–76, 178, 180–82, 191
Châlons-sur-Marne, 53n128, 165, 214n62, 227
Chambéry. *See* Savoy
Chambre, Captain la (pseudonym), 196, 206–7, 219
Chambre des Comptes, 27–28, 31n52, 32, 34, 36, 39, 43n90, 46–48, 53, 57, 64, 120–21, 129, 135n101, 161
Chambre des Monnaies, 17, 20–25, 27–28, 198n13, 202n27; at Tours, 37n69, 44n92, 53–54, 57, 59, 161
Champagne, 47, 51, 131
changers, 27, 40, 105, 148
Chantal, Jehan, 24, 35–36
Charles VIII (king of France), 181
Charles IX (king of France), 3, 43n88, 48, 49n114, 88n97, 93, 113–14, 119, 129–31, 140, 193–96, 205–6, 223, 234, 236, 238
chartalism, 5–6, 12, 74n50
Chartres, 143–45
Chaucer, Geoffrey, 241–42, 255
chevauchées, 40–41, 99, 129–30, 143–44, 146–47
Choul, Guillaume du, 174, 181–82, 189, 254
Clerc, Guillaume le, 43n89, 46n104, 53, 57, 178, 184–85
Clermont, 146n136, 161
clipping, 111, 114, 128, 197–98, 200–201, 203, 205, 208, 212, 214, 217, 221, 227, 233
Colas, Jacques, 49, 116–26, 129, 154, 173–75, 179
Colom, Pierre, 20–22, 26n33
Columbus, Christopher, 60–61, 188
comedy, 43, 197n8, 260–61, 267, 269–70, 280
commonwealthmen, 63–64, 85, 94, 151
Comporion family, 217n70, 221–22, 226–27, 233
concubinage, 217–19, 221–22
Conseil Privé, 29, 34n57, 36nn65–66, 131n78, 158n14, 167n39, 171n53
copper coinage, 4, 8, 106, 148, 151, 161–62, 182–83, 185–86, 232n110. *See also* billon
Coquerel, Nicolas, 37n68, 53, 58, 75–76, 164, 174n69, 176–77

Corneille, Pierre, 15, 261–64, 270, 281
cosmetics, 237, 240, 250, 255–57, 272
Cour des Aides, 28, 35n59, 42, 52n122, 53, 220n79
Cour des Monnaies, ceremonial precedence, 34–35, 171, 283, 285–87; of Lyons, 58–59; subsidiary generals of, 20–21, 65, 167n38, 206, 231. *See also* Chambre des Monnaies; sovereign courts; individual members
credit and debt, 5–6, 12, 44–45, 86, 106, 137–39, 149–50, 162, 218, 253, 272, 280
Croumet, Barbe, 211, 218–19, 223n88
Cyrano de Bergerac, Hector-Savinien de, 265n72, 271, 273–75

Dain, Hilaire, 45, 112n22, 115n33, 129nn73–74, 132n82, 143n127, 202n26, 215n66, 216
Dassoucy, Charles, 265n72, 274
Dauphiné, 27n38, 31, 142, 160, 167n38
Deanebonne, Marie, 210–11, 220
death sentences, 17, 20, 35–37, 110, 203, 228, 232–34
debasement of coinage, 22, 29n44, 106, 148–52, 158, 160–64
debt. *See* credit and debt
Dee, John, 122
Derrida, Jacques, 71–73, 83n76
Des Jardins, Pierre, 49, 54–55, 112n22
Dewald, Jonathan, 45
Dijon, 23n23, 144
diplomacy. *See* international relations
Domayron, Antoine, 240–44, 247–48, 254–57, 259, 262, 273

écu. *See* money of account, écu
England, 3, 61n4, 63–64, 86–88, 94, 99, 102, 125n61, 137, 199n11, 204, 208, 234–36, 272, 286–87; coinage of, 8n14, 9, 11n21, 18, 29, 44, 106, 110–11, 129, 133, 143, 148–52 179
engravers, 9, 111–13, 143, 156, 181, 183, 185, 190, 202, 228, 272n90
Epernon, Jean Louis de Nogaret de la Valette, duc d', 164–5, 231, 283
Estates General, 57, 90, 100n127, 163, 166; of Blois, 87, 90, 125, 131–32, 137; of Orléans, 87–89, 118, 128. *See also* assemblies, advisory
Estoile, Pierre de l', 54n132, 58, 132, 135, 170–72
Etuves. *See* Paris, mints
executions. *See* death sentences

family economy, 196, 216–17
Fauchet, Claude, 41, 48–49, 51–53, 57, 65–66, 230
Faucon, Alexandre, 26, 47, 54
Faustina the Younger (empress of Rome), 255–56, 259
Favier, Jean, 42, 51n119, 165n31, 231–32
Flamel, Nicolas, 246
foreign coinage, 7, 108–9, 116–18, 122–26, 129, 131–32, 135–37, 144, 148, 167–69, 176–79, 191, 197
foreign trade, 63–64, 78, 90, 101, 107, 138, 166, 176, 184
Foulon, Abel, 113–14
franc. *See* money of account
François I (king of France), 21–22, 48n110, 87–88, 105, 258, 282
François II (king of France), 3, 119, 128, 204
Furetière, Antoine, 15, 200n19, 270n85, 278–81

Garrault, François, 51n119, 53, 120, 127, 134, 136, 173, 175, 179n78
Gelée, Vincent, 64–65
Geneva, 54, 102
Germany, 3, 18, 93n108, 110–11, 137n108, 150, 199n17, 206, 228, 244. *See also* Habsburg dynasty
Godefroy, Denys, 51, 167n40, 174n59, 176, 178, 180n82
Gohory, François, 51–52, 120
Gohory, Jacques, 51–52, 184n96, 186–88, 190, 229–31, 246
gold, 6–7, 13, 18, 27, 61, 70, 77–79, 86, 88, 91, 97, 116, 156, 168, 171, 180–81, 184, 186–91, 210, 237–39, 247–59, 268, 270, 273, 275, 277, 288. *See also* alchemy; bimetallic ratio; nobility of gold
Golden Age, 251–52, 270
goldsmiths, 7, 10, 14, 28, 34, 38, 40, 50, 98–99, 109, 142, 200–201, 203–4, 211–13, 218, 223, 230, 234
Grand Conseil, 22n17, 25–26, 31–33, 36, 53, 231
Grenoble, 23, 31n52, 156
Gresham, Thomas, 63; "Gresham's law," 8, 23n20, 27, 101, 125
Grolier, Jean, 47
Guesle, Jacques de la, 145
Guicciardini, Francesco, 76–77, 81
Guise family, 55, 58, 81, 155, 157, 236. *See also* Lorraine, Charles cardinal de; Mayenne, Charles de Lorraine, duc de

Guyenne, 21, 135n90, 143, 171
Guzmán de Alfarache, 261–64, 269

Habsburg dynasty, 2, 21, 35n59, 110, 158, 171, 184n93, 234
Haye, Jehan de la, 162
Hennequin, Loys, 47, 54, 115n33
Henri II (king of France), 2, 14–15, 22–23, 25–30, 32–34, 48, 55, 64–65, 87, 98, 105, 109–13, 118, 135, 181, 193, 249, 251, 259–60, 285. *See also* Poitiers, Diane de
Henri II d'Albret (king of Navarre), 21, 44, 110
Henri III (king of France), 3, 48, 49n114, 55, 57–58, 79, 87, 95, 131–32, 134–37, 144, 148–49, 155, 158–59, 236, 281
Henri IV (king of France), 3, 37, 54–55, 58–59, 63, 78, 85, 87–88, 100–103, 154–55, 160–65, 177, 180–82, 191, 204, 206n38, 239n6, 246, 259; assassination of, 14, 56, 282–85
henrique d'or, 27, 48, 177, 181, 259
Herail, Guillaume de, 176
Hermite, François Tristan l', 15, 265n72, 271–73, 277, 280
Holy Roman Emperors. *See* Habsburg dynasty
Hotman, Charles, 55, 120n46
Hotman, François, 51–52, 55, 134n3, 174, 179n78, 180n82
Hotman, Jean, 51–52, 55–56
Huguenots. *See* Protestants
humanism, 66–68, 78n61, 93–94, 101, 105–6, 120, 154, 179, 185, 244, 248, 258

inflation, 2, 15, 23, 30, 70, 89–91, 96, 100, 105–9, 114, 116, 120–21, 123–26, 128–39, 148–49, 151, 154, 161, 165, 184, 232n110
international relations, 4, 23, 28–29, 110–11, 123, 149–50, 152, 154, 158, 178–79, 150, 186, 188–92, 204n33, 207, 232–33, 235, 282. *See also* foreign coinage; foreign trade
Italy, 15, 76–77, 81, 87, 181–82, 206–7, 211, 217n72, 228, 247, 258, 267–69

jetons, 113n24, 165, 274, 276
Jonson, Ben, 257

La Rochelle, 23n23, 156, 212, 226
Lacanie, Antoine, 211–12, 215–16
Laffemas, Barthélemy de, 61, 102–3, 169

Laffemas, Isaac de, 71, 98n122, 102n130
Lambin, Denys, 66–67, 69, 71n39, 74
Languedoc, 157–59, 164
Lauthier, Philippe de, 23n22, 26, 46
legislation, 62, 75–76, 87, 90, 94–95, 97,
    116–17, 127, 136, 139, 179, 183, 188;
    publication of, 142–45, 147, 170. *See also*
    Bodin, Jean; sumptuary laws
letters of remission, 20n8, 22, 35, 165,
    202n25, 203
Lieur, Jehan le, 31n52, 37–38, 54
livre. *See* money of account
Locke, John, 60–61, 71, 179
Longuet, Germain, 44n95, 56, 115
Longuet, Pierre, 56, 227n97
Lorraine, Charles cardinal de, 42n85, 193,
    195–96, 236, 244, 251
Louis XIII (king of France), 15, 100n127,
    177n69, 181, 265, 283
Louis XIV (king of France), 15, 59, 98n120,
    149n142, 259, 278, 280
Loyer, Pierre le, 247–48, 273
luxury, 86, 88, 90–91, 94–95, 100n127,
    142, 167
Lyons, 23n23, 24, 34n58, 41, 58–59, 88n95,
    99, 102, 114n30, 131, 135, 142n124, 149,
    157, 159–61, 163–64, 167n38, 208
Lyons, François du, 132–33

magic, 227–28, 247, 262, 275, 281. *See also*
    alchemy; treasure hunting
Maignet, Joseph du, 25, 32, 208n50
Malestroict, Jehan Cherruyl de, 120–21,
    123–25, 173, 175
Malus, Martin, 115–16
marc d'or, droit de, 35n59, 281
Marie de Médicis (queen of France), 111,
    168n42, 282–88
Marillac, Charles de, 110, 112n21, 114n31
Marillac, Guillaume de, 47–48, 54, 109–10,
    130
Marlowe, Christopher, 234–36, 273
marriage, 47, 51, 54, 203n30, 210, 212–13,
    216–23, 266, 268–70, 278–79, 288. *See*
    also concubinage
Marseilles, 23
Marx, Karl, 1–2, 4, 11, 72n42, 77n59
Mayenne, Charles de Lorraine, duc de, 58,
    155, 160–62, 164
medals, 113n24, 180–86, 189n108, 240,
    254–59, 280
mercantilism, 61, 70, 78n61, 88, 167, 191
merchants, 15, 20, 26n33, 47, 57n141, 63, 89,
    89–90, 93n110, 102, 104, 114–15, 129,

133, 145–46, 155n4, 159, 166–68, 172–73,
    184, 205–6, 209–11, 213, 216, 221, 250,
    266, 272n90. *See also* bourgeoisie
Mercoeur, Philippe Emmanuel de Lorraine,
    duc de, 163, 165
Mestayer, Jehan le, 32, 46, 54, 115n32,
    143n127
Mestrelle, Eloi, 110, 112n21N
mining, 3, 18–19, 102, 107, 190
mint price, 107, 131n78, 139, 149, 169
mints, 7–11, 14, 27, 30, 38–40, 43–47,
    49–50, 52–53, 59, 64, 98–99, 106–7,
    113–16, 118, 123–24, 133, 135–36,
    141–43, 146, 148, 156–66, 215, 231; fraud
    at, 17–26, 34–35, 105, 109, 199, 231–32;
    mechanization of; 27, 109–14, 132, 165;
    outside France, 7, 18, 29, 44, 149–50, 197,
    268n77. *See also* individual cities
Molière (Jean-Baptiste Poquelin), 15, 261
monetization of economy, 2, 12, 79, 185
money of account, 5–6, 24n20, 89, 106–8,
    117, 119–20, 128, 131–32, 148, 166,
    176, 232n110; écu as, 126, 129–30, 139,
    167–68, 176–77
moneyers, 39, 165
moneychangers. *See* changers
monkeys, 15, 260, 274–77, 281
Monnaies, Chambre des; Cour des. *See*
    Chambre des Monnaies; Cour des
    Monnaies
Montaigne, Michel de, 73n46, 82–84,
    188–91, 228–29, 276
Montchrestien, Antoine de, 62, 102–3, 176,
    178n71
Montmorency, Anne, duc de, 21, 32, 42n85,
    109–10
Montmorency, François de Damville, duc
    de, 81, 156n8, 157–59, 161n22, 163–65,
    206, 231, 236, 284
Montpellier, 23n23, 157, 159, 164
Montperlier, Claude de, 41, 54n130,
    167n38, 226n95
More, Thomas, 77–78, 90, 121, 123
Morvilliers, Jean de, 134–35

Naudé, Gabriel, 236n120, 271, 275
Navarre (kingdom), 7, 20, 110, 113
nesles. *See* pinatelles
Netherlands, 100, 102, 149n142, 199n17,
    214, 228, 234–35, 282
Nevers, Louis de Gonzague, duc de, 245
New World. *See* Americas
nobility, 14–15, 21, 57, 87–88, 97, 151,
    195–96, 200, 203, 206–7, 209–11, 216,

219, 226, 239–41, 250, 255–57, 261–64, 266–72, 275; of gold, 239, 247–53; of the robe, 46–50, 54, 88, 266
Normandy, 142, 199, 207–9, 226n95

Olivier, Aubin, 112
Oresme, Nicole, 4n15, 117, 121, 123, 150n144
Orléans, 56n139, 114n28; edict of, 31n52, 38n72, 115, 134, 145n134, 213. *See also* Estates General of Orléans
Ottoman Empire, 240

Palais de Justice de Paris, 38–39, 162, 233n113, 283
Palissy, Bernard, 223–24, 230, 248
pardons. *See* letters of remission
Paris, 10, 35, 38–39, 53, 58, 98–99, 131, 133, 144, 155, 158, 162, 167, 198–200, 203, 207–8, 212–15, 221–22, 233, 244–45, 265–66, 271, 282; Arsenal, 162, 169, 172; livre of, 6; mints, 9n16, 23–24, 27, 45n96, 47–48, 110–13, 118, 165, 272n90; municipal government, 35n59, 43n91, 45, 58, 104, 115–16, 120, 134n94, 162, 169, 285; "Sixteen," 53–54, 57. *See also* sovereign courts; *individual institutions*
Parlement of Paris, 21n12, 22n17, 26, 29, 35–37, 42, 46–47, 49, 51n122, 53–54, 99n125, 125, 132, 135, 141–48, 161, 168, 170–71, 198, 204, 245n21, 249, 265, 279n105, 283; of Dijon, 144; of Rennes, 85, 233–34; of Rouen, 45, 167n39, 171; of Toulouse, 21n12, 164
Parliament, 86–87
Pasté, Michel, 212, 225–26, 228–29
patronage, 5, 7, 161n22, 206, 216–17, 245, 252, 278
Perrière, Guillaume de la, 80–81, 93–94
picaresque, 15, 195, 229, 260–68, 270–73, 278
Piètre, Roland, 84–87
Pilon, Germain, 258–59
Pinatel, Jacques, 17–19, 22, 24–26, 30, 34–35, 43, 46–47, 161, 202n25, 231
pinatelles, 161, 164–65, 231
pistole, 7, 138, 202, 210, 214, 235, 274, 277
Plato, 67, 72, 75n53, 122, 124, 126, 139
Pléiade, 120, 249, 251n39, 253, 260–61. *See also* Baïf, Marc-Antoine de; Ronsard, Pierre de
Poitiers, 23n23, 58, 134
Polanyi, Karl, 1, 11, 68n29

police, 65, 76, 92–94, 102n130, 109, 142, 144, 168n42, 176, 187, 198, 200
political economy, 2, 4, 11, 61–62, 64, 66, 68, 79, 82n74, 101–3, 105, 117, 239, 287
Polybius, 171–72
Potosí. *See* silver, American
Poulain, Henri, 55n136, 173–76, 184
presidial courts, 28, 51, 140, 143, 145n134, 146, 148, 157
Prevost, Charles le, 23
Primaudaye, Antoine de la, 23
printers, 143, 201, 258n56, 280–81
prisons, 9, 20n6, 22, 26, 45, 201, 203, 218, 226n95, 232, 235, 265, 273
Protestants, 3, 47–49, 51–55, 58, 63, 83–84, 86, 92, 94, 100, 103, 114, 131, 137, 152, 155–56, 158, 169, 171, 212, 224, 269
publication. *See* legislation, publication of
pyxes, 11, 38–39, 43–44, 53, 115n34, 156n7, 232

Quintilian, 73

Rabelais, François, 253
Radin, Simon, 23, 26, 46, 207n46
Rascas de Bagarris, Pierre-Antoine de, 176, 182–84, 254, 259, 280
real. *See* pistole
Regin, Jehan, 284, 286
Rennes, 23n23, 43, 163
Riberolles, Bernard de, 9n16, 112n22
Riberolles, Jehan de, 56
Riberolles, Sébastien de, 22n17, 24n24, 47, 56
Ribier, Louis, 46, 49, 54
Richelieu, Armand-Jean du Plessis, cardinal duc de, 173, 265n72
Robineau, Jacques, 38n74, 56n138
Roland, Nicolas, 79, 81
Roland du Plessis, Nicolas, 37n67, 55–56, 134–35, 139n114, 161, 175–76, 232n109
Rome, Empire, 180, 181–85, 187–90, 246, 254; Republic, 65, 71, 91–92; coinage of, 123, 126, 153, 180–81, 183, 189, 258
Ronsard, Pierre de, 78–79, 195, 249–53, 259
Rouen, 23n23, 166, 167n40, 211–12, 272
Roy, Loys le, 67, 69–71, 73n46, 78, 81

St. Germain-des-Pres, 200, 278
St. Malo, 163
Saintes, 156, 230
Sallust, 67, 84n82, 85, 172
Savoy, 20, 22–23, 160, 167, 169n47, 191, 194
secrecy, 55, 58, 65, 100, 106, 149, 228n99

seigniorage, 106, 113–14, 118, 137, 148–49, 160

silk, 86, 88, 90, 250

silver, 4, 6–7, 18–19, 24, 77–78, 86, 91, 99, 107, 119, 122, 131, 149, 151, 156–58, 165, 177, 204, 208, 214, 247, 250, 280; American, 2, 107, 125, 165, 177, 186. *See also* bimetallic ratio; teston

Simmel, Georg, 13

small change. *See* billon; copper coinage

Sorel, Charles, 15, 184n96, 264–70, 275–76, 278–79

sovereign courts, 25–35, 42, 46, 50, 52–53, 57–58, 64–65, 116, 145, 147, 170, 174, 183, 249, 266, 279n105, 280, 283, 285–86

sovereignty, royal, 4, 15, 75, 91–92, 105, 152, 154, 164–65, 168n42, 172–73, 178–79, 183, 191, 194–96, 234, 236, 238–40, 246, 251–54, 259–61, 269n81, 277–78, 281, 288

Spain, 61n4, 63, 83, 110, 161, 188, 190–91, 161, 207, 219, 261–63, 282; coinage of, 7, 18, 106, 124, 135, 184, 186, 197, 210, 232. *See also* Habsburg dynasty

Spondent (papal bull), 150n144, 224, 241–42, 243n15

Spooner, Frank, 136n105, 177

stoicism, 67, 70, 80, 84, 120n48, 246

Sully, Maximilien de Béthune, duc de, 47, 101n129, 102–3, 169–72, 174n59, 176n66, 178, 180, 283

sumptuary laws, 76, 86–92, 94, 96–97, 141n122, 250

Swiss Confederation, 131n80, 158, 232–33, 276

Symeoni, Gabriel, 258–59

taxation, 10–11, 23, 28, 39, 79, 149–50, 170, 274, 280–81

teston, 7, 24, 112, 138, 158n14, 181, 193, 235, 276

Thou, Jacques-Auguste de, 51, 136, 151, 182n87

torture, 36, 221n82, 223, 228, 268

Toulouse, 19, 21, 24n25, 58, 113–14, 164, 197, 244

Tourette, Alexandre de la, 23, 25, 31–33, 38, 44–45, 47n108, 48, 51–52, 65, 109, 115n33, 131n78, 135n99, 141–42, 144, 205n37, 229–31, 239

Tourette, Germain de la, 167n38, 206

Tranchetti, Andrea, 206, 211, 215, 218–19, 222–23

treasure hunting, 247–48

triage, 197, 200

triumviri monetales, 65, 92

Troyes, 10n19, 23n23, 51

Turnèbe, Adrien, 48, 66–67, 73–74

Turnèbe, Odet de, 48–49, 66, 261, 266

Turquam, Thomas, 36n66, 41, 51n122, 54n130, 115n33, 118, 129–32, 134, 138–40, 143–44, 147, 157, 174

Turquet, Louis de Mayerne, 102–3, 169

usury, 71, 94, 100, 288n13

Vachot, Loys, 21, 24–26, 31, 33, 46–47, 49

valets de chambre du roi, 47, 102, 113–14

Varade, Ambroise de, 56

Varade, Augustin de, 44n44, 53

Varade, Jerosme de, 49, 215n65

vellón. *See* copper coinage; Spain, coinage of

venality of office, 86, 100n127, 149, 170, 279, 281. *See also* marc d'or, droit de

Verdier, Antoine du, 271–72

Viau, Théophile de, 265, 269, 275

Vico, Enea, 182, 254

Villefranche-de-Rouergue, 17, 19–26, 199

Villeneuve-les-Avignon, 19, 23–25, 35, 39

virtue, 70, 74, 76, 79, 84–86, 92, 171–72, 189–90, 196, 238, 240, 252, 259, 261, 275, 288

Vries, Jan de, 2, 216n68

Wars of Religion, 2. *See also* Catholic Church; Protestants

Weber, Max, 1, 11–13, 287

Zachaire, Denis, 243–44